United States Bureau of Education

Industrial Education in the United States

A special Report

United States Bureau of Education

Industrial Education in the United States
A special Report

ISBN/EAN: 9783337185640

Printed in Europe, USA, Canada, Australia, Japan

Cover: Foto ©ninafisch / pixelio.de

More available books at **www.hansebooks.com**

INDUSTRIAL EDUCATION

IN THE

UNITED STATES.

A SPECIAL REPORT

PREPARED BY

THE U. S. BUREAU OF EDUCATION.

WASHINGTON:
GOVERNMENT PRINTING OFFICE.
1883.

47TH CONGRESS, } SENATE. { Ex. Doc.
2d Session. No. 25.

LETTER

FROM THE

SECRETARY OF THE INTERIOR,

TRANSMITTING,

In response to Senate resolution of December 15, information relating to industrial education in the United States.

DECEMBER 27, 1882.—Referred to the Committee on Education and Labor and ordered to be printed.

DEPARTMENT OF THE INTERIOR,
Washington, December 27, 1882.

SIR: I have this day received from the Commissioner of Education, and have the honor to forward for the information of the Senate, the following reply to the resolution of the Senate of the 15th instant, calling for information in regard to industrial education.

Very respectfully, your obedient servant,
H. M. TELLER,
Secretary.

The PRESIDENT OF THE SENATE.

DEPARTMENT OF THE INTERIOR,
BUREAU OF EDUCATION,
Washington, D. C., December 27, 1882.

SIR: I have the honor to acknowledge the receipt of the following resolution of the Senate of the United States, referred by you to me on December 19:

Resolved, That the Secretary of the Interior is directed to furnish to the Senate the latest and fullest information in the possession of the Bureau of Education in relation to technical or industrial education in the schools and colleges endowed in whole or in part by the Government of the United States, and also in other schools in the country reporting instruction in industry for either men or women.

Education, in its relation to industry, is a subject of earnest consideration in the public mind. Older countries, struggling with some of the severer problems of civilization, have found great aid in their solution by modifying the instruction given the children in their schools. Educated labor is found to be a prominent factor in national prosperity.

Recently industrial education in some form has been the subject of special inquiry in various foreign countries. Several of our own States,

S. Ex. 25——1

and a number of associations and institutions, have been making active efforts to gain further information upon the subject.

This office is compelled to make technical instruction a subject in regard to which it constantly collects and communicates facts; and I have the honor to submit the following reply to the resolution of the Senate, drawn from material already gathered in the office in response to previous demands.

I have the honor to be, very respectfully, your obedient servant,

JOHN EATON,
Commissioner.

The Hon. SECRETARY OF THE INTERIOR.

REPORT.

It will be seen that the information called for by the Senate resolution is concerned with a wide educational field. Colleges of agriculture and mechanics, and institutions affording instruction similar to that of agricultural colleges, as well as those which give opportunities to women for industrial education, come within the sphere of inquiry. In other words, the educational training of the farmer, the mechanic, and the housekeeper, so far as it is attempted by organized effort, is the subject on which information is required to be given. In the West provision is usually made for the education of these three classes in the same schools; for, in the newer States, it is the generally accepted belief that those who are to be coworkers in actual life may well be associated in the preparation for it; that man and woman are entitled to equal and similar, if not identical, educational privileges. In the more conservative regions of the East and South the sexes are not so frequently educated together.

In Massachusetts the colleges of agriculture and mechanic arts are distinct from each other, so that not only the education of the housekeeper is entirely separated from that of the farmer and mechanic, but even these latter classes are trained in independent institutions. This separation exists to a less extent in Missouri, where the school of mines and metallurgy is distinct from the other departments of the university.

It has been necessary, in order to cover the entire ground contemplated by the resolution, to extend the report beyond the limits of a single class of schools, and to present information respecting varied institutions other than those endowed by the national land grant. The colleges of agriculture and the mechanic arts are entitled to and receive the most prominent place in both resolution and report for many just reasons. They are doing a great proportion of the work of industrial education. The number of students attending them in 1880 was more than double that of the students in the schools of science not aided by the land grant, if the institutes affording only evening instruction, special teaching, or general lectures, such as the Cooper Institute of New York and the Wagner Institute of Philadelphia, be excluded. It is true that some of these individual schools of science are munificently endowed, and afford their students most excellent opportunities for obtaining a technical education, but this has come to be true of some of the schools, colleges, and universities which have received national aid, and many of those that are less richly endowed are occupying fields which otherwise would be destitute of institutions for educating men in the practical sciences and arts, and consequently without educated men to foster and direct their industries and utilize their resources. As the fruits of these institutions appear, they show that in all sections the education of persons to be engaged in staple industries is being obtained largely within their walls.

It is evident [said an eminent educator after an extended tour among our agricultural colleges] that the American technical colleges are rapidly taking the idea that their usefulness will depend, not on solving an abstract problem as to what sort of education would most benefit a farmer, for example, but on solving a problem much more practical, though really harder, namely, what sort of an education does the farmer want or can be induced to receive in order to fit him for his work of farming.

The thinking farmer and mechanic have wanted and will ever desire to see a system of schools established and in operation for the benefit of the classes to which they belong. The farmer, striving to improve his land and crops and stock, asks himself a thousand questions, and is obliged to confess his inability to answer half of them satisfactorily. There is a latent, deeply-rooted belief in his mind that it is possible that his son may be so taught as to know not only the innumerable details and the practical working of the farm, where he himself is the best teacher, but also the things which have been beyond his comprehension. The peculiarities of soils, the causes of deficiencies in crops, the insects that injure them, the unproductiveness of his orchards, the diseases of his stock, the inconveniences of his buildings, these and similar things attract his attention, give rise to questions which he knows not how to answer correctly, and fix in his mind the thought that if education is education it can and should teach how to avoid or remedy the evils which are robbing him of his profits and impairing his prosperity. There are also those who take a more comprehensive and far-reaching view of the subject. They remember that agriculture feeds the world and gives employment to a multitude of its inhabitants; that it is an art founded on science, and that as the departments of science on which it is based are more thoroughly known, and the art itself is carried to greater perfection, the world will be better fed and the services of those that till the earth more richly rewarded. They regret that agriculture is slow to advance. Oldest of the arts, it is almost last to come into deserved prominence, and to receive systematic and liberal encouragement and aid.

This lack of adequate development [says a recent writer] is due to two main causes: To the rarity of scientific investigation into the principles upon which the tilling of the ground (and the care of cattle) ought to be carried out, *i. e.*, into the laws governing the growth of crops and of beasts, and to the want of adequate scientific training on the part of the farmer. If we look at the other arts, we shall find the numbers of the respective guilds enthusiastically bent on two thin s: On the advancement of scientific inquiry and the scientific education of the practitioner. * * * Of all human occupations, the one which most of all stands in daily need of a sound scientific judgment and of wide scientific knowledge, is that of tilling the ground and feeding cattle. The problems of agriculture are scientific problems of the highest difficulty and complexity. The question how, under given conditions, to feed a beast in the cheapest and best way is one which involves the most profound physiological considerations; is one which can only be satisfactorily answered by prolonged and exact experimental inquiries. The adequate preparation of the ground for the growth of a given crop is a subject which, seriously examined, expands into a whole series of problems, taxing to the utmost the fullest and most advanced chemical and botanical knowledge.

An idea prevails with the mechanics similar to that entertained by the individual farmer. He, too, sees in a suitable education the advancement of his position and the elevation of his children. A proof of this is furnished by the answers given by employés in various kinds of factories and shops to questions concerning education, asked of them by the New Jersey Bureau of Statistics of Labor and Industries. A laborer in a glass factory writes: "Technical education should be made compulsory for the laboring class." A silk worker says: "Industrial schools as they exist in Europe should be set up." A carpenter believes that "There should be appropriations for technical schools in every city." The idea of education for business and for labor penetrates, pervades, and permeates the masses. It has compelled recognition in political circles, and statesmen have sought means whereby it might be satisfied. To use the words of President White, of Cornell University:

It is not to be scolded out of existence by solid review articles or pooh-poohed out of existence by pleasant magazine articles. Evidently the idea is rooted in our planet and will hardly be pulled up by narrow literary men who hold the time-honored studies the most eminently respectable; or by narrow practical men who disbelieve in "book learning"; or by narrow religious men who fear that geology may harm Genesis.

It was in conformity to this practical, popular, and controlling idea of educating men for their work that colleges of agriculture and the mechanic arts were established, and are arranging and putting into operation their courses of study, training, and experimentation; and what is being done to satisfy a popular educational demand should be plainly set before the people, that they may know that their wishes are regarded and their expenditure in this direction is applied for their own benefit.

Again, the colleges of agriculture and mechanic arts deserve prominence in a report of this kind because they are distinctively American. No other country possesses a similar class of institutions, which freely open their doors to the youth of the regions in which they are situated and provide for their students wise, liberal, and appropriate courses of study adjusted to their peculiar wants. Nowhere else is there a system of schools affording parallel lines of instruction, doing the same kinds of work, and covering so wide a ground. The countries of Europe have their schools of agriculture and of polytechnics, but they are more specialized than ours. Education is not so much directed toward preparation for citizenship in the monarchical governments of Europe as with us. There the end of teaching has been reached when it has produced a skilled specialist in some branch of science, art, or industry; here the work is to be done by the pupil is not taught to the exclusion of his social and political obligations. Our system of agricultural colleges recognizes the fact that the American laborer has duties to perform, both as a workman and as a ruler. They seek to educate him for leading industries, so that our fields may be carefully tilled and our trades skillfully followed. They aim, also, to prepare him by a general education for his share in the government of the people, so that the prosperity and intelligence of the nation may be increased through his efforts.

The agricultural and mechanical colleges of the United States not only differ as a class from foreign schools in being less specialized, but are also dissimilar to the schools of particular nations and to individual schools in many points of detail. They differ from the agricultural colleges of England in being open to all youth; while at Cirencester, where the tuition is £50 per annum, and presumably at its sister agricultural college, Wilts and Hantz, only the sons of the wealthy are educated. They are unlike the agricultural colleges at Altnarp, Sweden, and at Hohenheim, Württemberg, for in those the sons of the wealthy and titled receive other instruction than that given to the sons of peasants. "Every great agricultural college in Europe," says President White, "must either be cut into two parts, with peasants' sons in one and the gentry in the other, as at Hohenheim, or they must exclude peasants' sons altogether, as at Cirencester." Our colleges are not in name a part of a graded system of schools teaching the same subjects like those of Ireland, nor even links in a chain of institutions laboring for the same ends, like those for agricultural education in Sweden. In that country the agricultural colleges are aided in their work by agricultural schools, model and experimental dairies, and agricultural societies. In Ireland there is a graduated system of instruction from the public schools, in which a text book on agriculture is used, to the farm schools, and finally to the Albert Institute at Glasnevin. In France there are farm schools, departmental schools of agriculture, and a national agricultural institute.

Elsewhere there is a similar classification of schools. Our agricultural colleges are not a part of a system of agricultural schools. To be most useful they must be connected with some tributary institutions. The public schools are the only available ones with which to make connection, and this connection is being made close and firm, and by it agricultural colleges are becoming a part of the national system of education. This intimate relation of our higher institutions with public schools is illustrated by a law passed by the legislature of Minnesota, by which it binds its high schools closely to its university, which receives the benefit of the land grant of 1862. Aid is provided for them by the State; in order that it may be bestowed judiciously, its distribution is intrusted to a board of commissioners, one of whom is the president of the university. They must require each school desiring aid to comply with the following conditions:

1. That there be regular and orderly courses of study embracing all the branches prerequisite for admission to the collegiate department of the University of Minnesota.

2. That the said schools receiving pecuniary aid under this act shall at all times permit the said board of commissioners, or any of them, to visit and examine the classes pursuing the said preparatory courses.

After inspection, report, and approval, each school receives $400. The president of the university has charge of the required examinations when a study in a college preparatory course is about to be completed. Examination papers are furnished by the examining officer of the board, and every pupil that passes the examination receives through his principal a certificate on which is the following indorsement: "On applying for admission to the University of Minnesota, present this certificate and you will be excused from examination in the study named."

There are colleges of agriculture in Europe giving instruction in more advanced studies and requiring greater previous training than do any of the colleges of the United States. A single illustration will suffice. In Bavaria higher agricultural education is afforded by the central school, at Weihenstephan, and the agricultural department of the polytechnic school at Munich. The candidate for admission to the central school must complete the course of study either of the Gewerbeschule or the Realgymnasium. The student from the former school has carefully studied his mother tongue; mathematics, including trigonometry and descriptive geometry; the natural sciences, especially chemistry and zoölogy; the French language; and all the usual studies of an elementary course, such as drawing, arithmetic, geography, and history. The student coming from the Realgymnasium has pursued similar studies, except that he has not obtained an actual knowledge of the sciences, but has studied Latin seven years. In either case the applicant for admission to the central school must have a practical acquaintance with farm work. The course of study in this school is such as to require this amount of preparation. Applicants for admission at Munich must spend two years more at their books, though they are not required to have a practical knowledge of farm operations. These requirements for admission are equivalent to the completion of an ordinary collegiate course, and the studies pursued are on a par with a graduate professional course.

In touching upon other differences between American and foreign technical schools, I cannot do better than to quote the language used by Prof. John D. Runkle, in an account of some institutions with which he became familiar during a recent visit to Europe:

The teaching force in all of them, particularly in the professional subjects, is much larger than with us. The result is that there is a much greater subdivision of subjects, and more time given to each. The theoretical subjects are treated with much more fullness than is possible here, and a much wider range of instruction is included in each department.

There is also a marked contrast in the methods of instruction. In the foreign schools all the instruction is given by lectures, and the professor, as a rule, takes no means to learn whether his students understand the subject or not. They are expected to take sufficiently full notes during the lecture to be able afterwards to write it out fully. For those students who have the ability and industry to do this work faithfully the method is a good one; but from all the information I have been able to gain, with a large number it fails. While most of the programmes of instruction refer to periodic examinations for testing the student's progress and proficiency, I know that in some of the German schools such examinations are entirely discontinued, and the only examinations held are those for degrees. The reason given me was that it entailed too much work upon the teachers.

Another strong contrast between these schools and those at home is in the freedom of the student in the choice of studies. There the student enters his name for certain courses of lectures, and then attends or not, as he likes. Of all the polytechnic schools we have visited, that at Zürich is the only one which prescribes a fixed course of studies and holds stated test examinations for progress and promotion; and even in this school the agitation has begun for the adoption of the German method. The great advantage to the student of the German freedom is that it enables him to concentrate all his time and energies upon those studies which are vital to the end he has in view. This course is only allowable after the student has acquired a good general education, equivalent to the under-graduate course in the best American colleges and technical schools, which I consider a far broader and more substantial education for the mass of students than that furnished by the German schools of the same grade. It may be that the German student enters the polytechnic school with technically a better preparation than the majority of our students; but this by no means justifies the removal of all further restraints in the manner and matter of the subsequent education. Even the best students are aided by the moral support of frequent examinations and a fixed course of studies until they are able to work with a good degree of independence, and only need the guidance and advice of teachers in connection with proper opportunities. After the student has the ground-work of his profession laid he can profit by a period of freedom to fill out the plan and make up deficiencies of which he will then begin to be conscious.

A final reason for devoting the larger part of the report to the colleges of agriculture and the mechanic arts is that they have been given endowment funds by Congress; those who have received money from the government should furnish reports of the methods and results of its expenditure. This duty was required in the act granting aid to agricultural colleges in the following words:

An annual report shall be made regarding the progress of each college, recording any improvements and experiments made, with their cost and results, and such other matters, including State industrial and economical statistics, as may be supposed useful.

SECTION 1.

COLLEGES OF AGRICULTURE AND THE MECHANIC ARTS.

Many of the colleges of agriculture and mechanics made full and satisfactory replies to a circular letter addressed them some time since for the purpose of obtaining direct statements about their educational aims, methods, and appliances. Where these statements were incomplete they were filled out from material in this office, such as catalogues and annual reports. In the absence of any special statement from a college officer, facts have been gleaned from available sources. In this way a brief sketch of each institution has been prepared, and is presented, usually after revision by the head of the institution it describes, in Appendix A, accompanying this report. In Appendix B are statistics of the same institutions.

There remains, therefore, little to be said concerning agricultural colleges except in the way of a general review of their sphere and work.

OBJECTS.—The usual form of stating the objects these colleges are endeavoring to accomplish is to say that they are those specified in the act of Congress of July 2, 1862, by which the grant of land for the endowment of these institutions was made. This act says:

> The leading object shall be, without excluding other scientific and classical studies and including military tactics, to teach such branches of learning as are related to agriculture and the mechanic arts in such manner as the legislatures of the States may respectively prescribe, in order to promote the liberal and practical education of the industrial classes in the several pursuits and professions of life.

The real intent of the act has been considered to be not only the establishment of schools for professional training in agriculture and in trade, but particularly " to promote the liberal and practical education of the industrial classes."

1. Education which prepares persons for the occupation they are to follow is practical. The instruction of the dissecting room and that of the lecture room are equally practical to the medical student. The instruction of a young mechanic in arithmetic and in reading is as much a part of his practical education as his labor in the shop beneath the eye of a master. The former kind of instruction is everywhere afforded in our public schools; the latter is not provided for the multitude of laboring men. With the disappearance of apprenticeship and the multiplication of artistic manufactures has come a great need of training for mechanics, but no direct way has been opened by which they can learn their trades. The truth of this statement is shown by the answers given by New Jersey workmen of different trades to the question "Is there any system of teaching apprentices in the factory where you work?" which had been asked by the statistical bureau of that State.

Glass-blowers.—"None."

Iron workers, iron moulders.—"Very loose system; taken without indenture, and are discharged at their own pleasure or that of the employer, with the trade only half learned." · "They work at what they can do and gradually learn." "Pick it up the best way they can." "If they are smart boys we teach them." "They are not indentured; a verbal agreement is all." "Take them for five or six years, paying them at first $2.50 a week."

Core-makers.—" No one teaches them; they work up themselves." "Merely verbal agreement, which is not often regarded." "If they have ability and aptness anyone is willing to teach them." "Learners must serve a term of two years."

Nail feeders.—"The system is to keep one from learning the trade." "They give us no chance to."

Iron roller.—"They work up."

Saw maker.—"Yes. Hire them by the week, with the understanding that if they are steady they will have the first chance to learn. The time thus occupied is allowed if they are taken on."

Printers.—"Boys are taken on a three years' apprenticeship, and are taught the trade by the foreman." "Go in as a 'devil' and work up." "It has been successfully taught in technical schools."

Weavers in cotton factory.—"Weavers take new hands for about three weeks, after which they become spare hands until they are good weavers and work for themselves. They receive nothing while learning." "Taught to fix looms; go under instructors for two or three weeks."

Woolen mills operatives.—Weaver: "Learn by practice in a few weeks, with an old weaver." Wool sorter: "Yes, there is a regular system. We set the apprentice to work assorting until he can, in a measure, tell the qualities. It is all eye practice."

Carriage makers.—"Work them up gradually." "Generally they are taken during the busy part of the season and then sent off." "A cutthroat plan."

Chair makers.—"The boys are used to the best advantage of the employer. The work is so subdivided that a boy cannot learn how to make a complete chair in four years."

Potter.—"The foreman teaches them." "They are taught by being shown." "They learn by watching and being instructed in the different branches."

Silk weavers.—"Yes. Apprentices are taken and sent to some experienced hand for three or four weeks to help and get instructions. This is without pay. Then they obtain looms for themselves." "Yes and no. The weaver is at liberty to take in apprentices whenever he chooses. As soon as they are able to tend a power loom they can fill vacancies, if there are any." "The employés ought to have control of the apprentices, in order that the bosses may not take their friends and favorites to teach them the trade, and send off those of the employés." "Learners must stand by and look on for three or four weeks without pay, until they can weave." "Take children under 14 years and let them learn for one or two weeks." "Sometimes they are taught. In order to understand perfectly they must work for six weeks. They work three out of the six without pay."

Silk workers.—"School girls are taken for three or four weeks, until they understand how to tend six or twelve ends; till they are able to run a machine." "Experienced silk workers are instructed little by little, until finally they are able to twist perfectly." "Girls taken in learn how to handle silk and start the machine." "Boys are taken on small wages to help, and in course of time become skilled workmen." "The method here adopted is to take in fresh hands, let them look on for a week or less, then help one or two weeks without pay, and then discharge them. If they desire to come back they are taken from $3 to $5 a week." "There are not sufficient opportunities offered to the girls to learn the other branches of the business."

Jewellers.—"Boys come in at low wages and work up until twenty-one." "No system; they learn all they can." "During a period of from three to five years, until he knows how to scroll." "Boys are placed between men and sometimes put on the same jobs, and are watched by them." "Almost every shop has its own system, and the majority a very bad one. The trouble is that our trade is not sufficiently organized to compel employers to have a fair plan of taking in boys. In a good many shops most of the work is done by teams of boys or green hands. This is the curse of our trade and keeps us down." "To get all the work possible out of the apprentices, so that the journeymen will lose all the time possible, is the only method in my shop."

The educational opportunities of an apprentice at the present time compared with those he possessed in the days when apprenticeship was the accepted way of admission to trades and had the protection and support of wise laws are discouraging. This is well illustrated by an extract which Mr. Twining gives in his Technical Training from a writer on technical education in France, from which I take the following:

The old guilds, with their antiquated rules and rage for public banqueting, were not perhaps progressive bodies; but in their own rough way they kept an eye on apprentices, reproved and even punished the masters who were remiss in instructing them, and maintained among the apprentices themselves a wholesome emulation by means of frequent examinations, badges, and money prizes. There were, in fact, trade degrees like those in a university; and an apprentice, however rich he might be, could only become a master and set up shop after having obtained three certificates of proficiency. The first was bestowed after two years of apprenticeship; the second, with a colored badge, at the end of the fifth year; and the third, with a silver badge, when the apprenticeship was concluded in a brilliant manner. * * * In the guild times care was taken that every tradesman who accepted apprentices should be thoroughly qualified to teach them. Nowadays, no qualifications being needed, it is naturally the most incapable tradesmen who are keenest in trying to secure apprentices by low premiums. They take in a boy as pupil and treat him as a servant, send him out to carry parcels, make him sweep the shop, wash up plates and dishes, and let him pick up many more bad habits than good lessons.

The reasons for the decay of apprenticeship are numerous and many of them of long standing. Among objections advanced by Adam Smith and his school to the system are interference with the property which every man has in his own labor, encroachment on the liberties of employer and employé, restraint of competition, unnecessary duration, and its failure to allow the rewards of faithful labor to be enjoyed as they are earned. Mr. Stetson, in his work on technical education, says:

This decay of apprenticeship is mainly due to the subdivision of labor which is now observed in the manufacture of nearly all things, from pins to locomotives, because it is found to yield the best results. The use of machinery, the character of which is often such as to put an end to small enterprises, has promoted this subdivision by accumulating workmen in large groups. The beginner, confining himself to one department, is soon able to earn wages. This gratifies both himself and his parents; and so he usually continues as he began.

Now that apprenticeship is actually gone, the question of the practical education of the industrial classes in their handicrafts and occupations is more than ever one for the public consideration. There is no prospect of a revival of old-time apprenticeship. Foreign skilled labor ought not to be made a reliance. Our own youth ought to be, and must be, trained to occupy leading places in the arts and manufactures, by means of special instruction given in schools organized for the purpose. Any system of schools or instruction which fits pupils to enter intelligently upon the duties of life and the work of a trade promotes the practical education of the industrial classes.

Occasionally some form of apprenticeship is devised by a single firm, or by an association of manufacturers or mechanics, by which workmen may be prepared for places in which they need more than ordinary skill. An illustration of this is found in an attempt made a few years since by a firm in Springfield, Mass., to obtain and discipline such a force of mechanics as they needed in their work as designers and manufacturers of machinery. Applicants were to be at least sixteen years old. The term of apprenticeship was six years for those under twenty who had had no previous experience, and five years for those over twenty. Those who had worked in a shop were advanced according to proficiency. Fifty-eight hours a week of work in the shop and nine hours of evening study were required. The rates of pay for labor varied from five to thirteen cents an hour, depending upon age and length of service. Two cents an hour additional were paid into a reserve fund and kept for the apprentice until he had finished his term of work. Then it would amount to some $400. This scheme of apprenticeship promised success, but the firm were compelled by business changes to dissolve partnership, and so the plan was abandoned.

The necessity of industrial training to the advance of individuals and the prosperity of a nation has been well shown by Mr. J. S. Russell.* An abstract of portions of his work will show vividly the real objects for which technical schools are being established, and for which the institutions endowed with the national land grant ought to labor as their circumstances will permit.

The mission of the book was to stir up a crusade against educational ignorance, disorganization, and neglect. "It was written under the conviction that the power, wealth, influence, and moral character of the English people were dependent on systematic, elementary, scientific, and technical education." The earlier parts of the work are devoted to a description of the organization by which the best educated nations of the continent have reached their present distinction. After a few chapters the author comes to the consideration of technical education as a national want. It interests a man in the work done by himself and his neighbor. It makes workmen better, both in themselves and as aids to each other.

An intelligent community of workmen will get through their work quicker, will fit its parts more nicely, will finish off everything more sharply, will waste less material by trial and error, and so give higher value as well as quality and durability to all their work, than ignorant, unrefined, ill-educated men.

The highest value in the world's markets will be obtained by that nation which has been at most pains to cultivate the intelligence of its people generally, and afterwards to give each the highest education and training in this special calling.

These propositions axiomatic to his mind are sustained by the lessons of the world's improvement as shown by expositions, in each of which the nations which had educated their mechanics excelled those which had not. Quotations are given from officials and workmen who attended the Paris Exposition of 1867. A china painter says:

The present prosperity of this country is so unmistakably interwoven with its manufactures, and the pre-eminence of these depends so much upon new adaptations, discoveries, and improvements, as to demand for the workers in iron, china, and other departments the readiest and best educational training and enlightenment this nation can give them.

Others speak in the same manner.

The technical education of the industrial classes has also social and moral effects, drawing master and workman into closer and more sympathetic relations, and inducing each to aim at good work rather than mere pecuniary success.

When education has given to each man a knowledge of all the branches of his work, and there remains no difference of rank, excepting superior skill and intelligence, then each man's individual work will be weighed in the balance, and the true share of his merit will be appraised in the scale of wages.

Equality will be then, as now, impossible, but the scale of each man's life may be one of steady, continual, meritorious rise.

After a few chapters on English and continental education the author discusses the kinds of technical training which various industrial classes require, in addition to a fundamental education, saying substantially:

The farmer should be educated in sciences, elementary engineering, mechanics, and agriculture; the miner, in mineralogy, geology, chemistry, and his own work; the merchant, in geography, history, foreign languages, political economy, and laws. The machinist must master all the known powers of material nature: heat and cold, weight and impulse, matter in all conditions—liquid, solid, and gaseous, standing or running, condensed or rare, adamantine or plastic—all must be seen through and comprehended by the master of modern mechanics. Architects, engineers, teachers,

---

*Systematic Technical Education for the English People, by J. Scott Russell, esq., M. A., F. R. S. London, 1869.

and all classes of workers require technical education, which is defined to be "that special training which renders the talents of the educated man directly useful to that society in which its youthful member is destined to pass his life."

The details of a proposed technical university, and other matters pertaining to the application of general principles rather than the discussion of the principles themselves, occupy much of the latter portion of the work. In one chapter, nevertheless, the author makes general remarks on the *present* need of technical education, summarized as follows:

The world is now the field in which men must compete. Therefore they ought to know its languages, that they may go from one country to another as better opportunities for them to labor are offered. They should be acquainted with its manufactures and markets, that they may be successful in competition with home producers and foreign importers. The proper education of mechanics enables them to dispense with the services of expensive agents and middlemen and to adapt themselves to the changes and progress in industries. In this progress agriculture is becoming chemistry; husbandry, machinery. All that is done without skill is going to be done, not by intelligent men, but by dead machinery. Yet intelligent, educated, conscientious men are needed to invent and manage this machinery. For the time when such men are required in every occupation the working man should be fitted. But above and over him will arise the class who, in their turn, are to instruct, guide, and think for him. However skilled to work his machine, he will still depend on a superior to invent or make it; on a man who shall come after him to complete it. These are the higher departments which form the higher ranks of crafts; in short, above the skilled doers we must have the skilled thinkers. * * *

In this view of an intelligent, skilled nation it is plain that we shall be able to do without the unskilled, the unintelligent, the uneducated. * * * The men of the future must have one of two qualifications: skill to do, education to know, or both.

Conclusions as to the value of technical education have been drawn by Mr. C. B. Stetson from the opinions of manufacturers, mechanics, educators, and statesmen. They are stated in a concise and comprehensive form in his work already referred to, and deserve the consideration of all thinkers upon the subject. They are as follows:

(1) The person who has general charge of any business should understand that business both theoretically and practically. His knowledge of principles should be such as to enable him to instruct any subordinate requiring instruction, to determine at once the comparative value of different processes of work, or to invent new ones when emergencies require it. In a word he should be able to reach just conclusions at once by his knowledge of principles, and not slowly by trial and error. He should be workman enough to know when work is well done that he may not be cheated by those under him, and that he may be able to render justice unto all by duly discriminating between the skilled and unskilled laborer. He should understand his business as a whole, and the relation of each part to the whole. Neither skilled workmen nor tariffs can compensate for stupidity on the part of the superintendent. Only the very few exceptional geniuses, like Stephenson, become thus qualified to take charge of enterprises, great or small, without special school instruction.

(2) The workman should not only be dexterous in manipulation, he should certainly know so much of the theory of his business as will enable him readily to comprehend all instructions, verbal or graphic, given for his guidance. The more extended and thorough his knowledge of principles the better. Such a workman requires very little supervision; he executes with rapidity; he wastes the least possible; he adapts himself readily to new methods; he devises novel and better ways for doing even the simplest things; he is the first to be promoted; he is the last to be discharged; he always commands the best wages, and yet his labor is the cheapest in the market. On the other hand the workman who works only by "rule of thumb," though he may be dexterous, lacks logic, lacks invention, lacks adaptability; indeed, is only a better kind of machine.

(3) The workman should be better instructed because of the machinery used, since it is the rude or dexterous workman rather than the really skilled workman, who is supplanted by machinery. Skilled labor requires thinking, but a machine never thinks, never judges, never discriminates. Objects which have a simple and regular form and require high finish or not, may be made with advantage by machinery if the objects are produced in large numbers. Most kinds of work which demand little besides strength for their execution can usually be best done by machinery too. Though the employment of machinery does, indeed, enable rude laborers to do many things now which formerly could be done only by dexterous workmen, yet, after making allowance for all the bearings of the question, it is clear that the use of machinery has decidedly increased the relative demand for skilled labor as compared

with unskilled labor, and there is abundant room for an additional increase, if it is true, as declared by the most eminent authority, that the power now expended can be readily made to yield three or four times its present results, and ultimately ten or twenty times, when masters and workmen can be had with sufficient intelligence and skill for the direction and manipulation of the tools and machinery that would be invented.

(4) All those persons whose business it is to produce new combinations of matter—such as the farmer, miner, dyer, bleacher, founder, maker of machinery, and numerous others—should have a knowledge of chemistry. Without such knowledge, which is an essential element of skilled labor in these departments of industry, neither rude nor dexterous labor can produce satisfactory results.

(5) The utmost effort should be made to produce articles of beautiful design, whether in form or in color, or both. The difference between good design and poor design is the difference between success and failure in the market of the world. When the beauty of the object depends, as it usually does, upon its own form, or upon the form of the applied decoration, the workman should be one who has been thoroughly instructed in artistic drawing and designing. Not only should the originator of the design have been thus instructed, but also the reproducer of the design in wood, metal, earth, or other substance.

(6) For the most successful prosecution of any great enterprise in land or naval architecture, in the construction of railroads, canals, machinery, there should not only be an abundance of thorough and expert draughtsmen, but each workman should be draughtsman enough to make a drawing of any object he is required to construct. Of two competing establishments, the one having such workmen, the other not, the former would not only win, but would distance the latter every time.

Says President E. P. Tenney, of Colorado College:

The means for industrial education will certainly prove a part of the endowment of any well-ordered college in the new West. It is essential for aiding needy students, for promoting a manly independence, for training those who will develop the material interests of the country, and for preparing young men to induct semi-barbarous populations into the mysteries of civilized life.

2. It was not an easy question to determine the best mode of placing the benefits of the endowment fund provided by the nation within reach of the people for whom it was designed. Should the money be granted to existing institutions or made the basis of establishing new ones? Should the courses of study be closely confined to the wants of the artisan or enlarged by studies more purely disciplinary? Should agriculture or mechanics predominate?

The industries of each State, the wealth of its inhabitants, and their sentiments with regard to education determined largely the solution of these problems. In California and Missouri, States abounding in mineral resources, there are courses in mining and metallurgy provided in the institutions receiving national aid. In manufacturing States, the colleges have generally lent their aid to the prevailing interests.[1]

In the manufacturing State of Pennsylvania the institution receiving the national endowment is chiefly agricultural, and it is in the farming region of that State. In the great grain-producing sections of the Mississippi Valley, the colleges are rarely devoted principally to agriculture. It does not require skill to obtain remunerative crops from the rich prairies; and it is in the States where the soil is less fertile by nature and more impoverished, the climate less favorable, and the rural population more dense, that the need of scientific agriculture is felt. In accordance with this rule, good types of agricultural schools are found in the

---

[1] A college which leans strongly toward some form of industry that does not attract the intelligence and wealth of the section of country from which it would naturally draw its students, will meet with opposition or negligence that will impair its usefulness and possibly end its existence. Maryland is largely a commercial State. One-third of its population is in the single city of Baltimore. The drift of the State is toward the commerce and manufactures of that city, and the president of its agricultural college, an institution where peculiarly ample facilities for the study of agriculture have been offered, has been compelled to confess that "few fathers desire their sons to become farmers."

cold and forbidding climate of Maine, on the exhausted soil of Virginia, and in the thickly-populated State of Massachusetts. This same influence is readily perceived in the distribution of agricultural schools in European nations. Those of Russia are found rather in its cold northern sections than its southern grain-producing areas. The wealth of the English land-owners and the poverty of Irish farmers find expression in the schools established for their education, those of England being few, expensive, and exclusive, and those of Ireland numerous, public, and elementary.

The wealth of States affects the character of all their institutions of learning. When the procuring of the bare necessities of life engrosses the attention of the people, only the most elementary forms of education are possible for their children. The Southern States, from which the tide of war swept not only wealth but the producers of wealth, cannot largely use, much less sustain, such expensive, advanced, and specialized institutions as the circumstances of the North permit and require. The frontiersmen must have schools more elementary and more industrial in their nature than those of the cities and villages in the East. In accordance with this principle it is found that all of the institutions aided by the land grant in the Southern States, with two exceptions, have preparatory departments, or else require for admission proficiency in those studies only which are pursued in the public schools. Several of them also have normal departments. The characteristic feature of the schools of Kansas and Iowa is the prominence given to industries. The wealth of the patrons of agricultural colleges has also largely determined the place which manual labor occupies in them.

The sentiments prevalent in a State with reference to education have greatly influenced the legislatures in determining the objects for which the money intrusted to them for disposition by Congress should be expended. The States of the West had cherished the idea of building up within their borders universities which should be centers of learning. By their creation was realized what Mr. Cushing once called "a noble and beautiful idea of providing wise institutions for the unborn millions of the West, of anticipating their good by a sort of parental providence, and of associating together the social and territorial development of the people." Upon the title page of the register of an institution of this class is the following quotation:

One university, at least, should stand like a pillar of light in every State, the glory of the community and the constant object of its care, on which the watchful eyes of the State should be ever set, and to which its hand of bounty should always be extended. Bounty we have said, with all carefulness, instead of patronage; for such an institution patronizes the State far more than the State can patronize it.

For the establishment of these universities lands were set apart while the States were as yet only prospective Territories, and donations of money were made as needed. After the first establishment of the university almost yearly appropriations were made to it from the State treasury. The action of the legislature expressed the prevalent belief that the State university was the educational institution most needed, most beneficial, and therefore most worthy of public benefactions. It was in keeping with this idea that the fund placed at the disposal of the legislature should be turned in many cases toward the State university. Other arguments were not wanting. The general intelligence and elevation of the people is the most practical end of education. He who has learned to think has the key to success even in the industries; for thought can fertilize farms, produce beautiful fabrics, and give perfectness to every species of handiwork. To increase intelligence and nourish the power of thought is a burden which the university undertakes to bear in the education of the masses; therefore it should receive the funds donated for that purpose. Again, the university is an existing institution. It has buildings and apparatus especially designed for educational purposes. It has a corp of trained teachers. Consequently it can best promote the objects contemplated by Congress when it gave of the public domain for educational purposes. The real reason why the fund arising from the national land grant was in so many cases given to existing institutions was the belief that they were doing the work most valuable to the people, and that the attainment of the results they were accomplishing was the virtual object for which the aid was given rather than the compulsory establishment of schools for which the people were not prepared and of which the people might be suspicious. Whether this belief was sound or not is for individual judgment. It was not universal. Those believing in special training for a particular occupation were not lacking in strong arguments, and these had the letter of the Congressional act on their side. For such training separate institutions were required. The atmosphere of classical education was not congenial to this practical work. Mental discipline would be pitted against manual skill, theory against practice, culture against knowledge. In short, those who believed in the possibility of a special training for the common industries saw the necessity of providing institutions which could carry out the new and growing idea untrammelled by the antagonistic tendencies of classical education. A compromise between the two parties was in some cases effected. But where the champions of industrial training, pure and simple, prevailed, the institutions receiving the national aid had one dominating object, namely, the education of those engaged in agriculture or manufactures. In the education of the former class have been attempted (1) the education of young men who were inclined to agricultural pursuits; (2) the enlightenment of the community on agricultural subjects by means of lectures, written articles, and experiments; and (3) the establishment of a clearing house for agricultural information. The aid rendered to those pursuing the mechanic arts has been practically confined to the training of young persons in the leading branches of industry and in the principles underlying all of them. And the arts of the household, not being wholly unlike or less important than these, obtained in many schools a just recognition.

The Kansas State Agricultural College proposes to carry out the objects of its endowment in the following ways:

First. It teaches the sciences applied to the various industries of farm, shops, and home. Chemistry, botany, entomology, zoölogy, and mechanics are made prominent means of education to quick observation and accurate judgment. Careful study of the minerals, plants, and animals themselves illustrates and fixes the daily lesson. At the same time, lessons in agriculture and horticulture show the true applications of science.

Second. It gives a substantial education to men and women, among farmers and artisans, and in business life. Such general information and discipline of mind and character as help to make intelligent and useful citizens are offered in all its departments.

Third. It trains in the elements of the arts themselves, and imparts such skill as makes the hands ready instruments of thoughtful brains. The drill of the shop, garden, and farm is made a part of the general education to usefulness, and insures a means of living to all who make good use of it. At the same time, it preserves habits of industry and manual exertion and cultivates a taste for rural and domestic pursuits.

Fourth. It strives to increase our experimental knowledge of agriculture and horticulture. So far as means and circumstances permit, experiments are undertaken with a view to more definite results than ordinary experiments can give. At the same time, the students themselves are trained to a more accurate observation and judgment in such practical tests of principles in farming.

Fifth. It seeks to disseminate such practical truths as have stood the test of scientific inquiry. For this purpose it publishes the weekly *Industrialist;* and its officers share in the debates and consultations of farmers and horticulturists throughout the State.

Funds.—The principal source from which our colleges of agriculture and the mechanic arts derive an income is the endowment resulting from the land grant of 1862. Some colleges have received large appropriations from their States and munificent gifts from individuals. The amount of land given and the sum of money realized from it appears as follows in The Public Domain, by Thomas Donaldson:

Name and location of institution.	Amount derived from sale of United States land or scrip.	Number of acres received from the United States in land in place, or scrip in lieu, by the several States.
Agricultural and Mechanical College of Alabama, Auburn, Ala	$216,000	240,000, scrip.
Arkansas Industrial University, Fayetteville, Ark	135,000	150,000, scrip.
University of California, Berkeley, Cal	750,000	150,000, place.
Agricultural College of Colorado, Fort Collins, Colo *a*		90,000, place.
Sheffield Scientific School of Yale College, New Haven, Conn	135,000	180,000, scrip.
Delaware College, Newark, Del	83,000	90,000, scrip.
State Agricultural College, Eau Gallie, Fla. (location questionable; college not yet organized)	110,806	90,000, scrip.
Georgia State College of Agriculture and the Mechanic Arts, Athens, Ga. (department of University of Georgia)	243,000	
North Georgia Agricultural College, Dahlonega, Ga *b*		270,000, scrip.
Illinois Industrial University, Urbana, Ill	319,494	480,000, scrip.
Purdue University, La Fayette, Ind	212,238	390,000, scrip.
Iowa State Agricultural College, Ames, Iowa	500,000	240,000, scrip.
Kansas State Agricultural College, Manhattan, Kans	290,000	90,000, place.
Agricultural and Mechanical College of Kentucky, Lexington, Ky	165,000	330,000, scrip.
Louisiana State Agricultural and Mechanical College, Baton Rouge, La	(*c*)	210,000, scrip.
Maine State College of Agriculture and the Mechanic Arts, Orono, Me.	116,350	210,000, scrip.
Maryland Agricultural College, College Station, Md	112,500	210,000, scrip.
Massachusetts Agricultural College, Amherst, Mass	157,538	} 360,000, scrip.
Massachusetts Institute of Technology, Boston, Mass	78,769	
Michigan State Agricultural College, Lansing, Mich	275,104	240,000, place.
University of Minnesota, Minneapolis, Minn	*d*178,000	120,000, place.
Agricultural and mechanical department of Alcorn University, Rodney, Miss	113,400	} 210,000, scrip.
Agricultural and Mechanical College of the State of Mississippi, Starkville, Miss	115,000	
University of the State of Missouri:		
Agricultural and Mechanical College, Columbia, Mo	5,000	} 330,000, place.
School of Mines and Metallurgy, Rolla, Mo		
University of Nebraska, Lincoln, Nebr		90,000, place.
University of Nevada, Elko, Nev	90,000	90,000, place.
New Hampshire College of Agriculture and the Mechanic Arts, Hanover, N. H.	80,000	150,000, scrip.
Rutgers Scientific School of Rutgers College, New Brunswick, N. J.	116,000	210,000, scrip.
Cornell University, Ithaca, N. Y	602,792	990,000, scrip.
University of North Carolina, Chapel Hill, N. C	125,000	270,000, scrip.
Ohio State University, Columbus, Ohio	507,913	630,000, scrip.
State Agricultural College, Corvallis, Oreg		90,000, place.
Pennsylvania State College, State College, Pa	439,186	780,000, scrip.
Brown University, Providence, R. I	50,000	120,000, scrip.
South Carolina Agricultural College and Mechanics' Institute, Orangeburg, S. C.		180,000, scrip.
Tennessee Agricultural College, Knoxville, Tenn	271,875	300,000, scrip.
Agricultural and Mechanical College of Texas, College Station, Tex.	209,000	180,000, scrip.
University of Vermont and State Agricultural College, Burlington, Vt.	122,626	150,000, scrip.
Virginia Agricultural and Mechanical College, Blacksburg, Va	190,000	} 300,000, scrip.
Hampton Normal and Agricultural Institute, Hampton, Va	95,000	
West Virginia University, Morgantown, W. Va	90,000	150,000, scrip.
University of Wisconsin, Madison, Wis	244,803	240,000, place.

Total of 9,600,000 acres. In place, 1,770,000 acres; scrip, 7,830,000 acres.

a Prospective endowment is the Congressional grant to agricultural colleges, amounting in Colorado to 90,000 acres; not yet in the market.
b Receives annually from the University of Georgia $3,500, part interest of the land scrip fund.
c $327,000 of State bonds, scaled to $196,200 of new State bonds.
d Estimated.

There appears to be no ground for criticism of the financial management of the colleges of agriculture and the mechanic arts or of the other institutions receiving the benefits of the national land grant, since their organization, the selection of trustees and faculties, and the commencement of instruction. The sums originally obtained by the several States from the sale of their land scrip have remained unimpaired, with a few exceptions. In no State are the productive funds of the institution to which the national aid was allotted more than $5,000 less than the total proceeds of the land sales as given in a report made to Congress in 1875. In Kentucky and Maryland the exact sum realized and the amount of productive funds reported are the same. In Rhode Island the sum received is kept intact and separate, and its income used for scholarships.

The universities and colleges which have received the benefit of the grant have a total amount of funds largely in excess of the amount obtained from this source. How far they have kept this fund distinct from others cannot be answered by the data at hand. The amounts received by the institutions established or reorganized solely or primarily in furtherance of the purposes of the Congressional land grant have been largely augmented by individual donations and State appropriations. The original grant formed but a nucleus, around which funds for building purposes, for the purchase of libraries and educational appliances, for buying and stocking farms, have gathered. Sometimes the gifts have been princely; oftener they have been in accordance with the moderate fortunes of those for whose benefit the institutions were created. That such men have given is gratifying evidence of their favorable opinion of these institutions. But their gifts, though so acceptable, have not been sufficient to provide the expensive outfit which any school of applied sciences must have. As the president of the trustees of the Maine State College of Agriculture and the Mechanic Arts recently said:

How to establish and maintain colleges to promote the liberal and practical education of the industrial classes in the several pursuits and professions of life, and accomplish this in a manner to meet the exacting requirements of the times without the expenditure of a considerable amount of money, is a problem no board of trustees has ever been able to solve.

The expense of teaching theoretically the industries and the related sciences is no greater than that of teaching mathematics or languages. The average ratio between the expense of instruction in ten colleges and universities and their entire expenses in 1877–'78 was 67.2. It is the greater capital which must be unproductively invested that makes technical schools expensive. Shops, farms, laboratories, and museums are not furnished without large outlay. The shop of the Worcester Free Institute, three stories in height and covering an area of 6,600 square feet, is equipped with machinery and tools from cellar to roof. The basement of the building occupied by the Stevens Institute of Technology, having an area of nearly one-fourth of an acre, is well filled by machinery; the first story is largely occupied by laboratories and museums. Such extensive provisions do private technical schools deem necessary to the proper fulfillment of their work as teachers of the mechanic arts.

Public institutions cannot do similar work without similar opportunities and appliances. These have not been given the colleges of agriculture and the mechanic arts. No part of the national aid can be used for obtaining them. Complaints because the institutions receiving an annual stipend of a few thousand dollars do not occupy the same ground and afford the same facilities for mechanical instruction as munificently endowed polytechnic institutes, whose appliances have cost hundreds of thousands of dollars, and whose instruction is sometimes embraced in a single course, are unreasonable and unjust. Those institutions which have attempted instruction in the mechanic arts are doing good work considering their means and the numerous other branches of instruction to which they are required to give attention. Only one agricultural college has as great an amount of productive funds as the former of the institutions mentioned, and but four have as large an endowment as the latter.

The expensiveness of technical institutions is also shown by the amounts expended by foreign schools. For example, the annual expenditure of the Imperial Technical School of Moscow in 1878 was about $140,000; its receipts, $160,000; its capital, $2,030,000.

Reference has already been made to the ratio between the expense of instruction and the total expense of educational institutions. It is impossible to give this ratio, as it exists in agricultural colleges, with the accuracy which is necessary to give exactness and authority to the figures. The reported sums expended for all purposes and for the single purpose of paying salaries, and the per cent. which the latter is of the former are given by States in the following table:

States in which the several colleges are located.	Total expenses.	Expenses for salaries.	Per cent.
Alabama	$22,500	$17,600	78
Arkansas	17,500	15,500	89
Connecticut	45,118	40,816	90
Illinois	61,876	28,184	46
Indiana	33,213	15,957	48
Iowa	41,000	26,000	63
Kansas	18,000	8,000	44
Kentucky	27,000	16,000	59
Maine	16,885	10,068	60
Maryland	12,000	8,500	71
Massachusetts:			
Agricultural College	22,581	11,127	49
Institute of Technology	60,758	41,055	68
Michigan	29,000	18,000	62
Minnesota	49,000	30,000	61
Missouri:			
University	23,805	18,000	75
Agricultural College	8,600	6,000	70
New York	105,802	74,886	71
North Carolina	17,000	16,000	94
Ohio	48,526	26,461	55
Pennsylvania	30,000	12,457	42
Tennessee	30,884	19,800	64
Texas	19,280	12,000	62
Virginia:			
Agricultural College	21,000	14,000	67
Hampton Institute	32,500	20,000	61
Wisconsin	80,000	40,200	50

The lower percentages are due to expenditures during the year for which the report was made which were outside of the usual current expenses. For example, the Pennsylvania State College, during or near the time for which the above-mentioned outlay was made, devoted $10,000 to the heating of its building, $2,000 to the improvement and extension of its laboratories, and $5,000 to building a professor's house. A considerable share of the $22,581 expended by the Massachusetts Agricultural College was in ways not common to educational institutions, and which produced an income that contributed largely to the reduction of the net expenditure. Its farm account in 1881 exceeded $3,000, and the receipts from farm produce were $1,614; the botanical account was $2,326, while the income from plant-house and nursery was $2,481. Probably $15,000 of the $80,000 expended by the University of Wisconsin were expended for repairs and permanent improvements to buildings. The expenses of its experimental farm are also large. The Ohio State University paid into the State treasury nearly one-fourth of the money disbursed by it, which sum went to swell the permanent fund held by the State for the university. The Illinois Industrial University, Purdue University in Indiana, and the Kansas State Agricultural College are still growing institutions. They expend for growth as well as for continued existence. This and the industrial departments which they maintain account for the relatively small sums expended by them directly for instruction. Their wide variance from the average of $2 for instruction and $1 for contingent and current expenses is not indefensible; neither is the tendency of some institutions to the other extreme censurable. These are mostly southern colleges, where the present desideratum is the spread of elementary education among the masses rather than the higher and more technical education of professional men.

Faculties.—The faculties of the institutions under consideration are able, and when the income warrants they have a sufficient number of members to give instruction in all the branches which go to make up a practical education. Nothing need be said of those instructors whose work it is to teach languages, mathematics, philosophical sciences, and other branches not directly pertaining to industrial pursuits. Though more numerous, they occupy a field of labor not distinguished from that of ordinary college professors. The peculiar work of the colleges of agriculture and the mechanic arts is done by a comparatively small body of men, and is, in some particulars, unlike anything heretofore undertaken. Forty-three professors are known to this office to be giving instruction in agricultural science. Twelve of them are strictly professors of agriculture, and that alone. The remainder unite some other branch with agriculture or occupy chairs named after some allied science. Eight professors give instruction in chemistry and agriculture; four in horticulture and agriculture; six in botany and horticulture; three in botany, with special reference to agriculture; four in agriculture and natural history; four in entomology; and others occupy nominally chairs of horticulture, geology, and zoölogy, but do the work usually assigned to professors of agriculture. The practice of employing lecturers on topics of interest to farmers has not been generally pursued, though several institutions have done this. The New Hampshire College of Agriculture and the Mechanic Arts employs as lecturers men prominent in that State or in Vermont as successful farmers or as students of agriculture in some of its special departments. Each winter they deliver lectures in a continuous course, open to farmers as well as students. Much practical instruction is given by the several farm superintendents. Ability to impart information ought to be, and usually is, one of the qualifications sought in those who have charge of the work in the gardens and nurseries and on the farms. In some institutions the persons occupying these places are ranked as members of the faculty. In the State Agricultural College of Michigan six members of the faculty are in charge of departments of labor. They are the foreman and assistant foreman of the farm, the superintendent of the horticultural department, the foreman of the gardens, the vegetable gardener, and the florist.

Six colleges of agriculture have professors of veterinary science or special lecturers upon the subject.

The mechanic arts are not being taught in the majority of the institutions endowed with the national land grant. Fourteen professors give instruction in mechanical engineering, applied mechanics, industrial art, or industrial mechanics. Several of these are in charge of shops. In other schools the shops are in charge of separate individuals, so that the number of persons giving instruction in shop work is nearly or quite twice the number of professors in the departments of mechanics. In a single institution, the State Agricultural College of Kansas, there are four superintendents of industrial departments ranking as members of the faculty, which leads to the inference that they give instruction as well as oversee labor. Six professors of metallurgy and mining or chemistry, and about the same number in architecture, are to be counted as doing work as valuable and as industrial in character as that of the instructors in shop work or mechanical engineering.

It was not an easy task for the colleges of agriculture and mechanic arts to obtain instructors in the particular subjects engaging their attention. Especially was this the case when an efficient professor of agriculture was demanded. A theorist would not meet the expectations of those who sought practical results from professional training. An intelligent and successful farmer could not always adapt himself to the changed position which he would occupy as a professor of his favorite occupation. Foreigners might have had the kind of education which would fit a person for the position; but they labored under the disadvantage of having to deal with soils, climates, and systems of labor different from those of their own countries. Nothwithstanding these difficulties, there are instances of persons of foreign birth and education filling chairs of agriculture and kindred sciences with great ability and doing work acceptable to all interested parties. Yet the general rule was well stated by President Abbott, of the Michigan Agricultural College, in his remark that—

Professors of agriculture, agricultural chemistry, and horticulture had to be made, or, rather, in the face of adverse criticism, with every failure through inexperience open to the world, to make themselves.

The hindrances to obtaining suitable professors of agriculture are now removed. The disciples of the pioneers in agricultural instruction long since began to take up the work of their predecessors, and the graduates of the leading schools of agriculture have received a training which is sufficient to make them capable of giving instruction in all the work of the farm and conducting its practical operations. Many have gone out to fill these places in the agricultural schools of our own country, and some have carried the benefit of their training to other nations. Two of the professors in the Japanese Agricultural College are graduates of the Massachusetts Agricultural College.

Students.—Many remarks are made about the number of students pursuing the technical studies pertaining to agriculture and the mechanic arts that are based upon partial and sometimes untrustworthy information. It is impossible for the best informed to make complete and satisfactory statements on this delicate yet important matter. The returns to this office, though made out as fully and correctly as statistical returns can be, do not point out all the particulars as to the classification of students in agricultural colleges, nor do their reports and catalogues show how many are pursuing studies directly preparatory to industrial pursuits. Some facts are shown. Nine institutions, having each a single course of study, were attended in 1880 by nearly 1,500 students. As there is more or less of agricultural instruction incorporated in their several courses, those in attendance upon these nine schools are in some measure students of agriculture, and in every sense they are preparing for industrial work. Twelve colleges give the number of students pursuing the special agricultural courses which they offer as 145. Eight institutions, having distinct courses in mechanical engineering or some other department of applied mechanics, are known to have 146 students pursuing these courses. Seven institutions report 92 students in chemistry; two have 91 students in mining and metallurgy; three have 27 students of architecture; one has a course in industrial art attended by 25 students; two report 9 students of mining engineering; and one has 6 taking a specific metallurgical course. The total number of students reported as in attendance in 1880, upon schools endowed by the national land grant was 6,039.

Tuition and scholarships.—The tuition fees of the agricultural colleges are in most cases nominal. They are given in the statistics found in Appendix B, and few comments are necessary. There are a few colleges only in which there are fees, other than those for incidentals, which are not covered by scholarships. Exceptions are found in the institutions located in Connecticut, Massachusetts, and Vermont. All the students in Cornell University pursuing prescribed courses in agriculture and intending to complete the same are granted free tuition; and provision is made for the admission of one student from each of the assembly districts of the State. The appointee is selected by means of a competitive examination. Thus 128 of the most scholarly youth of the State may enjoy the privileges of the university free of charge.

The mode of assigning scholarships and the help they furnish are worthy of further illustration, although the usual practice is simply to remit tuition to those desiring to be relieved of that expense. In North Carolina the commissioners of each county may select annually a native of the State, resident in the county, possessing ability and good character, and being in indigent circumstances; and he "shall be admitted to any classes in the university for which he may be prepared, free of all charges for tuition and room rent." The first section of the act authorizing the appointment of students to Purdue University, Indiana, and defining their privileges therein, is as follows:

The board of commissioners of each county in this State may appoint, in such manner as they choose, two students or scholars to Purdue University, who shall be entitled to enter, remain, and receive instruction in the same, upon the same conditions, qualifications, and regulations prescribed for other applicants for admission to or scholars in said university: *Provided, however,* That every student admitted to said university by appointment by virtue of this act shall in nowise be chargeable for room, light, heat, water, janitor, or matriculation fees, and said student shall be entitled in the order of admittance to any room in the university then vacant and designed for the habitation or occupancy of a student; and such student so admitted shall have prior right to any such room, subject to the rules of the university, over any student not appointed and admitted as aforesaid.

In Kentucky each legislative representative district is allowed to send, on competitive examination, one properly prepared student each year, between the ages of twelve and twenty-five, to the State Agricultural and Mechanical College, free of tuition charge. The examination is held by a board appointed by the court of claims. Applicants are either those who come of their own choice or those selected by the trustees and teachers of the several common school districts, each district being entitled to send one. Preference is given in examination to energetic, moral, indigent young men. The words "properly prepared student" mean one who can pass a satisfactory examination in reading, writing, spelling, arithmetic as far as decimal fractions, geography, and English grammar.

A recent enactment of the legislature of Texas provided for the maintenance and instruction at the Agricultural and Mechanical College of three students from each senatorial district. The districts are thirty-one in number. One of the students was to be appointed by the senator and the other two by the representatives holding office within the district. One-half of the beneficiaries were to be compelled to take an agricultural course, and the other half a mechanical course of study. They are entitled to board, fuel, lights, washing, and tuition free of charge. The directors of the college, for the purpose of carrying the statute into effect, resolved to request the members of the legislature to determine their appointments by the results of a competitive examination, to require the applicants to be over sixteen years of age, and to assign the appointment of two students in agriculture and one in mechanics to the districts bearing odd numbers, and the appointment of two students in mechanics and one in agriculture to the districts bearing even numbers. In this institution the students reside in the college building and are charged for all their necessary living expenses and tuition at the rate of $130 a year. A similar arrangement is in force in the Maryland Agricultural College, the charges being $142.50 a year; and in the Hampton (Va.) Institute, the charges there ($70 for board and tuition) being met by scholarships. The prevalent custom among agricultural colleges is to furnish rooms at nominal cost, and in one of their buildings to furnish board at actual or estimated cost. Other ways of helping students to make satisfactory arrangements for board are practiced by various colleges. A dormitory accommodating seventy students is turned over rent free by the Ohio State University for the use of a university club. Board, furnished room, fuel, lights, and washing are supplied for less than $3 a week. A system of licensing boarding-houses has been adopted by the South Carolina College. Each house desiring a license must engage through a responsible proprietor, first, that a lady shall always preside at the table; second, that the meals shall be punctually furnished at prescribed hours; third, that intoxicating liquors shall not be furnished or permitted to be used in the house; and fourth, that misconduct will be reported and the house be kept subject to visitation by the faculty. In the Virginia Agricultural and Mechanical College there are two clubs occupying quarters in college buildings, called the farmers' mess and the mechanics' mess. The cost of board is in each reduced to a minimum of five or six dollars a month, room rent being free.

The students of agricultural colleges are encouraged in economy, not merely because their present circumstances require it, but because it will be necessary for them to practice it throughout their lives if they follow industrial pursuits and wish to secure a competence from the results of their labor. As President White, of Purdue University, said to the last graduating class:

> Extravagance in an industrial college is subversive of its chief purpose. Success on the farm or in the shop requires simple habits and wise economy in living, and the young farmer who has not learned this lesson has not completed his preparatory training. A thorough education unfits no one for industrial pursuits, but the acquiring of extravagant tastes and habits may render such an education of little practical value. The spending of money needlessly during four years of college life is certainly a poor preparation for the life of self-denial and thoughtful saving which awaits nine-tenths of our industrial students.

The aid rendered students in agricultural colleges by furnishing them rooms free of charge, and by helping them to accommodations of many kinds, is one reason why these institutions do not seem to be economically managed. Private institutions do little for their students beyond supplying instruction. Their rooms are rented at paying prices, and advantages gratuitously offered in the case of agricultural colleges are made a source of unreported revenues. The income of ordinary colleges and universities is much smaller, in comparison with the number of students in attendance, than that of the institutions endowed by the land grant. In three States, Maine, Massachusetts, and New Jersey, this rule fails. The average income per student of the colleges of Maine is only slightly in excess of that of the agricultural college. The average Massachusetts college has an income of nearly $300 per student, while its colleges of agriculture and the mechanic arts have only a little more than $170. In New Jersey the comparative incomes of the schools aided by the land grant and of other colleges do not materially differ. From seventeen other States sufficient data have been received to enable a comparison to be made between the amount of income per student received by both classes of institutions. In ten States the income per student of the endowed institution is more than double that of ordinary unaided colleges. There are two additional reasons for this apparent lack of economical administration besides the generous aid rendered to their students already mentioned. These are the character of the work done and the disinclination of private institutions to report their revenues. Single illustrations of both these reasons will suffice. In Massachusetts the income of scientific and industrial institutions of collegiate rank and not endowed by the land grant was nearly $450 per student in 1880, while the corresponding income of the colleges and universities is, as has been stated, in the vicinity of $300. The relative income per student in these classes of institutions in New Jersey is as $300 to $160. This goes to show that scientific and technical training under private administration is more expensive than classical instruction. In illustration of the second reason, namely, that private institutions are not willing to report their income, any State may be chosen. Taking Illinois as an example, it appears that the full incomes of only 18 of the 28 colleges in the State were reported to this office for 1879, while in only one case was the number of students withheld. If private institutions reported their financial condition as faithfully as they do the number of their students the ratio between students and incomes would be much nearer that existing in agricultural colleges than a casual observation of the figures upon which such ratios are usually based would indicate.

Graduates.—None of the colleges of agriculture and mechanic arts have a very large number of alumni. They have not been in existence twenty years, and many of them are of more recent origin. Consequently their graduates are still young, and many of them have not entered upon their permanent occupations. Large numbers have devoted themselves to teaching. In the South the call for teachers is urgent, and it is to the credit of the universities and colleges aided by the national land grant that they have sent out so many thoroughly equipped teachers. In the North and West the occupations chosen by graduates are various and largely industrial. Of 1,000 graduates of institutions located in Northern States, 168 are following agricultural or horticultural pursuits; 141 are teaching; 128 are engaged in civil engineering and similar work; 92 have gone into active mercantile life, and 85 are manufacturers. From these figures it is inferable that at least 60 per cent. of the living graduates of agricultural colleges are engaged in those pursuits which the aid given to their alma maters was intended to promote. The heads of institutions are inclined to estimate the proportion of graduates in industrial colleges even higher. The president of the Kansas State Agricultural College writes, "Of graduates, a few are teachers, and the rest farmers, business men, or mechanics." The graduates of the Maryland college are said to be devoting themselves to teaching and agricultural pursuits. The president of the board of trustees of the College of Agriculture and the Mechanic Arts in Maine, an institution eminently practical in its purposes and methods, makes the following interesting and significant statement:

Besides these (156 graduates) nearly 200 young men have had the benefit of its instruction from one term to three and one-half years, making an aggregate of 356 who have enjoyed its advantages more or less fully. As nearly as can now be ascertained, less than 12 per cent. of this number have entered, or are preparing to enter, the liberal professions. On the other hand, 88 per cent. have entered, or propose to enter, other employments. But few of them remain long unemployed after leaving the college. Many are at once sought for responsible positions—some of them before they have finished their course of study. They may be found on farms and in work-shops. Their services are sought as civil and mechanical engineers, surveyors, draughtsmen, foremen of shops, superintendents of mills, agents of business houses, instructors in technical departments of industrial institutions of other States, and in public schools.

The last report on graduates of the Hampton Normal and Agricultural Institute gives interesting statistics. There are 397 living graduates and *senior* under-graduates, a term which seems to be applied to those who left the institute during their senior year. Of this number 363 had been heard from directly. Nearly all had taught more or less, more than half of them in Virginia. One hundred and fifty-three own land or other property; 13 are pursuing studies at other institutions; 10 are in mercantile work; about the same number are clerks and book-keepers; 5 are carpenters; and a large number are scattered among a great diversity of employments. Of those owning land, 7 have above 100 acres; 18, from 50 to 100 acres; 4, from 20 to 50 acres; 14, from 5 to 20 acres; and 59, less than 5 acres. The value of property reported by 2 is $3,000 each; by 10, $1,000; by 17, from $500 to $1,000; by 16, from $200 to $500; and by 6, less than $200.

Courses of study.—The institutions which have received aid from the land grant of 1862 have either single prescribed courses of study or several courses from which a selection may be made. Those in Colorado, Kansas, Massachusetts (agricultural college), Michigan, Mississippi, New Hampshire, South Carolina, and Virginia belong to the former class. One of the schools in Virginia, the Hampton Normal and Agricultural Institute, has a course which embraces few studies not usually pursued in public schools of intermediate grades. Of the remaining eight institutions, six have four-years' courses and two three-years' courses. The studies pursued during the first year by one-half or more of these eight institutions are, algebra in 8 institutions; history, 7; geometry, 6; botany, 6; English studies, drawing, agriculture, 5 each; rhetoric, 4; arithmetic, physics, physiology, and book-keeping come next in order. During the second year the studies are more varied. Chemistry is prescribed by six institutions. Geometry, trigonometry, surveying, botany, and English studies are each pursued in five institutions; drawing and mechanics in four; algebra and agriculture in three; physics, mineralogy, zoölogy, literature, horticulture, entomology, and modern languages in two institutions.

In the third year chemistry is a part of the course of all the colleges. Agriculture (including horticulture) and mechanics are each prescribed by six institutions; English studies, by five; geometry, surveying, physics, geology, entomology, and physiology, by three.

Mental science and agriculture are studies common to the senior year of the six institutions, having single prescribed courses of four years in length. Logic is pursued in four; constitutional law, political economy, history, botany, geology, astronomy, veterinary science, and engineering in three each.

This statement shows the general scope of the instruction afforded by agricultural colleges of the kind under discussion. It reveals the fact that agriculture, mathematics, the natural sciences, and English branches have overshadowing prominence as departments of study, and that languages and practical mechanics (a far different thing from theoretical mechanics) are not receiving great attention. The course of study in the State Agricultural College of Colorado, which is outlined in Appendix A, is worthy of notice.

The direct industrial instruction afforded is most often in the line of agriculture and horticulture. The studies pursued in these subjects are not always given. Four of the colleges under consideration do not give an extended course in agriculture. Its principal subjects are presented by lectures, and agricultural chemistry is given a fair share of attention. In the State Agricultural Colleges of Kansas, Massachusetts, Michigan, and Mississippi agriculture is made a prominent and characteristic feature of the course. In Kansas its study is confined to the second and fourth years. In the second year stock-breeding, the cultivation of crops, implements and their use, drainage, and the history of agriculture are considered; in the fourth year stock feeding, rotation of crops, fertilizers, experimentation, and diseases of animals are among the subjects treated. Lectures are given on horticulture, forestry, pomology, and vegetable gardening. In the Agricultural and Mechanical College of Mississippi agricultural instruction is continued throughout the four years. All the leading subjects are presented at considerable length and with commendable thoroughness. In the State Agricultural College of Michigan agricultural chemistry, practical agriculture, horticulture, and landscape gardening are classed as separate departments of instruction, and all that is needed for proficiency in these branches of industry is taught. The formation and composition of soils; the nature and source of food of plants; chemical changes attending vegetable growth; the improvement of soils by chemical means and by the usual fertilizers; the chemistry of the dairy—these and similar topics form the course of work in agricultural chemistry. The subjects of study in practical agriculture, many of which have just been mentioned in connection with another institution, are brought before the students theoretically and practically. Horticulture receives special attention. All the work, from the location of the garden to the choice of a time and place of marketing its products, is carefully taught. The selection of sites for orchards, the kind of trees to set out, pruning, the destruction of injurious insects, and the care of fruit are studied in the department of pomology. In the Massachusetts Agricultural College the instruction in agriculture and horticulture includes every branch of farming and gardening practiced in the State, and is both theoretical and practical. Each topic is discussed thoroughly in the lecture-room, and again in the plant-house or field, where every student is obliged to labor six hours a week, and may do additional work for wages if it does not interfere with his study.

Prominence has been given to the subjects pursued in institutions where no selection of courses and little or no opportunity for election of studies were allowed, because all the students in them take up the work prescribed, and become more or less familiar with the agricultural subjects presented. The number of these institutions is not as great as of those which offer an agricultural course as one of several open to the student. Few students in colleges of the latter class choose the agricultural course. Probably seventy per cent. of those who pursue systematically the study of agriculture in their collegiate course are found in the nine institutions of the former class. Yet there are at least twenty schools which have agricultural courses and one which provides a course in horticulture. The courses in agriculture are of a grade similar to that of regular college courses. They substitute agriculture for studies which may be omitted from a course without impairing its industrial value, or which are technical or professional in character. The remaining studies furnish a good general education, a foundation for a wide range of investigation in the departments of agriculture, and a facility in imparting and applying special knowledge. History, literature, mathematics, modern languages, and natural sciences form the ground-work of every course. The importance of these studies, their place in a liberal education, and the advantages which familiarity with them gives to persons of every calling are known to all intelligent men. All agricultural courses have a line of general studies such as has been indicated.

In the Royal Agricultural and Forestry Academy at Hohenheim, in Württemberg, [says Professor Runkle] the general studies include the elementary mathematics, with trigonometry and descriptive geometry, physics, and chemistry, and the natural sciences which apply in farming, fruit, and forest culture, and the raising and training of domestic animals. The practical studies include the history and literature of farming, farm productions in general, with special instruction relating to the culture of hops, grapes, fruits, and vegetables, the breeding, rearing, diseases and uses of domestic animals, the production of wool and silk, and bee culture, farm management, with practice in the drawing of plans and specifications for such management, and farm book-keeping. Farming technology is taught through practice.

The studies which are considered by Mr. J. Scott Russell as necessary to an agricultural education are the following:

Farming knowledge.	Technical teaching.
Nature of soil	Surface geology.
Structure of plants	Anatomical botany.
Food of plants	Physiological botany.
Manures	Agricultural chemistry.
Structure and constitution of animals	Comparative anatomy.
Rearing of animals	Animal physiology.
Diseases of animals	Veterinary medicine and surgery.
Laying out of farms	Land surveying.
Draining and irrigating	Surveying and levelling.
Gates and fences	Practical mechanics.
Construction of farm buildings	Agricultural economics and plan drawing.
Improvement of seeds and breeds	Agricultural geography.
Ploughs, wagons, implements	Theoretical mechanics.
Steam engines and machinery	Elements of mechanism.
Fruit trees and timber	Technical botany.

The course of study for graduation in agriculture in the Virginia Agricultural and Mechanical College requires four years of English studies and of mathematics; three years of agriculture and horticulture and of history; two years of chemistry and of French or German; and one year or less of natural philosophy, book-keeping, drawing, geology, and mineralogy, botany, zoölogy, and moral philosophy.

The peculiar studies of an actual agricultural course are not matters of common knowledge with the people, either as to the extent to which they are pursued or the preparation they give for farm work, and information on these points is difficult to obtain. A few facts have been brought out with regard to the extent to which agriculture is taught in the United States by special courses.

Twenty-one institutions endowed with the national land grant offer twenty-three courses in agriculture. Seventeen of the twenty-three are four years in length, four are three years, one is five years, and one two years. Of the seventeen having courses four years in length, seven introduce agricultural studies into every year of the course, four require one year of general study before special branches are taken, five two years, and one three years. Of the four courses which are three years in length, one only has any part exclusively devoted to general study. The agricultural instruction given in those institutions in which it is continuous during four years includes nearly every subject taught in connection with agriculture. Shorter courses either omit some branches or abridge instruction in them. None of them bears any marked similarity to any other. No relation seems to have been discovered between one branch of agricultural study and another by which some classification of them for the purposes of consecutive study can be made. The studies found in senior year in one college are almost as often in the freshman year of others. The topics pursued during freshman year by the greatest number of institutions are general agriculture, entomology, horticulture, and agricultural botany; in sophomore year horticulture, landscape gardening, agricultural chemistry, agricultural botany, and animal anatomy and physiology; in junior year farm economy and management, veterinary science, rural law, farm machinery, crops, and farm engineering; in senior year, rural economy, rural architecture, history of agriculture, botany, horticulture, and chemistry.

Manual labor is required of the students in several agricultural colleges. In the State Agricultural College of Colorado they are required to spend at least two hours of each day in labor on the farm or in the shop, under the direction of their instructors. A labor system is connected with the course in agriculture of Purdue University, Indiana, by which each student is to labor two hours daily in the experimental field, green-house, or campus, during the fall and spring terms, while in the winter term an abbreviated course in the mechanic shop is provided, consisting of wood-work and iron-work, in which forge-work is made a leading feature.

One hour of daily practice is required in the industrial departments of the Kansas State Agricultural College. Students are encouraged to work more, and most of the labor needed on the farm and in the garden, shops, and offices is performed by students. Nearly all of it is under the direction of superintendents, and is instructive. The provisions with regard to manual labor in the Maine State College of Agriculture and the Mechanic Arts are as follows:

> The maximum time of required labor is three hours a day for five days in the week. In the lowest class the students are required to work on the farm, and they receive compensation for their labor according to their industry, faithfulness, and efficiency, the educational character of the labor being also taken into account. The maximum price paid is ten cents an hour. The labor is designed to be, as much as possible, educational, so that every student may become familiar with all the forms of labor upon the farm and in the garden. The students of the three upper classes carry on their principal labor in the laboratory, the drawing-rooms, the work-shops, or in the field, and for it they receive no pecuniary consideration, since this labor is of a purely educational character.

In the Massachusetts Agricultural College six hours a week of work in the plant-house or field are required. In the Michigan State Agricultural College all the students labor three hours daily, except when exempt on account of physical disability. (See appendix A.) The same rule exists in the Agricultural and Mechanical College of Mississippi. The labor is arranged as far as practicable to illustrate studies and lectures. The junior class generally is assigned work in the gardens and orchards and on the grounds, the sophomore class on the farm, the freshman and senior classes on the farm or in the garden, or wherever their studies may find best illustration. The Agricultural Colleges of South Carolina and Virginia require manual labor. The trustees of the Iowa Agricultural College have made the following rules regulating manual labor:

(1) The manual labor required by law of students in the college is divided into two kinds, viz: uninstructive labor, which shall be compensated by the payment of wages; and instructive labor, which shall be compensated by the instruction given and the skill acquired.

(2) Uninstructive labor shall comprise all the operations in the work-shop, garden, upon the farm, and elsewhere in which the work done accrues to the benefit of the college and not to the benefit of the student. Instructive labor shall embrace all those operations in the work-shop, museum, laboratories, experimental kitchen, upon the farm and garden, in which the sole purpose of the student is the acquisition of skill and practice.

(3) Students shall engage in instructive labor in the presence and under the instruction of the professor in charge. * * *

(4) The labor furnished by the school of agriculture, of veterinary science, and of engineering is given by each exclusively to its own special students.

Manual labor has a large place in the system of instruction of the Hampton (Va.) Normal and Agricultural Institute. For the sake of discipline, as well as instruction, all its students are required to labor. Day scholars work an hour a day, without compensation, at such industries as may be assigned them. Boarding students usually work one school day each week and the whole or half of Saturdays. Suitable young persons who are eager for an education, but have not the means for procuring it, are furnished work and taught in the evening, so that they can be gaining some knowledge while accumulating the money necessary for pursuing a more complete course of study. The student earnings for the year ending June 30, 1881, were almost $25,000.

There are physical, mental, and moral results which are expected to come from manual labor. President T. C. Abbott, of the Michigan Agricultural College, enumerates the following: First, physical strength and endurance, which are necessary to the farmer, are promoted by it; second, a wide range of practice in farming, horticultural, and other practical operations is given; third, a working familiarity with the sciences whose principles are involved in the processes of agriculture is acquired; fourth, the opinion and the sentiment that farm labor is not degrading, and that labor and culture are not mutually incompatible, are inculcated. The benefits of manual labor in the State Agricultural College of Colorado are held to be financial aid, instruction in methods of work, health derived from regular exercise, and a correct idea of the importance of labor. Evidence of the propriety of giving manual labor a recognized place in agricultural colleges is furnished in that the institutions which have given it a permanent and prominent place have been eminently successful. Recently established agricultural colleges have adopted after due consideration the manual labor system, and persons who have had experience with the operation of the system and observation of its results are ready to testify in its favor.

A large part of the manual labor of students has been utilized in the work of agricultural experiment, and their laboratory practice has turned toward the solution of chemical problems of importance to the farmer. In either case the improvement of the student and the information of the public were objects to be attained. Agricultural colleges have commonly done more in the line of field experiments, under the direction of skillful superintendents, than in the determination of questions immediately answered by chemistry, except in the analysis of fertilizers. Where agricultural experiment stations have been maintained at State expense they have chosen the laboratory as their principal workshop. When the Connecticut agricultural experiment station was established in 1877 it was given not a farm, but a laboratory. Its first and prominent work was the analysis of fertilizers. The testing of seeds, the analysis of feeding-stuffs, the relation of soils to water, and the improvements of methods of agricultural analysis were soon made subjects of experiment. The work required of the North Carolina experiment station was the analysis of fertilizers, minerals, mineral waters, well waters, articles of food and drugs, and the examination of cases of supposed poisoning. The station has also analyzed marls and chemicals used in composting, identified plants and insects to ascertain their useful or injurious character, and tested the germinating power of seeds. The results of such work done originally for individuals and of investigations of general interest have been given to the public, and thereby the station has become an educational agency.

The New Jersey agricultural experiment station is located in connection with the Rutgers Scientific School at New Brunswick. It is actively engaged in benefiting practical and scientific agriculture and encouraging land improvement in the analysis of soils and fertilizers, in the trial of experiments, and the publication of bulletins and reports.

The field experiments conducted under the supervision of agricultural colleges are directed principally toward the determination of questions relating to grains, roots, and forage plants. The varieties which are the most hardy and productive are ascertained. Various methods of culture, including the preparation of the soil and the time and manner of sowing and harvesting, are tried. The effect of different fertilizers and different soils is determined. Experiments are extended from the feeding of plants to the feeding of animals, and the comparative effects of early and late cut hay, of grass and other forage plants, of roots and grain, and of different grains are noted. The manufacturing processes of agriculture, dairying, sugar-making, &c., are experimented upon in several States. Irrigation and forestry receive a large share of attention in parts of the West. In fact there are few subjects affecting the farmer which have not been investigated and experimented upon in our colleges of agriculture. The work has been done at points scattered over the country and representing every variation in soil, temperature, moisture, and elevation; it consequently renders service to all kinds and sections of country. It has been done systematically and exactly. The methods of experimenting have been a miniature of the way in which agricultural knowledge is obtained. But instead of rough guesses there have been exact measurements. Instead of memory of circumstances there has been a record kept. Instead of hasty and prejudiced conclusions there have usually been deliberate judgment and impartial opinions. In this way many economical truths are quickly and correctly ascertained by which the farmer who intelligently applies them is saved from disastrous experiment and directly educated in his occupation.

The courses of study in the mechanic arts are not characterized by irregularity and diversity, but possess unity of plan and systematic arrangement. They embrace the courses in mechanical engineering, chemistry, mining, and metallurgy, and a few individual courses in industrial art, architecture, and kindred branches. Fourteen endowed institutions teach mechanical engineering or its equivalent. Two of them have no shops or mechanical appliances, and incorporate instruction in mechanics with a civil engineering course modified for the instruction of those wishing to engage in mechanical engineering. Four of them confine the professional studies to two years; five have courses in which technical studies are pursued for three years, and three have courses four years in length, with special studies and practice throughout. The scope of instruction in this branch of mechanic arts is indicated by the courses which are given at length in Appendix A. The practical work presents points of interest which may be properly noticed at some length. Ten institutions, at least, have shops and unite theory and practice in training for mechanical pursuits. Two others have more or less mechanical apparatus. The shop practice of the ten institutions which are known to give prominence to practical work may be considered in an order corresponding with the alphabetical arrangement of the States in which the several institutions are located.

A department of mechanics and drawing was opened in September last in the State Agricultural College of Colorado. A building has been erected and shops for bench-work in wood and iron and for forging have been equipped. The full furnishing of the department will be pushed forward rapidly, so that students may complete a course in mechanics similar to that provided in eastern schools.

In the Illinois Industrial University the student of mechanical engineering receives practice in five shops which are devoted to (1) pattern-making, (2) blacksmithing, (3) molding and founding, (4) bench-work for iron, and (5) machine tool-work for iron, respectively. In the first the practice consists of planing, turning, chiselling, and the preparation of patterns for casting. The shop has a complete set of tools, benches, and vises. The common operations of blacksmithing are undertaken in the second shop, and those of casting in the third. In the fourth shop there is first a course of free-hand bench-work, and afterward the fitting of parts is undertaken. In the fifth shop all the fundamental operations on iron by machinery are practiced. The actual work done is carefully outlined beforehand by drawings; and the designing of machines and their elements is required.

The school of mechanics of Purdue University offers the kinds of practice mentioned above. The course is taken in the freshman and sophomore years. Relatively more time is devoted to simple carpentry. The shop contains five benches for wood-working, with as many complete sets of tools, and machines for iron-work, such as lathes, planers, drill-presses, and emery-grinders. All the tools requisite for the work to be performed are supplied.

In the Iowa Agricultural College shop practice is required during freshman, junior, and senior years. The work of freshman year is of a general character, and occupies only two hours a week. No regular course is prescribed for the other years. An original design of a machine must be made, but it is not stated that the machine must be constructed.

In the Maine State College of Agriculture and the Mechanic Arts there are two shops equipped according to the Russian system, and work in them is required of all who take the course in mechanical engineering. In the second term of sophomore year a course in forge-work is given, by which familiarity with the methods in use in actual construction is gained. A similar course in vise-work is given in junior year. The facilities for practice are being increased as funds for the purpose are obtained.

In the Massachusetts Institute of Technology there is a course of two years in mechanic arts designed for those who have received a grammar-school education and wish to enter as soon as possible on industrial pursuits. The shop-work of the first year embraces carpentry and joinery, wood-turning, pattern-making, and foundry-work; of the second year, iron-forging, vise-work, and machine tool-work; the students in the course of mechanical engineering are required to devote considerable time to these kinds of work. It is intended that they shall learn principles rather than construct machines.

The shop practice in the department of mechanic arts of Cornell University embraces work requiring the use of all hand-tools and of the machines ordinarily employed in machine-shops, and requires two hours daily of the student of mechanic arts. The department occupies a three-story building and basement, 42 by 110 feet, with an engine-house, a brass and iron foundry, and a stereotype foundry in immediate connection. The first floor of the main building is occupied by a machine-shop and printing-office; a part of the basement by a forge-shop. The cost of the building and equipments was about $42,000. Among the equipments are hand and lathe tools of the usual kinds; instruments for mechanical experiments, and a collection of drawings from those of technical schools abroad. The instruction is given by two professors, one assistant, and one foreman. Skilled workmen are also to be employed.

The Ohio State University requires of students in the mechanical course three terms of elementary practice in the use of tools and one term of machine construction. The laboratory has been equipped recently, and this branch of industrial instruction is receiving increased attention.

The Agricultural and Mechanical College of Texas, which has recently been reorganized with reference to practical work in agriculture and mechanic arts, has a shop fitted up as completely as the State appropriation for the purpose would permit. A sufficient variety of tools has been furnished to enable the student to receive practice in carpentry, wood turning and sawing, vise-work, the operating of metal-working machinery, and steam engineering. The prescribed course of shop-work covers two years, and the work of the third year may be conformed to the student's chosen line of investigation.

The University of Wisconsin introduced a course in mechanical engineering in 1877, and a shop was provided and equipped. Practice is continued throughout four years. Machines are constructed and a variety of profitable work done, as well as many processes learned solely for their illustrative and disciplinary value.

Methods of shop-work are either instructive or constructive. The instructive method proceeds on the theory that there are certain elementary operations underlying the important branches of mechanical labor, and that skill in these opens the way for the ready acquisition of the minor details which make up the differences between trades. These elementary operations are classified according to their simplicity and their interdependence. The scientific principles which control their performance and the work itself are taught to classes by lectures and recitations, and the actual work is illustrative of the theoretical instruction. The fundamental idea of the constructive method is that completed work must be done by the student in order that his training shall be practical; therefore he is given work in the construction of machines or other articles of use, and is taught how to perform each branch of the work as it is reached, and is helped over difficulties which are actually in his way.

The instructive method is adopted in the main by the Russians in their system of instruction in mechanic arts. The principles which underlie this system are concisely stated by Prof. J. D. Runkle, of the Massachusetts Institute of Technology, as follows:

The ideas involved in the system are, first, to entirely separate the *art* from the *trade*, the *instruction* shops from the *construction* shops; second, to teach each art in its own shop; third, to equip each shop with as many places and sets of tools, and thus accommodate as many pupils as the teacher can instruct at the same time; fourth, to design and graduate the series of sample to be worked out in each shop on educational grounds; and, fifth, to adopt the tests for proficiency and progress.

The elementary operations are performed in their natural order and place, and learned not by themselves as isolated facts, but in their relations to each other and to details.

The number of institutions endowed with the national land grant which have special courses in chemistry is ten. They are mostly located in the East. This branch of instruction is of prime importance to those contemplating manufactures involving the use of compounds, and such industries are more developed in the North and East than in the South and West. Those institutions in the latter sections which have undertaken to give thorough chemical instruction are to be commended. By so doing they are contributing powerfully to the wealth of the State and the prosperity of its people. The work of those institutions which have special courses in chemistry is presented in Appendix F.

Mining and metallurgy are given special prominence in at least seven institutions endowed with the national land grant. The courses of instruction in these branches is outlined in the statements of work done by individual institutions as given in Appendix A. Into these courses, history, literature, political economy, and the branches of law connected with mining are introduced for the sake of the culture and information they afford. French and German have a place, as familiarity with them is necessary in order that the engineer may avail himself directly of the many valuable treatises and reports on engineering published in those languages. Leading branches of natural science, and particularly those which treat of minerals, are taught in all the schools. The courses differ chiefly in the kind and extent of purely technical study.

The course in mining engineering in the Alabama Agricultural and Mechanical College is three years in length, two of which are undergraduate, one graduate. The studies of the undergraduate years are not very different from those of the course in civil engineering. In the first year of professional study (the junior) laboratory work is taken by the students in mining, and the drawing and engineering study done by them differs slightly from that done by the civil-engineer students. The next year the courses differ chiefly in the kind and amount of scientific study and in the substitution of laboratory work for engineering studies. A statement of the course of study for the graduate year has not been received.

The Illinois Industrial University affords training in mining engineering and in metallurgy. The student of mining engineering takes the course in civil engineering, substituting for special studies not closely related to their profession portions of the metallurgical course. This latter does not differ greatly from the chemical course. The assaying and analysis of ores, and the analysis of metallic compositions, mineral waters, and coal are undertaken in place of work less important to the metallurgist. Provision is made in the general laboratory for metallurgical and assaying laboratories, with stamp-mill, furnaces, and other apparatus required for practical instruction.

In the Sheffield Scientific School, New Haven, Conn., those wishing to become mining engineers go through the regular course in either civil or mechanical engineering, and then devote a year to studies fundamental to the education of a mining expert.

The Ohio State University has a course in mining engineering. The studies of the first three years are nearly in common with the other engineering courses. Considerable time is devoted in the third year to metallurgy. In the last year the studies are distinctly professional, including theory of veins, mining, coal-washing, and the mechanical treatment of ores, metallurgy, assaying, mineralogy, and blow-pipe analysis, strength of materials, and plans, specifications, and estimates for metallurgical works. It is intended that the course shall secure to the student careful instruction in mining and in the preparation and metallurgical treatment of ores.

The University of Wisconsin offers special courses in mining engineering and metallurgy. The student that has pursued the civil engineering course for two years may choose either of them at the commencement of junior year. The studies of the mining engineering course are chiefly higher mathematics, theoretical and applied mechanics, physics, civil engineering, drawing, and geology. Mining engineering proper is taught during the last two terms of the senior year. The metallurgical course is principally composed of chemical work. Metallurgy itself is taught during the fall and winter terms of the senior year. The subjects taken up in order are general principles, fuels, furnaces, and metals. Excursions are made to smelting establishments and descriptions of actual operations required. Assaying is taught during the spring term of junior year to the students in mining engineering and metallurgy. The assay laboratory is provided with tables for eighteen students, six crucible furnaces, two roasting furnaces, two large muffle furnaces for cupellation and scorification, a Blake crusher, bullion rolls, &c. The laboratory work is so extensive that he who completes it is deemed an expert in assaying.

The college of mining of the University of California is intended to give thorough professional training in mining engineering. The full course leading to the degree of mining engineer is six years in length. The first two years are nearly the same as those of other scientific colleges. The instruction of the next two years is more directly connected with mining. The scientific studies are taught as far as possible with direct reference to their connection with mining and metallurgy. The last two years are post-graduate, and the course of study is yet to be perfected. The metallurgical laboratory furnishes the best facilities for assaying and metallurgical practice, and various collections aid the student by illustrating collateral branches of study.

The University of Missouri has a department, called the School of Mines and Metallurgy, located not at the same place as the university, but to the southward from it, at Rolla, in the district in which iron, lead, and zinc abound. Several courses of study, each three years in length, are provided, all of them giving prominence to studies in mining and metallurgy. The course in mining engineering is the standard one of the school. The others are identical with it during the first year and similar to it in many respects during the other two years. The engineering itself is taught principally by lectures and field practice, and the operations of metallurgy are performed in the laboratory.

In the Massachusetts Institute of Technology there are three courses of study which deal with mining. They are styled the courses in mining engineering, in geology and mining, and in metallurgy. The technical studies of each extend over three years. The special instruction in mining consists of a course of eighty lectures, delivered to students in the third year, on the general character of the various deposits of useful minerals and on the theory and practice of mining operations. In the fourth year, ore-dressing and metallurgy are taken in a course of sixty lectures, accompanied by a series of continuous practical exercises in the concentration and smelting of ores in the mining and metallurgical laboratories.

It has been the aim in outlining the instruction given in agricultural colleges to show what opportunities are afforded by them as a body for the acquirement of training for industrial pursuits. Agriculture, mechanics, chemistry, and mining have been considered in turn, and it has been seen that there are numerous schools in which each subject receives marked attention. To some the results of these national schools of science seem meager and discouraging. They are unwilling to wait for harvest, until there has been time for growth and ripening. The space between sowing and reaping is too wide for their patience. The truth of this is seen in movements that hasten to maturity more rapidly than can a new system of schools and a new line of education. A single score of years measures the life of these schools, a period not long compared with the time in which education has been coming to its present advancement, and none too long for a satisfactory trial of methods and studies. Earlier conclusions did not carry that weight which those reached now will have. Individual minds cannot but be convinced by the facts of this report that great benefits have accrued from the investment of public and private wealth in these schools. Certainly scientific training and investigation have been promoted as in no other way. Improved methods of instruction and enlarged facilities for experiment have been introduced by their influence and example. Theory has been more largely supplemented by practice. Abstract rules are learned by their application to practical affairs. The larger part of the technical training in this country at present is being done by institutions which have been stimulated, if not established, by national aid. They are paying the just debt with ample interest by sending out men and women to develop, utilize, and economize the resources of the country; to maintain the fertility and increase the productiveness of its fields; to construct and control its machinery; to improve its manufactures, augment their variety, and lessen their cost; and to bring its untold mineral wealth into the use of its people.

Section 2.

INDUSTRIAL EDUCATION IN SCHOOLS OTHER THAN THOSE ENDOWED WITH THE NATIONAL LAND GRANT.

SCHOOLS OF SCIENCE.

Besides the schools endowed by the national land grant, there are some thirty other schools and collegiate departments furnishing similar instruction. Extended statements concerning a few schools representative of this class are given in Appendix C, viz: The Worcester (Mass.) Free Institute, the Stevens Institute of Technology at Hoboken, N. J., and the Polytechnic and Manual Training Schools of Washington University, Saint Louis, Mo. A statement of the condition of industrial and technical education in the institutions of this class not named above, and other facts concerning these institutions which have a bearing upon the same subject, are briefly given below.

In San Francisco, Cal., there is an institution, conducted by the private enterprise of A. van der Naillen, for practical instruction in the departments of engineering, assaying, &c. There are 4 instructors, and usually from thirty to fifty students, many of them women. The several courses are wholly directed toward the immediate attainment of practical knowledge of the studies pursued, the time spent in the school being usually only a few months.

The State School of Mines, recently established at Golden, Colo., aims to adapt itself to the mining and metallurgical interests of that State. It is dependent on the State for its support, and received an appropriation of the proceeds of a State tax of one-fifth of a mill, amounting to $10,000 in 1880. The faculty has 7 members, and the students in attendance, 1880, numbered twenty-six, many of whom were ladies. Tuition is $20 a term, or $60 a year. There are two regular courses of study, one in mining engineering and one in metallurgy, each covering three years, and facilities are offered to those wishing to pursue special courses of similar study.' The school possesses a good library of standard scientific works, and is liberally provided with apparatus for regular work and for experimental illustration. A museum is in process of formation with a special department representative of the fossils and minerals of the State.

The Rose Polytechnic Institute has the following history: About twelve years ago Mr. Chauncey Rose, of Terre Haute, Ind., placed over half a million dollars in the hands of ten trustees for the endowment of an educational institution at that place. His only restrictive provision was that the school should be "for the promotion of technical education." He instructed the trustees to obtain the best light they could and then decide upon the character and scope of the school. European and American schools and methods were examined, and the conclusion reached was that the Worcester Free Institute was the best model upon which to construct the institution. A site of ten acres was secured, and a shop and an administration building erected. The next move on the part of the trustees was to obtain a president for the school, who should take charge of the incipient institute. Prof. C. O. Thompson, principal of the Worcester Institute, was decided upon, and, after several attempts, the trustees finally secured him. He will have personal supervision of equipping the shops, arranging a course of study, and purchasing a library, and of the details of organization. The institute has an annual income of $30,000 and reserve accumulations amounting to $75,000 which can be applied to the purchase of appliances.

The Boston University, Boston, Mass., announces that the place of its college of agriculture is supplied by the State Agricultural College at Amherst. A college of commerce and navigation is provided for by statute, and will be established as soon as the necessary funds shall be secured. The School of All Sciences connected with the university furnishes to specialists instruction in all the leading branches of advanced study.

The Massachusetts Normal Art School at Boston contributes largely to industrial education. It was established in 1873 for the purpose of affording opportunities for special instruction to those who intended to teach. There were at that time many who needed this instruction, as drawing had been recently included among the branches required to be taught in the public schools of the State, and free instruction in industrial or mechanical drawing was required to be provided by the larger cities and towns. The great obstacle to the carrying out of the law was the lack of suitable teachers. The training and influence of the normal school, under the management of Walter Smith, has been directed primarily to supplying this deficiency. Incidentally it has educated artists and designers and assisted in bringing art education into popular favor.

The attendance upon the school has been large and generally increasing. In 1880-'81 it was 294. Of these 179 ladies and 43 gentlemen attended the day classes, 32 ladies and 40 gentlemen the evening classes. The students now enter better prepared than formerly for the work of the school. This is a natural result of a general introduction of drawing into the schools, and it has enabled the normal school to advance the course of study. A few years since an examination in free-hand drawing of ornament from copy and in object-drawing from the solid was required to be passed upon admission. The work of the first year was devoted to elementary drawing. The subjects of study of the other three years were, respectively, form, color, and industrial design, the constructive arts, and sculpture and design in the round. These groups could be taken in the order preferred by the individual student, if he showed fitness for the work required.

The school receives its main support from the State, from which it has received annual appropriations. That for 1880-'81 was $17,000. The school year is from October to May, inclusive.

Harvard University, Cambridge, Mass., has two departments especially contributing to industrial and technical education, viz: The Bussey Institution and the Lawrence Scientific School. The Bussey Institution is at Jamaica Plain, Boston, Mass., and has been in operation for about twelve years. Its object is to promote and diffuse a thorough knowledge of agriculture and horticulture, and it aims to prepare young men for work as practical farmers, gardeners, florists or landscape gardeners. The teaching corps consists of professors of applied zoölogy and of agricultural chemistry, instructors in botany, horticulture, entomology, and farming, and a demonstrator in zoölogy. The course of study covers three years, one of them preparatory, one devoted to the regular course of study in the school, and the last spent in advanced study and practical research in some of the departments of science which receive special attention. The aim of the teachers is to give the student a just idea of the principles upon which the arts of agriculture and horticulture depend; to teach him how to make intelligent use of the scientific literature which relates to these arts, and to enable him to make accurate observations and experiments, and draw correct conclusions therefrom.

The Harvard Book says:

During the second and third years agricultural chemistry, useful and ornamental gardening, agriculture, and applied zoölogy are taught at Jamaica Plain. Instruction is given by lectures and recitations, and by practical exercises in the laboratory and green-house, and by the inspection of field work. In order to give the student a sound basis for a thorough knowledge of these arts, instruction in physical geography, meteorology, the elements of geology, chemistry, physics, botany, zoölogy, entomology, leveling and road building is given the first year at the Lawrence Scientific School, Cambridge.

The object of this latter school is to give complete courses of instruction in the leading departments of science. It is richly endowed, having productive funds amounting to some $730,000, and an income of about $50,000. Its faculty comprises, besides the president, eleven professors, three assistant professors, four instructors, one tutor, and eight assistants. The attendance of students in 1881-'82 was 30. Ample provision for instructing teachers and special students is made. The teachers' courses of study are one year in length, and may be selected from the elements of natural history, chemistry, and physics. The instruction is mainly given in the laboratories and museums of the university. Every student is taught to make experiments and study specimens. No examination is required for admission. A very worthy class of students enter both in the teachers' class and as special students. The regular courses of study, each four years in length, are (1) civil and topographical engineering, (2) chemistry, (3) natural history, and (4) mathematics, physics, and astronomy. The facilities for illustration, experiment, and investigation afforded to students in any department of Harvard University are, as is well known, very complete.

The University of Michigan offers courses in civil, mechanical, and mining engineering, each four years in length. The course in civil engineering is laid out so as to embody a close imitation of the requirements of active labor. The courses in mechanical and mining engineering are in part similar to the civil engineering course, but include such a range of special studies as enables the graduate to enter understandingly upon the practice of his profession. The studies pursued in the earlier parts of the course by all students of engineering comprise, in mathematics, algebra, geometry, plane and spherical trigonometry, general geometry, and the elements of differential and integral calculus; in French and German, an amount covering in all about two years of study, the choice depending on the language presented on examination for admission; in English, a course in higher English grammar and composition; in physics and chemistry, the elementary principles; in drawing, practice in geometrical and mechanical drawing and the study of descriptive geometry. The special studies which predominate in the latter part of the courses in engineering are those commonly pursued. Practical work accompanies each course. A peculiar feature of the instruction is a course of lectures on naval architecture, discussing the resistance of ships, the power necessary to secure a given speed, buoyancy, stability, wave motion, steadiness, determination of center of gravity and metacenter, and similar topics. Instruction in analytical and applied chemistry is given by accomplished teachers, and supplemented by practice in the excellent and extensive laboratory of the university. Combinations of particular courses are recommended for those seeking proficiency in mineralogical and metallurgical chemistry, medical chemistry and biology, and sanitary chemistry, as well as in general chemistry. The report of Mortimer E. Cooley, U. S. N., professor of mechanical engineering, made to the regents of the university at the close of his first year of service, shows that the course was established in the autumn of 1881 that a complete school of engineering might exist in the institution. The facilities for giving the instruction belonging to this course were insufficient; the demand for it great. A legislative appropriation of $2,500 was devoted to the purpose; and with this sum and slight aid from the university and private individuals a building was erected and equipped with machine and hand tools, an engine, forge, furnace, and other fixtures. Though the shop is limited in size and in variety of furnishing, it is a starting point for improvements and additions.

The Chandler Scientific Department of Dartmouth College, Hanover, N. H., was organized in 1851, in compliance with the conditions of a bequest of $50,000 for the establishment and support of a permanent department or school of instruction in the college in the practical and useful arts of life, comprised chiefly in the branches of mechanics and civil engineering, the invention and manufacture of machinery, carpentry, masonry, architecture, and drawing, the investigation of the properties and uses of the materials employed in the arts, the modern languages and English literature, together with book-keeping and such other branches of knowledge as may best qualify young persons for the duties and employments of active life. No other or higher preparatory studies are to be required in order to enter said department or school than are pursued in the common schools of New England. A course of four years has been established to carry out, as far as possible, the intentions of the founder. Instruction is given by four professors, six instructors, a lecturer, and a tutor, and the number of students in attendance, according to the catalogue of 1881–'82, is 48, all men. The income of the school is derived from tuition fees, at the rate of $60 a year, and the interest on its productive funds, which now amount to $100,000. The department is well supplied with approved instruments for surveying and engineering, and its students have free use of the college libraries, cabinets, and general appliances.

The Thayer School of Civil Engineering is an institution, also connected with Dartmouth College, which furnishes an essentially post-graduate course in civil engineering extending over two years. It has a productive fund of $55,000; the faculty consists of a president, a professor, and three instructors. The success of its graduates bears testimony to the thoroughness of its instruction.

The John C. Green School of Science of the College of New Jersey, at Princeton, owes its existence to the munificence of the gentleman whose name it bears, his gifts to it having amounted to some $330,000. It was organized as a department of the college in 1873, and aims to give thorough training in science and art, together with a liberal course in certain academic studies, and opportunities for the special pursuit of prescribed departments of study. These departments are three in number, as follows: (1) a department of general science, in which after the second year there are elective courses providing special instruction in mathematics and mechanics, biology and geology, chemistry and mineralogy, also a select course in physics; (2) a department of civil engineering; (3) a department of architecture. The studies of each of these departments cover four years. The extensive laboratories and collections belonging to the college furnish the student ample means for illustration and practice. There were in 1880 twenty instructors and fifty-six students (all males) connected with the school.

The Cooper Union for the Advancement of Science and Art is an institution unique in character, alike from the sagacious beneficence which marks its projection, organization, and administration and the results which it is steadily achieving. The name of the founder, Peter Cooper, has deservedly become a "household word" wherever a broad philanthropy, a genuine uprightness, and a wise conception of human needs and the wants imposed by civilization are understood and recognized. There is little need of extended remark. Mr. Cooper's benefactions have reached nearly or quite $1,000,000. The Cooper Union is now in its twenty-fourth academical year, having been organized and opened in 1857. At that time property was transferred to it by Mr. Cooper which cost $630,226. Since that date Mr. Cooper has given $150,000 as a special endowment for a free library and reading-room. He has also added a story to the building, and by other donations has increased his gifts to nearly or quite the sum named. Since 1857 the trustees have expended in the educational work alone some $898,000, derived largely from the rent of stores and offices connected with the building. The expenditure reported for 1880 was $50,974.

The means of instruction and schools of the Cooper Union consist of (1) the free library and reading-room; (2) free lectures during the winter; (3) an evening school of science; (4) an evening school of art; (5) a day school of art for women; (6) a school of art for amateurs; (7) a school of wood-engraving; (8) a school of telegraphy. The last four are designed for women students; all are based on practical principles.

The evening school of science embraces fifteen classes or studies, extending the ordinary (English) common school education in the direction of mathematics, mechanics, engineering, and chemistry. It was attended in 1882 by 936 students. While liberty is given them to pursue any branches taught in the school for which they are fitted, a regular course requiring five years for its completion is arranged. The Cooper medal and diploma are awarded to those who successfully complete the course, which is as follows:

First year: algebra, geometry, natural philosophy, and elementary chemistry. Second year: algebra, geometry, elementary chemistry, and astronomy. Third year: trigonometry, descriptive geometry, analytical geometry, and mechanics. Fourth year: analytical geometry, differential and integral calculus, and mechanical drawing. Fifth year: engineering and analytical chemistry. The night school of art embraces classes in rudimental, mechanical, architectural, form, figure, perspective and ornamental drawing, decorative designing, drawing from cast, and modeling in clay. Lectures to the classes are also given. The number of students in 1882 was 1,227.

The day school of art for women is perhaps the best equipped institution for its purposes to be found in the United States. It occupies large and well-arranged rooms, furnished with casts, models, copies, &c., and the teachers possess the highest qualifications. The school contains departments of drawing, painting, normal teaching, photography, and wood engraving. The earnings of the pupils for the year under review are reported at $28,932. The number of students was 756 in the general studies and 150 in the pottery class. The school of telegraphy had 60 pupils. The Western Union Telegraph Company maintains a teacher in the school of telegraphy. Prang & Co., art lithographers, have given $750 per annum for a teacher to the normal drawing class.

The School of Mines of Columbia College, New York City, was established in 1864 for the purpose of furnishing young men the means of acquiring a thorough knowledge of those branches of science which form the basis of the important industrial pursuits. Its system of instruction included, for some time, five courses of study, viz: (1) civil engineering, (2) mining engineering, (3) metallurgy, (4) geology and palæontology, (5) analytical and applied chemistry. A course in architecture has been added recently. The plan of instruction includes lectures and recitations, practice in the chemical, mineralogical, blowpipe, and metallurgical laboratories, and in operative mining; field surveying, projects, estimates, and drawings for the establishment of mines and for the construction of metallurgical and other works; and reports on mines, industrial establishments, and field geology. Each course is four years in length. A large amount of vacation work is done. Each student is expected to visit mines, metallurgical and chemical establishments, and to hand in on his return a memoir, with collections illustrating it. A class in practical mechanical engineering is formed for the vacation of students entering the third year of that course; one in mining for students entering the fourth year of the course in mining engineering; and in geodesy for those equally advanced in the civil engineering course. The class in mechanical engineering in 1881 visited iron works in the city, studying closely the machinery, processes, and methods used. It was limited to twenty members. The class in mining visited the copper mines of Lake Superior and the Marquette iron region of Northern Michigan. The professor in charge drew up a plan of study for both the copper, and the iron mines. The work outlined for the copper region required three weeks for its completion, and included the study of drifting and sinking with machine drills, stoping of copper rock, handling, breaking, and assorting copper rock, timbering, pumps, surface works, shops, stamping of copper rock, concentration of coarse and fine sands by jigs, and treatment of fine sands and slimes. The outline of work in the iron region was also elaborate.

The number of students in mining engineering in 1881–'82 was 111; in civil engineering, 28; in analytical and applied chemistry, 35; in architecture, 2. The first class, which pursues studies preparatory to the special courses, contained 95 members. The total attendance was 275. The degrees conferred are engineer of mines, civil engineer, and bachelor of philosophy.

The School of Civil Engineering of Union College was founded in 1845, for the purpose of giving such instruction in the theory and practice of civil engineering as will fit students for immediate usefulness in the field and in the office. Its faculty consists of a president, nine professors, and a registrar. Its students in 1880 numbered 26. The course of study is completed in four years, and gives special prominence to mechanical draughting, instrumental field work, and numerical calculation. The collection of appliances for illustration is extensive, and facilities for practical work are ample. Students are admitted to all the departments of the college without extra charge. Among these is the department of general culture and of fine art, in which instruction and practice in decorative landscape and figure drawing are afforded, as well as general instruction respecting sculpture, painting, and architecture.

The Rensselaer Polytechnic Institute, Troy, N. Y., offers a course of study in civil engineering extending over four years, and embracing a great variety of subjects, including mechanical, mining, and other forms of engineering. During each summer vacation it is intended, also, to give qualified persons a six-weeks' course in assaying. The institute has a faculty composed of 10 professors, 2 instructors, and 4 assistants, and reported in 1880 104 students and 739 graduates. The appliances for illustration and practice are very complete, and include an observatory, chemical and metallurgical laboratories, collections of birds, shells, minerals, &c., and approved apparatus in all departments of study. The long and successful career of this institute has given it a wide and honorable reputation, so that students come to it from the most distant nations of the world.

The Ohio Mechanics' Institute of Cincinnati was established in 1829 for the purpose of furnishing educational aids to mechanics, manufacturers, and artisans. For many years it has sustained a reading room, courses of lectures, and evening drawing schools. The branches of drawing pursued are three in number, mechanical, architectural, and artistic. The course in mechanical drawing is designed for machinists, founders, blacksmiths, and the like, and was taken by 117 students in 1881–'82; that in architectural drawing is for builders and those in their service, and attendance the last session was 58. The class in artistic drawing did not attract persons of any particular employments, but enrolled 78 from various stations and occupations. About two years ago there was a department of science and art created. Its work has been the publication of a scientific journal in which to publish its own transactions and such other information as it may seem best to include, the arrangement of meetings for the discussion of questions in science, and the maintenance of evening classes in geometry and mathematics, and in elementary physics and mechanics. These classes are held on Monday and Thursday evenings, the former from 7 to 8.15 o'clock; the latter from 8.15 to 9.30. Instruction is given by lectures. The total expenses of the institute for 1881–'82 were $8,253.34. An effort is now being made to organize a complete school of technology in connection with the institute.

The Case School of Applied Science, Cleveland, Ohio, was founded by deed of trust executed in 1877 by Mr. Leonard Case. It was incorporated after his death in 1880 and organized in October, 1881. The amount of property secured to the institution from his estate is estimated at $1,250,000. The design of the instruction is to give a thorough technical and professional training in the principles of natural and physical science and their applications to the arts. Four years of study will be required to complete its courses. Two of them will be devoted to general training and two to studies of a technical or professional nature. Five courses of this kind are now arranged, embracing mathematics and astronomy, chemistry, physics, civil engineering and mining engineering. Twelve freshmen and 4 special students were in attendance in May, 1882. The faculty had 6 members.

The Toledo (Ohio) University of Arts and Trades was organized in 1872 for the education of artists and artisans of both sexes. Instruction was suspended in 1877 on account of the unproductiveness of its endowment funds, and has not yet been resumed.

The Pardee Scientific Department of Lafayette College, Easton, Pa., was organized in 1866, in accordance with the provisions regulating the use of a generous gift intended for the promotion of scientific education. The gift was made $200,000 in the next year. In 1873 a magnificent building, costing, with its scientific equipment, nearly $300,000, was transferred by the same liberal giver (Ario Pardee, esq.) to the college trustees. It was replaced by him in 1880, after its destruction by fire. The department offers four courses of scientific study. One is a general course four years in length, with the latter part largely elective. By the choice of chemical studies, those wishing to make a special study of chemistry can become thoroughly acquainted with the subject. Provision is also made for advanced and special students who wish to make special researches. The third course is in civil engineering. The course is not strictly confined to that branch of the science, but introduces studies commonly brought under the head of mechanical engineering. The fourth course is in mining and metallurgy. It differs from the one just mentioned chiefly in the last two years. Then mine surveying, mining machinery, mineralogy, lithology, assaying, and similar studies are associated with the direct subjects of mining and metallurgy. Instruction is always supplemented by practice, and the observation and study of the mining, manufacturing, and engineering enterprises of the vicinity contribute largely to the student's education.

The Franklin Institute at Philadelphia was organized in 1824 for the encouragement of science and the mechanic arts. The methods by which it does this include the publication of a monthly journal, the maintenance of an evening drawing school, and a library, and the provision of lecture courses. The journal is intended to disseminate useful knowledge in all matters relating to the practical application of science, but more especially to engineering and the mechanic arts. Each number contains 80 pages of reading matter, and the amount of advertising done by it is very large, so that the journal is self-supporting. The drawing classes are a leading feature of the educational work of the institute. They are held three evenings a week. The course arranged for them is progressive, and includes instruction in mechanical, architectural, and topographical drawing, both free-hand and instrumental, extending over three years. Pupils, if sufficiently advanced, may select any subject of importance to them and receive in it individual instruction. Special classes in architectural and machine drawing have been started recently. The technicalities of drawing, such as the proper selection and use of instruments and materials, the making of clear and perfect lines in pencil and ink, the use of brush and colors, and the relative arrangement of the different views of an object are given particular attention. The library contains 15,968 volumes and a large number of pamphlets, and is said to be one of the most complete collections of works on science and the arts to be found in America. The lectures are intended to be on subjects connected with the callings of members of the institute. Among those delivered during 1881–'82 were four on geology, two on the rise and progress of manufactures in Philadelphia, four on hygiene, two on the microscope and its revelations, four on engineering, six on mechanics, eight on chemistry, two each on astronomy, " machine design and construction," and "drainage and disease and utilization of sewage," and single lectures on "modern photography and gelatine prints," "silk and its culture," "electrotyping," and "mechanical drawing." The lectures are open to the members, each of whom may bring a friend; and complimentary tickets are issued and distributed by members, which admit to the hall five minutes before the lecture commences. The institute has a membership of nearly 2,000, property valued in 1878 at $125,000, and an annual income of some $15,000. Says the president:

It is true that we neither feed the hungry, clothe the naked, nor heal the sick; but, on the other hand, our efforts are to dry up the sources of hunger, destitution, and disease, and to avert these evils by the diffusion of such knowledge as strengthens and directs the hands of the bread winner, cheapens the cost of food and habitation, and improves the construction of dwellings.

Another Philadelphia institution which aids industrial education is the Spring Garden Institute, which maintains a library and free reading-room, drawing-schools, and schools in mechanical handiwork, and provides courses of lectures and entertainments. The library contained 8,500 volumes in 1880, and was increasing rapidly in size and value. The books are loaned to members of the institute, and are at the service of the public during a large part of the day and evening. The drawing-schools furnish evening instruction in mechanical, free-hand, and architectural drawing, free to members of the institute. The pupils in mechanical drawing are more numerous than in either of the other kinds, and have been graded to some extent. In the schools of handiwork there are classes in vise and lathe work, pattern-making, and the elements of molding and steam-engineering. The course in vise-work includes chipping to line, filing, scraping, and polishing; that in lathe work includes turning, drilling, planing, and dressing of tools at the forge. These two courses constitute a term of study three months in length, with sessions two nights each week, and a tuition fee of $5. The course in pattern-making is similar in length and expense. The class in steam-engineering is instructed by lectures upon the physical properties of steam, methods of using it, construction of boilers and engines, methods of propulsion on sea and land, &c. The course is three months in length, sessions two evenings a week, and expense $10. The institute is supported by the income of productive funds and the dues required of members. They are of five kinds, viz, members *in perpetuo* (with right of succession), who pay $50; life members, who pay $30; stockholders, paying $10 per share of stock and $2 a year tax thereon; annual subscribers at $3, and junior subscribers at $2 a year. Each department of work undertaken by the institute is controlled by a special committee, and has been carried on so as to meet the approval and gain the aid of substantial business men.

The University of Pennsylvania in 1872 created a special department of scientific instruction called the Towne Scientific School. Its design is to give a thorough technical and professional training in chemistry, with its manifold appliances to the industrial arts; metallurgy and assaying; mineralogy and geology; civil, mechanical, and mining engineering; mechanical drawing and architecture, and studies preparatory to a medical course. The completion of any of these courses requires five years. The first two years are devoted to a thorough training in preparatory and elementary mathematics, chemistry, and the methods of scientific research in general, and to instruction in history, English composition, rhetoric, modern languages, and mechanical and free hand drawing. At the close of these two years the student selects one of six parallel courses and devotes himself to the professional training they are intended to give. The course most frequently chosen is that in mechanical engineering. In it students are required to give particular attention to the cinematics of mechanism, the conditions under which work and power act, and the means of regulating them, the problems of hydraulics, and the mechanical theory of heat, with its application to the steam-engine. Weekly visits of inspection are made during two years to furnaces, foundries, machine-shops, and rolling-mills. Recent provision has been made for instruction in marine engineering and naval architecture. The faculty of the school is composed of 17 professors and 6 instructors and assistants. The students in attendance in 1881–'82 numbered 171. The museums, laboratories, and collections of apparatus are extensive and well adapted to their several purposes.

The School of Technology of Lehigh University, South Bethlehem, Pa., offers young men every needed facility for studying civil, mechanical, and mining engineering, metallurgy, and chemistry. The studies of the first year and a half are preliminary to the several technical courses. The course in civil engineering includes so much of mechanical engineering as is of direct service to the civil engineer, thorough instruction in geology and mineralogy, practical work, and visits of inspection to engineering undertakings in the Lehigh Valley and its vicinity. The course in mechanical engineering is accompanied by shop instruction, not necessarily involving manual labor and the manipulation of tools, but rather aiming to familiarize students with those points in pattern-making, moulding, forging, fitting, and furnishing which they need to know as designers of machinery. The object of study is the acquisition of the knowledge required by foremen and superintendents rather than manual dexterity and skill in the use of tools. The course in mining and metallurgy includes studies in those subjects necessary to all technical education, and in mining, metallurgy, geology, mineralogy, dynamics, qualitative and quantitative analysis, blowpipe analysis, topographical and mine surveying, and drawing. The full course occupies five years, though the student may take the degree of bachelor of metallurgy at the end of four years, which is the length of the other courses. The course in chemistry exhibits no peculiarities. The laboratories in which the practical work is done are said to be unsurpassed in excellence by any in the country. Arrangements are made whereby graduate students may pursue advanced studies and after examination receive doctor's degrees. The university is so richly endowed that no tuition is charged, and many advantages are offered which would be beyond the means of poorer institutions.

Lewis College, Northfield, Vt., is the institution long known as Norwich University. It has but a small faculty and is not largely attended. The instruction is scientific and military in character, and of a grade comparing favorably with other scientific schools. The regulations of the college conform closely to those required by military usage.

The Virginia Military Institute, Lexington, Va., was organized in 1839 as a State military and scientific school on the basis of the United States Military Academy at West Point. In it is a special school of applied science, offering seven courses of study, the subjects being as follows: Architecture, civil engineering, machines, mining, metallurgy, analytical and applied chemistry, and agriculture.

The University of Virginia has no fixed course of prescribed study. Each student selects studies from its various schools. One of these is the Miller School of Agriculture, Zoölogy, and Botany. The studies in agriculture are either practical or scientific. The practical studies comprise the nature and formation of soils; their exposure and drainage; the best method of tillage; and the use of manures and fertilizers, and experiments to show their effects. Special instruction is given in the mechanical operations of the farm and in the management of teams. The scientific course comprises a review of what is known of the chemical composition of plants and the structure and functions of their organs, and of the atmosphere and soil, as related to vegetable production. The opportunities for studying the sciences are ample, and the chemical facilities are especially good. Degrees are conferred on students according to the kind and amount of their study.

After this summary of the work of our schools of science and industry, it is of interest to read the tribute paid to their efficiency by one of the directors of the Ohio Mechanics' Institute, in an address to the graduating class of 1880. He said:

> In the mechanic arts, and indeed in every department of busy practical life, the kind of training furnished by our industrial schools is of the highest importance, both to the industrial worker and the country at large; not only to the individual, by enabling him to command better prices for his work, but especially to the nation whose artisans are skilled workmen and whose productions secure prices in foreign markets and turn the balance of trade in its favor. The necessity for this special education was never so great in America as it is to-day. But a few years ago the United States contributed millions annually to the coffers of France and England in buying back as manufactured goods the very cotton our fields had grown, and, in the form of machinery and cutlery, the products of our ore banks.
>
> * * * *
>
> But now the trade is changing. The fostering effect of our free institutions, which place the humblest workingman on an equal plane with the millionaire, the wise protection thrown by the national government around our struggling industries, and lastly, perhaps not least important, the elevating influence of our industrial training schools, these have worked a mighty change, which is heard in the increasing hum of busy spindles and clank of iron arms once more saluting the rising sun over all this broad land.
>
> The superiority of American design and workmanship has steadily and surely compelled recognition against every obstacle. * * * We are to-day competing successfully in the markets of the world with older and wealthier nations because we are able to produce articles, implements, and machinery either better in quality, superior in artistic and mechanical design, or better adapted to the purposes of their construction than the products of our competitors, and this is directly attributable to the superior intelligence of our industrial classes. We make better wares because our artisans bring a higher intelligence to bear upon their work.

Evidences of the advantages which have accrued to cities on account of the establishment of schools for technical education may be obtained from the history of places within our own country. Better illustrations are to be found in foreign nations. For example, a town of Saxony, Chemnitz, is teaching by indisputable arguments the value of industrial training. Once forests grew up around it, and coal beds there kept their wealth of fuel. Through it streams abounding in water privileges flowed undisturbed in their natural channel. Within it lived people possessing only moderate powers of mind and body. Consequently forest trees fell uselessly into decay, coal mines were scarcely opened, and the rivers spent their force on the rocks that hindered their descent.

The scene is changed. The town has been filled with schools of industry. In them mechanics, architecture, weaving, agriculture, trade, and miscellaneous industries, as well as "the general knowledge required in daily life," are being taught. The State Technical Educational Institution receives into its new home, which cost some $400,000 in 1877, more than 600 students, and trains them in the highest forms of labor. A hosiery school near by contributes to the success of that industry. The weaving school sent out recently 40 students as its semi-annual quota of trained weavers and dealers in woven fabrics. Mercantile and trade schools teach the duties and rights of merchants and the branches of knowledge which aid in the prosecution of business.

But are not these schools expensive, some one asks. Certainly. The town is taxed for their support and for its own growth more heavily than any city but one in Germany. Yet the burden is cheerfully borne, for the people have learned that the industrial training of their children is the fountain of their prosperity, and prefer elementary schools to prisons, trade and technical schools to workhouses and emigration, and school rates to poor rates. This willingness of the people to provide instruction and this eagerness to establish technical institutions are due to the development of industries, which have extended themselves as they were able to obtain trained workmen. Their growth is the growth of the city. Year by year they attract to themselves laboring men, and thus add to the population citizens contributing to permanent wealth. The number of inhabitants has more than doubled in a score of years.

The manufacturing cities of other countries are finding that their specialties are being produced cheaply and artistically in Chemnitz, and their trade thereby seriously impaired. Already Nottingham has yielded to it the front rank in the production and sale of gloves. America drew from its mills goods to the value of $4,500,000 in a single year of the last decade. Such is the prosperity of this city of schools. And when other cities, whether in Germany or England or America, adopt similar measures for training their citizens and extending the variety and improving the quality of their industrial products, then will they also meet with similar prosperity.

PREPARATION FOR INDUSTRIES A FEATURE OF KINDERGARTEN WORK.

The aim of Kindergarten training is to develop the child according to the natural law of its being. Baroness von Marenholtz-Bülow says:

This is the kernel of Fröbel's method, that a way has been found to let the individual character of each one unfold itself in full freedom.

Fröbel himself remarks:

We must launch the child from its birth into the free and all-sided use of all its powers. That is just the aim of these plays and occupations, which exercise the yet unseen powers of the nursling on every side. * * * Steadily, and during the whole era of childhood, body and mind should be exercised and cultivated together.

The statement of Bertha Meyer is that—

Special talents find their opportunities better in the Kindergarten than elsewhere; for here the means of their development are presented in much greater abundance than in the family or anywhere else.

It is very often the case that this natural development discloses marked aptitudes for some industrial employment. Fröbel says:

The faculty of drawing is as natural to the child as the faculty of speech.

This belief in the constructive tendencies of the child is revealed in his statement that—

Man, the image of God, is, as such, a creative being; consequently the first principle of education is to make him capable of creativeness, able to create.

Miss Susan E. Blow gives especial emphasis to this outcome of Kindergarten methods when she says that—

The aim of the Kindergarten is to strengthen and develop productive activity. * * * Hence the first use of the gifts is to waken, by their suggestiveness, the mind's sleeping thoughts, and the first use of the occupations to train the eye and the mind to be the ready servants of the will. While the child is still imitative in the occupations, he becomes inventive in the gifts; but as he grows to be more and more a law unto himself, he turns from the coercion of his blocks, tablets, and sticks, to obedient paper and clay, and, ultimately outgrowing the simpler occupations, concentrates his interest in the exercises of drawing, coloring, and modelling.

Respecting the need of such training as the Kindergarten aims to give, Fröbel says:

When we ask for artistic industry, that our dignity may not be lost by the substitution of machine work, we find stiff and awkward fingers; we ask for a sense of beautiful form, harmony of colors, &c., in the workman, and find only dull eyes and senses, which cannot tell the crooked from the straight and know not how to put light and shadow in the right places. Indeed, when professional and art schools are opened for grown-up youth only, they cannot repair what was lost in childhood, let ever so much teaching be furnished. Technical skill must be given in early childhood if the human hand is not to be outdone by the machine, and the sense of beauty must be awakened in the soul in childhood if in later life he is to create the beautiful.

W. N. Hailmann, in his lecture on the specific use of the Kindergarten, speaks of its power to develop the artistic side of a child's nature thus:

Æsthetically, the Kindergarten reveals to the child the wonderful beauties of color, form, and sound, and enables him to control them within the ever-expanding limits of his intellectual power; thus making him an artist as well as a discoverer and inventor, a poet as well as a worker and thinker.

To this statement of what the Kindergarten can do may be added a statement by Miss Blow of what the Kindergarten has done:

In the Des Pères Kindergarten predestined engineers have built bridges as remarkable in conception as clever in execution; little mathematicians have discovered rather than learned all the simple relations of numbers; children with more than ordinary spiritual insight have intuitively seized the moral analogies of physical facts; tiny fingers have guided the pencil to trace beautiful decorative designs, and soft clay has been fashioned into flowers, fruits, and animals by the dextrous hands of embryo sculptors.

The preparation for industrial work afforded by the Kindergarten is ably discussed by Baroness von Marenholtz-Bülow, from whom the following is taken:

As the whole method of Fröbel rests upon spontaneous activity and has for its aim to teach the formation and production of things, its first condition is to form the hand. * * * The hands of the child make their earliest apprenticeship to the art of giving form by digging into the earth and sand. To dig holes, to build houses and bridges, to give shape to the little dirt-pie by the help of mamma's thimble, to build castles with cards, and the Swiss cottage with pieces of wood; later, to make buildings out of pasteboard or to draw them on card-board—all this flows from that instinct of transformation which is, properly speaking, the instinct of work. * * * This instinct is cherished and satisfied in the child-garden, where children build, make, and unmake in a thousand ways, and by means of every kind of material, always in the order indicated in the history of human development. Not only houses and tools are made, but also the hands are taught to weave and stitch. In weaving they make tissues similar to those fabricated by the inhabitants of New Zealand out of reeds and bark. Gradually the woven stuffs of our own times are reached. In learning to fold paper, in printing, pricking, cutting, not only skill necessary for making clothes is acquired, but that general dexterity which all manual labor demands. The hand is made ready for all those technical processes necessary to workmen in all professions as well as to those of which every one has need in practical life. At the same time the child is initiated early in industrial labor.

The facility with which children can acquire a familiarity with many industrial arts is well presented in a circular just issued by this office entitled "Industrial Art in Schools," by Charles G. Leland, of Philadelphia.

INDUSTRIAL WORK IN EVENING SCHOOLS.

Evening schools are emphatically for the working people. The wealthy have either received an education in their early years or have gained the training they desire by actual contact with men and things while accumulating and caring for their property. Their children are not driven to the necessity of devoting their evening hours to preparation for coming life. It is only the hope of a future prosperity, to be gained in no other way, that induces any one to call the currents of life away from the refreshment of the weary body to the solution of problems which contribute only indirectly and after long waiting to comfort and happiness. The studies of these schools are not usually directed to the immediate preparation of a workman for his trade. In this sense they have not often been industrial. In a wider sense they have been; for the faithful pursuit of even the simplest studies awakens that within a man which augments his value and capacity as a worker. Many years ago a clergyman, reporting on evening schools in a manufacturing city of New England, said:

The effect of only a little education has been an increase of self-respect, a quickening of the powers of action, a management of the physical powers to more advantage, an easier triumph over difficulties, an increase of skill and production. From the mills and work-shops of the city frequent testimony to this point has been proffered us.

A mechanic in New York City, who had accomplished so much in his trade as to have received a medal at the Paris Exposition of 1878, in a recent letter to this office refers to the starting point in his career as a thinking and educated workman as follows:

After serving my apprenticeship and working three years as a journeyman smith, I began to feel how ignorant I was, and how much I stood in need of culture and other matters which could only be gained through an education. And to lift myself out of this mediocre mine in which I had so long remained I attended night school twenty-eight nights at one of the public schools of this city, at which I mastered reading, writing, arithmetic, and book-keeping, single and double entry. Since that time I have been an ardent student.

Such results as these have come from the quiet elevating and dignifying of men and women through the pursuit of elementary and general studies. By the introduction of drawing and other subjects pertaining directly to an industrial education even more has been accomplished for artisans. They now take studies which prepare them for the better execution of their work. The report of the evening high school of New York City, 1877, says:

In most cases they (the pupils) attend in order to acquire that knowledge which they deem desirable and even necessary to enable them to pursue their various avocations with skill and intelligence.

The report for 1881, expressing the same truth, says:

Almost every industry of our city is here represented by those who are seeking that particular instruction the attainment of which will qualify them to perform more skillfully and in a more satisfactory manner the duties of their several vocations.

The large number of evening pupils who choose drawing, when such a choice is allowed, indicates that the working classes are coming to understand its importance and to agree with those who give it a prominent place in education, and who estimate its value, as did General J. C. Palfrey when he wrote the following sentences:

A knowledge of mechanical drawing is invaluable to all constructors, whether employers or employed, and of constant use in ordinary affairs. In all matters of construction, in the widest sense of the word, it takes the place of a knowledge of reading and writing in the other concerns of life, and is indispensable for giving and receiving intelligible ideas. A mechanic who is without it will almost always be subservient and inferior to one who has it, but is his inferior in all other respects. A man rarely becomes a competent master mechanic without some knowledge of it. It affords means of representing any combinations of forms with such accuracy and minuteness as to convey as clear an idea of the thing represented as the thing itself could if present to the senses, and thereby saves the delay and expense of experimental or tentative constructions, and the inconvenience or impossibility of using the thing itself for explanation or examination. It is the only way of directing one's own or others' labor in construction exactly to any desired result.

It is the place of evening schools to continue the work of the day schools, not only in drawing and other industrial directions, but also in imparting the fundamental studies of a general education. Many working people are unwilling to keep their children in school even during the time when attendance is compulsory. The small earnings which might be gained before a child is fourteen years of age, which is commonly the time when compulsory school laws allow children to leave school, seem too valuable to be lost or sacrificed to the requirements of the school-room. In Connecticut, in 1873, about 2,250 children under fourteen years of age were reported as kept from school to work. In New Jersey in 1880, while only 4 per cent. of the children between 10 and 11 enrolled in the census were out of school, the per cent. increased to 20 for those between 12 and 13, and to 67 for those between 14 and 15. So fixed are poor parents in the idea that their children must commence work at the earliest possible moment and so often does necessity compel this that it is doubtless true, as Mr. Huxley asserted of England:

That no scheme of technical education is likely to be seriously entertained which will delay the entrance of boys into working life or prevent them from contributing to their own support as early as they do at present.

However this may be, it is certain that the sons and often the daughters of the people who labor in our factories generally commence work soon after they arrive at the age when they are not compelled to attend school. Often their hours of labor are so many that little time is left for evening study. Doubtless many have not strength to labor and study at the same time. Yet it may be assumed that the cases of injury from overstudy at night are fewer than the instances of moral and physical injury received in evening hours upon the street or in the haunts of vice. When at length a pupil is found who possesses strength and ability to combine faithful and efficient work during the day with intelligent study at night, he is worthy of higher education. He has passed a test that would have shown any serious obstacles to progress in his trade, and enables his superiors to forecast the probabilities of his final success. He has acquired a practical knowledge of the matters which his technical studies would explain and illustrate, and thereby can pursue them to the best advantage. The gain obtained in this way is of great value. The keeper of the mining-records at the Royal School of Mines of England once said:

> If I could do it, no man should attend the school in Jermyn street (the school of mines) until he had worked three years under ground, so satisfied am I of the necessity of combining practical knowledge with scientific acquirement.

The technical school in Chemnitz, Saxony, which has hundreds of pupils studying the arts of milling, dyeing, tanning, and manufacturing, requires that each student shall have worked two years at his occupation before admission to the school, and attended an evening school during his years of actual work. An eminent writer, himself an advocate of ideas similar to those mentioned, commends such a course of education as should give a youth, first, instruction tending to strengthen his body, elevate his morals, and cultivate his intelligence; second, a period of actual service in a shop; and lastly, if deserved, a superior special training. In such a scheme for technical training, evening study must hold an invaluable place as the means by which the mind is kept fresh and mobile during the time employed in manual labor.

If such a method of growing toward and into leading places in industrial pursuits is best for the poor, it is also for the rich. And would it not be well for our industries, would it not contribute to the solution of social problems, might it not also benefit our young men themselves, if people of wealth could be led to believe that it is good for their children to bear the yoke in their youth, to be inured to such labors as workmen in our factories perform, to show by open competition their capacity and efficiency, and then to be educated for that branch of industry for which they have shown special aptitude?

As has been intimated, the actual instruction afforded by evening schools is chiefly in the most elementary branches; some introduce higher studies, and a few may be said to give industrial instruction, usually in the form of lessons in drawing. A brief statement of the attendance and studies in some of them indicates the bearing of these schools on industrial education. The evening high school in New York City during the winter of 1879-'80 had an average attendance of 1,054 pupils, of ages varying from fourteen to forty-seven. Among the studies pursued were freehand, architectural, and mechanical drawing, chemistry, and phonography. It is authoritatively stated that a large and deserving class of men are receiving the benefits of this school.

In two of the evening schools of Saint Louis, at which there was an average attendance in 1879-'80 of nearly 200, "the branches taught are such as form an elementary course in polytechnic studies."

Although the practical benefits derived from evening schools in general are questioned by school authorities in many of the cities in which they have been maintained, the value of evening drawing schools is almost invariably admitted and urged.

In Cambridge, Mass., while the results of the ordinary evening schools in 1878-'79 scarcely warranted their continuance, the drawing schools furnished a most favorable report. One of the two schools gave instruction in mechanical and the other in freehand drawing. The former was largely composed of those already engaged or about to engage in mechanical pursuits, and represented fourteen callings. Carpenters, cabinet-makers, and machinists predominated. The subjects of instruction were geometrical drawing, orthographic projection, and building construction. The principal subject studied by the class in freehand drawing was industrial design.

S. Ex. 25——4

In 1879–'80 there were six evening drawing schools in Boston, having seventeen instructors and an average attendance of 299, of whom 235 were males and 64 females. The usual number of sessions was 80 or 81. A plan of a two years' course in industrial drawing was arranged and adopted. The first year's instruction is general and elementary and for all students.

In the second year there is a choice of four courses, viz (1) freehand design; (2) machine drawing; (3) building construction; (4) ship drawing. Applicants being over 15 years of age are admitted to the first year's course without examination. For entrance upon the freehand course of the second year students are examined in drawing from the object; for entrance upon the instrumental courses, in plain geometry. Classes are open three evenings each week from 7½ to 9½, and students are required to sign an agreement to attend the whole session, punctually and regularly, unless prevented by sickness or removal.

Says a Boston newspaper:

One of the most gratifying features of this branch of our public education is that so many of the pupils are able to apply what they have been taught, both as a direct means and as an important aid in the acquisition of a livelihood. The manner in which one or more individuals have received a practical benefit from their public instruction in drawing has been brought to the attention, some time or other, of a majority of persons in the community. These cases are but types of a large body of workers in the same direction—a body whose numbers are rapidly increasing, and who have already exerted a positive moral and commercial influence among us. It is now not unusual for an employer to require of certain of his employés, as a prerequisite to an engagement, more or less familiarity with drawing, such as can be acquired in the evening schools. This, in some instances, is the case in the so-called purely mechanical occupations. More than this, it is frequently part of an apprentice's contract, in such trades as wood-carving, fresco painting, and the like, for him to attend some drawing school in the evening.

The superintendent of schools of Springfield, Mass., speaks of the success of the evening drawing school of that city during 1881 as follows:

This school has had an enrollment this term of 185, the largest number ever in attendance in one year. The steady patronage given to the school, year after year, is gratifying evidence of the practical work done there and of the estimation in which such a school is held by those who are willing, after laboring during the day, to devote their evenings to improvement in a branch which is so highly beneficial in increasing their preparation for better work in their several callings.

The superintendent of public schools of Worcester, Mass., made the following response to an inquiry about the evening drawing schools of that city:

The course of study in the evening drawing schools consists of beginners' and advanced classes in both free-hand and instrumental drawing. The students are young men and women for the most part engaged in mechanical or artistic callings or in teaching. In the advanced classes they are employed in construction, in the mechanical drawing and in drawing from the life in free-hand. All the students in these classes are earnest and industrious. There is no time wasted, no nonsense, and no unnecessary absence.

The following classes, open to both sexes, are proposed for the winter of 1882–'83. Each class will be formed in case twenty applicants appear:

Advanced free-hand drawing (class No. 1) for those who have had previous instruction. This class will draw from models and imported casts. The facilities for the study of figure and form from the valuable collection of casts are excellent.

A course in free-hand drawing for beginners (class No. 2). Instruction will be given from the blackboard in outline, principles of design, perspective, and elementary model-drawing, and in copying from imported examples of ornament and figure.

A course of instrumental drawing for beginners (class No. 3). The instruction will include the elements of plane geometry, the principles of plane projection, intersection of surfaces, &c.

Advanced course of instrumental drawing for machinists and iron-workers (class No. 4). This class will make working drawings of machinery. The work will be so arranged as to include all the processes and principles involved in making plans, elevations, and sections of combinations, and details, including coloring and lettering.

Advanced course in instrumental drawing for carpenters and wood-workers (class No. 5). This class will make details, working drawings, scale drawings, and elevations of a modern dwelling-house, store-front, or something similar. Attention will be given to coloring, lettering, and finishing the drawings. Instruction will be given from the blackboard and from practical working drawings used in the construction of buildings already put up or in process of construction.

The Technical School for Carriage Mechanics holds its sessions in connection with those of the art schools of the Metropolitan Museum, at 214 East Thirty-fourth street, New York City. It has been in operation over two years and has met with a good degree of success. The attendance has increased, and even distant portions of the country are now represented in the attendance. Drawing is the principal study. Lectures on subjects connected with carriage building are given, and a library is being collected. The annual report of the committee of the carriage builders' association on technical education, given in Appendix C, presents additional information respecting this school.

In connection with this effort the work of Mr. J. L. H. Mosier with the boys in the carriage factory of Brewster & Co., in New York, may be noted. He had acquired a good education in practical directions by improving his leisure time and was anxious to help others to advance by the same road over which he had come. Consequently he has been accustomed to encourage the workmen intrusted to him to read and study by gaining them admission to libraries, loaning books, and urging them to attend evening schools. Later he has gathered the boys in his office during the noon hour, given them reading matter relating to their trade, instructed them in elementary book-keeping, and in parliamentary rules and practice, and given copies for writing and drawing to be done at home. In this way the education which most of the boys received in their younger days in the public schools is put into use and increased, and their spare hours are made to contribute, not to their injury, but to their moral and intellectual progress and to their capacity as workmen. A short account of this peculiarly commendable effort from Mr. Mosier himself is given in Appendix C.

Other educational efforts in behalf of carriage builders have been made by Mr. J. Polya, in New York City (1295 Broadway), and Mr. George A. Hubbard, in New Haven. The latter gentleman has presented such a full account of his work that it has seemed best to present it nearly in full in Appendix C. It is a most noticeable statement, and should be read by all interested in industrial education. Mr. Polya's school is entitled "A Drawing School for Body-makers." It is open three evenings a week from 7.30 to 9.30, for five months. Its object is to teach the application of geometrical principles to the construction of carriages, with a special view to economy of labor and material. Problems are drawn on a blackboard, explained to the class, and copied by them. Each scholar is also given exercises on the blackboard. The school is conducted after a French model, the history of which Mr. Polya gives substantially as follows: The first school of this kind was established in Paris, France, in 1839, by Mr. Fablot, a bodymaker. It was abandoned several times in subsequent years because it was not a financial success. In 1872 it was reopened by the Paris Carriage-makers' Mutual Benefit Society, and received the promise of a yearly bounty of 2,000 francs from the local government. The monthly dues were placed at three francs. Five lessons a week at seven o'clock in the evening were given. In the succeeding years the attendance grew to be so large that many of the applicants could not be received. Consequently another similar school was established in 1878 by the Carriage-Builders' Association. Both schools are said to be successful.

Among the evening schools imparting industrial training may be mentioned the night school of art, Cooper Union, New York City, the Trenton (N. J.) Art School, and the schools of art and design of the Maryland Institute, Baltimore, Md. The first of these has been mentioned; the second, the Trenton Art School, was begun in October, 1879, by the master potters of that city for the purpose of giving apprentices opportunities of educating the eye to appreciate form and color and the hand to imitate. The school is open two evenings each week from 7.15 to 9 p. m., and has an enrollment of from 30 to 35. On account of the deficiencies of the pupils in acquirements in drawing, the instruction begins with elementary drawing, and is adapted to the increasing skill of the student. Classes in painting and modelling will be established as required. The progress thus far has been satisfactory, although the lack of copies is a considerable hindrance.

The schools of art and of design of the Maryland Institute have for the last thirty years been attended by an average of 417 students each year. Its managers, who are mainly engaged in the industries, and therefore interested in their development, have devoted time and energy to perfecting and enlarging the sphere of its educational operations.

The night school of design is especially intended for the adult industrial class. It is open three evenings each week from the middle of November to the middle of April, and provides a full course of elementary, artistic, industrial, mechanical, and architectural drawing. Premiums amounting to $500 annually are given to the seven students of highest rank.

Some of the leading art schools maintain evening classes in addition to their usual work; for example, the school of design of the Cincinnati University has classes from 7 to 9 p. m., as follows: wood-carving on Tuesday, Thursday, and Saturday; sculpture on Monday, Wednesday, and Saturday; pen-drawing on Thursday; drawing on Tuesday, Thursday, and Friday; decorative design on Monday and Wednesday. The Metropolitan Museum of Art in New York City maintains evening classes in (1) modelling and carving, (2) drawing and designing (instrumental and perspective, and technical), and (3) carriage drawing and construction. A nominal tuition fee is charged (from $8 to $15 a season). This pays for materials and models, and "has so far secured a superior class of intelligent workmen and students, thoroughly in earnest in practical or artistic improvement."

MISCELLANEOUS PROVISION FOR TECHNICAL TRAINING.

There are several schools of an industrial nature which are not included in the classes of which mention has been made. Their organization and methods of instruction are unlike those of other institutions and are, therefore, rich in suggestion to those seeking new channels through which industrial training may be carried to the people.

The industrial education of Indian youth is being successfully undertaken. An account of the schools at Carlisle, Pa., and Forest Grove, Oreg., will be found in Appendix G; and the work done in this direction at Hampton Institute, Va., is mentioned in Appendix A.

An attempt to connect shop work with the studies of the public schools was made at Gloucester, Mass., a few years since. A lady placed several hundred dollars at the disposal of the school committee to be expended for the industrial education of boys. A shop was fitted up with benches to accommodate twelve workmen; and, in addition to the fixtures belonging with the bench, the following set of tools was furnished: a rule, try-square, hammer, jack-plane, jointer, smoothing-plane, bitstock, bit, mortise-gauge, mallet, a one-half-inch mortising-chisel, a one-and-one-quarter-inch paring-chisel, chalk-reel, rip-saw, panel-saw, screw-driver, brad-awl, oil-can, oil-stone, bench-hook. The shop course was divided into forty lessons. The names and uses of the tools are first learned. Afterward the pupils are instructed in their use, and eventually taught box-making. The lessons were at first given on Saturdays; as the novelty wore off, the pupils wearied of giving their holiday time to shop work, and a change of plan was necessitated. The industrial department as it existed after the changes were made is described by Mr. L. H. Marvel, then city superintendent, as follows:

In October, 1880, arrangements were made to accommodate pupils in the carpentry class one-half of each afternoon session on Monday, Tuesday, Thursday, and Friday of every week (two classes each session). By this change regularity and punctuality in attendance have been secured; and from a membership of thirty pupils, in three classes, there was an immediate advance to a membership of ninety-six in eight classes, each receiving one hour per week. A few girls (six) were permitted to join one of the classes in 1878. There are now two full classes of girls, and there is one class composed partly of each sex. The work of the girls is equally as good as that of the boys, and they seem to enjoy it heartily. The attendance is entirely optional, nearly one-half the pupils in the first and second classes of the two larger grammar schools desiring to attend. There is no compulsion whatever, except that, while members of the industrial class, the pupils are required to be as attentive, industrious, and orderly as during any portion of their school work. There has been a training in the nature of the implements used, in the best methods of employing those implements, constant attention to those habits of method and system which are necessary to secure good work anywhere, and continued practice of the hand and eye in unison, requiring close application as well as clear perception and accurate manipulation. The result is tangible, and the proficiency is measured by no arbitrary standard of percentages, but is clearly defined, and may be estimated with much more precision than in any other line of school work. I do not know of any manner in which fifty to eighty hours can be employed in any form of education where the practical results can be more satisfactorily determined. If the pupil never sees saw, hammer, or plane again, the training he has received will be of value, whatever his vocation.

The Miller Manual Labor School, Batesville, Albemarle County, Va., is an institution recently organized for the purpose of affording poor children an opportunity to obtain a practical education. It was founded by the late Samuel Miller, who bequeathed the greater part of a princely fortune to trustees for its creation and endowment. The will was contested, and it was several years before the executor was enabled to transfer to the trustees the property designed for the school. An act of compromise was passed by the legislature in 1874, and in accordance with its provisions stock, bonds, and property, amounting to over $1,000,000, were put in the hands of the proper officers. The work of preparation was commenced in 1876. A building, costing $100,000, was erected the subsequent year, which realized the intention of the donor to have accommodations at once provided for one hundred pupils and their teachers. The first pupils were received in the fall of 1878; now there are over one hundred in attendance. The number of pupils is not limited, except by the sufficiency of the income to pay their expenses, not only for tuition, but also for board, clothes, medical attendance, and "everything incident to and connected with the school." The instruction is to be in " all the branches of a good, plain, sound English education, the various languages (both ancient and modern), agriculture, and the useful arts." A superintendent and four teachers are engaged in the work of supervision and instruction.

Manual labor is required of all the pupils in several departments of industry. Carpentry, printing, telegraphy, farming, and gardening are already introduced. An extensive machine-shop is being built. In it practical training will be had in wood and iron working. The farm connected with the school consists of 600 acres of land. It has good buildings, and is being stocked with the best animals procurable. An orchard, a vineyard, and a garden are furnishing opportunities for work and instruction.

Efforts have been made to introduce elementary manual training into the public schools of Boston. In 1879 the subject was brought before the city council by a petition from intelligent and influential citizens. The matter was referred to the school committee. They appointed a select committee to consider the question and report upon it. This committee thought that a free industrial institute should be established consisting of a developing school and school shops, to be supported by the city, at least in part, and permanently ingrafted on our school system. The proposition was not sustained by the city council, but the friends of the project considered it postponed rather than defeated. The prevailing opinion of the school committee is expressed in their report for 1881, as follows:

> The school committee has again repeated its formal vote of desire to test the feasibility of imparting to grammar scholars some of the elements of mechanical skill, by whose final application so many of them must, by and by, earn their daily bread. The term industry, as applied to manual labor, is far too large to be adequately comprehended under any use of carpenter's, machinist's, or blacksmith's tools. These are but portions of a vast field, which only a great number of special schools could make any pretension of properly traversing. But it is possible to meet some of the complaints which are so frequent that the public education is so exclusively intellectual as to unfit the majority of youth from entering heartily into the ranks of manual labor, by directing certain pursuits of the school hour to the especial end of training the hand and the eye, so that whatever the future occupation of the child, he shall not be utterly awkward and helpless in the every-day responsibilities of earning his living. Education may and ought to help youth to be self-reliant and handy, as a mere bookish student is not likely to be.
>
> The eminent success of the sewing instruction in the girls' school, a branch of school work for a long time looked upon with great distrust by most persons who had given any thought to matters of education, has afforded convincing evidence that it is possible to impart special manual skill without interfering with the established routine of study. The teaching of industrial drawing, now pretty firmly seated among the essentials of instruction, is quite within the line of training for the practical life of the manual worker; and so those who have watched the shop work of the Massachusetts Institute of Technology and the smaller experiment of the Boston Industrial School Association in teaching boys the manipulations of a few varieties of mechanics' tools (from which training some have been known to go into successful positions in trades) have continued to feel, notwithstanding the disapproval of their plans by the money-appropriating authorities, that it would be no unwise venture to devote a small portion of the week in a few boys' grammar schools to an experiment of using hammers, saws, chisels, and like tools, under a competent instructor, with the design of enlarging the work as fast as its smaller operations should be shown to be of advantage.

In the Boston Industrial School a course of 24 lessons in wood-carving was taught in such a manner as to afford the greatest amount of instruction and involve the least possible expenditure. The lessons were given from 7 to 9 o'clock on two evenings of each week. The tools used were the flat chisel, the gouge, and the veining tool. Smooth blocks of white wood, 6 inches long, 2 or 3 broad, and 1½ thick, were the material used. Specific articles were not made. Manipulations common to leading wood-working trades were taught. The school proved the practicability and value of doing this, and thus has become a foundation in fact for arguments in favor of giving youth instruction of the kind imparted by it during its existence. Rev. George L. Chaney, the president of the association which had the school in charge, says:

A single ward-room like the one used by the school in Church street, in any city, for the six months from December to May, during which time it usually lies idle, with very little expense beyond the original plant and a moderate salary to the teacher, would meet all the needs of three or four of the largest grammar-schools for boys.

Three such supplementary schools, if used in turn, would amply satisfy all the rightful claims of industrial education of this kind upon the school system of such a city as Boston. At so small an outlay of attention and money might the native aptitude of American youth for manual skill be turned into useful channels. In so simple a way might the needed check be given to that exclusive tendency toward clerical rather than industrial pursuits, which the present school course undoubtedly promotes.

The organized charities of Boston have used their influence in favor of the introduction of manual instruction into the public schools by the appointment of a committee on industrial training and the publication of its report, in which five articles of belief were presented. The substance of them is as follows: First, industrial training is the proper complement of a literary education, and as such should be adopted as a part of the public school system; second, public industrial training should be general, not special; third, education, not production, should be sought; fourth, elementary training might commence in the primary school and be continued through the higher grades; fifth, such training is feasible and not unwarrantably expensive.

The co-operation of the people of Boston and the inducements offered by the Industrial School Association have at length enabled the school committee to make a practical trial of a shop in connection with a public school. One of the rooms of the Dwight school building was fitted up for the purpose. A carpenter was employed as teacher. The session continued from January to May, 1882. The total expenses incurred in equipping and continuing the shop were $712. A report of the success of the enterprise was made by James A. Page, principal of the Dwight school, soon after the close of the session. From it the following extract is taken:

On the first Thursday of January the instructor gave his opening lesson to a class of eighteen boys, all who could be accommodated at the three benches at one time. These boys had been selected by myself from the graduating class, without reference to their standing, and no conditions were made with them except that they should not fall behind in their regular school-work. Another class of the same number was selected from the second, third, and fourth classes, in order that the experiment might be tested by a wider application to ordinary grammar-school material. Many of these latter had already handled tools, to a certain extent, either at home or in their fathers' work-shops.

In arranging the practical details of the school with Mr. Bachelder it had been agreed that school discipline should be maintained throughout the sessions; that the programme should be carefully written out on the blackboard; that each boy should be marked on the work done, and that a record of it should be kept. All this was faithfully carried out, and contributed, as I think, largely to the final success. From this beginning to the close the school went on with unbroken and successful regularity. The teacher was promptly on hand; the order was good; the pupils interested.

It was delightful to see the eager desire manifested everywhere in the room to do the day's work well. There was no absence, no tardiness. On one occasion a count was made, and seventeen out of eighteen pupils were found at work at one o'clock when two was the hour for beginning. It was feared that the noise of many hammers and other tools in use at once (as was necessary in giving the same lesson to a whole class) would be so great that the other rooms on the same floor might be seriously disturbed. It was arranged, therefore, that the school in the adjoining room should proceed to the hall whenever a lesson in the training-room was going on. Practically, however, no trouble was felt from this source. The walls in the school-room were found to be so thick as to deaden the sound almost completely. It was thought also that taking a part of a class away from its regular school-work would result in more or less detriment to its progress in the prescribed studies. Here and there a complaint was made by the teacher of some second class boy, that he was not doing his work well in his own room; but the pupil, in every case, was so anxious to remain in the "carpenter's class" that a word or two of warning was sufficient to bring his performance up to the standard again.

* * * * * * *

I consider that the results go far to prove that manual training is so great a relief to the iteration of school-work that it is a positive benefit, rather than a detriment, to the course in the other studies.

Immediately in this line are the recommendations of the committee on industrial education of the American Institute of Instruction presented at the meeting of the institute in July last. They are the following:

First. The introduction into schools of broader provisions than now exist for the development of the sense of perception of pupils in regard to color, form, proportion, &c., by contact with models and with natural objects.

Second. The more general introduction into schools of simple physical and chemical experiments, for the purpose of acquainting pupils through observation with the elements of chemical and physical science and their application in the arts.

Third. The teaching of drawing, not as an accomplishment, but as a language for the graphic presentation of the facts of forms and of objects, for the representation of the appearance of objects, and also as a means of developing taste in industrial design.

Fourth. The introduction into schools of instruction in the use of tools, not for application in any particular trade, but for developing skill of hand in the fundamental manipulations connected with the industrial arts, and also as a means of mental development.

A recent paper by Prof. H. H. Straight, of the Oswego (N. Y.) State Normal School, contains many practical and well-digested thoughts on industrial education and the public schools. The following elements are given by him as necessary to a person educated industrially:

(1.) An industrial disposition, which leads to a cheerful and even happy devotion to some chosen employment as the avenue through which to make his contribution to the world's wealth.

(2.) Industrial knowledge—such general and special knowledge as will put him in possession of the best human experience in the direction of his chosen vocation.

(3.) Industrial power—such development of physical, intellectual, and artistic power as will remove as far as possible the chances of failure, and, by giving a just consciousness of strength, will enable him to work always with the hope and expectation of success.

The means by which Professor Straight would have the public schools develop this industrial power are the following:

(a.) *Physical power*—They must take the best physiological knowledge the age affords, and under its guidance develop a body capable of enduring all the strains and fatigues likely to be brought upon it by at least the ordinary exigencies of life.

(b.) *Intellectual power*—They must impart the knowledge which it is their duty to give according to the laws of mental assimilation, as discovered and interpreted by the best students of mental growth, to the end that mental dyspepsia may be avoided, and that the best intellectual conditions may exist for the quick and accurate solution of at least the ordinary problems of life.

(c.) They must give such a development of the sense of the beautiful as will enable our people not simply to enjoy the beautiful in the objects about them, but such as will give a *finesse* and finish to whatever work they undertake, whether it be the culture of corn, the making of a coat, the building of a house, or the painting of a picture. Every workman should have, to the largest possible degree, the fine feeling of the artist, while every artist should be recognized as a working man.

This basis for special industrial training is to be obtained by associating materials, forms, and processes with the common studies of the public school. A workshop may be equipped at small expense in which considerable may be accomplished. What might be gained by an industrial course involving only inexpensive illustrations and aids, and carrying out the principles stated, is summed up as follows:

(1.) The cultivation of observation and judgment, the discipline of hand and eye, obtained in this way, would not be second to that obtained in any other way.

(2.) The course in mathematics, together with the course in language and geography, could be made the means of acqainting them with those natural products and forces which underlie all industries and all arts.
(3.) They would learn in a general but efficient manner the fundamental industrial processes which underlie the more special processes of the common arts.
(4.) This general but genuine knowledge of materials, forces, and processes will enable each student to choose, with a fair degree of intelligence, the industry for which he or she is fitted by special taste and power.
(5.) Such a course would make far easier than now the change from one occupation to another, which must ever remain an incident of growing industries.
(6.) It would give to each person, as employer, some power to judge of the work of the employed.
(7.) It would furnish a basis in intelligence for general sympathy and appreciation among different classes of workers.
(8.) The last and greatest good would be the cultivation of the industrial disposition. * * *

SECTION 3.

INDUSTRIAL AND SCIENTIFIC EDUCATION OF WOMAN. *

The education of woman in science, arts, and industries is undertaken by many of our schools of science and agricultural colleges. Following the example of ordinary colleges and universities, more than half of which extend equal advantages to both sexes, the institutions endowed by the nation for the practical education of the people have generally afforded women the benefits of the instruction given men and frequently have provided special training for them in spheres peculiarly their own. The institutions of this class which are not known to admit women are the State Agricultural and Mechanical College of Alabama, the Georgia State College of Agriculture and Mechanic Arts, the Southwest Georgia Agricultural College, the South Georgia College of Agriculture and the Mechanic Arts, the Louisiana State University and Agricultural and Mechanical College, Maryland Agricultural College, Alcorn Agricultural and Mechanical College (Mississippi), Agricultural and Mechanical College of the State of Mississippi, New Hampshire College of Agriculture and the Mechanic Arts, Rutgers Scientific School, Agricultural and Mechanical College (University of North Carolina), agricultural and scientific department of Brown University, South Carolina College of Agriculture and the Mechanic Arts, University of Tennessee and State Agricultural College, State Agricultural and Mechanical College of Texas, Virginia Agricultural and Mechanical College, and agricultural department of West Virginia University.

The greater portion of the remaining agricultural colleges open their recitation-rooms, lecture-rooms, museums, libraries, and laboratories alike to men and women. There may be minute differences in the regulations under which the sexes come, but they are not sufficiently important to be mentioned in the reports and catalogues of the individual institutions, and therefore are hardly worthy of general notice. A few colleges and universities understand the full needs of woman's practical education and have felt themselves able to undertake it. Older countries have deemed it necessary to give such instruction. The making of garments, the economical management of the household, and the care of the sick are among the home industries that have been taught in special schools. Mr. J. Scott Russell gives special prominence to fire, food, clothes, and health as subjects for woman's study. After discuss-

---

* The material for this Report was originally collected in conformity to a Senate Resolution introduced by Senator Morgan, of Alabama. That resolution made special mention of efforts for the industrial education of women. Consequently much attention has been given to that subject in preparing this document.

ing the need of instruction in them and other subjects of kindred utility, he says:

It is for the woman whose husband works hard to earn money that I propose this special and superior education to enable her to spare and spend his money as well and wisely as he earns it. It is most necessary for the poor man's wife to know the value of money and the nature of money's worth. The cost, value, and wise way of using fuel is to her and hers a first need. The first principles of cookery are to her vital conditions of existence. She, above all, should know how to select good food, to cook it wholesomely and nutritiously, to mix good drinks, to buy cheaply, and to get good measure and exact quantities of all she wants; to make all her markets wisely and well; to buy all of the best, and all at a moderate price; that is her special wisdom. How to clothe her children, her husband, and herself with good, lasting, warm stuffs; to select them herself, to cut them herself, to sew them herself—there is occupation, enjoyment, virtuous work. Then to be able to teach her children all she knows; to be able to train them to be wise, virtuous, and useful like herself—there is work and also happiness; and then to be able to receive from them grateful help in return—there is reward. Then look at the poor man's leisure in a home illuminated by such an educated woman; look at an evening fireside where books can be interestingly and well read aloud; where songs can be sung correctly and well in parts in which all can join; where stories can be well told and games of intelligence played, and where each can benefit by another's knowledge. See how the evils and gloom of a humble lot vanish before the sunshine of an educated mother's home organization. It is to the poor man that the educated wife is the great prize of life.

The efforts which are being made for the technical and industrial education of women, not only in agricultural colleges but also in all other institutions in which they are being practically trained, may be combined under the following heads:

(1.) The opportunities afforded them for general scientific training.

(2.) The instruction given in art which, though often intended only to give the pupil a valuable accomplishment, may be utilized for the purposes of earning a livelihood.

(3.) Instruction in sewing, dress-making, millinery, and kindred pursuits.

(4.) Instruction in household economy; that is, in subjects pertaining to the health and comfort of the family, including kitchen garden training, cookery, and nurse training.

(5.) Instruction in special industries, such as telegraphy, phonography, horticulture, wood and other engraving, decorative work, wood carving, lace work, designing textile fabrics, lithography, photography, and other related occupations.

THE EDUCATION OF WOMAN IN SCIENCE.

Universities and colleges furnish scientific instruction, either incorporated in a classical or literary course, or brought into a distinct course, or in both these ways. The general work of the distinctively scientific schools is given at length elsewhere, and the facilities they offer to women may be seen by referring to the accounts of the various schools. But there are special schools which call for notice in this connection.

Fifty-one courses of study, each constituting a full collegiate curriculum, are offered by professors and other instructors in Harvard College to those who pass the Harvard examinations for women. The number availing themselves of some or all of these courses is not large. The instruction afforded is well adapted to make highly educated teachers and specialists of those who are long in attendance.

Summer institutes are held in many places, and in some of them scientific and practical education receives prominent attention. The Martha's Vineyard [Mass.] Summer Institute in 1879 had courses in botany, zoölogy, geology, and mineralogy, in industrial drawing, and in phonography among the considerable number which it offered. There were about 170 students in attendance.

Scientific training in the majority of the institutions for the higher education of women is confined to the most elementary instruction in a few of the most prominent branches. Some of these institutions having the funds requisite to the furnishing of appliances illustrative of scientific studies, and patrons who demand such a course of study for their daughters, offer extended instruction, supplemented by laboratory practice and illustrated by the best apparatus in use. A few institutions only will be needed to represent this latter class. Rockford Seminary, Rockford, Ill., offers a scientific course, in which, in the first year, physiology and hygiene and botany are taken; in the second year, physics; in the third year, chemistry; in the fourth year, geology. The means of practice and illustration comprise a chemical laboratory, physical apparatus, a valuable herbarium, and cabinets of geology, mineralogy, etc.

The collegiate course of Milwaukee College (which is for women) gives prominence to scientific subjects, and the appliances in this direction include a finely equipped observatory; physical and chemical laboratories, each having special reference libraries; apparatus designed not only to illustrate, but to encourage investigation; and cabinets representing five branches of natural history. Original investigation is made the objective point toward which every student labors throughout the course.

A statement respecting the scientific instruction given in Wellesley College (Massachusetts) in 1880 has been furnished, and will be found in Appendix E.

Smith College, Northampton, Mass., and Vassar College, Poughkeepsie, N. Y., may be taken as the typical institutions providing the highest general education for women. Smith College has an extended course of study covering four years, equal in character and scope to that of the university as understood in this country. It employs a staff of 22 professors and teachers, accords degrees on graduation, and includes, besides the higher English branches of polite education, studies in Latin, Greek, German (early and modern), French, Anglo-Saxon (early English), mathematics, geometry, calculus, theoretical surveying, navigation, and astronomy. The scientific studies include chemistry (with laboratory work), geology, mineralogy, physiology, psychology, zoology, botany, and biology. The art courses embrace music, drawing, painting, modelling, with lectures on architecture, sculpture, art, and household decoration.

Besides general studies the courses at Vassar embrace the Greek, Latin, German, and French languages; in mathematics, geometry, calculus, surveying, navigation, and astronomy, with the use of observatory; in science, chemistry (with laboratory practice and lectures), physiology and hygiene, geology, and mineralogy. The art classes can be made elective or special studies. The college has a fine gallery of art, anatomical cabinet, and museum of natural history. The last contains collections of fossils, minerals, rocks, etc., and the zoölogical museum is rich in ornithology. A considerable number of the Vassar graduates engage in teaching.

INSTRUCTION IN SEWING.

Sewing has been successfully undertaken in the public schools of several cities, among them Baltimore, Newark, Boston, and Providence.

In the report of the school commissioners of Baltimore for 1879 it is stated that at the request of the president of the board some of the teachers commenced teaching sewing, knitting, embroidery, and other useful branches, one afternoon each week being devoted to this instruction of the female pupils. The experiment was satisfactory to both pupils and patrons, and a general wish for its continuance was expressed.

In Newark five primary industrial schools are established for poor and destitute children. The pupils in them spend a portion of their time in work, a portion in regular class-room duty, and another portion in receiving a dinner. The dinner and the materials for work are provided by a society of ladies, while the board pays the educational expenses, not exceeding $200 for each school. The superintendent says:

Nothing in our schools gives me more pleasure than to witness the sewing exercise of the girls. Many receive here all the instruction in this most useful art they ever obtain.

The rules for the department of sewing in the public schools of Boston give a good view of the scope and requirements of the system employed there. They are as follows:

(1) Two hours a week, as appointed by the regulations of the school committee, shall be given to each scholar of the fourth, fifth, and sixth classes of the grammar schools, one hour at a time, for instruction in sewing. This time should not be shortened for other studies or examinations, or any other purposes, without the consent of the committee on sewing especially obtained.

(2) Each scholar shall be requested to bring work from home prepared, as far as possible. But in any case where it is not so provided, the sewing teacher will be expected to have work on hand, that there may be no excuse for an unoccupied hour, and that time may not be wasted in sending home for work.

(3) A sufficient supply of needles, thread, and thimbles shall be kept on hand by the sewing teacher to furnish to any child who is without them from carelessness or inability to supply them, or who has not the proper needle or thread for her work.

(4) The sewing teacher is requested to make all preparation and fitting of work out of school, that she may give the whole hour to the oversight of the work. Any fitting that requires time should be laid aside to be attended to out of the hour, and other work supplied in its place.

(5) Every effort should be made to vary the instruction, that every girl may learn thoroughly the varieties of work. If she has learned one kind of work the sewing teacher is requested to furnish her with some other variety, that she may be made efficient in all kinds of work. In this way, patchwork should be discouraged after a scholar has learned thoroughly what can be learned from it. Every effort should be made for promotion in work, from plain sewing through the darning of stockings to nice stitching and button-holes, from the simpler to the more difficult, in order to give an interest and desire for perfection in such work. It is a good plan to keep pieces of cloth for practice in making button-holes, stitching, or any other such special work, which can be given whenever there is want of work, or if other work has been completed in the course of the hour, to carry out the idea of promotion.

(6) The sewing teacher may find assistance from any charitable society with which she is connected, which would willingly furnish garments prepared and fitted, to be returned to the society when completed. Or she can suggest to any scholar who has not provided material for her work, that she show to her mother the garment she has finished at school, and offer it to her for the price of the material. Many a mother would like to buy such a garment for its use or for a specimen of work, if it is well done.

(7) The regular teacher of the class is expected to take entire charge of the discipline of the class, as she is more thoroughly acquainted with her scholars; also to see that the work is distributed promptly, at the beginning of the hour, either by herself or through monitors, and to assist in keeping each scholar diligently occupied through the sewing hour. It is recommended that she should give credits or marks for efficiency and inefficiency in sewing, in the same manner and according to the methods pursued in other lessons in her class.

The history of sewing in the public schools of Boston begins as far back as 1835. In that year an order was issued allowing the girls of the second and third classes of the public writing schools to be instructed in sewing by their regular teachers one hour a day. In 1854 this branch of instruction was included among those taught in the lowest class of the grammar schools. Lessons of not less than an hour in length were given twice a week. Materials for sewing, to an amount not exceeding twenty dollars annually, were furnished each school in which instruction in sewing was introduced. A reaction occurred the subsequent year, through the influence of the masters of the schools, and an order was passed permitting the discontinuance of the instruction when the interests of any school should be subserved thereby.

The introduction of instruction in advanced needlework was due to the philanthropy of a lady, who was allowed to provide materials and teachers for a class of older girls connected with the Winthrop school. This was in 1865 or 1866. The results of the experiment were satisfactory, and after some eight years the work was adopted by the school board. In 1875 it was decided by the city solicitor that it was not competent for the board to employ a special teacher of sewing. This difficulty was overcome by procuring an act of the legislature allowing sewing to be taught in the public schools of the State. Since that time the work has prospered. Exhibitions of sewing have contributed to awaken interest. Though poorly attended at first, they are now oftentimes crowded. They are so planned as not to interfere with the regular work of any school. Says a recent report:

> The sewing committee, and doubtless other members of the [school] board, have from time to time interesting proofs of the practical value of this industrial training. Not infrequently young girls, fresh from school, find steady and remunerative employment, thanks to their skill with the needle. Others are now able to keep their own garments, and those of younger sisters and brothers, neat and tidy, when formerly rents and rags prevailed. And many graduates of our schools, in more favored positions, admit that they owe their skill in fine needlework entirely to the teaching received at school.

The cost of material supplied by the city in 1880–'81 was $208.23.

The following extracts are from a newspaper account of an exhibition of plain sewing done at one of the Boston schools:

> Several long tables were placed lengthwise in the room, and these were filled with garments and articles of household use, which had been made by the girls, whose ages ranged from eight to sixteen. There were shirts with plaited bosoms stitched by hand, every stitch set with the utmost precision; undergarments very prettily made and trimmed, in some cases entire sets trimmed with lace, which was also the work of the youthful seamstresses; dainty flannel skirts with embroidered edge, and seams done in a regular "feather stitch" or "herring bone," the old stitches that our grandmothers used so much and that are coming in vogue again with many other old fashions. One ambitious girl had made herself an entire suit of lace bunting; it was a pale shade of blue, and was made with short round skirt trimmed with a double row of side-plaiting, the upper one edged with lace, prettily-arranged draperies, lace trimmed and held in place with loops of satin ribbon, and a blouse waist with three plaits at the back and in the front. Every stitch was made by hand; there wasn't a touch of machine work about it, and the whole costume was stylish and jaunty. Dressing-sacks and wrappers were among the articles exhibited, and there were the cunningest of all little baby dresses and sacks. It is evident that the girls do a good deal of the home-work in those few hours each week. The specimens of lace-work were very handsome, a part of it being most exquisitely done, every stitch set with an evenness that was remarkable. During the afternoon half a dozen girls from the upper classes fitted dresses and drew patterns; they do this with ease and accuracy, and are very good fitters indeed. * * *
>
> The progress that has been made since the plan of having yearly exhibitions was carried out two years since is very marked. Not only has there been an improvement in the work, but individual taste has been cultivated as well. One sees it in the knots of ribbon that adorn the garments, in the very way in which they are folded, the quality of material, the dainty laundering, and the sheets of colored tissue paper set underneath the folds to show the work to better advantage. Not only are the

children taught to make, but to mend as well, and the manner in which some of these girls keep their garments in good repair is very gratifying. It is a good thing in more ways than one, this teaching; it makes the girls careful and tidy and gives them economical habits. Not a girl graduates from that school but may earn her own living by needlework if the necessity meet her, and she is not compelled to give time that she can ill-afford in learning to use the needle properly. If she has not to do this she becomes invaluable at home.

Specimens of work done by girls in the Winthrop School, Boston, are permanently on exhibition in the museum of the National Bureau of Education, and attract the favorable notice of visitors.

The teaching of sewing in private educational institutions has been generally limited to directing and assisting the young ladies for an hour or two each week while they do any necessary mending or other work with the needle. A few schools now have regular and thorough instruction in this department; for example, in the Kansas State Agricultural College "young ladies are taught in all the ordinary forms of sewing with needle and machine, and in cutting, fitting, and trimming dresses and other garments. They may furnish materials and work for their own advantage during the hour of practice under the direction of the superintendent." In Lasell Seminary opportunity is given to learn dress cutting and millinery, and many pupils gladly avail themselves of the offered instruction. The report of the industrial work of this institution, given in Appendix E, shows the results of this training, and plainly indicates its utility and success.

ELEMENTARY INSTRUCTION IN HOUSEHOLD ARTS.

Kitchen gardens.—Closely allied to the Kindergarten is the kitchen garden, a school which applies the principles of the Kindergarten to the instruction of young girls in various branches of household work. The end it has in view is the preparation of its pupils for practical work in the household, either as servants or as members of families. The instruction is given by means of toys illustrating domestic operations, and the children are directed in their play with these toys so that they learn many household duties and come to associate housework with pleasure and enjoyment. The course is divided into six lessons, to each of which a month's time is devoted. The first lesson embraces, among other subjects, fire-kindling, paper-folding, and waiting on the door; the second, the setting and clearing of the table and house-cleaning; the third, making beds and sweeping; the fourth, laundry-work; the fifth, the dinner-table and the names and uses of different kinds and pieces of meat; the sixth, the moulding of bread, biscuit, &c.

This system of instruction was originated by Miss Emily Huntington, of New York City, and the first "kitchen garden" opened there in 1877. Since that time the system has been introduced into schools in many prominent cities, and is welcomed by people of wealth and culture as a means of introducing order and intelligence into the homes of the poor, and of inspiring an early love for domestic work; and, as a prominent paper remarks, "It seems to be a step toward solving the old problem of how to obtain a supply of skillful, intelligent, and contented household servants."

The latest report received gives an account of eleven different schools or classes in progress, with 200 children under instruction. There were several classes or lecture courses in progress for the training of teachers. This development of the Fröbel methods of object-teaching seems to be peculiarly adapted to the practical character of our people and to the needs of the times.

INSTRUCTION IN DOMESTIC SCIENCE.

Instruction in domestic economy forms a considerable part of a young lady's education in several of the European nations, and is coming into prominent notice in this country. In Germany the instruction and the methods of imparting it conform to the social position of the parties instructed; but in England, as in this country, the instruction is given in schools established for the training of any who may wish to avail themselves of their advantages. The most prominent of the English schools is the National Training School for Cookery, at South Kensington; it was maintained by subscriptions, donations, and fees until the government gave it, in 1873, the use of a building and in 1874 an endowment.

The establishment of schools of cookery in this country is largely due to the efforts of a few efficient ladies who realized the imperative need of the general adoption of more economical and healthful methods of cookery. Successful schools have been opened in many leading cities. A historical sketch of the New York School of Cookery and an account of the work of Miss Maria Parloa are given in Appendix E.

In addition to the distinctive schools of cookery there are several institutions which provide instruction in this and in other equally important household arts. The schools in which young ladies are required to share in the domestic work for the sake of health, discipline, and the reduction of expenses are not included among them. They usually assert that it is not their intention to teach the industrial pursuits of the home. For example, the catalogue of Mount Holyoke Female Seminary, South Hadley, Mass., in which it is well known that there are labor requirements, says:

> It is no part of the design of this seminary to teach young ladies domestic work. This branch of education is exceedingly important, but a literary institution is not the place to gain it. Home is the proper place for the daughters of our country to be taught on this subject, and the mother the appropriate teacher.

If it be conceded that a majority of mothers have the opportunity, ability, and disposition to teach their daughters household arts, yet it must be allowed that there are many who have not the power to become teachers of such things. Some are ignorant of the subjects to be taught. Some are not strong enough to undertake the task. Others are too much engaged in undertakings which have no direct connection with the home. It seems no more than fair that mothers busied by a multitude of calls and duties, or deprived by sickness of the privilege of keeping their place in the family, or consciously deficient in skill themselves, should be able to find schools in which their daughters could be trained in those things which lie peculiarly within the province of the mother. A great end of primary schools is to aid and extend home instruction, and it is not a valid objection that lessons are learned in them which mothers might better teach. The mother is the appropriate religious teacher of children of tender years, yet the instruction of such children in Sunday school is not generally objected to by Christian people. Brief mention may be made of instances in which this principle of teaching what belongs especially to the mother is carried out in relation to home labors and duties.

In the Elizabeth Aull Seminary, Lexington, Mo., there is a school of home-work where "are practically taught all the mysteries of the kitchen and laundry, such as the making of pastry, pickles, sauces, cakes, ornamental icing, and the washing of flannels, ruffles, and laces."

The degree of mistress of home work is conferred upon graduates in this school.

The ladies in the Kansas State Agricultural College are given during their third year a course of lectures on the laws of life and health. The course is ten weeks in length, and brings up questions pertaining to personal health, such as food, air, exercise, clothing, and temperature of rooms. There is also a series of lectures on household economy, accompanied by practical illustration in the kitchen laboratory, continuing through a term and a half. These cover the general ground of economical provision for the household, marketing, cooking, preserving, order, neatness, and beauty in table service, comfort of family, and care of sick room. These are supplemented by the lectures upon household chemistry and dairying.

In the Pennsylvania State College female students substitute a course in domestic economy for the practical instruction on the farm and campus taken by the men. This course is intended to give a knowledge of the application of science to the work of the kitchen and laundry, a further acquaintance with drawing, and some familiarity with the principles and practice of house decoration. The studies included and the time devoted to each may be seen by reference to the statement respecting the college, found in appendix A.

At the Hampton (Va.) Normal and Agricultural Institute instruction in sewing and household industries is continued through the course, special attention being given in the middle year to plain cooking and sewing.

In Missouri University a course of lectures on domestic chemistry is given to students intending to graduate in the girls' course in arts. The instruction is given upon the general topics of air, water, food, and cosmetics. Under the head of air such subjects are considered as respiration, ventilation, heating of houses, clothing, and the germ theory of disease. All the properties of food, the methods of its preparation, and its nutritive and hygienic values are discussed. In this way the young ladies receive correct ideas of the subjects which pertain to the health, comfort, and happiness of the human family.

Extended accounts of what has been accomplished in the industrial training of women in Lasell Seminary, Auburndale, Mass., in the Iowa State Agricultural College, and in the Illinois Industrial University are to be found in Appendix E.

TRAINING SCHOOLS FOR NURSES.

The establishment of training schools for nurses is a wisely directed, philanthropic effort; and all who need the skilled hand and accurate judgment of an experienced nurse, or are interested in enterprises the purpose of which is the alleviation of suffering and the recovery of health, will allow that these schools furnish a considerable element in the promotion of the practical education of woman. They are preparing suitable women for the onerous and responsible duties of nursing in both hospital wards and private residences, and they are working with most commendable zeal and thoroughness. The statistics of these schools are presented in the table given herewith; and facts which indicate the general features of the schools, such as requirements of admission, nature and methods of instruction, success of pupils and graduates, etc., are set forth in the subsequent statements. Schools other than those which the statistics and statements here given represent are either organized or about to be organized in many other cities.

INDUSTRIAL EDUCATION IN THE UNITED STATES. 65

Statistics of training schools for nurses; from replies to inquiries by the United States Bureau of Education.

	Name.	Location.	Date of incorporation.	Date of organization.	Superintendent.	Number of instructors.	Present number of pupils.	Graduates in 1880.	Total number of pupils since organization.	Graduates since organization.	Number of years in full course of study.	Number of weeks in lastto year.	Salary paid pupils.	Conditions of admission.
	1	2	3	4	5	6	7	8	9	10	11	12	13	14
1	Connecticut Training School for Nurses (State Hospital).	New Haven, Conn.	1873	1873	Gertrude Barrett	4	24	8	*116	43	1½	50	$174 yearly, with board and washing.	Age, 22-40; good health and character, and common school education.
2	Illinois Training School for Nurses.	Chicago, Ill.	1880		M. E. Brown						2		$8 a month for first year; $12 a month for second.	Age, 25-35; sound health and good education.
3	Boston City Hospital Training School for Nurses.*	Boston, Mass.		1878	Alice C. Davis	a16	42	17	70	19	2	52	$10 a month for first year; $14 a month for second; $20 to $30 head nurses (graduates).	Preference given to applicants between ages of 25 and 35; if otherwise good, applicants between 21 and 25 may be admitted.
4	Boston Training School for Nurses (Massachusetts General Hospital).	Boston, Mass.	1875	1873	Jane E. Sangster		42	16	247	73	2	50	$102 a month for first year; $14 a month for second.	Preference given to applicants between 25 and 35 years of age.
5	Training School for Nurses (New England Hospital).	Boston, Mass. (Codman avenue, Roxbury district).	b1863	1872	H. F. Kimball, chairman of nurse committee.	c1	16	6	83	40	1½	50	$1 a week for first 6 months; $2 a week for second 6 months; and $3 a week for the last 4 months.	Age, 21-31; satisfactory references of character and capacity and a month's probation.
6	Missouri School of Midwifery.	St. Louis, Mo.	1875	1875	Wm. C. Richardson, M.D., president.	3	16	21	*180	*173	1	16	None.	A common school education.
7	Brooklyn Training School for Nurses.	Brooklyn, N. Y.	1880	1880	M. E. Snyder	1	10	0	10	0	2	62	$9 a month for first year; $15 a month for second year.	Age, 21-35; sound health, good education and character.
8	New York State School for Training Nurses.*	Brooklyn, N. Y. (46 Concord street).	1873	1873	A. H. Wolhrupter	8	7	5	66	47	1	52	Boarded and lodged during the entire course of instruction.	Age, 21-40; satisfactory references as to moral character and general health, ability to read and write, and an agreement to remain one year.

*From Report of the Commissioner of Education for 1879.

a These are 1 matron and 15 head nurses.   b Date of incorporation of hospital.

S. Ex. 25——5

Statistics for training schools—Continued.

	Name.	Location.	Date of incorporation.	Date of organization.	Superintendent.	Number of instructors.	Present number of pupils.	Graduates in 1880.	Total number of pupils since organization.	Graduates since organization.	Number of years in full course of study.	Number of weeks in scholastic year.	Salary paid pupils.	Conditions of admission.
9	Charity Hospital Training School.a	New York, N. Y. (Blackwell's Island).		1875	Harriet L. Clute	(d)	40	28	120	57	2	52	$10 a month for first year; $15 a month for second year; $15 a month for second.	Age, 20-35; good health and character, and good English education.
10	Training School for Nurses (Bellevue Hospital).	New York, N. Y. (426 East 26th street).	1872	1873	E. P. Perkins	6	63	29	209	148	2	50	$9 a month for first year; $15 a month for second.	Age, 25-35; satisfactory references from clergyman and physician, and a knowledge of simple arithmetic, reading, penmanship, and English dictation.
11	Training School of New York Hospital.a	New York, N. Y. (West 15th street).		1877	Eliza Watson Brown	4	20	14	52	14	1½	52	$10, $12, and $16 a month for the first, second, and third 6 months respectively; graduate, $25.	Age, 25-35; sound health, perfect senses, good moral character, and good common school education.
12	Training School for Nurses (House and Hospital of the Good Shepherd).	Syracuse, N. Y.	1873	1872	Mary D. Burnham	8	10						$10 a month and board and lodging.	
13	Nurse Training School of the Woman's Hospital.a	Philadelphia, Pa. (North College avenue and 23d street).	b1861	1863	Anna E. Broomall, M. D.	c1	17	10	117	c46	2	52	$5 a month for first 6 months; $10 a month for second 6 months; $16 a month for second year.	Age, 21-45; intelligence, good character and habits.
14	Philadelphia Lying-in Charity and Nurse School.	Philadelphia, Pa.		1828										
15	Washington Training School for Nurses.	Washington, D. C.	1877	1878	J. M. Toner, M. D., president.	7	10	3	24	3	2	50	None	Must not be under 21; must furnish certificates of health, good moral character, and possess a common school education.

*From Report of the Commissioner of Education for 1879. b Date of incorporation of hospital. d Instruction given by hospital physicians.
a These are 1 matron and 15 head nurses. c Also lecturers. e Since 1873.

Admission.—It is recognized in all schools for the training of nurses that the duties of a nurse are such that only those who have peculiar aptness for the work and who possess mental, moral, and physical strength, should be encouraged to undertake it. In order to make an estimate of an applicant's fitness, it is the custom of several schools to send her a list of questions the answers to which will enable the authorities to estimate her suitability for the vocation of nurse. The list sent out by the New York Hospital Training School, which fairly represents the usual questions, is as follows:

(1) Candidate's name in full, and address; (2) condition in life, single or a widow; (3) present occupation or employment; (4) place and date of birth; (5) height; (6) weight; (7) where educated; (8) are you strong and healthy, and have you always been so? (9) Are your sight and hearing perfect? (10) Have you any tendency to pulmonary complaint? (11) Have you any physical defects? (12) If a widow, have you children? How many? How old? How are they provided for? (13) Where (if any) was your last situation? How long were you in it? (14) Names in full and addresses of two persons to be referred to. State how long each has known you. If previously employed, one of these must be the last employer. (15) Have you read and do you clearly understand the regulations?

In the Connecticut Training School, the secretary corresponds with the applicants, and thereby becomes sufficiently acquainted with their character and capacities to discern any special improbability that they would pass successfully through the course of training. If this is the case, the applicant is advised to seek employment elsewhere.

The suitable age of applicants is generally placed at from twenty-one to thirty-five years. The reason given is that those younger have not ordinarily sufficient mental and physical development, and those older do not readily acquire new habits. The necessity of good character in a nurse is obvious, and the need of sound health is equally so, for none are ignorant of the sacred trusts and arduous duties which devolve upon her. The amount of education required of applicants is not very great, as natural ability and willingness to learn are the chief requisites. Often pupils are admitted without examination on the statement that they have acquired a common school education; but in at least one school —the one connected with Bellevue Hospital, New York—an examination is required in reading, penmanship, arithmetic, and English dictation.

The various requirements for admission and limited accommodations preclude the reception of the majority of applicants in many instances.

The New York State School makes up a class each year of only six from the large number of applicants. Of thirty-three who applied at Bellevue in December, 1879, only three were received. At the New England Hospital, in 1878, eighteen of forty applicants were admitted to probation. Of the remaining twenty-two, nine withdrew their applications, eight were not of proper age, and five were for various reasons considered unsuitable.

Probation.—The pupils of the nurse-training schools are usually admitted to a probation of one month, during which they receive no compensation for their services beyond board and lodging. A large portion of those thus admitted fail to meet the demands made upon them during this time. In one school, sixteen out of one hundred and five left during the probationary month. Of the eighteen mentioned above as admitted to probation in the New England Hospital, only nine were approved. Of the other nine, one left on account of death in the family, six were not thought strong enough, one was dismissed for disobedience, and one because unreliable. It could not be otherwise than that the first month's experience of a nurse should be full of difficulties and discouragements. The secretary of the Connecticut Training School makes a clear presentation of this point in the following well-advised remarks:

> A severe test it (the month of probation) is to most of the young women who come to us from quiet homes where they have led for years a sedentary life. The active work required in the wards—bending over the beds of the sick, bearing patiently the caprices and exactions of invalids, witnessing surgical operations and other painful sights, dressing wounds and sores—presents hospital life under a different aspect from the one drawn by their imagination; and some, for want of strength, patience, or perseverance, fail to carry on the work on which they so hopefully entered. Others come to the school with a real self-consecration, and, although they may be almost discouraged by the recognition of all that is expected of them, yet if they faithfully discharge their duties as they meet them one by one and seem desirous to embrace every opportunity for improvement, they are encouraged to persevere, and soon acquire a skillfulness which enables them to do their work acceptably and with comparative ease to themselves.

Those fulfilling the conditions and expectations of the probationary month are usually required to enter into a written agreement to remain in the school, subject to its authority during the time allotted to a complete course, and sometimes to remain at the call of the school superintendent for a specified period after graduation. Without such an agreement, pupils would be drawn away before completing the course by tempting offers from other sources.

Maintenance.—Pupil nurses are maintained, with one or two exceptions, at the expense of the school, or the hospital to which it belongs, during the time of their training. The sums paid in addition to board and lodging are given in the table. These sums are not looked upon as a remuneration for services performed, as the instruction and experience are considered a sufficient compensation. But it seems desirable that the pupil should not be dependent on any one outside of the hospital for money to meet her expenses for at least dress and text-books, and therefore an allowance is made for them. The dress is often required to conform to rules relative to material, to plainness, and to other things which make it suited to the sick-room. Thus one of the regulations of the nurse training school at Philadelphia is:

> Nurses, while on duty, shall wear cotton dresses without crinoline and without trains, and soft shoes without heels. * * *. White aprons must be worn. The utmost simplicity is enjoined both in outer and under clothing, as no ruffled, tucked, or flounced skirts nor trimmed garments are allowed to be sent to the hospital laundry.

In another school—

> They are required after the month of probation to wear the dress prescribed by the society, a gray woolen dress in winter and seersucker in summer, *simply made*, white apron and cap, and linen collars and cuffs.

The text-books are not numerous, being usually limited to a few works upon nursing, such as Domville's Manual for Hospital Nurses, Dr. Frankel's Manual, the Bellevue Hospital Manual, the Connecticut Training School Handbook, Florence Nightingale's Notes on Nursing, Mrs. Lee's Handbook, Miss Veitch's Handbook, and Smith's Notes.

The information in the possession of the office does not render it possible to state positively what provisions are made for the board and lodging of pupils in all cases, but it may be stated, as a general rule, that they have quarters in or connected with the hospital building, and removed as far as possible from the sick wards. It is most desirable that they should have, not a bare living place in a corner of the hospital, but a comfortable and attractive home, furnishing surroundings that rest, revive, and animate those that are weary and discouraged from excessive toil and care, and that give opportunities for undisturbed sleep in the daytime to night nurses, and entire immunity to all from suggestions of the hospital. The Nurses' Home of the Bellevue Hospital provides for all these wants, and it has been said that the noticeable exemption from illness which the nurses of that institution have enjoyed is largely owing to their cheerful and healthy surroundings.

The maintenance of pupil nurses suggests an inquiry into the support of the schools or hospitals to which they are attached. Two schools make no report or statements that bear upon financial questions; two, which are connected with public hospitals, are supported in the main by city appropriations. The income for 1879 of the Bellevue Hospital Training School for Nurses was: services of nurses, $13,142; annual dues of members, $2,920; donations, $3,230.

The Connecticut Training School for Nurses received, in 1877, $1,003.55 for the services of nurses, while its entire expenses were $1,922.12. It has an endowment of $12,000.

The school at the Woman's Hospital of Philadelphia, in 1879, received enough for services of nurses to pay the expenses incurred by the hospital for its support.

The New England Hospital receives its income mainly from payments for yearly free beds, receipts for board, treatment, and medicine, income of funds, and subscriptions and donations.

The Boston Training School is supported by receipts for nurse services, subscriptions, and donations, and income of funds.

The New York State School is a part of the Brooklyn Maternity (hospital), which derives its income from contributions and collections, city appropriations, pay of patients, etc.

The Missouri School of Midwifery has fees of $75 for the entire course, and $10 extra if the pupil be admitted to the dissecting rooms.

Instruction.—The instruction afforded in nurse training schools seems to divide itself naturally into practical, or that received at the bedside of patients; theoretic, or that obtained from text-books and lectures; and auxiliary, or that which is useful in nurse-training, but not specifically a part of it.

Practical nursing must be learned at the bedside, and the beds of a hospital offer the best opportunities. There the nurse may observe the treatment of persons suffering from the various medical and surgical diseases, or who have undergone surgical operations, and thus she acquires an extensive and valuable experience in a short time. Sometimes there may be only a special class of patients treated in the hospital where the pupils of the nurse schools do their work, as is the case in the Brooklyn Maternity, but within any such class there is a wide variety of diseases and dangers. Usually there are several departments requiring nursing adapted to the cases included in each, in which pupil nurses serve in turn.

In the Connecticut Training School for Nurses "each has a special place assigned to her, and remains several weeks in charge of that department. In the course of the year she acquires experience in medical, surgical, fever, and confinement cases."

In the Boston Training School for Nurses the time is divided between medical and surgical cases, and between day and night duty, and each nurse has two months in the lying-in hospital.

At Bellevue Hospital, all the female wards, two male wards, the Sturges Pavilion for the treatment of acute surgical cases, and the lying-in hospital, attached to Bellevue, are nursed by pupils of the school.

Another principal advantage in hospitals is the frequent presence of skillful physicians to give counsel and directions, and furnish instruction at a time when it will make a lasting impression on the pupil's mind. Then the advice and assistance of experienced nurses, especially on critical occasions, prepares the nurse for similar emergencies in the future, while the constant oversight of both head nurses and physicians stimulates the pupil to form habits of accuracy, fidelity, and attentiveness to patients. Although the practical drill obtained at the bedside under the supervision of experienced persons is of principal value, yet systematic instruction from carefully written manuals of nursing, and by lectures and talks on subjects pertaining to nursing, is not neglected. The course of instruction is very similar in the majority of the schools, and that of the Connecticut Training School for Nurses may be taken as a representative. The instruction includes (1) the dressing of blisters, burns, sores, and wounds; the application of fomentations, poultices, and minor dressings; (2) the application of leeches; (3) the administration of enemas; (4) the use of the catheter; (5) the keeping of temperature records; (6) the best method of applying friction to the body and extremities; (7) the management of helpless patients; removing, changing, giving baths in bed, preventing and dressing bed sores, and managing positions; (8) bandaging, making bandages and rollers; (9) making patients' beds and removing sheets while the patient is in bed; (10) the keeping of all utensils, sponges, bed, tables, etc., perfectly clean.

Other subjects of instruction mentioned in courses of training elsewhere are warming, ventilation, and care of sick rooms; the making of accurate observations and reports to the physician on the state of the secretions, expectoration, pulse, skin, appetite, temperature of the body, intelligence, as stupor or delirium, breathing, sleep, condition of wounds, eruptions, formation of matter, effects of diet or medicine; management of convalescents; attention during confinement and care of new-born infants; management of trusses and other appliances; the giving of baths; the stopping of hemorrhages; disinfectants. Some of the schools specify that examinations in the studies pursued are held either at appointed intervals or at the option of the examining officers. The annual report of one institution says that there have been 146 class recitations to the lady superintendents and five formal examinations conducted by members of the hospital staff. Another, "Our superintendent teaches the nurses from the best manuals we can procure, and examines them on the lesson. There are quarterly examinations by the lecturers and by the medical men among the directors."

The theoretic instruction in several of the schools is received only by lectures on the fundamental subjects of training. The Washington Training School announced for 1880–'81 six lectures upon each of the following subjects, viz: Anatomy, physiology, surgical nursing, medical (hospital) nursing, obstetrical nursing, medicines and dietetics, and nursing of children. The Boston City Hospital had provided 46 lectures for the training school in 1879–'80, as follows: On nursing of insane patients, circulation of the blood, care of surgical instruments and appliances, one lecture each; on poisons, common sense in the sick room, nursing and care of skin diseases, nursing and dressing of fractures, two lectures each; on eruptive fever, administering of medicine, nursing in confinement, physiology and food, care of nervous patients, three lectures each; on care of the eyes, four lectures; on anatomy and surgical dressings and appliances, five lectures each; on general diseases and emergencies, six lectures.

The education of pupil nurses in branches collateral to their profession is not extensively attempted in the training schools. Usually they are taught how to prepare delicacies for the sick, attractive articles of diet, and the drinks and stimulants in common use. On the subject of medical instruction the secretary of the Connecticut Training School for Nurses remarks:

> Whilst far from wishing our nurses to be so learned as to think they know as much as the physicians, we are desirous to have them understand the structure of the human body and all its functions; for this purpose they study from text books on physiology, anatomy, and midwifery, reciting to, and receiving valuable instruction from, the head nurse, who also conducts quarterly examinations in these studies in the presence of the ladies of the executive committee.

Results.—The success of these training schools may be seen in the excellent work done by the pupil nurses in both hospitals and private houses, in the thorough preparation they give for a life work in a noble calling, and in the appreciation in which their services are held by the medical profession and others after their graduation. A report speaks thus of the benefits which the establishment of the nurse training school brought to the inmates of the Charity Hospital of New York:

> The change wrought in the hospital was sudden and radical. The nurses themselves were of a better class than it was thought possible to secure, many of them being ladies of culture and refinement. Abuses which had existed since the foundation of the hospital were at once swept away. The care and sympathy received by the patients promoted their recovery, while the presence among them of the pupils of the school so improved the moral tone of the institution that the calls for punishment were no longer necessary and were removed. The death rate of the hospital has steadily diminished since the introduction of the training school. * * Other causes have contributed to diminish the mortality, but none so much as the increased efficiency in nursing, due to the careful training of intelligent nurses.

Quotations from two reports will indicate the excellence of the work done by the pupils in private families and the constant demand from that direction.

A recent report of the Connecticut Training School for Nurses says:

> We have been able to respond this year to thirty-six applications for the services of trained nurses, and in each case the one sent has returned to us with a certificate from the patient or the attending physician which testified to her efficiency and the value of the school as an educator.

The Bellevue Training School says:

> The demand for nurses in private families has increased far beyond the ability of the school to supply. One hundred and forty persons have been attended by nurses from the school, and twenty-nine graduated nurses have been fully employed during the year in New York and the vicinity. The managers have been much gratified by the satisfactory reports which the nurses have brought back from physicians and employers.

The following paper is sent with pupils that go out from this school for the purpose of private nursing.

> New York Training School for Nurses, 426 East Twenty-sixth street.
>
> ——— ——, 18—.
>
> This day the nurse ——— ——— has been sent on the recommendation of ——— ——— to nurse in case of ——— ———.
>
> ———— ————,
> Superintendent.
>
> REGULATIONS.
>
> The charge for the services of a nurse is $3 per day, or, if employed one week or more, $16 per week. Traveling expenses and washing to be paid by the family employing the nurse.
>
> All applications must be made personally, or in writing, to the superintendent.
>
> When the nurse's services are no longer required, this sheet of paper is to be returned, sealed up, with a candid statement, on the fly-leaf, of her conduct and effi-

ciency, either from one of the family or the medical attendant, together with information of the amount to be paid, and whether it is inclosed or will be paid at the office of the society.

The nurse is to be allowed reasonable time for rest in every twenty-four hours; and when her services are needed for several consecutive nights, at least six hours in the day out of the sick room must be given her.

Except in cases of extreme illness the nurse must be allowed opportunity to attend church once every Sunday.

When on duty the nurse is always to wear the dress prescribed for her by the regulations of the society.

Patients and their friends are invited to contribute to the general funds of the society, and thus assist in enabling it to afford the advantages of gratuitous nursing to the poor, which is one of the objects the association hopes to accomplish.

Where it is possible, a few days' notice of the nurse's return to the home should be sent to the superintendent.

Copy of paper to be returned by employers.

———, 18—.

The services of the nurse ——— ——— being no longer required, she is this day set at liberty to return home, and the sum of $———, being the remuneration for her attendance, is ———

(Signed) ——— ———.

Remarks as to conduct, efficiency, etc.

The post graduate success of educated nurses, which is the evidence of their training, is manifest from the continued call for their services in preference to those of any others, and receives further proof from letters written by those who have observed their work; and the same may be said by the citizens of any city possessing a nurse training school that Felix Adler said of the one at Bellevue:

It is one of the beneficent institutions of our city, in which every New Yorker may take a legitimate pride, and of which there can be no doubt that it is destined to become a source of inestimable blessing to the community.

EDUCATION IN MISCELLANEOUS INDUSTRIES.

Telegraphy.—Women may receive instruction in telegraphy in at least thirty-three business colleges and commercial departments; in five or six colleges not having such a department; in a few institutions for the superior instruction of women; and in several special schools, among which the Cooper Union School of Telegraphy is pre-eminent. The following is its report for 1882:

This school admitted 60 pupils this year. About 160 applied at the regular examination and passed, but they could not be admitted to the class for want of room. The Western Union Telegraph Company has so far interested itself in this school as to pay a teacher, who trains the pupils in the thorough methods of that company. They can thus draw competent operators for their offices from this school, and have provided a large proportion of the graduates of this school in times past with employment on their lines, although they are under no special obligation to provide a place for any. At present the supply of operators is less than the demand; and the extension of lines going on rapidly over this vast country will always make a steady demand for the employment of women in telegraphy. Their fidelity, intelligence, and patience will always give them the larger share of this kind of work, from which the young men are drawn away by a more active and ambitious life. The number of pupils remaining at the end of six months' instruction was 55, and the number receiving certificates was 28.

Stenography.—There are a few institutions for higher instruction furnishing training in some form of short-hand writing, among them Oskaloosa (Iowa) College and Battle Creek (Mich.) College. The usual places of instruction are private classes, of which the office has no information, and business colleges, some twenty of which offer this branch of instruction to ladies as well as gentlemen.

Practical design for manufactures.—A school of practical design is connected with the Massachusetts Institute of Technology. The art of making designs for fabrics is taught by means of practical work done under the personal direction of a skilled designer. The course embraces technical manipulations, copying and variation of designs, original designs or composition of patterns, and the making of working drawings. A weaving department is associated with the school, and observation of manufacturing on a larger scale is made during occasional visits of inspection. The expense to pupils is about $5 a year for instruments and material. Applicants are required to show some acquaintance with free-hand drawing and the use of drawing instruments.

Printing.—The employment of women in printing offices is increasing, and, in order to encourage them in fitting themselves for remunerative positions in these offices, the Kansas Agricultural College remits the fees of women taking the courses of instruction in printing. Two courses are pursued in this art. In one the student is given a general view of the rise and progress of printing, of type-founding, stereotyping, electrotyping, and lithography. He (or she) is taught the implements or tools employed in typography and how to use them, composition, imposition, principles and practice in plain and ornamental job-work, presses and their working, technical terms, and general duties of a first-class workman. The second course, the lessons of which alternate with those in the first, embraces instruction in spelling, capitalization, punctuation, proof-reading, and correcting, preparation of essays and criticisms on the same, and such other miscellaneous work as will make the student accurate and expert in language.

Dairying.—During the spring term daily instruction and practice in the different branches of dairying is given the ladies of the second year in the Kansas State Agricultural College by the professor of agriculture.

Horticulture.—It has seemed proper to several institutions to provide instruction in horticulture with special reference in some cases to the training of women. The Agricultural College of Missouri justifies the existence in it of an extended horticultural course, on the ground that it is but a fair recompense to the women of the State, who have succeeded in creating a taste for the cultivation of fruits and flowers and for ornamental grounds, that their daughters, as well as their sons, be provided with a school where they may perfect themselves in these pursuits. The course extends over four semesters, and includes propagation of plants, pruning and training, gardens and gardening, floriculture and transplanting, pomology and forestry, ornamental trees and shrubs.

Facilities for the study of horticulture are provided in Cornell University, Ithaca, New York, the instruction being given throughout the third year in the agricultural course. During the first term, attention is given to fruit culture and forestry; during the second, to vegetable culture; the third, to floriculture, including landscape gardening. The general subject (of floriculture) is divided into the following topics: window-gardening, general management of house plants, hanging baskets, climbing vines, flowering bulbs, ferneries, wardian cases, etc.; outdoor flower-gardening, lawns, ornamental shrubs and trees, commercial flower-gardening.

Similar horticultural courses exist in many of the other institutions endowed with the national land grant, and one or two colleges have also introduced instruction in horticulture, but the office has no information from which it can judge of the success of their work.

SECTION 4.

CONCLUSION.

The results expected of industrial education, and foreshadowed already by past achievements, are found in the improvement of our manufactures, the elevation of the producing classes, the removal of obstacles to learning a trade, the diminution of crime, the popularization of education, and the dissemination of peculiarly American ideas.

The manufacturer is aided by industrial education through the improvement of his products. His success depends on the demand for his goods at reasonable prices. This demand is regulated by the needs of customers. They ask for durability of material, attractiveness of design, and excellence of workmanship in whatever they purchase for permanent use. Manufactures improve as they become possessed of these and similar qualities, which can be economically secured only by the application of technical knowledge. Durability arises from excellence of raw material and is retained by the selection of the right processes by which to convert it into the state in which it finally appears. The quality of raw materials is not unfrequently to be determined by chemical tests, and many of the processes of its manufacture are regulated by chemical principles. The science which guides in the determination of these processes must be the one which will lead to their improvement and perfection. Hence courses in chemistry are established in our principal polytechnic schools as well as in colleges of agriculture (to which science chemistry makes liberal contribution), and in schools of mining and metallurgy. For a similar purpose engineers are taught to determine the strength of materials used in building railroads and bridges, houses and machines. Investigations in the domain of physics and chemistry have frequently taught the skillful application of new and serviceable agents to the production of labor. Efforts to render products more attractive in design are being made through schools and school systems by the introduction of drawing. From this art architects and designers acquire the power to represent the forms and patterns which, according to their judgment, will be most acceptable. Whether utility or elegance is the end to be obtained, it matters not. Either calls for the draughtsman's best production. In fact, the presentation of proofs that increased attractiveness in manufactured goods comes from excellence in drawing would be needless.

The end to which drawing contributes most frequently is accuracy of mechanical construction. The pencil precedes the hand and the machine. It leaves little for them to do but to execute with exactness the most minute details. In order to do this the workman must be able to interpret the drawings and reproduce the indicated forms. He must understand the language in which they are described, and acquire by education and experience the ability to obey it. Men of this class have laid out our railways, opened our mines, started and improved our manufactories, and built our houses. They have aided in increasing our industries 35 per cent. in the last decade and in compelling an English confession that "the United States will probably pass us in the ensuing decade" in the value of her industries.

The elevation of the working classes is an inevitable result of educating them in industries. The direct effect upon the intellect is great and beneficial. The immediate moral influence is of the best. A manly feeling is awakened and kept alive by the consciousness of power and skill to do. An incentive to enterprise and frugality is set forth. It has been laid down as a rule by Prof. Edward Atkinson that—

> Other things being equal, high wages coupled with low cost are the necessary result of the most intelligent application of machinery to the arts, provided the education of the operative keeps pace with the improvement of the machinery.

In this way wages are increased and the cost of living diminished. Things consumed are not made expensive through waste caused by ignorance. It is a fact, recognized by manufacturers, that more highly skilled and better paid laborers produce goods at lower cost. Under these circumstances a laboring man can reasonably entertain hopes that he may possess, by careful industry and economy, the things which his better nature most craves, a home, the implements of his trade, a few books, some dollars in the bank. The time seems to have come when a poor man's family need not be his misery. Property may accumulate; wealth possibly be attained. The moral value of such possibilities is incalculable; and therein lies the elevating power of industry well paid and well performed, and of education toward some of its branches. Few will deny that the training for a legitimate calling, and the pursuit of it with earnest application and perseverance, though done for the express purpose of gaining a competency, contributes to morality and virtue, and lays no stumbling blocks in the way of intelligence and education. There are the soundest reasons for believing that the instrumentalities in operation for the promotion of industrial education are silently yet powerfully lifting the laborer to a higher position. The immediate future will reveal this truth clearly. The well known statistician Col. Carroll D. Wright cautiously and significantly says:

> There is a slow but constant decrease in the number of laborers who seem to be doomed to remain at the bottom; a decrease in the number who are able to employ nothing but muscle. If this be true, and all my own observations indicate it, the status of what is now unskilled labor will be vastly improved during the next generation.

A recent writer on Holland represents the peasants around Gröningen as wandering about the city after their produce is sold and their purchases made "casting compassionate glances at all that population of shop-keepers, clerks, professors, officials, proprietors, who, in other countries, are envied by those who till the ground, but here are regarded by them in the light of poor people." It is not impossible that the industrial classes of our country may be brought by suitable education to occupy, and realize that they do occupy, a place to be envied by many of those engaged in mercantile and professional pursuits. George MacDonald is credited with saying:

> I would gladly see a boy of mine choose rather to be a blacksmith, or a watchmaker, or a book-binder, than a clerk. Production, making, is a higher thing in the scale of reality than mere transmission, such as buying and selling. It is, besides, easier to do honest work than to buy and sell honestly.

The entrance to industrial occupations has been beset by difficulties and discouragements. The apprenticeship system first degenerated and then died. Scarcely any one but a father will direct a novice in mechanical labor, and he rarely has ability and opportunity. Now the defect is being remedied. Boys are going from our manual training schools and departments of mechanical engineering to honorable and responsible positions in mills, foundries, and factories. Three or four years of study and practice have given them a broad intelligence and more training than the customary seven years' of apprenticeship ordinarily gave to boys of the olden time. By these schools, whose work has been reviewed in the preceding pages, the question of how to obtain preparation for industrial employment has been answered.

Industrial education dignifies labor as well as opens doors to its skillful and remunerative performance. If labor has a noble end and purpose, if it employs intellect, if it abundantly rewards its servants, then it is worthy to be crowned.

The perfection of our manufactures, the facilitating of commerce, the unearthing of mineral wealth, the economizing of the fertility of farms, the dissemination of practical knowledge, these are ends which are being served by the graduates of our industrial institutions. These ends do not lack nobility. These forms of labor require the exercise of high intellectual powers. The attainments are of no mean order which enable a man to perform the great feats of engineering for which our country is becoming known or which are required of superintendents of extensive factories. Even the doing of a single thing understandingly and well brings the doer respect from himself and his neighbor and dignifies his calling. "It is the privilege of any human work which is well done," says Emerson, "to invest the doer with a certain haughtiness. He can well afford not to conciliate whose faithful work will answer for him."

The diminution of crime is to be expected from the diffusion of industrial education. The percentage of criminals who have received even the elements of an education is small. An authority on the subject has said that "one-third of all criminals are totally uneducated, and that four-fifths are practically uneducated." Yet when the relative number of convicts who are illiterate is compared with the number of those who have not learned a trade it is found to be much smaller. It is stated by Dr. Wines that in Baden only 4 per cent. of the prisoners are unable to read when received, and that they are for the most part fond of reading, but that 50 per cent. have not learned a trade; in Bavaria 12 per cent. are illiterate, 29 per cent. ignorant of a trade. Mr. Charles F. Thwing a few years since claimed that 60 per cent. of the inmates of the Michigan State prison had no trade, while less than 25 per cent. could not read, write, and cipher; that in the prison of Minnesota 37 of 235 prisoners could not read and write, 130 never learned any business; and that in the Iowa penitentiary the ratio of illiterate convicts to those unskilled in a trade was about 1 to 6.

Whatever may be the reliability of these figures it cannot be denied that the lack of technical training is a prolific cause of crime. This lack is being supplied to some extent by recently established schools, which both afford opportunities for such training and draw public attention to the existing need of it.

The introduction of industrial features into educational institutions has a tendency to relieve education of the accusation that it is unpractical. There are those that ask of our schools more than they are intended to furnish. Their voice in years past called into being manual-labor and half-time schools. Since the failure of these means to realize the expectations of their advocates, believers in education for industrial labors have been uncertain what course to adopt in carrying out their views. Now it may be said with safety that the mass of our citizens are convinced that the educational systems and institutions of the country are above reproach, and will be modified by the introduction of new features as they are needed. A minority are disposed to be critical and assert that education is unwisely conducted, and that governmental aid might be applied more reasonably to the establishment of public farms and work-shops for training purposes than to public schools.

That which has seemed better to them than existing methods is taking place. It may be anticipated that as the day approaches when training in mechanic arts and agriculture shall be as possible as in literature and science the sounds of complaint will be fewer and prejudice less frequently will dull the weapons by which the forces of ignorance are being destroyed.

Finally, the protection of American institutions demands the industrial education of our youth, that they may carry our ideas of obedience to law and our republican principles into the midst of the multitude of foreigners that crowd our factories and our mines and perform much of our labor.

Ours is a peculiar nation. In it the principles of morality prevailing in civilized countries are upheld with warmth and reason. Our political principles are distinctive and characteristic. Daniel Webster enumerated them in one of his great speeches. They are the establishment of popular governments on the basis of representation; the recognition of the will of the majority, fairly expressed, as having the force of law; the supremacy of law as the rule of government for all, and the existence of written constitutions founded on the authority of the people. He asserted his belief that the influence of town meetings in which American principles were recognized and followed made those who went from them to dig gold in California " more fit to make a republican government than any body of men in Germany or Italy." If there be added to the lessons of our political gatherings and elections education in the essentials of government, instruction in the sciences contributing to human prosperity, familiarity with the languages of civilization, sound rules for the conduct of life, and training for an ennobling and enriching occupation, then American youth will be prepared oftener to fill leading places in industries, will win respect for their skill, learning, and wisdom, and, being respected and trusted, will be enabled to enshrine American liberty more securely in the hearts of laboring men. So our land shall be the home of a safe and permanent nation, "where an industrious population advances like a victorious army, where the poor find work, the laborer becomes a proprietor, the proprietor grows rich, and all have the hope of a prosperous future;" and the ends of our industrial education will be accomplished.

APPENDIXES.

APPENDIX A.

STATEMENTS RESPECTING THE INDIVIDUAL INSTITUTIONS ENDOWED WITH THE NATIONAL LAND GRANT.

ALABAMA.

STATE AGRICULTURAL AND MECHANICAL COLLEGE.

[Report of President I. T. TICHENOR, D. D.]

In compliance with your request, I have the honor to submit the following report of the Agricultural and Mechanical College of Alabama.

It was designed that this college should conform, as nearly as its means would permit, to the demands of the law of Congress: that without excluding other scientific and classical studies and including military tactics, its leading object should be to teach those branches of learning which relate to agriculture and the mechanic arts, with a view to furnishing a liberal and practical education to the industrial classes.

If in any respect we have come short of this design, it has been because we lacked the means for its full accomplishment.

Our endowment is derived entirely from the sale of lands donated by act of Congress, and consists of Alabama State bonds amounting to $253,500, bearing 8 per cent. interest, payable semi-annually. The only other source of income is an incidental fee of $15 per annum charged each student. Our annual income from these sources averages about $22,500.

The grounds and buildings were donated to the college by the trustees of the East Alabama College. The cost of the main building, which was erected in 1858, was about $65,000.

A farm, donated by citizens of Auburn, to which additions have been made by purchase, comprises about 100 acres, with farm-house, stables, &c.

The annual expenses of the college are equal to its income of $22,500. The salaries of professors and instructors amount to $17,600 per annum.

The faculty of the college (1880) consists of (1) a president, who is professor of moral philosophy, (2) a professor of engineering, who is also commandant, (3) a professor of ancient languages, (4) a professor of chemistry, (5) a professor of mathematics, (6) a professor of agriculture, (7) a professor of natural history, (8) three instructors, two of whom are engaged as teachers in the preparatory departments.

The number of students for the year ending June, 1879, was 279. The number in classes last year was: First class, 13; second class, 31; third class, 51; fourth class, 78; preparatory department, 104; post-graduates, 2.

The number of graduates of the college since its organization in 1872 is 42; of these there have been graduates in the literary course, 14; scientific course, 7; engineering course, 14; agricultural course, 7.

The inability of many of our students to remain at college long enough to accomplish the entire course has greatly diminished the number of graduates. Seven hundred and fifty young men have received instruction here since the organization of the college; many of these who did not graduate are engaged in useful and honorable vocations.

Of those who have terminated their connection with the institution whose employment we have been able to ascertain, there are engaged in agriculture, 222; mechanical pursuits, 40; teaching, 30; the professions, 40; and commerce, 90; while the occupation of 94 others is unknown.

There are now (1880) in college 228 students in classes, as follows: first class, 20; second class, 18; third class, 57; fourth class, 59; preparatory department, 74.

No law of the college excludes women, but public opinion prohibits them from sharing its benefits. The faculty have brought this matter to the attention of the board of trustees, and have expressed their almost unanimous desire that women should be invited to enter the college; but the board has not seen proper to adopt their recommendation.

For information as to the means for practical application of instruction, you are respectfully referred to the reports of the professors of chemistry, agriculture, and engineering, and the commandant of the college, herewith submitted.

Very respectfully, your obedient servant,

I. T. TICHENOR,
President.

The following statements accompany President Tichenor's report:

Statement of the professor of agriculture.

I present herewith an outline of the course of study in the agricultural department of this institution. The course requires four years for its completion, entitling the student who stands an approved examination in all the studies embraced in it to the degree of "bachelor of scientific agriculture."

The first two years of the course are devoted to studies which are common to the usual college course in the freshman and sophomore years, except that modern languages (French and German) may, if the student elects, be substituted for Greek and Latin. The last two years are devoted to technical instruction, embracing the following subjects:

(1) Mechanics and physics, in which the class makes daily recitations during the first term (five months) of the junior year.

(2) Botany, two recitations weekly during the second term of the junior year.

(3) Descriptive astronomy and meteorology, three recitations weekly during the first term of the senior year.

(4) Geology and mineralogy, three recitations weekly during the second term of the senior year.

(5) Zoölogy and entomology, two recitations throughout the first and second terms of the senior year.

(6) Agricultural chemistry, with practical instructions in qualitative and quantitative analysis of soils and fertilizers, to which two hours are devoted daily throughout the first and second terms of the junior year.

(7) Vegetable physiology, embracing the structure and habits of plants and their relations to the soil and atmosphere, occupying two recitations weekly during the first and second terms of the senior year.

(8) Practical agriculture, embracing the subjects of soils, drainage, cultivation, irrigation, fertilization, farm-crops, farm-implements, farm-animals, fruit-culture, market-gardening, floriculture, and landscape gardening; in which daily recitations are required during the whole of the two years.

In addition to the technical studies embraced in this course, the class in agriculture is required to make three recitations weekly in the second term of the senior year in political economy, and to attend weekly lectures upon constitutional law, the law of contracts, conveyancing, and landlord and tenant, in which it is designed to furnish such instruction on these subjects as will be of service to the practical agriculturist.

For the purpose of illustrating and applying the principles taught in the text-books and lectures, the college is furnished with the following appliances:

(1) Extensive mineralogical and geological cabinets, and a museum of natural history.

(2) A commodious laboratory, fitted up for lectures and work in analysis, supplied with furnaces, balances, gas and water, and twenty-five work tables, each furnished with necessary chemicals and apparatus.

(3) An experimental farm of twenty acres, devoted to soil-tests of fertilizers and experiments in the cultivation of field crops, grapes, fruits and flowers, conducted under the supervision of the professor of agriculture, with practical instructions to the class during the junior and senior years.

Respectfully submitted.

W. H. CHAMBERS,
Professor of Agriculture.

Statement of the professor of engineering.

In the first year of the course of four years we teach practical drawing on the plan pursued in the English schools; in the second year, the practical use of the chain, compass, theodolite, and engineers' leveling instruments is thoroughly taught in the field for farm and land surveying, ditching, and leveling.

Drawing, in the second year, includes practical work on farm maps, drawing from models, shades, shadows, structural drawing, and topographical delineation; in the third and fourth years, at least two hours each day in completing a course in projection and perspective. Graphical skill is cultivated in depicting, in conventional colors, machines, bridges, furnaces, water, gas, and railway structures. Plans, profiles, and sections of railroad surveys complete a very full and practical course of industrial drawing.

The practical work in surveying begins in the second year of the course. All students of this year are exercised in the use and adjustment of the plain and solar compass, of the theodolite, sextant, engineer's leveling instruments, and the various styles of leveling rods. Individual practical instruction is given to each member of the class in the practice of surveying, locating, and division of lands, and in leveling ditches, gradients, terraces, farm, water, and railroad levels. Tracing railroad curves and subterranean lines in mining work is practically taught as part of the general course for all students of the second year.

Technical engineering is taught only to those students who have completed the general course of two years. A full course in chemistry, physics, and pure mathematics, with an elective course in either ancient or modern languages, is the basis of the course in engineering.

Mechanics, particularly the theory of strength of materials and of strains in roofs and bridges, with full instruction in regard to the construction of roads, railroads, bridges, canals, improvements of rivers and harbors, complete the work of the last two years of the course.

In aid of the practical studies of the college, and as a means of familiarizing students with the actual details of work, the second class in engineering devote two weeks in December, and the first class four weeks in April, to field work and to visits of inspection to machine-shops, mills, mines, furnaces, and engineering constructions within convenient reach. Geological students are afforded in vacation each year an opportunity of accompanying the State geologist in his excursions. In the past scholastic year the second class in engineering has visited and inspected the cotton and woolen mills, founderies, machine-shops, bridges, and gas works in and near Columbus, Ga. The first class in engineering inspected the founderies, workshops, gas and water works of Montgomery, and the iron region lying along the South and North Railroad.

R. A. HARDAWAY,
Professor of Engineering.

Statement of the professor of chemistry.

This department occupies four rooms: a lecture-room, a working-room, a furnace-room, and a balance-room.

The lecture-room is 40 by 40 feet, and is provided with a counter, pneumatic trough, copper gasometer, water basins, blackboards, shelves with glass cases, gas jets, blow-pipes, and all the necessary apparatus for illustrating a general course in theoretical chemistry.

The working-room is 36 by 24 feet and has 24 work-tables, each one supplied with a full set of reagents, a drawer, a gas jet with Bunsen's burner, and such other apparatus as is necessary to make all the analyses required in a full course on agricultural science. The balance-room contains two sets of balances with weights, one made by Becker of New York, the other by Oertling of London. The furnace-room is provided with a temporary furnace, furnishing an air-bath, water-bath, sand-bath, and a still for distilling water. There are also small furnaces for assaying and organic analysis.

Water and gas are supplied in every part of this department; and a constant Watson's battery, furnishing electricity to all the bells of the college, is kept in the lecture-room.

The instruction given in this department consists of (1) a general course in chemistry to all students; (2) qualitative analysis, given to students in agriculture and science; (3) quantitative analysis, including both gravimetric and volumetric, given to students in agriculture and science, and (4) agricultural chemistry, given only to agricultural students. The text-books used are Bloxam's Chemistry, Church's Laboratory Guide, Caldwell's Agricultural Analysis, Mott's Manual of Chemistry, Johnson's How Crops Grow and How Crops Feed.

The course in general chemistry requires five hours a week to complete it; that in agricultural chemistry three hours a week; three years are required.

Respectfully submitted.

WM. C. STUBBS,
Professor of Chemistry.

Statement of the commandant and military instructor.

The practical work in the military department consists of daily drills in the school of the soldier, squad, company, and battalion; guard duty is required of all cadets capable of bearing arms.

The text of Upton's Report on Tactics, revised edition, through the "school of the soldier" is learned by heart by every cadet, and each is required to repeat it verbatim. The school of the company and battalion, the parades, honors, &c., are recited by all cadets, illustrated by demonstrations on the blackboard, but only the "school of the soldier" is required to be recited literally.

In addition to recitations in Upton's Tactics, lessons in organization, supply, transportation of armies, fortification, strategy, target-practice, and ordnance are recited by the cadets and illustrated by the professor. This is a four years' course.

R. A. HARDAWAY,
Colonel Commanding.

Supplementary information.

From the catalogue of 1880–'81, it appears that a professor of English literature has been added to the faculty. The number of students registered is 182, in classes as follows: first class, 15; second class, 23; third class, 34; fourth class, 63; fourth class, section A, 47. The twenty graduates in 1880 make up the whole number of alumni to 62; of these twenty, six took the degree of A. B.; two B. S.; three, B. S. A.; and nine, B. E.

The requirements for admission to the college embrace the common-school studies, elementary algebra, and English history; to these must be added, by those who are candidates for the degree of bachelor of arts, in Latin, four books of Cæsar and six of Virgil's Æneid; in Greek, two books Xenophon's Anabasis. All students pursue the same course for two years, except that those in other than the literary course may take French and German in place of Latin and Greek, and must take drawing. At the end of the two years the students choose between courses in agriculture, civil engineering, mining engineering, literature and science.

There appears to be a recent modification of the course in civil engineering for the purpose of giving students an opportunity to become familiar with mining. Special instruction is introduced in mining, preparation of ores and their metallurgical treatment. Geology and mineralogy receive considerable attention. An additional year of study is required of those who would obtain the degree of mining engineer, that of bachelor of mining engineering being given at the end of the fourth year.

ARKANSAS.

INDUSTRIAL UNIVERSITY.

FAYETTEVILLE, ARK., *March 30, 1881.*

SIR : The chief end of the Arkansas Industrial University is to afford a cheap practical education to the industrial classes, but especially to teach them agriculture and the mechanic arts.

The endowment funds consist chiefly of the grant of land by the general government, in the donations of $100,000 by the county of Washington, Ark., and $30,000 by the town of Fayetteville. The grounds and buildings are valued at $170,000. The annual income is $10,400 from the bonds of the county and town aforesaid, $2,000 from tuition fees, and an average of about $5,000 from the legislature; annual expenditure, about $17,500. Professors' salaries consume about $15,500 of this sum.

The professors and instructors are as follows: (1) president and professor mental and moral science; (2) principal of normal department; (3) professor of mathematics (instructor in tactics); (4) professor of natural sciences and chemistry; (5) professor of civil and mechanical engineering; (6) professor of natural sciences; (7) professor of military science and tactics (not appointed as yet); (8) professor of physics and astronomy; (9) teacher of drawing and painting; (10) professor of ancient and modern languages; (11) professor of English literature and history; (12) professor of music, aided by competent assistants; (13) principal of preparatory department; (14) preceptress of preparatory department; (15) first assistant preparatory department; (16) second assistant preparatory department; (17) third assistant preparatory department.

The number of enrolled students this session (including the medical department) is 473; of these, two-thirds are males. The college fees are almost nominal, the majority not paying more than $5. All expenses, including boarding, clothing, books, &c., do not exceed $200 to the majority of the students. The board grants free tuition to 600 beneficiaries and 400 normal students sent from the various counties according to population. Not more than one third of these appointments are claimed by the respective counties. Our graduates do not exceed eight or ten annually. They take generally the A. B. or B. S. degrees, though a few take the normal degree. About one-fourth of the graduates are females.

We have a classical course differing not materially from that in most colleges; an agricultural course identical with that in the agricultural and mechanical colleges, giving agriculture prominence in the curriculum; a scientific course, prominence being given to mathematics, engineering, and mechanical philosophy; and a normal course specially devoted to the training of teachers.

There is not now, nor has there been, any special instruction for young women. I have felt the need of a curriculum adapted to their mental characteristics. Some of them have been found with taste and talent for the higher mathematics.

We have no workshops, and practical mechanics receive no illustrations. In fact the farm work itself is on a small scale. The State in its poverty has not felt able to build workshops or suitably to equip a farm.

Very truly yours,

D. H. HILL, *President.*

Hon. JOHN EATON,
Commissioner of Education.

It will be observed that the first nine instructors specified in the foregoing list are more related to the college of agriculture and the mechanic arts than the remainder.

From the annual catalogues of the university the following facts are gathered:

STUDENTS.

The number of enrolled students for the year ending June, 1881, was 441, of whom 411 were from Arkansas, 8 from Missouri, 8 from Louisiana, 5 from the Indian Territory, 2 from Texas, and the rest (1 each) from several other States. The "academic" (collegiate) department enrolled 120, and the normal classes 82. Many students are enrolled in two or more branches of the institution.

TUITION.

The fees are $5 for matriculation; students other than normal or beneficiary also pay $10 per term; there are three terms each year, covering forty weeks in all. Tuition in the university proper is free.

FREE SCHOLARSHIPS.

The trustees, under legislative authority, have created 600 beneficiary and 430 normal appointments. In addition each county can appoint each year one honorary scholarship from among the meritorious students of the public schools therein. Sixty scholarships are also open to scholars from any part of the State.

STUDIES.

Particular notice of the studies of the classical, Latin, letters, modern languages, English, and normal courses would not be in the province of this report. The scientific, the two engineering, and the agricultural courses are industrial in their direct bearings. The studies of the subfreshman year preparatory to these courses are the same, namely, algebra, French, German, drawing, and English composition. The studies common to the four courses during freshman year are English, algebra, geometry, physical geography, physics, drawing, and German. Those not in other than the agricultural course take French, and those in the civil engineering course omit botany. Sophomore year the courses continue nearly parallel. Their common studies are trigonometry, general and analytical chemistry, blowpipe, analytical geometry, surveying and navigation, and German. The civil engineering course omits botany and zoölogy, which are common to the others. The common studies of the junior year are analytical geometry, geology, mineralogy, and analytical chemistry. The other studies are as follows: Scientific course, physiology, biology, and anatomy; civil engineering course, applied mathematics and calculus; mining engineering course, applied mathematics; agricultural course, physiology, stock breeding, entomology, anatomy, astronomy, book-keeping, agricultural chemistry, and machinery. In the senior year the studies of the civil engineering course are natural philosophy, industrial chemistry, and applied mathematics. The mining course added analytical chemistry to these studies, and the scientific course substituted it for applied mathematics. The studies of the agricultural course are more numerous, including, besides analytical and industrial chemistry, physics, agriculture, landscape gardening, and veterinary surgery.

Degrees are given to those who have successfully completed the several courses, as follows: Classical course, A. B.; scientific course, B. S.; agricultural course, B. Agr.; civil engineering course, C. E.; mining engineering course, M. E.; Latin letters course, B. Lat. letters; modern languages course, Bach. Letters; English course, Bach. Eng. Letters.

The following additional information, gathered from the annual reports, gives the general scope of the technical and special work pursued:

Military: Instruction in this department is designed to impart to each male student not physically incapacitated to bear arms practical instruction in the school of the soldier, of the company and of the batallion, the duties of guards, outposts, and pickets. The drills occur not over three times a week, and being short they involve no hardship, while it is manifest that they afford a good health-giving exercise and aid in the development of the physique and manly carriage of the student.

Chemistry: Chemical physics is studied by the students of all the courses during the first term of the sophomore year; it embraces the physical principles requisite to the pursuance of chemistry.

Inorganic chemistry: The course embraces three hours a week recitation and ten hours a week laboratory work. The important chemical elements and their principal compounds are considered as to their occurrence in nature, physical and chemical properties, methods of manufacture, prominent uses. About three hundred experiments illustrating important chemical principles are individually performed.

Organic chemistry is pursued by applicants for all the degrees excepting the A. B. (bachelor of arts).

An experimental farm of excellent character has been provided, immediately contiguous to the university, for agricultural and horticultural purposes. The labor system will be under the direction of the board of trustees, but students will not be required to labor more than ten hours per week. Compensation for labor will be from 2 to 10 cents per hour, according to ability.

All male students appointed as beneficiaries are required to take a course in agriculture or mechanics, "with permission to select such other studies as circumstances may allow."

Students in all departments are required to pursue not less than three distinct studies. The university library, though small, is increasing and comprises some valuable works. The legislature makes small appropriations, the last being $1,000 in 1879–'80.

The cabinet and museum are small as yet, but the collections slowly increase. The philosphical apparatus, though not large, is excellent. Female students are admitted to all the departments. There were in 1880 in the classical course, 3 in the senior class, 1 in the junior class, 0 in the sophomore, and 21 in the freshman. In the preparatory department there were 67.

CALIFORNIA.

UNIVERSITY OF CALIFORNIA.

[Statements from the recent registers and bulletins.]

The University of California was established by a law which received the approval of the governor early in 1868. It was opened at Oakland in the autumn of the following year. In 1873 it was transferred to its permanent home at Berkeley. The college of California, which had been organized several years before, transferred its property and students to the new university, and closed its work of instruction when that of the university began.

The university has for its object general instruction and education in all the departments of science, literature, art, and industrial and professional pursuits, and special instruction in military science and for the professions of agriculture, the mechanic arts, mining, civil engineering, law, and medicine.

The funds by which the university is maintained are derived from various sources and include the following endowments: (1) The seminary fund and public building fund, granted to the State by Congress. (2) The property received from the College of California, including the site at Berkeley. (3) The fund derived from the Congressional land grant of July 2, 1862. (4) The tide land fund, appropriated by the State. (5) Specific appropriations by the legislature for buildings, current expenses, &c. (6) The gifts of individuals. The amount received from the sale of the Congressional land grant of 1862 was $750,000.

The latest information received (1880) gives the following financial exhibit: Value of grounds, buildings, and apparatus, $805,000; amount of productive funds, $1,671,204; income from productive funds, $90,216; receipts from tuition fees, $200; receipts for the last year from State appropriations, $36,600.

COLLEGES.

The scientific departments are five in number, and consist of the colleges of agriculture, mechanics, mining, engineering, and chemistry.

The faculty is as follows: President of the university (also professor of physics); professors of the Latin language and literature; of the Greek language and literature; of history and political economy; of the English language and literature, of industrial mechanics; agriculture, agricultural chemistry, and botany; geology and natural history, chemistry; civil engineering and astronomy; mathematics; instructors in Latin, English, French, German, engineering, chemistry (2), quantitative and qualitative analysis; industrial drawing, mining, metallurgy; mathematics (2); mineralogy, physics and mechanics, and chemistry. Also a superintendent of the physical laboratory, assistant in agricultural laboratory, lecturer on practical agriculture, and lecturer assistant in chemistry. Besides these there are seven instructors in the literary branches.

The academic senate consists of all the faculties of all the colleges of the university.

STUDENTS.

The number of students who have been in attendance at the university in each year since its opening in 1869 is as follows:

Years.	Science.	Letters.	Special and at large.	Total.	Ladies.
1869–'70	14	21	5	40	
1870–'71	28	24	26	78	8
1871–'72	75	28	50	153	27
1872–'73	93	44	48	185	30
1873–'74	100	44	47	191	22
1874–'75	95	73	63	231	38
1875–'76	134	138	38	310	42
1876–'77	126	140	39	305	45
1877–'78	117	149	52	318	51
1878–'79	122	142	68	332	55
1879–'80	79	120	69	268	55
1880–'81	71	96	79	246	59

Of the 71 in the colleges of science in 1880–'81, 21 were in the freshman class, 17 in the sophomore class, 18 in the junior class, and 15 in the senior class. The course of study during freshman year is common to all the colleges of science.' At the beginning of the second year choice of course is usually made. Those continuing in science beyond the first year numbered in 1880–'81 4, of whom 2 were sophomores and 2 juniors. The students in the college of agriculture were 9. Of these 4 were sophomores, 3 juniors, and 2 seniors. Two sophomores, 2 juniors, and 7 seniors took the course in mechanics. The students in mining were: sophomore, 1; juniors, 3; seniors, 2; in all 6; in engineering: sophomore, 6; juniors, 4; senior, 1; in all, 11; in chemistry: sophomores, 2; juniors, 4; seniors, 3; in all, 9.

The students at large numbered 21, of whom there were in the college of chemistry, 2; mechanics, 1; general scientific course, 3; engineering course, 1.

The special students numbered 23, of whom there were in the college of agriculture, 2; chemistry, 5; mining, 5; engineering, 1; general course, 2; in all the scientific courses, 15. There were 35 pursuing partial courses, of whom 6 were taking agriculture; 1, engineering; 2, chemistry; and 2, general science. Tuition is free to residents of California; students from other States pay a matriculation fee of $25 and a tuition fee of $50 per year.

The following degrees have been conferred (to 1879 inclusive): bachelors of arts, 73; bachelors of philosophy, 137; total, 210.

By a recent bulletin it appears that the degree of bachelor of science is now given to those completing the undergraduate courses in science. Higher professional degrees are given to those who complete prescribed courses of higher study.

Women are admitted to all the colleges. Their attendance is chiefly in the classical and literary courses.

UNIVERSITY APPLIANCES AND COLLECTIONS.

Laboratories.—A large amount of space is devoted to the chemical laboratories. They are planned after the very best models. A physical laboratory is already organized.

Philosophical apparatus.—The cabinet of apparatus for the experimental demonstration of the laws of physics and mechanics is very complete.

An observatory has been provided for, through the benefaction of the late James Lick, esq.

The library contains about 20,000 books and pamphlets.

The collections illustrative of science which belong to the university are large and valuable and are adapted to the wants of students seeking a scientific or technical education. They are made up from material derived mainly from the State geological survey;

the Voy collection of California fossils, minerals, and rocks; the Pioche collection of rocks, ores, minerals, shells, &c., gathered in all parts of the world, but largely in South America; and the Hanks collection of minerals. These collections are given the names of their collectors. Current donations and purchases by the university do much to increase the value and extent of the means of illustration. The collections are divided among museums of classical archæology, ethnology, zoölogy, botany, geology, mineralogy, and ore deposits. The museum of ore deposits was founded in 1879. It is expected that it will fulfill the twofold purpose of rendering possible a course of instruction to mining engineers in ore deposits, and of affording an opportunity for the general study of the deposits of the Pacific coast. The museum of classical archæology contains a cabinet of medals and coins. There are also sets of ancient war maps and pictures of ancient life, customs, and architecture.

The museum of ethnology contains stone implements, skulls, ancient wooden tools, and Peruvian pottery.

The museum of zoölogy embraces a small collection of mammals, birds, reptiles, fishes, mollusks, and radiates.

The museum of botany has a valuable herbarium of Australian plants, collections of native wood cones, cereals, and photographs of California trees.

Professor Hilgard has placed his private collection of some 12,000 specimens of American and foreign plants in the lecture room of the college of agriculture for the use of students.

The museum of geology is divided into departments of paleontology and lithology. The first comprises the Whitney collection of California animal fossils and the collection of plants recently made by Mr. Lesquereux.

The lithological collection embraces extensive representations from notable localities, and especially of the rocks of California, eruptive and stratified.

The museum of mineralogy contains many specimens from the Eastern States and Europe, and a very full exhibit of minerals of the Pacific coast.

An agricultural museum is now being arranged, and already contains many indigenous and exotic woods and specimens of the flora of the State. A cabinet of the soils, agricultural products, and manufactures of the State is being formed.

The plants, &c., of the State geological survey are also in possession of the university and available for agricultural students. The agricultural grounds are being prepared and occupied as rapidly as the finances permit. A standard orchard, embracing 600 varieties, is now bearing. An experimental station, embracing 13 acres, is in use. Part of it is permanently occupied as a garden of economic plants. A garden of general botany is being laid out. There are three propagating houses, with other necessary buildings.

The regents have recently appropriated funds to commence an industrial survey of the State, under the direction of the professors of agriculture, chemistry, &c.

The college of mining has been further equipped (during 1879) with a complete metallurgical laboratory. Its students have full access to the chemical and physical laboratories and collections.

The college of mechanics is being equipped with a special laboratory and model room, which will also be open to the students in mining.

The college of engineering possesses a suitable collection of surveying instruments, models in wood of walls, bridges, arches, &c.; also in joints in carpentry and frame work, of bridge and roof trusses, diagrams of famous structures, and the hypsometrical and surveying apparatus formerly belonging to the State geological survey.

The college of chemistry possesses the necessary appliances, laboratories, &c., to make the work of study effective and practical.

The course in military science, required of all the students not physically disqualified, includes tactical instruction in book and field, lectures on the art of war, and practical study of fortification, &c., as afforded by the United States post at San Francisco and its extensive forts, garrisons, arsenal, and other appliances.

The opportunity for field and operative study in agriculture, mining, mechanics, engineering, and manufacturing chemistry afforded by the great industrial resources and enterprises of California are being freely made available by organized visits of inspection and other modes of study and observation.

The United States Coast and Geodetic Survey, the surveys and operations of United States engineers in the harbors of the coast, and the extensive works of the hydraulic mines, the irrigation, engineering, &c., are all used for illustration and instruction.

STUDIES.

There are eight regular courses of study in the university proper, namely, classical, literary, letters and science, and five scientific courses, and three irregular courses, namely, student at large, special, and partial. The classical course leads to the degree of bachelor of arts and corresponds to the usual academic course of the leading American colleges. It is designed to offer the best preparation for professional study and to furnish a liberal education.

Both Latin and Greek are required for this course.

The literary course leads to the degree of bachelor of letters and has the same general purpose as the classical course. It is designed for students who wish to study Latin and to enjoy a fuller course in English, French, and German than that offered by the classical. Greek is not required.

The course in letters and science leads to the degree of bachelor of letters, and in it special attention is given to the English language and literature, to modern languages, history, and political science. It is especially intended for students who wish a liberal course in general culture. Neither Latin nor Greek is required.

The student-at-large course does not lead to a degree; but students in it may, by vote of the faculty, be recommended to a degree upon the satisfactory completion of studies equivalent to those pursued in one of the regular courses. It is designed for students who wish to take a full but a purely elective course. They select studies from any of the courses, provided they satisfy the faculty that they are fitted to take the studies selected. Candidates for it are required to pass one of the regular admission examinations, and upon admission to take studies enough to make up the full number of exercises required of students pursuing a regular course. Students who fail to maintain their standing as regular students are not admitted.

The special course does not lead to a degree; but students in it may, upon leaving the university, receive a certificate of proficiency in the studies which they have pursued and in which they have attained marked scholarship. It is designed for students who are mature, and who wish to pursue some line of special study and correlated branches. Students under age are not ordinarily admitted. Applicants who fail on the admission examinations or students who fail to maintain their standing as regular students are not admitted.

The partial course does not lead to a degree; but students in it may, upon leaving the university, receive a certificate of proficiency in the studies which they have pursued and in which they have attained marked scholarship. It is designed for students who, because of ill health or other disability, are able to pursue only a limited number of studies or to remain at the university only a short time.

Applicants are not admitted to this course until they have passed a satisfactory examination on such preparatory subjects as may be thought necessary to fit them for the studies they wish to pursue.

The courses in science are those of agriculture, mechanics, mining, engineering, and chemistry. They are designed to give the student a good English education and an introduction to the principles of modern science, together with special instruction preparatory to a fuller course of professional study in the particular department he may choose. Neither Latin nor Greek is required in them, but a preparatory course in Latin is recommended.

The course in agriculture is designed for students who wish to familiarize themselves with the sciences which underlie the farmer's calling and with the best practice of its several branches. It is arranged with a view to preparing them for the intelligent and successful exercise of their profession as practical farmers or agricultural experts. The instruction obtained from text-books, recitations, and lectures is supplemented by visits to orchards, vineyards, farms, and dairies, and by the experiments conducted on the university farm.

The special instructors of the college of agriculture are a professor of agriculture and related subjects, a lecturer, who has charge of the experimental grounds, and two assistants in the laboratories.

The course of study under the regular professor begins with botany in the sophomore year. Much time is given to the description and study of plants useful and injurious to agriculture. From economic botany the student passes to agricultural chemistry and the theories of culture and the maintenance of fertility, which are the special studies of the junior year. During the senior year lectures are given and studies pursued which treat of the fundamental branches of agriculture, such as stock breeding, dairying, farm machinery, drainage and irrigation, and general field crops. The laboratories of the college are intended to aid in the investigation of questions in practical agriculture, principally by the examination of soils and products. In this way the best methods of increasing fertility, the value of manufactures relating to agriculture, the nature of the diseases of crops, can be ascertained, and adaptation of plants and the usefulness or injuriousness of insects can sometimes be determined. The benefits of the practical work of the college are available to farmers, as the professor in charge is ready to give prompt answer to inquiries that come within the sphere of his labors.

The course in mechanics is designed for students who intend to become mechanical engineers or machinists (so far as they are constructors of machinery) or to devote their energies to such technical and industrial pursuits as involve a knowledge of machinery. The course of study peculiar to the college commences with the junior year. Its special studies during that year include the applications of differential and integral calculus, the laws governing the rest and motion of points, bodies, and systems of bodies, and the determination of strains in structures. In the senior year hydrostatics, hydrodynamics, the regulation and accumulation of motion, and the determination of forces are considered; and a post-graduate year is devoted largely to the theory and construction of machines and to steam and steam engines. The acquaintance with drawing which the student has acquired during the previous years of general study is now utilized in drawing plans for machinery and in representing motion and the means for modifying it. No mention of a shop appears in the reports received from the university. It is presumed that actual work on machines is conducted in the mechanical laboratory, which is well equipped for practical instruction.

The course in mining is designed for students who wish to become mining or metallurgical engineers, or to engage in one of the many pursuits connected with the mining industries, such as the surveying and mapping of mines, the assaying and working of ores, the designing and use of mining machinery, or the exploitation of mines. The first two years of the undergraduate's course are nearly the same as that of the other scientific colleges of the university. A certain amount of the second year is, however, devoted to more special work, such as qualitative analysis, blowpipe analysis, land and mining surveying and leveling, industrial drawing, &c. The instruction given in these studies is practical as well as theoretical, the laboratories, instruments, and grounds of the university furnishing excellent facilities for this purpose.

During the last two years the instruction is more directly connected with mining, attention being given to analytical chemistry, analytical and applied mechanics, mineralogy, geology, mining, metallurgy, and assaying. While the scientific studies are not taken up in a merely technical way, they are taught as far as possible with reference to their applications to mining and metallurgy, and the entire course of the last two undergraduate years is overlooked by the instructor of mining and metallurgy, under whose special guidance the mining students come.

Students are encouraged throughout the course to visit the industrial establishments of San Francisco, Oakland, and vicinity, and to visit and study on the spot mines and smelting works at greater distances during vacations.

The course of study for post-graduate students in this department is being organized as fast as the means of instruction become available. It will include the studies of petrography, economic geology, crushing, separating, and mining machinery, political economy, and mining law, together with original work on the part of the students with ores, metallurgical processes, machinery, &c., for which the metallurgical and mechanical laboratories will offer excellent facilities.

The course in engineering is arranged for students expecting to adopt civil engineering as a profession, and to engage in such work as the survey of lands, leveling, topographical engineering, geodetic surveying, the location and construction of roads, railways, and canals, the designing and construction of bridges of wood, iron, or stone, the building of dams, reservoirs, and systems of water supply, drainage and sewerage, and the improvement of rivers, harbors, and seacoasts.

The special instruction in engineering begins in the sophomore year with the surveying course. This includes land and topographical surveying, leveling, the use of the plane table, road and railroad surveying and construction, with computation of earthwork required by excavations, tunnels, and embankments. A liberal amount of time is allotted, to practice in the field and to the use of instruments and in the working up and plotting of field notes.

Topographical drawing and map making are taught, and sketches made of the surrounding country. The work of the fourth year is chiefly professional. The subjects treated include the characteristics and properties of the various building materials, their strength, uses, and different methods of employment in structures; the rules governing the construction of works of masonry; problems relating to the more difficult constructions, such as groined, cloistered, rampant, and skew arches and domes, and walls bounded by warped surfaces; and the principles and practice of framing, bridge and truss building, the preparation of estimates and working plans. The solution of a problem in engineering terminates the undergraduate course.

The post-graduate course is three years in length, and leads to the degree of civil engineer (C. E.). The appliances are well chosen and sufficient for the practical illustration of the branches pursued.

Surveying instruments, models of structures, and the apparatus belonging formerly to the geological survey make up a large part of the collection.

The course in chemistry is designed for those who wish to become professional chemists, either as teachers or investigators, or manufacturers in chemical industries; and also for those intending to become expert chemists preparatory to the pursuit of medicine or pharmacy. Special teaching begins with the second term of the sophomore year, during which elementary instruction in general and theoretical chemistry is given by means of lectures, recitations, and laboratory practice.

In the junior year the course is continued, and the application of the science to mineralogy and metallurgy is made prominent.

Senior year is specially devoted to organic chemistry. The laboratory work is required to be carefully and systematically performed. After a satisfactory completion of the work in qualitative analysis by the blowpipe and in the wet way, the student passes to quantitative work, and receives practice in the analysis of gases, salts, ashes, mineral waters, and other substances, and in the preparation of organic and inorganic compounds. Special attention is paid to the analysis of mineral waters and agricultural fertilizers, and to electrometallurgy. The students are encouraged to visit the chemical and metallurgical works in the vicinity, and have many advantages in the way of lectures and laboratory practice in the various departments of the university.

COLORADO.

STATE AGRICULTURAL COLLEGE.

[From letters, circulars, &c., received by this office.]

This institution, located at Fort Collins, Colo., is founded on the national land-grant benefaction, and its leading object is to impart a thorough and practical knowledge of all those branches and sciences that pertain to agriculture and the mechanic arts. The endowment consists of 90,000 acres of land, selected "in place" by the State under the agricultural college land grant acts of 1862, 1864, and 1866. The land remains unsold, and if properly disposed of will doubtless result in the establishment of a large permanent fund.

The college is now supported by a biennial appropriation of the State legislature. The appropriation made in 1881 was ⅛ mill tax on State valuation, or about $20,000 annually.

LOCATION, BUILDING, AND APPLIANCES.

The college building at Fort Collins is well arranged and ample for present uses. The locality has many advantages, and is thus described: Fort Collins is located on the southern bank of the Cache la Poudre, about 6 miles east of the foot-hills of the Snowy Range and 35 miles south of the State line; it is surrounded by a fertile and well-watered region, including some of the best agricultural lands of the State. Its elevation of 5,100 feet above the level of the sea gives it a pure, dry atmosphere, while its proximity to the mountains brings it within the limit of occasional rains, thus rendering the climate pleasant and salubrious and adapting the soil to the cultivation of the cereals. This region, comprising the counties of Larimer, Weld, Boulder, and parts of Arapahoe and Jefferson, is rendered accessible from the north and south by the Colorado Central Railroad, which passes directly through Fort Collins, and the Greeley, Salt Lake and Pacific, just completed from Greeley, both of which roads connect with the Union Pacific at Cheyenne and with the Kansas Pacific at Denver. The streams draining this region, the Cache la Poudre, Big Thompson, and other tributaries of the South Platte, furnish an inexhaustible supply of water for purposes of irrigation. It is estimated that the great irrigating canal, now in process of construction and supplied from the Cache la Poudre, will bring at least 100,000 acres of unproductive land under cultivation. The college has been most judiciously located with reference to this large extent of farming land, in the midst of communities refined and progressive and very fast surrounding themselves with all the comforts of the most advanced localities in the West.

The president writes, under date of April, 1880, that, "during the winter vacation, the faculty of the college, and such members of the State board of agriculture as can accompany them, travel over the State, holding farmers' institutes at eligible places. These institutes consist of a course of lectures by members of the State board, the faculty, and resident farmers on topics connected with farm or garden work. Five of these institutes were held during the past vacation at Fort Collins, Greeley, Longmont, Monument, and Del Norte, and were well attended by farmers and others."

A more complete account of this branch of the work of the college, given in the catalogue for 1881, is as follows: "To give a clearer idea of the work at these institutes, we append a programme of places and topics: Fort Collins, November 26 and 27, 1879, and December 9 and 10, 1880; Del Norte, December 30 and 31, 1879; Monument, January 2 and 3, 1880; Greeley, January 15 and 16, 1880; Longmont, February 5 and 6, 1880; Loveland, December 16 and 17, 1880; Denver, January 5 to 8, 1881. All the members of the faculty attended these institutes and read papers or gave lectures on the following topics: Ex-President Edwards, the utility of trees, tree culture, relations of the Agricultural College to the State, book farming and hygiene of the farm; Prof. A. E. Blount, corn and its culture, seeds, wheat culture, injurious and friendly insects, milling properties of wheat, hybridization and cross-breeding; Prof. F. J. Annis, soils and their analysis, relative food value of flour, the farmer's home; Secretary H. Stratton, dairying, amber cane. The following members of the board furnished lectures on the annexed topics: W. E. Watrous, fruit culture, strawberries; B. S. La Grange, construction of ditches, irrigation; J. S. Stanger, relation of grasses to agriculture, Colorado as a home for farmers, diversification and marketing of crops, the necessity of improved farming; S. W. Homer, irrigation; P. M. Hinman, wheat.

The dormitory was erected in 1881, and will accommodate 30 students, or 25 students with officers assigned for care and duty.

A small building now used for chemical laboratory is well fitted and supplied with all needful apparatus for work. It will accommodate 12 students, classes working in two sections.

Ample work in qualitative and quantitative analysis is given, while with the new assay furnace just added excellent work in that line can be done.

The department of mechanics and drawing was opened to students September 12, 1882. The shop is fitted for doing bench work in wood and iron, while an adjoining room is used for forge work. Sixteen students are now taking this work, and more would be pleased to do so were there an opportunity. A building has been erected containing basement and one and one-half stories, which is soon to be used for mechanics. Within two months power will be supplied and machinery put in, which will give an opportunity for our students to complete the course in mechanics by taking wood-turning, scroll and fret sawing, while pattern making will lead to the course in iron work upon lathes and planes.

FACULTY.

The faculty consists of a president, who is professor of logic and political economy; professor of agriculture and botany, who is also superintendent of the farm; professor of chemistry and physics; professor of mechanics and drawing, who is superintendent of the shops; a secretary; a superintendent of the department of horticulture; a superintendent of floral department; and a matron of the ladies' dormitory.

STUDENTS AND TUITION.

The first college class was formed November 28, 1879, and consisted of 23 students, of whom 7 were women. The number of students in attendance in the year ending in 1881 was 57, of whom 25 were ladies; in 1882, 56.

Tuition is free to all residents of the State. A matriculation fee of $5 and an incidental fee of $1 per term entitle the student to all the privileges of the college.

There are as yet no scholarships provided.

STUDIES.

Preparatory year.—First term: Arithmetic, United States history, physical geography, English analysis. Second term: Arithmetic, United States history, physical geography, elementary physiology, English analysis. Third term: Elementary algebra, elocution, elementary physiology, word analysis. Throughout the year two hours of daily labor are required on the farm or garden.

Freshman year.—First term: Algebra, elementary rhetoric, drawing, agricultural lectures. Second term: Geometry, bookkeeping, drawing, botany. Third term: Higher algebra, ancient history, drawing, botany. Two hours of daily labor on the farm or garden are required throughout the year.

Sophomore year.—First term: Geometry completed, history continued, drawing, elementary chemistry. Second term: Trigonometry and surveying, English literature, drawing, organic chemistry, and blowpipe analysis. Third term: Physics, English literature, drawing, zoölogy. Throughout the first and second terms there are two hours of daily shop practice in mechanics; in the third term, field surveys and levelling.

Junior year.—First term: Physics, rhetoric, geology, agricultural chemistry. Second term: Chemical physics, floriculture, anatomy and physiology, agricultural chemistry. Third term: Meteorology, horticulture, physiology, entomology. During the first and second terms there are two hours of daily laboratory work in chemical analysis; during the third term, two hours on the farm or garden.

Senior year.—First term: Botany, stock breeding and food stuffs, veterinary science, psychology. Second term: Astronomy, household economy, veterinary science, logic. Third term: Moral science, landscape gardening, United States Constitution, political economy. Throughout the year there are two hours of daily shop practice in mechanics.

THE FARM AND GROUNDS.

The college farm includes 240 acres, most of which is under cultivation, the work being chiefly experimental, and including the culture of trees, small fruits, cereals, garden vegetables, &c.

The trees under successful cultivation include the standard varieties of apple, pear, plum, and cherry; and of forest trees, the ash, box-elder, chestnut, elm, locust, maple, and willow. The small fruits are represented by blackberries, currants, gooseberries, grapes, raspberries, and strawberries.

The floral department is an interesting and attractive feature of the college. The grounds adjoining the building have been terraced and grassed, and adorned with the choicest varieties of shrubbery and flowers. The farm has been surveyed by an experienced landscape gardener, with a view to the irrigation of its highest portions, its division into fields and parks, and the setting out of fruit and forest trees.

MANUAL LABOR.

The college embodies with a liberal course of study practical training in the work of the shop and the farm, its students being required to spend at least two hours daily in labor under the direction of their instructors. Although this labor is directly in the line of their studies, they are paid for it when not purely instructional. This manual labor is held to be beneficial by the financial aid it gives to the student, by instruction in methods of work, by the health derived from moderate exercise, and by the correct ideas imparted as to the dignity and importance of labor.

Military drill has been introduced, and all male students are required to participate. The State has furnished the college with thirty stand of arms for equipment. These are not sufficient for our present needs, to say nothing of future prospective growth. The drill is for twenty minutes each day, as the faculty believe a short time daily to be better than a longer time at longer intervals.

LATEST INFORMATION.

School opened September 7, 1882, with the college reorganized and a full line of work added to the course, which includes two years of drawing. The instruction in this is made supplementary to the course in the mechanic shop.

The attendance is good, there being 35 young men and 21 young ladies enrolled—total 56. The school is in a most prosperous condition; there being more students in attendance than at any previous period in the history of the college, and all are doing good, earnest, and thorough work.

The experimental work has been extended very much. One hundred varieties of wheat, 12 of barley, and several of oats were grown on the grounds this year, and the products tastefully arranged by the professor of agriculture, after which they were exhibited at the Denver Exposition and afterward at the Colorado State Fair. This exhibit was awarded the highest honors, and was conceded by all to be the finest agricultural exhibit ever seen.

CONNECTICUT.

SHEFFIELD SCIENTIFIC SCHOOL.

[Statements from the most recent reports received by this office.]

HISTORY AND OBJECTS.

The Sheffield Scientific School at New Haven, Conn., is one of the departments of Yale College, and was made, in 1863, by action of the State legislature, the beneficiary of the fund created by the national land-grant endowment for the founding of a college of agriculture and the mechanic arts. The scientific school proper was founded by the Yale College corporation in 1846 and operations begun in 1847.

A chair for instruction in agricultural chemistry was founded; then followed one in chemistry in its applications to the arts. The chemical laboratory then established was the beginning of this great scientific school.

In 1852 a section of civil engineering was provided for and a professor appointed. In 1855 a special course in metallurgy was established, and later several professors and instructors were added. At this period, the importance of the school being established, endowments were solicited. Quite a number of benefactions were made, and at last Mr. Joseph E. Sheffield, who had already bestowed $10,000, came forward with a munificent offer of a building and permanent fund. He purchased a building, refitted the same, added two wings, and gave $50,000 in addition, making the total benefaction over $100,000. Since then the school has been known by the name of its benefactor. The enlarged work began in 1859–'60.

Under the agricultural college act of 1862, Connecticut received scrip for 180,000 acres of public lands. As no part of this fund created by the sale thereof could be used for building purposes the State accepted the offer of the Sheffield Scientific School to receive the grant and fulfill its conditions. As a result of this endowment the State arranged for a board of visitors and provided for free scholarship. The faculty proceeded at once to meet the requirements of the United States statutes, by providing competent instruction in agriculture and the mechanic arts. The latter subject was embodied in the engineering section. The curriculum has been steadily strengthened and enlarged in the direction of technical science and arts as applied to industry.

Mr. Sheffield has since largely increased his endowments by enlarging the building, &c., and other important benefactions have been received.

The Sheffield school, as now organized, provides for "instruction and researches in the mathematical, physical, and natural sciences, with reference to the promotion and diffusion of science, and also to the preparation of young men for such pursuits as require especial proficiency in these departments of learning." This instruction is designed "especially for undergraduates who desire a training chiefly mathematical and scientific, in less part linguistic and literary, for higher scientific studies, or for various other occupations to which such training is suited," and also for post graduates of Yale or other colleges, and other persons qualified "for advanced or special scientific study." It is, therefore, a technical school of high character and also one for higher scientific study, investigation, and research.

ENDOWMENTS, FUNDS, AND INCOME.

The proceeds of the land grant amount to $135,000. The State pays interest on this sum at 6 per cent. to the school. The other funds of the school have in 1882 a face value of about $530,000. The total income for 1881 was $47,010, of which $17,798 were received from tuition fees. The expenses amounted to $48,796, of which sum $43,207 was expended for instruction. There are two buildings, with fixtures, costing in the aggregate somewhat over $200,000.

THE FACULTY.

The Sheffield Scientific School maintains a faculty of seventeen permanent professors, and in addition twelve instructors and assistants. The list is as follows: President; a professor of mineralogy, who is also executive officer and chairman; professor of civil engineering; of physics and astronomy (theoretical and practical); of linguistics and French; of theoretical and agricultural chemistry; of agriculture; of mathematics; of botany; of English; of political economy and history; of analytical chemistry and metallurgy; of zoölogy and geology; of comparative anatomy; of chemistry; of physiological chemistry; and of dynamical engineering. These permanent professors compose the governing board. Additional instructors and assistants are provided for in German, elocution, free-hand drawing, mathematics, French, cinematics and machine design, analytical chemistry (2), mineralogy, descriptive geometry, and projection drawing.

STUDENTS AND FEES.

There are no female students; the following is the number of students for 1882–'83: Graduates (students), 16; seniors, 47; juniors, 56; freshmen, 83; special, 5; total, 207.

The undergraduate tuition fees are $150 per annum, the graduate $100. The special student in chemistry pays $70 per annum, additional, for chemicals and use of apparatus; he is required to pay for breakage, gas, &c., the annual cost of which is about $20. A fee of $5 is charged the members of the freshmen and other classes taking laboratory practice in chemistry, mineralogy, and zoölogy; the same amount to all undergraduates for the use of the college reading room and gymnasium.

There are thirty free scholarships, twenty-seven being provided by the State and three by the governing board.

AGRICULTURAL PRACTICE.

The State of Connecticut was the first to establish an experimental station in agriculture. This was originally located in the Sheffield Scientific School and one of the professors of the institution was constituted its director. For several years the station had the free and exclusive use of the first story of the eastern wing of Sheffield Hall. The laboratory apparatus and the materials of the school have also been used when needed. But the enlargement of the chemical work of the school last year compelled the discontinuance of aid to the station, which has now ample quarters of its own in the vicinity. The New Haven Farmers' Club has had the free use of a room for its meetings, which have been held on the first and third Fridays of the month for half the year, and on the first Friday of each month during the summer. The New Haven County Agricultural Society has had free use of rooms for its business meetings. The professors of agriculture and of agricultural chemistry have from the very first co-operated with the various agricultural societies and farmers' clubs throughout the State, and the establishment of a permanent experimental station was largely due to their influence. In various other ways, the school has, according to its opportunities, given such aid and assistance as it could to the farming and gardening interests of the State.

BUILDINGS AND APPLIANCES.

The buildings are known as Sheffield Hall and North Sheffield Hall. All instruction in mineralogy, geology, zoölogy, and comparative anatomy is now given in the Peabody Museum. These halls contain a large number of recitation and lecture rooms, a hall for public assemblies and lectures, chemical and metallurgical laboratories, an astronomical observatory, museum, a library and reading room, besides studies for some of the professors, where their private technical libraries are kept. The following is a summary statement of the collections belonging to the school: (1) laboratories and apparatus in chemistry, metallurgy, physics, and zoölogy; (2) metallurgical museum of ores, furnace products, &c.; (3) agricultural museum of soils, fertilizers, useful and injurious insects, &c.; (4) collections in zoölogy; (5) astronomical observatory, with an equatorial telescope, by Clark & Sons, of Cambridge, a meridian circle, &c.; (6) a collection of mechanical apparatus, constituting the Collier cabinet; (7) models in architecture, geometrical drawing, civil engineering, topographical engineering and mechanics, diagrams adapted to public lectures, instruments for field practice; (8) maps and charts, topographical, hydrographical, geological, &c. The herbarium of Professor Brewer and the astronomical instruments of Professor Lyman are deposited in the buildings. Professor Eaton's herbarium, near at hand, is freely accessible. Students also have access to the various laboratories and collections in natural science in the Peabody Museum. The students of the Sheffield School have also at command the libraries, school of fine arts, museums, &c., belonging to Yale College.

STUDIES AND COURSES.

The courses of instruction, occupying three years, are arranged to suit the requirements of various classes of students. The first year's work is the same for all; for the last two years, the instruction is chiefly arranged in special courses. Those most distinctly marked out are the courses in chemistry; civil engineering; dynamical (or mechanical) engineering; agriculture; studies preparatory to mining and metallurgy; natural history; biology preparatory to medical studies; and select studies preparatory to other higher studies. The arrangement of the studies is as follows:

(1) Freshman year, introductory to all courses. In addition to the usual academic studies attention is paid especially to analytical geometry and spherical trigonometry, physics, chemistry, botany, and elementary drawing.

(2) The course in chemistry for the junior year embraces recitations and lectures in theoretical chemistry, qualitative analysis and laboratory practice; mineralogy—blowpipe analysis and determination of species; French; German. The course of study for senior year embraces the following subjects: Organic chemistry; agricultural chemistry (optional); laboratory practice—volumetric and mineral analysis, assaying; zoölogy; geology; metallurgy (optional); mineralogy (optional); French.

(3) The course in civil engineering is as follows: Mathematics—elements of the theory of functions; numerical equations; differential calculus, integral calculus, rational mechanics; surveying—field operations, topographical work; descriptive geometry, drawing, warped surfaces, shadows, perspective, and topographical drawing; German; French.

The senior year embraces the following courses: Field engineering—laying out curves, location of line of railroad, with calculations of excavation and embankment, Henck's Field Book for railroad engineers; civil engineering—resistance of materials, bridges and roofs, stone-cutting, with graphical problems, building materials, stability of arches and walls, Mahan's Civil Engineering; geology—Dana's; mineralogy—blowpipe analysis and determinative mineralogy; dynamics—principles of mechanism, steam-engine; hydraulics and hydraulic motors; drawing—graphical statics, Loomis's Astronomy with practical problems; French.

(4) The course in dynamic (or mechanical) engineering is as follows: For the junior year: Mathematics—elements of the theory of functions, numerical equations, differential calculus, integral calculus, rational mechanics; surveying—field practice; drawing—descriptive geometry; cinematics—general theory of motion and principles of mechanism, elementary combinations of pure mechanism, pulleys and belts, gearing and forms of teeth for wheels, parallel motions; German; French.

For the senior year: statics—the application of the principles of statics to rigid bodies, elasticity and strength of materials, forms of uniform strength, stability of structures, theory of the arch, construction of roof trusses, girders and iron bridges; machine drawing—bolts and nuts, riveting, journals, axles, shafts, couplings, pillow blocks, shaft hangers, pulleys, connecting rods and cranks, cross-heads, pipe connections, valves, cylinders, stuffing boxes, glands; proportioning of machine parts; designs for machines with working drawings; designing of hoisting engine, shearing and pumping engine, high speed steam engine; blowpipe analysis; shop visits and reports; hydrostatics—equilibrium and pressure of fluids, hydrometers, manometers, gauges, &c.; hydrodynamics—water-pressure engines and water wheels, construction of water reservoirs and conduits, measurement of water supply, discharge of pipes; thermodynamics—general principles of heat employed as a source of power, theory of steam engines, hot air engines, gas engines; metallurgy.

(5) The course in agriculture is as follows: For the junior year, lectures and recitations; theoretical and organic chemistry; qualitative analysis; laboratory practice; mineralogy—blowpipe analysis and determination of species; physical geography; physiology; botany; French; German. For the senior year: Agriculture—cultivation of the staple crops of the Northern States; tree planting and forestry; laws of heredity and principles of breeding; rural economy—history of agriculture and sketches of husbandry in foreign countries; systems of husbandry, agricultural and organic chemistry; geology; zoölogy; botany; microscopy; English; French.

(6) The mining course is additional, and young men desiring to become mining engineers may pursue the regular course in civil or mechanical engineering and at its close spend a fourth year in the study of metallurgical chemistry, mineralogy, &c.

(7) Lectures on military science and tactics are annually given by General Abbott and other officers of the Engineer Corps of the United States Army.

The course in drawing extends through the three years. During the first term of freshman year, the students practice free-hand drawing at the art school building. After the completion of the course in free-hand drawing, instruction is given during the second term in the elementary principles of instrumental drawing, embracing elementary projection drawing, isometric drawing, and descriptive geometry as far as warped surfaces. This course is obligatory upon all.

During the junior and senior years, instruction in drawing is obligatory only on the students in civil and mechanical engineering. In the former year the system of instruction embraces shades and shadows, tinting, perspective, and warped surfaces. By this method, all the problems in descriptive geometry are required to be worked out on the drawing-board instead of the black-board. The course extends through the entire year. In senior year students are required to apply the principles of drawing already obtained to works of construction, under the general supervision of the professors of civil and of dynamic engineering.

(8) In addition to these courses and studies, which may properly be esteemed as falling within a comprehensive conception of the purposes of Congress in creating an endowment for colleges of agriculture and the mechanic arts, the Sheffield Scientific School has courses of highest scientific studies, as follows:

(9) In natural history, either geology, mineralogy, zoölogy, or botany may be made the principal study, some attention in each case being directed to the other three branches of natural history. For the junior year, the course embraces chemistry, qualitative analysis, laboratory practice, mineralogy, blowpipe analysis, and determinative mineralogy; botany—Gray's manual, laboratory practice; zoölogy—laboratory practice, recitations, excursions (land and marine); botany—laboratory practice, excursions; physiology; physical geography; German; French.

For the senior year: geology—Dana's, excursions; zoölogy—laboratory practice, lectures, recitations, excursions; botany—herbarium studies, comparative cryptogamous orders, botanical literature; essays in descriptive botany, excursions; anatomy of vertebrates—Huxley's; zoölogy—laboratory practice, recitations, lectures; meteorology; French. Besides the regular courses of recitations and lectures on structural and systematic zoölogy and botany and on special subjects, students are taught to prepare, arrange, and identify

INDUSTRIAL EDUCATION IN THE UNITED STATES.

collections, to make dissections, to pursue original investigations, and to describe genera and species in the language of science. For these purposes large collections in zoölogy and paleontology belonging to the college are available, as are also the private botanical collections of Professor Eaton.

(10) The course in biology, preparatory to medical studies, embraces two years and covers theoretical and organic chemistry, mineralogy, physiology, toxicology, physiological chemistry, botany, zoölogy, geology, comparative anatomy and histology; the laws of heredity and breeding, with laboratory practice as needed; also German and French.

(11) A course of select studies preparatory to other higher studies, is also provided and embraces mineralogy, English history and literature, English history, physical geography, botany, political economy, geology, zoölogy, linguistics, meteorology, German, and French.

DEGREES.

The degrees which are conferred are bachelor of philosophy, civil engineer, dynamical engineer, and doctor of philosophy. The degree of bachelor of philosophy is conferred upon those who complete any of the three years' courses of study, passing all the examinations in a satisfactory manner and presenting a graduation thesis. Those upon whom this degree has been conferred may obtain the engineering degrees at the end of two academical years by pursuing a course of higher study and obtaining professional training through special investigations or actual practice. The course of study for the degree of civil engineer comprises higher calculus, higher geometry, theory of numerical operations, analytical and applied mechanics, practical astronomy, and a course of construction and design. The course of study for the degree of dynamical engineer is slightly varied from that just given, astronomy being omitted, and other studies so pursued as to bring mechanics and mechanical engineering into prominence. The degree of doctor of philosophy is conferred upon those who, having already taken a bachelor's degree, engage in assiduous and successful study in the department of philosophy and the arts for not less than two years.

DELAWARE.

DELAWARE COLLEGE.

[Statements from the most recent reports received by this office.]

This college, located at Newark, Del., has been made the beneficiary by the State of the fund arising from the national land grant in behalf of agricultural colleges.

The catalogue for 1879-'80 states that "It is the design of the college to give to young men of proper age and acquirements such a course of instruction, directly pertaining to agriculture, as will enable them to conduct the operations of a farm both intelligently and profitably, and at the same time, by the introduction of such other studies as constitute a substantial education, to secure thorough mental discipline."

ENDOWMENT AND INCOME.

The proceeds of the land scrip sales form the permanent fund of this institution; it amounts to $83,000; the annual income therefrom is $4,980; income from tuition fees (1881), $500; total income, $5,520. The grounds, buildings, and appliances are valued at $75,000.

Faculty.—The number of professors is five, and includes the president, who is also professor of mental, moral, and political science, and the professors of agriculture, physics, and civil engineering; of chemistry, mineralogy, and natural history; of mathematics and modern languages; and of ancient languages and classical literature. There are also several lecturers.

Students.—The return for 1880-'81 reports 54 students, 11 of whom were young ladies. There are 30 State scholarships in the gift of the members of the State assembly. The fees are $5 for matriculation and $60 a year for tuition.

Studies.—The agricultural and scientific department embraces the following: In the freshman year, besides usual collegiate studies, anatomy, physiology, the laws of health, modern and constitutional history, and practical mathematics are taught.

The sophomore class study, in addition to English, Latin, and literature, agriculture, inorganic chemistry, zoölogy, higher algebra, geometry, botany, and political economy.

The course of the junior class includes organic chemistry, mineralogy, French or German, trigonometry, mensuration, agriculture, surveying, and navigation.

The senior class, in addition, study astronomy, physics, civil engineering, geology, differential calculus, elements of law, international law, and also use the laboratory.

S. Ex. 25——7

There is a special course given in chemistry. The recitations and lectures in agriculture embrace the following subjects : the formation of soils, their chemical and physical qualities, their suitability for different kinds of crops, and the industrial and commercial effects of the varied distribution of soils in the United States; the constituents and chemical agencies of the atmosphere and of the water, and the composition of manures; farm implements, principles of construction and use; the botany of agriculture, classification of plants, a knowledge of the crops cultivated for food and for other special purposes; the anatomy of domestic animals; rotation of crops, improvement of soils by manuring and draining; methods of conducting experiments; and a consideration of the history of agriculture, and the State and national policy in relation to the development of agricultural interests.

Women are admitted and a special literary course is arranged for them. As to special appliances, beyond small library, laboratory, and usual philosophical apparatus, no information is given.

Experimental and practical work.—The college does not own a farm, but students are instructed on that owned and worked by the professor of agriculture, who is also under a State law regulating the manufacture and sale of fertilizers ex-officio State chemist; "it is his duty to inspect by analyses samples of all the fertilizers offered for sale in the State. As a consequence of the performance of this duty, many worthless articles have been driven from the market, and the fertilizers remaining have been greatly improved in quality. From the analyses made by the State chemist, farmers have learned the necessary constituents of plant food, and, profiting by this knowledge, have been enabled to make their purchases to the best advantage.

Hon. W. H. Ruffner, of Virginia, in narrating a recent visit to Delaware College, for the State Agricultural College of Virginia, says: "The department of agriculture in the Delaware College is conducted by means of expositions in the class room and visits to the farm of the professor of agriculture, who carries on a system of mixed husbandry on private account, and is himself a skilled and laboring farmer, as well as a man of scientific education. He keeps a liberal supply of tools and takes his class not only to witness the various operations of farming, fruit growing, and trucking, but to handle the tools and implements. Nothing very systematic, however, is required. The professor also takes his class to visit the machine and implement shops, of which there are many in Newark."

GEORGIA.

THE STATE UNIVERSITY AND ITS BRANCHES.

[Statements from catalogues and letter.]

HISTORY OF THE DISPOSITION OF THE GRANT.

The entire proceeds of the sale of agricultural college scrip ($242,202.17) were given to the University of Georgia in 1872.

A college of agriculture and the mechanic arts was then established as a department of the university. In the same year the United States mint building at Dahlonega was donated to the university by the general government, and a department of the university opened there under the name of the North Georgia Agricultural College. Two thousand dollars are annually appropriated to it from the income of the agricultural fund of the university. In 1878 branch institutions were added, one of them at Cuthbert, called the Southwest Georgia Agricultural College, and the other at Thomasville, called the South Georgia Agricultural College. Each college receives $2,000 a year from the land-grant fund.

In 1879 the Middle Georgia Military and Agricultural College, at Milledgeville, having the old State buildings for its use, was made a part of the system. It also receives $2,000 per annum.

The State legislature pays to the industrial department of Atlanta University $8,000 per annum, as in lieu of all claims of colored citizens upon the land-grant funds. The total disbursed under this head is as follows: Total income from fund created by sale of the land-grant scrip given by the United States to the State of Georgia for the use of a college of agriculture and mechanic arts, as per secretary's report 1880, $17,914.14; appropriated annually by legislature for use of colored students to the Atlanta University, $8,000; total income for industrial and technical education, $25,914.14. This is disbursed as follows: State College of Agriculture and Mechanic Arts, at Athens, $9,914.14; North Georgia Branch College, at Dahlonega, $2,000; Middle Georgia Branch College, at Milledgeville, $2,000; South Georgia Branch College, at Thomasville, $2,000; Southwest Georgia Branch College, at Cuthbert, $2,000; Atlanta University, $8,000.

GEORGIA STATE COLLEGE OF AGRICULTURE AND THE MECHANIC ARTS.

The leading object of the department of the University of Georgia known as the State College of Agriculture and the Mechanic Arts is to teach scientific agriculture and afford young men opportunities for instruction in practical departments, such as engineering, analytical chemistry, and mechanics.

The annual income consists of the remainder of the income of the land grant after deducting the sums devoted to other branches of the university, or about $8,000.

The faculty consists of chancellor of the university and seven professors, teaching the following subjects: English literature, modern languages, mathematics (pure and applied), chemistry, geology, and mineralogy, physics, astronomy, engineering, and military tactics, and agriculture and horticulture.

The number of students in 1882 was 39. The number taking agriculture as a study was 29. Tuition, in July, 1881, was made free. But every student pays $10 matriculation and $5 library fee—$15 annually.

The number of graduates from the organization of the college in 1872 until and including 1880 was 53, of whom 25 were civil engineers, 11 bachelors of engineering, 11 bachelors of chemical science, and 6 bachelors of agriculture. The number of bachelors of agriculture does not fairly represent the number of students who have attended the college for the purpose of preparing themselves for farming as a profession. Many of them have taken degrees in engineering or chemical science.

APPLIANCES AND APPARATUS.

In addition to instruction by recitation and lectures in the class room students in agriculture visit frequently the experimental farm connected with the university, which is under the direct supervision and management of the professor of agriculture, and there receive practical instruction.

The new laboratory building for the use of the college of agriculture and mechanic arts, now constructed, is 100 by 50 feet, three stories with basement. The entire first floor and basement are appropriated to the department of chemistry, containing analytical laboratories, balance rooms, an assay room, a room for microscopic and spectroscopic work, an industrial museum, store room, engine room, workshop, printing office, &c. The second floor contains a lecture room and museum for the department of agriculture, and apparatus room, working room, and lecture room for department of natural philosophy. The third floor contains a model room, lecture room for students in engineering, and drawing hall.

Under an appropriation made by the State legislature of $15,000 this building has been equipped with the modern apparatus requisite for chemical and physical laboratories and models, &c., required in the department of engineering.

The university chemical laboratories are located therein; they comprise rooms for elementary work, for qualitative, quantitative, and volumetric analysis. These are connected with convenient balance rooms, an assay room, evaporating chambers, &c., and are completely fitted with all necessary appliances for chemical work, and furnished with gas, water, rapid filtration apparatus, &c.

The appliances in the department of physics are worth about $10,000. Three-fourths of this value represent new and modern apparatus recently bought. All the apparatus is in excellent condition, and is constantly kept in perfect working order. The selection has been made carefully, every piece being bought from that maker with whom its manufacture is a specialty. The apparatus illustrating optics was purchased of Duboseq; that illustrating acoustics, from Koenig; for heat, from Salleron; for electrical tests, from Elliott—all European makers. The general apparatus was procured of Ritchie of Boston and Queen of Philadelphia. Students pursuing the courses for the degrees of B. S. and B. E., and others who desire to do so, take a special course in practical physics in addition to the general course. In it students perform under the professor's direction the experiments, and explain them as they proceed or submit their results for criticism. They are thus taught to handle apparatus, to improvise and construct apparatus of their own, to make their own verifications of the truth of principles, and to perform such tests as belong to physical work. The department occupies a well arranged lecture hall, an apparatus room, a laboratory, and a workshop for the construction and repair of apparatus.

The department of engineering, in addition to full sets of surveying instruments, possesses a very fine collection of working models of engineering structures and of machinery, by the aid of which the actual construction of bridges, roofs, &c., can be thoroughly illustrated. Amongst them are found working models of high and low pressure steam engines; models of steam boilers; of roofs and bridges; of water wheels; of railway tracks; of machinery; of the orders of architecture, &c.

To the department has lately been added a fine machine for testing the strength of materials, made by Riehle of Philadelphia; this machine works up to 41,000 pounds, and materials can be tested for tensile, crushing, or transverse strength. There are also a large number of plates and drawings illustrating engineering works.

A large hall, 50 by 84 feet, well lighted, is used by the students in drawing.

The legislature has granted to the university 200 stand of arms. All students, both in the State college and academic departments of the university, unless exempted by the faculty, are required to take part in the regular drills; these are conducted on three afternoons of each week of the session, when the weather is favorable, between the hours of half past four and half past five.

STUDIES AND DEGREES.

Every student who enters the college is required to take one of the prescribed courses. He can elect either the course of agriculture, or of engineering, or of applied chemistry, or a partial course. He can also add to the studies of the prescribed course those of the schools of the university for which he may be prepared, provided that his election does not interfere with the daily schedule of recitations and lectures.

The agricultural course is as follows:

In the freshman class, besides English studies, algebra, geometry, linear drawing, and botany are pursued.

In the sophomore class book-keeping, geometrical drawing, elements of mechanics, trigonometry, mensuration, and surveying, with field and practical work, zoölogy, botany, and agriculture are studied.

In the junior class the following studies are pursued: Chemistry; agricultural chemistry, with six hours per week laboratory practice; natural philosophy; mechanics of solids, liquids, and gases; acoustics; heat; natural history; surveying and drawing; agriculture, its principles, its methods, its products, methods of propagating plants, general nursery management, practical illustration on experimental farm; French or German; English literature.

The senior class has the following course: Industrial chemistry; agricultural chemistry, including the chemical composition of the plant, the laws regulating its growth, the physical and chemical properties of the soil, the composition and manufacture of fertilizers, laboratory practice in agricultural analysis of six hours per week; natural philosophy; light; magnetism; electricity; meteorology; descriptive anatomy; agriculture, implements, crops, farm management, stock breeding, economy of labor, preparation of manures and composts, taught practically on the experimental farm; geology and mineralogy; rural engineering and building construction; English literature.

The entire course entitles graduates to the degree of bachelor of agriculture.

It is the design of the school of agriculture to give a thorough knowledge of theoretical and practical farming, so that the agriculturist may do his work carefully and skillfully. With this view the students are instructed by text books and professors' lectures in the following subjects:

Classification of soils, their mineral ingredients, chemical composition, and physical properties; how these properties may be changed and improved; the best mode and implements of tillage; the advantages of subsoiling and drainage, and how these may be best performed, and the various kinds and properties of manures.

Plants, botanically, economically, and geographically considered; those adapted to the food of man, how and where produced, their properties and value, which can be produced best at home, and which purchased from abroad.

The design, use, location, arrangement, kind of soil, culture, and implements of the vegetable garden and orchard; pruning, transplanting, and propagation of fruit, ornamental, and forest trees.

The anatomy and physiology of the domestic animals, their breeding, management, and adaptation to farm economy.

Insects, their classification, history, and habits; which are noxious and should be destroyed, and which beneficial and should be preserved.

Farm buildings and farm machinery.

Landscape gardening, laying out gardens and lawns and their ornamentation, and the culture and propagation of flowers and shrubs.

Students in agriculture meet with the classes in engineering in some studies; they become draughtsmen, and are enabled to make necessary plans. Attention is particularly turned to the construction of farm buildings. They also study surveying and join in all field exercises.

Special instruction is given on the drainage of land, and the manner of laying the lines of drainage is thoroughly illustrated by practice in the field.

Instruction is also given in strength of materials; in framing and building; in the construction of roads.

The engineering course embraces for the freshman and sophomore classes the same studies as those of the agricultural course. The studies pursued by the juniors and seniors lead to the degree of bachelor of engineering, and embrace the following subjects: Analytical and descriptive geometry; geometrical, topographical, isometrical engineering, and plan drawing; tinting, lettering, shades and shadows, and perspective; surveying with chain, compass, and transit; leveling; natural philosophy; mechanics of solids, liquids, and gases; acoustics; light; heat; magnetism; electricity; meteorology; elements of astronomy; French or German; differential and integral calculus; mechanics of engineering; chemistry; mineralogy and geology; laboratory practice; mechanics, theoretical; astronomy, spherical and descriptive; analysis of engineering constructions; thesis.

A special course of one year for the degree of civil engineer includes the following subjects: Weisbach's or Mosely's Mechanics of Engineering; Stoney on Strains; Warren's Machine Construction and Draughting; chemical laboratory work; French or German; thesis.

The department of engineering has also organized a partial course in "building and architecture;" it includes the studies of the first, second, and third years in engineering, omitting a part of the higher mathematics, and instead thereof giving attention to architectural drawing, structures of wood, stone, and iron, foundations, walls, arches, trusses, roofs, &c.; the application of descriptive geometry to masonry and carpentry; strength of materials; ventilation, warming, acoustics; building materials, woods, stones, mortars, cements, paints, &c.

Upon the satisfactory completion of this course a certificate will be given stating the time spent at the college and the progress made.

The school of engineering is organized for the benefit of the following classes of students, namely: (1) Those who intend to make engineering a profession, the course of instruction enabling the student to acquire such a practical knowledge of the science as to be qualified for entering, upon graduation, upon the duties of the profession; (2) those who desire to study applied mathematics, to complete the scientific course.

The students in the regular course of agriculture not able to complete one of the regular courses confine themselves to the study of such subjects as they may elect.

The mode of instruction is partly by means of text books, but principally by lectures. Throughout the course the application of the theory is enforced by requiring the solution of practical problems, by exercises in the field, and by the construction of original drawings, with necessary bills of materials and specifications.

In the course of surveying each student has abundant opportunity to manage and use the instruments himself. Every operation is illustrated by actual field work.

The course of drawing includes all the principles required in the practice of the professional engineer and architect. Each student of the State college is employed in drawing during a part of the course from one to two hours each day. During the first year all are required to take linear drawing, and the work done is intended to be auxiliary to the study of geometry.

The full course includes orthographic and isometrical projections; development of surfaces; practical perspective; linear, free-hand, and object drawing; building and architectural drawing; masonry drawing; drawing for carpenters; mechanical drawing, including drawing from rough sketches, drawing and shading from solid objects, drawing of machinery.

The course in chemistry leads to the degree of bachelor of chemistry and embraces, for junior and senior classes, the following studies:

For the junior class—general chemistry; laboratory practice, including chemical manipulations; blow-pipe analysis and qualitative analysis; physics; mechanics of solids, liquids, and gases; acoustics, light, heat; English and English literature; French; German.

For the senior class—industrial chemistry, including mining, metallurgic processes for the extraction of the useful metals, the manufacture of important commercial chemicals, acids, salts, fertilizers, &c.; the manufacture of glass and porcelain; agricultural chemistry, the composition and use of crude and manipulated fertilizers, &c.; the manufacture of cane and beet sugar, of alcohol, wine, beer, vinegar, &c.; bleaching, dyeing, calico printing, and tanning; gunpowder and other explosives; soap and candles; gas and illuminating oils; printing, photography, &c.; laboratory practice; quantitative analysis; gravimetric and volumetric analysis of soils, fertilizers, blood, urine, metals, ores, &c. (the student will be employed in this laboratory work for five hours each day during six days of the week); mineralogy; geology; physics, magnetism, electricity, meteorology; astronomy; French; German.

Besides lectures and recitations, a certain amount of time to be devoted to practical work is required of each class, but facilities are offered each student to increase the amount if desired.

A preliminary course of instruction is given in manipulation, and constant practice is required, that students may familiarize themselves with such portions of the laboratory work as require mechanical skill, with glass blowing, handling and care of apparatus, use of blow-pipe, &c.

A course of blow-pipe analysis is next given; then a thorough course in qualitative chemical analysis is pursued, until the student is competent to determine the chemical constituents of an unknown substance presented to him.

The remainder of the course is devoted to quantitative analysis, gravimetric and volumetric, the quantitative determination of the chemical constituents of a substance the composition of which has been previously determined by qualitative analysis. After passing the regular course to the necessary extent, the students will be allowed considerable latitude in the choice of substances for examination, whether of soils or fertilizers, in connection with the study of scientific agriculture; of blood, urine, &c., by the medical student; of metals and ores, by those interested in mining, mineralogy, and metallurgy.

NORTH GEORGIA AGRICULTURAL COLLEGE.

This college, opened January, 1873, is located in Northern Georgia, at Dahlonega. Its building was destroyed by fire in December, 1878, but has been rebuilt on the old foundations. It has a front of 122 feet, with an extension in the rear of 87 feet, and is three stories high. It contains a chapel room, society halls, fourteen recitation rooms, library room, and chemical laboratory.

No special age or preparation is necessary for admission to the college. While it is desirable that all pupils should enter at the beginning of the term, yet they are received at any time, and such is the scope of instruction that a grade can at all times be found for those entering late. Tuition is free, but a matriculation fee of $5 a term or $10 a year is required of each student.

The session commences first Monday in September, and is continuous for two terms. Spring term commences February 1 and ends June 15. Military drill is compulsory, and students are required, when on drill, to wear uniforms.

The military department is under the management of a United States officer, especially detailed by the Secretary of War as commandant of cadets at this institution.

The educational intelligence afforded by this institution has especially in view the preparation of the pupil (1) for the business and for the enjoyment of practical home and farm life, (2) for the higher classes in the University of Georgia, and (3) for the profession of teaching and as a passport for the same. Certificates of proficiency in the studies of the several departments and of qualifications to teach will be granted by the trustees to students showing diligence, aptitude, and progress in their education.

The faculty, by express authority of the legislature, can grant licenses to the students of this institution to teach in the State schools without examinations. It consists of five professors, two adjunct professors, and one assistant. Number of students for the session of 1881: males and females, 177. Of this aggregate there are in the college classes 48, viz: seniors, 6; juniors, 11; sophomores, 13; freshmen, 18. The balance, 129, are in the preparatory and primary classes.

MIDDLE GEORGIA MILITARY AND AGRICULTURAL COLLEGE.

This college, opened January, 1880, is located at Milledgeville, Baldwin County, Georgia.

The old State capitol buildings and grounds, donated to the trustees of the State University for the purpose of establishing this college, furnish ample accommodations.

The faculty consists of 5 professors and 5 teachers. Number of students (1882), 355; 37 are in college grade. Under college grade there are 318, viz: 151 boys and 167 girls. Military exercises form a part of the instruction, and the boys are required to wear a uniform.

The college has recently come into possession of a library consisting of about 3,000 volumes.

SOUTHWEST GEORGIA AGRICULTURAL COLLEGE.

This college, opened in September, 1879, is located at Cuthbert, Randolph County, Georgia. The college building is spacious and well arranged, with capacity to accommodate from two hundred to two hundred and fifty students.

The real estate belonging to the college embraces an area of 30 acres. The situation is beautiful, pleasant, and well adapted to such an enterprise.

No charge is made for tuition, but an incidental fee of $5 per session is required of every student able to pay, making $10 for the year.

The faculty consists of 3 professors and 1 assistant. The number of students for the present session (all males) is 155, of whom 25 are in college grade, viz: 7 in the sophomore class and 18 in the freshman. The remainder, 130, are under college grade.

Military exercises form a part of the scheme of instruction, and the students are required to wear a uniform.

SOUTH GEORGIA AGRICULTURAL COLLEGE.

This college, opened in September, 1879, is located at Thomasville, Thomas County, Georgia. The buildings, all brick, are three in number, capable of accommodating about one hundred and seventy-five or two hundred students. The main building has recitation rooms below and four rooms above used for sleeping rooms for students. The recitation rooms are all comfortably furnished.

Tuition is free, but a matriculation fee of $5 per term is required, making $10 a year.

Session begins first Wednesday in September and continues forty weeks.

The faculty consists of 5 professors. Number of students (all males) was, in 1882, 185, of whom 14 are in college grade. The remainder, 171, are under college grade.

All students are required to drill and to wear uniform.

ATLANTA UNIVERSITY.

Atlanta University was chartered in 1867 and organized in 1869. It is designed to afford the colored people opportunities for obtaining such education as shall be most profitable to them. It has three courses of study, the college, college preparatory, and the normal. A grammar school is also connected with the university.

In the year 1880–'81 the number of students in the college course was 17; in the college preparatory course, 14; in the normal course, 83; in the grammar school, 227. Of the 341 students, 158 were boys, 183 girls; 215 were boarders and 126 day pupils.

The faculty consists of the president, 3 professors, and 11 instructors and teachers. The graduates previous to 1881 in the college course (A. B.) numbered 22; in the normal course, 49.

The expenses for tuition are $2 a month in the college course and $1 per month in the other courses.

The board is estimated at $3 per month, and all pupils are required to work for the institution at least one hour a day.

The university has only $5,300 permanent fund, a little physical apparatus, and a library of about 500 volumes. The $8,000 annually given by the State is its chief income. There are three commodious buildings.

ILLINOIS.

ILLINOIS INDUSTRIAL UNIVERSITY.

[From report by the regent, supplemented by material from catalogues.]

The leading objects of the Illinois Industrial University are those expressed by the terms of the act of Congress of 1862, under which the State received the endowment that supports the teaching force of the university.

ENDOWMENT AND FUNDS.

The State of Illinois received from the United States, in accordance with the provisions of the act of 1862, scrip for 480,000 acres of land. Scrip for 454,460 acres was sold, yielding $319,178.17, and the proceeds were invested in approved State and county securities in the State of Illinois. The remaining scrip, 25,440 acres, was located in Minnesota and Nebraska upon lands which are yet part of the property of the university, but unproductive. There is no other endowment.

The real estate of the university situate in Urbana, its farms and public grounds, with the buildings thereon, and its other property in machinery, apparatus, library, stock, &c., have been obtained partly from donations of the cities of Urbana and Champaign and their residents, and partly from appropriations made in successive sessions by the State. The total value of such property may be estimated (1882) at $400,000 to $450,000.

Receipts and expenditures for the years ending at the dates given.

	September 30, 1880.	September 30, 1881.
RECEIPTS.		
Balance from last year:		
State	$10,618 66	$5,582 91
Current	7,298 93	7,168 23
Interest on endowment	21,398 40	20,660 00
From State appropriations	8,605 50	26,610 37
From fees and room rent	10,619 21	9,908 67
Gross receipts from departments of labor	15,053 34	16,100 41
Illinois Central Railroad freight donation		2,199 60
Miscellaneous	943 24	981 98
Total	74,627 28	89,212 17
EXPENDITURES.		
On account of salaries	28,184 22	28,392 54
On account of State appropriations	13,842 88	15,712 91
On account of departments of labor	12,595 62	16,188 67
Miscellaneous	7,253 42	7,763 54
Total	61,876 14	68,057 66
Balance:		
State	5,582 91	16,451 85
Current	7,168 23	4,702 66
	74,627 28	89,212 17

ORGANIZATION.

The organization of the university provides instruction in these colleges and schools: The college of agriculture, the college of engineering, school of mechanical engineering, school of civil and mining engineering, school of architecture, the college of natural science, school of natural history, school of chemistry, the college of literature and science, school of English and modern languages, school of ancient languages. Additional schools: The school of military science, school of art and design.

In each of the schools enumerated above instruction has been given continuously throughout the year. The question as to which of them are "leading" will be best answered by the list of professorships, and by describing the facilities, including buildings, farms, workshops, laboratories, apparatus, &c., furnished and in use as the equipment for instruction.

FACULTY.

The faculty consists of the regent, who is professor of mechanical engineering and physics; professor of botany and horticulture (vice-president), professors of mathematics, modern languages, geology and zoölogy, English language and literature, architecture, history and ancient languages, chemistry, agriculture, veterinary science, industrial art and designing, military science and tactics, civil engineering, and agricultural chemistry; assistants in mechanical engineering, English and ancient languages, and laboratory work, instructors in right-line drawing, elocution, mathematics and botany, and natural science; a teacher of vocal and instrumental music, and foremen of carpenter and machine shops.

STUDENTS.

Three hundred and fifty-two students were in attendance in 1881–'82, classified as follows: Resident graduates, 9; seniors, 35; juniors, 49; sophomores, 91; freshmen, 87; preparatory, 71; special, 10. The course in agriculture was pursued by 21 students; mechanical engineering, by 41; civil engineering, 41; mining engineering, 3; architecture, 14; chemistry, 42; natural history, 14; art and design, 4; English and modern languages, 105; ancient languages, 16; elective, 14; miscellaneous, 35. There were 76 ladies among the number, one of whom studied chemistry; 1, art and design; 4, elective courses; 7, courses not specified; 9, natural history; 50, English and modern languages; and 4, ancient languages.

Tuition is free in all the university classes. A matriculation fee of $10 entitles the student to membership in the university until he has completed his studies. Fees for

INDUSTRIAL EDUCATION IN THE UNITED STATES. 105

incidental expenses amount to $22.50 annually. Students are charged for material used or apparatus broken in the laboratories, but not for the use and ordinary wear of instruments.

The legislature of Illinois in the act founding the university provided that no degrees should be conferred nor diplomas awarded, but that certificates might be given which should set forth the studies pursued and the proficiency attained therein during the residence of students at the university. A full certificate, deemed equivalent to evidence of graduation, was evidence of satisfactory attainment in thirty-six university studies covering one term each. In 1877 the legislature gave authority to confer degrees, and pursuant to that authority degrees of bachelor of science, bachelor of letters, bachelor of arts, master of science, master of letters, master of arts, civil engineer, and mechanical engineer have been conferred.

The total number of graduates to 1882 holding full four years' certificates is, men 179, women 34, total 213. Graduates from 1877 to 1881: bachelor of arts, men 4, women 2, total 6; bachelor of letters, men 33, women 17, total 50; bachelor of science, men 71, women 11, total 82. Total number of graduates 347, men 280, women 67.

A list of the graduates with their occupations and residences is given in the catalogue for 1881–'82. According to it, 52 are engaged in teaching, 37 in farming, 33 in law, 27 in engineering, 18 as clerks and agents, 15 in household duties, 14 in medicine, 12 are merchants, and 11 architects or draughtsmen, and the remainder are distributed among a score of different occupations.

OUTLINE OF PLAN OF INSTRUCTION.

Each school has a well-defined course of study, peculiar to itself in certain technical branches. The full time for each of the courses of study is four years; but students take a longer time if necessary, or if competent they may complete a course in less time. A student may, under certain conditions, arrange a course of study for himself, and when he shall have completed thirty-six terms of university subjects he is entitled to a full certificate setting forth the facts.

THE COLLEGE OF AGRICULTURE.

The object of the College of Agriculture is to lead the student toward a thorough understanding of all that man can know about soils and seeds, plants and animals, and the influences of light, heat, and moisture on his fields, his crops, and his stock, so that he may both understand the reason of processes he uses and may intelligently work for the improvement of those processes. Theory and practice are united in the method of instruction. The technical studies are taught mainly by lectures, with careful reading of standard agricultural books and periodicals and frequent discussions, oral and written, by students, of the principles taught. These are also illustrated by demonstrations and observations in the fields, stables, orchards, gardens, and plant-houses.

The requirements for admission to the agricultural course are that the candidate be at least fifteen years of age and pass satisfactory examinations in common school branches and the studies of the preliminary year, which are algebra, geometry, natural philosophy, botany, physiology, and studies in English. For admission to a "farmer's" course of one year examination in common school branches only is required.

There are two courses of study, one covering four years, the other one year. The former is the regular course leading to the degree of B. S. Its studies are as follows:

First year: elements of agriculture and horticulture, vegetable physiology, chemistry, trigonometry, rhetoric, British authors or free-hand drawing, and shop practice.

Second year: agricultural chemistry, economic entomology, zoölogy, botany, and German.

Third year: agricultural engineering and architecture, animal anatomy and physiology, animal husbandry, veterinary science, landscape gardening, geology or ancient history, and physics or mediæval and modern history.

Fourth year: meteorology and physical geography, history of agriculture and rural law, rural economy, political economy, constitutional history, mental science, history of civilization, and laboratory work.

Special horticultural branches may be substituted for agricultural or veterinary studies by those so desiring. The shorter course is called the farmer's course. Its studies are taught in the following order: First term: elements of agriculture, agricultural engineering and architecture, animal anatomy and physiology, shop practice. Second term: animal husbandry, rural economy, veterinary science. Third term: history of agriculture and rural law, veterinary science, practical entomology or landscape gardening.

The studies of the second or winter term are arranged so as to be profitably studied by those who can be in attendance only during that term.

As will be seen by the courses given above, the agricultural studies are included under the heads elements of agriculture, agricultural engineering and architecture, which includes drainage, irrigation, water supply, fencing, building, and machinery; animal husbandry, including breeds and breeding; rural economy, history of agriculture, and rural law. The special studies in horticulture are (1) elements of horticulture, in which are briefly discussed nursery work, orcharding, ornamental trees and shrubs, flower gardens, vegetable gardens and their accessory hot beds and houses, vineyards, and small fruits. Instruction and practice is given in grafting, budding, and propagation. (2) landscape gardening, in which the principles and history of the art, the laying out of grounds, the construction of buildings, the use of water, and many other similar things are taught. Practice in designing grounds is given. (3) floriculture, or the kinds, propagation, growth, and care of flowering and other ornamental plants. (4) pomology and forestry, which are each accompanied with practical work. (5) plant-houses and management. This study includes gardening and landscape architecture, and the construction, heating, ventilation, and general management of plant-houses so as to secure the best growth. Practice is afforded in the plant-houses of the university.

The class-room work consists of lectures and architectural designing and drawing.

Veterinary science is taught during the third year. In the first term the anatomy and physiology of the domestic animals is taught by lectures, demonstrations, and dissections. Post-mortems of healthy and diseased animals are made, so that the student may become practically acquainted with the tissues in health and disease. The first six weeks of the second term are devoted to the study of medicines, their actions and uses; the remainder of the term, to lectures on the principles and practice of veterinary science. During the third term, practical instruction is given in clinical work, as cases present themselves at the veterinary infirmary, where animals are treated or operated upon, free of charge, for the instruction of students. Lectures are also given on veterinary sanitary science and the principles and practice of veterinary surgery.

The apparatus and appliances which are used in the aid of instruction are described a few pages further on.

COLLEGE OF ENGINEERING.

The three schools embraced by this college are designed to thoroughly train students of engineering and architecture. The instruction in the school of mechanical engineering, while severely scientific, is thoroughly practical.

The mechanical laboratory is in use at every stage. Principles are imparted by lectures, text-books, and illustrations. Test experiments in machines and motors are tried. Practice is acquired by the production of elementary forms and the execution of projects. Designing is a necessary part of every term's work, and accompanies all studies. Shop practice is carefully arranged in order to fully familiarize the student with tools, machines, and the mode of their production. This practice represents four branches: Pattern-making, blacksmithing, bench-work for iron, and machine tool work for iron. The course fits the student for the advanced shop practice in designing and constructing complete machines, which is undertaken after finishing the elementary work of the first year.

The students in the course leading to the degree of bachelor of science in the school of mechanical engineering are, in the first year, trigonometry, analytical geometry, calculus, descriptive geometry and lettering, freehand and projection drawing, French or German, and shop practice. Second year: The advanced study of algebra, analytical geometry and calculus, the designing and construction of machines, astronomy, and French or German. Third year: Analytical mechanics, advanced descriptive geometry, physics, chemistry, with laboratory practice, mechanism, laboratory work, and modern history. Fourth year: Resistance of materials, hydraulics, prime movers, mill-work, construction drawing, designing and laboratory work, geology, mental science, constitutional history, political economy, and thesis.

The student is trained in the school of civil engineering by a combination of theoretical instruction with practical work. In the first three years the student is trained to undertake engineering operations, while the fourth year is designed to fit him to plan and direct such works as making geodetic surveys, building arches, trestle bridges, and all supporting frames.

In the second year the class makes a complete topographical survey of a locality with preparation for a railroad survey, executed at a later date. A project in geodesy is executed by the seniors. Great attention is paid to surveying in its highest branches. Astronomical studies, with use of the observatory, are encouraged.

The courses of the first and second years are the same as in the mechanical school, with the exception that shop practice is omitted, and in the second year the designing and construction of machines are superseded by land and topographical surveying, with theory of instruments and topographical drawing. The third year includes advanced descriptive geometry, chemistry, and laboratory practice, railroad engineering, analytical mechanics, astronomy, and physics.

The fourth year embraces resistance of materials and hydraulics, geodesy and practical astronomy, geology, bridges and bridge construction, stone work, constitutional history, political economy, mental science, and thesis. Students in mining engineering take a course in metallurgy in place of geodesy and practical astronomy, bridges and bridge construction. There are well-furnished cabinets of geological and mineralogical specimens, and the chemical laboratory embraces assaying and metallurgical departments, with stamp mill, furnaces, &c., for practical instruction.

The school of architecture prepares students for that profession. Among the subjects in which practical instruction is given are office work and shop practice in such work as constructing joints in carpentry and joinery, cabinet-making, turning, &c.; also modeling in clay. The courses in mathematics, mechanics, physics, &c., are nearly identical with those in the schools of engineering. The technical studies embrace drawing from casts, modeling in clays, elements of construction; wood, stone, brick, and iron constructio ; tinners' work, slating, plastering, painting, and plumbing, architectural drawing and designing; history and esthetics of architecture, estimates, agreements, and specifications, heating and ventilation, graphical statics. The shop practice and the method of instruction are similar to those of the Russian system. The students' work from scale drawings occupies three terms; in the first, carpentry and joinery are taught; in the second, turning and cabinet-making; in the third, metal and stone work, pattern-making, &c. There is a large shop well arranged and fitted up for the carpenter and cabinet work. A course known as the builders' is provided for those who can take only a single year.

COLLEGE OF NATURAL SCIENCE.

This is divided into schools of chemistry and of natural history. A school of domestic science was formerly included. It has been abandoned for the present.

The school of chemistry is designed to equip students for work in the related arts, as well as for the field of original research and the practical business of pharmacy and chemistry. There are four distinct courses: chemical, pharmaceutical, agricultural, and metallurgical, each of which has a special laboratory work arranged for it.

The studies required to be completed by candidates for the degree of bachelor of science in the school of chemistry are, in the first year, chemistry and laboratory practice, free-hand drawing, trigonometry, analytical geometry, literature and rhetoric, or French; in the second year, agricultural chemistry, laboratory practice, physiology, or botany, microscopy, zoölogy, and German; in the third year, laboratory practice, minerology, physics, and German; in the fourth year, laboratory work, meteorology, and physical geography, geology, logic, mental science, constitutional history, and political economy.

The text book instruction in the principles of chemistry and chemical physics occupies the first term of the first year. The remainder of the year the recitations alternate with laboratory practice. During the remaining years each student is expected to work two hours daily in the laboratory, five days in the week. There are four courses in laboratory practice, viz: Chemical, pharmaceutical, agricultural, and metallurgical. The work of the first year is common to all the courses, except that the qualitative analysis of brass, solder, and type metal is added to make up the metallurgical course. The work of the remaining year is especially devoted to the end indicated by the names of the courses. The special work of the agricultural course includes the analysis of soils, ashes of plants, fertilizers, and agricultural products, and the preparation of organic and inorganic salts and compounds.

THE SCHOOLS OF NATURAL HISTORY, MILITARY SCIENCE, AND ART.

The aim of this school is to give a liberal scientific education. As its name testifies, it teaches the sciences connected with man and his habitation. The special studies are botany, vegetable physiology, anatomy and physiology, zoölogy and taxidermy, geology, paleontology, microscopy and fungology, and osteology. The school has a large collection of specimens in the departments of botany, entomology, zoölogy, and geology.

In addition to these colleges and schools properly related to technical and other pursuits, there are schools of military science, of art and design, of ancient languages, and of English and modern languages.

The courses in the school of military science are as follows:

First year.—School of the soldier and company; bayonet-fencing.

Second year.—School of battalion; skirmish drills; ceremonies and reviews; military signaling; sword-fencing; guard, outpost, and picket duty.

Third year.—Military administration; reports and returns; theory of fire-arms; target practice; artillery drill; organization of armies; art of war; field fortification.

The school of art and design furnishes instruction in free-hand drawing, and offers facilities for pursuing studies in industrial designing and other branches of the fine arts. Music is not a part of the university course, but a proper arrangement has been made for students who desire tuition and practice.

THE COLLEGE OF LITERATURE AND SCIENCE.

This is divided into two schools: English and modern languages, and ancient languages and literature. The purpose is to give a good general and liberal collegiate education; also to enable special students in the technical schools who may determine to become instructors, as teachers or writers, to acquire that command over languages and literature which most readily puts the work at their disposal and command. A prominent aim of the university is "the furnishing of teachers to the industrial schools of the country, and investigators and writers for the arts."

THE BUILDINGS AND THEIR USES.

The special report of the regent continues: The university main building, 214 feet in front by 122 feet in flank, occupies three sides of a quadrangle. It is five stories high, including basement and mansard; at the principal angles are two lofty towers, carrying a clock and a bell. The structure is well built of pressed brick upon a stone basement; its cost was $175,000. The main front is occupied by class rooms and offices; in the wings are several spacious apartments, 60 by 80 feet, used respectively for chapel, laboratory for physics, drawing room, museum of natural history, library, art gallery, and museum of engineering art. There are ample dressing rooms, work rooms, offices, and rooms for storage; and in the mansard story halls for literary and scientific societies. The entire building is lighted with gas and heated by steam.

The chemical building is 126 by 74 feet, and four stories high. It contains two laboratories, two lecture rooms, &c.

The mechanical building is 124 by 80 feet. In the lower story is the machine shop, with pattern room, machine room, and engine room; the carpenter's shop, with bench room and machine room, and a room for storing two field pieces. The second story is a drill-hall, with space sufficient for the evolutions of a company of infantry or a section of artillery. This room is supplied with gymnastic apparatus. This building also contains an armory and a printing office.

The greenhouse is 70 by 24 feet, with adjacent class room, work room, and propagating pits. The buildings also comprise a veterinary laboratory, hospital, and dissecting room, two spacious barns, two dwelling houses, two small dwellings used as dormitories, a small astronomical ob-servatory, lately rebuilt, a dairy house, and a farmer's cottage.

LABORATORIES, WORKSHOPS, AND COLLECTIONS.

The library contains over 13,000 volumes, selected by the various professors for reference in their several departments. The apartment is used also for a reading room, where books are consulted, but whence they cannot be taken, except by special permit. The reading room is opened during the daytime, and is greatly frequented.

The museum is well supplied with cases, which contain specimens of all the larger mammals of the United States, with very considerable collections in all the departments of zoölogy, geology, and mineralogy, and a set of Ward's casts of celebrated fossils. The specimens in the museum have mostly been prepared and mounted by the students, under the direction of their instructors. The students have been employed to mount specimens for the State museum and other cabinets.

The art gallery contains in statues, full size and reduced, busts, bas-reliefs, &c., 400 casts. It has also photographs, autotypes, and other copies of masterpieces of painting from all the noted modern schools of art. This collection represents no part of either the Congressional or the legislative grants, but is the donation of the citizens of Champaign and Urbana and of the faculty of the university. It attracts many visitors and renders notable service to the school of art and design.

The physical laboratory has a collection of apparatus which has cost over $5,000. The room is newly arranged and is well adapted for practical experimenting by pupils. The lecture room adjoining will seat 350 persons; it can be made available for experimenting by day or evening.

Special collections for illustration in mechanical, civil, and mining engineering, and in architecture, are found in their respective class rooms. They include models of mechanical movements made in the university shops; mining models and metallurgical apparatus from Freiberg; engineering and surveying instruments in abundance; models of bridges, trusses, roofs, and stairs, also made in our own shops, &c. This material will soon be gathered in the museum of engineering art.

The chemical laboratories are arranged in the latest and most approved manner. Each student has a desk furnished with closets, reagents, water, gas, and gas-hood, so that his researches may go on without inconvenience to any other. The rooms are ventilated by a powerful fan, furnishing warm or cold air as the season may require. There are 104 desks in the qualitative room and 64 in that for quantitative analysis, and all are occupied. The number of desks can be nearly doubled. There is also a private laboratory for professors; a balance room; room for gas analysis; a suite of rooms for photography; a pharmacy; and, in the basement, rooms and power for metallurgical purposes. These rooms have all been occupied. The building is heated by steam.

The machine shop has a steam engine of 16-horse power; two engine and three plain lathes; a planer; a large drill press and smaller drills; all needful bench-rooms; a pattern shop; a blacksmith shop, &c.

The students in this department have, during the freshman year, an elementary drill in wood and iron work with the cold chisel, the file, at the anvil, and at the machine tools. Afterwards they are employed in simpler and more complex designs in work for the shop or for customers.

The engine, the large drill press, three of the lathes, and other machines or parts of machines now in use were built in the shop, as were the engine, pump, and other mechanism under the chemical laboratory.

The carpenter's shop is similarly supplied with necessary machine tools, as saws, planers, tenoning machine, whittler, &c. Its power is furnished by the machine shop. A course of elementary wood construction is followed by such actual practice as occasion may offer. This shop has hitherto found abundance of work in building cabinets for the museum, cases for the library, and other work demanded in the development of other departments.

Drawing, free-hand, projection, mechanical, and architectural, and in the departments of botany and zoölogy, is taught as the handmaid of every science. One of the larger rooms is devoted to this purpose, having a large supply of models, casts, and similar material. Special rooms are set apart for architectural, mechanical, and engineering drawing. A room is given to modelling in clay and casting successful designs in plaster.

The botanical work-room has a supply of compound microscopes; the objectives and four stands have been bought abroad; a larger number of cheaper but thoroughly serviceable stands were made in the university machine shops. A tract of land is set apart for culture of rare or otherwise desirable plants. Experiments in horticulture, with practice in tree planting, grafting, budding, and other means of propagation are regularly performed or taught to classes.

The university grounds make a good study in landscape gardening. An arboretum has about 100 varieties of exotic and indigenous trees. An orchard has been planted with 1,000 varieties of apples, now bearing fruit, besides pears, peaches, grapes, and other small fruit.

The stock farm occupies about 400 acres; the experimental farm about 70 acres. The stock barn has the form of an L, the longer sides being 80 feet, and the breadth of each wing 40 feet. It is of wood, over an ample stone basement. Another barn nearer the house of the professor of agriculture is specially adapted to the housing and care of the small herd of choice cattle of recorded pedigree, chiefly short-horns and Jerseys.

A farmers' institute is held at the university in January of each year, occupying about a week. The labor is done mainly by the professors, in addition to their ordinary duties. The attendance is large, and each year the interest is greater. The information disseminated is bearing good fruit in the improved intelligence of the farming community in the vicinity.

MISCELLANEOUS.

Women are admitted to any of the university courses; most choose the course of literature and science. A course of studies under the general head "Domestic Science" was arranged specially for women, and was in use for five years. Thirty-one persons have chosen this course, and six have taken the degree of bachelor of science in this school.

Unless excused for actual physical disability, all the male students of the university are drilled during the first three years of their college course by an officer of the Regular Army, detailed for this duty by authority of an act of Congress.

The armory contains 300 Springfield cadet breech-loading rifles, with the necessary equipments, side arms for officers, and two six-pounder field pieces. A campus of about 10 acres, beautifully levelled and fringed with evergreens, furnishes space for evolutions in the season for out-of-door exercise. At other times the drill is conducted in the hall, already mentioned. A band of about fifteen pieces, the players being students, furnishes music for the drill, for marching to the chapel daily, and for the various other occasions which arise.

The university maintains a close connection with the public schools of the State. Such of the high schools as desire, after an examination by a committee of the faculty and a satisfactory report, are placed upon an "accredited list." Graduates from these schools are admitted to the freshman class of the university without any examination. About one-third of the last class (1880) were admitted in this way, upon exhibition of their diplomas. * * *

In every department of life, as professional men, teachers, merchants, engineers, farmers, naturalists, our graduates, and those who have gone out from us after a shorter residence without remaining to finish any distinct course of study, are doing honest and faithful work, serving their country and adorning the fair fame of their *alma mater*.

It will be remembered that the university was organized but fourteen years prior to the date at which this report ends, and that but eleven classes have passed out as graduates.

The Illinois Industrial University, as it stands to-day, whether considered with reference to its outlined plans of study, scientific, practical, esthetic; its present standards of scholarly attainment; its generous equipment in lands, buildings, laboratories, museums; the character and learning of its able corps of instructors; or the manly and womanly earnestness and high purposes which pervade the whole body of its under-graduate members, all these characteristics which are the sources of gratified surprise to whoever examines its present condition, attest the wisdom of its founders, and particularly emphasize the eminent success of its first president, under whose vigorous hand and fertile brain its destinies were guided for twelve years.

To John M. Gregory, LL. D., its first regent, the university and the people of Illinois owe a debt which can never be discharged, but whose magnitude will be more fully appreciated with each revolving year.

INDIANA.

PURDUE UNIVERSITY.

[Statements from the latest reports received by this office.]

HISTORICAL STATEMENT.

Purdue University is located at La Fayette, Ind., and has been in operation since September, 1874. It was first organized exclusively upon the basis of special schools for technical studies, but after two years' experience the institution was reorganized on the plan described below, which, though more fully developed, has remained substantially unchanged.

John Purdue, after whom the university is named, donated $150,000 on condition that the institution should be located within Tippecanoe County; the county gave $50,000, and four citizens 100 acres of land.

ENDOWMENT.

The proceeds of the sale of the land (390,000 acres) amounted to $212,238.50. This endowment has been increased largely, and now amounts to $340,000. The buildings and grounds are valued at $250,000. The university has received State appropriations, from 1873 to 1882, amounting to $148,000.

Receipts and expenditures for 1880–'81.

Interest on land grant endowment	$17,161 25
State appropriations	4,500 00
Current receipts from fees, etc	3,084 48
Current receipts from farm	2,053 85
Balance in treasury July 1, 1880	7,548 77
Total receipts	34,348 35

The expenditures were as follows:

Salaries of instructors	$16,483 35
Other running expenses	11,015 03
Improvements	3,489 35
Running expenses of the farm	1,571 51
Total expenditures	32,559 24

INDUSTRIAL EDUCATION IN THE UNITED STATES. 111

Boarding House. Ladies' Hall. Laboratory. Engine House. University Hall. Men's Dormitory.
Industrial Art Hall. Mechanics' Shop. Military Hall.

The State appropriations prior to 1881 were made for definite purposes. In 1881 the legislature appropriated $20,000 for 1881 and $20,000 for 1882, to be expended at the discretion of the trustees.

THE FACULTY.

The faculty consists of 11 professors and instructors in the collegiate department and 2 in the preparatory, with 3 assistants; in all, 16 instructors. They are the president, who is also professor of intellectual and political science, the professors of chemistry and physics, of the natural history sciences, of mathematics, of industrial art, of agriculture and horticulture, of English and history, of German, the instructors in mechanics, and in Latin and elocution, the principal and assistant in the academy, an assistant chemist, and two assistants teaching one class each.

The employés are a librarian and registrar, farmer, horticulturist, and engineer (who is also superintendent of buildings), a janitor, and assistant workmen in the engine house on the farm and in the experimental station.

STUDENTS.

The total number of students in the college proper (1881–'82) was 99; in special schools, 61; in the preparatory department, 129.

Fifty-one of the students in the special schools were also enrolled in the college or academy, so that the total number of different students is 238. There were 68 appointed students in attendance. No distinctions on account of sex are made. The university contained during the school year 1880–'81, 30 women students in college, 13 in special schools, and 52 in the academy. Of those in special schools, 10 were in the industrial art school, 2 in the school of mechanics, and 1 in the school of chemistry. The fees are small, and it requires an annual expenditure of only $160 to meet them and to pay for board and necessary expenses. The students appointed by counties (2 may be appointed by each county) are relieved from expenses to the amount of $33 a year.

DEPARTMENTS AND WORK.

Purdue University embraces three departments, designated as follows:
1. The college of general science.
2. Special schools of science, agriculture, and the mechanic arts.
3. The university academy.

The college provides four general courses of study, viz: The scientific course and three industrial courses, designated as the agricultural course, the mechanical course, and the industrial art course. These courses are so arranged that they include nearly the same instruction in science, mathematics, industrial drawing, English history, and political and intellectual science; and the completion of any one of them entitles a student to the degree of bachelor of science.

These four regular courses are as follows:

1. *Scientific course.*

The aim of the scientific course is to give a thorough scientific education as a general preparation for all industrial pursuits; and, secondly, as an adequate preparation for special courses of study. The natural and physical sciences are the *leading* branches in the course, requiring about one-third of the student's time for the entire period of four years. It also gives unusual prominence to industrial art.

The regular course is as follows:

FRESHMAN YEAR.—(*a*) Biology and botany; (*b*) geometry and algebra; (*c*) industrial drawing; (*d*) Latin or German or English.

SOPHOMORE.—(*a*) Zoölogy and physics; (*b*) higher algebra, trigonometry, and surveying; (*c*) ancient, mediæval, and modern history; (*d*) Latin or German.

JUNIOR.—(*a*) Chemistry; (*b*) analytical geometry and astronomy; (*c*) rhetoric and English literature; (*d*) Latin or German.

SENIOR.—(*a*) Higher physiology and geology; (*b*) political economy, United States Constitution, and intellectual science; (*c*) the calculus and logic, or an advanced course in chemistry or botany or zoölogy.

The university has a well-equipped chemical laboratory, a good biological laboratory, a choice museum of natural history, a large geological cabinet, and other first-class appliances for scientific instruction and training.

2. *Agricultural course.*

The agricultural course aims not only to give a good scientific education, but also to impart a thorough and practical knowledge of the principles of agriculture and horticulture. It gives special attention to scientific experiments.

The regular full course is as follows:

FRESHMAN YEAR.—(a) *Stock, stock breeding, comparative anatomy, veterinary obstetrics,* and *veterinary science;* (b) biology and botany; (c) geometry and algebra; (d) industrial drawing.
SOPHOMORE.—(a) *Crops* (methods of tillage, rotation of crops, &c.), *meteorology, drainage,* and *farm management;* (b) zoölogy and physics; (c) higher algebra, trigonometry, and surveying; (d) ancient, mediæval, and modern history.
JUNIOR.—(a) *Pomology, floriculture, forestry, entomology, landscape gardening,* and *market gardening;* (b) chemistry; (c) analytical geometry and astronomy; (d) rhetoric and English literature.
SENIOR.—(a) *Agricultural chemistry* and *special studies and experiments in agriculture;* (b) higher physiology and geology; (c) political economy, United States Constitution, and intellectual science.
Due attention is given to English composition.
The students who take the above course are required to work two hours daily in the experimental field, campus, nursery, orchard, &c., during the fall and spring terms (receiving pay for satisfactory work), and in the mechanics' shop during the winter term. This manual labor not only imparts increased skill but it also fosters an active interest in industrial pursuits.
The first two years of the full course outlined above constitute a short course in agriculture. The young man who completes this course will acquire a good knowledge of the principles and methods of agriculture, and at the same time he will obtain a higher practical education for all the duties of life.
The branches of study printed in italics in the above course constitute a special course in agriculture and horticulture. All students who take this special course are required to pursue the corresponding natural and physical sciences. Students who have a fair knowledge of botany and zoölogy can complete the first two years of this special course in one year.
The agricultural department of Purdue University is well equipped for thorough instruction and practice. It occupies a commodious building ("Agricultural Hall"), recently erected, and its means of illustration include the university farm, experimental station, conservatory and propagating house, nurseries, orchards, &c.
The experimental station of a ten acre plat is well laid out and devoted to experiments in agriculture and horticulture with promise of great success and marked utility. The experiments in 1881 included thirty-two varieties of wheat, forty-nine varieties of potatoes, twenty-three varieties of grapes, and a number of varieties of strawberries, raspberries, and other small fruits. Twenty plats of corn were used for experiments with fertilizers. This department is supplied with a full set of meteorological instruments purchased through the United States Signal Service Office. The weather observations are carefully made and recorded, and a full statement of the same is published in the annual report of the university.

3. *Mechanical course.*

The regular mechanical course is as follows:
FRESHMAN YEAR.—(a) Shop practice in *carpentry, wood turning, pattern making,* and *vise work,* with instruction in *carpentry, pattern construction, casting* and *founding* and *machine drawing;* (b) geometry and algebra; (c) industrial drawing; (d) English.
SOPHOMORE.—(a) Shop practice in *forging* and *machine work,* and instruction in *machine drawing, mill work,* and *machinery;* (b) higher algebra, trigonometry, and surveying; (c) physics.
JUNIOR.—(a) *Mechanical engineering,* or German; (b) chemistry; (c) analytical geometry and astronomy; (d) rhetoric and English literature.
SENIOR.—(a) *Mechanical engineering,* or German; (b) higher physiology and geology; (c) calculus and logic; (d) political economy, United States Constitution, and intellectual science.
The first two years of this course furnish an excellent technical training for a mechanic or machinist, and also afford a good preparation for a course in mechanical and civil engineering. The course provides two years of shop practice (two hours daily) in the use of hand and machine tools for working in wood and iron; one year's instruction (one hour daily) in the elements of carpentry, pattern making, founding, mill work, &c., and one year's instruction in mechanical drawing, thus including the elements of all the common trades; and, at the same time, the course for these two years provides instruction in mathematics, physical science, and English.
This may be followed with two years' instruction in mechanical engineering, taken in connection with the branches in the corresponding terms of the scientific course.
The branches of study and practice printed in italics in the first two years of the above course constitute a special course in practical mechanics, and may be taken by those who have the necessary knowledge of algebra, geometry, and drawing.

The shops are supplied with tools and machines of a superior quality and specially adapted for the work for which they are used. They include complete appliances for bench work in wood, machine work in wood, vise work in iron, machine work in iron, and forging.

The method of mechanical instruction and training employed in Purdue University is clearly set forth in a statement by Prof. M. F. M. Goss, instructor in mechanics, which is presented by Prof. John D. Runkle, Ph. D., LLD., of the Massachusetts Institute of Technology, in a paper on "The Manual Element in Education." Professor Goss's statement is given below.

The shop instruction is divided as follows:

Bench work in wood_____12 weeks (120 hours)
Wood-turning_____4 weeks (40 hours)
Pattern-making_____12 weeks (120 hours)
Vise-work in iron_____10 weeks (100 hours)
Forging in iron and steel_____18 weeks (180 hours)
Machine tool work in iron_____20 weeks (200 hours)

The object of the shop instruction is, first, to prepare students for a course of mechanical engineering, and, second, to provide a preparation for some industrial pursuit.

Method of instruction.—We have series of unchanging principles which must be taught practically through the use of corresponding sets of tools; and, while series of models are principally used, we vary these with each class in form and dimensions, always keeping in view the principles to be taught. Another feature is to make the models assume a form which may, if possible, afterward be utilized. The principles involved will always be of prime and the utilization of secondary consideration.

Course in carpentry and joinery.—1, exercise in sawing and planing to dimensions; 2, application, a box nailed together; 3, mortise and tenon joints; a plain mortise and tenon, an open dove-tailed mortise and tenon (dovetailed halving); a dovetailed keyed mortise and tenon; 4, splices; 5, common dovetailing; 6, lap dovetailing and rabbeting; 7, blind or secret dovetail; 8, mitre-box; 9, carpenter's trestle; 10, panel door; 11, roof truss; 12, section of king-post truss roof; 13, drawing model. Elements applied in simple forms in each case.

Wood-turning.—1, elementary principles—first, straight turning; second, cutting in; third, convex curves with the chisel; fourth, compound curves formed with the gouge; 2, file and chisel handles; 3, mallets; 4, picture frames (chuck work); 5, card-receiver (chuck work); 6, match-safe (chuck work); 7, ball. The articles present good forms for learning the art, and each of the last four a new and difficult feature of chucking.

Pattern-making.—The student is supposed now to have some skill in bench and lathe work, which will be increased; but the direct object is to teach what forms of patterns are in general necessary, and how they must be constructed in order to get a perfect mould from them. We have not thought it necessary that each student should do the same examples to accomplish this object. In this way the work has been much more varied; each student learns the peculiar features in the work done by his neighbor, and gets a much broader knowledge than could in the same time be acquired in any other way. The work is, consequently, somewhat different each year; for the year just passed, besides simple patterns easily drawn from the sand, such as glands, ball-cranks, &c., there followed a series of flanged pipe-joints for $2\frac{1}{2}$-inch pipe, including the necessary core boxes, in which all took part; then pulley patterns from 6 to 10 inches in diameter, built in segments for strength, and to prevent warping and shrinkage; lastly, a complete set of patterns for a three-horse power horizontal steam engine, all made from drawings of the finished piece.

"*Vise work in iron.*—1. Given a block of cast iron 4 inches by 2 inches, by $1\frac{1}{2}$ inches in thickness, to reduce the thickness $\frac{1}{4}$ inch by chipping and then by finishing with the file. 2. To file a round hole square. 3. To file a round hole into elliptical. 4. Given a 3 inch cube of wrought iron to cut a spline 3 inches by $\frac{3}{8}$ inch, by $\frac{1}{4}$ inch, and second, when the under side is a one-half round hollow. These two cuts involve the use of the cape chisel and the round nose chisel, and are examples of very difficult chipping. 5. Round filing, or hand vise work. 6. Scraping. 7. Some special examples of fitting.

"*Forging.*—1. Elementary processes, drawing, bending, upsetting. 2. A course in welding. 3. Miscellaneous forgings, intended to represent different principles in forming. 4. Steel forging, including hardening and tempering in all its details.

"*Machine work.*—In this course we have used few set models, the work varying more or less with each class. But the aim is to teach centring, plain and taper turning, taper fitting, screw cutting, to bring in all the adjuncts of the machines, and to give practice in their use. All students are not upon the same work at the same time; but each during his course has an opportunity of learning the use of all the tools and appliances. Nor is a given time allotted to each piece. The slow ones must work extra time to keep up, while those who are quick are given extra work. All students are required to devote all the time allotted to each shop course, and not allowed to pass from one to another in advance of the class, unless they are proficient and can enter a regular class in an advanced branch.

"The shop instruction is supplemented by a course of lessons on the theory of the hand and machine tools, more or less use being made of Shelley's Workshop Appliances, Holly's Laws, Rose's Pattern Maker's Assistant, Rose's Practical Machinist, and notes notes found in the first two volumes on Building Construction, published by Rivingtons."

4. *Industrial art course.*

Instruction in industrial drawing has been provided for from the beginning of the university, and such instruction is made an important element in all the regular courses of study. The more advanced instruction has been given to special students, or to regular students who have been able to continue industrial art as an extra study.

The importance of this training and the interest of students in it have resulted (1882) in the adding of an industrial art course to the regular industrial courses. It is as follows:

FRESHMAN YEAR.—(*a*) *Industrial drawing* (1 year); *clay modelling* (15 weeks) and wood carving; (*b*) geometry and algebra; (*c*) biology and botany; (*d*) English.

SOPHOMORE.—(*a*) *Industrial art* (see below) and *industrial design;* (*b*) higher algebra, trigonometry, and surveying; (*c*) zoölogy and physics.

JUNIOR.—(*a*) Chemistry; (*b*) analytical geometry and astronomy; (*c*) rhetoric and English literature; (*d*) Latin or German.

SENIOR.—(*a*) Higher physiology and geology; (*b*) political economy, United States Constitution, and intellectual science; (*c*) Latin or German; (*d*) *special study in industrial art.*

The course in industrial drawing in the freshman year includes geometrical drawing (about 100 problems), perspective, orthographic projection, isometric projection, and model and object drawing.

The course in clay modelling includes the modelling of geometrical solids, followed by architectural ornaments, fruits, flowers, parts of the human body, &c.—an excellent preparation for work in wood, iron, glass, plaster, stucco, &c.

The course in wood carving includes diaper carving, incised carving, low relief carving, and higher relief carving, including tablets, panels, sculptured ornaments, &c.

The course in industrial art in the sophomore year includes drawing in light and shade, light and color, and historical ornament; and the course in industrial design includes the analysis of plant forms for purposes of design, and the making of original designs for prints, carpets, lace, wall paper, oil cloths, tiles, china ware, &c.

Students who do not wish to take the full course, outlined above, can take a special course, made up of branches printed in italics in the above full course, and devote all their time to it.

The industrial art department is provided with a suit of rooms specially fitted for the different courses, and is well supplied with casts, models, copies, charts, and other appliances required for thorough art instruction and practice. It is believed that no industrial college in the country has a better equipped or more successful art department than Purdue University.

Conditions of admission.

Applicants for admission to the freshman class (to take any one of the four courses given above) must pass a satisfactory examination in spelling, geography, English grammar, arithmetic, elementary algebra (including quadratic equations), the history of the United States, physical geography, and physiology. An applicant's knowledge of the common branches must be sufficient to entitle him to a teacher's certificate of good grade, and his knowledge of the elements of algebra should be thorough. Applicants who have completed their course of preparation in high schools that hold the certificate of the State board of education will be admitted without examination.

Entrance examinations are held in the several counties of the State, under the direction of county superintendents, and also at the university.

Special schools.

The several departments of the university which provide special instruction for students who wish to pursue branches as *specialties* are called *special schools.* The following special schools have been organized:
1. School of agriculture and horticulture.
2. School of practical mechanics.

3. School of industrial art.
4. School of chemistry.
5. School of natural history.
6. School of mechanical and civil engineering.

The courses of instruction and practice in the special schools of agriculture and horticulture and practical mechanics include the studies printed in italics in the regular courses given above, and correspond to what are there designated "special courses." The conditions of admission to either of these schools are the same as the conditions of admission to the freshman class.

The course of instruction and practice in the special school of industrial art takes a wider range of art studies than the regular course. The course in clay modelling and wood carving is similar to this element of the regular industrial art course, but is more extended and thorough.

The course in industrial design (drawing) covers two years. The first year is the same as the sophomore year of the regular industrial art course. The second year is mainly devoted to the designing of articles of manufacture and their ornamentation.

The course in mechanical drawing for the first year is the same as the first year's course in industrial design, except that the details of machinery form part of the instruction in instrumental drawing.

The instruction in the second year includes drawings made to scales of engines and other machines; drawings of machines from measurements; drawings from given data; original designs for machines, giving plans, elevations, sections, &c.; and orthographic projection, development of surfaces, descriptive geometry, &c.

The special school of chemistry is open to students who have completed the first two years of one of the regular courses of the college or an equivalent. The first year of the course is the same as the course in chemistry prescribed for the junior year of the scientific course.

The course for the second year includes lectures on qualitative and quantitative analysis, including minerals, soils, fertilizers, &c., with laboratory practice ten hours per week.

The third year's course is arranged under the three divisions of mineralogy, metallurgy, and organic chemistry. The students in metallurgy are required to take the course in mineralogy. The practice includes from six to eight hours of daily work in the laboratory.

Students who complete a three years' course in this school are entitled to the degree of analytical chemist (A. C.).

The chemical laboratory is well equipped for thorough work in each branch of study, and the instruction looks to direct practical applications. The professor of chemistry is the State chemist, and as such is charged with the duty of analyzing all fertilizers offered for sale in the State. The laboratory also renders the State board of health important assistance.

The special school of natural history provides two courses of two years each, one in botany and one in zoölogy, each course being open to students who have a knowledge of biology, botany, and zoölogy, as taught in the scientific course, or an equivalent.

The course in botany in the first year includes advanced instruction in structural and systematic botany, histology, organogeny, and embryology of phanerogams. The first term of the second year is devoted to cryptogams, and the second and third terms are devoted to original work preparatory to a thesis.

The course in zoölogy during the first four terms is a study of the comparative anatomy of the various classes of animals by dissection. During the last two terms students devote themselves to special original work and are required to present a thesis.

The biological laboratory is supplied with simple and compound microscopes, reagents, and dissecting tables, thus furnishing ample facilities for practical work. The geological cabinet contains valuable collections of minerals, fossils, archæological specimens, &c. The zoölogical museum contains important collections in conchology, entomology, ornithology, and other branches. The herbarium has over 2,000 specimens, and is specially well supplied with sets of State grasses, sedges, and ferns.

The school of mechanical and civil engineering was to be organized in September, 1882. It will be open to students who have completed the first two years of the regular mechanical course, or an equivalent. The course of instruction will cover a period of three years. The first two years may be taken in connection with junior and senior studies in the regular college course.

The university academy.

The academy has the two-fold object of preparing students for admission to the freshman class and of providing thorough instruction in the higher common school branches for those who cannot take a more extended course. It thus fills the gap between the common country school and the college. It is in charge of first class teachers, and is provided with commodious rooms and other appliances necessary for thorough and practical instruction.

Applicants for admission must have a fair knowledge of spelling, geography, arithmetic, and English grammar as taught in the better class of country schools. Students who have a thorough knowledge of the common branches can prepare for the freshman class of the college in one year.

Other advantages.

The *military department* is in charge of Lieut. W. R. Hamilton, U. S. A., detailed by the War Department as instructor in military tactics in Asbury University and permitted by the Secretary of War to occupy the same position in Purdue University. The cadets receive two to three drills a week.

Four *literary societies*[1] are open to students: the Irving, the Philalethean, the Carlyle, and the Periclean, the first and third for young men, the second for young women, and the fourth for academy students of both sexes. The exercises are an efficient means of improvement in writing and speaking. The college societies have commodious halls, neatly carpeted and furnished. A branch of the Young Men's Christian Association was organized in 1880, and is well sustained by the students.

The *library* occupies a commodious and well-lighted room, appropriately fitted and furnished. It contains a valuable collection of books of reference in each department and a goodly number of miscellaneous works, many of standard value, the number of volumes being over 2,000. It also contains many periodicals, scientific, industrial, and literary.

BUILDINGS AND GROUNDS.

The main college building, "University Hall," contains a chapel or assembly hall, an academy hall, two large society halls, a library, and fifteen other rooms used for recitations and other college purposes. The other buildings are the laboratory, containing also the mechanics' shop, the "boarding house" (containing the ladies' dormitory, a complete suite of rooms for the department of industrial art, and a spacious dining hall and other rooms for boarding purposes), the young men's dormitory, the Agricultural Hall, the Military Hall, the boiler, engine, and gas house, and the Peirce Conservatory. There are also a dwelling house for the engineer, a farm house, barn, stables, and other buildings. The entire group of college buildings is heated by steam and lighted by gas.

---

[1] The regulations of Purdue University forbid its students from joining or having any active connection with college secret societies. The regulations upon the subject are as follows:

"No society is permitted to be organized by the students, except by consent of the faculty, and the public exercises of the societies thus organized are subject in time, place, and character to the approval of the faculty.

"No student shall join or have any active connection as a member, or otherwise, with any so-called Greek fraternity or other college secret society or with any other students' society not authorized by the faculty; and, as a condition of graduation or honorable dismission, students shall be required to sign a written statement that they have complied with this regulation."

As a condition of admission to the university or any department therein or of re-entrance, students shall be required to subscribe to the foregoing regulations, and all other regulations of the university relating to the obligations and duties of students, and promise a faithful compliance therewith during their connection with the university; that is, until dismissed or graduated.

PLEDGE.

"I hereby subscribe to the foregoing regulations and all other regulations of Purdue University which relate to the duties and obligations of students, and I promise on my honor a faithful compliance therewith during the university year ending June 30 next."

The power of the Purdue authorities to prohibit the connection of students with college secret societies is thus affirmed by the supreme court of Indiana in an opinion revised August 15, 1882:

"It is clearly within the power of the trustees, and of the faculty when acting presumably or otherwise in their behalf, to absolutely prohibit any connection between the Greek fraternities and the university. The trustees have also the undoubted authority to prohibit the attendance of students upon meetings of such Greek fraternities or from having any other active connection with such organizations, so long as such students remain under the control of the university, whenever such attendance upon the meetings of or other active connection with such fraternities tends in any material degree to interfere with the proper relations of the students to the university. As to the propriety of such and similar inhibitions and restrictions, the trustees, aided by the experience of the faculty, ought and are presumed to be better judges, and as to all such matters, within reasonable limits, the power of the trustees is plenary and complete."

The special reasons for the exclusion of the Greek-letter fraternities from Purdue University were given in a report by the president to the board of trustees in December, 1878, as follows:

"The membership of these societies is almost exclusively in the classical colleges, and they necessarily represent the classical and professional spirit. Purdue University is an *industrial* institution and its students must be imbued with an industrial spirit. Its success requires that the dominant, controlling influence of the institution be scientific and industrial, not classical. The multiplication of Greek societies, in close alliance and under the influence of the chapters in the classical colleges, would antagonize and supplant the industrial spirit in Purdue and give its agricultural and mechanical departments the 'dry rot.' No industrial school can prosper if secretly sapped by the adverse influence of the classical system."

The campus and horticultural grounds contain 20 acres, and are so laid out and cultivated that they well illustrate landscape gardening and horticulture. The nursery and grounds contain some 2,500 trees and shrubs, and the conservatory and propagating house are filled with choice plants. The lawns and ornamental plats are kept in excellent condition. The university occupies one of the handsomest, as well as healthiest, college sites in the country.

IOWA.

STATE AGRICULTURAL COLLEGE.

The objects of the Iowa Agricultural College are clearly set forth in the language of the Congressional law, which declares that its course of study and organization shall be made "to promote the liberal and practical education of the industrial classes in the several pursuits and professions of life," and the entire management and policy of its officers have, from its opening to the present time, aimed to secure this important purpose.

ENDOWMENT AND FUNDS.

The endowment consists of the proceeds from the sale and rent of 204,309 acres of land, and the annual income therefrom amounts to $41,000.

The regular annual expenditure is the same as the income, viz: $41,000. The annual expense of teaching staff is $26,000.

THE FACULTY.

There are 22 instructors, divided so as to give the school of agriculture 1; of horticulture, 1; of veterinary science, 2; of domestic economy, 1; of military tactics, 1; of literature and language, 2; of mathematics and physics, 2; of chemistry, 2; of biology, 3; of philosophy, 3; of mechanical engineering, 2; of civil engineering, 2.

STUDENTS AND GRADUATES.

In 1881 the attendance was as follows: Number of young men, 159; young women, 67—total, 226. Tuition is free. There are no scholarships. The number of graduates was, in 1880, as follows: Young men, 122; young women, 43—total, 165.

Classified according to degrees conferred, they stood as follows: Agricultural course, B. S., 83; mechanical engineering, B. M. E., 8; civil engineering, B. C. E., 31; ladies' course, B. S., 43—total, 165.

The occupations of graduates as far as ascertained are: Teachers in agricultural colleges and agricultural departments, 10; farmers, 20; ministers, 2; book-keepers, 10; principals of schools, 18; teacher in Deaf and Dumb College, 1; inventor, 1; business men, bankers, merchants, &c., 6; physicians, 7; veterinary surgeons, 2; lawyers, 21; engineers, surveyors, and architects, 10; editors, 2; deceased, 6; unknown, 1; printers, 2; students, 3; ladies' pursuits, unknown, 43—total, 165.

ORGANIZATION OF CLASSES AND INSTRUCTION.

The several branches taught are arranged in courses known as general and technical. The general course aims to give a liberal culture in the sciences and other branches of learning, without especially confining it to any particular pursuit or profession. The technical course aims to direct a liberal culture, so as to meet the requirements of some particular industrial pursuit or profession. The technical courses are pursued as follows:
I. The school of agriculture.
II. The school of engineering, embracing two courses—mechanical and civil.
III. The school of veterinary science.

In addition to these defined courses there "are certain lines of technical and scientific study, which include either a single prominent science or several closely-related ones, which may be pursued exclusively by students properly qualified. These, however, do not lead to any degree, but any student completing the studies of any such line may receive the college certificate showing his standings in such studies." These are designated: 1, domestic economy; 2, military science; 3, literature and language; 4, mathematics and physics; 5, chemistry; 6, biology; 7, philosophy.

The two terms of the freshman year and the first term of the sophomore year are filled with certain required and antecedent studies, common to all the schools, except that of veterinary science. There are certain "additional studies" which increase the efficiency of the preparation. The general "course in sciences related to the industries" provides for the degree of bachelor of science and embraces the following studies: In the freshman year, besides algebra, geometry, book-keeping, drawing, composition, elementary botany, and descriptive zoölogy, with optional studies of Latin, German, rhetoric, or moral science, there are, for young men, practical agriculture and horticulture, with military drill; and for young women, domestic economy and work.

The first term of the sophomore year provides for botany, chemistry with laboratory practice, zoölogy, and physics (mechanics of solids, liquids, and gases). The additional studies are: for young men, plane trigonometry, land surveying, and drill; for young women, plane trigonometry, history, domestic economy, and lectures.

For the second term, the regular course for both sexes is zoölogy and entomology, laboratory practice, physics (light and sound), botany, and vegetable anatomy. For young men, additional besides drill, general chemistry and laboratory practice, analytical geometry (optional), stock-breeding. For young women, general chemistry, with practice, or analytical geometry.

For the junior year, besides English literature, botany, vegetable anatomy and physiolgy, comparative anatomy, physics (heat), laboratory practice, and political economy; the additional studies for young men are quantitative chemistry, calculus, physics (electricity, magnetism, meteorology), landscape gardening and farm engineering, organic chemistry and practice.

For young women are the following optional studies: Quantitative chemistry and practice, calculus, physics (magnetism, electricity, and meteorology), landscape gardening, domestic economy and chemistry, kitchen practice, and French. Both classes have to prepare two essays and two dissertations during junior year.

The senior year embraces geology and mineralogy; psychology; two dissertations; science of languages; classification of the sciences; and sociology, with thesis. The young men have in addition agricultural chemistry; anatomy of domestic animals, with clinics and dissections; also, veterinary medicines and lectures on food. French is the special study for young women.

The omissions and substitutions allowed to those who wish to specialize in certain sciences, are as follows:

The special student in chemistry may omit, junior year, botany or physics, comparative anatomy or landscape engineering; senior year, geology or veterinary science or science of language.

The special student in botany may omit: junior year, physics; senior year, geology or veterinary science or science of language.

The special student in zoölogy may omit: junior year, chemistry or physics, and French; senior year, geology or veterinary science and French.

The special student in mathematics and physics may omit: sophomore year, botany or zoölogy; junior year, botany, comparative anatomy, or landscape engineering; senior year, geology, or veterinary science, or agricultural chemistry, or science of language.

The special student in veterinary science may omit, senior year, geology, science of language.

THE SCHOOL OF AGRICULTURE.

Its special faculty, besides the president, embraces professors of practical and experimental agriculture, of horticulture, of veterinary science, of chemistry, of physics, of botany, of zoölogy, and of entomology.

The design of the course is to furnish a broad and thoroughly practical education, giving it such direction as will be especially applicable to the life and duties of the farmer. It has been framed to combine that knowledge and skill which will best prepare the pupil for the highest demands of agricultural industry, and to meet the requirements of of an educated citizenship. Particular attention is paid to the problem of economic production and to the reduction of farm improvement and management to a science which shall eliminate, as far as practicable, elements of uncertainty, and foster well-defined principles of assured success. In this special line of instruction it is the purpose to evolve the science in agriculture as distinct from pure skill and from the sciences relating to agriculture. This course includes four years of college work. The distinctive work of the school is divided into two departments: agriculture and horticulture.

During the freshman year especial attention is paid to descriptive zoölogy and the management of live stock; also to dairy work. To illustrate and demonstrate the various problems, there is upon the farm a dairy of 70 cows, composed of pure shorthorns, Holsteins, and Jerseys, and grades of the same breeds. The dairy barn will accommodate 80 cows. There is a large creamery, supplied with improved apparatus. In the sophomore year special attention is given to stock breeding and the laws of heredity, &c.

During the junior year, farm economy in all its branches is thoroughly studied. The senior year is devoted to experimental agriculture and cognate studies.

The study of horticulture and forestry begins, the former in the second term of the freshman year, and the latter with the second term of the sophomore year.

The means for practical work are: Extensive vegetable and flower gardens; ornamental grounds; experimental nurseries and orchards; small fruit plantations; forestry grounds; propagating grounds and pits under glass; collections of native and cultivated woods, and of injurious and beneficial insects; sets of abnormal and diseased growths, with fac simile fruits, casts, and a growing horticultural museum. Labor of from one to four hours a day, with usual compensation for similar work, is provided for the students.

The course of studies for the two terms of the freshmen year embraces agriculture and horticulture, in addition to elementary botany; descriptive zoölogy; algebra; geometry; drawing, &c. Garden work for twelve hours each week is added, with domestic economy and work for the young women students.

The sophomore year embraces: General chemistry; plane trigonometry; land surveying; physics; mechanics of solids, liquids, gases; horticulture; stock breeding; systematic and economic botany; entomology; general and vertebrate zoölogy; light and sound, and *analytical geometry* (optional). This year also includes practical work on the farm and grounds and in the laboratory.

The junior year embraces, besides English literature, political economy; commercial law; essays and dissertations; drill; farm economy; horticulture, with six hours practice each week; how crops feed and grow, with agricultural practice of six hours each week; vegetable anatomy and physiology, with laboratory practice; physics; heat; landscape gardening; farm engineering, and organic chemistry.

The senior year embraces agricultural chemistry and experimental agriculture, with laboratory practice; veterinary science, anatomy and physiology, diseases, treatment and medicine, with clinics and dissertations; geology and mineralogy; lectures on foods; philosophy of science; psychology, and sociology; thesis.

THE SCHOOL OF ENGINEERING.

This includes the two departments of mechanical engineering and civil engineering. The department of mechanical engineering includes a special course of instruction in architecture. For the freshman year the course of study in mechanical engineering is the same as that in the sciences related to the industries, except practice in the workshop and the study of drawing and workshop tools and appliances; the former occupies three forenoons of two and a half hours each per week, the latter one hour two afternoons per week. The workshop practice is of a general character; it is not pursued with a view to any particular trade or calling. Each student is required to make a complete set of elementary forms and to execute a series of problems which will give a general training, with excellence of finish and correct fitting.

The sophomore year is devoted to leading scientific studies, and those of the junior year are in the line of the profession.

In the junior year, the studies are more strictly technical. During the first term the various methods of laying out railway curves, putting in switches and side tracks, and setting slope stakes, are taught, together with the principles of the construction of waterworks, sewers, retaining walls, and other combined structures. Data are also taken for problems in earthwork, both excavation and embankment, and the cubic contents calculated. In pure mathematics, calculus is taught; descriptive geometry is continued, dealing with stereotomy, shades, shadows, and perspective, and isometric drawing. In the second term, analytical mechanics and the strength of materials are made prominent. During this term, also, a practice survey of a portion of a line of railway is undertaken.

The faculty consists of the president, with professors of mechanical and civil engineering (3); of pure mathematics; of physics and mechanics, and of chemistry. The degrees are B. M. E. (bachelor of mechanical engineering) and B. C. E. (bachelor of civil engineering).

The studies pursued for the last two years in the course of mechanical engineering are as follows: In the junior year, stereotomy; shades, shadows, and perspective; model drawing; differential and integral calculus; the principles of analytical, theoretical, and applied mechanics; physics, heat, electricity, magnetism and meteorology; political economy; French; and dissertations.

During the senior year they embrace principles of mechanism, theory of motors, mechanical drawing, French, psychology, geology, and mineralogy (optional), dissertations, prime movers, mechanical designing, philosophy of science and sociology, preparation of thesis. Shop practice and laboratory work are required during both years. Throughout the entire year, lectures and experimental work are added as the class advances in the different subjects. The student determines, from experiments, the laws and coefficient of elasticity and the modulus of strength of different materials. The work in the mechanical laboratory has in view its usefulness to the mechanical engineer.

In the senior year the study of prime movers and thermo-dynamics occupies the greater part of the time. For the purpose of making tests, a fifteen-horse power Harris-Corliss engine has a Richards indicator fitted to it; a four-horse power slide-valve engine has also the indicator, a friction brake, and calorimeters fitted to it. A given amount of fuel is placed in the hands of the student, he making all the tests and determining the efficiency of furnace and engine.

The civil engineering course is begun by systematic drill in algebra and geometry during the freshman year, while plane and spherical trigonometry and land surveying, descriptive and analytical geometry are taught later in the class-room and the field if necessary. Drawing also forms part of the course.

SCHOOL OF VETERINARY SCIENCE.

This is the only distinct school of the indicated character yet formed in an agricultural college. Similar studies are followed in all such institutions, but none besides the Iowa College has made a regular school and provided for the issuing of degrees. The two years' course leads to the degree of bachelor of veterinary medicine (B. V. M.) and with a post-graduate course of one year additional that of doctor of veterinary medicine (D. V. M.).

The purpose is to furnish a practical and theoretical training in the veterinary specialty of medicine and surgery. It aims, furthermore, to prepare young men for the practical work of the veterinary profession. The course of study includes two years and embraces a portion of the studies of the course in the sciences related to the industries, together with the lectures on the technical and special topics of the course and practice in the microscopical and anatomical laboratories and the veterinary hospital.

The course of study is announced as equal to the best American schools. The departments include anatomy of domestic animals; zoölogy and comparative anatomy; histology and physiology; general and comparative pathology; pathological anatomy and histology; instruction in botany; chemistry, general and applied; laboratory therapeutics; veterinary medicine and surgery and clinics. There is a well-furnished dissecting room, a laboratory for the zoölogical class, also a microscopical laboratory. The college claims abundant conveniences for chemical and pathological lectures, studies, &c. In the course of medicine and surgery, the students assist in a large practice. Those of the senior class are made familiar with the use of instruments and the administration of medicines. Several hundreds of animals, including horses, cattle, swine, and sheep, are kept on the college farm, a large portion of there being breeding stock. Frequent inspection of these flocks and herds affords the student most valuable opportunities for observing sanitary conditions and gaining experience in obstetrical practice. The course includes about one hundred and eighty lectures. A collateral course of reading, embracing some of the best approved English works on the subjects taught, is required. In the clinics, advanced students are required to examine animals for certificates of soundness, diagnose diseases, and prescribe for the same. Hundreds of animals are presented at these examinations, for which medical or surgical advice is required; the student must exercise judgment as to the course of treatment to be pursued in these widely differing forms of disease.

Candidates for admission must be at least sixteen years of age. Before entering the classes they must pass an examination in reading, orthography, geography, English grammar, and arithmetic. The course occupies two years. Sessions begin the 1st of March and continue to the middle of November, with a vacation of two weeks in July. Candidates for graduation must be eighteen. Graduates of the science course can enter the veterinary course, and on completion receive a degree as D. V. M.

For the junior year (two terms) the studies are: General chemistry, laboratory practice; general zoölogy, laboratory practice; anatomy of domestic animals; dissections and clinics; materia medica; elementary botany; comparative anatomy; anatomy of domestic animals; veterinary medicine; dissections, and clinics.

The senior year embraces the study of medicine and surgery; medical botany; therapeutics; organic chemistry and toxicology, laboratory practice; histology and physiology, laboratory practice; comparative and general pathology, laboratory practice; veterinary obstetrics; pharmaceutical chemistry, laboratory practice; veterinary sanitary science, and police.

DEPARTMENT OF DOMESTIC ECONOMY.

The studies comprised in this course have been selected with reference simply to their value as prerequisites to a thoroughly practical education, embracing a well-balanced variety of subjects. Besides antecedent studies, the course embraces the most approved branches of science and literature in the last five terms, and the study and practice required for systematic housekeeping.

One division of young ladies, from the freshman class in the science course, practice in the experimental kitchen from 10 to 12 every morning, helping to get dinner for the students. Each member of the class thus gives two hours a week to the study of domestic economy, and they thus learn to prepare plain food in an economical, skillful, and appetizing manner. The sophomore class receive one lecture a week on subjects connected with household management, the preservation of health, care of the sick, &c. The juniors practice two afternoons a week in the experimental kitchen, receiving instruction in the more difficult operations of the culinary art.

The freshman and sophomore years are the same as those for young women in the general scientific course, with certain additions, as above indicated. A standing of at least three (four being perfect) and a final thesis, as required by college law, are the conditions of graduation in this course. The degree is that of bachelor of science.

The studies for the junior year are as follows: Vegetable physiology, cryptogamic botany, physics, heat, English literature, quantitative chemistry, differential and integral calculus, domestic economy, domestic chemistry, French, comparative anatomy, landscape gardening (optional), physics (electricity, magnetism, and meteorology optional), political economy, and dissertations.

The senior year has the following studies: French, geology and mineralogy, psychology, dissertations, philosophy of science and sociology, science of language, and thesis.

MILITARY SCIENCE.

Lectures on military subjects are delivered throughout the course and regular military drill takes place every Wednesday afternoon as follows: First year, first term, school of the soldier; second term, school of the company. Second year, first term, school of the battalion; second term, field artillery drill. Third year, first term, broad-sword exercise and artillery drill; second term, small-sword exercise. Fourth year, first term: cavalry drill and small-sword exercise.

THE DEGREES CONFERRED.

The degree of bachelor of science (B. S. C.) is conferred upon the graduate in the course in sciences related to the industries.

The degree of bachelor of scientific agriculture (B. S. A.) is conferred upon the graduate in agriculture.

The degree of bachelor of mechanical engineering (B. M. E.) is conferred upon the graduate in mechanical engineering.

The degree of bachelor of civil engineering (B. C. E.) is conferred upon the graduate in civil engineering.

The degree of bachelor of veterinary medicine (B. V. M.) is conferred upon the graduate in that study.

The higher degrees are conferred upon the following rules and the recommendations of the faculty:

That of master of science (M. S. C.) is open to bachelors of science, who are graduates of the course in sciences related to the industries, and spend one year additional in such higher studies as may be indicated.

That of master of scientific agriculture (M. S. A.) is open to bachelors of scientific agriculture after pursuing a post-graduate course of one year.

That of mechanical engineer (M. E.) is open to bachelors of mechanical engineering under similar regulations.

That of civil engineer (C. E.) is open to Bachelors of civil engineering in the same way.

That of doctor of veterinary medicine (D. V. M.) is open to bachelors of veterinary medicine. This requires an extra year.

That of master of philosophy is open to graduates of any of the four-year courses of study, the candidates to reside one year and pursue during that time a course of study embracing at least two studies, selected with the approval of the faculty, of which the science of language, psychology, social science, or higher mathematics shall constitute the principal subjects.

GENERAL INFORMATION.

The Iowa Agricultural College has completed its thirteenth year since the formal opening in March, 1869. From its dedication at that date to the cause of industrial learning to the close of its last commencement, it has been striving steadily and successfully to accomplish the purpose set forth in the national law, which at once constitutes its charter and supplies its endowment. Whoever studies its brief history will not fail to find therein all the indications of a uniform and healthy advancement.

Manual labor is divided into uninstructive labor, which is paid for by wages, and instructive work, which forms part of the course of study and practice. The first embraces all work accruing to the benefit of the college.

Instructive labor embraces all operations in work-shop, museum, laboratories, experimental kitchen, upon farm and garden, in which the sole purpose pursued is the acquisition of skill and practice. The labor furnished by the school of agriculture, of veterinary science, and of engineering is given by each exclusively to its own special students.

The current expenses of students, board, light, heat, &c., per week is $2.86; room rent per term, 75 cents to $1.50; washing, 50 cents; janitor's fee per term, $3.

The library numbers about 6,000 volumes. It is made up almost entirely of new books, purchased since the opening of the college.

There are large and well furnished chemical laboratories, wherein a hundred students at once may engage in experimentation and analysis. They cover a space of 4,500 feet. The quantitative laboratory has filter pumps to each desk. The physical laboratory is supplied with a lecture-room furnished with all modern appliances. Rooms are fitted up for those who desire to do special work in experimental physics. Lectures and the text-book are combined, illustrated by numerous experiments throughout the course. There is a very complete cabinet of philosophical apparatus; a large dynamo-electric machine, for producing powerful electric currents, can be used for producing the electric light, as a motor for driving machinery, or to illustrate all the effects and uses of electricity. An electric engine in the college workshop is of sufficient power to drive sewing-machines and other pieces of light apparatus, and was planned and constructed by a post-graduate student. The laboratory has an excellent galvanometer and set of resistance coils, so that good work can be done in the way of electrical measurements.

The zoölogical museum includes mounted specimens of a few mammals, several hundred birds (mounted), representing the *avian fauna* of the State, a large collection of reptiles in alcohol, a few fishes, and a small but typical collection of invertebrates. A set of the "Ward models," illustrating the principal larger fossils, is of service in this study, as well as in geology. There are besides the following collections in process of formation: an entomological cabinet, sets of the eggs and nests of birds, the brains of vertebrates, skulls of mammals, and skeletons of vertebrates. The museum is used during part of the year as a laboratory.

The geological museum possesses a good collection of the common rocks and minerals to which the student has access. Among other advantages for pursuing this study, the museum contains a set of the Ward series of geological casts.

A horticultural laboratory and green-house occupy separate buildings. The botanical collections, now rapidly increasing, are made mainly by students. There is a vegetable garden of 10 acres and experimental orchards occupying 20 acres; also a farm of 860 acres, with the various breeds of cattle, swine, and sheep, all supplied with the requisite stabling. An experimental farm of 30 acres is taken from this, wherein new varieties of grains, roots, grasses, etc., are tested.

The college buildings consist of main structure, boarding cottage, chemical and physical hall, horticultural building, south hall (used as boarding-house and for the college of domestic economy), the farm-house, creamery, workshop, laundry, and gas works. The workshops embraced for some time a printing-office, with steam-press, jobber, type, and all necessary fittings; and still include a shop for working in wood and one for iron work. The machinery is run by steam, and there is a good equipment.

KANSAS.

THE KANSAS STATE AGRICULTURAL COLLEGE.

[Statement by the president.]

OCTOBER, 1882.

This institution, located at Manhattan, Riley County, Kansas, was organized originally as Blue-Mont College, under the auspices of the M. E. Church; but upon Kansas receiving the national grant of 30,000 acres of land for each of its three members of Congress, the new three-story college building, completed in 1863, with 100 acres of land, was presented to the State and endowed with the 82,313.35 acres of land received under the act of July 2, 1862.

For ten years the management of the college remained essentially with the original founders, Rev. J. Denison, president, and it retained largely the character of a classical college and preparatory school, for which it had been designed.

The State had loaned funds for current expenses till the endowment should become productive, and in 1870 provided that these funds, amounting to over $30,000, should be repaid, as soon as the income became sufficient to warrant it, by investment in permanent improvements. An issue of scrip in anticipation of expected surplus income procured the purchase of a fine farm of 155 acres, and the erection, at a cost of $11,000, of one wing of a huge barn.

In 1873 the organic law of the college was revised, a new board of regents appointed, and a new president, Rev. J. A. Anderson, selected, since which time the college has been maintained upon a thoroughly industrial basis, in that all students are required to learn the elements of some industry, while the course has been modified from time to time to correspond, by excluding the classics and including more complete instruction in the sciences related to agriculture and the mechanic arts.

In 1875 the erection of buildings upon the new farm was begun, and the "barn" was made the principal college building, leaving the old college, one mile distant, to serve as a dormitory, so that the principal part of its growth, as now existing, has been within the last eight years, more than half of which were years of struggle against local opposition and with poverty, debt, and general lack of comfort or convenience. Five substantial buildings had been provided at a cost of $35,000, and considerable improvement upon the farm had been made, when, in 1879, President Anderson resigned to take a seat in Congress, and the present president, George T. Fairchild, who had been fifteen years a professor in the Michigan State Agricultural College, was chosen.

The college has now, October, 1882, a productive endowment of $386,164.87 invested in school and municipal bonds at an average interest of 8 per cent., received wholly from the sale of 69,723.15 acres of the original land grant. There remains to be sold 12,590.37 acres, rapidly selling at an average price of nearly $8 an acre, and the State still claims from the national government 7,686.47 acres deficiency in the lands patented to the State under the act of 1862.

The income for the last financial year, closing June 30, 1882, was $28,890.76, of which $25,779.82 was from interest upon the invested endowment; the rest was from rent, fees, and sales of stock. The expenses during the same year for all college purposes were $24,701.42. The year closed with a balance in the treasury of cash $10,969.23, and uncollected interest overdue, $6,461.37. There were unexpended balances of appropriations for library and other specific purposes of $1,276.92. These particulars of the financial condition are given to show how fully this State has met the requirements of the act of 1862, in making the fund as large as possible and in guarding it from loss, and to emphasize the prosperity of the past three years, during which the income has increased from $18,000 to nearly $29,000.

The college has received from the State for all purposes, besides the mileage and fees of regents and commission of land agent, $212,482.02, $77,000 of which has been for the buildings now in use. These, all of the famous Manhattan limestone, stand upon a sightly elevation, overlooking the city and giving a fine view of the most beautiful part of the Kansas valley. The principal building, or college hall, yet incomplete, contains now a chapel to seat six hundred people, society room, offices, library, reading room, and class rooms for agriculture, mathematics, English history, and drawing. When fully completed the building will be 130 by 250 feet in extreme dimensions, arranged in three different structures, with connecting corridors. The other buildings answer the following description: Chemical laboratory, one story high, 36 by 99 and 46 by 75 feet, in the form of a cross. It contains eight rooms, occupied by the department of chemistry, physics, and mineralogy, and the printing office.

Mechanics' Hall, 39 by 103 feet, of two stories, occupied by the carpenter shop and finishing room, telegraph office, sewing rooms, music rooms, and kitchen laboratory.

Horticultural Hall, 32 by 80 feet, one story and cellar, with cabinet room, class room, work room and storage, with small greenhouse attached.

Armory Hall, 46 by 96 feet, and two stories high. It was originally designed for a barn, and once served as the chief building of the college, but is now used for the armory and drill room, the dwelling of the farm superintendent, and rooms for the janitor and a few students.

The barn, of stone, 48 by 96 feet, with side-hill basement stables, granary, tool room, &c.

The piggery, of wood, contains six pens, with yards attached.

A farm house, purchased with the farm, is still occupied as the president's house. The original college buildings, a three-story hall and a dormitory, are but partially occupied on account of the distance from the principal work and machinery.

Both farms are surrounded by substantial stone wall, and both have considerable plantations of forest, fruit, and ornamental trees.

The total property of the college is inventoried at a trifle over $125,000. This includes, besides the buildings above mentioned, various means of illustration and instruction, as follows:

Two farms of 171 and 100 acres. Eighty-five acres in crops; 30 acres in tame grasses;

81 acres in prairie pasture and mowing land of native grasses. Samples of special crops and experimental plots in grains, grasses, and forage crops.

A well planned barn for grain, hay, horses, and cattle; and a piggery with ten pens, with separate yards.

Shorthorn, Jersey, Polled Angus or Aberdeen, and Galloway cattle, Berkshire and Essex swine.

Farm implements of approved patterns.

Orchards, containing apples, peaches, pears, plums, cherries and apricots, of many varieties.

Small-fruit garden, with varieties of blackberries, raspberries, gooseberries, currants, and strawberries; and vineyard with fifty varieties of grapes.

Forest plantation of 5 acres, containing twenty varieties of trees of from ten to fifteen years' growth.

Ornamental grounds, set with a variety of evergreens and deciduous trees. Sample rows of ornamental and useful trees and shrubs, labeled.

Vegetable garden, with hot and cold frames and experimental beds. Practice rows for students' budding, grafting, cultivating, and pruning.

A small greenhouse, with collection of bedding and house plants. Chemical laboratory, with seven rooms, fitted with tables and apparatus for a class of forty students; also, physical apparatus and meteorological instruments.

Mathematical instruments, models and patterns for drawing, and charts for illustration.

Cabinets of mineral and geological specimens, including the collections of Professor Mudge; and growing collections in botany, entomology, and zoölogy, with some interesting illustrations in ethnology.

Collections of grains, grasses, and forage plants, and of native and foreign woods.

Carpenter shop, with separate benches and tools for twenty students in each class, besides lathe, mortising machine, scroll saws, and general chest of tools for fine work.

Shop for iron work, with forges, vises, drill, &c.

Printing office, with twenty-five pairs of cases, a good assortment of type, and a half-medium Gordon press,

Telegraph office, with six miles of line, connecting thirty-two branch offices and as many instruments.

Sewing rooms, with five machines, models and patterns.

Kitchen laboratory, with range, cooking and table utensils, dining-room furniture, and dairy apparatus.

Music rooms, with three pianos, an organ, and other instruments.

Library and reading room, containing over 3,600 volumes and 150 periodicals, to which all students have access during college hours.

Armory, containing seventy-five stand of arms (breech-loading cadet rifles, caliber 45) with accouterments.

The course of study, essentially the same to all classes of students, except for variations in industrial training requires four years of training in English and the natural sciences with applications in agriture, horticulture, mechanics and domestic arts. Students are admitted upon examination in the elements of common school studies and pursue their studies in the following order:

First year.—Fall term: Arithmetic, English analysis, geometrical drawing. Winter term: Book-keeping, English structure, United States history. Spring term: Algebra, English composition, botany with drawing.

Second year.—Fall term: Algebra completed, elementary chemistry, horticulture, 14 lectures in military science. Winter term: geometry, practical agriculture, (household economy for ladies), organic chemistry and mineralogy, 12 lectures in military science. Spring term: Geometry completed, with drawing, entomology and anatomy, analytical chemistry.

Third year.—Fall term: Trigonometry and surveying, physiology, general history. Winter term: Mechanics, agricultural chemistry, rhetoric. Spring term: Civil engineering, with drawing, (hygiene for ladies), chemical physics, English literature.

Fourth year.—Fall term: Agriculture (literature for ladies), meteorology, psychology. Winter term: Logic (deductive and inductive), zoölogy, structural botany. Spring term: Geology, United States Constitution, political economy.

These studies are taught with especial reference to an accurate use of knowledge in every-day life, and a habit of keen and precise observation as students.

The scope of special studies is shown in the following outline:

PRACTICAL AGRICULTURE.—*Second Year.*—History of agriculture, showing the successive steps by which the art has attained its present position. History and characteristics of breeds; their adaptation to the varying conditions of soil, climate, and situation; study of the forms of animals as shown by the different breeds belonging to the college;

the relation of stock-raising to general farming. Cultivation of hoed crops; management of corn and roots with reference to stock-feeding and the growth of finer grains. The growth of the "tame grasses" in Kansas, the best sorts for the State, and their management as shown by experience on the college farm and elsewhere. Implements of simple tillage; mechanical principles involved in their construction. Application of labor. Draught; different adjustment as affecting draught. Use of the dynamometer. Plows for soil and sub-soil. Drainage; soils that need draining; how to lay out a system of drains. *Fourth Year.*—General principles governing the development of domestic animals. The laws of hereditary disease; of normal, abnormal and acquired characters; atavism; correlation in the development of parts; in-and-in breeding and cross-breeding; influences affecting fecundity. The selection and arrangement of the farm with reference to the system to be pursued. Rotation of crops; general advantages of a rotation; the best rotation for the distribution of labor, production of manure and extermination of weeds; planning farm buildings—barns, piggeries, and stables; manure—how best housed and applied; composting; commercial fertilizers. Agricultural experiments; field and feeding experiments. Stock-feeding and meat production; stall-feeding; soiling. In this Miles's Stock Breeding is supplemented by a course of lectures.

HORTICULTURE.—It is the aim to teach this art from a botanical basis. The student applies his knowledge of the prime facts in botanical physiology to the various operations of the nursery, orchard, and garden. Barry's Fruit Garden is used, supplemented by a series of lectures upon the following topics, among others: The scope of horticulture. General principles of propagation by buds, by seeds. Production of improved varieties, by careful selection of seeds, by interfertilization of known kinds. Perpetuation of valuable sorts of fruits by bud propagation, budding, grafting, layering, &c. The important points in nursery manipulation. The orchard, conditions of site, soil, exposure, elevation. Special treatment of different kinds of fruit trees. Pruning. Gathering and storing fruits. Small-fruit culture; lists of varieties suitable for Kansas planting. Vegetable garden; selection and preservation of seeds; planting and transplanting. The management of the hot-bed and cold-frame. Forest plantations. Wind breaks. Hedges. Trees and shrubs for ornamental purposes.

BOTANY.—During the course two terms are given to the study of botany.

Elementary botany.—In the first year the student is familiarized with the aims of botanical classification to a sufficient degree to enable him to appreciate differences and resemblances in the plant kingdom, and is made acquainted with the salient points in plant physiology. Gray's Manual and Lessons is the text-book.

Advanced or higher botany.—In the fourth year, the intimate structure of plants, a more detailed study of plant physiology (in the germination of seed, the growth of cellular substance, and the fertilization of the ovule), variation and improvement of varieties, parasitic fungus, are among the topics studied. The text-book used in this part of the course is Bessey's Botany. This study is made more practical by the use of the compound microscopes belonging to the department, of which there are fifteen, with suitable accessories for a high grade of work.

CHEMISTRY.—*Inorganic chemistry*, which occupies fourteen weeks in the second year, includes a consideration of chemical forces and of the laws of chemical combination, with nomenclature and formulæ, and a careful study of the history, manufacture, physical and physiological properties, tests and uses of the various elements and their compounds. Especial attention is given to those substances having extended application in the arts.

Organic chemistry comprises a six weeks' course of lectures upon the theory of organic types and compound radicals, and the preparation and properties of those organic substances most useful to man.

In *chemical analysis* each student has his stand in the qualitative laboratory, completely furnished with apparatus and chemicals for his own use. His work includes the analysis of more or less complex mixtures of chemicals, minerals, ores, soils, mineral waters, well waters, &c.

Agricultural chemistry.—This includes a thorough consideration of the application of chemical principles to the economy of the farm; the origin and formation of soils; the classification and composition of soils, the analysis of soils, and their adaptation to the purposes of production; the composition and use of manures; composting; chemistry of farm operations, such as plowing, fallowing, draining; chemistry of plant growth. Text-book, Johnson's How Crops Feed.

MINERALOGY AND GEOLOGY.—For six weeks in the second year, two hours a day are given to mineralogy. This includes the study of crystallography, with the properties, forms, and uses of the principal minerals of the United States. Blow-pipe analysis forms an important part of the course, each student being required to name and identify a large series of minerals.

A term's study in the fourth year gives a view of the causes which have produced the geologic changes in the past, of the general arrangement of the earth's crust, and of special peculiarities of the various strata. Attention is given to the formation of soils and deposits of valuable minerals, especially in Kansas.

PHYSICS AND METEOROLOGY.—Two terms' work gives an opportunity for experimental study of the laws of light, heat, electricity and magnetism, the constitution of the atmosphere, the measurement of temperature and humidity, atmospheric pressure. This course also includes a careful study of instruments and methods employed in taking meteorological observations.

ANATOMY AND PHYSIOLOGY.—A full term's study is preceded by a course of lectures on anatomy. The study of physiology embraces a thorough consideration of the functions of the organs of the human body, and the relation these sustain to the conditions of health and disease. Among the topics discussed these, may be mentioned: food and digestion; assimilation; secretion and excretion; the circulation of the blood; the nervous system; the special senses; reproduction.

SPECIAL HYGIENE.—To the ladies of the third year, a course of daily lectures is given by the lady superintendent of the sewing room upon the laws of life and health. The course extends over a period of ten weeks, and covers questions pertaining to personal health and the health of the household, such as food, air, exercise, clothing, temperature of rooms, &c.

ENTOMOLOGY.—This science is studied with especial reference to its economic relations with agriculture and horticulture. A brief course in the principles of classification is followed by a more extended study of the life history of beneficial and injurious insects and means of encouragement of one and control of the other.

ZOÖLOGY.—In this study Packard's Zoölogy has been adopted as the text-book. The intention of the course is to familiarize the student with the characters of some type of each class, and then by comparative study with the chief modifications of the type chosen. Especial attention is directed to comparative anatomy and physiology, as underlying all logical classification.

HOUSEHOLD ECONOMY.—A series of lectures to the ladies of the second year class, accompanied by practical illustration in the kitchen laboratory, continues through a term of twelve weeks. These cover the general ground of economical provision for the household, marketing, cooking, preserving, order, neatness, and beauty in table service, comfort in the family, and care of a sick-room.

SPECIAL COURSES.—Persons of suitable age and advancement who desire to pursue such branches of study as are most directly related to agriculture or other industries may select such studies, under advice of the faculty. Assaying and pharmaceutical chemistry may be provided for by special arrangement when students are qualified to pursue them.

POST GRADUATE COURSES.—Arrangements can be made for advanced study in the several departments at any time. Special opportunities for investigation and research will be afforded to resident graduates.

All other branches of study are so taught as to give most thorough work in the time allotted to them.

INDUSTRIAL ARTS.—The training in these departments is designed to be systematic and complete in each, so that any student following a single line diligently through a four years' course gains the essentials of a trade and a reasonable degree of skill. Those who wish only a general acquaintance with the arts can take shorter courses in several of them; but all are to select with definite purpose. All are required to give at least five hours a week to some course of training, and most of these are so adjusted as to occupy a single hour each day in the regular routine of classes; a few take two and a half hours in the afternoon of two days each week.

Young ladies are required to give the necessary time for practice in the kitchen laboratory, and are expected to show some facility in the practice of the sewing room, though other industrials may occupy their course.

DAIRYING.—During the spring term daily instruction and practice in the different branches of dairying is given the young ladies of the second year by the professor of agriculture in a dairy well equipped with improved appliances for the manufacture of butter and cheese. The course of instruction given on this subject embraces the following cognate subjects: Dairy products as human food; influences affecting the quantity and quality of milk; the factory system, and household plans of cheese making; butter making; creameries; "deep and shallow" setting systems; packing and preserving butter. This instruction is enforced by regular and systematic work in the dairy.

Work in the farm and gardens is required of young men during one term of the second year and one term of the third year. Every young man thus gains acquaintance with the methods of the college and with the work itself.

CARPENTRY, &c.—On entering the shops all are enrolled as carpenters, and take the same first lessons in sawing, planing, and dressing lumber, making mortises, tenons, and joints, and in general use and care of tools. Later, one who chooses a trade is provided with work in the line chosen; while the farmer's course provides for general training in a great variety of operations, rather for ingenuity than for skill. In the full course of a carpenter, special instructions are given in the whole range of work, from framing to stair-building. Students are allowed, after attaining sufficient skill, to work upon their own materials, under the advice of the superintendent. All are required to take at least one term of practice in the shop during the first year at college. In iron work, instruction is given in ordinary forging, filing, tempering, &c.

PRINTING.—Two courses are pursued in this art. In one the student is taught the implements or tools employed in typography and how to use them; composition, imposition, correcting proof, technical terms, presses and their workings, and the general duties of a first-class workman. The second course of lessons alternates with those in the first, and embraces instruction in spelling, capitalization, syllabication, punctuation, proof-reading, preparation and criticism of essays, and such other work as will make the student accurate and expert in language. *The Industrialist*, a weekly paper edited by the faculty as an exponent of the work of the college, is printed by the students in the department.

TELEGRAPHY.—The course of training involves for beginners the characters that compose the alphabet and combinations of these characters into words and sentences—attention being paid to spelling and to short and precise expression in messages—abbreviations, signals, forms of messages, train orders, reports, &c. To the more advanced is given regular line business, as press reports, messages, cipher messages, and orders in all forms used by prominent telegraph companies, together with the necessary book-keeping on exact copies of the blanks in actual use, thus giving the student an understanding of the work of an operator. A portion of the time is devoted to instruction in the use and management of lines, batteries, instruments, &c. The elementary principles of electricity, magnetism, and electro-magnetism evolved in telegraphy are taught and illustrated by experiments. The more recent inventions relating to the art are discussed and explained. Pope's Hand-book of the Telegraph is used as a text-book.

SEWING.—Young ladies are taught in all ordinary forms of sewing with needle and machine and in cutting, fitting, and trimming dresses and other garments.

MUSIC.—Provision is made for the teaching of instrumental music. The college furnishes instruments for daily practice, but the teacher depends upon his fees for income. Instruction in vocal music for beginners and for advanced students is furnished at a very slight expense.

MILITARY TRAINING.—During the second year a course of twenty-six lectures is given. These are designed to show what an army is for, its relation to the country, and, in a general way, to describe its organization and duties. To those who desire it an opportunity is given to obtain a fair practice in the ordinary infantry drills, including bayonet exercise. Although drill is thus made optional, students are not allowed to take it for periods shorter than one term.

Classes are in session from 9 a. m. to 1 p. m. of every week day except Saturday, and no student may be absent without excuse. A full and permanent record of attendance, scholarship, and deportment shows to each student his standing in the college, and after each monthly examination a report of advancement is made to parents. Chapel exercises occupy fifteen minutes before the meeting of classes each morning, and unnecessary absence from them is noted in the grades.

Twice in each month the whole body of students gather for a lecture from some member of the faculty, or for the rhetorical exercises of the third and fourth year classes. On alternate weeks all the classes meet at the same hour in separate class rooms for exercise in elocution and correct expression.

LABOR.—The general drift of instruction and training is such as to encourage habits of manual labor during the course. The work of the college is done chiefly by students at wages ranging from eight to ten cents per hour, and every effort is made to encourage those who depend largely upon their own earnings for an education. The amount paid to students for labor during the last year was $1,611.70.

Expenses of students are at the same time limited by the general economy of surroundings. Tuition is free except in music; to young men in telegraphy and in printing for the first year, and to all in analytical chemistry a small fee each term is charged to cover incidental expenses.

Of the students attending the college 75 per cent. are from farmers' homes, and a very large proportion of the rest from the families of mechanics and tradesmen.

Since the organization in 1863, there have been in attendance 2,072 different students—1,369 male and 703 female.

The attendance of the last college year was 312 (224 male and 88 female). The average age this year was 19.35 years, and the students were gathered from 54 counties of Kansas and from 13 other States. The present year shows an increase of 40 over the attendance of last year at this date, and a better preparation for the course.

The graduates of the college number 74 (46 male and 28 female). Twenty-four of these received the degree of A. B., and 50 that of B. S. Seven have taken a second degree in course.

The general influence of graduates and students of shorter course is widely felt in the general improvement of the State in all departments of industry.

The college is now under the control of a board of regents, 6 in number, appointed by the governor of the State, subject to the approval of the State senate, and commissioned for a term of three years. All interests of the college, including the sale of lands and care and investment of funds, are committed to their charge. The president of the college, elected by the board, becomes *ex officio* a member of that body.

The faculty is composed of the president, professors, and superintendents regularly appointed by the board; and all methods of instruction and discipline within the prescribed course are intrusted to their direction. This body has now 14 members, employed at salaries ranging from $600 to $2,200, and amounting to $14,800 a year. The members are as follows: President and professor of logic and political economy, professor of mathematics and engineering, professor of practical agriculture and superintendent of the farm, professor of chemistry and physics, professor of botany and zoölogy and superintendent of the orchards and gardens, professor of elementary English and mathematics, professor of military science and tactics detailed by United States War Department, instructor in English and history, instructor in industrial drawing, superintendent of telegraphy, superintendent of printing, superintendent of sewing and instructor in hygiene and domestic economy, superintendent of workshops, teacher of music.

Besides the work of instructing the youth of the State who gather at the college, the faculty have undertaken various experimental researches of direct interest in agriculture and other industries. The results have been disseminated through the columns of The Industrialist, a weekly paper edited by the faculty and widely circulated, and by publication of official reports. Recently a series of farmers' institutes has been organized to reach and co-operate with the farmers of different sections of the State. These have proved efficient means of advancing the interests of both the college and agriculture throughout the State.

Members of the faculty are prominent in the various educational associations of the State, as well as those for the promotion of agriculture, horticulture, and science in general. The college is generally recognized throughout the State as serving well the purposes of the national land grant and working out profitably the problem of industrial training with a liberal education, though, as yet, only an encouraging beginning has been made.

The improved facilities and extended means of the immediate future must help to more complete success and larger usefulness in the same direction.

GEO. T. FAIRCHILD, *President.*

KENTUCKY.

AGRICULTURAL AND MECHANICAL COLLEGE OF KENTUCKY.

OBJECTS.

The leading aim of this college is to teach the branches that are related to agriculture and the mechanic arts. During our connection with Kentucky University, which existed from 1866 to 1878, but little success was attained in that direction. This was due to the failure of Kentucky University to meet the obligations it had contracted.

In 1878 the State of Kentucky detached this college from Kentucky University and by action of the legislature it was placed upon an independent footing. The State has added a classical to the former course of scientific study, and also a normal school department. The preparatory department of the college works in connection with and subordinate to the normal school department.

INCOME AND EXPENDITURE.

The annual income is $9,900 from the Congressional land fund of 1862, $16,000 from tax levied by the State for the benefit of the college, $2,500 from tuition fees; total, about $28,400.

THE FACULTY.

The faculty consists of the president, who is also professor of civil history and metaphysics, professors of mathematics and astronomy, natural history, Latin and Greek,

French and German, chemistry and physics, English language and literature, and a principal of the normal department (with three assistants), practical mechanics, and military tactics.

STUDENTS.

There were last year (1881–'82) 320 students in the college, of whom 249 were males and 71 females. Last year there were six graduates. The whole number of graduates since 1878 is fifteen. Women have access to all the classes of the institution. Each legislature representative district is entitled to send *four* properly prepared students free of tuition, and each county four normal school pupils.

THE COURSE OF STUDY.

The time given studies is as follows: history, two years; mental and moral philosophy, one year; mathematics (exclusive of preparatory), four years; Latin and Greek, four; chemistry and physics, two; natural history, four; English language, four; French and German, each, two; normal school, three; bookkeeping course, two; tactics and military science, two. Instruction is mainly from text books.

SCHOOLS AND STUDIES.

The instruction is classified, according to its nature, into schools, as follows:
1. School of civil history, embracing studies in European history, that of the United States, Germany, England, the constitutions of the United States and of England, and political economy.
2. School of English language and literature, with an excellent course.
3. School of mental and moral philosophy.
4. School of mathematics, covering algebra, geometry, trigonometry (plane and spherical), analytical geometry, calculus, mathematical physics, and astronomy.
5. School of chemistry, embracing elementary physics, practical chemistry, with application to agriculture, mechanic arts, and medicines; there are lectures and laboratory illustrations.
6. School of natural history, embracing physical geography, botany (general and economic), anatomy and physiology, forestry, zoölogy, microscopy, geology, and palæontology.
7. School of modern language, embracing French, German, Spanish, and Italian.
8. School of military tactics and civil engineering.

A normal department has been added by the State, and it is proposed to endow a professorship of the "theory and practice of teaching."

The technical value of the institution has been enlarged by an advanced course on agricultural chemistry; by special lectures on the relation of geology to soils, of forests to agriculture, and of insects to vegetation.

There is an evident desire to increase the efficiency of the college in every branch of instruction.

The grounds upon which the college buildings are situated were given by the city of Lexington to secure the location of the college, and comprise 52 acres within the city limits. The bulk of the money expended in the erection of buildings was given by the city and county of Fayette. The estimated value of the grounds is $25,000, and of the buildings, $85,000.

President Patterson adds also the following:

HISTORY OF THE COLLEGE.

The proceeds of the land grant were first applied to the creation and maintenance of an agricultural and mechanical college of the Kentucky University, a denominational institution. When this college was detached from its former connection in 1878 a commission was appointed to determine its future character and location. After a provisional existence for two years the legislature of 1879–'80, in accordance with the recommendation of the commission, established it upon the grounds offered to the State by the city of Lexington. After a long contest the legislature also agreed to give the college the proceeds of a tax of one-half cent on each hundred dollars of taxable property in the Commonwealth, said tax to continue until repealed. The principal opposition to this additional endowment came from friends of the Kentucky University, who fancied that their institution would be injured by the establishment and success of the State college.

A board of trustees was appointed, nominated by the governor, and confirmed by the senate, and the college was by them reorganized in accordance with the terms of the charter on a basis entirely undenominational.

The success of the first year under its reorganization more than exceeded expectations.

But when the legislature of 1881–'82 met the college found itself forced into a struggle for existence. All the denominational colleges of the State, Presbyterian, Baptist, Methodist, and Christian, formed a combination to procure the repeal of the one-half cent tax voted by the preceding legislature for its aid. Their chief ground of complaint was that the State college because of the aid secured by the State was making education so cheap and so comprehensive that they were unable to compete with it. After a contest of nearly three months, in which all the resources and menaces of ecclesiasticism were evoked and used, the bill for repeal was laid on the table of the house of representatives by a vote of 51 to 38. The contest is, however, not yet ended. The presidents of the aggrieved colleges have carried the question of the constitutionality of the tax into the courts, where it is now pending.

If let alone the State college will do a good work and supply a want long felt in Kentucky.

LOUISIANA.

STATE UNIVERSITY AND AGRICULTURAL AND MECHANICAL COLLEGE

The institution which is now receiving the income of the fund arising from the national land grant made to Louisiana for the establishment of an agricultural college is the result of combining the old State university and the Agricultural and Mechanical College. The State university was founded in 1853, and opened at Alexandria in 1860, under the superintendence of General (then Colonel) W T. Sherman. In 1869 its building was burned, and the institution moved to Baton Rouge. In 1877 the Agricultural College, which had been in operation in New Orleans since its opening in 1874, was made a part of the university.

The object of uniting the institutions was to provide a seat of learning where literature, science, and the arts should be taught, and where the citizens should be fitted "to perform skillfully and magnanimously all the offices, both private and public, of peace and war." To carry out its object the law requires it to provide "general instruction and education in all the departments of literature, science, art, and industrial and professional pursuits," and "special instruction for the professions of agriculture, the mechanic arts, mining, military science and art, civil engineering, law, medicine, commerce, and navigation."

The productive funds of the institution are $318,313. Two sources from which they have been obtained have been the seminary fund, which had its origin in grants of land made by the general government in 1806 and 1811, and the agricultural college fund, which was originally $327,000. It was reduced in 1875 to $196,200. The income of these funds is about $14,500. An annual State appropriation of $10,000 nominally makes up the entire income to an amount sufficient to enable the university to carry on efficiently the work which has been assigned to it by State legislation. But the $10,000 appropriated have realized to the university a sum much less, the net value of it being $6,700 in 1880 and in 1881, though the outlook for the present year is more favorable. Nothing is derived from fees toward the support of the institution, as tuition is free to all.

There are 8 professors and 159 students. The work of both is being performed thoroughly and satisfactorily. The full courses in agriculture and the mechanic arts cover three years each of undergraduate study. The subjects pursued are arranged for the purpose of educating those who propose to devote themselves to agriculture and the industrial arts in Louisiana. It is considered as presenting an opportunity nowhere else to be had for intelligent training in the cultivation of the semi-tropical staples, sugar, cotton, and rice. Special studies are added in horticulture and the domestic arts.

The college maintains no extensive laboratories or costly farm, but utilizes the practical opportunities for study found in the cotton fields and gin-houses, the sugar plantations and mills, the rice fields, oil mills, &c., which are open for study and investigation around Baton Rouge.

The agricultural course embraces French, chemistry, physics (including the theory of the steam engine), animal and vegetable physiology and anatomy, with scientific agriculture and rural economy, and engineering. These latter include farm architecture, hygiene, veterinary surgery, surveying roads, bridges, levees, ditches, &c. There are also added short courses of social and industrial history, English rhetoric and literature, bookkeeping, political economy, and ethics. One hour a day is devoted to labor in the field, garden, or workshop.

In the mechanical course the instruction is full, both theoretical and practical. The studies embrace mathematics, analytical and descriptive geometry, a short course in engineering; also drawing, French, chemistry, physics, social and industrial history, and other studies similar to those in the agricultural course. The workshop has (1880–'81) been opened, and contains tools, engine, lathes, forge, &c., to illustrate and teach both wood and iron working. It has proved both useful and successful, and has enlisted the public interest largely.

Students in the Agricultural and Mechanical College have access to the cabinets, collections, and chemical and physical apparatus, but the chief design of the instruction pursued is to familiarize students with the practical knowledge grounded on the sciences underlying industrial occupations.

The State topographical survey was made under the general direction of the university.

The attention devoted to the sugar cane and other tropical staples makes the Louisiana State University and its agricultural instructors an authority, and it is the special aim of the faculty to steadily increase this usefulness.

A station for the production of vaccine lymph was established in February, 1882, and an apiary is suggested by the president as a proper addition to the practical appliances of the college.

The experiments and the actual work are carried on largely by the students, under the direction of the professor in charge, and thus the educational and scientific character of this branch of the college is brought into prominence. The vaccine establishment has been self-sustaining, besides gratuitously distributing more than 20,000 ivory points, with very satisfactory results, and has met the hearty approval of the physicians of the State.

Owing to its origin as a military academy, for a long time almost exclusively devoted to the education of State students, this institution is carried on under a strictly military system. The discipline is exact, though not severe, and all cadets drill one hour daily. The larger portion of the corps reside in the barracks, but a considerable number live with their parents or guardians in Baton Rouge, and under the same regulations as others from 8 a. m. until 5 p. m. This somewhat anomalous system is adapted to the needs of the students.

MAINE.

THE STATE COLLEGE OF AGRICULTURE AND THE MECHANIC ARTS.

[From special statement of the president and annual catalogues.]

"The object of the institution is to furnish to the young people of the State (those from other States not excluded) who may desire it the advantages of a thorough, liberal, and practical education, and especially instruction in such branches of learning as are related to agriculture and the mechanic arts."

ENDOWMENT AND FUNDS.

Its endowment, which is much too small for its purposes, was derived from the sale of land donated by the national government by act of Congress in 1862. The amount of land to which this State was entitled was 210,000 acres. By direction of the legislature of the State the land scrip was sold by the governor and council, and at a ruinously low figure, the price received for the greater part of it being but 53 cents per acre. As a result the endowment secured was less than $120,000. From interest which accumulated chiefly before the institution was opened to students, this sum was increased to $132,500, which is the present endowment. The larger part of this is invested in State 6 per cent. bonds, and has yielded a revenue of about $8,000 per annum.

Considering the low rates at which safe investments can now be made, the revenue from this source is estimated at $7,500.* For other assistance the institution is obliged to look to the State.

The annual expenditure is about $11,000; the annual expense of teaching force, $10,000. Several of the instructors recently entered upon duty at moderate salaries. With increasing efficiency of service their compensation must be increased. The prospective annual expense of teaching staff is $12,500, and the prospective ordinary annual expenditure, $14,000. These figures presuppose the maintenance of the institution on its present basis. Any considerable enlargement of plan would involve necessarily an increase of annual expenditure.

The value of grounds and buildings is $120,000; of library, apparatus, &c., $25,000.

---

* By direction of the State legislature, since August, 1881, a moderate tuition has been charged, yielding an annual revenue of something above $2,000.

The site was given by the towns of Orono and Oldtown, and cost $11,000. The buildings have been erected principally by means of appropriations made by the State. Citizens of Bangor contributed something over $12,000 for the benefit of the college in its early years.

THE FACULTY.

The number of instructors is nine (not including the farm superintendent, who gives no class room instruction), namely: President (who is professor of physics and mental and moral sciences), professor of chemistry, professor of civil engineering, professor of mechanical engineering, professor of natural history, professor of modern languages, professor of agriculture, instructor in vise work and forge work, and professor of military science, assigned by the United States Government.

STUDENTS AND GRADUATES.

The number of students in 1881–'82 was 90, 3 of whom were young women. No charge for tuition has been made until recently, except for students from without the State, who are charged the nominal sum of $12 per term. Tuition is now $30 a year. Only one scholarship has yet been provided; others are earnestly desired.

The number of graduates is 156, 140 young men and 16 young women. Of these, 50 have graduated in the course in civil engineering and 22 in mechanical engineering. Upon 84 has been conferred the degree of bachelor of science, which includes those who have taken the course in agriculture, in chemistry, and in literature and science. The course in science and literature is the course in agriculture with certain modifications adapting it more especially to the wants of young ladies.

Besides the 156 graduates, there have been connected with the institution for periods of time, ranging from one term to three and a half years, 210 students.* Of the 366 who have received training at the college the vocations of 250 are known. Of this number 27 per cent. are engaged in agricultural pursuits and 27 per cent. in the mechanic arts; 11 per cent. are in professional life and 89 per cent. are engaged in non-professional callings.

The graduates have been very successful in passing early to worthy and lucrative positions, and, so far as known, have maintained themselves with credit in the positions secured.

THE COURSE OF STUDY.

The plan of instruction embraces five courses of study, namely: A course in agriculture; a course in science and literature, which is the course in agriculture with certain modifications; a course in civil engineering; a course in mechanical engineering, and a course in chemistry. The subjects taught and the time given to each may be best understood by an examination of a condensed outline of the courses, together with brief explanatory statements.

COURSE IN AGRICULTURE.

For the first year the course embraces physical geography, physiology, algebra, rhetoric and botany, geometry, French, bookkeeping, and labor on farm.

For the second year it includes botany, horticulture and arboriculture, general and qualitative chemistry, physics, French, English literature and surveying or (L) history of England, trigonometry, freehand and mechanical drawing, field work and forge work (elective with a part of the mechanical drawing).

For the third year, it requires farm drainage, mechanical cultivation of the soil and physics, agriculture and organic chemistry with principles of plant feeding, mechanics, agricultural engineering and farm implements, zoölogy and entomology, German, laboratory work and experimental farming, or analysis of English authors (elective).

For the fourth year are required landscape gardening, stock breeding, and veterinary science, cultivation of cereals, care and feeding of animals, dairy farming and sheep husbandry, comparative anatomy, mineralogy and geology, history of civilization, United States Constitution and political economy, logic, mental and moral science, with experimental farming and agricultural botany or historical readings and analysis (elective).

COURSE IN CHEMISTRY.

For the first year the following studies are included: Physical geography, physiology, algebra, rhetoric and botany, geometry, French, bookkeeping, and labor on farm.

For the second year: General and qualitative chemistry, botany, horticulture and arboriculture, physics, French, English literature, surveying, trigonometry, freehand and mechanical drawing with field work.

---

* Not including those now in the college.

For the third year: Chemistry, physics, German, zoölogy and entomology, American literature, laboratory work.

For the fourth year: Chemistry, comparative anatomy, mineralogy and geology, history of civilization, United States Constitution and political economy, laboratory work, logic.

COURSE IN CIVIL ENGINEERING.

For the first year the following studies are included: Physical geography, physiology, algebra and geometry, rhetoric and botany, French, bookkeeping, and labor on farm.

For the second year: Trigonometry, botany, horticulture and arboriculture, general chemistry, analytical geometry and calculus, English literature, surveying, physics, French, freehand and mechanical drawing, with field work.

For the third year: Henck's Field Book, mechanics, calculus, descriptive geometry, physics, descriptive astronomy, German, field work and drawing, isometric and cabinet projection and perspective.

For the fourth year: Civil engineering, designs and specifications, stereotomy, practical astronomy, mineralogy and geology, logic, United States Constitution and political economy, topography and railroad work, machine drawing and designing.

COURSE IN MECHANICAL ENGINEERING.

For the first year the following studies are included: Algebra and geometry, physiology, physical geography, rhetoric and botany, French, bookkeeping, and labor on farm.

For the second year: Trigonometry, analytical geometry and calculus, French, English literature and surveying, general chemistry, physics, botany, horticulture and arboriculture, free hand and mechanical drawing, field work and forge work.

For the third year: Machinery and mill work, calculus, descriptive geometry, German, shop work and machine drawing, isometric and cabinet projection and perspective.

For the fourth year: Hydraulic motors, steam engine, designs and specifications, practical astronomy, mineralogy and geology, logic, United States Constitution and political economy, applied descriptive geometry, machine drawing and designing.

THE AGRICULTURAL INSTRUCTION.

Instruction is given largely by lectures, and embraces the subjects of most marked importance to the farmer. The following defines the leading topics: Mechanics and farm implements, embodying use and principles of construction; agricultural engineering, roads, culverts, masonry, strength of materials; mechanical cultivation of the soil; principles of plant feeding; landscape gardening; cultivation of cereals; care and feeding of animals; dairy farming; sheep husbandry; botany, horticulture, arboriculture; chemistry; zoölogy and entomology, with bee keeping; comparative anatomy, including illustrated lectures on stock feeding and veterinary science; mineralogy and geology; law, international and rural.

INSTRUCTION IN SCIENCE AND LITERATURE.

The course in science and literature includes French and German, the general mathematical and most of the scientific studies of the agricultural course. Instead of certain branches quite purely technical in the latter course, history and English and American literature are substituted.

WOMEN STUDENTS.

In the special laws of the State, passed in 1872, it is provided that young ladies, "who possess suitable qualifications for admission to the several classes may be admitted as students in the college." In arranging the course in science and literature, reference has been had to this enactment. From this course, however, young men who desire it are not excluded, as, on the other hand, young ladies are not excluded from any of the other courses.

INSTRUCTION OF THE CIVIL ENGINEER.

The object is to give the student a thorough knowledge of higher mathematics, mechanics, astronomy and drawing, and at the same time a thorough drill in the use of instruments and in the application of mathematical principles and rules, so that the graduate can at once be made useful in engineering work, and be fitted after a limited amount of experience in the field to fill positions of importance and trust. The course is also arranged so as to afford the education required to prepare the graduate for a responsible position among *men* as well as among engineers.

In the first term of the third year, Henck's Field Book is used as a text book, from which the student obtains methods of running railroad curves, calculations of earthwork, &c. This is supplemented by many examples, worked by the student, and by lectures on preliminary and final surveys and on the resistance to trains offered by curves and grades.

The subject of mechanics is taken up the last term of this year, in which the students receive a thorough training in the principles underlying construction, illustrated as far as may be by practical examples, in which these principles are applied.

Most of the time is given to statics, as being the branch of mechanics most applicable to civil engineering, enough of dynamics being taught to meet the requirements of the civil engineer. During the senior year Rankine's Civil Engineering is the text book, though other works are used for reference.

The course of study is thorough and practical, applied directly to materials and their use, together with engineering problems. Drawing is made a permanent and marked feature of every term. Field work in surveying, general, road, and railroad engineering, with topographical surveying, are its main features. Mineralogy, geology, and astronomy are carefully taught.

INSTRUCTION OF THE MECHANICAL ENGINEER.

It is the design of this course to give such a knowledge of mathematics, mechanics, principles of mechanism, drawing, and manual art, as shall enable the student successfully to enter practical life as an engineer with the same thorough education in subjects required to fit him for the general duties of life as is afforded by the other courses.

The work of the first two years is similar to that of the civil engineer's course, except that forge work is added in the second year.

There are now two shops equipped according to the Russian system, and work in these is required of all students in this course.

In the second term of the sophomore year, a course in forge work is given, in which the student becomes familiar with the methods in use in actual construction. A similar course in vise work is given during the first term of the junior year, in which a corresponding knowledge is obtained. It is the intention to add more shops at the earliest possible moment. It should be understood that it is the object in these shops to teach operations in use in a number of trades, rather than the details of any one trade.

INSTRUCTION OF THE CHEMIST.

This course aims to supply a want felt by students who wish to enter certain industries in which a somewhat extensive knowledge of chemistry is important. The first two years are mainly like those of the other courses, qualitative analysis being, however, obligatory for these students in the second term of the sophomore year.

During the junior year, daily recitations are held in agricultural chemistry and elementary organic chemistry, and the study of advanced inorganic chemistry is begun. In the senior year, advanced inorganic chemistry is concluded and advanced organic chemistry is taken up.

The afternoons are devoted to quantitative chemical analysis by the junior and senior students of the course. The work consists of the most useful gravimetric and volumetric methods, beginning with simple estimations, which are followed by more complex analyses of alloys, minerals, fertilizers, farm products, &c. A short course in the assay of gold and silver is also given.

DEGREES.

In the courses in agriculture, science and literature, and chemistry the degree of bachelor of science is given.

In the engineering courses the degrees are bachelor of civil engineering and bachelor of mechanical engineering. The master's degree in any of the courses may be conferred after three years.

LABOR.

It is a peculiarity of the college that it makes provision for labor, thus combining practice with theory, manual labor with scientific culture. The maximum time of required labor is three hours a day for five days in the week.

In the lowest class the students are required to work on the farm, and they receive compensation for their labor according to their industry, faithfulness and efficiency, the educational character of the labor being also taken into account. The maximum price paid is 10 cents an hour. The labor is designed to be as much as possible educational, so that every student may become familiar with all the forms of labor upon the farm and in the garden.

The students of the three upper classes carry on their principal labor in the laboratory, the drawing rooms, the work shops, or in the field; and for it they receive no pecuniary consideration, since this labor is of a purely educational character.

MILITARY INSTRUCTION.

Thorough instruction in military science is given by an officer detailed by the Secretary of War from the active list, United States Army.

All able-bodied male students receive instruction in the school of the soldier, company, and battalion drill.

Artillery drill is limited to the senior class.

Arms and equipments are furnished by the United States Government.

FARM AND BUILDINGS.

The college farm contains 370 acres of land of high natural productiveness and of great diversity of soil, and is therefore well adapted to the experimental purposes of the institution.

White Hall, the building first erected, affords excellent accommodations for a limited number of students. The lower rooms of this building are appropriated to general and class purposes.

Brick Hall contains 48 rooms and has connected with it a boarding house for students. In these buildings the institution furnishes desirable accommodations for 125 students.

The laboratory contains two apparatus rooms, a lecture room, a cabinet, a library and weighing-room, a recitation room, and rooms for analytical and other purposes, and is in all respects admirably adapted to the wants of the chemical and mineralogical departments.

APPARATUS.

The college is furnished with new and valuable apparatus for the departments of physical geography, chemistry, physics, surveying, civil engineering, and mechanical engineering, to which additions will be made as the exigencies of the several departments require. Models have been obtained from the United States Patent Office and others have been purchased that serve for purposes of instruction.

LIBRARY.

The library contains above 4,000 volumes, some of which have been obtained by purchase, while others have been kindly given to the college. The volumes secured through the liberality of Ex-Governor Coburn and the gifts of other friends are a valuable addition to this department. It is earnestly hoped that so important an auxiliary in the education of students in the college will not be disregarded by the people of the State, and that liberal contributions will be made to the library, not only of agricultural and scientific works, but also of those profitable to the general reader.

CABINET.

Rooms have been fitted up with cases of minerals and specimens of natural history, and several hundred specimens have been presented to the college. The valuable private cabinets of Prof. C. H. Fernald and Ex-President C. F. Allen are placed in these rooms and are accessible to the students. All specimens presented will be properly credited and placed on exhibition. Rocks illustrating the different geological formations and minerals found within the State are particularly solicited.

MARYLAND.

MARYLAND AGRICULTURAL COLLEGE.

[Statement of the president, 1880.]

The leading object of the Maryland Agricultural College is to promote agricultural education under the resolution of Congress of 1862.

ENDOWMENT AND FUNDS.

The United States land scrip invested by the State yields annually $6,978; the State gives annually, $6,000* additional; the grounds, buildings, and apparatus are estimated at

---

*The State withdrew the donation of $6,000 at the last session of the legislature.

$100,000, one-half owned by the State. Students from the State and District of Columbia, in consideration of the above yearly endowment, are admitted free of tuition. The only other income is from board, which at $200 a year yields an average income of $12,000. The annual expenditures, including repairs, improvements, and necessary working expenses, cover the whole income; the annual expense of teaching staff is $8,500.*

THE FACULTY.

The instructors and lecturers occupy the following chairs: President and professor of engineering and astronomy; registrar and professor of physics; professor of English literature, mental science, and history; of ancient and modern languages; of agriculture and natural history, architecture, &c.; of chemistry, and the instructor in military science.

STUDENTS' FEES—DEGREES.

For the last five years the students have averaged 75, all males. Students pay, in addition to a board bill of $200, $75 a year for tuition. There are no scholarships. Since 1875 there have been 20 graduates. During the war the college was closed.

The degrees conferred are bachelor of arts, bachelor of science, master of arts, and bachelor of agricultural science. Graduates are devoting themselves mostly to teaching and to agricultural pursuits. Nearly 1,400 students have registered since the college was founded.

Women are not admitted to any of the departments, since military instruction is one of the requirements of the government.

THE PLAN OF STUDY.

The course of instruction extends over four years, embracing all subjects under the chairs enumerated. The plan of instruction is by a systematic series of recitations, each one hour in length, accompanied by oral lectures and reviews. All the departments run through the four years.

APPLIANCES AND APPARATUS.

The theoretical outfit of the department of agriculture is complete, embracing all necessary charts, anatomical exhibits, seeds, minerals, and text books. There have never been sufficient appropriations for workshops. The laboratory is in good working order, and students are required to work four hours a week in practical chemistry; analyses of soils, ores, and metals are frequently made during the course, which extends from the sophomore year to the close.

TECHNICAL LABOR AND APPLICATION.

Students of the freshman and practical classes practice four hours a week upon all necessary farm work, under the charge of the professor of agriculture. Students in this class are divided into details for garden, field, yard, and grounds, and, under competent supervision, are instructed in whatever work the season may offer in these divisions. At the commencement of each week the respective details rotate, thus changing the work to each class.

A suitable compensation is paid to students on special volunteer detail, on Saturdays, during vacations, and during the hours from 4 to 6 p. m.

The laboratory work comprises work in agricultural chemistry; work in the microscopic department of botany and zoölogy; work in geological, mineralogical, and osteological cabinets; work in the veterinary dissecting and other rooms.

SPECIAL METHODS.

Especial attention is directed towards a cultivation of veterinary knowledge. A class of special agriculturists studying for farm superintendents, farmers, and teachers has been organized.

By an act of the last legislature the Commissioner of Agriculture was placed upon the board of trustees and tendered such portions of the farm, of 286 acres, as may in his judgment be necessary for the benefit of the government and State. Several plats are now devoted to a trial of the cereals.

COLLEGE BUILDING.

This is an imposing structure of brick, 120 feet long, 54 feet wide, 6 stories high, relieved by an east and south portico. The basement contains the dining room, kitchen,

---

*The annual expense for teaching staff is now $4,000, and is being reduced.

pantry, wash room, and bakery. On the first floor are the laboratory, museum, chapel, bath room, and department of languages. On the second floor, the parlor, visitor's room, president's room, registrar's office, commandant's office, room of officer of the day, English, agricultural, and mathematical rooms, society hall, and library. The chambers above are large, well ventilated, well heated, and lighted throughout with gas.

[Additional statements from latest reports received in this Office.]

THE SCHOOL OF AGRICULTURE.

It has been the aim of this institution, under the present direction, to make the school of agriculture the leading one in the college course. The acquisition to the faculty of Prof. A. Grabowskii has done much to make this possible. In the report of 1880 the professor states that an increased interest has been aroused, 41 students taking the course of agricultural studies.

The veterinary studies of this college have received a special evidence of approval in the offer of the New York Veterinary College of a free scholarship for an appointee of the Maryland institution, and the crediting also of the time spent at the college by all students entering therefrom.

The fair (for 1880) of the National Agricultural Society, held at Washington, was utilized by the Maryland college, the students visiting the fair and listening to explanatory lectures and statements.

THE FARM AND APPLIANCES.

The farm consists of 286 acres, with artificially drained meadows, also dry bottom and rolling uplands. There is a well selected herd of stock, animals for use and breeding.

The vegetable garden embraces ten acres, and several acres are laid down in fruit and flowers.

The national Department of Agriculture is utilizing the farm for experimental purposes to some extent.

THE COLLEGE COURSE.

The branches of study included in the college course are grouped under the following departments:
1. Civil engineering and astronomy.
2. English literature, mental science, and history.
3. Pure mathematics.
4. Physics and applied mathematics.
5. Agriculture, architecture, and natural history.
6. Chemistry.
7. Ancient and modern languages.

Physical geography is classed with civil engineering and astronomy; constitutional law with English literature, mental science, and history; calculus and mechanics with physics and bookkeeping; lectures on shades, shadows, and perspective and descriptive geometry with pure mathematics.

The studies of the school of agriculture are: *Freshman year*, general agriculture; *sophomore year*, geology, animal anatomy and physiology, botany, and zoölogy; *junior year*, horse and cattle raising, animal therapeutics, climatology, agronomy and manuring, general and special plant culture, diseases of animals and animal obstetrics; *senior year*, raising of swine, sheep, poultry, and bees, horticulture, vegetable gardening, agricultural implements and machines, agricultural technology and architecture, arboriculture and landscape gardening.

The practice comprises work on the farm and in the laboratories. For farm work, students are divided into garden, field, yard and grounds details, and instructed in whatever work the seasons may offer in these divisions. At the commencement of each week the "details" rotate, thus changing the work to each class. The special agricultural class is on practice detail daily from 2 to 4 p. m.; all freshmen, on Tuesdays and Thursdays from 2 to 4 p. m. For work done during the time from 4 to 6 p. m., during vacation and on Saturdays, a suitable compensation is paid to volunteer students.

The laboratory work comprises practice in the chemical laboratory (agricultural chemistry), in the microscopic department of botany and zoölogy, in the geological, mineralogical and osteological cabinets, and in the veterinary dissecting rooms.

MASSACHUSETTS.

MASSACHUSETTS AGRICULTURAL COLLEGE.

[Statement prepared from the latest reports in this office and from other sources.]

OBJECT.

Professor Levi Stockbridge,* president of the college, writes that "the leading object of this institution is education, as required by the act of Congress which gave us our endowment fund, but, technically, everything is made to contribute to science and practice in agriculture."

ENDOWMENT AND FUNDS.

The permanent college endowment consists of two-thirds of the fund created by the sale of the land scrip granted by the United States and held in the State treasury, and of certain donations from private benefactors, with the income therefrom derived. The full endowment fund, as derived from this sale and increased by the State, is as follows:

From sale of land scrip	$236,307 40
Profits on bond investment	10,067 40
Added by the State	141,535 35
	387,910 15

Of this total the State has expended $27,778.40 for an experimental farm, leaving the total permanent fund $360,067.67.

Of this amount, invested by the State so as to produce a little over 5 per cent. per annum, the agricultural college is endowed with two-thirds, or	$240,045 20
Value of farm purchased by State	27,778 40
Donated by the town of Amherst, for building purposes	75,000 00
Donation for constructing and stocking plant house	20,000 00
For herbarium	2,000 00
For scholarships, prizes and books (various)	7,751 00
By State appropriations from 1864 to 1879†	240,000 00
	612,574 60

The present income outside of legislative aid is derived from the land scrip fund and some additional sources (1881), and is as follows:

Income from State treasury	$12,958 00
Income from other funds	907 00
Income from tuition, &c	4,601 00
Income from all other sources	6,379 00
	24,845 00

Expenditures for 1881 were:

Salaries, &c	$11,137 00
Other expenses	11,444 00
	22,581 00

Value of realty, &c.

Buildings, farm, &c	$202,747 00
Other property	3,024 75
	205,771 75

THE FACULTY.

According to the catalogue of 1881 the college staff consisted of the president (professor of agriculture), professors of modern languages, chemistry, physics and civil engineering, botany and horticulture, military science, lecturers on veterinary science, geology, zoology, and entomology, and the superintendent of nurseries—10 in all.

---

*Since succeeded by Hon. Paul A. Chadbourne, D. D., LL. D.
†Of this amount, $150,000 were designed for buildings and equipments.

DEGREES, STUDENTS, AND GRADUATES.

The college course continues four years. On graduation the degree of bachelor of science is received. An advanced course is open for college graduates and licentiates of scientific schools. The degrees are doctor of science or doctor of philosophy.

The number of students registered in the catalogue of 1881 was 113, 80 of whom were in the regular classes.

The tuition fees are $12 per term—$36 per annum. One free scholarship is awarded to each Congressional district in the State, the value of which is $144 per annum. The income from the bequest ($1,000) of Miss Mary Robinson, of Medfield, Mass., is bestowed by the faculty on such needy student as is deemed most worthy.

The number of graduates previous to 1882 was 181, to whom the degree of bachelor of science was given. A list of the graduates, with their occupations, is published from time to time. That given in the last report shows that some 37 graduates are engaged in farming; 28 as clerks, agents, salesmen and the like; 24 have entered the "learned professions" or are taking professional studies; 11 are in mercantile business; 10 are in manufacturing work; 10 are teachers, 5 of whom are in agricultural colleges; 9 are engineers or surveyors, 6 florists, 3 veterinary surgeons, 3 druggists, 3 chemists, and the remainder are occupied in a diversity of employments. Over 400 others have taken partial courses.

Professor Stockbridge writes: "By vote of the trustees of this institution females are invited here as students. In but one instance, however, has the opportunity been availed of." In the catalogue for 1879 a report of meteorological observations for 1878, by Miss Snell, is given.

COURSE OF STUDY.

Each collegiate year is divided into three terms. The studies for the first year are as follows: Chemistry, general and inorganic; human anatomy, physiology, and hygiene; algebra; English; agriculture; declamation; botany, general and systematic; geometry; elocution; freehand drawing; French; military drill; and manual labor for six hours each week, except in the second term.

For the second year: Systematic botany; geometry; French; English; agriculture; declamation; geology; lectures in history; trigonometry; drawing; zoölogy; surveying; levelling; military drill, and manual labor as before.

For the junior year: Mechanics; entomology; market gardening; horticulture; physics; practical chemistry; German; drawing; agricultural debate; astronomy; roads and railroads; stock and dairy farming; military drill four hours, and manual labor as before.

For the senior year: English literature; lectures in history; practical chemistry; bookkeeping; roads and railroads; military science; original declamation; thesis; mental science; agriculture; veterinary science; microscopy; botany; landscape gardening; rural law; lectures on English language; agricultural review; military drill.

APPLIANCES AND APPARATUS.

The students have the advantage of contiguity to Amherst College and its collections, library, and appliances, from which, though there be no direct connection, there cannot but be beneficial aids obtained to the students of the Agricultural College. The library property of the Agricultural College consists of over 2,000 volumes, mostly on technical subjects, embracing every department of agriculture and the natural sciences.

The Knowlton Herbarium contains more than 10,000 species of catalogued plants and botanical specimens.

The State cabinet of geology, ornithology, and entomology is complete in its illustration of the natural history of Massachusetts.

The chemical laboratory has accommodations for 70 students, and is in a high state of efficiency. Practical laboratory work is required of each student daily for an entire year.

The department of physics and civil engineering is fully equipped. Practical field work in surveying, laying out roads, &c., is required of every student sufficient to give him a knowledge of the most approved instruments and methods, to be pursued under a great variety of circumstances.

The military department affords facilities for valuable discipline, and is educating far more thoroughly and completely than any militia system can be expected to do a large number of young men, who go out capable of serving as officers or soldiers in case of emergency. This feature of the course of study and training is far more important than is generally supposed, and has from the first received the most careful attention by the college authorities, and has been eminently successful.

The horticultural department contains extensive plant and propagating houses, peach, pear, and apple orchards, vineyards, and nurseries, thus affording ample facilities for in-

INDUSTRIAL EDUCATION IN THE UNITED STATES. 141

struction and for the labor of students, who are paid by the hour for all work beyond the limits of what is called "class work," which is required of all students six hours a week as a part of the educational course.

The farm of nearly 400 acres must be regarded as an important adjunct of the college, as it affords facilities for observation and labor which could not be had without it. It has been somewhat cramped for means, and has been required to do a vast amount of work in the way of grading grounds, building roads and walks, and teaming of various kinds for the college, so that its accounts have not shown its actual working; but its capacities for usefulness in connection with other departments of the college are quite obvious.

The farm stock, though considerably diminished, owing to sales in order to meet indebtedness, still consists of 25 head, old and young, all but two of which are pure Ayrshires.

PRACTICAL RESULTS.

The farm is largely self-sustaining, and is in many ways profitable to the college. Its benefits experimentally considered are very great. The horticultural department is also nearly self-sustaining. The crops in 1880, with one or two exceptions, were good. The vineyard produced very well, and the crop yielded about $150. The nursery is in good condition, and contains a very large stock of peach and other fruit and ornamental trees, consisting of apple, pear, plum, and peach seedlings (root grafted or budded), quince stocks budded with pear, grape vines from cuttings, evergreens (mostly Japanese) from cuttings, a large stock of the umbrella pine, Japanese maple, &c.

The catalogue of 1880 says: "Though the education and training of young men must be regarded as the primary object, the contributions of the college to the science and practice of agriculture have been extensive and valuable, and they are universally recognized throughout the country as in the highest degree creditable to the institution and to the State; they have, indeed, in repeated instances been taken as the basis of important legislative action in other States. The following may be stated as a few of the subjects that have been investigated, most of them exhaustively and with valuable practical results:

"1. The growing of sugar beets, the manufacture of sugar from them, and trials of their value for cattle foods. This industry is soon to grow up in our midst and to absorb large amounts of capital.

"2. The sources of supply and the quantity and quality of our manurial agents. These careful scientific investigations have been the prime means of revolutionizing the manufacture and trade in fertilizers not only in this State but throughout the country.

"3. Laboratory and physical examinations of the South Carolina phosphates, and trials of their agricultural value in the raw state and after treatment with acids.

"4. On the use and effect of common salt on the grain and root crops.

"5. The chemical and physical condition of the salt marshes of the State, and the devising of methods by which they can be made available for agricultural purposes.

"6. Experiments with compound commercial fertilizers to test their comparative agricultural value and their value as compared with single elements.

"7. To determine what elements will make practically a complete manure on our average soils.

"8. Investigations of the quality and composition of commercial fertilizers offered for sale, and the protection of the community by legal control and inspection from frauds in them.

"9. Observations and study of the phenomena of plant life.

"10. The circulation of sap in plants, and their expansive power during growth.

"11. To determine the proportions of different elements of nutrition in feeding substances to be used to save needless expense and to produce the most certain results.

"12. Experiments on the continuous growth of crops on the same soil with chemical fertilizers alone.

"13. The influence of different kinds of fodder plants fed to milch cows on the quantity and quality of their milk and butter.

"14. Examinations and trials to test the comparative value of different methods of setting and treating milk in the butter dairy.

"15. Practical trials of new implements and a great variety of farm machinery.

"16. Investigations as to the effect of girdling fruit trees and plants to hasten the time of ripening and to improve the quality of the fruit.

"17. The effect of chemical salts on the carbo-hydrate contents of plants and the quality of fruits.

"18. The construction and repair of common roads.

"19. The growing of early amber cane and the manufacture of sugar from its juice.

"20. The influence of temperature on the vital functions of plants, and temperature of soils and air on the changes in forms of water in soils and plants and vapor in air.

"21. Investigations in relation to the evaporation and percolation of water from the soil.

"22. The tilling of soils of different characteristics as affecting the loss of water by evaporation.

"23. The determination of the elements of plant nutrition lost from the soil by leaching and of those it retains.

"24. Investigations in relation to the comparative temperature of the soil and air by day and by night.

"25. The establishment of true meridian lines to regulate the practice of surveying.

"26. The comparative study of the milk of different breeds of cows.

"27. Accurate investigations of the comparative nutritive and feeding value of northern, southern, and western varieties of Indian corn."

In further illustration of the work achieved in this direction, as well as in that of practical training, the following testimony is given:

Dr. James R. Nichols, editor of the Journal of Chemistry, chairman of the examining committee for 1878, says: "A prominent aim was to ascertain if the young men were really qualified to go upon a farm and conduct its operations in an intelligent and practical manner."

After a recapitulation of the range of knowledge required and information possessed by the students, Dr. Nichols says: "Upon these points and many others the young men were examined sufficiently in detail to bring out what they really knew; and it is gratifying to report that the answers showed marked proficiency in these departments of study."

In 1870, Professor Agassiz, acting as chairman of the examining committee, reported that the "theory of scientific agriculture is thoroughly taught, and the application of such knowledge is made on the farm, * * * and all students are compelled to work at the details of husbandry; so that manual labor becomes a valuable adjunct to mental application."

In 1873, Professor Agassiz declared, in reference to one of the papers referred to in the foregoing schedule: "Let me say to those who have not thought that the Agricultural College was doing anything worth its expense, that the production of this one paper has amply paid for every dollar which the State has thus far bestowed upon the institution."

MASSACHUSETTS INSTITUTE OF TECHNOLOGY, BOSTON.

[Statement from the latest catalogue and reports received at this office.]

OBJECTS.

This institution was organized under State charter in 1861 as an "institution devoted to the practical arts and sciences, having the triple organization of a society of arts, a museum or conservatory of arts, and a school of industrial science and art," and as a means of aiding "the advancement, development, and practical application of science in connection with arts, agriculture, manufactures, and commerce." The Congressional land grant for the State of Massachusetts and in aid of a college of agriculture and the mechanic arts was divided between the Agricultural College at Amherst and the Institute of Technology, the latter institution receiving one-third.

ENDOWMENTS AND FUNDS.

The endowment was obtained from the gifts of individuals and from the grant by the State of one-third of the land-grant fund. The latter amounted to $120,000 and the private donations were about $515,000. Of this latter sum $316,000 were invested in real estate, $54,000 in permanent property, and $145,000 are still regarded as productive funds, which, with the national endowment of $120,000 and a small additional sum, makes up $267,000 of permanent funds. The annual income and expenditure are each about $60,000, two-thirds of which is paid for salaries.

THE FACULTY.

The faculty of the institute has 40 members, divided as follows: President, professor emeritus of physics and geology; professors of mathematics (2), civil and topographical engineering, mechanical engineering, mining engineering, metallurgy and industrial chemistry, general chemistry, analytical and organic chemistry, physics, theoretical and

INDUSTRIAL EDUCATION IN THE UNITED STATES. 143

applied mechanics, architecture, geology and geography, zoölogy and palæontology, modern languages, and English history; assistant professors of architecture, architectural design, and modern languages; instructors in practical design, mechanical and free-hand drawing, physics, geology and mineralogy, military tactics, and civil engineering, with two others in the school of mechanic arts; and assistants in mechanical engineering, quantitative analysis (2), physics, general chemistry and qualitative analysis (3), chemistry and biology, drawing, and applied mechanics. There are also four instructors and assistants in the shops.

STUDENTS AND GRADUATES.

The number of students for 1880–'81 is given as follows:

Graduate students	15
Regular students:	
Fourth year	24
Third year	20
Second year	33
First year	87
Special students	138
In school of mechanic arts	39
In Lowell School of Practical Design	49
Deducting 15 (twice named) the total is	390

The number of graduates previous to 1880 was 244, whose occupations are approximately stated as follows: Civil engineers, 45; teachers, instructors, &c., 26; chemists, 22; draughtsmen, 16; manufacturers, 13; in business, 13; superintendents of mills, &c., 11; mining engineers, 10; mechanical engineers, 8; deceased, 14; miscellaneous employments, 54; not reported, 12. There were 8 graduates in 1880 and 28 in 1881.

Tuition is charged as follows: The institute proper, $200; school of mechanic arts, $150; average expense per scholar, $254.22. There are ten free scholarships: five in the advanced or graduate course, three undergraduate, and two in the school of mechanic arts. On the 1st of February, 1881, there were 35 young women in attendance, of whom 14 were in the scientific department and 21 in the Lowell school of practical design.

THE COURSE OF INSTRUCTION.

Five of the regular courses open to students are purely professional in character and are designed to train for active careers therein. These courses are: 1, civil and topographical engineering; 2, mechanical engineering; 3, mining engineering, or mining and geology; 4, building and architecture; 5, chemistry.

THE STUDIES OF THE PROFESSIONAL COURSES.

The studies of the first year are common to all the courses, and embrace the following subjects: Algebra, geometry, plane and spherical trigonometry, chemistry, qualitative analysis, laboratory work, rhetoric, English composition, English history and literature, French, drawing, military drill.

COURSE IN CIVIL ENGINEERING.

The studies of this course are:
Second year.—Surveying, leveling, field practice, plotting from notes, topography, analytic and descriptive geometry, differential calculus, physics, descriptive astronomy, physical geography, English history and literature, German.
Third year.—Roads and railroads, engineering drawing, integral calculus, statics, general hydraulics, rivers and harbors, locks, dams, and canals, field practice, strength of materials, cinematics and dynamics, physics, lectures and laboratory work, constitutional history, political economy, German.
Fourth year.—Framed structures, water supply, sewerage of cities and towns, drainage and irrigation, details of construction, study of actual works, specifications and contracts, theory of elasticity, dynamics, strength of materials, building materials, metallurgy, history of engineering, thesis work.

COURSE IN MECHANICAL ENGINEERING.

Second year.—Setting of machines, transmission and production of power, cinematics of machines, machine drawing, analytic and descriptive geometry, differential calculus, physics, descriptive astronomy, physical geography, English history and literature, German, pattern and foundry work (shopwork), carpentry.

Third year.—Combustion of fuel, steam generators and steam engines, machine drawing, machine design, elements of thermodynamics, steam engineering laboratory, integral calculus, general statics, strength of materials, blacksmithing (shopwork), physics, lectures and laboratory work, constitutional history, political economy, German, cinematics and dynamics, chipping and filing (shopwork).

Fourth year.—Machine design, measurement and regulation of power, machine drawing, thermodynamics of steam and other heat engines, pumping engines, hydraulic motors, machines and regulators, abstracts from memoirs, steam engineering laboratory, strength of materials, hydraulics, metallurgy, theory of elasticity, dynamics, building materials, blacksmithing (shopwork), engine lathe work (shopwork), thesis work.

COURSE A IN MINING (ENGINEERING).

Second year.—Blowpipe analysis, crystallography, and determinative mineralogy, qualitative and quantitative chemical analysis, lectures and laboratory work, use of survey instruments, surveying, field practice, drawing, analytic geometry, differential calculus, physics, physical geography, English history and literature, German.

Third year.—Quantitative chemical analysis, mining engineering, sinking, timbering, hoisting, pumping, ventilating, etc., integral calculus, general statics, strength of materials, cinematics and dynamics, physics, lectures and laboratory work, assaying, structural, chemical and historical geology, constitutional history, political economy, German.

Fourth year.—Quantitative chemical analysis, mining laboratory (work upon gold, silver, copper, and lead ores in quantity), metallurgy lectures, ore dressing lectures, drawing, strength of materials, building materials, dynamics, welding and tempering, memoirs, thesis.

COURSE B IN MINING (GEOLOGY AND MINING).

Second year.—Blowpipe analysis, crystallography, and determinative mineralogy, quantitative chemical analysis, use of surveying instruments, surveying, field practice, drawing, physical geography, zoölogy, palæontology, botany, physics, German.

Third year.—Mining engineering, sinking, timbering, hoisting, pumping, ventilation, etc., quantitative chemical analysis, assaying, industrial chemistry, zoölogy, palæontology, physics (lectures and laboratory work), structural, chemical and historical geology, constitutional history, political economy, German.

Fourth year.—Quantitative chemical analysis, mining laboratory (work upon gold, silver, copper, and lead ores in quantity), metallurgy lectures, ore dressing, drawing, applied physics, building materials, welding and tempering (shopwork), memoirs, thesis work.

COURSE IN ARCHITECTURE.

Second year.—Greek, Roman, and medieval architectural history, the orders and their applications, drawing, tracing and sketching, analytic geometry, differential calculus, physics, descriptive geometry, descriptive astronomy, botany, physical geography, English history and literature, German.

Third year.—Theory of decoration; color, form and proportions; conventionalization, symbolism, modern architectural history, the decorative arts, stained glass, fresco painting, tiles, terra cotta, etc., original designs, sketching, specifications, integral calculus, general statics, strength of materials, cinematics and dynamics, bridges and roofs (descriptive), stereotomy, structural geology, physics, lectures and laboratory work, constitutional history, political economy, German.

Fourth year.—The history of ornament, the theory of architecture, style and composition, drawing, original design, sketching, specifications, strength of materials, building materials, stability of structures, flow of gases, carpentry (shopwork), thesis work.

COURSE A IN CHEMISTRY.

Second year.—Qualitative analysis, quantitative analysis (lectures and laboratory work), blowpipe analysis, crystallography, and determinative mineralogy, chemical philosophy, analytic geometry, differential calculus, physics, English history and literature, German.

Third year.—Quantitative a analysis, special methods and laboratory work, industrial chemistry, lectures, work with the microscope, assaying, physics (lectures and laboratory work), physical geography, drawing, constitutional history, political economy, German.

INDUSTRIAL EDUCATION IN THE UNITED STATES.

Fourth year.—Organic chemistry, lectures and laboratory work, metallurgy, lectures, abstracts of memoirs, applied physics, optional studies.

Studies for the second term, including thesis work, will be specially assigned to each student.

COURSES B AND C IN CHEMISTRY.

Second year.—Qualitative analysis, quantitative analysis (lectures and laboratory work), blowpipe analysis, crystallography, and determinative mineralogy, chemical philosophy, botany, physical geography, physics, descriptive astronomy, English history and literature, German.

Third year.—Quantitative analysis (laboratory work and special methods), industrial chemistry lectures, biology, assaying, physics, lectures and laboratory work, structural, chemical and historical geology, drawing, constitutional history, political economy, German.

Fourth year.—Course B: Organic chemistry (lectures), chemistry (laboratory work), metallurgy (laboratory work), abstracts of memoirs, applied physics, optional studies. Course C: Organic chemistry (lectures), chemistry (laboratory work), industrial chemistry (laboratory work), metallurgy (lectures), abstracts of memoirs, applied physics, optional studies.

Studies for the second term, including thesis work, will be specially assigned to each student.

THE STUDIES OF THE NON-PROFESSIONAL COURSES.

The course in metallurgy is similar to that in chemistry, but has more particular reference to the production and working of the metals. The course in natural history affords an appropriate general training for those whose ulterior object is the special pursuit of geology, mineralogy, botany, zoölogy, pharmacy, or rural economy. It is specially suitable for those who intend subsequently to enter upon the medical profession.

The course in physics is based on the mathematical and physical sciences, and offers a suitable preparation for persons desirous of fitting themselves to teach physical science, as well as for those desiring to enter upon the pursuit of the various practical applications of physics, as making physical tests of materials.

In view of the rapidly increasing development of the various branches of electrical engineering, and the consequent demand for persons conversant with the theory and applications of electricity, a course of instruction has just been established bearing more directly upon this subject than any of those which have hitherto been offered. It constitutes an alternative course in physics differing from the one previously existing chiefly in the continued study of electricity, instead of a pursuit of other branches of physics, and in the introduction of a considerable amount of practice in the laboratory of mechanical engineering and the workshops, in place of chemical analysis. A knowledge of the theory of electricity will be given sufficiently extensive to prepare for ordinary electrical work and advanced study. Instruction in the various methods of electrical testing, and special instruction regarding land and submarine telegraphy, the telephone, electric lighting, the electrical transmission of power, and acoustics as involved in telephony will be given.

Certain general courses have been established for such as may not intend to adopt a distinctly scientific profession and yet desire to obtain an education through studies of a predominantly scientific character. Each of these courses contains a solid body of scientific study and of scientific field or laboratory work. In the first, physics, with the requisite mathematics, predominates among the scientific studies; in the second, chemistry, with the closely related sciences of botany and physiology; in the third, geology, with botany and zoölogy, forming a thorough course in biology, with field work and laboratory practice, especially with the microscope.

All the regular courses of the institute, whether professional or general, extend through four years, and for proficiency in any one of them the degree of S. B., bachelor of science, is conferred.

Advanced courses of study may be pursued, and the granting of the degree of doctor of science has been authorized by a vote of the corporation.

INDUSTRIAL INSTRUCTION.

INSTRUCTION OF WOMEN.

The Lowell School of Practical Design, described further on, though open free to both sexes, seems to be adapted more directly to the female students, so that a majority in attendance are young women. They have also become members of various other classes, and largely availed themselves of the opportunities for technical education. Special laboratories have been provided for their instruction in chemical analysis, industrial chemistry, mineralogy, and biology. This instruction is arranged for those who by reason of other engagements can spend only a few hours a week in these exercises as well as for such as can devote their whole time to the work. Other instruction is given so far as suitable arrangements can be made.

SCHOOL OF MECHANIC ARTS.

The School of Mechanic Arts is designed for industrial education as distinguished from that given professional engineers and chemists. It embraces manual and technical instruction in the shop as well as an opportunity to continue elementary literary and scientific studies. It is designed for students who have completed the ordinary grammar school course. Students continue their elementary literary and scientific studies while receiving instruction in the use of tools and machines. The plan of shop work adopted is the same as that of the Imperial Technical School at Moscow, Russia. The studies are, in addition to shop work:

For the first year, algebra to equations of the second degree, plane geometry, mechanical drawing, and English composition.

For the second year, algebra, physics, mechanical drawing, and English composition.

The shop courses of the school are as follows: for the first year, carpentry and joinery, wood-turning, pattern-making, foundery work; and for the second year iron-forging, vise work, and machine tool work.

Two years cover the full course. It begins with simple lessons in carpentry and gradually goes on to more difficult exercises requiring accuracy and judgment. Beginning with the chalk-line and a piece of rough board, the pupil proceeds with sawing, planing, squaring, jointing, mitering, nailing, boring, dove-tailing, mortising, and framing, receiving intermediate lessons in the design, structure, and care of tools. * * * Wood-turning and pattern-making come next to round out his instruction in the working of wood. The use of the pattern is illustrated by a series of lessons in moulding, core-making, and casting. In the second year of the course the pupils enter the blacksmith's shop, where they are first taught how to build and manage the fire; next how to heat and how to strike the iron; then, consequently, how to bend, draw out, upset, shape, weld, punch, bore, and rivet; how to heat, weld, and temper steel, how to case-harden iron. The articles made for illustration are required to be of the precise forms and dimensions given in drawings, and made with the fewest possible heatings. The aim is to teach the pupil to accomplish what is wanted with the fewest blows and the least waste of material. In forty-five lessons of three hours each the pupil has practice in operations of every kind that a blacksmith is called upon to perform, and he is enabled to do work that would not be discreditable to the practical journeyman. The material used is of inconsiderable cost, and the articles made are of interest to the worker to call to mind just how the work was done in each case. If he used due diligence he is justly proud of his work and is allowed to keep it. After a short course in chipping and filing cast-iron, wrought-iron, and steel, the pupil finishes his course with a series of exercises in lathe and plane work. It is desirable to extend the course and include some other branches, such as soldering, brazing, plumbing, painting, varnishing, &c. To all these arts, and many more, the method of instruction may be adapted, keeping constantly in view the main purposes, elementary instruction, moderate expense for tools, and very little expense in the cost of material consumed.

FREE TECHNICAL INSTRUCTION.

The trustee of the Lowell Institute has established, under the supervision of the Institute of Technology, courses of instruction, generally in the evening, open to students of either sex free of charge. These courses are more or less varied from year to year by the omission or interchange of particular subjects, but include in their entire scope instruction in mathematics, physics, drawing, chemistry, geology, natural history, physiology, English, French, German, history, navigation and nautical astronomy, architecture, and engineering. They have also made provision for a course of free instruction in practical design for manufactures, open to a limited number of pupils of either sex. Students are received at the beginning of the school year in September, to whom is taught the art of making patterns for prints, delaines, silks, paper-hangings, carpets, oilcloths, &c. The course embraces original design or composition of patterns, secondary design or variation of patterns, the making of working drawings, and technical manipulations. This school is doing excellent work, and is especially availed of by young women. It is under the personal direction of Mr. Charles Kastner, formerly of the Atelier Le Bert, Paris, and for fourteen years designer at the Pacific Mills, Lawrence, Mass. The school is provided with pattern looms.

The Massachusetts Charitable Mechanics' Association has founded two free scholarships in the School of Mechanic Arts, for sons of past or present members of the association. The Public Library of Boston is placed at the full use of professors and students.

APPLIANCES AND APPARATUS.

The institute is amply provided for its work. Laboratories, well fitted and fully equipped, are devoted to chemical studies, mineralogy, metallurgy, and to industrial chemistry. In the new buildings there is a properly arranged laboratory for the women students, with balance and reception rooms. The industrial chemical laboratory and the microscopic and spectroscopic laboratory are in the same building; also the organic chemical laboratory.

In physics the institute is provided with ample apparatus and the Rogers Laboratory for advanced students. There are also laboratories of steam engineering, of mining and metallurgy, of biology, and the museum of architecture; also the observatory. The last named is used to great advantage in connection with instruction in geodesy and is a means of studying practical astronomy. The laboratory of steam engineering provides practice in testing, adjusting, and managing steam machinery and apparatus. The appliances in connection with mining and metallurgy include a five-stamp battery complete, Blake crusher, automatic machine jigs, a spitzkasten, also engine pulverizer, a Root and a Sturtevant blower, with blast, reverberatory, wasting, cupellation, and fusion furnaces, and all other necessary machinery for reducing and smelting ores. There is a large collection of models. The architectural museum contains several thousand models, casts, photographs, prints, and drawings. The museum of fine arts, whose collection is close by, is open to students. The biological laboratory has a full outfit of microscopes and accessory apparatus.

The shops for handwork, recently fitted up, are quite large and well arranged. They include a vise-shop, forge-shop, machine, tool, or lathe shop, foundery, rooms for pattern making, weaving, and other industrial instruction. The vise-shop contains four heavy benches, with 32 vises attached. This gives a capacity for teaching 128 students the course every ten weeks, or 640 students in a year of 50 weeks. The forge-shop has eight forges. The foundry has 16 moulding benches, an oven for core baking, and a blast furnace of one-half ton capacity. The pattern weaving room is provided with five looms, one of them a twenty-harness and four-shuttle loom, and another an improved Jacquard pattern loom.

SCHOOL OF MECHANIC ARTS.

The attention which has been directed to manual training schools makes it desirable to present a further and more extended account of what is being done in this direction in the Massachusetts Institute of Technology. The following extracts, taken from the Forty-fifth Annual Report of the Massachusetts Board of Education, were written by Prof. John D. Runkle.

This school was founded by a vote of the corporation of the institute dated August 17, 1876. Since October 1, 1878, it has been in charge of a committee of the faculty, Prof. John M. Ordway, chairman, upon whom has devolved the main direction of the school. While adhering to the spirit and method of instruction, the aim has been to make the work in all departments as practical as possible, by selecting useful forms, if equally good, to teach the particular manipulation. The accompanying pages of cuts showing series of samples used in the shops are given as a general illustration, and not as the only, or even necessarily the best, series, for teaching the manipulations in each case. Every qualified teacher will naturally design his own course, and will also modify it from time to time as experience suggests. There is obviously the same freedom here as in the teaching of other subjects.

The mechanic art courses are as follows: In *wood:* (1) carpentry and joinery; (2) wood-turning; (3) pattern-making. In *iron:* (1) vise-work; (2) forging; (3) foundry-work; (4) machine-tool work.

While these shops are used for the practical instruction of our students in mechanical engineering, and for such other professional students of the institute as desire it, they are most largely used by students in the school of mechanic arts. This school, in which special prominence is given to *manual* education, has been established for those who wish to enter upon industrial pursuits rather than to become scientific engineers. It is designed to afford such students as have completed the ordinary grammar-school course an opportunity to continue the elementary, scientific, and literary studies, together with mechanical and free-hand drawing, while receiving theoretical and practical instruction in these various arts, including the nature and economic value of the materials with which they deal. Nine hours per week—three lessons of three hours each—of the students' time are devoted to shop work, and the balance to drawing and other studies, only one shop course, except in the case of special shop students, being carried on at a time.

It may be well now briefly to indicate the steps necessary to be taken in fitting up a shop and in working out the course of study.

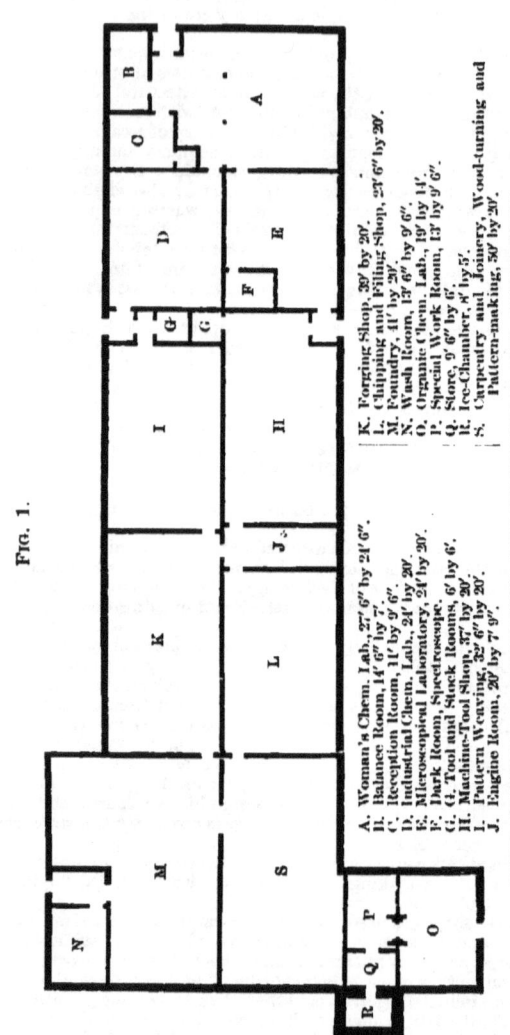

Fig. 1.

A. Woman's Chem. Lab., 27' 6" by 24' 6".
B. Balance Room, 14' 6" by 7'.
C. Reception Room, 11' by 9' 6".
D. Industrial Chem. Lab., 24' by 20'.
E. Microscopical Laboratory, 24' by 20'.
F. Dark Room, Stereoscope.
G. Tool and Stock Rooms, 6' by 6'.
H. Machine-Tool Shop, 37' by 20'.
I. Pattern Weaving, 32' 6" by 20'.
J. Engine Room, 20' by 7' 9".
K. Forging Shop, 39' by 20'.
L. Chipping and Filing Shop, 23' 6" by 20'.
M. Foundry, 41' by 20'.
N. Wash Room, 13' 6" by 9' 6".
O. Organic Chem. Lab., 19' by 14'.
P. Special Work Room, 13' by 9' 6".
Q. Store, 9' 6" by 6'.
R. Ice-Chamber, 8' by 5'.
S. Carpentry and Joinery, Wood-turning and Pattern-making, 50' by 20'.

NEW TEMPORARY BUILDING FOR SHOP-WORK AND CHEMISTRY.

INDUSTRIAL EDUCATION IN THE UNITED STATES. 149

FIG. 2.

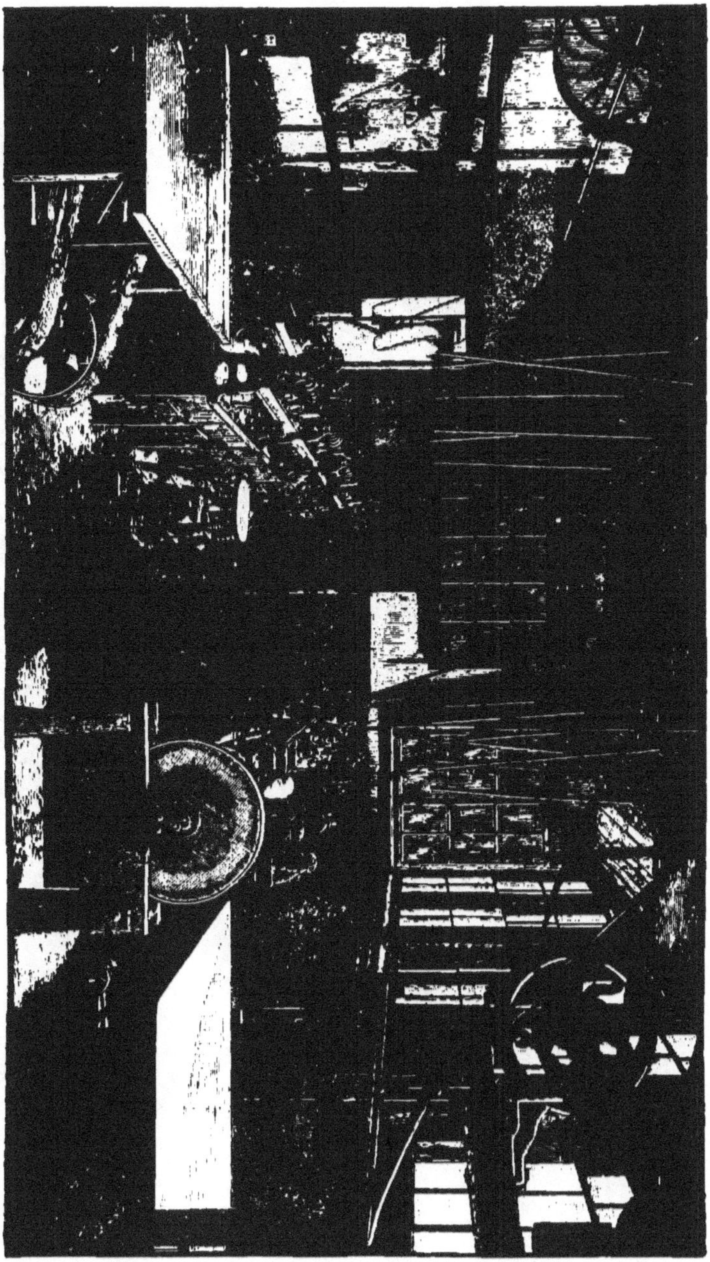

CARPENTRY, JOINERY, WOOD-TURNING AND PATTERN SHOP.

150   INDUSTRIAL EDUCATION IN THE UNITED STATES.

The shop.—1. Settle upon the tools and appliances to be used during the course. 2. Decide how many students can be taught in a section. 3. Design the fitting up of the shop, giving each student the proper space and facilities, and so arrange that each stu-

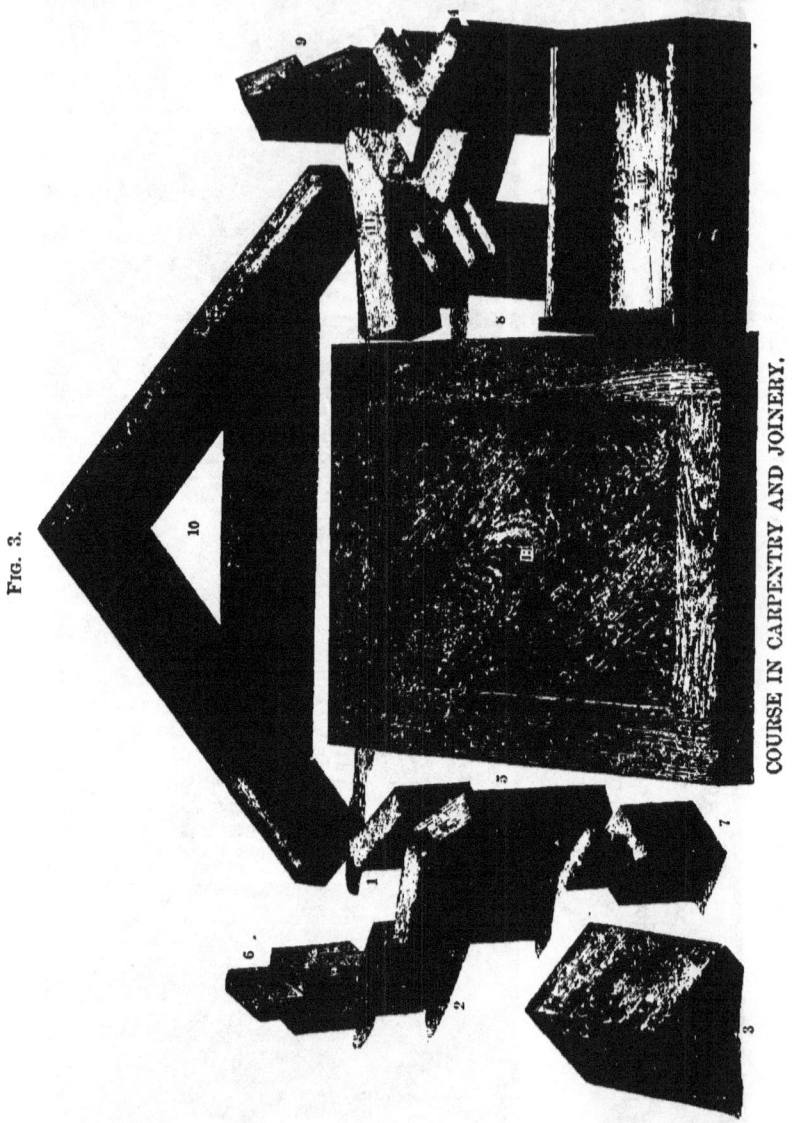

Fig. 3.

COURSE IN CARPENTRY AND JOINERY.

dent in each section can lock up and control his own tools and instruments, which are not to be used in common.

The course of study.—1. Design a series of progressive lessons, especially adapted to teach the use of the set of tools and appliances pertaining to each course. 2. Let the master work each lesson or sample, that he may settle clearly in his own mind the best method of solution, with a statement of the reasons therefor. 3. A system of inspection upon which the quality of the work can be based and each student given his proper percentage, and which shall also be the means of educating the judgment of the student, that it may keep pace with his skill of hand to execute.

We find, then, that in this practical part of the problem there are three distinct educational steps. First, the best method of solution; second, skill of hand to execute the work; third, the capacity to judge of the quality of the work.

The theoretical studies are arithmetic, algebra, geometry, English, physics, and drawing. The shops are arranged for teaching sixteen in a section, except that for forging, which contains only eight forges, on account of the smallness of the room. The deficiency has been remedied as far as possible by enlarging the foundry and using portable forges.

All our shops are entirely to small for the work we are endeavoring to do in them, and the present temporary building must soon be replaced by a larger and better adapted one if the purposes of the school are ever fully realized.

The carpentry, joinery, wood turning, and pattern shop.—This shop is 50 by 20 feet, one end containing the carpentry and joinery benches and the other the wood turning lathes shown in the cut. The lathes are placed four on each side of two benches, and under each lathe are four drawers to hold the tools of the four sections. The carpentry and joinery benches at the other end of the room are similarly arranged. In the middle of the room the cut shows the saws for cutting up the lumber to the dimensions needed in the courses of instruction.

FIG. 4.

The first instruction in carpentry and joinery is the use of the saw and plane in working wood to given dimensions, and then a series of elements follow in order (Fig. 3): No. 1, a square joint; 2, a mitre joint; 3, a dovetail joint; 4, a blind dovetail; 5, a mitre dovetail; 6, a common tenon; 7, a key tenon; 8, a tusk tenon; 9, a brace tenon; 10, a pair of rafters with collar-beam; 11, a truss tenon; 12, a drawer; 13, a panel. In addition to the above, each student makes a small frame, to apply several of the elements of the previous lessons. A sample is given in Fig. 4.

The instruction in turning (Fig. 5) and circular section pattern making is given in the following series of models: Nos. 1, 2, and 3 represent a series of manipulations in simple turning; 4, 5, and 12, pulleys; 9, a globe valve; 6, 7, 8, 10, 11, 13, and 14, patterns for various forms of pipes. Corresponding core patterns form part of the course. Bench patterns and bench and lathe combined are not included for want of space.

The instruction in this shop is given by Mr. George Smith, assisted by Mr. Z. Nason.

The foundery.—The cut representing the foundery shows a part of the sixteen moulding benches, combined with troughs for holding the sand, with the cupola furnace at the other end of the room. Over the furnace is seen the Sturtevant fan, which exhausts the heat and dust from the blacksmith's shop beyond. The furnace connects with a flue, which passes out of the shop, thence underground, into a chimney in the rear end of the main institute building. The blast for the furnace is taken from the pipe shown over the door, in the rear right hand corner of the room. An average charge of the furnace is about 500 pounds.

Foundery course.—Nos. 1, 2, 3, 4, and 5 are pieces used in the course of filing and chipping; 6 and 7, curved castings; 8, a sheave; 9, a pulley; 10, a pulley; 11, an eccentric; 12, a clutch; 13, 14, 15, 16, 17, 18, and 21, parts of a loom; 19 and 20, cog wheels; 22, a rack; 23, a shield.

The forging shop.—This shop is fitted with eight forges. The Sturtevant pressure blower, which furnishes the blast for the forges, is placed in the engine room. The hoods over the forges are connected with a 16-inch pipe, which runs longitudinally near the ceiling of the shop and enters a No. 4 Sturtevant exhaust blower in the foundery. This exhaust blower removes all smoke and dust and much of the heat. This shop was planned and fitted by Mr. B. F. Sturtevant, of Boston, at his own expense. The school is also indebted to him for other valuable assistance.

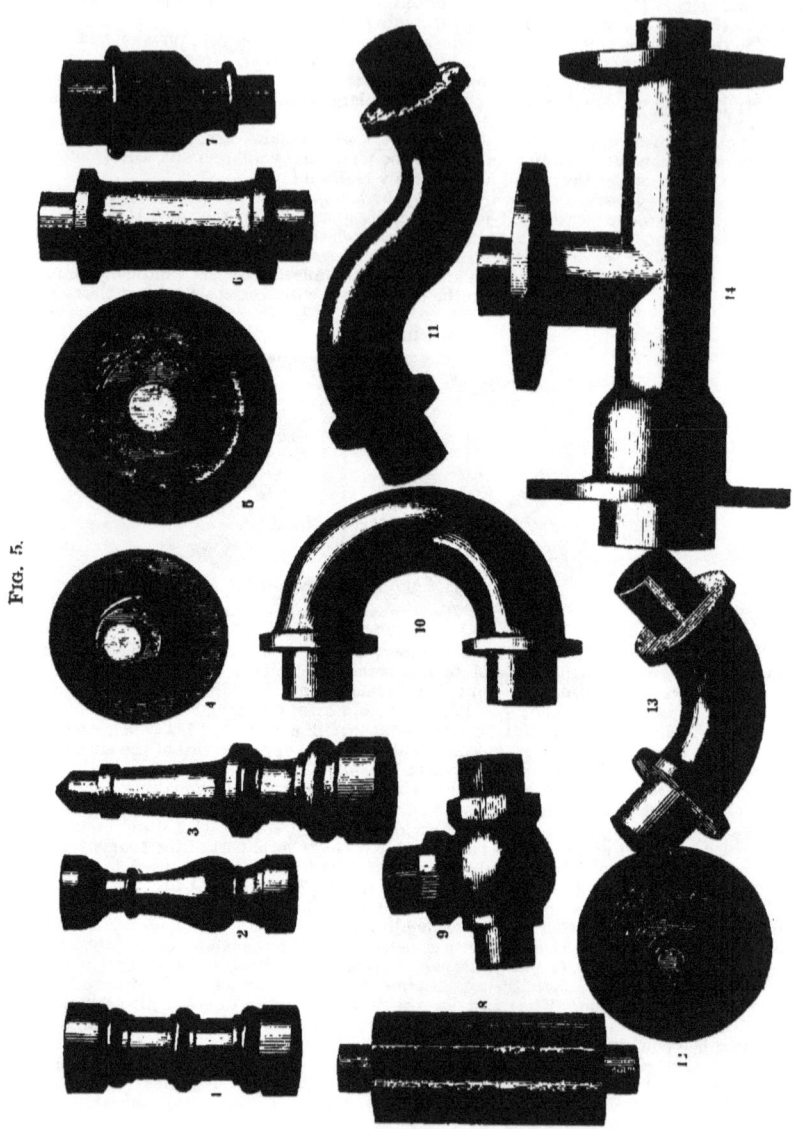

Fig. 5.

FIG. 6.—THE FOUNDERY.

154 INDUSTRIAL EDUCATION IN THE UNITED STATES.

FIG. 7.   COURSE IN FOUNDRY WORK.

INDUSTRIAL EDUCATION IN THE UNITED STATES. 155

FIG. 8.

THE FORGING SHOP.

The machine tool shop.—This shop contains sixteen engine lathes of $4\frac{1}{2}$[1] bed, four speed lathes, and a Brainard milling machine. The engine lathes were made for the school by the Putnam Machine Company, of Fitchburg, Mass., from new designs, and furnished at a greatly reduced cost, and have proved in all respects first class tools. Under each lathe is a chest of drawers to hold the tools belonging to the student using it. A bench under the window holds the requisite number of vises. The shop needs a variety of additional tools, which are not furnished for want of room.

The chipping, filing, and fitting shop.—This shop contains benches with sixteen vises and other needful appliances, with a planer, grindstone, &c., for which there is no room in the machine tool shop. The instruction in forging, vise work, and machine tool work is in charge of Mr. Thomas Foley, a thorough and skillful mechanic, who has served his seven years' apprenticeship, and has had, besides, a long and varied experience in his profession. He has a clear comprehension of the problem of mechanic art education, and has during the past five years shown equal capacity as a teacher. He recognizes that the student should acquire something besides simple manual training in this department of education. A want of method, a want of appreciation of the ends to be gained on the part of the teacher, are both fatal to the best results. Mr. A. W. Sanborn, a graduate of the school, is Mr. Foley's assistant.

A report from Mr. Foley accompanies Professor Runkle's paper. From it the following statements are taken:

"The system of apprenticeship of the present day, as a general rule, amounts to very little for the apprentice, considering the length of time he must devote to the learning of his trade. He is kept upon such work as will profit his employer, who thus protects himself. If the apprentice should be thoroughly taught all branches in the shortest time, he would be likely to leave as soon as he could do better, letting his employer suffer the loss of time devoted to his instruction.

"Now, it appears like throwing away two or three years of one's life to attain a knowledge of any business that can be acquired in the short space of twelve or thirteen days by a proper course of instruction. The dexterity that comes from practice can be reached as quickly after the twelve days' instruction as after the two or more years spent, as an apprentice, under the adverse circumstances spoken of above. The plan here is to give to the student the fundamental principles in such lessons as will teach them most clearly, and give practice enough in the shortest time to acquire a knowledge of the different kinds of tools and various ways of using them. For instance, if a man can make a small article in iron, steel, or any other material perfectly by such methods, he can make it of larger proportions with the additional time and help required for such an undertaking. The same in degrees of heat required for fusing or welding metals: if he can do it well in a lesser degree, he can certainly do so in a greater, with the additional facilities.

"After nearly five years' experience in the workshops in my charge, with the valuable suggestions of the professors so much interested in the success of the school, we find the best results in the time allowed accomplished by the method now in use in the institute workshops, viz, three lessons per week of three hours each.

"The time is just sufficient to create a vigorous interest without tiring; it also leaves a more lasting impression than by taxing the physical powers for a longer period. We have tried four hours a day, and find that a larger amount of work and of better quality can be produced in the three-hour lessons.

"In order to give each student the proper credit and to show him the most important points in each piece, the following method has been adopted for inspection. Take case of bending, the points to be noted by the student are rated as follows:

Dimensions	25
Form	70
Finish	5
	100

"The most important point in this lesson is the form, the next the dimensions, and the last the finish. Through all the iron working and other metals in each shop the same method is carried out. Every piece is made to certain dimensions laid down upon the drawing. The object of working to dimensions is to establish the necessity of correctness in measurement, and is followed throughout the course as a very essential point. The most of the exercises convey the idea of the necessity of straight lines in drawing or lengthening iron and graceful curves in bending."

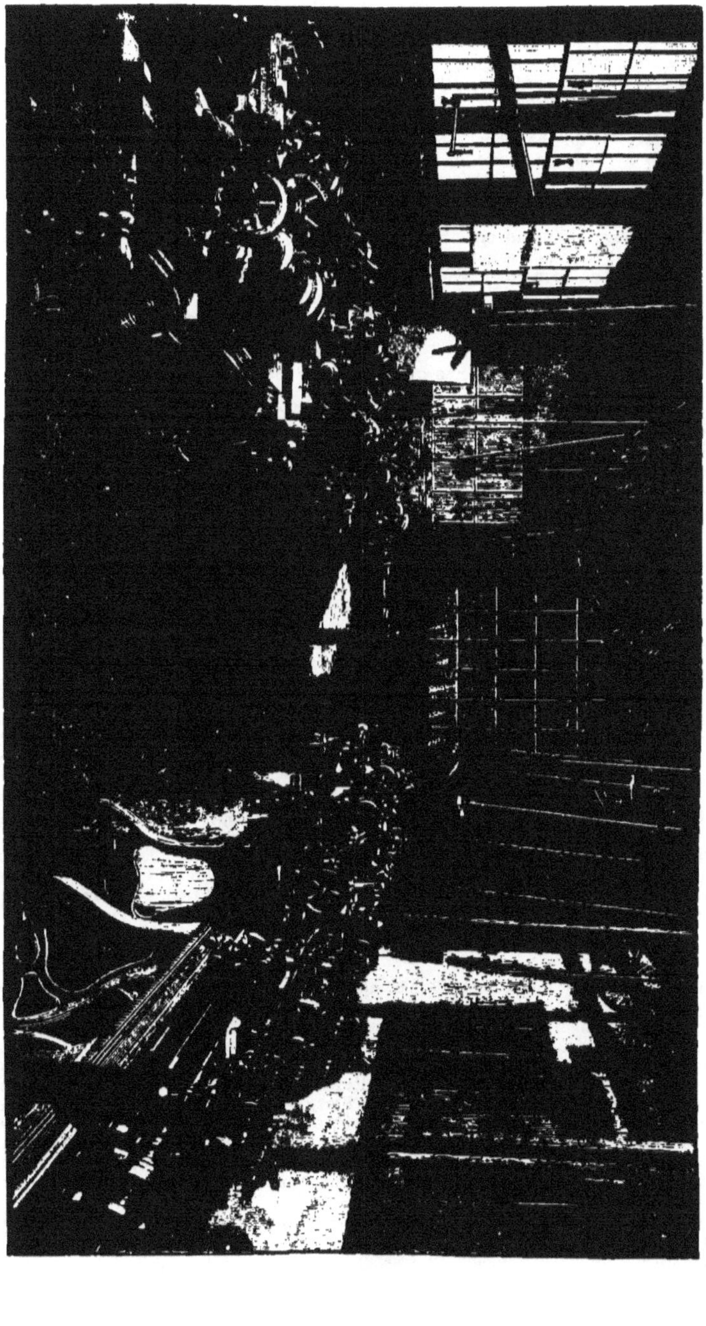

INDUSTRIAL EDUCATION IN THE UNITED STATES.

FIG. 9.

THE MACHINE TOOL SHOP.

MICHIGAN.

STATE AGRICULTURAL COLLEGE.

The constitution of Michigan, adopted in 1850, directed the legislature to encourage agricultural improvement and to provide for the establishment of an agricultural school. In obedience to this direction, the legislature in 1855 authorized officers of the State Agricultural Society to select, subject to the approval of the State board of education, a site near Lansing for the school, and to purchase for it not less than five hundred, nor more than a thousand, acres of land. It appropriated twenty-two sections of salt spring lands, or the money arising from their sale, for the purchase of land, erection of buildings, and the payment of necessary expenses. Few months passed before a site three miles from Lansing was selected and the erection of buildings commenced. In May, 1857, the college went into operation. It then had a faculty of six and sixty-one students. During the first years of its existence the institution underwent severe trials. The buildings had been poorly constructed and needed expensive repairs. The price of building and furnishing materials was unexpectedly high. Efficient agricultural instruction could not be afforded. The question whether the institution should continue to afford a general education or be so modified as to give professional training alone was earnestly debated until in 1859 the advocates of the latter idea were victorious. The course of instruction was cut down from four years to two. The professors resigned and discontent prevailed.

In 1861 a State board of agriculture was created for the management of the State Agricultural College. The board consists of six appointed members, and the governor of the State and the president of the college members *ex officio*. The appointed members receive their appointment from the governor of the State and are confirmed by the senate. One-half of them must be practical farmers. Their term of service is six years, two going out of office every second spring.

The course of study is four years in length, and embraces agriculture in all its departments, the sciences on which agriculture depends, and the elements of a general education such as citizens of the State ought to possess. Foreign languages are not taught.

ENDOWMENT AND FUNDS.

The endowment of the college arises from the sale of lands donated to the State for that purpose by the United States. The total number of acres of land given to the State was 235,673.37 acres. The number of acres sold up to September 30, 1882, was 100,203.50. The number of acres remaining unsold, and held for sale at $5, was 135,469.87.

The fund from the sale of these lands is held by the State as a trust fund for the institution, and the State pays 7 per cent. interest on it, quarterly, into the treasury of the college. The State also collects 7 per cent. interest on the amount due from purchasers, and pays that also quarterly into the college treasury.

The legislature each biennial session makes such appropriations for buildings, improvements, and current expenses as it sees best. The appropriations for 1881 and 1882 amounted to $67,164.

The grounds and buildings are valued (October 1, 1882) at $240,928. The inventory of all the property, not including lands for sale and the endowment funds, is (September 30, 1882) $338,471.55, being an increase in two years of $64,091.49. The annual current expenses amount to $29,000. The annual expense of teaching staff is about $21,000.

FACULTY.

The faculty as laid down for 1883 is composed of professors of mental philosophy and logic, chemistry, zoölogy and entomology, botany, horticulture, mathematics and civil engineering, practical agriculture, and English language and literature, history and political economy, a librarian, assistants in chemistry, in mathematics, in agricultural experiments, and in horticultural experiments, a lecturer in veterinary, a florist, a steward, the foreman of the farm and of the horticultural department, an instructor in military science and tactics, and the secretary of the State board of agriculture. The president of the college is professor of mental philosophy and logic. Nearly all of the professors have charge of some auxiliary department of the institution. One is farm superintendent, another the superintendent of the horticultural department, another in charge of experiments in sorghum, another of surveys and repairs in iron; others are in charge of museums and the laboratories.

Additional work is performed by the professors and their coadjutors in conducting farmers' institutes, six each winter, in different parts of the State, at which topics relating to agriculture, domestic economy, and social life are discussed.

INDUSTRIAL EDUCATION IN THE UNITED STATES. 159

STUDENTS AND THEIR EXPENSES.

The number of students in attendance in 1881–'82 was 216. Of these 2 were resident graduates, 29 seniors, 31 juniors, 56 sophomores, 81 freshmen, and 17 special students. Less than 5 per cent. of the students were women.

Matriculation, incidental, laboratory, and graduation fees are charged, but tuition is free. The rent of heated rooms is $3.50 a term for each student. Board is furnished at cost in the college boarding hall, where all students are required to board. The average price of board for the year 1881–'82 was $3.05 a week.

Students receive remuneration for most of their labor in the quarterly settlement of accounts at a rate depending on their ability and fidelity, the maximum being eight cents an hour.

GRADUATES.

The completion of the full college course entitles the student to the degree of bachelor of science. The number of graduates, up to and including 1881, was 244, of whom 230 are living. One hundred and forty-three are engaged in pursuits related to industrial arts. Among these are 96 farmers, 16 instructors or professors of agriculture or allied sciences, 7 engineers, 6 horticulturists, 6 machinists and mechanics, 3 fruit culturists, 2 agricultural editors, 2 housekeepers, 2 artists, 2 in United States Signal Service, and 1 printer. Of the remainder 24 are business men (mercantile), 24 lawyers or students of law, 17 physicians or students of medicine, 14 teachers or general students, 3 ministers or students of theology, 2 editors, 1 a lecturer, and 2 not reported.

Thus it appears that about 60 per cent. of the graduates are employed in industrial labor. The interest taken by the alumni in each other and in their alma mater is evidenced by the fact that 86 graduates came back to enjoy the reunion of August 16, 1882, though many of them resided in distant States.

INSTRUCTION.

The college year is divided into three terms of nearly equal length. A vacation of about three months intervenes between the autumn term and the spring term. This arrangement enables students to employ the winter months in teaching and be present at the college during the time of the most important farm labor. Instruction is given daily, Saturdays and Sundays excepted.

Elementary chemistry is taught by lectures during the first term of the second year, organic chemistry during the second term, each student being employed daily in blowpipe analysis. The same class studies analytical chemistry three hours a day during the third or summer term. The juniors have lectures during the autumn in agricultural chemistry; during the spring term they study chemical physics; and in the summer term they hear lectures on meteorology. Further instruction is frequently given, the above being a minimum amount.

The study of botany is commenced in the summer term of the freshmen year and continued into the autumn term of sophomore year. It is resumed senior spring, two or three hours of laboratory practice with the compound microscope being had daily for six weeks. A three months' course of lectures on horticulture is given to the juniors, and a half term each of landscape gardening to the juniors and seniors. Practical instruction is given the juniors in connection with their three hours' daily labor in the horticultural department of the college during the entire year.

Entomology, zoölogy, anatomy, physiology, veterinary science, and geology occupy four terms in the junior and senior years. Students have practice in the management of the apiary and the opportunity of dissecting and other laboratory work for two hours daily for one term, an opportunity of which they generally avail themselves.

In practical agriculture the subjects of drainage and breeds of cattle occupy one term of the freshmen year. Lectures are given during one term of senior year on stock breeding, and the principles of general husbandry and of special systems of husbandry. Many of the scientific principles of agriculture are taught by the professors of chemistry and botany. Students receive practical instruction in agriculture during their hours of daily labor throughout sophomore year.

The students receive instruction in rhetoric three terms and in history one term in the freshman and sophomore years. Higher rhetoric (conviction and persuasion) occupies a term in the junior year, and English literature another. Class readings in Shakspere and Milton and in masterpieces of senatorial discussion, in voluntary classes, under instruction, are of continual occurrence. Instruction is given to the seniors one term in psychology, one-half term in moral philosophy, one term in logic, with special attention to induction, one term in political economy and political philosophy, and one-half a term in the constitution of the United States.

APPLIANCES AND APPARATUS.

The college is located on a farm of 676 acres, in which are included swamp lands, pasture lands, fields in rotation of crops, orchards, vineyards, an arboretum, fruit, vegetable, and botanical gardens, a wild garden of native and foreign plants growing on rocky soil, and a park of eighty acres. The farm has cattle, sheep, and pigs of various breeds, and buildings for the protection of stock and the storage of farm produce.

The mechanical department has a carpenter's shop and a blacksmith's shop. There is also a museum of mechanical inventions, illustrating most of the industrial arts, especially agriculture, manufactures, architecture, and engineering. It is intended to enlarge this department greatly another year, and to appoint a professor of practical mechanics.

The botanical department has a laboratory containing the study of the professor of botany, a lecture room, a drying room, a store room, the Cooley herbarium of about 20,000 plants, a museum of vegetable products, and about thirty compound microscopes. A green-house of seven rooms contains a choice collection of the best ornamental plants and of those used in the arts. The botanic garden, the arboretum, beds of grasses, and the labeling of trees and shrubs in the park furnish further facilities for botanical study.

The chemical laboratory has a lecture room for 150 students, analytical rooms fitted with evaporating hoods and tables for 68 students, the professor's private laboratory and study, and rooms for researches in higher chemistry. It contains the chemical apparatus and stores, apparatus for illustrating chemical physics, and a full set of instruments for meteorological observations.

The zoölogical laboratory contains a lecture room for 80 students, rooms for anatomical study and histological work, and a private study.

A general museum contains the usual variety of collections. The library has more than 6,000 bound volumes exclusive of duplicates, and the reading room is supplied with 100 periodicals.

A VISITOR'S REMARKS.

The distinctly agricultural character of the college has attracted much attention, excited many comments, and induced many students and promoters of agricultural education to visit it. Hon. W. H. Ruffner, of Virginia, did so, when inspecting institutions for industrial training, in obedience to the request of the board of visitors of the Virginia Agricultural and Mechanical College. The following paragraphs make up the body of his report:

"The farm contains 676 acres. This includes the ample grounds about the building, which are used for instruction as well as ornament. The barns are large, well planned, and well stocked with horses, cattle, sheep, and hogs, and are kept astonishingly clean. There are six breeds of horned cattle, four of sheep, and four of hogs. But as heretofore intimated, the plan now determined is to breed only one variety and buy samples of others for study. The short horns are the favorite cattle everywhere. I saw a shorthorn heifer at the college for which $1,000 had been paid. The Duchess and Oxford families are preferred, and yet the Rose of Sharon cattle are highly spoken of. * * *

"Besides these appliances there are an apiary, a green-house, flower garden, sample grounds for trees, hedge plants, herbs, grasses, and clovers; also gardens of small fruits and orchards; also a botanical laboratory containing lecture room, drying room, herbarium, and museum of vegetable products. This is close to the gardens and grounds. Besides these are other laboratories and museums and a library and reading room. The buildings of this, as of the colleges generally, are large, handsome, and well furnished. The discipline of the institution is managed chiefly by the students themselves.

"The afternoons of five days in the week are devoted to labor by the entire body of students, 232 in number. Dinner at the college boarding-house is at 12. At 12.45 the students report at the tool rooms for orders. Every one who receives an implement is charged with it, and must return it clean and otherwise in good order. The body is divided off into squads, each squad under a leader, who may be one of the senior students. At 1 o'clock they go to work, and are kept busy until four.

"Driving into the grounds through a self-opening gate, I first passed through a gang of students paving the gutters. Next I came to a gang engaged in a very heavy and disagreeable job of ditching and under-draining the lawn. Another party was working in the botanical garden. A large party was husking corn, another cleaning off new ground, &c. Generally they were stout, cheerful fellows who were neither afraid nor ashamed of work, and who are said to become much interested in their jobs, and never to complain so long as their bosses will lay hold and work with them.

"As to compensation for labor, the principle here is the same as elsewhere, and is the plan likely to prevail—namely, to require unpaid labor when strictly under instruction, and for the rest graduated pay, according to the kind of work and the skill and industry of the worker."

MINNESOTA.

THE STATE UNIVERSITY.

The University of Minnesota is located in Minneapolis, on the east side of the Mississippi River, about one mile below the Falls of Saint Anthony, on an elevated bluff overlooking the thriving city and the falls. Its site had been acquired as early as 1857, and a building commenced. Financial disturbances and the effects of the war prevented the opening of the institution, and its practical organization was delayed until the legislature of 1868 passed an act to reorganize the University of Minnesota and to establish therein colleges of agriculture and of the mechanic arts. The act stated that the object of the university "shall be to provide the means of acquiring a thorough knowledge of the various branches of literature, science, and the arts, and such branches of learning as are related to agriculture and the mechanic arts, including military tactics and other scientific and classical studies." A faculty consisting of a president and eight professors was formed in 1869, and the first college class organized in September of that year. A preparatory department had been opened two years before. The same privileges are extended to women as to men.

ENDOWMENT AND FUNDS.

When, in 1849, the Territory of Minnesota was created, two townships of public lands (46,000 acres) were set apart for the endowment of a university. When the Terrritory became a State in 1857 two more townships were added, and the grant of 1862 (120,000 acres) was retained for the university. Thus it had 212,000 acres at its disposal. That which has been disposed of has sold at good rates. The price obtained for the earlier sales of agricultural college land was $5.62 an acre. The regents of the university have no control of the lands. They are in charge of the State land commissioner, who is also State auditor. He is required by the law to manage them as he does the State school lands. The annual income from them is received by the regents from the State treasury.
The financial condition of the university in 1881 was:

Value of grounds, buildings and apparatus _____ $220,000
Amount of productive funds _____ 575,000
Income from productive funds _____ 35,000
Receipts from the last year's State appropriation _____ 23,000

FACULTY.

The officers of instruction in 1881–'82 were the president, who is instructor in political science, and professors of mathematics and astronomy, chemistry, geology, mineralogy and biology, English language and literature, German language and literature, French language and literature, Greek language and literature, mental and moral philosophy and history, rhetoric and elocution, public health, military science, engineering, and theory and practice of agriculture; assistant professors of Greek and mathematics, and of Latin, and instructors in English and German, vocal music, practical horticulture, field work and drawing, and shopwork, and physics.

Students in 1881–'82.

College or department.	Class.	Gentlemen.	Ladies.	Totals.
Science, literature, and arts	Senior	18	14	32
	Junior	8	7	15
Mechanic arts	Senior			
	Junior	4		4
	Special	14		14
Agriculture	Senior	1		1
Collegiate department	Sophomores	39	11	50
	Freshmen	25	8	33
	Subfreshmen	44	27	71
	Special	24	9	33
Total		177	76	253

There are also 9 candidates for masters' degrees, 42 attending summer school of science, 51 attending evening drawing school, and 191 attending the farmers' lecture course. The grand total of students is, therefore, 546.

The only university charge is an annual fee of $5 required of regular students for incidental expenses.

GRADUATES.

The degrees which have been conferred in course up to and including 1882 are as follows: Master of arts, 3; bachelor in arts, 56; bachelor in science, 58; bachelor in literature, 34; bachelor in civil engineering, 8; bachelor in mechanical engineering, 1; bachelor in architecture, 1; bachelor in agriculture, 1; total, 162. Nine persons have taken two degrees.

The whole number of women who have been graduated is 42, viz: 6 B. A.; 14 B. S.; 22 B. L.

A statement of the occupations of 74 graduates was made in 1882. Of that number 31 were teachers, 26 lawyers, 8 farmers, 11 physicians, 10 ministers, 8 manufacturers, 9 merchants; and there were in banking, 2; journalism, 3; milling, 2; mining, 2; library work, 3; building, 2; real estate, 3; engineering, 4; 2 were naturalists; 1 an architect; 1 a government clerk, and 1 a florist. Seven ladies were married. Those who leave before graduating return usually to the employments they formerly pursued, and as half the students are farmers' sons, many return to a farmer's life.

GENERAL PLAN OF THE UNIVERSITY.

Under the organic law the board of regents are authorized to establish *any* desired number of departments or colleges, the following, however, being specified:
A department of elementary instruction.
A department of science, literature, and the arts.
A college of agriculture.
A college of mechanic arts.
A college or department of medicine.
A college or department of law.
The colleges of law and medicine have not yet been organized.
The relative position of these colleges or departments is illustrated by the following diagram:

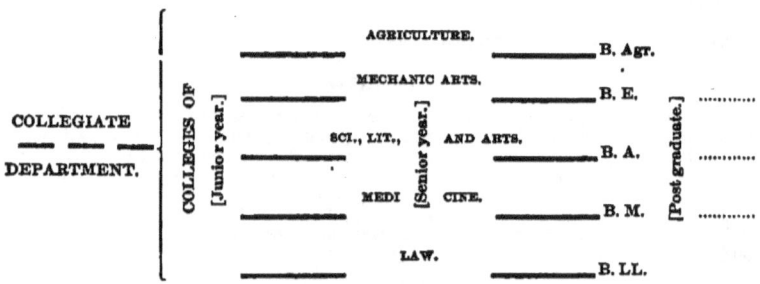

The department of elementary and collegiate instruction, known for short as the collegiate department, is introductory to the permanent colleges of the university. It includes that part of the preparatory department which is retained, and two years of the usual collegiate work. The following remarks on this plan of organization appear in the calendar of 1881–'82:

"This arrangement of departments emphasizes and formulates the growing tendency and custom of American colleges and universities to make the close of the second or sophomore year a branching point for the introduction of optional studies and for certain professional or technical courses. It presupposes a separation of the secondary and superior epochs of education, and a corresponding assortment of studies. The high schools and other fitting schools of the State are thus invited to extend their work substantially up to the junior year. When at length this shall have been generally done, the university will, as provided by law, dispense with the whole of the department of elementary instruction, and will extend her work on post graduate ground. Among the advantages claimed for this general plan may be named the following:

"1. A faithful adherence to the letter and spirit of the laws, State and national, which have established and endowed the university, and which contemplate it as a federation of literary, professional, and industrial colleges, having each its own organization, faculty, buildings, and equipment.

"2. That while offering the old college curriculum and discipline in their best forms to the literary and professional classes, the university will provide for the industrial classes that 'liberal and practical education' required by law and public sentiment.

"3. The separation of the natural epochs of secondary and superior education, and the ultimate liberation of the university from the elementary work of the former; and, coinciding with this division, an advantageous assortment of studies, methods, and discipline suitable to the two periods respectively.

"4. A close and vital articulation of the university with the public school system of the State; the elevation of the high schools by enlarging the recognized sphere of their instruction.

"5. The elevation of the professional schools by requiring of candidates for degrees a good general education as a prerequisite for admission, while not insisting upon the impossible condition that all shall have gone over the whole of the old college course.

"6. The elevation in particular of the colleges of agriculture and mechanic arts to equal rank and standing with other university courses, and the separation of the studies and exercises properly belonging to them from the elementary branches taught in primary and secondary schools."

There are three courses of study in the collegiate department, (1) classical, (2) scientific, and (3) modern. The requisites of admission common to all courses are arithmetic, elementary algebra, plane geometry, geography, history (United States and general), physiology, and either English grammar or Latin grammar. The additional requirements for the classical course are Greek grammar, three books of Cæsar, and two orations of Cicero; for the scientific course, physical geography, the elements of astronomy and physics, and either English history and English composition and word analysis, or the Latin for the classical course; for the modern course, composition, word analysis, English history, and either the scientific or the Latin subjects mentioned.

All successful examinations on entrance studies in the high schools under the State high school board are accepted in lieu of entrance examinations at the university.

The work of the classical course is mostly confined to the ancient languages, mathematics, and the elements of science. The modern course has chiefly to do with modern languages (German and French), mathematics, sciences, and English or Latin studies.

The scientific course is distinctly preparatory to the colleges of agriculture and mechanic arts. The required studies of sub-freshman year are, first term, elementary chemistry, ancient history; second term, drawing, algebra; third term, botany, geometry, English studies. German and Latin are optional studies throughout the year. Drawing and higher algebra, physics, trigonometry, and mediæval history, and general chemistry, botany, and surveying are the required studies of the three terms of freshman year. The optional studies are of the same nature as those of the previous year. In sophomore year French is substituted for German in the optional list; and the required studies are, first term, applied chemistry and physics; second term, descriptive geometry, rhetoric, and analytical chemistry; third term, zoölogy, conic sections, history (modern), and analytical chemistry.

The members of the subfreshman class and all students lately admitted are required to attend courses of lectures as follows: (1) On the use of the library, and on their relations to the university, to be delivered by the president, in alternate weeks during the first term of each year; (2) on books and reading, by the professor of English, in alternate weeks during the second term; and (3) on health and hygiene, by the non-resident professor of public health, in alternate weeks during the third term. Each student must have as a general rule three recitations a day (fifteen a week), besides rhetorical, military, and other exercises.

COLLEGE OF AGRICULTURE.

Instruction in agriculture and the sciences relating thereto is imparted through the following channels:

1. An elementary course to such as may choose it upon entering the university, which affords special technical instruction from the beginning.
2. The regular undergraduate course, which is open to those who have pursued the elementary course or one of the courses of the collegiate department.
3. Special courses of one, two, or three terms, which may be pursued without any entrance examinations.
4. A farmers' lecture course, for admission to which no fees, examinations, or other conditions are imposed.
5. Labor of students upon the farm, which though done primarily for pecuniary gain does not fail to impart manual skill and a knowledge of better methods, together with some theoretical insight.
6. The publication of the results of experiments which have been pursued.

The elementary course agrees in the main with the scientific course of the collegiate department, differing from it chiefly in the substitution of natural sciences and practical instruction for a portion of the mathematics and languages. Students are admitted to it on the same conditions and are required to engage in the same general exercises. During their course they have sufficient practice on the farm and in the garden to give them skill in the different operations. The prescribed studies of sub-freshman year are algebra, mechanical drawing, elementary chemistry, elementary botany, how crops feed and grow, and English studies or German. Freshman year: Soils and manures, farm crops, general chemistry, physics, botany, drawing, and English or German. Sophomore year: Horticulture, practical agriculture (farm animals), applied chemistry, analytical chemistry, meteorology, climatology, zoölogy, and English or French.

The regular undergraduate course is as follows:

Terms.	Junior year.	Senior year.
I	Composition and physiology of plants—How Crops Grow. Horticulture Mechanical physics, or other elective.	Practical agriculture—soils and fertilizers. Comparative anatomy and physiology. Geology, or other elective.
II	Agricultural chemistry. Mineralogy and chemistry. Mineralogy, or other elective.	Practical agriculture—farm crops. Veterinary medicine and surgery. Civil government, or other elective.
III	Atmosphere and soils—How Crops Feed. Horticulture. Psychology, or other elective.	Practical agriculture—farm animals. Economics—"Accounts, markets, &c." Political economy, or other elective.

The special courses in agriculture are arranged for three terms, each of which may be taken separately. They are as follows:

First term.—Agricultural chemistry, how crops grow; agriculture, soils and manures; horticulture, fruits.

Second term.—Agricultural chemistry, how crops grow; agriculture, farm animals; arboriculture.

Third term.—Farm drainage and accounts; agriculture, farm crops; horticulture, vegetables.

The scope of instruction in agriculture can be understood more clearly by presenting some of the important topics included under the general headings given above.

In *agricultural chemistry* a study is made of the elements of the volatile parts of plants, as carbon and oxygen; of the organic compounds of plants, as water, starch, and sugar; of the elements of the ash of plants and their compounds, as potassium, calcium, iron, sulphates, and phosphates; and of the atmosphere and the soil as related to vegetation and as sources of food to plants. A course in the analysis of soils, fertilizers, grains, and fodders is taken.

In *horticulture* subjects of study are relations of heat, light, moisture, and food to plant growth, and the means of controlling their supply and intensity; plant-houses and hotbeds; soils and manures and their manipulation; propagation of plants; grafting, budding, pruning, and training; planting and transplanting; hybridizing, crossing, and selecting; cultivation of fruits; kitchen, market, and landscape gardening and floriculture.

In *arboriculture* the reasons for planting forest trees are considered, as are also the kind of trees to plant, methods of propagating, care in the nursery, and special culture of each species.

In *practical agriculture* the topics are the history of agriculture; composition, classification, properties, peculiarities, treatment, and adaptations of soils; reclamation and improvement of soils, including drainage, subsoiling, trenching, tillage, &c.; road making and fencing; manufacture, preservation, and application of manures and stimulants; green manuring and irrigation; farm implements and machinery; production, management, and sale of crops; the different breeds of domestic animals, their characteristics and adaptations, breeding, rearing, feeding, and management; selection and purchase of farms; and the location, construction, and arrangement of farm buildings.

The students in agriculture have the benefit of the library and apparatus of the university. Of these appliances the museum of agriculture, the plant-house, and the farms belong especially to the College of Agriculture.

The *museum of agriculture* contains models of agricultural implements; seeds of garden vegetables, grasses, grains, and noxious weeds, in jars; grains and grasses in the straw; drawings and lithographs of machines; fruits in alcohol; woods, from the United States Department of Agriculture; and miscellaneous objects and materials used in agriculture.

The *plant-house*, covering an area equal to 34 by 45 feet, supplies plants and flowers for the study of botany and the apparatus of instruction in the propagation and care of plants.

The *experimental farm* has been divided up by the extension of the city and the construction of a railroad, and consequently is unfitted for advantageous use. A new farm of 155 acres has been procured, which is said to be one of the finest pieces of land in the State.

A fruit farm is under the care of the regents. Upon it experiments chiefly in acclimatization are being tried.

The farmers' lecture course is specially designed to meet the wants of farmers and others who desire practical and scientific information on agricultural subjects, and who cannot devote an entire year to study. The *scientific* instruction includes agricultural chemistry, botany, physiology, entomology, geology, and mechanics. It is given by the professors who have these departments in charge in the university. The practical instruction includes the improvement of soils by drainage, subsoiling, trenching, plowing, rotations, manures, grain raising, dairying, fruit culture, forestry, farm accounts, and rural architecture. This instruction is given by the professor of agriculture and by men who have become successful and noted in these special departments. One hundred and ninety-one persons, many of them from distant parts of the State, were registered in the course given in February, 1882. A large additional number were in occasional attendance. The course was opened by a valuable address by Hon. George B. Loring, United States Commissioner of Agriculture.

THE COLLEGE OF MECHANIC ARTS.

The aim of the instruction given in the College of Mechanic Arts is to lay a broad and solid foundation in mathematics, mechanics, and drawing, so that, with the practice in field, shop, and office work, students shall be fitted for immediate usefulness upon graduation, and after a moderate amount of subsequent practice and experience be capable of taking charge of important works.

There are five courses of study, three regular and two special. The regular courses are in mechanical engineering, civil engineering, and architecture; the special, in shop work and drawing, and in mechanical drawing, an evening course. Students are admitted to the last two courses if deemed competent by the professors giving instruction. Applicants for admission to the regular courses must either have completed the scientific course of the collegiate department or be examined in its studies.

The course in civil engineering is as follows:

Junior year.—First term: (1) Curves, leveling, and earthwork; (2) analytical geometry; (3) history of civilization and comparative philology or other elective; (4) field work and drawing. Second term: (1) Mechanics (statics); (2) differential calculus; (3) mineralogy; (4) drawing (descriptive geometry). Third term: (1) Mechanics (statics) and strength of materials; (2) integral calculus and theory of equations; (3) English literature, or other elective; (4) topography and drawing.

Senior year.—First term: (1) Arches, retaining walls, and hydraulics; (2) stereotomy; (3) geology or astronomy; (4) railroad work and drawing. Second term: (1) Roofs, trusses, and lectures on motive power; (2) practical physics (testing strength of materials); (3) civil government, or other elective; (4) drawing. Third term: (1) Designs and specifications; (2) practical astronomy; (3) political economy, or other elective; (4) drawing on designs.

The course in *mechanical engineering* differs from that in civil engineering in the following particulars:

1. Shop work is offered every term except the last, and field and railroad work is omitted.

2. In the junior year elements of mechanism is substituted for curves, leveling, and earthwork, and dynamical mechanics for statical.

3. In senior year machinery takes the place of arches, retaining walls, and hydraulics; applied descriptive geometry, the place of stereotomy; and steam engine, the place of roofs, trusses, and lectures on motive power.

The course in *architecture* coincides with that in civil engineering except as follows:

1. The drawing throughout the course is especially arranged for architecural work.

2. In the first term of the junior year history and orders of architecture are substituted for curves, leveling, and earthwork.

3. In the second term of the senior year lectures on decoration and color are substituted for lectures on motive power.

4. In the third term senior year the designs and specifications are those of buildings instead of bridges, &c.

The course in *shop work, drawing,* &c., is intended to give a thorough drill in the use of tools, teaching methods and processes common to different trades, and also a practical working knowledge of drawing and such branches of mathematics as may be studied. It is one year in length. Instruction in drawing and mathematics is continued throughout. Vise work is undertaken in the first term, forge work in the second, and wood work in the third.

This course has been rendered possible by the equipment of shops for the practical work of the course in mechanical engineering. These shops are three in number, and each has its room in the basement of the Agricultural College building. (1) The vise shop contains two benches, with double sets of drawers, so that thirty-two students can be accommodated in two reliefs. It has ten vises and the necessary tools for giving instruction and practice in chipping and filing. (2) The forge shop is provided with eight forges and anvils and the tools required for the manipulations of the blacksmith, a six-horse power engine, and the usual accessories of such a shop. (3) The wood shop contains benches and vises sufficient for accommodating thirty-two students in two sections. Shops for instruction in the use of machine tools and in foundery work will be equipped when the building for the college of mechanic arts is completed.

An evening course in *drawing* is arranged for the winter of 1882–'83, consisting of twenty-five lessons. Those who have received instruction in drawing are given advanced work. Beginners first receive instruction in geometrical and projection drawing; afterward the work is varied as far as possible to meet individual requirements.

COLLEGE OF SCIENCE, LITERATURE, AND ART.

The College of Science, Literature, and the Arts is intended to furnish higher courses of liberal studies, leading to the customary academical degrees. Accordingly there are classical, scientific, and modern courses. About one-third of the work of each is prescribed, two-thirds elective. The studies of the courses are as follows:

JUNIOR YEAR.

First term.—Required: In the classical course: Greek—Homer; in the scientific course: Physics—mechanics; in the modern course: German—Goethe. Elective: History of civilization, comparative philology, analytical chemistry, analytical geometry, zoölogy.

Second term.—Required: In the classical course: Latin—comedy; in the scientific course: Mineralogy; in the modern course: German—Lessing. Elective: Psychology, differential calculus, analytical chemistry, and theoretical chemistry.

Third term.—Required: In all courses: English literature. Elective: Logic, integral calculus, analytical chemistry, Latin (philosophy), German (literature).

SENIOR YEAR.

First term.—Required: in all the courses: Geology. Elective: History of philosophy, English literature (British and American oratory), analytical chemistry, astronomy, French.

Second term.—Required: In all the courses: Ethics. Elective: Civil government, French, analytical chemistry, economic geology, sanitary science, international law.

Third term.—Required: In all the courses: Political economy. Elective: Practical astronomy, French, analytical chemistry, English literature, natural theology, anthropology.

The instruction closes with the tenth week of the term; the examination takes place in the eleventh week.

DEGREES.

The completion of the classical course of the College of Science, Literature, and the Arts entitles the student to the degree of bachelor of arts; of the scientific course, bachelor of science; of the modern course, bachelor of literature. The courses of the College of Mechanic Arts lead, respectively, to the degrees of bachelor of civil engineering, bachelor of mechanical engineering, and bachelor of architecture; that of the College of Agriculture, to bachelor of agriculture.

The degrees of civil engineer, mechanical engineer, and architect will be conferred upon those who have received bachelor's degrees in those callings who shall, not sooner than two years after attaining a first degree, pass a satisfactory examination on (1) some special professional subject and (2) any three subjects on a prescribed list, and shall present a design and a thesis.

On similar conditions, the furnishing of a design excepted, masters' degrees in science, literature, and arts are conferred. The examination of the candidate for the degree of master of arts is upon two classical authors (Latin and Greek) and on three subjects chosen from a list. The characteristic subjects of examination are two distinct branches of natural or physical science for candidates for the degree of master of science; two modern authors (German or French) for the candidates for a master's degree in literature. These candidates must also undergo examination upon three other subjects chosen from a list, and all must submit a thesis.

INDUSTRIAL EDUCATION IN THE UNITED STATES. 167

BUILDINGS AND APPLIANCES.

The general plan of the university buildings contemplates a central academic building, and grouped around it additional structures for the separate departments or colleges. The main edifice and the agricultural college building have been erected, and an appropriation aggregating $180,000 is intended to supply a farm-house, a building for the College of Mechanic Arts, a military building (including a gymnasium), an astronomical observatory, a museum, and a library.

The main or academic building is built of blue limestone, is 186 by 90 feet, and three stories in height. The rooms, 53 in number, as well as the corridors, are heated by steam and thoroughly ventilated. Water is supplied from the city mains, and is amply available in case of fire.

The *agricultural college* building is a brick structure with a central portion two stories in height and one story wings, in one of which is the chemical laboratory. The other is a plant house. Rooms in the central building are used for recitations in agriculture and chemistry and for the museums of technology and agriculture.

The *chemical laboratory* occupies five rooms, as follows: (1) A large room for students' work, fitted up for 64 persons working in two sections; (2) a smaller quantitative laboratory; (3) an apparatus room; (4) the professor's private laboratory; (5) a room in the basement fitted up for assay and furnace work.

The *physical laboratory* is so arranged and furnished that students desiring to make a specialty of physics can have an opportunity to use the apparatus and perform their own experiments. One of the rooms has been set apart for a lathe and work bench.

The *mineralogical laboratory* is furnished with three double tables, accommodating eighteen students. Each table is provided with all the apparatus and reagents necessary for a complete series of blow pipe tests and for all the qualitative chemical work done in the determination of rocks and minerals. The room is also used for the practical work in zoölogy and botany.

Three of the *museums* of the university have not been described. They are the general museum, the classical museum, and the museum of technology. The general museum contains the collections of the geological and natural history survey of the State, sets of collections of the United States Fish Commission, and a large display of zoölogical specimens. The classical museum is to be composed of material illustrative of classical geography and history, coins and medals, ancient books and manuscripts, specimens of inscriptions, implements of writing, and similar objects of interest. The museum of technology will be composed, among other things, of fuels, ores, furnace products, textile materials, earthenware, and the processes and products of applied chemistry.

The *library* now contains about 15,000 volumes, and is open eight hours a day, Sundays and holidays excepted.

GEOLOGICAL AND NATURAL HISTORY SURVEY.

Among the kinds of work carried on under the supervision of the university which are indirectly educational are the geological and natural history survey of the State and the trial of agricultural experiments. The survey was commenced in 1872, but has been confined principally to geological work. The collection of botanical specimens has recently been ordered, with a view to the creation of a full herbarium of the flora of the State. Systematic observations and reports on the birds of the State have also been commenced. A recent calendar says:

"The law creating this survey is comprehensive. It embraces not only a strictly geological survey, including a complete account of the rocks and minerals of the State and their chemical analysis, but also a natural history survey, comprising an examination of all species of trees, shrubs, herbs, grasses (native or naturalized), and a complete account of the animal kingdom, as represented in the State, including all mammalia, fishes, reptiles, birds, and insects. It also orders the tabulation of meteorological statistics and au investigation of the climatic peculiarities of Minnesota. It orders the collection of topographical and hypsometrical data, and the compilation of an accurate map which, with the approval of the governor, is to be the official map of the State. The law also requires an exhibition made during the progress of the survey, in the building of the university, for public inspection free of cost, in well warmed and furnished rooms. The regents make annual reports of progress, and on the completion of any portion of the work a final report thereof is made to the governor."

FARM EXPERIMENTS.

The experimental work of the university has been extensive, important, and practical. Almost all varieties of garden vegetables have been tested for determining their comparative value and their characteristics. Varieties of corn have been tried with reference to time of ripening and productiveness. Wheat, rye, oats, and barley have been subjects of experiment. Fertilizers, methods of culture, fruit trees, ornamental and forest trees, the working value of implements and machines, and the germination of seeds are also among the matters of experiment. The results of experiments are often exhibited at fairs, and seeds produced are kept for sale at low prices, so that a wide distribution and a careful trial of them are secured.

SUMMER SCHOOL OF SCIENCE.

Courses of instruction in botany, chemistry, and geology were given during July, 1881 and 1882. They were designed to afford teachers and all others interested in the practical study of science an opportunity to become acquainted with the methods of original investigation and of teaching from actual specimens.

The course in botany was substantially as follows: (1) the general histology of plants, five days; (2) the structure of cryptogams, seven days; (3) the structure of phanerogams, six days; (4) the special physiology of the higher plants, several days. The course consisted to a great extent of laboratory work, preceded each afternoon by a lecture.

The lectures in chemistry comprised a presentation of the main points in the modern theories of the science and a review of its practical applications.

The course in geology included (1) a statement of some recent theories in dynamic geology, (2) an outline of historical geology, and (3) lectures on the geology of Minnesota.

Museums, laboratories, and the conservatory were in constant use. A laboratory fee of $1 a week was charged; the lectures were free.

The summer school of 1882 was extended in its scope to embrace rhetoric and elocution, English literature, and the German language.

Over two hundred persons, chiefly teachers, attended. The instruction was given by professors of the university, without extra compensation.

MISSISSIPPI.

THE AGRICULTURAL AND MECHANICAL COLLEGE.

The Agricultural and Mechanical College of Mississippi is located near Starkville, in Oktibbeha County. It was opened October 6, 1880, receiving national aid formerly given to the State University for the endowment of an industrial college as one of its departments. The objects and character of the institution are presented in the first annual catalogue as follows:

"The legislature of Mississippi, in accepting the endowment or trust fund from the general government, prescribed in the powers given to the board of trustees " the establishment and maintenance of a first class institution at which the youth of the State may acquire a common school education and a scientific and practical knowledge of agriculture, horticulture, and the mechanic arts, also the proper growth and care of stock, without, however, excluding other scientific and classical studies, including military tactics. They shall regulate the course of study, rates of tuition, management of experimental farm, manner of performing labor, and the kind of labor to be performed by students. These two acts of the general and State governments plainly define the objects of the college. The 'leading object' must be to benefit 'agriculture and the mechanic arts.' Should other studies be taught than those relating to these interests they should be considered secondary and rather as instruments to more readily comprehend the sciences which underlie agriculture and the mechanic arts.

"The complexion of the college must be such as to familiarize students with the leading objects as set forth in the acts: to educate and direct their minds and tastes to agriculture, horticulture, care and growth of stock, management of farms, manner of performing labor, and the mechanic arts. The college is not to be, in the strictest sense, either literary, classical, or military, but rather a college intended for special technical training in agriculture and the mechanic arts.

"This necessitates that special stress should be laid on the sciences, such as chemistry, botany, geology, zoölogy, entomology, physiology, mechanics, mathematics, physics, &c., which underlie agriculture, as this is the predominant interest of Mississippi. To understand properly these sciences, a very liberal culture, especially in English, is requisite. The foundation of this liberal culture must be proportionally as systematic and thorough as that required to comprehend what are sometimes called the learned professions. The varied conditions contributing to an intelligent understanding of agriculture as a science

INDUSTRIAL EDUCATION IN THE UNITED STATES.

and an art comprehend an education as broad and liberal as that needed in mastering any profession. The education must necessarily, however, differ in kind. Students whose education is intended to promote the interests designated in the acts must omit some studies taught in other colleges looking to general or special trainings. The education, too, is to be practical and industrial; students must be familiar not only with farms and labor, but must also labor themselves, and this labor is a part of their education. It is educational in so far as it is in illustration of studies taught in the lecture or recitation room."

FINANCIAL CONDITION.

The status of the agricultural land scrip fund donated by the United States Government is as follows: The scrip represented 207,920 acres of public land, which was sold for about ninety cents per acre, realizing in currency $188,928. This amount, by judicious management, has been increased to $227,150, which is now in the State treasury, represented by twenty year bonds running from 1876 to 1896, bearing five per cent. interest per annum. This fund, by the terms of the act of the State legislature of February 28, 1878, is equally divided between Alcorn University and the Agricultural and Mechanical College, giving to the college $113,575, or an annual interest of $5,678.75.

With the means furnished by the legislature in their first appropriation for the years 1880 and 1881 ($85,000), they finished the college building, erected a dormitory for 200 students, a president's house, together with temporary barns and stables for stock.

They have bought and partially equipped a farm of 840 acres and paid the expenses of conducting the college for one and one-half years, including pay of the faculty and the partial equipment of the academic and scientific departments.

The recent legislature (1882–'83) has made a most liberal appropriation ($120,000) to put the college on a permanent basis.

The board of trustees now have the means and are proceeding to erect all needed buildings, such as additional dormitory room, a hospital, professors' houses, barns, stables, &c.* Books for library are provided, as also the means to thoroughly equip the scientific, agricultural, and horticultural departments, to exemplify varied and diversified agriculture to the best advantage. The legislature has also given permission to remove from the State capitol to the college the splendid cabinet of minerals and soils illustrating the different sections of the State.

The legislature of the State has indicated its intention, by its acts, of supplementing liberally the means furnished by the general government and to make the college a first-class institution.

FACULTY AND OFFICERS.

The collegiate faculty as now constituted consists of a president, who is the executive officer of the board of trustees, professors of English language and literature, biology, scientific and practical agriculture, scientific and practical horticulture, chemistry and physics, mathematics and civil engineering, military science and tactics, and a tutor of English and mathematics.

This faculty intends to give a practical and scientific knowledge of agriculture and the mechanic arts.

The board of trustees provided also for a preparatory department, which will afford the youth of the State the means of acquiring a thorough elementary education. The faculty of this department consists of a professor in charge and two assistants.

Other persons included in the faculty and officers are the secretary and treasurer of the board of trustees and college, writing instructor, a steward and foreman of the farm.

STUDENTS AND COLLEGE EXPENSES.

Students in attendance the first year numbered 354; during the second year, 304. The session of 1882–'83 opened with nine students in the senior class, twenty in the junior, forty in the sophomore, eighty in the freshman, and eighty in the preparatory department, a larger number than at the opening in either of the previous years. Only those who have older brothers are admitted under fifteen years of age.

Before admission all applicants must submit to an examination. If for the freshman class, they must be thorough in arithmetic, geography, grammar, reading, spelling, and writing.

Students will be admitted into the freshman class or any more advanced class at any time, provided they can stand an examination in all the previous studies of the course.

---

* All of the new buildings are about completed, viz: 8 professors' houses, 2 large cattle barns, a mess-hall to accommodate 300 students, engine-house, sorghum mills and evaporators, sub-earth ventilating dairy (in process of construction), and a hospital building. A new laboratory for chemistry is going up, to cost $9,000.

No one will be admitted into the preparatory department unless he is able to read ordinary prose readily, to spell words of common use, to write simple English sentences, and to read and write numbers with facility; he must also be thoroughly acquainted with the four fundamental rules of arithmetic.

A matriculation fee of $5 is required. Tuition is free to residents of Mississippi. Owing to large numbers of applicants no students, at present, are received from other States.

The average cost of board is $9 per month. The college has accommodation for boarding 250 students.

The students wear a neat and serviceable uniform of cadet gray. The annual expense of students (not including clothing and traveling expenses) is from $80 to $125.

Students are required to work on the farm, in the horticultural department, or under the master mechanic for three hours for five days in the week, and are paid 8 cents an hour for the work faithfully performed. They are marked in their work as in their recitations, half work only gives 4 cents an hour. Work on Saturday is not compulsory as during the week, but at the pleasure of the students. Some twenty-five students during the session of 1880-'81, by means of their work, paid all their expenses with less than fifty dollars from outside resources.

INSTRUCTION.

There is a single course of study extending over two years preparatory and four years collegiate. Only common English studies are required in the preparatory department. The collegiate course is as follows:

Freshman class.—Algebra, geometry, outlines of history, English language, natural philosophy, botany, agriculture (lectures), book-keeping, and writing.

Sophomore class.—Geometry, trigonometry, surveying, English language, rhetoric, elementary chemistry (lectures), blow-pipe and wet analysis, organic chemistry (lectures), and agriculture (lectures).

Junior class.—English language and literature, mechanics, mechanical drawing, anatomy and veterinary science, agricultural chemistry, chemical physics, physiology, physical geography, horticulture, and free-hand drawing.

Senior class.—Astronomy, civil engineering, English literature, meteorology (lectures), agriculture (lectures), entomology (lectures), political economy, Constitution of the United States, botany with microscope, moral philosophy, and zoölogy.

Preparatory department course of study.

First year.—Arithmetic (mental and practical), elementary grammar, composition, spelling, reading, writing, and declamation.

Second year.—Arithmetic reviewed, English grammar and composition, geography, writing and declamation, algebra, analysis, and United States history.

The energies of the college are at present centered in agricultural education, as shops and conveniences for instruction in mechanics are not yet supplied. This deficiency is made up by the employment of a first class master mechanic, who has charge of the students inclined in this direction, and they are engaged in building, repairing, and shop work done on the premises.

In the industrial department the farm and horticultural departments are separated, and each is in charge of a professor. The professor of horticulture is now establishing a large commercial nursery for supplying fruit trees to the people of the State. He has also a large garden of 20 acres, which supplies vegetables for the students. The mess hall of over 200 students is a market for sale of supplies from the farm and horticultural department.

The principal topics of instruction in agriculture are the following:

Freshman class, second term.

Instruction is given by lectures, embracing the history, characteristics, breeding, and care of the most valuable breeds of cattle, horses, sheep, and swine; dairying; the feeding and care of the cow; manipulation of the milk in shipping or making into butter and cheese. To illustrate the course of lectures the college is breeding pure and grade Jerseys, Holsteins, Galloway, and short-horn cattle, Merino sheep and Berkshire swine. Other breeds will be added; also a dairy herd of 50 cows. During the present year a model dairy house, with all the appliances for making butter and cheese, will be erected and put in operation.

Sophomore class, third term.

Lectures on the principles of drainage, effect of an excess of water in the soil on the cultivation and growing of crops, contamination of well and cistern water, surface and subsoil drainage, laying tile and sewers, side-hill ditching, controlling streams, and preventing soil from washing.

Principles and mechanical construction of farm implements and machinery, draught, care of and repairs, with practical instruction in the field in the use of the plow, cultivator, mower, reaper, &c.; also the care of the steam engine, corn mill, evaporator, threshing machine, feed mill and fodder cutter.

The college now owns and is using a complete set of farm machinery and implements, procured from the leading manufacturers of the country.

Senior class, second term.

Lectures on farm economy and management, stock feeding, value of different kinds of food and manures, management and application of manures and fertilizers, composting, green manuring, adaptations of soils to crops, special crops, rotation of crops, different methods of cultivation, planning and erecting farm buildings. The course of lectures is based on the standard agricultural literature of the day and practical experience gained in farming. The instruction, while embracing the theories and sciences relating to agriculture, is practical and will be illustrated by the work of the farm as far as possible. As a means of illustration the college has a farm of nearly one thousand acres, embracing a great variety of undulating land, both fertile and exhausted, with commodious barns and out-buildings, planned with especial reference to exhibit special and mixed husbandry on a sufficiently large scale to enable the student to become conversant with all the details of the business. The crops grown include the different grains, grasses and forage crops, corn, cotton, sugar cane, sorghum, &c., besides experimental plats of all the plants that can be obtained that promise to be of value for any purpose. At present the college owns over two hundred and fifty head of pure bred, grade, and native cattle.

The growing of food crops and their preparation for feeding in an economical manner by cutting, grinding, and cooking, and the feeding of cotton seed and its products, and the making of barn yard manure is one of the special features of the farm department.

The breeding and rearing of the several most noted breeds of stock, both for milk and meat, and experiments in comparative tests in feeding, will acquaint the student with the desirable qualities of the several breeds for various purposes. Nearly all the work of the farm, except driving the teams, is performed by students.

At the close of the course in agriculture, questions pertaining to the details of the entire work of the farm department will constitute a part of the regular required examination.

MILITARY DEPARTMENT.

Few agricultural colleges give as much prominence to military regulations and instruction as does the Agricultural and Mechanical College of Mississippi.

Drills are compulsory on all who are not specially excused by the surgeon, day scholars equally with others. Companies are drilled by student officers, under the supervision of the commandant. Battalion drills take place similarly. Artillery drill is by classes. A new guard is mounted every morning, and there is a parade every day about sundown. In the evening, during study hours, sentinels are posted along the halls of the dormitory to maintain order. At the change of reliefs, each sentinel inspects the rooms on his post to see that no one is visiting, sleeping, or absent without authority.

Members of the guard are not excused from study or recitation because of having been on duty. Just before 10 o'clock sentinels are relieved and all retire, except officers, who inspect at that hour. Early in the morning all students are wakened and immediately attend roll call.

Half an hour later their rooms must be ready for inspection. Then study is required until 7 o'clock, the breakfast hour. In like manner a ceaseless watch is kept over students; and their delinquencies subject them to mild but certain punishments.

The professor of military science and tactics delivers a three months' course of lectures to the senior class on subjects pertinent to his department.

ALCORN AGRICULTURAL AND MECHANICAL COLLEGE.

The fund for the education of the people of Mississippi in agriculture and mechanics is divided equally between the white and colored races. The institution through which the latter race receives the benefit of this is now called the Alcorn Agricultural and Mechanical College, formerly Alcorn University. It is located near Rodney, in Jefferson County, which lies on the Mississippi River, just below Vicksburg. Little has been reported recently from the college, and only a few general facts can be given.

The university was charted in May, 1871; it had been opened some months before. There are collegiate and preparatory departments, each having agricultural and literary courses. The collegiate courses are four years in length; the preparatory, two. The faculty in 1881 consisted of the president, Rev. H. R. Revels, D. D., who was professor of mental and moral philosophy; professors of mathematics and natural philosophy, and ancient and modern languages and literature; tutors of English branches and penmanship; and the foreman of the farm. The students numbered 185. Only 15 of these were in the collegiate department. Of those preparing for college 50 had a classical course in view; 90, a scientific. Tuition is free, and expenses are made as low as possible. Further figures are presented in the table in Appendix B, which will show the financial condition and other facts relative to the college.

MISSOURI.

UNIVERSITY OF THE STATE OF MISSOURI.

The University of the State of Missouri is located at Columbia, in a beautiful and picturesque limestone region, on an elevated rolling table land lying back from the north side of the Missouri River. It was chartered by the legislature of 1838–'39, and went into full operation on the 4th of July, 1840. Only a collegiate department was established at that time, though a medical school at Saint Louis was associated with the university. Agricultural instruction was commenced in 1859, in connection with the teaching of chemistry. No new departments were added until after the close of the war. During that period it had a precarious existence. The constitution adopted by the State in 1865 required the general assembly to "establish and maintain a State university, with departments for instruction in teaching, in agriculture, and in natural science, as soon as the public school fund will permit." The condition of the university at a time little later than this is stated in one of its publications as follows:

"When Dr. Read came on the ground (in 1866) with a view of determining his course of action as to accepting the position to which he had been elected, he found the university largely involved in debt; its officers paid in university warrants, inconvertible except at a large discount; the payment of the income of the endowment fund suspended during the process of the conversion of the bank stock into United States bonds, as required by the new State constitution; the university building greatly defaced and injured in consequence of its occupation by United States troops, and some of the rooms unfit for use; the roof leaky and the plastering fallen from the ceilings of many of the rooms. * * * Upon the first week of the opening of the session not a single student appeared to matriculate, there being a county fair in the neighborhood, and on the second less than forty came forward for that purpose."

The prosperity of the university dated from the subsequent year. The State then began to render aid. A normal college was opened in 1868, and other colleges have been added since. The university now has suitable buildings, all necessary apparatus, and a valuable library of about 13,000 volumes and as many pamphlets. It has been governed by a broad and liberal policy, the principles of which were stated a few years since to be as follows:

"1. To keep the university perfectly free from complications of party politics and sectarian religion.

"2. To adapt the university to the peculiar needs of Missouri by giving it that scientific cast required by our special circumstances; also, while furnishing the highest instruction in various departments for the scholar, to afford instruction to a large class who require shorter courses to prepare themselves for specific pursuits.

"3. To give the largest practicable liberty of choice in the selection of studies, according to the most advanced ideas of the day, a system commenced in the University of Virginia. * * *

"4. To admit women students to classes as they may desire; to keep the expenses of university education at the lowest practicable point to the student by diminishing the rate of tuition one-half and providing the means of cheap boarding.

"5. To aid and encourage our local and denominational colleges by opening the doors of the university, without money and without price, to their graduates, in order that they may avail themselves of the larger educational means afforded by the State in the university. In short, it has been a settled policy to make the university an institution for the whole of Missouri, and not for any section, party, or partisan clique."

INDUSTRIAL EDUCATION IN THE UNITED STATES. 173

FINANCIAL CONDITION.

The two townships received by Missouri when admitted into the Union in 1820, for the support of a university were sold at $2 an acre in 1832. The net sum realized was about $70,000. This was kept at interest, and amounted to $100,000 before the end of the decade. Then it was determined to establish a university, and a bonus of $117,500 was offered by Boone County for its location at Columbia. These funds were used for the erection of a building and other necessary expenses, and the endowment of the university. Missouri received nominally 330,000 acres of land by the grant of 1862 for agricultural colleges. Really it was somewhat less, in consequence of a provision requiring that one acre taken within the railroad belt should be counted as two. After a long struggle it was decided that the State University should have the benefit of the grant. Most of this land remains unsold. Some of it is leased. The income from rents and the interest on amounts realized from land sales has not been large. The land is increasing in value, and will eventually provide a handsome endowment. The recent reports of the property and income of the university, as made to the Bureau of Education, are as follows:

	1880.	1882.
Value of grounds, buildings, and apparatus	$150,000	
Amount of productive funds	227,000	$480,000
Income from productive funds	13,620	27,500
Receipts from tuition fees	11,295	
Receipts from State appropriations	27,000	

ORGANIZATION.

The organization of the Missouri University is unlike that of ordinary colleges and universities. A general plan was adopted fifteen years ago, and has been adhered to since. It was as follows:
 I. To retain substantially the usual college curriculum for those who desire that course.
 II. To enlarge and perfect the scientific course.
 III. To establish and maintain—
  1. A college of agriculture and mechanic arts, which, in addition to instruction in agriculture, horticulture, military tactics, etc., shall embrace schools of engineering, analytical chemistry, and mining and metallurgy.
  2. A normal school.
  3. A law school.
  4. A preparatory school.
 IV. To expand the university by instituting colleges of applied science or professional departments, as its means will permit or the wants of the State demand.
 V. To accumulate the materials of education, as books, apparatus, cabinets, models, etc.
 VI. To adjust the different departments of instruction so as to economize labor and material, and thus render the institution the most effective to the largest number, and save means for the enlargement of the university and the increase of its facilities.
 VII. To exercise judicious economy in all departments, that there may be improvement in all, and the accumulation, year by year, of those educational means and appointments which belong alike to all departments and increase the general prosperity.

In pursuance of this plan the university is organized into a college, in which the subjects of instruction are arranged in academic schools of (*a*) science and (*b*) language and professional schools. The schools of (1) physics, (2) chemistry, (3) natural history, (4) mathematics and astronomy, and (5) metaphysics constitute the schools of science; those of (1) Hebrew and Semitic literature, (2) Greek, (3) Latin, (4) modern continental German, French, Spanish, and Italian, and (5) English form the schools of language. The first three schools of science are closely related to industrial education, and consequently deserve more than simple mention.

The *school of physics* is under the charge of a single professor. In it not only academic, but agricultural, normal, medical and special students are instructed. The study of the assigned text-book and the recitation are supplemented by laboratory work and by lectures. The laboratory work familiarizes the student with physical apparatus, of which the university has a fair supply, and fixes in his memory the principles and the processes which he sees illustrated. The lectures elaborate more fully subjects of special difficulty or interest, as, for example, the steam engine.

The *school of chemistry* is under the supervision of a professor and his assistant. In it there are distinct courses of study in (1) phenomenal, (2) rational, (3) domestic, and (4) agricultural chemistry, and (5) toxicology. The course in phenomenal chemistry is elementary, and must be pursued by all the students of the university, except those in law, before they can receive a diploma or be admitted to other classes in the chemical department. The course in rational chemistry is a continuation of it. Organic and applied chemistry largely enters into this course. Domestic chemistry is taught the students in the ladies' department by lectures on the general subjects of air, water, food, and cosmetics. Agricultural chemistry is also taught by lectures treating of the structure and functions of plants, the properties of soils, the composition and value of fertilizers, and other subjects similarly related to agriculture. The instruction in toxicology is given principally to medical students by a course of lectures lasting about two months. The chemical laboratory is furnished in the most approved style, with working tables, reagents, and general apparatus.

The *school of natural history* is in the charge of two professors, and their instruction is supplemented by lectures by other members of the university faculty. The subjects of instruction include geography, botany, entomology, anatomy and physiology, zoölogy, comparative anatomy, mineralogy, paleontology, geology, and physical geography. The last subject is taught at the end of the course, as it is more readily understood after a study of the individual branches of natural history, and is a review of that whole subject. Especial attention is given to zoölogy, botany, and entomology.

The other academic schools do not contribute directly to industrial education. They furnish general culture and discipline, and their studies make up the larger part of the courses which must be pursued by undergraduates seeking a degree. These courses are four in number, namely: Course in arts, in science, in letters, and girls' course in arts. Each covers four collegiate and two preparatory years, and it is estimated that four hours a day five days in the week will be required for recitation and eight hours a day for study. The course in arts is the old-time classical course slightly modified, and leads to the degree of bachelor of arts. The course in science gives prominence to mathematics and sciences; that in literature, to Latin and the modern languages. Their degrees are respectively bachelor of science and bachelor of literature.

LADIES' DEPARTMENT.

The girls' course in arts is made up substantially of studies selected from the other academic courses, with additional work in literature, composition, and criticism, and diversified by studies peculiarly adapted to the culture of woman, such as calisthenics, music, physiology, and domestic chemistry and economy. The degree of bachelor of domestic arts is conferred upon those successfully completing it. Young ladies may choose any academic course, but this one is the most popular with them. Its establishment has tended to increase their number, which has already reached nearly a hundred. The ladies are required to wear a prescribed dress and are expected to engage in calisthenics. The opportunities for the study of music are good, and it is thought that they will be greatly increased in the immediate future.

PROFESSIONAL SCHOOLS.

There are nine professional schools connected with the Missouri University. They are the law school, attendance in 1881–'82, 38; medical school, 36; normal college, 83; commercial school, 105; school of art, 140; school of military science and tactics, 53; engineering school, 42; agricultural and mechanical college, 21; and the school of mines and metallurgy at Rolla, 82. Each has a faculty of its own, or else is in charge of a single professor, who is aided in the work of instruction by other members of the university faculty as may be necessary.

The *engineering school* has a faculty of nine members, composed of the president of the university, who is professor of the science of mind, and professors of mathematics and astronomy, civil and topographical engineering, free-hand and topographical drawing, military science and tactics, geology, chemistry, economic botany, and law. Instruction is also given by visiting lecturers on engineering. Fees are $40 a year. Forty-two students were in attendance in 1881–'82. In their professional preparation they are instructed in the following subjects, among others: The location and construction of roads, railroads, canals, and water-works; the surveys and improvements of coasts, harbors, rivers, and lakes; the determination of astronomical and geographical coördinates on land and at sea; the design and construction of roofs and trusses, girders, and suspension bridges; drawing and constructing the various kinds of arches; the design, application, and construction of wind and hydraulic motors, air and steam engines; blow-pipe analyses of minerals, and economic geology, mineralogy, chemistry (elementary and applied); the art of war; the preparation of the various kinds of projections and drawings used by the military, topographical, civil, and mine engineer; the selection, tests, and applications of materials used in constructions; and papers and essays on professional subjects. In order that the student may pursue those branches which are preparatory to special departments of engineering, courses of study covering the last two years of a six years' course are offered in (1) civil engineering, (2) topographical engineering, (3) surveying and astronomy, and (4) military engineering. The college course in science prepares the student for the professional study of any of these branches. Instruction is given by text books, lectures, and field and observatory practice.

AGRICULTURAL AND MECHANICAL COLLEGE.

After a discussion, continuing seven years, the Agricultural and Mechanical College of Missouri was located at Columbia in immediate connection with the university. The county of Boone and the city of Columbia gave land costing $60.000 and $30,000 in bonds for the sake of having the college within their limits. Three-fourths of the income of the land grant belongs to the college, and the State cares for those wants which the income from fees and productive property cannot supply, as it does for the university. The attendance of students has not been uniformly large. In 1873 there were 138; in 1881–'82, 21. A few students have taken the degree of bachelor of agriculture; a considerably larger number have received certificates of proficiency in horticulture. The fees are the same as the ordinary university fees, namely, an annual entrance fee of $10, and $10 a year for incidentals and use of library.

The course of study has been made strictly professional and reduced to two years, the first, horticultural; the second, agricultural. Those completing the first year are entitled to the certificate in horticulture. The full course leads to the degree of bachelor of agriculture. The requirements for admission are very slight. The studies of the first year are: *First semester*, propagation, pruning, training, soils, fertilizers, tillage, and drainage; pomology, nursery business, forestry, and meteorology; physics and mechanics; and nursery work at the discretion of the professors. *Second semester*, gardens and gardening; entomology; orchards, vineyards, fruit gardens, ornamental trees, and landscape gardening; botany; work in gardens and vineyards. The studies of the second year are: *First semester*, zoölogy and veterinary science, farm crops, surveying, agricultural chemistry, mineralogy, mechanical drawing, and field work or feeding and care of stock: *Second semester*, farm buildings, machinery, fences, and water supply; domestic animals, geology, roads and bridges, and farm law, with out-door work.

Six prizes are offered, as follows: To the junior class (1) for best essay on pruning, Loudon's Encyclopedia of Gardening; (2) for best specimens of propagation, including apples, pears, grapes, gooseberries, and strawberries, 20 plants each, $10; and (3) for best show of garden vegetables, including tomatoes, cabbages, onions, pease, and beets, 20 plants each, $10. To the senior class (1) for best corn culture, ¼ acre, $10; (2) for best reaping, binding, and stocking, ¼ acre, $10; and (3) for best specimen of plowing, ¼ acre, $10. The college furnishes land and materials; the contestant must do all the work.

The college farm contains some 640 acres, has a variety of soils, and is well watered. It offers opportunities for student labor, practical work, and agricultural experiment. The value of different varieties of wheat, corn, and potatoes has been tested. Gardens, vineyards, and orchards have been planted, and will be closely observed. A commercial nursery is a special source of profit. A plantation of forest trees has been commenced.

SCHOOL OF MINES AND METALLURGY.

The School of Mines and Metallurgy is located at Rolla, Phelps County, in the midst of an extensive and rapidly developing iron section and near districts abounding in lead and zinc deposits. The institution was established in February, 1870, and opened in November, 1871. Its design is to unite with the agricultural college in carrying out the purposes of the national grant in aid of industrial education. This object has been kept in view in arranging the studies of the school, in selecting its apparatus, and in organizing its faculty.

The school has a one-fourth interest in the agricultural college lands. It still receives its chief support from State appropriations, that for 1881 being $7,500. It also received in that year $800 from students' fees and $3,300 interest on its productive funds, which amount to $55,000. Its buildings, grounds, and apparatus are valued at $46,600.

The faculty of the school is composed of professors of mathematics, civil and mine engineering and graphics, analytical chemistry and metallurgy, physics and natural history, and languages. The last is principal of the preparatory department, and has an assistant. The number of students reported for 1881 was 82. Of these 25 were preparatory students, 45 in partial courses and 12 in regular courses. The annual fees are $20.

The graduates previous to 1882 numbered 24; the licentiates, 25. They are engaged largely in teaching, studying, and professional work of kinds for which the school furnishes preparation.

Great freedom is allowed students in the choice of studies, and five courses of study are arranged in addition to the preparatory course of one year. There is a teachers' course, two years in length, which includes the usual English studies of a high school and normal instruction. Those completing it are assured of a first-class teacher's certificate, good for two years, from the State superintendent of public schools. A girls' course in arts extends over four years. The professional courses are three years in length, and lead to the degrees of mining engineer, civil engineer, and bachelor of philosophy, respectively. Analytical chemistry, mineralogy, geology, metallurgy, pure and applied mathematics, artistic and mechanical drawing, and civil and mine engineering form the main branches of study.

The school is well furnished with apparatus, instruments, and other appliances for practical instruction and demonstration. It has a full supply of excellent surveying and engineering instruments, physical apparatus, embodying the newest forms for illustration and research, together with diagrams and models for the illustration of metallurgy and for engineering, topographical and ornamental drawing. The geological, mineralogical, and technical collections are all rapidly increasing, and are already rich in specimens and products illustrative of the mineral industries of Missouri. The laboratories for analysis and assaying have been increased in working capacity, and are amply furnished with apparatus and reagents necessary for practical instruction and for any line of chemical and metallurgical research. The library of 2,750 books and pamphlets has been selected with special reference to supplementing the labors of the class and lecture room, and consists, therefore, largely of standard reference works on the physical sciences, mathematics, and technology. A good selection of technical periodicals is supplied to the reading room. Earnest efforts are constantly made to increase the efficiency of all the means of practice and illustration.

The rooms of the school building are comfortably furnished, well lighted, and well ventilated. The first floor is occupied by the analytical laboratory, the chemical lecture room, and the room of the professor of geology. On the second floor are the public hall, the office, library, reading and engineering rooms; and in the third story are the rooms of the professors of mathematics and English and a large drawing room, with ample accommodations for upwards of eighty students. The basement contains the assay furnaces and other appliances for metallurgical work.

A recent report of the School of Mines and Metallurgy gives the following quotations concerning the organization, equipment, and effective character of the school, taken from an official report of the visit and examination of the legislative committee on mines and mining:

"We do not intend to eulogize this institution with high-sounding phrases, nor do we mean to underrate the difficulty that each undertaking meets with during its incipient stage; but with pride we acknowledge the unanimous opinion of your committee that this school is highly worthy of the people of the great State of Missouri and in full coincidence with the intent which led to its creation. We may look forward with well-founded hopes that by the practical working of this school our dormant mineral wealth will meet the attention of the entire civilized world.

"The force of professors employed to teach the various branches of learning has been selected with more than usual care, and their ability and devotedness justify the highest expectations.

"Analytical chemistry, mineralogy, geology, metallurgy, mathematics (pure and applied), drawing (artistic and mechanical), civil and mine engineering, military tactics, etc., form the main branches of study in this institution.

"The apparatus, mathematical and philosophical instruments, are all of the latest and most approved kind, and their selection shows excellent tact; the laboratory is in good working order, and the library, consisting mainly of technical works, contains a large number of rare volumes.

"The morals of the students are vigilantly looked after, and the remarkable progress made by them is not only noteworthy, but also a source of gratification to your committee.

"The maps of surveys and mines, the drawings of furnaces and reduction works, prepared by the more advanced students, display art and mastery on the subject of their study and labor.

"A remarkable feature of the school consists in combining theory with practice."

NEBRASKA.

THE UNIVERSITY OF NEBRASKA.

[Statement by Prof. S. R. Thompson.]

The University of Nebraska exists by virtue of an enactment made by its first legislature soon after it became a State. This act, passed in 1869, provided for the organization of six colleges, as follows: 1. A college of literature, science, and the arts. 2. A college of agriculture. 3. A college of law. 4. A college of medicine. 5. A college of practical science, mechanics, and civil engineering. 6. A college of fine arts. Only the two first named could be opened without consent of the legislature.

The regents appointed under this act organized, elected a chancellor and faculty, and opened the college of literature, science, and art in September, 1871. During this year a professor of agriculture was chosen and arrangements made to open the agricultural college in the autumn of 1872. The plan was to have students in the agricultural college take their scientific and literary studies in the college of literature and science, so that only special and technical instruction need be provided in the other.

In 1874 an improved farm of 320 acres was procured and provided with a fair outfit of stock, teams, and tools. In 1875 a dormitory to accommodate about 20 students was erected, and henceforward all students in agriculture were to reside on the college farm. In 1877 the law was amended so as to consolidate the second and fifth colleges of the original scheme into one to be called "The Industrial College, embracing agriculture, practical science, civil engineering, and mechanic arts." In 1881 a professor of horticulture and a tutor in civil engineering were appointed; these, with the professor of agriculture, who is dean of the industrial college and superintendent of the farm, now constitute the teaching force of this department.

The classes in both colleges use the same building for recitation and general purposes. Students in the agricultural course reside on the farm and work an average time of two hours a day. Part of this labor is compensated and part not. All other students find boarding in or near the city as they prefer.

The course of study in the department of civil engineering is not materially different from that of other schools of like character. The studies of the first four years are substantially the same as those of the scientific course, most of the special and technical studies being assigned to the junior and senior years.

The course in agriculture is of the same length and difficulty as other courses in the university, viz: four years, with two of preparatory work, which may be taken in the university if desired. The following is a list of the studies which are taught to students in the agricultural college only: Practical agriculture, book-keeping, horticulture, laying out and improving farms, farm implements and machinery, entomology, anatomy and physiology of domestic animals, stock raising, meteorology, rural and domestic sanitation, vegetable physiology applied to farm crops, landscape gardening, bee keeping, agricultural chemistry, cryptogamic botany, sorghum manufacture, and the history and literature of agriculture.

As regards means of illustration of subjects peculiar to the industrial college there is now provided a farm of 320 acres, all improved, with good buildings, orchards, timber plantation, a nursery, the beginning of an arboretum, a vineyard, five breeds of cattle, two of hogs, thirty stands of bees, and an agricultural reference library of 300 volumes. There is also a fair outfit of meteorological instruments for making observations on the weather. The State volunteer weather-service has its central station at the college and publishes a monthly bulletin.

A considerable amount of experimenting has been undertaken, and it is intended to enlarge that work as fast as possible.

The mechanical department has not been organized, but the legislature which meets the coming winter will be asked to provide for it.

Since its opening in 1872, in all about 60 students have attended the industrial department. Four have graduated, three in agriculture and one in engineering. Of these one is now professor of horticulture in the institution, two engaged in farming, and one is in charge of an engineering party of the Union Pacific Railroad in Wyoming. At present there are enrolled 3 seniors, 5 juniors, 3 sophomores, 4 freshmen, and 7 in the preparatory. This number, though small, is all that can be accommodated on the farm with boarding and rooms until additional buildings are erected.

Besides the special facilities for study and instruction above enumerated, students in this department have access to the university library of 4,000 volumes, to the cabinet containing some 70,000 mineralogical and geological specimens, to the herbarium with 25,000 species of plants, and to the entomological collection of 5,000 specimens. Facilities for teaching analytical chemistry and physics are good, and the engineering department has a good level, transit, and other apparatus for field work.

The number of students enrolled in all departments of the university for the year 1881–'82, according to the catalogue soon to be issued, was 284, of whom 101 were in the colleges classes and 183 in the preparatory school.

The whole number of professors and instructors now employed in the university is sixteen. The entire support of the university has hitherto depended on appropriations by the State legislature. Within two years some of the endowment lands have been sold and more leased, but the income cannot be used till authority is granted by the legislature. The funds arising from sales of educational lands are made by the constitution trust funds and cannot be granted by the legislature for any but educational purposes. No part of the school or university lands can be sold for less than $7 an acre.

The appropriation made in 1880 to the university was $28,000 per annum for two years.

NEVADA.

STATE UNIVERSITY.

[Prepared from latest reports on file in this office.]

The State University of Nevada has received from the general government, by act of Congress, the usual grant of land for university purposes, 46,080 acres, and also 90,000 acres as endowment for college of agriculture and the mechanic arts.

The agricultural land from the grant has been sold, and the fund, $90,000, is set aside for the college, not yet organized. The interest, 8 per cent., is being added to the principal.

The university is located at Elko, in the eastern part of the State. A preparatory department has been organized.

In 1880, the faculty consisted only of the principal and one professor. The pupils numbered 48, 26 of whom were girls.

Tuition is free. Board and expenses at university dormitory, about $30 per month.

The value of buildings, grounds, and apparatus is stated at $25,000. Annual income by State appropriation, $6,000.

NEW HAMPSHIRE.

COLLEGE OF AGRICULTURE AND MECHANIC ARTS, DARTMOUTH COLLEGE.

[Prepared from latest reports and catalogues on file in this office.]

HISTORY AND OBJECTS.

The New Hampshire College of Agriculture and the Mechanic Arts is an institution associated with Dartmouth College, Hanover, and has for its object, "the liberal and practical education of the industrial classes in the several pursuits and professions of life." It was founded in 1866, by the State legislature, in accordance with the provisions of the agricultural college legislation.

ENDOWMENT AND FUNDS.

The original endowment of the institution ($80,000) was derived from the proceeds of the Congressional land grant, which, on being sold, was invested in New Hampshire State bonds, the interest (6 per cent.) on which constitutes the chief source of annual income.

The scrip received, representing 150,000 acres, was sold at 53½ cents per acre. The endowment has been increased to $100,000. Total annual income therefrom, $6,000; State appropriations (1880) for two years, $3,000; total, $9,000.

The tuition fees are stated at $30 per school year, but, as there are 34 free scholarships and an average annual attendance only slightly more than that number, the income from this source is small.

The total valuation of the college property, farm, buildings, apparatus, &c., is given at $100,000.

STUDENTS AND DEGREES.

According to catalogue of 1881–'82, the number of students was 41, of whom 10 were seniors, 13 middlers, and 18 juniors. No women are admitted.
In 1881 the degree of bachelor of science was conferred upon 14 young men.

THE FACULTY.

The staff of the College of Agriculture and the Mechanic Arts consists of the president, professors of chemistry, natural history, mathematics, and English language and literature, instructors in elocution and drawing, with lecturers (occasional) on the history of agriculture, farming as a profession, irrigation and drainage, veterinary science, stock-breeding, theoretical and practical farming, dairying, ensilage, fruit culture, and sheep husbandry. The lectures are arranged in a course which is given each winter and are open to all.

COURSE OF STUDY.

There is but a single course of study, covering a period of three years. The studies of the first or junior year include algebra, geometry, trigonometry, Grecian, Roman, mediæval and modern history, physiology, zoölogy, botany, drawing, and bookkeeping.
The studies of the second year are mechanics, surveying, and field work; physics and chemistry, with laboratory work; rhetoric and English literature; business law. The optional studies provided for the first term of the year are theory of equations, entomology, and history of civilization.
The regular studies of the senior year are physics, blowpipe analysis, astronomy, meteorology, geology, mineralogy, mechanics, English and American literature, constitutional law, and political economy. The optional studies include assaying, general geometry, analysis of farm products, and international law.
The assignment of agricultural lectures to the different years is: *Junior year*, lectures on history of agriculture, forestry, drainage, and irrigation; *middle year*, lectures on soils, plant growth, stock feeding, stock breeding, ensilage, and fruit culture; *senior year*, dairying, diseases of animals, sheep husbandry, and general methods of farm management.

APPLIANCES, FARM TOOLS, STOCK, AND POLICY.

The library belonging to this institution contains about two thousand volumes, chiefly valuable scientific works. The students also have access to the library, the cabinets, and the observatory of Dartmouth College upon the same terms as the students of the latter.
A State museum of general and applied science has been established. The specimens accruing from the State geological survey have been devoted to this institution by the legislature. Various contributions have also been made by persons interested in this object, and others are solicited.
The chemical laboratory is commodious, well lighted, and well ventilated, and is furnished with appliances for instruction in general, analytical, and agricultural chemistry.
The college is provided with instruments for practical surveying and with apparatus for illustration. The students also have the benefit of the valuable philosophical apparatus belonging to Dartmouth College, and attend the lectures on physics and other subjects.
A valuable tract of land of 360 acres in the immediate vicinity of Culver Hall (the principal college building) was secured, and for several years it has been under cultivation as a college farm. In convenience of access and in the character of the soil it is admirably suited for the purposes of agricultural experiment.
It is the intention to keep upon the farm a full line of such agricultural implements as promise to be of practical value, and their use has reduced the manual labor employed to a minimum.
The stock consists of 50 cattle, pure (milk producing) Durhams and Ayrshires, and their grades; 40 Cotswold sheep, 3 horses, &c.
The farm policy is to pass from the conservative rule of "small areas richly tilled" to larger areas; but these are well supplied with fertilizers, by means of rich foods given to the stock, such as meal, bran, cotton seed meal, &c. Chemicals are also used in the nutrition of crops.

CROPS, EXPERIMENTS, LABOR.

The crops for 1880 consisted of 6 acres of sugar beets; one-quarter of an acre of sorghum; 3½ acres of barley; 7 acres of oats and pease; 24 acres of corn; 8 acres of clover; 4½ acres are devoted to experiments, and the remainder of the tillage is in grass. Corn yields 60 to 70 bushels per acre; oats, 60 to 80 bushels; grass, 2 to 3 tons.

Experiments are always being carried on. They are so conducted as to be of direct use to the practical farmer as well as to the agricultural scientist.

Among the recent experiments have been those respecting root feeding, the comparative merits of different corn-meals and brans, early and late cut hay, the preparation and use of fertilizers and the value of foods.

Student labor is employed at 12½ cents per hour, instruction being at the same time afforded in the use of farm machinery and in the experiments and work of the farm.

The scientific and engineering departments of Dartmouth College, known respectively as the Chandler Scientific School and the Thayer School of Engineering, are accessible in a general way to the students of the Agricultural College, and afford facilities for the study of the mechanic art.

Mention of these schools has been made in this report among the institutions grouped as not endowed by the agricultural land grant.

NEW JERSEY.

RUTGERS SCIENTIFIC SCHOOL, NEW BRUNSWICK.

Rutgers College is one of the few institutions of its kind which were organized before the revolutionary war. Its life during that period and through many years of the present century was surrounded with peril. A few decades only have passed since its ultimate prosperity was assured. In the early part of the civil war the attention of its officers was called to the importance of introducing scientific instruction, and in 1863 a new department was organized for this purpose and named the Rutgers Scientific School. It was determined by the State legislature in 1864 that this school should receive the benefit of the national land grant of 1862. The act of the legislature directed the interest on the proceeds of the land scrip to be paid to the trustees of Rutgers College, "to be used wholly and exclusively for the maintenance of such courses of instruction as should carry out the intent of the act of Congress," *i. e.*, those relating to agriculture and the mechanic arts and adapted "to promote the liberal and practical education of the industrial classes in the several pursuits and professions in life." It required the trustees to furnish instruction free to a designated number of students from the several counties of the State; to erect additional and adequate buildings when they should become necessary, without charge to the State; and in like manner to provide a suitable tract of land, conveniently located, for an experimental farm. It also prescribed the appointment of visitors, made it their duty to visit the college at least twice a year and report to the legislature, and gave them general powers of supervision and control. Thus Rutgers Scientific School became the "State College for the benefit of Agriculture and the Mechanic Arts."

The relations which exist between the old college proper and the State college are stated in a recent account of Rutgers College, as follows:

"The two are served by the same professors; their classes, though distinct, unite in many subjects in the same recitations and are known by the same designations. The interests of the two departments, in short, are made to harmonize with and to aid each other, and the reciprocal benefits derived from this intercommunication and union can hardly be exaggerated. The young men in the literary department are allowed to pursue practical chemistry by making actual analyses in the laboratory along with the scientific students; and the latter in turn compete with the former in elocution and composition, in mental and moral philosophy, in political economy and constitutional law, and in biblical recitations. The scientific students are thus preserved from the narrowing process of a purely technical education. They do, indeed, get enough of technical training to prepare them, when a little experience has been added to their theoretical knowledge, for entrance at once upon civil engineering and analytical chemistry and into various mechanical and industrial spheres; but along with this they absorb the refining and liberalizing influences which spring from the enlarged culture alluded to above. * * * In addition to this the students of both departments join the same literary societies, and thus confer upon each other all the advantages resulting from the generous emulation and contact of minds engaged at many points on different subjects and having different objects of ambition."

The opportunities for education offered by the State college have been increased by the extension of two regular courses of study from three to four years, and by the provision of special agricultural and chemical, and post-graduate courses.

ENDOWMENT AND PROPERTY.

The direct endowment and income of the scientific school are derived from the proceeds of the national land grant. The land scrip received represented 210,000 acres and was sold for $116,000, 55 cents an acre. This amount is invested in New Jersey State bonds at 6 per cent. per annum, and thus produces $6,960 a year. This sum is devoted to the payment of salaries. The amount received from tuition fees is small, as nearly all students have the benefit of the State scholarships.

The trustees of the college had expended for the school previous to 1874 $30,000 for a farm, $50,000 for buildings, and $13,000 for equipment and miscellaneous expenses.

The financial report of the college to the Bureau of Education for the year ending March 31, 1881, presents the following items:

Value of grounds, buildings, and apparatus	$400,000
Amount of productive funds	303,129
Income from productive funds	20,215
Receipts from tuition fees	3,270

FACULTY.

The faculty of the Rutgers Scientific School is composed of the president (professor of moral philosophy) and professors of geology and agriculture, rhetoric, logic, and mental philosophy, mining and metallurgy, history, political economy and constitutional law, French and German, inorganic and organic chemistry, mechanics and physics, mathematics and engineering, mathematics and graphics, mathematics and astronomy, analytical and applied chemistry, and military science and tactics, and an assistant in analytical chemistry. The college has also professors of the Latin, Greek, and English languages and literatures.

COURSES OF STUDY.

There are four years' courses of study in (1) civil engineering and mechanics and (2) chemistry and agriculture, two years' courses in (1) chemistry and (2) agriculture, and post-graduate courses.

The studies of the two full courses are the same during the first year, and are designed to furnish either a suitable introduction to the pursuit of the several courses, or a course complete in itself, suitable for those who desire to fit themselves for land surveying. During the last three years the subjects of higher mathematics, mechanics, and engineering, in the engineering course, are replaced by analytical chemistry, practice in the laboratory, and agriculture in the other course. The studies of the sophomore year are alike in the two courses, except the special professional branches. The common studies are chemistry, history, mental philosophy, descriptive geometry, shades and shadows, perspective, and the graphical solution of problems in these subjects and in solid geometry and the intersection of surfaces and solids. The special studies of the course in chemistry and agriculture for this year are qualitative and blowpipe analyses and laboratory practice; of the engineering course, railroad curves, analytical geometry, and essays in literary criticism.

The junior year in chemistry and agriculture embraces the following: German; analytical chemistry, by text book; laboratory practice and lectures; agriculture: lectures at the farm, vegetable physiology; natural philosophy; history of civilization; political economy; international law; constitutional history of United States; drawing, lettering, tinting, with ink shading, flat and graded; constructions; mineralogy.

The senior embraces organic, applied, and other departments of chemistry and chemical work; geology; principles of agriculture: its methods and products, animal physiology: care and management of domestic animals; laboratory practice and theory; moral philosophy; drawing; thesis.

The junior year in civil engineering and mechanics includes the following studies: German; natural philosophy; history of civilization; constitutional history of the United States; political economy and international law; differential and integral calculus; astronomy; drawing, lettering, tinting, with ink shading, flat and graded; construction, &c.

The senior year embraces mechanics; engineering; bridge building; railway practice; geodesy; geology; organic chemistry and chemical physics; indeterminate analysis; moral philosophy; drawing: mechanical, architectural, and engineering; thesis.

SPECIAL COURSES.

The special course in chemistry extends over two years. The first year is devoted to inorganic chemistry; qualitative, quantitative, and blowpipe analyses; chemical physics; stoichiometry; French; a thesis and a journal of travel and observation.

The work of the second year includes organic and applied chemistry; chemical physics; quantitative analysis; assaying; mineralogy and geology; German, and thesis.

The special course in agriculture requires the following studies:

During the first year, algebra; geometrical problems; inorganic chemistry; physiology and zoölogy; geometry; coloring and topographical drawing; analytical chemistry; mineralogy; bookkeeping; trigonometry; mapping; analytical chemistry; botany; farm accounts.

During the second year, surveying; projections; natural philosophy; study of domestic animals; systematic agriculture; navigation and nautical astronomy; architectural drawing; physics; geology; how crops grow; leveling and roadmaking; machine drawing; meteorology; botany; how crops feed. Composition and declamation throughout the whole course.

The hours of lectures or recitations are four each day, besides work in the chemical laboratory.

Post-graduate courses may be arranged in chemistry; geology and natural history; geology, metallurgy and engineering; agriculture; mathematics (geodesy, pure mathematics, astronomy, theoretical and applied, and the use of physical apparatus); modern languages; and political and social science. Students completing a full course of two years, in any two of these lines of study, are entitled to the degree of doctor of philosophy. Those completing either of the four years' courses receive the degree of bachelor of science. The practice of giving the degree of master of science as a matter of course to all graduates of three years' standing has been discontinued.

Partial students may enter at any time and elect, under the advice and direction of the faculty, such studies as they are qualified to pursue with classes already formed. Such students are required to have their time fully occupied and receive certificates at the close of their study showing the amount and kind of work performed.

STUDENTS.

The number of students in attendance at Rutgers College in 1881 was 143. Of these 6 were post-graduates, 10 special students, 87 members of the classical department, and 40 in the scientific department, 10 being seniors, 8 juniors, 4 sophomores, and 18 freshmen. Nearly all the counties of the State are represented in this scientific school. Forty students are admitted free of expense for tuition on the recommendation of the superintendent of schools, each county having the right to nominate a number of candidates proportional to its representation in the legislature.

In filling these State scholarships the trustees have, from the first, interpreted the law liberally, and adopted the policy of allowing any vacant scholarship to be filled temporarily by applicants from another county, provided the superintendent of the county entitled to the scholarship gives his consent. Tuition is habitually remitted to students who are unable to pay that in addition to the other expenses of procuring an education.

GRADUATES.

The occupations of 158 persons who have been educated in the scientific school are known to be as follows: Engineering, 47; business, 32; manufacturing, 20; farming, 19; teaching, 13; medicine, 12; law, 10; architecture, 5.

APPLIANCES AND COLLECTIONS.

The students in the State college have the freest access to apparatus, appliances, library, and all other aids and agencies at the disposal of Rutgers College. These include a large variety of apparatus to illustrate the domain of physics, and ample laboratory and other appliances for the courses in chemistry; a large and well-lighted drawing room; a fine observatory, the gift of Daniel S. Schanck, a two-story building, with revolving dome, containing a large equatorial telescope, a fine meridian circle, sidereal clock, and other appliances; a museum, located in Geological Hall, and containing collections in mineralogy, metallurgy, paleontology, conchology, and geology.

There are special cabinets of minerals, iron ores, and products, birds, fossils, and existing animals.

The general library, containing 10,500 volumes and 4,500 pamphlets, is open to students. There are also special collections numbering 4,300 volumes.

THE COLLEGE FARM.

The trustees of Rutgers purchased for the State College of Agriculture and Mechanic Arts 97 acres of land for a college farm, at an original cost for the land of $16,712.60. Up to

1873 the amount expended on this for improvements and expenses was $43,846.06. Up to the same date $23,386.61 were received from sales.

The land was in a wet and unprofitable condition. It has been thoroughly drained with seven miles of under-drains. The former swamps are now the most productive fields. The plans of working have been in the highest degree experimental and the results have been in the best sense of value to the agriculturist.

The farm is well equipped with buildings, stock, and tools, and the work done in the way of technics—theoretical and practical—is of sterling character.

The State legislature established an agricultural experiment station in 1880 and placed it mainly under the control of the board of visitors of the State College. "It has only just begun its work; but it is receiving the hearty coöperation and support of the farmers of the State, and is sending out to them bulletins containing the results of analyses and investigations on fertilizers, cattle foods, fodders, milk, &c., thus stimulating them to study their own calling and to find profit in it. The farm of the Agricultural College affords the opportunity for making proper experiments, and the rooms of the Scientific School and of Rutgers College furnish the places for the necessary chemical laboratories and experiments." So that the experiment station may be fairly considered a part of the Scientific School, and the 3,500 farmers who regularly receive its investigations and results are its students. The Scientific School teaches the "branches of learning related to agriculture and the mechanic arts," and the experiment station applies that learning to the practical operations of the farm.

NEW YORK.

THE CORNELL UNIVERSITY, NEW YORK STATE COLLEGE OF AGRICULTURE AND THE MECHANIC ARTS.

[Compiled from various official sources.]

HISTORY AND OBJECTS.

The establishment of the Cornell University is due to the combined bounty of the general government and of Ezra Cornell.

Under the act of July 2, 1862, the State of New York received for the benefit of instruction in agriculture and the mechanic arts, scrip representing about 990,000 acres of land. Determining to concentrate the fund, it was first offered to the People's College on certain conditions. Failure having been made in the observance of these conditions, in 1865 the State transferred the scrip to the Cornell University on granting the institution a charter, provided the university should admit one student from each assembly district without the payment of tuition and that Mr. Cornell should give half a million dollars as an endowment fund. This he did, adding two hundred acres of valuable farming lands contiguous to Ithaca then, and making the university from its organization in 1868 the object of most generous benefactions and watchful solicitude as long as he lived. Besides gifts of cabinets, libraries, &c., amounting to several hundred thousand dollars, Mr. Cornell bought from the State the entire land scrip to which the university was entitled at the price for which a single acre could be obtained, viz, 60 cents, agreeing to locate the scrip and sell the land, and, after deducting expenses, turn over the balance to the university. Under this arrangement the land was carefully selected and a considerable portion of it has been sold at $5 an acre.

"I would found an institution" (said Mr. Cornell) "where any person may find instruction in any study," and the charter of the university is conceived in the same broad spirit. Providing that a majority of the governing body shall never be of any one religious denomination or of no religious denomination, the charter granted by the State left the trustees at liberty to provide any instruction they might see fit in addition to that contemplated by the act of Congress establishing the colleges of agriculture and the mechanic arts. Women are admitted to all courses on the same terms as men, except that they must be one year older. They are not required to drill or to study military tactics.

ENDOWMENT.

The following information has been taken from the report of the treasurer of the university for the year ending June 1, 1881:

PRODUCTIVE FUNDS.

Cornell endowment fund	$628,596 61
Land scrip fund	473,412 87
Sage College endowment	100,000 00
Dean Sage sermon fund	30,000 00
Sibley endowment	30,000 00
Woodford medal fund*	1,500 00
Horace K. White prize fund*	500 00
Total amount of productive funds	1,264,009 48

OTHER PROPERTY.

Real estate, exclusive of western lands	$689,465 48
Equipment of departments of university	253,509 42
	942,974 90

WESTERN LANDS.

Number of acres of Congressional land grant remaining unsold June 1, 1881:

Pine land	271,952.23
Farm land	37,863.53
Land from which pine timber has been sold	27,500.00
	337,315.76

During the year ending June 1, 1881, land and timber were sold to the amount of $153,278, the average price of land being nearly $7 an acre.

The income from the various funds reached $105,435.26; from tuition it was $14,750, including rents, &c.; the total income was $128,182.95. The disbursements, including $84,609.94 for salaries, amounted to $118,987.03.

FACULTY.

The number and classification of professors and instructors given in the Register, printed in 1882, were as follows: Whole number in the faculty, 48:28 resident professors, 16 assistant professors, and 4 non-resident professors. In addition to 5 instructors and lecturers not included above, there were also various university officers employed as curators, assistant librarians, &c. There were 7 teachers employed in agriculture and its related sciences, 2 in architecture, 3 in chemistry, 3 in ancient languages and 7 in modern, 5 in history and political science, 4 in mathematics, 3 in civil engineering, 6 in mechanics and physics, 1 in philosophy and 1 in military science, 1 in physiology, and 2 in palæontology and geology.

STUDENTS.

The number of students present in 1882 was 384, 22 of them being graduate students. The attendance is considerably less than it was during the earlier years of the university—a result in part, probably, of the gradual but material elevation of the standard of admission that has been effected, and in part of the increase in the rate of tuition, which is now $75 a year.

Applicants for admission to the university (who must be at least 16 if boys and 17 if girls) are examined in English grammar; political and physical geography; physiology; arithmetic; algebra, through quadratic equations and including radicals and the theory of exponents; and plane geometry.

Holders of certificates or diplomas issued by the regents of the university or the State superintendent, or of diplomas of the State normal schools or academies and high schools whose requirements for graduation have been approved by the faculty, may waive the examination except as to algebra.

For admission to the various courses of science, literature, arts, &c., further examinations are required in French, German, Latin, Greek, mathematics, &c.

---

*Funds remaining in the hands of donors, interest regularly paid.

INDUSTRIAL EDUCATION IN THE UNITED STATES.

Energetic young men desirous of defraying the expenses of their education by means of manual labor are given work in the printing office, on the farm, and about the buildings, for which they are paid at current rates; but after a somewhat extended trial of the system, the university authorities have reached the conclusion that the physical and mental stamina of few young men is such that they can safely pursue a course of study to advantage while providing entirely for their own support, and they therefore encourage applicants to come not wholly unprovided for.

SCHOLARSHIPS.

In accordance with the provisions of the act of incorporation 1 free student from each of the 128 assembly districts is admitted. The certificate of scholarship is granted after a successful competitive examination, but the usual entrance examination is not waived in the case of successful competitors.

GRADUATES.

The following table shows the number of graduates and the degrees taken for each year since the organization of the university in 1869 to 1881 inclusive:

Degrees.	1869.	1870.	1871.	1872.	1873.	1874.	1875.	1876.	1877.	1878.	1879.	1880.	1881.	
A. B	8	8	7	4	17	4	8	8	5	9	7	12	18	115
A. M					1			4	2	1				8
Agr. B					2	2	1	1	2	1		3	8	20
Arch. B					1	6	4	6	7	2	4	2		32
B. C. E			7	16	18	15	3	12	15	14	10	7	9	131
B. M. E					3	1	5	6	7	12	5	3	3	45
B. S		8	16	38	45	30	21	26	24	24	33	40	35	340
B. V. M				1										1
B. V. S			1								1			2
C. E		1			1	4		2	2	2	2		2	16
Lit. B					3	4		1	2	3	7	5	5	30
M. S				1		3	3	4	3		1		1	16
Ph. B			7	9	9	6	3	5	3	8	2	4	4	60
Ph. D					1	1	1			1		1		5
	8	24	40	70	98	73	55	73	78	70	71	76	85	821

No information as to advanced degrees conferred in 1880 has been available.

No record is kept of the occupations of those who have graduated, but the Ten-Year Book of the Cornell University, first published in 1878, is expected to give all needful information about graduates.

SPECIAL COURSES OF STUDY—AGRICULTURE.

I. APPLIED AGRICULTURE.

In applied agriculture five hours weekly during the fourth year are devoted to technical instruction in all its leading and most of its minor branches. The student is also required to spend three hours a day, two days in each week, in field practice, and in the handling and feeding of domestic animals.

The instruction by lectures begins with the fourth year and continues through three terms.

FIRST TERM.—Wheat: Culture, varieties, preparation of the soil, seeding, injurious insects, harvesting, threshing, marketing. Swine: The history of breeds, feeding, general management, piggeries. Farm buildings: Location, plans, material, construction, repairs and preservation, contracts, liabilities of contractors. Fields: Shape and size. Fences and gates: Construction, number, kind, repairs, durability of woods used. Farm and public roads, bridges, and culverts: Location, construction, repairs. Farms: Selection and purchase with regard to remoteness or nearness to markets, agricultural capabilities, roads, improvements, schools, and society. Titles, deeds, judgments, and mortgages. Farm-yard manures: Composition, manufacture, preservation, application. Commercial fertilizers: Composition, application, utility.

SECOND TERM.—Farm accounts. Principles of stock breeding: Law of similarity, of variation as caused by food, habit, and climate, atavism, relative influence of male and female, prepotency, sex, in-and-in breeding, crossing and out-crossing, grading up or breeding in hue. Races and breeds: Pedigrees, leading breeds of neat animals treated as to history, markings, characteristics, and adaptation to uses, soil, climate, and locality. Breeding, feeding, and management of cattle. Butter, cheese, and milk dairies, and beef production. Sheep husbandry treated in detail same as cattle.

THIRD TERM.—The horse: Breeds and breeding, education, care, driving, stables. Farm drainage: Mapping of drains, material, construction, utility. Plows and plowing. Farm implements and machinery: Use, care, and repairs. Corn, oat, barley, and flax culture. Grasses and forage plants. Weeds and their eradication. Business customs, rights, and privileges. Notes, contracts, and obligations. Employment and direction of laborers.

II.—AGRICULTURAL CHEMISTRY.

The study of agricultural chemistry comprises analytical practice in the laboratory, and 75 lectures, embracing the following subjects:

The general principles of chemical science, accompanied by introductory laboratory practice; the chemistry of the elements and their compounds that constitute soils, plants, and animals; agricultural chemical investigators and their methods and means of working, and the literature of agricultural chemistry; the chemistry of vegetable life, and the production of vegetable substance in general; the physical and chemical properties and agricultural resources of the soil; tillage, drainage, &c., and amendments and manures; the composition of crops and other materials used for fodder; animal chemistry and nutrition; fermentation and putrefaction; milk and its manufactured products and residues; food, water, and air in their relations to human and animal life; the chemical analysis of fodder and food; farm crops and their manufactured products and residues.

The analysis of agricultural materials and products is treated in a course of chemical practice.

III.—ECONOMIC ENTOMOLOGY.

The course of twenty lectures presents the characteristics of the orders of insects, the more important families, and the species which are injurious, beneficial, or otherwise especially interesting. The lectures are illustrated by specimens of the stages and works of insects, and due prominence is given to the practical treatment of forms having an economic importance.

In the laboratory and field practice, students are instructed in all kinds of practical entomological work, involving drawings and notes of observations, with methods of collecting, breeding, destroying, preserving, arranging, &c.

IV.—HORTICULTURE.

The instruction comprises two courses of lectures during the first term, supplemented by experimental or practical work.

In the *third year* there is a course of lectures on arboriculture and landscape gardening; in the *fourth*, one on the principles of horticulture.

Additional time is given to experimental work in the garden or conservatories. The instruction in botany, both in the laboratory and in the several courses of lectures, is intended to afford a scientific basis for the special instruction given in horticulture.

V.—VETERINARY SCIENCE.

The regular course for students in agriculture, natural history, &c., embraces five lectures a week during an entire academic year; laboratory work on the bones, plastic models, pathological preparations, and parasites of domestic animals; clinical instruction on cases occurring in practice.

FIRST TERM.—Lectures on the anatomy and physiology of the animals of the farm. Attention is given to the principles of hygiene as affected by genus, breed, climate, soil, exposure, buildings, ventilation, drainage, food, and water; to the varying anatomical peculiarities which imply special aptitude for particular uses; to the data for determining age; to the principles of breeding, of shoeing, &c.

SECOND TERM.—Lectures on general comparative pathology; on specific fevers and other contagious diseases; on the parasites and parasitic diseases of domestic animals; and on constitutional diseases. An important feature in this course is the subject of veterinary sanitary science and police, embracing as it does the prevention of animal plagues by legislative and individual action, the improvement of unhealthy localities, and the destruction of animal poisons and parasites which are intercommunicable between man and the domestic animals.

THIRD TERM.—Lectures on the local diseases of the various systems of organs in the different animals and on veterinary surgery.

Opportunities are afforded to students who desire it to pursue the study of veterinary medicine and surgery further than is provided for in the regular courses of study.

INDUSTRIAL EDUCATION IN THE UNITED STATES. 187

THE COURSES IN AGRICULTURE.

I.—A FOUR YEARS' COURSE.

(Leading to the degree of bachelor of agriculture.)

First year.

FIRST TERM.—French *or* German, 5; rhetoric, 2; geometry and conic sections, 5; free-hand drawing, 3; hygiene, 6 lectures.

SECOND TERM.—French *or* German, 5; rhetoric, 2; algebra, 5; free-hand drawing, 3.

THIRD TERM.—French *or* German, 5; rhetoric, 2; trigonometry, 5; general chemistry and laboratory work, lectures, 3.

Second year.

FIRST TERM.—French *or* German, 3; agricultural chemistry, 5; zoölogy, lectures and laboratory work (vertebrates), 3; anatomy, laboratory work, 2. Elective, 3.

SECOND TERM.—French *or* German, 3; agricultural chemistry, lectures, 4; chemistry, qualitative analysis, 5; anatomy, laboratory work, 2, Elective, 2.

THIRD TERM.—French *or* German, 3; land surveying, 4; botany, lectures, 3, field work, 2; entomology, lectures, 2, laboratory work, 2.

Third year.

FIRST TERM.—Experimental mechanics and heat, 3; compositæ and gramineæ, 2; arboriculture and landscape gardening, 2; entomology, 3; veterinary anatomy and physiology, 5.

SECOND TERM.—Electricity and magnetism, 3; chemistry, quantitative analysis, 4; vegetable physiology, 3; vegetable histology, 2; veterinary pathology, sanitary science and parasites, 5.

THIRD TERM.—Acoustics and optics, 3; chemistry, quantitative analysis, 9; veterinary medicine and surgery, 5.

Fourth year.

FIRST TERM.—Agriculture, lectures, 5; field-work, 3; botany (fungi), 4; horticulture, lectures, 2; geology, 3.

SECOND TERM.—Agriculture, lectures, 5; field-work, 2; systematic and applied botany, 3. Elective, 5.

THIRD TERM.—Agriculture, lectures, 3, field-work, 3; building materials and construction, 2; American law, 5.

II.—A THREE YEARS' COURSE.

(Not leading to a degree.)

First year.

FIRST TERM.—Geometry and conic sections, 5; free-hand drawing, 3; agricultural, chemistry, lectures, 5, laboratory work, 3.

SECOND TERM.—Algebra, 5; agricultural chemistry, lectures, 4, laboratory work, 6.

THIRD TERM.—Trigonometry, 5; botany, lectures, 3, field-work, 2; entomology, lectures, 2, laboratory work, 2.

Second year.

FIRST TERM.—Experimental mechanics and heat, 3; compositæ and gramineæ, 2; arboriculture and landscape gardening, 2; geology, 3; veterinary anatomy and physiology, 5.

SECOND TERM.—Electricity and magnetism, 3; chemistry, laboratory work, 4; vegetable physiology, 3; vegetable histology, 2; veterinary pathology, sanitary science, and parasites, 5.

THIRD TERM.—Acoustics and optics, 3; land surveying, 4; chemistry, laboratory work, 4; veterinary medicine and surgery, 5.

Third year.

The same as the fourth year of the four years' course.

MECHANIC ARTS.

Each student in this department is required to devote two hours a day to work in the shop; but such students as have, before entering, acquired sufficient practical knowledge are admitted to advanced standing. Attendance is required upon ten lectures or recitations a week, or their equivalent, in addition to two hours daily drawing, two hours daily shop-work, and the passing of the examinations at the close of each term.

THE COURSE IN MECHANIC ARTS.

(Leading to the degree of bachelor of mechanical engineering.)

First year.

FIRST TERM.—German, 5; geometry and conic sections, 5; freehand drawing, 3; shop work, 3.
SECOND TERM.—German, 5; algebra, 5; freehand drawing, 3; shop work, 3.
THIRD TERM.—German, 5; trigonometry, 5; geometrical drawing, 3; shop work, 3.

Second year.

FIRST TERM.—German, 3; rhetoric, 2; analytical geometry, 5; experimental mechanics and heat, 3; shop work, 3.
SECOND TERM.—German, 3; rhetoric, 2; calculus, 5; electricity and magnetism, 3; shop work, 3.
THIRD TERM.—Calculus, 5; descriptive geometry, text and drawing, 4; mechanical drawing, 2; building materials, 3; shop work, 3.

Third year.

FIRST TERM.—Calculus and analytical geometry, 5; descriptive geometry, text and drawing, 6; mechanism, 3; shop work, 3.
SECOND TERM.—Mechanics of engineering, 5; mechanism, 3; physics, laboratory work, 8; chemistry, 3; shop work, 3.
THIRD TERM.—Mechanics of engineering, 5; mechanical drawing, with shades, tinting, and perspective, 3; physics, laboratory work, 3; chemistry, 3; shop work, 3.

Fourth year.

FIRST TERM.—Mechanics of engineering, 5; mechanical and working drawings, 3; physics, laboratory work, 3; steam engine, 3; shop work, 3.
SECOND TERM.—Mechanical drawing, 4; steam engine, 3; metallurgy, 2; experimental work with indicators, governors, pumps, and injectors, 3; shop work, 3.
THIRD TERM.—Graphical statics, 3; field practice and the use of instruments, 3; industrial chemistry, 3; technical reading and preparation of thesis, 3; shop work, 3.

Graduate course.

FIRST TERM.—Machines for regulating, counting, &c., 3; mechanical *or* physical experiments, *or* chemistry, 3; riparian laws, contracts, Patent-Office laws, &c., 2. Elective, 7.
SECOND TERM.—Machines for change of form, 3; mechanical *or* physical experiments, *or* chemistry, 3; technical reading, 2. Elective, 7.
THIRD TERM.—Locomotive machines, hoists, cranes, &c., 3; mechanical *or* physical experiments, *or* chemistry, 3; shop systems and accounts, 2. Elective, 7.
The elective studies are hydraulics, assaying, mineralogy and blowpipe analysis, chemical laboratory practice, physics (acoustics and optics), motors other than steam, architecture, civil engineering, shop work, mathematics, botany, French, rhetoric, history, literature.

MILITARY SCIENCE.

The practical military exercises include:
Infantry tactics.—To comprise the schools of the soldier, company, and battalion; with skirmishing, the forms of parade, and the duties of guards.
Artillery practice.—To comprise at least the school of the piece and section for the field guns, with such further artillery instruction as may be found practicable.
Special exercises.—To comprise recitations at such times as may be prescribed.
The advanced course of instruction in military science is optional, and is open to all

undergraduates and to such special students as have sufficient scientific and practical preparation.

It requires an attendance upon a class exercise or lecture of one hour on three days of the week during one year. The subjects are:

Military engineering.—To comprise the principles of military topography; the effect of projectiles; the principles of fortification, with their application to field works; military mining; the attack and defense of works; and the construction of military roads and bridges.

The art of war.—To comprise the history and principles of special tactics; the organization of armies, with some account of the administrative arrangements of our own army; strategy; grand tactics; and accessory operations of war.

Military law.—To comprise the origin, principles, and limitations of military law; the nature and force of the articles of war and the general regulations for the army; a summary of the rules of evidence; the constitution, jurisdiction, and procedure of courts-martial, courts of inquiry, military commissions, and military boards.

ARCHITECTURE.

The course in architecture is so arranged as to give the student instruction in all subjects which he should understand in order to enter upon the practice of the art.

The instruction is given by means of lectures and practical exercises. Its object is not merely to develop the artistic powers of the student, but to lay that foundation of knowledge without which there can be no true art. Drawing is taught during the first two years, and afterwards thoroughly used and applied in mechanics, stereotomy, and designing.

Architectural mechanics occupies a part of each term for one year. The lectures are each supplemented by at least two hours of work on problems. In developing the subjects and in solving problems analytical methods are used, but for practical use special attention is paid to the application of graphical statics.

The study of the history of architecture and the development of the various styles runs through five terms. The lectures are illustrated by photographs, engravings, drawings, casts, and models.

Proper attention is paid to acoustics, ventilation, heating, decoration, contracts, and specifications. The whole ground of education in architecture, practical, scientific, historical, and æsthetic, is covered as completely as is practicable in a four years' course.

THE COURSE IN ARCHITECTURE.

(Leading to the degree of bachelor of architecture.)

First year.

FIRST TERM.—French or German, 5; rhetoric, 2; geometry and conic sections, 5; freehand drawing, 3; linear drawing, 1; hygiene, six lectures.

SECOND TERM.—French or German, 5; rhetoric, 2; algebra, 5; freehand drawing, 3; projection and tinting, 1.

THIRD TERM.—French or German, 5; trigonometry, 5; descriptive geometry, text and drawing, 4; botany, 3.

Second year.

FIRST TERM.—French or German, 3; composition and elocution, 1; analytical geometry, 5; descriptive geometry, text and drawing, 6; experimental mechanics and heat, 3.

SECOND TERM.—French or German, 3; composition and elocution, 1; calculus, 5; drawing, 3; electricity and magnetism, 3; chemistry, lectures, 3.

THIRD TERM.—French or German, 3; composition and elocution, 1; drawing, 3; acoustics and optics, 3; chemistry, lectures, 3; building materials and construction, 3.

Third year.

FIRST TERM.—Mechanics, strength of materials, 3; shades, shadows, and perspective, 3; drawing, 3; Egyptian, Greek, and Roman architecture, 3; designing, 4.

SECOND TERM.—Mechanics, trusses, 3; Byzantine and Romanesque architecture, 5; designing, 3; construction, 2; lithology and determinative mineralogy, 2.

THIRD TERM.—Mechanics, arches, 3; freehand drawing, 3; Gothic architecture, 5; designing, 3; construction 2.

Fourth year.

FIRST TERM.—Renaissance architecture, 3; decoration, 3; designing, 6; stereotomy, 3.

SECOND TERM.—Modern architecture, 3; designing, 4; stereotomy, applied to stone-cutting, 5; economic geology, 3.

THIRD TERM.—Decoration, acoustics, ventilation, warming, professional practice, measuring, contracts, specifications, &c., 5; designing, 7.

CIVIL ENGINEERING.

The instruction is given by means of lectures and recitations, with drawing and field and laboratory practice. The field work embraces the usual operations and the more recent methods of land, railroad, and subterranean surveying, together with hydrography and geodetic practice; and since 1874 the department of civil engineering has been engaged in the surveys of the hydrographic basin of Central New York as a contribution to the geodetic surveys of the United States Government.

Laboratory practice is provided in chemistry, mineralogy, metallurgy, geology, physics, and civil engineering.

The students of this department receive instruction in an extended course of mechanics as applied to engineering, and their professional preparation comprises the following subjects: The location and construction of railroads, canals, and water works; the construction of foundations in water and on land and of superstructures and tunnels; the surveys, improvements, and defenses of coasts, harbors, rivers, and lakes; the determination of astronomical coördinates; the application of mechanics, graphical statics, and descriptive geometry to the constructions of the various kinds of right and oblique arch bridges, roofs, trusses, and suspension bridges; the design, construction, and application of wind and hydraulic motors; air, electric, and heat engines, and pneumatic works; the drainage of towns and the reclaiming of lands; the preparation of plans and specifications, and the proper selection and tests of the materials used in constructions. As a part of their instruction, students have frequent practice in the preparation of papers on subjects of professional importance.

An elementary course of lectures is given in engineering and mining economy, finance, and jurisprudence.

To meet the growing demand for special training, a five years' course has been arranged allowing considerable option and diversity of studies to students wishing to pursue special lines of study in bridge architecture, or in railroad, mining, topographical, sanitary, geographical, electrical, or industrial engineering. This course also offers lines of continuous study of a historical, literary, or scientific character, which may alternate with the prescribed studies, and with architecture, general science, and technology.

THE COURSES IN CIVIL ENGINEERING.

I.—A FOUR YEARS' COURSE.

(Leading to the degree of bachelor of civil engineering.)

First year.

FIRST TERM.—French *or* German, 5; rhetoric, 2; geometry and conic sections, 5; freehand drawing, 3; hygiene, 6 lectures.
SECOND TERM.—French *or* German, 5; rhetoric, 2; algebra, 5; freehand drawing, 3; linear drawing, 2.
THIRD TERM.—French *or* German, 5; trigonometry, 5; descriptive geometry, text and drawing, 4; botany, 3.

Second year.

FIRST TERM.—French *or* German, 3; analytical geometry, 5; descriptive geometry, text and drawing, 6; experimental mechanics and heat, 3.
SECOND TERM.—French *or* German, 3; calculus, 5; pen topography, 2; tinting and shading, 2; electricity and magnetism, 3; chemistry, 2.
THIRD TERM.—Calculus, 5; land surveying, 4; acoustics and optics, 3; chemistry, 3; technical essays, 1.

Third year.

FIRST TERM.—Calculus, 5; shades, shadows, and perspective, 3; topographical mapping and sketching, 2; lettering, 1; cinematics, *or* physics, laboratory work, 3; technical essays, 1.
SECOND TERM.—Mechanics of engineering, 5; detail drawing and graining, 2; physics, laboratory work, 3; mineralogy *or* metallurgy, 2; geology, 3.
THIRD TERM.—Mechanics of engineering, 5; railroad surveying, 5; colored topography, 3; lettering, 2.

Fourth year.

FIRST TERM.—Mechanics of engineering, 5; spherical astronomy, 5; practical astronomy, night observations, 2; Egyptian, Greek, and Roman architecture, *or* physics, laboratory work, 3; stereotomy and original problems, 3; civil engineering, 2; technical essays, 1.
SECOND TERM.—Hydraulics, 5; higher geodesy, 5; mineralogy *or* metallurgy, 2; stonecutting and original problems and practice, 5.
THIRD TERM.—Hydraulic motors, 2; civil engineering, 3; engineering economy, 2; bridge stresses, 5; hydrographic surveying, chart-making, and geodesy, field work, 3; preparation of thesis.
Students in the courses in civil engineering are required to write memoirs upon professional subjects of their own selection, before the close of the spring term, and these memoirs are presented on the first Friday of the following term. The memoir of the last two years must contain original investigations.

II.—A FIVE YEARS' COURSE.

(Leading to the degree of civil engineer.)

The first four years are the same as in the four years' course. The choice of electives in the fifth year is subject to the approval of the dean of the department.
Students in the fifth year pay no tuition fees and have all the privileges of resident graduates.

Fifth year.

FIRST TERM.—Riparian rights and law of contracts, 3; bridge construction and details, 3; projects, designs, and specifications, 3.
Elective, 9: Greek history, 2; modern history, 3; psychology, 2; American history, 2 or 3; physiology and zoölogy, 5; languages, 2; technical reading, 2; renaissance architecture, 3; chemistry, laboratory work, 3; engineering, laboratory work, 3; physics, laboratory work, 3; rock drills and air compressors, 3; the steam engine, 3; mining projects, 3; geology, 3; industrial chemistry, 3; mathematics, 3.
SECOND TERM.—River and harbor improvements, 3; advanced astronomy and geodesy, 3; technical reading, 2; projects, designs, and specifications, 2.
Elective, 8: Roman history, 2; American history, 2 or 3; political economy, 2; languages, 2; pure or applied mathematics, 5; zoölogy, 3; metallurgy *or* mineralogy, 3; chemistry, laboratory work, 3; engineering, laboratory work, 3; physics, laboratory work, 3; Romanesque architecture, 3; the steam engine, 3; mining projects, 2; industrial chemistry, 3; geology, 3.
THIRD TERM.—Sanitary engineering, 3; locomotive machines, etc., 3; projects, designs, and specifications, 2.
Elective, 6: Roman history, 2; modern history, 3; American history, 2 or 3; languages, 3; pure or applied mathematics, 4; historical or technical reading, 3; geology, 3; chemistry, laboratory work, 3; engineering, laboratory work, 3; physics, laboratory work, 3; Gothic architecture, 3; pumps and small machinery, 2; industrial chemistry, 3; mining projects, 4; arch ribs, 3; geodesy, field work.

MINING ENGINEERING.

Although no department of mining engineering has yet been formally established, all the main instruction required by a mining engineer is now given, as follows: The professor of civil engineering and his associates pay special attention to the needs of those intending to connect themselves with the mining industries, giving lectures on tunneling and on the theory and practice of such constructions as are common to the professions of the civil and mining engineer. The professor of mechanical engineering and his associates pursue a like course, giving instruction in mining machinery. The professors of general chemistry and mineralogy, of analytical chemistry, and of industrial chemistry give instruction in metallurgy, assaying, chemical analysis, and cognate subjects. The professors of geology and palæontology give instruction in the theory and classification of ores and in those branches relating to chemical geology.
It is intended, at an early day, to supplement the existing force by the appointment of such additional professors and lecturers as are necessary to the establishment of a mining school for the most advanced work, both as regards theory and practice. As it is, the university, by its existing provision in the departments named above, is enabled to give such instruction that a student graduating in them can, in a very short time, make him-

self acquainted with the practical processes; and, in all probability, by the time any student now entering the existing departments shall be sufficiently advanced to need instruction in the more elaborate special processes connected with mining, provision will have been fully made to give it.

FREEHAND DRAWING.

Instruction in freehand drawing is given by means of lectures and general exercises from the black-board, from flat copies, and from models. The work embraces a thorough training of the hand and eye in outline drawing, elementary perspective, model and object drawing, drawing from casts, and sketching from nature.

The effort is to render the student familiar with the fundamental principles underlying this art, and to enable him to represent any object he may desire correctly and rapidly. The course is largely industrial, and the exercises are arranged, as far as possible, with special reference to the drawing required in the work of the different departments.

All students in the departments of agriculture, architecture, civil engineering, mechanic arts, mathematics, and natural history devote two hours a day to freehand drawing during the first two terms of the first year; and students in architecture, in addition, two hours a day during one term of the second and one term of the third year. Students in the other courses may take drawing as an elective study.

MATHEMATICS AND ASTRONOMY.

Undergraduates in all the regular courses except natural history have the mathematics of the first year, namely, geometry, algebra, and trigonometry; those in mechanic arts, architecture, and civil engineering have two or four terms of analytical geometry and calculus; those in most of the general scientific courses have analytical geometry and astronomy; and all students have the privilege of electing these and the higher branches. The full course is designed for those intending to teach mathematics in academies and colleges, or to use it as an instrument of investigation. Most of the studies are either directly mathematical or closely connected with mathematics. Substitutes are allowed for nearly all others, so that no exact course is actually pursued by students of mathematics.

PHYSICS.

The instruction comprises a general course of lectures designed as an introduction to the study of the subject, an elementary laboratory course, designed to give a general knowledge of the science, and an advanced laboratory course.

The general course occupies one year, the exercises consisting of two experimental lectures and one recitation weekly. The subjects are pursued as follows: first term, experimental mechanics and heat; second term, electricity and magnetism; third term, acoustics and optics. A knowledge of mathematics through plane trigonometry is required for registration in either of the subjects; and for registration in electricity and magnetism and in acoustics and optics a knowledge of experimental mechanics and heat is also required.

The elementary laboratory course consists of a series of simple experiments arranged to perfect and fix the student's knowledge of physical facts and laws, and at the same time give him some experience in physical manipulation. The course occupies seven and one-half hours a week (equivalent to three hours of lectures) for one year.

Students are admitted to the laboratory to pursue only such subjects as they have completed in the general course of lectures.

The advanced laboratory course consists of a series of experiments for the establishment of physical laws and the determination of constants. Many of these experiments involve the most refined methods of measurement. Students entering this course are expected to devote to it at least seven and a half hours a week. They may enter for one or more terms at their option, and may, within certain limits, elect the line of work they wish to pursue. Special students will devote a part of their time to an original investigation.

CHEMISTRY AND MINERALOGY.

I.—DESCRIPTIVE AND THEORETICAL CHEMISTRY.

The instruction begins with lectures on inorganic chemistry. Three lectures a week are given on the theoretical principles and the general study of the chemistry of inorganic bodies. During the first term of the third year a course of lectures is given on the chemistry of organic bodies.

INDUSTRIAL EDUCATION IN THE UNITED STATES. 193

For laboratory instruction in this branch of the subject a course of introductory practice is given in the third term of the second year. This introductory practice consists in the performance by the student of a series of experiments illustrating the more important general principles of the science. The details of the manipulation of each experiment are carefully described, but the results to be obtained are not given. For the better cultivation of the student's powers of observation he is required to observe and describe these results for himself, and trace their connection with the principles which they are intended to illustrate.

The instruction in theoretical chemistry is continued in the course in chemistry and physics by recitations in chemical philosophy and by lectures on organic chemistry.

Metallurgy and mineralogy.—During the second term two lectures a week are devoted to each of these subjects in alternate years. The course in metallurgy is intended to give the students in the technical courses a general idea of fuels, ores, and the most important methods of extracting the various metals which are especially used in construction, the metallurgy of iron claiming naturally the most attention. A certain amount of laboratory work in blowpipe analysis, with practice in the identification of crystalline forms, is required in connection with the lectures on mineralogy.

II.—ANALYTICAL CHEMISTRY.

The course in analytical chemistry, beginning in the second year, comprises qualitative and quantitative analysis both in the wet way and in the dry way (blowpipe analysis and assaying), and is adapted in respect to length and completeness to the special course of study the student is pursuing.

In the course of chemistry and physics, leading to the degree of B. S., the qualitative analysis in the wet way and the blowpipe analysis are taken in the first two terms, beginning with the second term of the second year. This work may or may not, according to the proficiency attained in these two terms, extend into the following term. In connection with the quantitative work, which occupies at least a large part of the time devoted to chemical practice in the third and fourth years of this course, some practice in qualitative analysis is continued.

The quantitative work begins with general practice in the determination of bases and acids by gravimetric and volumetric methods, after which follow the analysis of minerals, ores, and technical products in the wet way, and dry assaying, organic ultimate and proximate analysis, the analysis of gaseous mixtures, the chemical examination of waters and articles of food, spectroscopic analysis, the preparation of substances, and, finally, the thesis for graduation, to which most of the time of the last two terms of the course should be devoted.

In the course in agriculture the analytical practice of agricultural chemistry begins in the first term of the second year, and comprises analysis in the wet way only; it is confined to those substances that may occur in agricultural materials and products. The qualitative analysis should be completed in two terms of this year, so that all the time given to the subject in the third year may be devoted to quantitative analysis. This quantitative work begins, as in the course in chemistry and physics, with general practice in the determination of bases and acids by gravimetric and volumetric methods. The chemical examination of fertilizers, soils, and agricultural products occupies the remainder of the course.

In the course in civil engineering a course of practice in blowpipe analysis is provided, which is intended to give to engineers such facility in the use of the blowpipe in determinative mineralogy as will enable them to avail themselves of this useful instrument in their field work, for the determination of the character of rocks and minerals.

In the medical preparatory course a short course of qualitative and quantitative analysis in the wet way is given, which may carry the student far enough to qualify him to examine animal liquids by chemical methods for assistance in the diagnosis of disease. The amount of practice necessary for acquiring merely the rudiments of chemical analysis renders it impracticable to accomplish more than this in the time allotted in the course. Students intending to study medicine who have more time for chemical practice can take a longer and more thorough course, which includes a better foundation in quantitative work and a wider application of the proficiency thus gained to the chemical examination of animal substances and articles of food and drink, and to medical jurisprudence.

III.—INDUSTRIAL CHEMISTRY.

A course of lectures is given in the third term of each year, and the subject is begun anew every second year.

The lectures relate to the applications of chemistry in the manufacturing industries and in daily life, and include among others the following subjects: acids and heavy

S. Ex. 25——13

chemicals, soaps, oils, coal gas, coal tar and its derivatives, glass, pottery, mortar and cement, leather, paper, paints, dyes and dyeing, alcoholic liquors, food, water, and air.

The treatment of these subjects embraces the consideration of the chemical nature of raw materials and the changes which they undergo in the course of manufacturing processes, the apparatus used and its resistance to chemical agents, the utilization or economical disposition of wastes, and the perfection and purity of finished products. The subjects of food, water, and air are also considered from a chemical standpoint with reference to their sanitary and industrial relations.

In connection with these lectures a course of laboratory work is provided, which bears upon the industrial applications of chemistry; and special courses are laid out for students with reference to the needs of any branch of industry they may select. This work consists of analyses of raw materials and commercial products, determinations necessary to the chemical control of a technical process in its different stages, and, when the student is sufficiently prepared, of original investigation with a view to the improvement of some industrial method.

Practical illustration of the different subjects treated is furnished not only in the collections belonging to the department, but also by means of excursions to mills and manufactories.

THE COURSE IN CHEMISTRY AND PHYSICS.

(Leading to the degree of bachelor of science.)

First year.

FIRST TERM.—French, 5, and German, 3, *or* German, 5, and French, 3; rhetoric, 2; geometry and conic sections, 5; hygiene, 6 lectures.
SECOND TERM.—French, 5, and German, 3, *or* German, 5, and French, 3; rhetoric, 2; algebra, 5.
THIRD TERM.—French, 5, and German, 3, *or* German, 5, and French, 3; rhetoric, 2; trigonometry, 5.

Second year.

FIRST TERM.—French *or* German, 3; composition and elocution, 1; analytical geometry, 5; experimental mechanics and heat, 3; chemistry, laboratory work, 3.
SECOND TERM.—French *or* German, 3; electricity and magnetism, 3; chemistry, lectures, 3, laboratory work, 8.
THIRD TERM.—French *or* German, 3; acoustics and optics, 3; chemistry, lectures, 3, laboratory work, 5; botany, 3.

Third year.

FIRST TERM.—Physics, laboratory work, 3; chemical philosophy, 3; chemistry, laboratory work, 7; geology, 3.
SECOND TERM.—Physics, laboratory work, 3; chemical philosophy, 3; organic chemistry, 1; chemistry, laboratory work, 5; mineralogy *or* metallurgy, 2; economic geology, 3.
THIRD TERM.—Physics, laboratory work, 3; chemical philosophy, 3; industrial chemistry, 2; chemistry, laboratory work, 7.

Fourth year.

FIRST TERM.—Physics, laboratory work, 4; organic chemistry, 1; chemistry, laboratory work, 8; history of philosophy, 3.
SECOND TERM.—Physics, laboratory work, 4; organic chemistry, 2; chemistry, laboratory work, 8; metallurgy *or* mineralogy, 2.
THIRD TERM.—Industrial chemistry, 2; chemistry, processes, 2, laboratory work, 8; organic chemistry, 1.

NATURAL HISTORY.

I.—BOTANY.

A course of lectures occupying 5 hours a week for 2 years is given upon each of the following subjects: physiological botany, gramineæ and compositæ, vegetable physiology, vegetable histology, systematic and applied botany, higher cryptogamia, fungi, and algæ. Most of these courses of lectures are given in connection with laboratory work, which is further supplemented, whenever desirable, by field work or class excursions.

II.—GEOLOGY AND LITHOLOGY.

Instruction is given in general and economic geology and lithology by means of lectures, laboratory practice, and field work. The lectures consist of a course on general geology, a course on economic geology, and a course on physical geography, designed to show the action of geological agencies in fitting the earth for human habitation.

The laboratory work consists of a progressive series of exercises in determinative mineralogy and lithology, and of exercises in the preparation of geological sections and maps from the data furnished by government reports. There are frequent excursions and lessons in field work.

To advanced students opportunities are offered for the microscopic investigation of minerals and rocks, and for the extended study of important mineral districts, with the preparation of reports thereon and discussions of the metallurgical methods and appliances adapted to their products. The rocks of Ithaca and its neighborhood afford ample material for study and original research.

III.—PALÆONTOLOGY.

Instruction is given as follows: By laboratory work throughout the year; by excursions to the rich fossiliferous localities in and about Ithaca; and by lectures on systematic palæontology.

The elementary work comprises the observation and recording of facts, the collecting of material in the field, the critical study of the literature and the classification in the laboratory of invertebrate fossils from all parts of the world.

Exceptional facilities are offered for advanced work in the interpretation of fossil forms as marks of geological age and sequence; in the study of faunas, their conditions and distribution; and in the critical study of species and genera, their characters, relations, and modifications, as exhibited in the faunas and floras of the past.

IV.—ZOÖLOGY.

1. *Hygiene.*—Early in the first term are given six lectures upon the personal care of health and upon emergencies. Among other practical matters, students are shown how to check bleeding and how to practice the best methods for resuscitating the drowned.

2. *Human physiology.*—The thirty-six lectures treat chiefly of the subjects not included in the entrance examination, the phenomena of nervous and muscular action, the vaso-motor system, and the structure and functions of the brain. They are illustrated by a life-sized manikin and other models, by numerous anatomical preparations, by diagrams, and by painless experiments upon the frog and cat. Each student also examines, through the microscope, about thirty preparations of the tissues, including the living amœba, cilia in action, and the circulation in the frog's foot and menobranchus's gill.

3. *General zoölogy.*—At one-third of the sixty-six exercises the students examine and dissect representative forms, including amphioxus, lamprey, shark, perch, menobranchus, frog, turtle, squid, crayfish, insect, clam, bryozoön, ascidian, starfish, &c. The lectures are illustrated by a full set of Auzoux models, by diagrams, and by the free use of the zoölogical collections.

4. *Comparative anatomy.*—A course of twenty lectures is devoted either to the brain or to some special group of vertebrates. In either case, practical work is done both in dissecting and in the examination of the literature of the subject.

5. *Anatomical, microscopical, and experimental technology.*—The forty lectures upon these subjects are accompanied by practical demonstrations of all the methods presented, and these methods are employed by the students in the laboratory.

LABORATORY PRACTICE.—The laboratory practice varies with the needs of the student and the extent of his preparation. Usually, as a basis for other work, the skeletons of man and the domestic cat are studied, and some of the bones drawn and described by the student. He then dissects some of the muscles, vessels, and nerves. In the second term, the methods of microscopic manipulation are learned, and the tissues of the cat, frog, and menobranchus are examined. In the third term the student examines the brain, heart, and other viscera of the cat, and performs for himself the simpler physiological experiments. Ordinarily this work can be commenced only at the beginning of the year, and the student must have had instruction in drawing.

After the first year the student, according to his purposes, dissects other vertebrate animals or human subjects, or insects and other invertebrates. There are special facilities for the study of the vertebrate brain.

FIELD WORK.—During the first and third terms students are occasionally accompanied by their instructors to the field or lake in order to observe living animals and learn the methods of their capture and preservation.

THE COURSE IN NATURAL HISTORY.

(Leading to the degree of bachelor of science.)

First year.

FIRST TERM.—French, 5, and German 3, *or* German, 5, and French, 3; rhetoric, 2; freehand drawing, 5; hygiene, six lectures.
SECOND TERM.—French, 5, and German, 3, *or* German, 5, and French, 3; rhetoric, 2; chemistry, lectures, 3, laboratory work, 3.
THIRD TERM.—French, 5, and German, 3, *or* German, 5, and French, 3; rhetoric, 2; chemistry, lectures, 3, laboratory work, 3.

Second year.

FIRST TERM.—French *or* German, 3; composition and elocution, 1; organic chemistry, lectures, 2; human physiology, 3; zoölogy, lectures and laboratory work (vertebrates), 3; anatomy, laboratory work, 2; anatomical technology, 1.
SECOND TERM.—French *or* German, 3; composition and elocution, 1; zoölogy, lectures and laboratory work (invertebrates), 3; laboratory work in physiological anatomy and histology, 5; microscopical technology, 1; blow-pipe determination of minerals, 3.
THIRD TERM.—French *or* German, 3; composition and elocution, 1; botany, lectures, 3; field-work, 2; comparative anatomy of the brain, lectures, 2; laboratory work, 3; museum methods and experimental technology, 1.

Third year.

FIRST TERM.—Experimental mechanics and heat, 3; higher cryptogamia, lectures and laboratory work, 2; compositæ and gramineæ, 2; geology, 3; psychology, 2; essays, 1; English literature, 3.
SECOND TERM.—Electricity and magnetism, 3; vegetable physiology, *or* systematic and applied botany, 3; vegetable histology, 2; economic geology, 3; palæontology, lectures, 2, laboratory work, 1; essays and orations, 1.
THIRD TERM.—Acoustics and optics, 3; algæ, lectures and laboratory work, 2; palæontology, laboratory, and field work, 3; geology, laboratory work, 3; entomology, lectures, 2; laboratory and field work, 3.

Fourth year.

FIRST TERM.—Fungi, 4; the anatomy, physiology, and hygiene of domestic animals, lectures, 5; palæontology *or* geology, laboratory and field work, 3; history of philosophy, 3.
SECOND TERM.—Descriptive astronomy, 3; physics *or* natural history, laboratory work, 2; systematic and applied botany *or* vegetable physiology, lectures, 3; geology or palæontology, laboratory work, 2; advanced work in natural history *or* veterinary science, 5.
THIRD TERM.—Physical astronomy, 3; physics or natural history, laboratory work, 2; advanced work in natural history *or* veterinary science, 8.

PRELIMINARY MEDICAL EDUCATION.

There is no medical department of the university, but special facilities are provided for those who wish their course to be of direct use in the study of medicine. A course of preparatory studies two years in length is offered. Its principal studies are French, German, physics, chemistry, botany, anatomy, and physiology.

Upon the completion of this course the student is entitled to a certificate countersigned by the professor in physiology, or to one covering an equivalent amount of similar work done in either of the full four-year courses or in one of the graduate courses. These certificates usually exempt the holder from one of the three years of study, under the direction of a physician, commonly required of the candidate for a medical degree.

LANGUAGES AND LITERATURE.

The departments of languages and literature provide thorough and comprehensive instruction in all branches connected with those subjects. There are courses in (1) the ancient languages; (2) the Oriental languages; (3) the Germanic languages; (4) the romance languages; (5) Anglo-Saxon and English literature; and (6) rhetoric, general literature, and oratory.

In turning from the scientific to the literary courses of Cornell University, it may not be out of place to introduce some remarks from a recent article in the Unitarian Review by the Rev. Henry C. Badger:
"No error is greater than to suppose that Cornell University is but a training school for mechanics. Many believe, with Matthew Arnold, that 'the university of Mr. Ezra Cornell, a really noble monument of his munificence, yet seems to rest on a provincial misconception of what culture truly is, and to be calculated to produce miners, or engineers, or architects, not sweetness and light.' But Mr. Cornell knew the full meaning of his words now set on the college seal, and the 'instruction' he wished any person might find here in any study was to be all-embracing, nor yet surface-building, with no attempt to dig to the rock. And instruction was to be but one step in education. Culture was a word of which Mr. Cornell was not afraid nor ashamed. He knew its best meaning.

"Studies are practical here. A brass foundry Mr. Sibley's generosity has just annexed to Sibley College. Young women may set type and cast stereotype plates. Young men build steam-engines and electrical machines. The telephone speaks from the president's house to the library, the business office, the professors' houses, and to the far-off village. The water power, singing in the gorges which bound the college grounds, by day turns the machinery in Sibley College and at night keeps a grand electric light gleaming high above the campus and far over the surrounding country. It may soon light all the great college buildings and the many professors' houses scattered about this hundred-acre campus. So a very few young men learn, on the college farm, how to repress diseases and develop the finer qualities of animals, grains, and fruits. But the thorough studies in anatomy (justifying the future founding here of a medical college) or in botany, chemistry, physics, architecture, engineering, mathematics, and in all allied branches, with their separate professors and colleges, make but the lower section of the studies here happily pursued. In certain particulars, like the ancient languages, the university meets the demand, in others it creates the demand. Probably nowhere else in America is the study of history, with all that it involves, carried on with greater method and thoroughness than here."*

The truth of the last sentence is brought out as we proceed with the courses of study.

MORAL AND INTELLECTUAL PHILOSOPHY.

Instruction in philosophy begins in the first term of the third year. During that term it comprises a study of the physiology of the nervous system in relation to mental phenomena, and the nature and origin of knowledge; and during the second term, the study of moral philosophy, theories of morals, and the development of moral sentiments.

It is resumed the third term, the subject being logic, including the laws of thought, the formulæ of reasoning, and the various methods of proof and refutation, together with the methods of investigation and the grounds of certainty.

The subject during the first term of the fourth year is the history of philosophy, and the progress of knowledge from its beginning in Greece to the present day, with criticisms on the methods of philosophy and transcendental logic.

HISTORY AND POLITICAL SCIENCE.

1.—HISTORY.

The aim in the courses of instruction in history is to present in logical and chronological sequence:
1. General history, ancient, mediæval, and modern, with especial reference to the political and social development of the leading nations.
2. The constitutional history of England, as that which has most strongly influenced our own.
3. The comparative constitutional and legislative history of various modern states, as eliciting facts and principles of use in solving American problems.
4. The history, political, social, and constitutional, of the United States, with a systematic effort to stimulate the student to original research into the sources of our national history.
5. The philosophy of history, as shown by grouping the facts and thoughts elicited in these various courses.

General history.

The instruction in general history extends through four years, as follows:
1. General ancient, Grecian, and Roman history, beginning with the third term of the first year and continuing through the three terms of the second year.
2. Mediæval history: General history of the social and political development of Europe

---
*Unitarian Review, October, 1882, pp. 320-321.

during the Middle Ages, mainly by instruction in general English history during the first and second terms of the second year, and by special lectures in the third year.

3. Modern history: The history of the political and social development of Europe from the close of the Middle Ages to the present day, with especial reference to the Reformation, the Reaction, the French Revolution, the Napoleonic era, and the recent period, divided as follows:

FIRST TERM.—The history of Germany begun.

SECOND TERM.—The history of Germany concluded, and the history of France begun.

THIRD TERM.—The history of France concluded, with incidental lectures on important points and periods in the history of Italy and Spain.

English history.

The instruction in English history is given by recitations from text-books during the entire second year, and by courses of lectures on the growth and principles of the Constitution during the third year. The student is expected to supplement these lectures by the use of some standard work for general details, and of monographs on particular subjects and epochs. While avoiding the more obscure technicalities, the aim is to present the great bases of law and policy on which the structure of the English Government rests. The early Saxon institutions are described at some length; and the lectures follow the development of the system from this germ through its leading phases down to modern times. Special attention is paid, during the whole course, to such topics as illustrate the institutions and constitutional history of the United States.

Comparative, constitutional, and legislative history.

This subject is treated, as far as possible, in the courses of lectures upon modern history in the third year, and in a special course of lectures during the fourth year.

American history.

The study of American history extends through the third and fourth years. The topics to which particular attention is paid are the following: The native races, especially the mound builders and the North American Indians; the alleged pre-Columbian discoveries; the origin and enforcement of England's claim to North America as against competing European nations; the motives and methods of English colony-planting in America in the seventeenth and eighteenth centuries; the development of ideas and institutions in the American colonies, with particular reference to religion, education, industry, and civil freedom; the grounds of inter-colonial isolation and of inter-colonial fellowship; the causes and progress of the movement for colonial independence; the history of the formation of the national Constitution; the origin and growth of political parties under the Constitution; the history of slavery as a factor in American politics, culminating in the civil war of 1861-1865.

In the presentation of these topics the student is constantly directed to the original sources of information concerning them and to the true methods of historical inquiry. The effort is also made to use American literature as a means of illustrating the several periods of American history.

Philosophy of history.

The lectures on this subject are given in the second term of the fourth year. Their object is to trace the origin and progress of civilization, and to point out the causes and institutions, civil, social, and religious, which have contributed to its advance or tended to retard its progress. The first half of the course treats of general principles, and the latter half, of the historic progress in civilization, beginning with the settlement of the Aryan nations in Europe.

II.—POLITICAL AND SOCIAL SCIENCE.

This division includes the following topics:

1. Political economy and the history and principles of finance.
2. Theoretical politics, or the state philosophically considered.
3. Systematic politics, or the state practically considered in respect to the organization of the various functions.
4. International law, including American diplomatic history, policy, and organization.
5. American law and jurisprudence.

Political economy.

The instruction in political economy is given by recitations from text books in the elements of the science, and by a course of lectures in which practical questions arising in the study of industrial society receive attention. A course of lectures upon the science of finance, embracing a study of the comparative financial administration of constitutional nations and the various sources of public revenue, is given. Both these courses of lectures are to be supplemented by private reading.

Theoretical and systematic politics.

The aim of the instruction in political science proper is to present both the philosophical and the practical side of the subject in a logical order of treatment. It comprises the two general topics of theoretical and systematic politics.

Theoretical politics treats of primitive societies, the growth of states, forms of government, history of political literature and speculation, and the philosophy of the state.

Systematic politics treats of states in their concrete relations, and includes such subjects as constitutional organization, legislation, administration, and civil-service methods, justice, revenue, military systems, and a comparative survey of existing governments. The historical and the analytical methods are both used, and the object of the course is to make the student acquainted in a scientific sense with the true principles of political organization and practice, as well as with the existing institutions of the great civilized states.

International law and diplomacy.

Instruction in this department consists of a course of lectures given daily during the third term of the fourth year. The course treats, among other subjects, of the history and literature of the law of nations, rules of war, neutrality, prize, embassy, forms of diplomacy, history of American diplomacy, together with descriptions of some of the more famous international disputes in which the United States have been concerned.

American law and jurisprudence.

The course consists of about forty lectures. The first three are devoted to the more general relations of man to government; then follow twelve lectures on the Constitution of the United States, and five on the origin and development of international law; then lectures on the rights of persons and of property, with a general discussion of the nature of contracts, partnerships, and corporations; then lectures on crimes and criminal law; and the course concludes with four lectures on the legal maxims relating to sovereignty, legislation, customary law, and the judiciary.

THE COURSE IN HISTORY AND POLITICAL SCIENCE.

(Leading to the degree of bachelor of philosophy.)

First year.

FIRST TERM.—French or German, 5; Latin, 4; rhetoric, 2; geometry and conic sections, 5.
SECOND TERM.—French or German, 5; Latin, 4; rhetoric, 2; algebra, 5.
THIRD TERM.—French or German, 5; Latin, 4; rhetoric, 2; pre-historic times, 2; plane trigonometry, 3.

Second year.

FIRST TERM.—French and German, 6; essays, 1; Grecian history, 2; English history, 3; Greek, Latin, modern languages, mathematics, or natural sciences, 3.
SECOND TERM.—French and German, 6; essays, 1; Roman history, 2; English history, 3; Greek, Latin, modern languages, mathematics, or natural sciences, 6.
THIRD TERM.—French and German, 6; essays, 1; Roman history, 2; English history, 3; theory of probabilities and statistics, 3.

Third year.

FIRST TERM.—Mediæval and modern history, 3; English constitutional history, 2; American history—pre-historic America and the period of discovery, 3; psychology, 2; sanitary science, labor laws, and penal discipline, 2; essays, 1; elective, 3.

SECOND TERM.—Modern history, 3; American history—the planting of the American colonies, 3; political economy, 2; moral philosophy and political ethics, 2; essays and orations, 2; elective, 3.

THIRD TERM.—Modern history, 3; American history—the institutions of the colonial times, 3; logic, 3; political economy, 2; essays and orations, 2; elective, 3.

Fourth year.

FIRST TERM.—American history—the period of the Revolution, 1765–1789, 3; history of philosophy and the natural sciences, 3; theoretical politics, 3; finance and political economy, 5; general literature and oratory, 3.

SECOND TERM.—American history—first national period, 1789–1820, 3; philosophy of history, 3; systematic politics, 5; comparative constitutional history, 2; general literature and oratory, 3.

THIRD TERM.—American history—second national period, 1820–1865, 3; comparative constitutional history, 2; American law and jurisprudence, 5; international law and diplomacy, 5; orators and oratory, 1.

GENERAL COURSES OF STUDY.

In addition to the special departments and courses which have been described there are general courses, partly made up from the various departments of study and partly elective. They are in (1) arts, (2) literature, (3) philosophy, (4) science, and (5) science and letters. Each is four years in length.

APPLIANCES.

I. THE UNIVERSITY BUILDINGS.

1. *The south and north buildings:* These two edifices, architecturally alike, are each one hundred and sixty-five feet by fifty, four stories in height. The south building cost $70,000; the north, $75,000. The south building contains the offices of the president, treasurer, &c., lecture rooms, and rooms for students. In the north building are fourteen lecture rooms and the hall of the literary societies.

2. *The McGraw building:* The central portion of the building contains one hall one hundred feet long, fifty-six wide, and nineteen in height; and another above it of the same length and breadth, but over thirty feet high, the latter containing three galleries, with an average height of twelve feet. In this part of the McGraw building are alcoves and galleries for the library on the lower floor; and in the galleries on the second floor are the various museums of the university. In the north wing is the anatomical theatre; in the south wing is the physical lecture room, and immediately over it the geological laboratory. This edifice is the gift of Hon. John McGraw, and was erected at a cost of $120,000.

3. *The laboratory building:* A new building for the department of chemistry and physics has recently been begun, and will be ready for occupation about January, 1883. This building will contain all the necessary space for a museum, a library, laboratories, lecture rooms, and other rooms, and will be thoroughly equipped with the most recent and approved appliances for the proper prosecution of the work of the department.

The chemical laboratory now in use contains, besides two lecture rooms and the private laboratories of the professors, laboratories for students, with accommodations for two hundred. It is provided with gas and a full supply of apparatus for wet analysis, dry assaying, blowpipe, spectroscopic, and all other branches of chemical analysis. Its reading room contains the best English, French, and German works of reference, and the current numbers of the chemical journals.

4. *The Sibley College:* Containing, on the first floor, the machine shop and the office of the university press; on the second floor, the lecture rooms of the professor of industrial mechanics and the mechanical museums; on the third floor, the mechanical and freehand drawing rooms. On the north side of the building are an engine room and a stereotype foundery. The building was erected by Hon. Hiram Sibley, at a cost of $30,000.

5. *The Sage College for Women:* This building will accommodate about one hundred pupils, and is used as a home for female students. Besides the dormitories it contains lecture and recitation rooms, a museum, laboratories for students in botany, with greenhouses, forcing-houses, and other facilities for the pursuit of floriculture and ornamental gardening. The building cost $150,000.

6. *The Sage Chapel:* Which contains two audience rooms, the larger of which will seat about five hundred persons. It cost $30,000.

INDUSTRIAL EDUCATION IN THE UNITED STATES. 201

7. *Cascadilla Place:* This is a large building, used for a boarding-house, in which many of the professors and students reside.

8. *The McGraw-Fiske Hospital:* In the year 1881, the sum of $45,000 was bequeathed by Mrs. Jenny McGraw-Fiske as a provision for the care of students who may fall ill during their attendance at the university. It is proposed that a portion of this sum be devoted to the erection of a cottage hospital, made comfortable and attractive, and thoroughly equipped in all respects; and that a trained nurse be attached to it, who shall be ready to give attention the moment it is needed.

II.—UNIVERSITY FARM.

The farm consists of 120 acres of arable land, the larger part of which is used for experimental purposes and the illustration of the principles of agriculture. Nearly all the domestic animals are kept to serve the same ends. Those portions of farm and stock not used for experiments are managed with a view to their greatest productiveness. Statistics of both experiments and management are kept on such a system as to show at the close of each year the profit or loss not only of the whole farm but of each crop and group of animals. Of the two barns with which the farm is equipped, one is largely devoted to the needs of the horticultural department; the other, containing steam engine, feed cutter, stationary thresher, and other necessary appliances, furnishes accommodation for the general crops and stock and for experimental work.

III.—LIBRARIES, LABORATORIES, MUSEUMS, ETC.

1. *The University Library.*—The library contains about 40,000 volumes, besides 15,000 pamphlets. It is made up chiefly of the following collections: A selection of about 5,000 volumes purchased in Europe in 1868, embracing works illustrative of agriculture, the mechanic arts, chemistry, engineering, the natural sciences, physiology, and veterinary surgery; the *Anthon Library*, of nearly 7,000 volumes, consisting of the collection made by the late Prof. Charles Anthon, of Columbia College, in the ancient classical languages and literature, besides works in history and general literature; the *Bopp Library*, of about 2,500 volumes, being the collection of the late Prof. Franz Bopp, of the University of Berlin, relating to Oriental languages, Oriental literature, and comparative philology; the *Goldwin Smith Library*, of 3,500 volumes, presented in 1869 to the university by Prof. Goldwin Smith, comprising chiefly historical works and editions of the English and ancient classics, increased during later years by the continued liberality of the donor; the publications of the patent office of Great Britain, about 3,000 volumes, of great importance to the student in technology and to scientific investigators; the *White Architectural Library*, a collection of over 1,000 volumes relating to architecture and kindred branches of science, given by President White; the *Kelly Mathematical Library*, comprising 1,800 volumes and 700 tracts, presented by the late Hon. William Kelly, of Rhinebeck; the *Cornell Agricultural Library*, bought by Hon. Ezra Cornell, chiefly in 1868; the *Sparks Library*, being the library of the late Jared Sparks, president of Harvard University, consisting of upwards of 5,000 volumes and 4,000 pamphlets, relating chiefly to the history of America; the *May Collection*, relating to the history of slavery and anti-slavery, the nucleus of which was formed by the gift of the library of the late Rev. Samuel J. May, of Syracuse.

By the establishment of the McGraw library fund, the income of which will be available after the present year, and which is to be applied to the support and increase of the University Library, the efficiency of the library both as regards the number of books and the facilities for their use will be greatly enlarged. Beginning with the year 1882, it is proposed to issue a serial containing classified lists of recent accessions and of books in various departments, as well as other bibliographical matter intended to assist students in their use of the library.

The library is a circulating one so far as the members of the faculty are concerned, and a library of reference for students. Undergraduates have free access to a collection of cyclopædias, dictionaries, and works of reference in the various departments of study, but they apply to the librarians for other works desired. Graduate students are admitted to the alcoves.

2. *Equipment.*—The White Architectural Library contains over 1,000 volumes, and the photographic gallery nearly 2,000 prints, all accessible to the student. Several hundred drawings and about 200 models in wood and stone have been prepared to illustrate the constructive forms and peculiarities of the different styles.

3. The library of the engineering department possesses many valuable works, among them the extensive publications recently presented to it by the French Government.

4. *Botanical herbarium and apparatus.*—The means of illustrating the instruction in botany include the herbarium, estimated to contain above 20,000 specimens; two series

of models, the Auzoux and the Brendel; two sets of maps, one by Achille Comte, the other by Professor Henslow; a lime lantern with 500 views, illustrating different departments of botany, but especially phytography; ten compound microscopes and several dissecting microscopes; a collection of fruits, barks, cones, nuts, seeds, fibres, and various dry and alcoholic specimens; a general collection of economic vegetable products, and above a thousand specimens of the woods of different countries. Besides these, the large conservatories and gardens and an uncommonly rich native flora afford abundant material for illustration and practical work.

5. *Veterinary Museum.*—The museum embraces the following collections:

(1) The Auzoux veterinary models, comprising elastic models of the horse, showing the relative position of over 3,000 anatomical parts; models of limbs, sound and with detachable pieces and their morbid counterparts, illustrating changes in diseases of the bones, joints, muscles, &c.; a set of obstetrical models, showing the virgin and gravid uterus in different animals, and the peculiarities of the female pelvis and its joints; models of the gastric cavities of domestic animals; an extensive set of models of jaws, showing the indications of age as well as of vicious habits and diseases; models of equine teeth in sections, showing structure and the changes effected by wear.

(2) Skeletons of the domestic animals, articulated and unarticulated.

(3) A collection of diseased bones, illustrating the various constitutional diseases which impair the nutrition of these structures, together with the changes caused by accidental injuries and purely local disease.

(4) Skulls of domestic animals, prepared to illustrate the surgical operations demanded in the different genera.

(5) Jaws of farm animals, illustrating the growth and wear of the teeth, age, dentinal tumors, caries, &c.

(6) A collection of specimens of teratology, consisting of monstrous foals, calves, and pigs.

(7) A collection of tumors and morbid growths removed from the different domestic animals.

(8) Some hundreds of specimens of parasites from domestic animals.

(9) A collection of calculi from the digestive and urinary organs, &c., of farm animals.

(10) Foreign bodies taken from various parts of the animal economy.

(11) A collection of surgical instruments used in veterinary practice.

(12) A collection of medicinal agents.

(13) In addition, a large number of diagrams, the property of Professor Law, available in illustration of different points in anatomy, physiology, and pathology.

6. *Zoölogical Collections.*—(1) *Vertebrates.*—There are about three thousand examples of about two thousand species of entire animals in alcohol. Half of the specimens are fishes collected in Brazil by the late Prof. C. F. Hartt; the remainder include series of named fishes from the Smithsonian Institution and the Museum of Comparative Zoölogy, representatives of the general North American fauna and of the local fauna, and rare specimens from various parts of the world. Among the last are the following:

(*a*) Orang, pangolin, sloths, ant-eaters, armadillos, jacana, sphenodon, monitor, crocodile, alligator, draco volans, axolotl, siren, amphiuma, pipa, ceratodus, polypterus, calamoichthys, chimæra, myxine, bdellostoma, and amphioxus.

(*b*) More than two thousand anatomical preparations, about one-half of which are skulls and skeletons; the remainder, brains, hearts, embryos, and other soft parts. Among them are more than two hundred and twenty preparations of the cat's brain, a large series of preparations of the lamprey and menobranchus, and embryos or young of opossum, kangaroo, manatee, dugong, peccary, lama, sea-lion, bat, alligator, menobranchus, amia, lepidosteus, shark, and skate.

(*c*) About four hundred microscopical preparations, chiefly from the cat, frog, and menobranchus.

(*d*) More than one thousand mounted skins of birds, most of which were presented by the late Green Smith, esq.

(2) *Invertebrates.*—The general invertebrate collection comprises a small but well selected series of forms representing all of the larger groups.

(3) *Shells.*—The Newcomb collection of shells embraces more than eighty thousand examples of more than twenty thousand varieties, representing at least fifteen thousand species.

7. *Museum of Palæontology.*—The museum comprises the following collections:

(1) The *Jewett Collection*, accumulated by the late Colonel Jewett when curator of the State Cabinet of Natural History. This collection is especially rich in New York fossils, containing many of the original specimens described in the State reports, and not a few unique specimens.

(2) A fair representation of the rich faunas of the cretaceous and tertiary formations

along the eastern and southern part of the Union, and a large number of characteristic English and European fossils.

(3) A fine series of English mesozoic fossils; of tertiary fossils from Santo Domingo: of preglacial fossils from Sweden; and numerous smaller collections from various typical localities in our own country.

(4) The Ward series of casts.

(5) The unique collections from Brazil, made by Professor Hartt and party on the Morgan expedition, containing the original specimens and a great number of duplicates.

The palæontological laboratory is furnished with the appliances needful for study. Among other thing, it has numerous maps, wall tablets, engravings of geological objects, and magic lantern slides.

Large and important additions have also been made to the lithological collections.

8. *Engineering Museum.*—This museum contains the following collections, which receive regular additions from a yearly appropriation:

(1) The Muret collection of models in descriptive geometry and stone cutting.

(2) The De Lagrave general and special models in topography, geognosy, and engineering.

(3) A nearly complete collection of the Schroeder models in descriptive geometry and stone cutting, with some of the Olivier models, and others made at the university.

(4) The Grund and Sohn collections of bridge and track details, roofs, and trusses, supplemented by similar models by Schroeder and other makers.

(5) A complete railroad bridge of one hundred foot span, the model being one-fourth of the natural scale.

(6) The Digeon collection of working models in hydraulic engineering.

(7) Several collections of European photographs of engineering works during the process of construction, and many other photographs, diagrams, and models.

(8) The following instruments of precision for astronomical purposes: A Troughton & Simmss transit, a universal instrument by the same makers reading to single seconds, three sextants, two astronomical clocks, chronographs, chronometers, two small equatorials, the larger of four and a half inch aperture, made by Alvan Clark, and other instruments necessary to the equipment of a training observatory.

(9) For geodetic work, a secondary base line apparatus, made under the direction of the Geodetic and Coast Survey Office, and all the portable astronomical and field instruments needed, including sounding machines, deep-water thermometers, heliotropes, &c.

(10) Among the coarser field instruments there is nearly every variety of engineers' transits, theodolites, levels, and compasses; such modern instruments as omnimeters tachometers, with a large number of special instruments, such as planimeters, pantographs, elliptographs, arithmometers, pocket altazimuths and sextants, hypsometers, and meteorological instruments of all descriptions.

9. *Physical Laboratory.*—Upon the completion of the new building now in progress, ample rooms expressly designed for laboratory work will be available. The collection of apparatus was increased by the expenditure during 1881 of about $15,000. The collection includes a fine gravity escapement clock, a chronograph for measuring tenths of seconds, and another for measuring short intervals of time to the ten thousandth of a second, two cathetometers, a dividing engine, a large spectrometer reading to seconds, a set of apparatus for electrical measurements, besides a large collection of illustrative apparatus.

10. *Mechanical laboratory and appliances.*—The machine shop is used for the sole purpose of giving instruction in practical work. It is supplied with lathes of various kinds, planers, grinding machinery, drilling machines, shaping machines, a universal milling machine fitted for cutting plane, bevel, and spiral gears, spiral cutters, twist drills, with additional tools and attachments for graduating scales and circles, and for working various forms and shapes.

In addition to the hand and lathe tools of the usual kinds there are tools of the greatest accuracy, consisting of standard surface-plates, straight-edges, and squares of various sizes, a standard measuring machine, measuring from zero to twelve inches by the ten-thousandth of an inch, a universal grinding machine for producing true cylindrical and conical forms, and a set of Betts's standard gauges.

In the iron and brass foundry and the blacksmith shop instruction is given in molding, casting, and forging. The cupola used is one of Colliau's improved, with a capacity of melting one ton of iron per hour.

For the purpose of instruction in experimental work there is a twenty-ton Riehle testing machine, arranged for testing the strength of materials by tension, compression, and transverse strain; Richards's and Thompson's steam-engine indicators, and Amsler's planometer; Schaeffer & Budenberg's revolution counter, steam-gauges, injector, inspirator, pop-valve, steam pump; Baldwin's link and valve motion, experimental valve motion, together with a large collection of brass, iron, and wooden models illustrative of mechanical principles.

Closely connected with the lecture rooms in the department of mechanic arts is the school of freehand and industrial drawing, in which there is a large collection of studies of natural and conventional forms, both shaded and in outline; of geometrical models, and of papier mâché and plaster casts, including a number of antique busts, casts of parts of the human figure, studies from nature, and examples of historical ornament.

NORTH CAROLINA.

THE STATE UNIVERSITY.

The original constitution of North Carolina, adopted in 1776, provided that all useful learning should be encouraged and promoted in one or more universities.

The fortunes of war were such as to delay the founding of an institution of the contemplated character until 1789, and its doors were not opened to students until 1795.

It prospered from its first opening until another war, more desolating than that of the Revolution, called away its students, diminished its property, and impoverished its patrons.

It was in this depressed condition when the State received the land scrip which had been issued by the national government, and the university was considered the proper institution for the benefits of the fund which should arise from this grant.

The scrip was disposed of in a manner which did not escape criticism. The university, at the time of the sale of the scrip, received $10,000, which was devoted to the payment of university debts. The trustees claimed the right to do this because they furnished a large tract of land, which might be available in agricultural instruction.

Not obtaining further aid, the university was compelled to suspend operations in 1872. In 1875 the remaining proceeds of the land grant were made available, and the university was reorganized and reopened.

Its objects, so far as they have a bearing upon industries, are "to afford theoretical instruction in the sciences relating to agriculture and the industrial arts."

As there have been no funds derived from the State or other sources which can be used for the establishment of an experimental farm, the university is at present enabled only, in the words of the act of Congress of July 2, 1862, donating the land scrip, "to teach the branches of learning relating to agriculture and the mechanic arts, without excluding the classics and other scientific studies."

The endowment of the university consists of the $125,000, realized from the sale of the land scrip, the Moore scholarship fund of $5,000 in United States bonds, and the Deems fund of $12,000 to be used for loan to indigent students. The former sum is invested in a North Carolina registered certificate, which yields an annual income of $7,500.

The State has recently appropriated $5,000 per annum, so that, with tuition money, the total income is about $19,000, and the expenses of the teaching staff about $16,000, the annual saving being devoted to the extinguishment of a small floating debt incurred for building and repairs.

The number of instructors and lecturers is thirteen. They occupy the following chairs: political economy, constitutional and international law; mathematics; Greek and French; moral philosophy; history and English literature; general analytical and agricultural chemistry; Latin and German; engineering, mechanics, and astronomy; geology, physiology, zoölogy, and botany; natural philosophy; the theory and art of teaching; law; anatomy and materia medica; geology of North Carolina (special).

The persons occupying the last four positions named are not charged with duties connected with the discipline of the university.

The number of students in attendance in the year 1881–'82 was 199. Of these 140 were pursuing the regular undergraduate courses, 8 were post-graduate students, 47 were optional students, and 30 were studying a profession. Several were in more than one department and therefore counted twice in the latter enumeration.

The graduates from the reopening of the university up to and including 1882 numbered 90, of whom 55 took the degree of bachelor of arts, 23 of bachelor of philosophy, and 12 of bachelor of science. No record is kept of their occupations.

The expense for tuition is $85 per annum; but there are ninety-six State scholarships and three created by private contribution; and indigent students who are worthy of aid are admitted upon giving their notes for tuition, and in extraordinary cases entirely free. The State scholarships are filled by appointment of the boards of commissioners of the counties, and secure to the person aided free tuition and room rent.

Only males are eligible to either the scholarships or the university.
The university offers three regular courses of study : the classical, the philosophical, and the scientific. The requisites for admission to the scientific course are only English studies, such as are pursued in the common schools; for admission to the philosophical course, algebra and Latin or Greek are added; and both Latin and Greek must have been pursued by those who would enter the classical course. The amount of reading in the classics is slightly less than that required for admission to most northern colleges.
The studies of the courses are as follows:

I.—CLASSICAL COURSE.

The figures in parentheses denote the number of recitations or lectures per week.
First Year.—Algebra and geometry (5), Latin (4), Greek (4), rhetoric and history (2).
Second Year.—Trigonometry, surveying and analytical geometry (4), Latin (4), Greek (4), zoölogy, physiology, and botany (3).
Third Year.—Physics (3), chemistry (3), logic and rhetoric (2), elocution (1), and any two of the following: Calculus (3), Latin (3), French (3), German (3), natural history (3), industrial and agricultural chemistry (3), Greek (3), surveying and engineering (3).
Fourth Year.—Mechanics and astronomy (3), geology and mineralogy (3), political economy, constitutional and international law (3), English literature (3), essays and orations (1), psychology and moral philosophy (2).

II.—PHILOSOPHICAL COURSE.

First Year.—Algebra and geometry (5), Latin or Greek (4), French (3), rhetoric and history (2).
Second Year.—Trigonometry, surveying and analytical geometry (4), Latin or Greek (4), German (3), zoölogy, physiology and botany (3).
Third Year.—Physics (3), chemistry (3), logic and rhetoric (2), elocution (1), and any two of the following: Calculus (3), Latin (3), German (3), natural history (3), Greek (3), French (3), industrial and agricultural chemistry (3), surveying and engineering (3).
Fourth Year.—Mechanics and astronomy (3), geology and mineralogy (3), political economy, constitutional and international law (3), English literature (3), essays and orations (1), psychology and moral philosophy (2).

III.—SCIENTIFIC COURSE.

First Year.—Algebra and geometry (5), English (2), Latin or Greek (4), physiology, zoölogy and botany (3), natural history, laboratory (2).
Second Year.—Trigonometry and analytical geometry (4), chemistry (3), French or German (3), rhetoric and history (2), advanced botany (2), book-keeping (1).
Third Year.—Surveying and engineering, or calculus (3), industrial chemistry and qualitative analysis (5), physics (3), French or German (3), business law (1).
Fourth Year.—Mechanics and astronomy (3), geology and mineralogy (3), political economy, constitutional and international law (3), English literature (3), and any one of the following: Calculus (3), surveying and engineering (3), quantitative analysis (3), psychology and moral philosophy (2).

IV.—TEACHERS' COURSE.

This course is intended to prepare young men to be teachers, either in the public or in private schools. It embraces all the studies required by law to be mastered by public school teachers, and several others that are indispensable to excellence in teaching. Students pursuing this course may also select, free of charge, any studies embraced in the other courses. Certificates will be awarded those who complete the course. It is believed that the studies embraced in this course and in the scheme of instruction offered in the University normal school, which is taught during the summer vacations and is free to all, will be of incalculable benefit, not only to professional teachers, but to all persons intending to enter into any business or profession and unable to complete one of the regular four years' courses of study in the university.
First year.—English, reading and elocution, arithmetic, algebra, geography (physical and descriptive), physiology and school hygiene, drawing and writing, Latin or Greek, theory of teaching.
Second year.—Rhetoric, history, reading and elocution, book-keeping, surveying, algebra, geometry, natural philosophy, business law, composition, theory of teaching.
The following synopsis of the work done in chemistry, natural history, natural philosophy, and engineering, shows in greater detail the course of instruction in the departments more nearly allied to agriculture and the mechanic arts:

In the department of chemistry there are four distinct classes. A student pursuing the regular course enters in his first year class of general chemistry. In that class he learns the laws of physics so far as necessary for a clear understanding of chemistry proper, then studies the philosophy of chemistry, the metalloids, the metals, their properties and compounds, and lastly organic chemistry (which includes the compounds formed in the process of vegetable and animal life). During the second year he pursues a course of laboratory work (six hours a week throughout the year) in which the substances of which he has heard the year before are placed in his hands so that he may investigate their properties and obtain a better knowledge of them. He is taught all the methods of detecting these substances and establishing their identity, whether alone or in compounds, the so-called qualitative analysis. During the same year he attends a course of lectures on the application of chemistry to the industrial arts, learning first about the extraction of the useful metals from their ores—their valuable properties and their uses; then methods of manufacturing the most important chemicals—potash, soda, salt, sulphuric acid, ammonia, &c.; then the manufacture of glass, porcelain, and earthenware; the production of foods, sugar, wines, and nervous stimulants. The subject of clothing engages his attention next, the dyeing and bleaching of cloth, tanning of leather, &c.; then the subject of building materials, artificial stone, lime, cements, paints, and preservation of wood; and lastly the manufacture of candles, soaps, inks, matches, &c. The last portion of the course is especially devoted to the application of chemistry to agriculture, the chemical constitution of plants, soils, and the atmosphere and the nature of plant-food, application of fertilizers, &c.

In his third year the student gives his time altogether to practical laboratory work. The course can be so varied as to suit the wants or aims of each student. If he desires to fit himself as a practical analyst, he is given instruction in the methods of analysis of minerals, soils, marls, mineral waters, fertilizers, &c.; if he wishes to become a teacher he is taught how to study the properties, constitution, syntheses, and decompositions of chemical compounds; if a physician or druggist, he can devote his time more especially to poisons, adulterations, and microscopical work.

All of these courses are fully carried out at present, but it is hoped that they can be made in time even fuller and more complete. Instruction is given by means of lectures, the training gained by taking notes being looked upon as very important. At the same time good reference books are recommended for use in the various classes. In order that the facts may be more clearly impressed upon the mind, numerous experiments are made in illustration of them, and that the knowledge may not be altogether one gained from mere descriptions, the various substances, as far as possible, are shown to the students, thus helping greatly to fix their nature in the memory. For purposes of illustration a very considerable number of specimens have already been collected and the collection is being continually added to.

The attempt to increase the usefulness of the course of lectures on industrial and agricultural chemistry by the collection of industrial specimens has met with pleasing success considering the necessarily small amount of time that has been given to it so far. These specimens illustrating the various steps in manufacturing processes and the resulting products serve as no mere description could to bring the whole subject clearly before the mind of the students.

GEOLOGY, MINERALOGY, BOTANY, ZOÖLOGY, PHYSIOLOGY.

The department of natural history embraces geology and mineralogy, zoölogy and botany, and the instruction is divided into three courses corresponding to these subdivisions, as will be seen below. The instruction in the several branches is intended to be practical. In all cases the economic bearings of the sciences will be considered as a prominent feature, and especially their bearing upon agriculture. The instruction will be given by lectures and text-books combined, supplemented whenever possible by work in the laboratory and in the field.

The course in geology and mineralogy will occupy three hours per week during one year. It will include mineralogy and lithology during the first session, general geology during the first half of the second session, and economic geology during the latter half of the second session. The instruction in economic geology will be devoted mainly to a consideration of geology in its relation to agriculture and mining, and special attention will be paid to the soils, marls, ore-deposits, and other economic geological products of North Carolina.

In zoölogy, in addition to physiology and hygiene, and general zoölogy, there have been added a course of lectures, laboratory, and field work on beneficial and noxious insects, and a course of laboratory work in general zoölogy.

In the course in physiology and hygiene there will be given also a course of special lectures on school hygiene.

INDUSTRIAL EDUCATION IN THE UNITED STATES. 207

In botany a course of instruction will be given during the spring session in physiological botany, including a study of the plant, structure, the relation which the different parts bear to one another, and plant analysis; and an advanced course, extending through one year. The advanced course will include a study of (*a*) rusts, smuts, and other fungi parasitic upon field crops, (*b*) grasses and forage plants, and (*c*) vegetable physiology, or the growth and cultivation of plants.

NATURAL PHILOSOPHY.

The studies are:
1. Rational mechanics, including statics, dynamics of a particle, and an introduction to rigid dynamics.
2. Astronomy, including spherical and practical astronomy and cosmical physics.
The theory of central forces is studied in connection with mechanics.

PHYSICS.

This class has completed during the term the subjects of mechanics, hydrostatics, pneumatics, and heat. To test the student's thorough comprehension of the laws and facts of physics, numerous examples are given out in every branch of the subject. It is the aim to require the students to perform for themselves, as far as practicable, the experiments given in the text, and thus familiarize themselves with the principles and construction of the instruments used. The experience of those engaged in teaching this subject shows that a few hundred dollars' worth of apparatus to be thus used by the students will be productive of better results than ten thousand dollars' worth which the students are allowed to look at only.

SURVEYING AND ENGINEERING.

The first portion of this course is devoted to mechanical drawing. The student is taught first the principles of projections and shades and shadows; later he is required to execute working drawings of details used in wood, metal, and stone constructions, and also drawings of ordinary structures and machines. In the surveying proper, field practice is made the prominent feature, each student having abundant opportunity to use the instruments himself. Field practice extending nearly over the entire year is afforded in (1) *Surveying*: measuring land, dividing up land, laying off land of given shape and area, surveying roads and streams, and making accurate maps and plots from actual surveys; (2) *Engineering*, which includes leveling, with its application to making roads and ditches, laying out curves of any curvature on the ground, setting slope-stakes, the measurement and calculation of earth-work, and all the work of locating a railroad up to the point of actual construction.

Instruction is also given in the principles involved in and the drawings required of the best and simplest kinds of roofs and bridges.

While the instruments used generally in this work are of the best make and costly, methods are exhibited, when possible, by which many of the above operations can be carried on with simple instruments which can be made by any person possessing ordinary mechanical skill.*

BOOKKEEPING.

The subjects of single entry and double entry are thoroughly explained and illustrated.

Each student is required to write several sets, including, besides the principal books, various auxiliary books and business papers.

An effort is made to present the science in as simple and practical a form as possible, so that each one at any time may readily apply it to his own affairs.

AGRICULTURAL STUDIES.

By availing themselves of an optional course, students whose time and means are limited may obtain purely agricultural instruction in branches deemed of special value.

The appliances for instruction and illustration consist of apparatus, not of large amount at present, but of most improved make and being augmented every year, the contents of several museums, laboratories for chemical, mineralogical, zoölogical, and botanical work.

The museums contain geological, mineralogical, zoölogical, botanical, industrial, and

---

* A considerable amount of excellent apparatus has been recently purchased in Germany for the use of the department of physics.

chemical specimens; and a room has been devoted to the accommodation of valuable agricultural tools, machines, and implements.

The laboratories are supplied with appliances necessary for the prosecution of the work intended to be done in them, according to approved modern methods.

The university buildings are eight in number. They are of brick and can accommodate 500 students. One is five stories in height; another, four; three are three stories; two, one story; and one, one story with basement. The lecture and recitation rooms are large and commodious.

The information presented in this statement of the condition and work of the University of North Carolina has been chiefly supplied by the courtesy of its president, Hon. Kemp P. Battle. He has also outlined the practical work of the university in letters subsequent to the one which has been used in the preparation of this article. From them the following extracts are selected:

The instruction in this institution is confined at present to theoretical teaching in our lecture room, and to practical and field work in chemistry, botany, zoölogy, mineralogy, engineering, physics, &c., as explained above. It is expected at no distant day to conduct open air experiments in agriculture as ancillary to theoretical instruction, and we are ready to conduct field experiments on a larger scale for the benefit of the public, as soon as the means shall be placed at our disposal. Until last year (1881), the "State Agricultural Experiment and Fertilizer Control Station" was located in the university buildings, its establishment by the State and its very successful beginnings and working for several years being largely owing to the exertions and counsel of the officers of the university. Its publications in the press of the State and in books and pamphlet form have very greatly enlightened the people of the State in agricultural chemistry.

The influence of the station has been very great on the purchase and manufacture of fertilizers. It has driven inferior brands from the market, increased the quality and decreased the price of the brands now remaining, and has disseminated a vast deal of information among our people on the subject of fertilizers; so that they buy more commercial manures than ever before, and at the same time engage more extensively in the preparation of fertilizers on their own farms.

By thus creating an intelligent demand for fertilizers, the station has greatly increased the annual products of the soil, and there is reason to believe that its good effects will be lasting and will gather strength year by year.

The station has also driven fraudulent seedsmen out of the market by its tests for the purity and power of the seeds here offered for sale.

It has also given much attention to the analysis of mineral waters, and its influence in regard to the purification of water, both on the farm and in the cities, has been exerted constantly and beneficially. Specimens of marl have frequently been analyzed, and the production of marl for manure has been economized.

The scientific instruction given in the university relates to the following sciences: chemistry (general and applied), agricultural chemistry, physics, civil engineering, botany, zoölogy, physiology, geology, mineralogy.

No trades or industries are taught, but in an agricultural community like ours it is of the first importance that the foundation be laid for scientific observation through life.

Habits of attention, observation, analysis, and generalization of scientific phenomena are impressed upon our students early in life; and these, fortified by an exact and intelligent acquaintance with the general principles of the sciences, cannot fail to produce more useful citizens and more productive workmen.

The structure, habits, and diseases of animals, the uses, growth, and nature of plants, the various sorts of food and their special uses, the value of minerals and their distinguishing features, and the various applications of the forces of nature to the service of man, are among the subjects that are presented to our students during their period of study.

The university had been in a state of suspension for several years, when it was reopened in 1875, in consequence of the restoration of the land-grant fund by the State.

Its revival has been the beginning of a new life in the education of the State.

Its normal school has had an attendance during its six sessions of nearly two thousand teachers, and the courses of instruction and methods of teaching have been greatly improved, while the attendance on the schools has much increased.

Several hundred more North Carolina boys are now students in our colleges than were before. By the aid of the land grant the university began its new career.

OHIO.

STATE UNIVERSITY, COLUMBUS.

[Statements from circulars and reports.]

The chief object of the Ohio State University is to promote the liberal and practical education of the industrial classes within the State in their several callings and pursuits.

The subjects commonly included among college studies are taught, and special provision has been made for extensive and practical instruction in the various branches of natural science and their applications.

The leading industries of the State—agriculture, mechanics, mining, and engineering—have each a separate department and special course of study, and the sciences which underlie these industries also have special departments, and are taught theoretically and practically by eminent instructors, who have ample means for illustration and for practical work at hand.

UNIVERSITY FINANCES.

The grounds, buildings, and apparatus of the university are valued at $500,000, and its endowment fund amounts to $559,628. The sources from which the latter was mainly derived were the proceeds of the national grant of 630,000 acres of public land and the net proceeds of certain tracts known as the Virginia military lands. The proceeds of the national grant were $342,450. This sum was put at interest and the interest added to the principal until the fund amounted to a little more than $500,000.

The sum realized from the sale of Virginia military lands up to the time of making the report for 1880 was $39,031.49. A gift of $300,000 from Franklin County, in which it is located, and frequent appropriations from the State treasury (among which the proceeds of the Virginia military lands are included) have done much to swell the property of the university to its present amount.

The special appropriation for 1880 amounted to only $3,350, of which $1,500 were for farm improvements and stock.

The cash receipts of the university for 1880 from the permanent endowment fund were $27,866; from incidental fees, $3,798; from State appropriation, $6,701; from military lands, $7,285; from miscellaneous sources, $987; cash on hand at the beginning of the year, $4,987; total cash receipts, $51,624.

The disbursements for the same period amounted to $48,526, of which $26,461 were paid for salaries.

FACULTY, STUDENTS, AND GRADUATES.

The faculty are 16 in number. Of these 12 are professors, including the president; 1 is an officer of the United States Army, on duty as commandant of the university cadets and professor of military science and tactics; 1 is an officer of the United States Navy, on duty as professor of steam engineering; 1 is assistant professor of industrial art, and 1 is instructor in French and German languages.

The professorships are of philosophy and political economy, geology, general and applied chemistry, agriculture and veterinary science, mathematics and civil engineering, zoölogy and comparative anatomy, mechanics, physics, mining and metallurgy, history and English language and literature, Latin and Greek, horticulture and botany. These 12 professorships are here named in the order of appointments of the present incumbents, with the exception of the first chair, which is occupied by the president.

In addition to the professors and assistant professors a number of tutors are employed in primary work.

The number of students increased from 27 in 1873 to 330 in 1882.

No tuition fees are required, but an incidental fee of $15 per annum is charged; and advanced students in chemistry are required to pay $10 a term for materials consumed in laboratory work and the deterioration of instruments. Students in physics pay $7 per term laboratory fees.

The first graduates reported to this bureau were those of 1878. The class of that year numbered 6 and all but 1 took the degree in science.

The graduating class of 1879 had 7 members, and one post-graduate degree was given in course, that of Ph. D.

The class of 1880 had 9 members; 6 of them received the degree of bachelor of arts, and 1 each bachelor of science, mining engineer, and mechanical engineer.

The class of 1881 had 9 members; 2 of them received the degree of bachelor of arts,

5 the degree of bachelor of science, 1 the degree of bachelor of philosophy, and 1 the degree of mining engineer. There was conferred also one post-graduate degree (of mining engineer) upon a bachelor of science.

The other degrees given by the university are bachelor of philosophy, bachelor of agriculture, and civil engineer. Certificates of work done are also granted.

There are seven courses of study preparatory to the seven degrees which have been mentioned. Three of them are general and four technical.

The general courses are in arts, philosophy, and science. The technical courses are in civil engineering, mechanical engineering, mining engineering, and agriculture.

Of the general courses that in science alone has a special industrial bearing. Its studies may be outlined as follows:

Freshman year: Analytical geometry, differential and integral calculus, chemistry, mineralogy, freehand drawing, and French.

Sophomore year: Botany, zoölogy, French, and an elective course in botany, chemistry, or physics, continuing through the year.

Junior year: Geology, astronomy, and two elective courses in the sciences above mentioned with the addition of vertebrate anatomy and physiology.

Senior year: Rhetoric and logic, and two elective courses in sciences, or one in psychology and ethics and the other in science.

The three engineering courses agree with the course in science for the freshman year, and are similar to each other in all but the special studies during the remaining three years.

The course in civil engineering has roads, drawing, geodesy, and civil engineering for special studies; the course in mining has an extended course in geology and chemistry, and furnishes thorough instruction in metallurgy, mineralogy, assaying, the treatment of ores, the theory of veins, mining engineering, and the construction of metallurgical works; the course in mechanical engineering gives prominence to physics and drawing, and is especially arranged for the purpose of giving instruction in thermo-dynamics, prime movers, mill work, and mechanism, with practice in the mechanical laboratory.

The course in agriculture differs from all the others. Its freshman year is devoted to work in the mechanical laboratory and the study of chemistry, mineralogy, surveying, civil engineering, and the construction of roads, drains, &c. The next year is wholly taken up with botany, zoölogy, and veterinary anatomy.

The special agricultural studies, commencing in the junior year, include a discussion of soils, manures, crops, and tillage, and farm improvement and management. The other branches pursued are geology and physiology.

In the senior year rhetoric and logic are the general studies; and the special studies include domestic animals, stock breeding and feeding, dairy products, and the diseases of animals and their treatment.

The practice of electing courses of study is so common to the students and so much encouraged by the university that an account of the institution would not be complete which did not give a view of the departments of instruction from which selection may be made and the character of the work done in them, so far as it has relation to industrial education.

The departments are fourteen in number, viz: Physics, chemistry, zoölogy and comparative anatomy, geology, agriculture, botany, mathematics, civil engineering, mechanical engineering, mining engineering, military science and tactics, modern languages and English, Latin and Greek, and history and philosophy. Of the last three departments no further mention is necessary.

In physics there are elementary and advanced courses. The latter occupies two years, and includes the application of graphics and mathematics to physics, lectures on the use of instruments and the details of observation and experimental work. The laboratory is supplied with expensive and well selected apparatus designed for illustration and for the purposes of original research.

Chemistry is required to be studied two terms and a half by all who are candidates for a degree. In this time organic and inorganic chemistry and the relation of chemistry to the arts are considered, and the student is prepared for the advanced course, which covers two years, and is required of students in civil and mining engineering. The work in qualitative analysis is supplemented by instruction in the use of the spectroscope and the blow-pipe. The volumetric and gravimetric methods of quantitative analysis are both taught; and after known compounds have been sufficiently investigated, assistance is given in doing work with substances which are employed in agriculture, medicine, pharmacy, or the arts. A full course in assaying, given in the mining laboratory, is open to students in chemistry.

The State has recently appropriated $20,000 for the erection of a new building for the chemical and mining laboratories. This building is now in process of erection, and will be completed before the beginning of the winter term. It is 160 feet long in front and

80 feet deep in the central portion. It will be two stories high, with basement and gable roofs. The upper floor will be devoted to the chemical department exclusively. The first floor will be occupied by the mining department. Ample space on this floor is reserved for agricultural chemistry.

In the department of zoölogy and comparative anatomy instruction in human anatomy and physiology is given to preparatory students; in zoölogy to the sophomores of all the courses, and in more special studies to junior and senior students at their election.

The object of the sophomore year course in zoölogy is to afford a general understanding of the animal kingdom as a whole, to illustrate the objects and methods of classification, to indicate the more important morphological relations on which classification is based, and to give an insight into the principles which underlie the phenomena of animal life.

The elective work of the junior year is in connection with comparative anatomy, and consists largely of practice in the laboratory and the dissecting room of the department. It may be so modified as to prepare the student for the advanced study, in the senior year, of either paleontology or physiology and histology.

Students in agriculture pursue the advanced studies in this department one year earlier than students in science, that is, during their sophomore and junior years; and special students take up such studies as they may be desirous of pursuing and are prepared to undertake.

The collections and appliances of the department have been carefully selected.

The laboratory is supplied with microscopes and other appliances for biological work; and the dissecting room affords ample facilities for performing the work incident to the study of veterinary and other branches of anatomy.

The department of geology presents no marked features. The collections made by the State geological survey are in the possession of the university, and valuable fossils and minerals have been added from various sources. Every geological formation in the State is represented in the collection.

In the department of agriculture work is provided for three years. The first and second terms of the first year's work are applied to the examination of soils, their origin, composition, organic relations, adaptations to particular crops and methods of culture, and the preservation and restoration of fertility; and to learning the character and value of forage plants, the approved methods of field culture, and the value and application of fertilizers.

The latter part of the year is devoted to the study of farm work and improvements. Under the latter head come drainage, irrigation, the construction and repair of roads and fences, and the erection of buildings. The second year is mainly spent on the following topics: the natural history, description, and adaptation of the various domestic animals; horse-training, cattle-feeding, wool-growing, dairy management, etc. The work of the third year is spent on veterinary science.

The State has established an agricultural experiment station, which is now located at the university. The station is sustained by appropriations from the State.

The experiments and investigations will be carried on both in the field and laboratory, and will deal with the following great agricultural interests, viz: (1) Grain raising. (2) Stock farming and dairy husbandry. (3) Fruit and vegetable culture. (4) Forestry.

The station is prepared to test varieties; to analyze and test fertilizers and manures; to examine seeds that are suspected of being unsound or adulterated; to identify and name weeds and other plants; to investigate, and describe when known, the habits of injurious and beneficial insects; and other work of a similar character that properly comes within its province.

Horticulture and botany have been provided for by the establishment of a separate professorship, the aim of which is to unite scientific knowledge and investigation with the most skillful practice in the important pursuits of fruit growing, gardening, forest culture, and other like divisions. The professor of horticulture and botany is the director of the agricultural experiment station.

An herbarium, representing quite completely the flora of the State, is accessible to students.

Mathematics are taught by two professors. One term is given to astronomy, and appliances for the use of students in this subject are being obtained.

Civil engineering has a prominent place, and the course in it includes practical surveying, the location and construction of railroads and bridges, strength of materials, geodesy, and studies of a more technical character. Varied and adequate field work is undertaken, for which a full set of finely-constructed instruments has been provided.

The department of mechanical engineering has recently been equipped, and is attracting many students.

The course of study includes the principles of mechanism, machine-drawing and designing, four terms of laboratory work, and the consideration of auxiliary branches. It is explained in a recent report as follows:

"In the principles of mechanism are studied the parts of machinery by pairs, or elementary combinations of mechanism. In this the form and arrangement of the parts necessary for securing the desired modification of motion are sought.

In the machine-designing the student takes up some problem in the shape of a particular machine for a special purpose. The forms, dimensions, and arrangements of the parts are decided upon, and then a drawing is carefully made of the whole. Detail drawings to regulation size are then made, and finished in shade lines, as done in the best shops. The quality of these drawings is sufficient for the requirements of photo-engraving for illustrations upon circulars.

In thermo-dynamics are studied the principles which form the groundwork of all heat-engines. In prime movers are studied all kinds of heat-engines, such as steam, hot-air, &c., and also wind and water wheels. Mill work and machinery takes up valve-gears, fly-wheels, governors, efficiency of parts of machines, strength of parts, &c.

The mechanical laboratory is intended for acquainting the student with the materials used in machine construction; with the forms customary in machinery; to impart a degree of skill in the use of tools and a knowledge of the operations and practices of the shop.

The first term consists of the actual use of tools in executing a set of forms chosen with a view to supplying the greatest possible amount of practical instruction for the time. This is combined with weekly lectures on tools and their use.

The second term carries the above practice to the fitting together of parts and to the use of machine tools, such as the lathe, planer, etc. This is combined with weekly exercises in designing and drawing of machine elements, such as cranks, bearing-boxes, stub-ends, etc.

The third term is fully occupied in fitting parts carefully together, as in the joints of machinery, and in finishing the surfaces by scraping, polishing, burnishing, etc. This is in combination with a weekly exercise in the invention of simple machines for specific operations, such as bending wire staples, cutting wool combs, &c.

The fourth term of mechanical laboratory practice is constructive. It is taken in connection with the principles of mechanism. In the latter, problems in mechanism are worked out, forms and dimensions assigned to the parts, and then these are executed in the laboratory, resulting in models of mechanical movements for the cabinet.

The course in mining engineering secures to the student careful instruction in mining, the preparation of the ore, and its metallurgical treatment.

Lectures, the study of text-books, preparation of maps and drawings, visits to existing works, and practice in estimates and designs form parts of the field of instruction. There is a collection of minerals such as are commonly met with in mining operations, a full equipment of furnaces and ores for assaying, and models exhibiting all the common forms of crystals.

The aid which the university directly renders to the agriculture of the State is given through the lectures on practical agriculture and the experiments conducted upon the farm. The lectures are given in the early part of each year, and are attended by intelligent farmers, who wish to obtain modern and correct scientific ideas of subjects related to their occupation.

The professor of agriculture not only contributes to this course of lectures (if he does not furnish the whole of it), but also attends the county institutes for farmers.

The university farm contains 320 acres of land. Valuable experiments are constantly being tried upon it. Those reported in 1880 were in wheat culture (including yield of varieties, effects of early and late sowing, late plowing, &c.,), corn culture, potatoes (yield, effect of fertilizers, etc.), forage crops, millet, rye, rice, corn, grasses, and clover; thorough drainage, and sorghum culture.

A circular of information on the classification of students, issued in June, 1882, is as follows:

CLASSIFICATION OF STUDENTS.

The attention of students is called to the following system of classification, which has recently been adopted by the faculty for the purpose of doing away with a large amount of unnecessary irregularity. There is no desire or intention on the part of the faculty to depart from its former liberal policy toward students seeking special facilities in any particular direction *for a definite purpose;* such students will, however, be in future required to state the ends which they have in view, and to pursue such studies as are, in the judgment of the faculty, conducive to the end designated. On the other hand, the faculty cannot escape the conviction that there is a great deal of purposeless irregularity, the result of mere whim or fancy in some instances, which they regard not only as detrimental to the progress of the institution but also to the welfare of the students themselves. It is this conviction which has led to the adoption of the plan herein described:

First. The various departments of the university will hereafter be classified in four schools, designated as follows:

The school of arts and philosophy, including those studies which enter into the courses leading to the degrees of bachelor of arts and bachelor of philosophy.

The school of science, including those studies which enter into the course leading to the degree of bachelor of science.

The school of engineering, including those studies which enter into the courses leading to the degrees of civil engineer, mechanical engineer, and mining engineer.

The school of agriculture, including those studies which enter into the course leading to the degree of bachelor of agriculture.

Second. Every student (resident graduates alone excepted) shall enter one of the above schools or shall be assigned to that one in which the majority of his studies are found (in case of irregularity). There shall be no unclassified students.

Third. Each school will be under the direction of a standing committee of the faculty, having power to act in all matters pertaining to the studies of students in such school and in matters of minor discipline. The following committees have been appointed for the various schools:

Arts and philosophy.—The president, the professors of Latin and Greek, history, geology, chemistry, and French and German.

Science.—The president, the professors of mathematics, chemistry, physics, geology, and zoölogy.

Engineering.—The president, the professors of civil engineering, mechanical engineering, mining engineering, physics, and drawing.

Agriculture.—The president, the professors of agriculture, horticulture, mechanics, metallurgy, and zoölogy.

Students will report at the beginning of the fall term to the secretaries of their respective committees, whose names will be announced at that time.

Fourth. All students in each school will be regarded as belonging to one of two groups; first, those whose purpose it is to enter upon one of the regular courses of study, with the expectation of taking its degree; second, those who come to the university for the purpose of pursuing some special study or line of work, and who do not expect to take a degree.

The courses of study leading to the various degrees having been arranged by the faculty in the order which they believe to be the best adapted to the general requirements of students, *all who do not belong to the second of the groups indicated* will be required to enter upon the regular work of the college classes to which they belong, or in case of present irregularity to remove such irregularity as speedily as practicable in the manner prescribed by the committee of the school in which they are classed, and no such student will be allowed to take more or other than his regular studies without presenting a request with reason therefor to his committee and receiving its consent. Such consent may be revoked at any time when it may seem advisable to do so.

Students belonging to the second group, viz: those coming to the university for a limited time with the definite purpose of pursuing some special line of work, will in each case enter the school in which their proposed work is chiefly included, and shall lay before the committee a statement of the end in view, the studies proposed for the accomplishment of that end, and the probable period of residence.

While it will be the purpose of each committee, in accordance with the well-established policy of the university, to allow to such students full freedom in the selection of the branches which they desire to pursue, subject only to the necessary limitations that they are prepared to take up the branches they select and that such branches are in accordance with the end proposed, it is also their intention to hold students as regularly to the performance of their accepted schemes of work as they do the members of the first group to their prescribed course of study; and they will refuse admission to this group to all of whose definiteness of purpose or fitness to undertake the work proposed they fail to receive satisfactory evidence.

OREGON.

CORVALLIS COLLEGE.

The legislature of Oregon accepted the national grant in behalf of agricultural education October 9, 1862. Nearly ten years later it gave the benefit of the grant to Corvallis College, at Corvallis, an institution established in 1865 and chartered in 1868 for the purpose of the preparatory and collegiate education of the youth of Oregon. The general character of the college has been maintained, although agricultural instruction is afforded. The object of this instruction is to give students a thorough knowledge of scientific and practical agriculture, and through them so improve the present system of crop culture that there shall be a minimum exhaustion of the soil and yet maximum crops.

The grant with which Corvallis College was endowed amounted to 90,000 acres. Part of this land has been sold for $50,000. The grounds, buildings, and apparatus are valued at $10,000. The annual income is about $6,000.

The faculty consists of the president, who is professor of moral philosophy and physics, professors of mathematics and languages, and teachers in the preparatory department and of drawing and painting. The subjects of instruction are arranged by schools. No regular courses of study are given in the catalogue. Agricultural studies treat of the composition and analysis of soils, the preparation of soils and manures, modes of drainage, construction of farm buildings, and stock raising. General, analytical, and agricultural chemistry are taught by the president; mineralogy, geology, and zoölogy, by the professor of mathematics; and botany and fruit culture, by the professor of languages.

The number of students enrolled in 1881–'82 was 150, of whom 90 were males and 60 females. Tuition for the scholastic year is, in the primary classes, $18; preparatory department, from $30 to $36; in the scientific and agricultural courses, $39; and in the classical college, $45. There are sixty free scholarships for young men over sixteen years of age. They are secured by application to the State senators or the president of the college.

The graduates of the college up to and including 1881 numbered 47, 35 males and 12 females. The men received degrees as follows: A. M., 3; A. B., 3; B. S., 29; the women, with one exception, took the degree of B. S. Farming is the favorite occupation among them. About five hundred young men, mostly farmers' sons, have received an education at the college.

PENNSYLVANIA.

PENNSYLVANIA STATE COLLEGE, CENTRE CO.

[Statement from catalogue, &c.]

The leading object of the Pennsylvania State College is, "without excluding other classical and scientific studies and including military tactics, to teach such branches of learning as are related to agriculture and the mechanic arts in such manner as the legislature of the State may prescribe, in order to promote the liberal and practical education of the industrial classes in the several pursuits and professions in life."

Since its opening in 1859 the college has sought to teach the various sciences in such a manner as to show their relations to the more common industries, and thus to combine the theory with the practice, the science with the art. The entire organization and equipment have, therefore, had these objects in view.

ENDOWMENT, ETC.

The income of the college is almost wholly obtained from a bond of the State of Pennsylvania for $500,000, upon which interest is paid semi-annually at the rate of 6 per cent. per annum. The property of the institution—its buildings, farm, farm stock, apparatus, &c.—is valued at $532,000. This property was in 1866 mortgaged for $80,000. For the payment of the mortgage provision was made by act of the legislature approved June 12, 1878. Owing to the expenditure during 1879 of $10,000 for steam heating apparatus, $2,000 for the extension and improvement of laboratories, and $5,000 for a professor's house, the floating debt was increased to $33,000; but that is now in process of extinguishment by regular additions to a sinking fund. The amount expended for instruction in 1882 was $17,500.

FACULTY AND STUDENTS.

The faculty consists of the president, who is professor of political and social science, and professors of English literature and ancient languages, botany and horticulture, agriculture and agricultural chemistry, mathematics and astronomy, military science and tactics, chemistry, modern languages, physics, civil engineering, geology and zoölogy, an assistant professor of ancient languages, and a lady principal in charge of the female department. There are also three other teachers in the preparatory department and an instructor of music.

There are superintendents of the college and experimental farms, the eastern experimental farm in Chester County, and the western experimental farm in Indiana County.

INDUSTRIAL EDUCATION IN THE UNITED STATES. 215

The students in attendance in 1880–'81 were classified as follows: Resident graduates, 5; graduates at last commencement, 3; seniors, 10; juniors, 9; sophomores, 10; freshmen, 18; special students, 8; preparatory, 85; males, 125; females, 23; total, 148.

Tuition is free. Incidentals, including room rent and all college charges except chemicals, are $40 per annum.

The whole number of graduates up to and including 1882 was 122. Of these 52 received the degree of bachelor of science, 46 of bachelor of agriculture, and 24 of bachelor of arts. Their occupations, as far as known, are lawyers and law students, 18; farmers, 18; teachers, 15; physicians and druggists, 11; chemists, 10; engineers (mining or civil), 6; manufacturers, 6; deceased, 5; miscellaneous, 33; total, 122.

COURSES OF STUDY.

The act of Congress of July 2, 1862, which the college regards as of binding authority, requires instruction to be given in a large number of subjects. In order to employ fully the large teaching force demanded, to meet as far as possible the wishes of its patrons, and to serve to the best advantage the interests of the State, the college has organized and offers to both sexes the following courses of instruction:

Preparatory course, classical and scientific; two general courses, general science and classics; and four technical courses, agriculture, natural history, chemistry and physics, and civil engineering. It also admits special students who do not intend to take all of any college course. It still further offers to farmers and others who cannot become students a farmers' institute or course of lectures, lasting two weeks in midwinter. Particulars concerning the studies are given below.

ADMISSION.

The college admits both sexes, on the following conditions:

First. Candidates for the preparatory department must be at least 14 years of age and have a fair knowledge of the ordinary common school branches.

Second. For admission to the freshman class, general science course, the candidate must be at least 15 years of age, and pass a further examination in United States history, Olney's Higher Algebra (to quadratics), Olney's Geometry (to section 7), Steele's Fourteen Weeks in Physics, and Houston's Physical Geography, or their equivalents. For the classical course the applicant will be examined in Cæsar, Cicero's orations, and Xenophon's Anabasis, instead of physics and physical geography. Candidates for either course should have some practical knowledge of drawing and bookkeeping. Students whose advanced knowledge of some subjects will enable them to make up their deficiencies in others may be admitted conditionally. Equivalents are accepted in all cases from candidates for admission.

PREPARATORY COURSES.

As many students come from districts where there are no advanced schools, it has been found needful to maintain a department which shall prepare such persons for admission to college, and shall, at the same time, give a good practical training to those who are unable from any cause to prolong their studies beyond the ordinary academic course.

Applicants should, as stated, be at least 14 years of age and have a good knowledge of the common English branches. Preparatory students, except those who are under the immediate care of their parents and guardians, are required to room in the building, where they are under the supervision of the principal of the department and his assistants during study hours; and every effort is made to incite in them a love of study and to create and confirm habits favorable to it.

As there are two general courses in the college, there are two preliminary courses, designed to prepare for these respectively. While these have much in common, clearness demands that they be given separately. They are as follows:

IN GENERAL SCIENCE.	IN CLASSICS.
First year.	*First year.*
Fall session.—Arithmetic, algebra, physiology, English analysis.	*Fall session.*—Arithmetic, algebra, physiology, Latin grammar and reader.
Winter session.—Algebra, English composition, physical geography, zoölogy.	*Winter session.*—Algebra, English composition, physical geography, Latin reader.
Spring session.—Algebra, English history, botany, English composition.	*Spring session.*—Algebra, English history, botany, Cæsar and Latin composition.

216   INDUSTRIAL EDUCATION IN THE UNITED STATES.

IN GENERAL SCIENCE.

Second year.

Fall session.—Algebra, English history, natural philosophy, German. Practicum, drawing one hour daily.
Winter session.—Algebra, geometry, United States history, physics or Latin. Practicum, bookkeeping one hour daily.
Spring session.—Geometry, United States history, geology or Latin. Practicum, drawing one hour daily.

IN CLASSICS.

Second year.

Fall session.—Algebra, English history, Cæsar and Latin composition, Greek grammar and reader. Practicum, drawing one hour daily.
Winter session.—Algebra, United States history, Cicero's orations, Greek grammar and render. Practicum, bookkeeping one hour daily.
Spring session.—Geometry, United States history, Ovid, Xenophon's Anabasis. Practicum, drawing one hour daily.

GENERAL COLLEGE COURSES.

The college offers, as already stated, two full courses, each of four years. That in general science embraces German and French, mathematics, and a fair outline of the natural and the metaphysical sciences. The classical combines with the essentials of the old time-honored "college course" a large amount of the scientific knowledge and the practical training which that course formerly lacked. Each course as here taught aims at the full development of the student's powers of observation and of reasoning.

At the close of the sophomore year the student in either course may enter one of the technical courses.

In the following schedules of studies a figure placed after any subject indicates the number of hours of recitation or of practice given to that study each week.

General science course.

FRESHMAN CLASS.

Fall Session.—Algebra (3), geometry (3), German (5), tactics (4). Practicum—drawing (4), horticulture (4).
Winter Session.—Algebra (4), geometry (2), rhetoric (4), German (5). Practicum—drawing (2), mechanic arts (6).
Spring Session.—Trigonometry (5), physiology (4), German (3), French (3). Practicum—drawing (4), horticulture (4).

SOPHOMORE CLASS.

Fall Session.—Trigonometry and surveying (4), chemistry (4), German (3), French (4). Practicum—surveying (6), chemistry (4).
Winter Session.—General geometry (4), chemistry (4), German (3), French (4). Practicum—chemistry (8), mechanic arts (2).
Spring Session.—Chemistry (3), descriptive botany (4), German (2), French (3), general geometry (4).* Practicum—chemistry (6), botany (4.)

Classical course.

FRESHMAN CLASS.

Fall Session.—Algebra (3), geometry (3), Virgil (5), Xenophon's Anabasis and Greek composition (4). Practicum—drawing (4), horticulture (4).
Winter Session.—Algebra (4), geometry (2), rhetoric (4), Virgil (3), Plato's Apology and Greek composition (3). Practicum—drawing (2), mechanic arts (6).
Spring Session.—Trigonometry (5), physiology (4), Sallust (3), Plato's Phædo (3). Practicum—drawing (4), horticulture (4.)

SOPHOMORE CLASS.

Fall Session.—Trigonometry and surveying (4), chemistry (4), Horace (3), Herodotus (4). Practicum—surveying (6), chemistry (4).
Winter Session.—General geometry (4), chemistry (4), Cicero de Officiis (3), Homer (4). Practicum—chemistry (8), mechanic arts (2).
Spring Session.—Chemistry (3), descriptive botany (4), Tacitus (4), Euripides' Alcestis (4). Practicum—chemistry (6), botany (4).

---

*For the general geometry of this session students preparing for the course in agriculture or that in natural history may substitute seven hours of practicum in chemistry.

General science course.

JUNIOR CLASS.

Fall Session.—Rational mechanics (4), chemistry (3), logic (3), animal physiology (4), or differential calculus (3), (elective). Practicum — mechanics (4), botany (4), physiology (4).
Winter Session.—Physics (4), chemistry (4), zoölogy (4), integral calculus (2), or natural theology (3) (elective). Practicum—physics (3), zoölogy (4), botany (4).
Spring Session.—Physics (4), mineralogy (3), civil government (3), English literature (5). Practicum—physics (3).

SENIOR CLASS.

Fall Session.—Physics (4), geology (4), mental philosophy (3), history of ancient philosophy (3), English literature (3). Practicum—physics (4), geology (3).
Winter Session.—Geology (3), political economy (3), astronomy (4), history of civilization (4). Practicum—geology (5).
Spring Session.—Geology (3), astronomy (3), ethics (3), history of English literature (3). Practicum—geology (5), thesis or oration.

Classical course.

JUNIOR CLASS.

Fall Session.—Rational mechanics (4), logic (3), Thucydides (4), botany (4), or differential calculus (3) (elective). Practicum—mechanics (4), botany (4), physiology (4).
Winter Session.—Physics (4), zoölogy (4), natural theology (3), Greek history and antiquities (3), Demosthenes (3). Practicum—physics (3), zoölogy (4).
Spring Session.—Mineralogy (3), civil government (3), English literature (5), Roman history and antiquities (3), Sophocles (3). Practicum—physics (3).

SENIOR CLASS.

Fall Session.—Geology (3), mental philosophy (3), history of ancient philosophy (3), English literature (3). Practicum—geology (3).
Winter Session.—Geology (3), political economy (3), astronomy (4), history of civilization (4). Practicum—geology (5).
Spring Session.—Astronomy (3), ethics (3), history of English literature (3), evidences of Christianity (3). Practicum—geology (5).

TECHNICAL COLLEGE COURSES.

The technical courses now offered by the college are four in number: Agriculture, natural history, chemistry and physics, and civil engineering. For admission to either of these courses with a view to graduation, the applicant must pass an examination on the studies of the freshman and sophomore classes of one of the general courses, or their full equivalent.

1. COURSE IN AGRICULTURE.—Agriculture involves the application of the sciences to a greater extent than any other human employment. The aim, then, of the college course of instruction in agriculture is to teach how the sciences are applied to the business of farming, to afford a thorough and comprehensive knowledge of its principles and methods. It explains the nature of soils and of manures, the reasons for and the best methods of tillage, the constituents and characteristics of plants and animals, and the conditions favorable to their development; and it combines theory and practice wherever the processes involve skilled labor, but it does not consume the student's time in the mere manual labor of plowing, planting, and feeding. For instruction in this branch there are the college farms of 400 acres, with nearly 20 acres of orchard, vineyard of about 500 vines, experimental grounds of more than 30 acres, barns, implements, &c.; the libraries, the laboratories of all the different departments, each of which is in certain respects subsidiary to agriculture; and the laboratory for agricultural work, with its special appliances for quantitative analysis of grain, grasses, fertilizers, &c.

In addition to purely technical studies, the schedule includes a few others, such as mental philosophy, political economy, ethics, &c., which are needful to fit the student for the right discharge of his duties as a citizen.

2. COURSE IN NATURAL HISTORY.—The design of this course is to give a practical knowledge of geology, zoölogy, botany, &c., and to train its graduates for the work of collecting and classifying objects in natural history, and for the superintendence of scientific explorations and investigations.

Instruction is derived not only from the text books and lectures and the work in the laboratories, but from the study of the various collections and from excursions in the vicinity of the college, the surrounding district being especially rich in material illustrative of geology and botany.

3. COURSE IN CHEMISTRY AND PHYSICS.—This course aims to prepare the student for work as a physicist or a practical chemist or pharmacist; it also seeks to fit him to enter the ranks of original investigators and discoverers.

The extensive and well-equipped laboratories afford opportunities for qualitative and quantitative work in both chemistry and physics; they enable the physicist to verify the laws of physical force, the assayist to determine the value of ores, and the agriculturist to ascertain the composition of his organic products.

4. COURSE IN CIVIL ENGINEERING.—This course was established at the opening of the collegiate year, 1881–'82. In general terms, its object is to combine thorough practical instruction and the higher mathematical training so essential to the success of the professional engineer; and to this end students are required, in addition to the ordinary class room work, to spend an unusual amount of time in the field and in the construction and drawing rooms.

SCHEDULES OF TECHNICAL COURSES.

1.—*Agriculture.*

JUNIOR CLASS.

Fall Session.—Rational mechanics (4), agricultural chemistry (3), cryptogamic botany (4), animal physiology (4). Practicum—Physics (4), chemistry (6).
Winter Session.—Physics (4), agricultural chemistry (4), zoölogy (4), agricultural engineering (3). Practicum—Zoölogy or physics, chemistry.
Spring Session.—Mineralogy (3), civil government (3), entomology (4), fertilizers (4), crops (1). Practicum—Agriculture, entomology.

SENIOR CLASS.

Fall Session.—Anatomy and breeding (4), Geology (3), mental philosophy (3), horticulture (3), crops (2). Practicum—Agriculture, dissection.
Winter Session.—Geology (3), political economy (3), feeding (4), veterinary (4), farm economy (1). Practicum—Agriculture.
Spring Session.—Dairy (3), sheep husbandry (1), ethics (3), history of English literature (3), history of agriculture (1). Practicum—Agriculture, geology, thesis.

2.—*Natural history.*

JUNIOR CLASS.

Fall Session.—Rational mechanics (4), cryptogamic botany (4), animal physiology (4), logic (3). Practicum—Mechanics (4), botany (4), physiology (4).
Winter Session.—Physics (4), zoölogy (4), phænogamic botany (4), natural theology (3). Practicum—Physics (3), zoölogy (4), botany (4).
Spring Session.—Physics (4), mineralogy (3), civil government (3), entomology (4). Practicum—Physics (3), entomology (9).

SENIOR CLASS.

Fall Session.—Anatomy and breeding (4), geology (3), mental philosophy (3), zoölogy (5). Practicum—Geology (3), zoölogy (8).
Winter Session.—Geology (3), political economy (3), astronomy (4), embryology (4). Practicum—Geology (5), embryology (6).

Spring Session.—Geology (3), astronomy (3), ethics (3), history of English literature (3). Practicum—Geology (5), thesis.

3.—*Chemistry and physics.*

JUNIOR CLASS.

Fall Session.—Rational mechanics (4), chemistry (3), logic (3), animal physiology (4) or differential calculus (3) (elective). Practicum—Mechanics (4), chemistry (8).
Winter Session.—Physics (4), chemistry (4), natural theology (3) or integral calculus (2) (elective). Practicum—Physics (3), chemistry (19).
Spring Session.—Physics (4), chemistry (4), mineralogy (3), civil government (3). Practicum—Physics (3), chemistry (9).

SENIOR CLASS.

Fall Session.—Physics (3), chemistry (1), geology (3), mental philosophy (3). Practicum—Physics (4), chemistry (18).
Winter Session.—Physics (3), chemistry (2), geology (3), political economy (3). Practicum—Physics (4), chemistry (16).
Spring Session.—Physics (3), chemistry (3), ethics (3), history of English literature (3). Practicum—Physics (3), chemistry (10), thesis.

4.—*Civil engineering.*

JUNIOR CLASS.

Fall Session.—Rational mechanics, differential calculus, descriptive geometry, shades, shadows, and perspective.
Winter Session.—Physics, integral calculus, descriptive geometry, analytical mechanics.
Spring Session.—Physics, analytical mechanics, mineralogy, civil government.

SENIOR CLASS.

Fall Session.—Geology, resistance of materials, principles of mechanism, railroad surveying.
Winter Session.—Geology, construction of bridges, astronomy, political economy.
Spring Session.—Geology, astronomy, hydraulics, ethics.

[Ten hours of practice a week throughout the two years.]

SPECIAL COURSES.

Students of mature years and younger students whose parents or guardians request it are permitted to choose such a special course as they may need. Of every such student it is required that he be prepared to enter upon and pursue with profit the studies chosen, that he have an equal number of hours of class-work with other students, and that he take part in the *practicum* to which he may be assigned. In order, however, to make a still more specific provision for the needs of those who are unable, for any reason, to pursue a full course, there were established in the early part of the year 1882–'83 a short special course in agriculture, of two years, and a similar course in chemistry. In these courses the studies are arranged with direct reference to the student's immediate aim, and of course cannot be largely educational in other directions.

PRACTICAL WORK.

The college has, from the first, sought to combine practical with theoretical instruction, and thus to fix in the student's mind a knowledge of both methods and principles. With this end in view a portion of the student's time has been set apart for this training, and the number of subjects in which such instruction is given and the apparatus for it have been added to until the range of topics is unusually extensive, as appears from the several schedules. A portion of this training is largely technical, and so is almost wholly confined to certain courses. Other parts, however, are so general in their character as to be appropriately required of all students. Among these *practicums* common to all, the following may be mentioned for the sake of illustration: Book-keeping, so important for the right conduct of all business; drawing, freehand and mechanical, needed by individuals in all employments and professions; military drill, required by the law of Congress and helpful in securing right habits of body and mind; mechanic arts, in which are learned among other things the making of plane surfaces, correct angles and joints, and the care and use of tools; horticulture, where instruction is given in all ordinary operations belonging to fruit culture, such as pruning, grafting, budding, and propagation by cuttings and layers; and surveying, which acquaints the student with the instruments of the art and trains him to determine points, distances, and areas. Some of these *practicums* not only give knowledge of almost universal use, but also serve a good purpose by developing, during the early part of the course, tastes and aptitudes which may determine the student's choice of a technical course and of his life work.

In each of the technical courses certain special lines of practice have a large amount of time given them proportionate to their importance or subsequent professional use. Each *practicum* is directed by an instructor who is familiar with both the theory and the practice and with their mutual relations.

FARMERS' INSTITUTES.

In order to meet the wants of farmers who desire to increase their knowledge of the theory of their calling a farmers' institute has been held at the college during the last two winter sessions. This two weeks' course comprises from thirty to forty lectures by the college professors or by others whose services are secured, that they may present to the farmers certain important specialties.

The following topics are among those included in the courses: Agricultural chemistry, botany, dairying, entomology, farm accounts, feeding, fertilizing, fruit growing, grain and forage crops, mechanics, roads and bridges, stock breeding, vegetable gardening, veterinary, drinkable waters, adulteration of foods, political economy for farmers, industrial education, &c. Besides this direct attempt to meet the wants of farmers who are engaged in the active pursuit of their occupation, the college has recently (November, 1882) begun the publication of occasional bulletins containing the results of agricultural experiments and investigations conducted by the professor of agriculture. These bulletins have reached a circulation of upwards of 5,000 copies, and are largely sought for by the most intelligent farmers of the State.

No charge is made for instruction or for the use of the public rooms of the college.

FREE SCHOLARSHIPS.

There have recently been established fifty free scholarships, one for each senatorial district in the State.

The scholar, male or female, is to be appointed by the senator of the district after a competitive examination in the studies required for admission to the freshman class; and must, therefore, fulfill the conditions requisite for admission to that class as given above.

The holder of the scholarship is admitted to the privileges of the institution free of the ordinary charges for incidentals, room rent, fuel, and furniture, this immunity to continue for the entire college course, provided that both conduct and class standing be satisfactory to the faculty. Other expenses, such as boarding, books, and light, must be borne by the student.

A vacancy may be filled after the opening of the college year if the appointee's attainments are sufficient for admission to the class at that time.

For information as to vacancies, time and place of examination, &c., candidates for a scholarship apply to their senator, in whose care the details of appointment are placed by the college.

MILITARY INSTRUCTION.

In addition to the exercises in the schedules of the several courses, all students, except those exempted because of conscientious scruples or physical disability, take part in military drill. The exercises occur, ordinarily, three times per week. Seniors and juniors are required to be present at but half the number of regular exercises assigned for members of the lower classes. The uniform used is of cadet gray cloth and of a standard pattern.

LABORATORY EXPENSES.—Students in the laboratories pay a small charge for their outfit; also, for apparatus destroyed and material consumed by them.

BOARDING.—The college does not maintain a boarding-hall, and most students depend upon the boarding-houses in the vicinity, the regular charge being $3 per week. The college offers special facilities to those who board themselves singly, and also to the College Boarding Club, which supplies its members, now numbering about twenty, with good boarding at about $2 per week.

FURNITURE.—The furniture provided for students who room in the building consists of a bedstead, mattress, table, washstand, and chair. The student provides all other articles, including bedding, wash-bowl and pitcher, mirror, lamp, &c.

MEANS OF ACCESS.—The turnpike from the college furnishes daily communication by stage with Bellefonte, which is connected by two trains daily with Tyrone, on the Pennsylvania Railroad, and with Lock Haven, on the Philadelphia and Erie Railroad.

Owing to the better accommodation and greater regularity of communications, the route by Bellefonte is now preferable for all those coming by railroad. The Lewisburgh and Tyrone Railroad runs within six miles of the college, and furnishes regular passenger trains from Tyrone.

EXPENSES.

Fall Session:
  Incidentals $6
  Room rent, fuel, and furniture 9
Winter Session:
  Incidentals 4
  Room rent, fuel, and furniture 11
Spring Session:
  Incidentals 4
  Room rent, fuel, and furniture 6

There is no charge for tuition in any course. The charge for incidentals is intended to cover the expenses of heating, lighting, and caring for the corridors and the recitation and other public rooms. This is the only charge made to pupils who do not room in the college.

The above charge for room-rent, fuel, and furniture is made to those who room in the building, and is on the basis of two persons to each room. In cases where a student rooms alone, he is charged $4 additional per session.

INSTRUCTION OF WOMEN.

Ladies are admitted to the preparatory and college courses on the same terms as gentlemen. For higher standing, also, the examinations are the same for both sexes, except in those instances in which a difference in studies is noted at the foot of a schedule. It is in contemplation, however, to establish at an early day a somewhat modified course for ladies.

APPLIANCES, ETC.

The building is a plain and substantial structure of magnesian limestone, situated on a pleasant rise of ground, in one of the most beautiful and healthful valleys of the Alleghany region, and is two hundred and forty feet in length, eighty feet in average breadth, and five stories in height, exclusive of attic and basement. It contains the public rooms, such as chapel, library, armory, cabinets, laboratories, society halls and class rooms, and a large number of dormitories.

INDUSTRIAL EDUCATION IN THE UNITED STATES.

The tract of land on which the building stands contains nearly three hundred acres. Of this about 50 acres in the immediate vicinity of the building constitute the campus and furnish recreation grounds, sites for the professors' houses and other needful buildings, &c.

The campus contains at present four of these residences of professors, and it is adorned with trees, shrubbery, flower-gardens, walks, and rustic bridges.

The college farm consists of 240 acres, of which 40 acres are woodland. The remainder, except so much as is occupied by farm buildings, orchard, and vineyard, is worked under a system of rotation of crops, in five divisions of 30 to 40 acres each. The soil is limestone, with a large admixture of flint, and is admirably adapted to the production of the various grains and grasses grown in this region. It responds freely to the use of lime, gypsum, and the various artificial fertilizers; but the chief dependence for increase of fertility is placed in barn-yard manure, which is obtained by fattening a large number of beeves each winter.

The farm-buildings include two dwelling-houses, a large and excellent over-shot barn, with double threshing-floor, threshing-house, corn cribs, root-house and stabling, a hog-pen, a slaughter-house, a tool-house, &c.

An orchard of about 14 acres, chiefly of apples, and a vineyard of five hundred vines, are in good bearing condition.

The greater part of the labor upon the farm, orchard, vineyard, and campus is done by paid laborers; but the professors in charge of instruction in agriculture and horticulture make use of all parts of the college grounds for their purposes, but require of each student under their charge only so much of the labor in each place as they deem needful for proper practical training.

EXPERIMENTAL FARMS.

The college has three experimental farms of about 100 acres each, situated in different sections of the State—one in Chester County, one in Indiana County, and one adjoining the college farm. These are intended to test practically some of the doubtful questions that vex agriculturists, to ascertain the value of new processes, to experiment in the breeding and feeding of cattle, to determine the relative value of fertilizers, and, in general, to further, through systematic and continued experiment under varying conditions of soil and season, the interests of progressive agriculture.

RHODE ISLAND.

BROWN UNIVERSITY, PROVIDENCE.

This venerable college was chartered in 1764 and organized in 1765. It received in 1863 the benefit of the national land grant to Rhode Island, and organized its "departments of practical science" in 1869, so as to give instruction in such "branches of learning" as are related to "agriculture and the mechanic arts."

Students who enter only for these studies, either in part or in full, are subject to the same conditions of admission as for any select course; and when they have duly pursued such studies they will be entitled to a certificate stating the time of their university residence and the amount of their acquisitions. They may, however, pursue these studies in connection with "the regular scientific and classical studies of the university," and when they have so pursued them as to fulfill the requirements for the degree of bachelor of arts or of bachelor of philosophy they will be entitled to these degrees.

The State received land scrip for 120,000 acres, which was sold for $50,000. This sum is invested in State securities at interest, and the income is turned over to the university to be expended in the education "of scholars, each at the rate of $100 per annum." Appointments to these scholarships are made on the nomination of the general assembly, by the governor and secretary of state, in conjunction with the president of the university.

The professors and instructors in the schools of practical science are as follows:

Rev. Ezekiel G. Robinson, D. D., LL. D., president, professor of moral and intellectual philosophy.
Samuel S. Greene, LL.D., professor of mathematics and astronomy.
Benjamin F. Clarke, A. M., professor of mathematics and civil engineering.
John Howard Appleton, A. M., Newport Rogers professor of chemistry.
Eli W. Blake, jr., A. M., Harvard professor of physics.
John W. P. Jenks, A. M., professor of agriculture and zoölogy, and curator of the museum.

Charles W. Parsons, M. D., professor of physiology.
Alpheus S. Packard, jr., M. D., PH. D., professor of zoölogy and geology.
Nathaniel F. Davis, A. M., assistant professor of mathematics.
William Whitman Bailey, B. P., professor of natural history (botany) and curator of herbaria.
William Channing Russel, LL. D., acting professor of history and political economy.
William Herbert Perry Faunce, A. B., instructor in mathematics.
Edwin Eddy Calder, assistant instructor in analytical chemistry.

The other professors in the university are those of the Latin language and literature, Greek language and literature, rhetoric and English literature, Elton professor of natural theology, modern languages, and elocution, as well as a librarian and assistant librarian.

The following is a summary of the students attending the present year (1882–'83): Seniors, 52; juniors, 59; sophomores, 68; freshmen, 85; total, 264.

The cost of living varies much according to circumstances; the ordinary expenses are as follows:

Tuition	$100 00
Room rent	20 00
Use of library	5 00
Registrar's salary	4 00
Public fuel, servants' hire, printing—charged at cost, but average about	22 00
Board, 41 weeks, at $3	123 00
Total	274 00

This amount may be much reduced by holding some one of the scholarships shortly to be mentioned, or it may be increased in various ways. If a student occupies a room alone, his rent and servants' hire are doubled; if he rents rooms or suites in Slater's Hall, he must pay from $25 to $155 per annum.

The foregoing estimate for tuition does not include the fees for instruction in analytical chemistry. The expenses of a student who takes a course of study of two hours daily in the chemical laboratory are as follows:

Tuition	$33 33
Gas, chemicals, &c.	36 67
Breakage (varying with student's care), about	6 00
Total	76 00

Students who take courses of four or six hours daily pay respectively double or treble the above amounts.

Allusion has been made to the "scholarships of the department of agriculture," as they are termed by the authorities of Brown University.

The amount received as interest is derived from $50,000 at 6 per cent., $501 at 7 per cent., and a variable amount on deposit at 7 per cent. If simple interest at these rates on the sums named be calculated from August 30, 1870, when the final payment for the land scrip was made, to August 30, 1881, it will be found to amount to $32,725, or about $3,000 per annum.

The treasurer of the university for the years ending the middle of April, 1873, 1877, and 1878 reports to the corporation as follows:

Year.	Income.	Disbursement.
1873	$3,381 22	$2,300 00
1877	3,287 32	3,300 00
1878	3,248 60	4,500 00

At the latter date there was a balance of income remaining and available of $4,859.33.

The expenditures seem to have been so kept within the income as to increase the fund at interest every year, and thus gradually increase the number of persons benefited.

In addition to these there are 66 scholarships of $1,000 each, the income of which is given, under the direction of a committee appointed by the corporation, to meritorious students who may need pecuniary assistance; but a scholarship is forfeited if the candidate incurs college censure or fails to secure at least seventy-five per cent. of the maximum mark.

There are also scholarships arising from the income of $12,300 given by Henry R. Glover, Mrs. E. S. Bartlett, and others, on various conditions.

Finally, a fund of something over $8,000 has been given to the university by two of its friends. The income of this fund is to be applied, either by loan or by gift, to the assistance of deserving young men of limited means.

It is needless to say that Brown University teaches a thorough classical collegiate course, after the conservative fashion. It is only necessary here to mention at some length its "departments of science," already alluded to.

I.—CHEMISTRY APPLIED TO THE ARTS.

The chemical laboratory is open to students (except on Sundays) from 8.30 a. m. to 2.30 p. m.

It is the design of this department to teach students analytical chemistry, and then to direct their studies to the practical applications of chemistry.

Attention is given to metallurgy, pharmacy, medical chemistry, agricultural chemistry, and the application of chemistry to manufacturing processes.

II.—CIVIL ENGINEERING.

The regular course in this department occupies four years, but a longer or shorter course may be pursued, according to the wants or abilities of students. Those who are unable to pursue a full course will find the studies so arranged that the knowledge and practice acquired in only a partial course will be practical and available. Ample provision will be made for the instruction of any who desire a more extended course than is here indicated in engineering and in higher mathematics.

III.—PHYSICS.

The laboratory of the department of physics provides instruction during the second half year to a limited number of students who show special aptitude for this study, and are desirous of familiarizing themselves with the construction and use of physical apparatus and with the means of investigation.

A course of experiments in sound, light, heat, and electricity, involving the principal phenomena and most important methods of measurement, has been arranged with reference to the needs of beginners. Apparatus available for more advanced students and for researches has been purchased recently, with the view of meeting the demand for special instruction in physics.

IV.—BOTANY.

Instruction in botany is given by means of lectures, in which free use is made of the blackboard and diagrams. The course embraces the necessary morphological and physiological subjects, and is supplemented by practical class work, in which each student employs the dissecting microscope in examining specimens.

Great stress is laid upon the importance of drawing from nature, and students are taught to make illustrative sketches.

Each student of botany is expected to pay a small fee for the cost of specimens used in class work.

At the proper season excursions are made, under the guidance of the professor, to neighboring points of botanical interest. At such times students are shown how to collect and preserve specimens.

V.—ZOÖLOGY AND GEOLOGY.

Zoölogy, with special reference to palæontology, is taught by lectures, laboratory work (forming a course of comparative anatomy), and by dredging and collecting excursions in Narragansett Bay and near the city, with special reference to the local fauna.

Instruction in geology is given by means of lectures and models, laboratory work, and field excursions, with special reference to the geology—structural and economic—of Rhode Island.

VI.—AGRICULTURE.

The course of instruction in agriculture includes the courses in the preparatory branches, chemistry and physics, botany, physiology, geology, and comparative anatomy.

It also includes special lectures on agriculture. These relate to the study of soils and applied economic geology. The course of instruction is illustrated by specimens from the museum of natural history and by field excursions.

It also includes practical instruction in obtaining and preserving specimens and in taxidermy.

SOUTH CAROLINA.

UNIVERTITY OF SOUTH CAROLINA.

The income of the proceeds of the land grant to South Carolina is now divided between the South Carolina College of Agriculture and Mechanics at Columbia and the Claflin College at Orangeburg.

These colleges, by the State law of March 22, 1878, are branches of a corporation styled the University of South Carolina, under the control of a board of trustees consisting of the governor, the State superintendent of education, the chairmen of the committees on education in both branches of the legislature, and seven other persons chosen by joint vote of the legislature. This board is created a body corporate and politic, with power to hold property, real and personal, and is the successor of the former University of South Carolina, of the College of South Carolina, and of the agricultural college at Orangeburg. It has the power to appoint and remove officers and professors in the colleges, to organize the colleges as shall be deemed best, and to confer degrees. The board may select ten professors and two presidents for service in the colleges at Columbia and Orangeburg, and these are paid from the treasury of the State.

The donation of land-scrip by the general government for the establishment of colleges of agriculture and the mechanic arts, under the act of July 2, 1862, was accepted by the State; and the law of December 10, 1869, directed that the proceeds of the sales of the scrip should be invested in Federal or State bonds bearing 6 per cent. interest. In 1870 the scrip was received, sold, and the proceeds, $191,800, invested in State bonds, on which the annual interest amounted to $11,508, the interest to begin July 1, 1870. The interest was not promptly or regularly paid, and the principal was irregularly used to meet the demands and obligations of the State treasurer, so that, ten years after, the legislature, on December 23, 1879, passed an act appropriating $191,800 in State stock, at 6 per cent. interest from July 1, 1879, to replace the principal; but the deficiency in interest, amounting to $58,736, was not reimbursed. The act just cited provided that the board of trustees should open a college for white students at Columbia as well as the one for colored students at Orangeburg, and use the property of the former State University as might be found necessary for this purpose. Tuition in the college was made free, and scholarships were also authorized.

COLLEGE OF AGRICULTURE AND MECHANICS.

The first session of the new college began Tuesday, October 5, 1880, with the following corps of instructors:
1. William Porcher Miles, LL. D., president and professor of English literature.
2. James Woodrow, PH. D. (Heidelberg), D. D., professor of geology, mineralogy, botany, and zoölogy.
3. Benjamin Sloan (U. S. M. A.), professor of mathematics and natural philosophy and secretary of the faculty.
4. William Burney, PH. D. (Heidelberg), professor of analytical and agricultural chemistry and experimental agriculture.
5. G. W. Connors, foreman of the farm.
6. Jesse Jones, foreman of the shop.

Two instructors, licensed by the college, give lessons in ancient and modern languages, the compensation therefor being a personal matter between the teachers and students.

The ordinary course of instruction in the college is open to applicants not less than fifteen years old who have passed a satisfactory examination in English grammar, geography, arithmetic, and algebra through equations of the second degree. Some familiarity with English and American history will be found useful. The following is the course of study, occupying three years:

First Year.—English history, rhetoric, composition and declamation, algebra, geometry.
Second Year.—Logic, political economy, declamation, mineralogy, botany, trigonometry, descriptive geometry, shades and shadows, surveying, inorganic chemistry.
Third Year.—Mental philosophy, English literature and language, zoölogy, geology, general geometry, differential and integral calculus, applied mathematics, organic chemistry, agricultural chemistry, analytical chemistry, both qualitative and quantitative.

The following extracts from a letter of President Miles shows something of the spirit and vigor with which the new college is working for the benefit of its pupils and the State at large:

"From the many letters of inquiry which I receive, it would seem that there has been little or no mention of this, our only State college for whites, in the local newspapers, and no attempt to present to our impoverished people the advantages afforded them of educating their sons gratuitously. I cannot but believe that if the course of instruction and the qualifications of our professors and instructors were more generally known, there would be many a poor young man—desirous of a liberal education, and at the same time unable to pay for his tuition—who would gladly seek our lecture rooms, where thorough instruction in so many of the most important branches of human knowledge is freely tendered him 'without money and without price.'

"For enabling our students to acquire practical acquaintance with planting and farming, and the methods of cultivating our staple crops, we have an ample area of land, where Mr. Connors, our farmer, an experienced and skilled agriculturist, gives his undivided attention to field and garden operations. Here the lectures on agricultural chemistry are supplemented and illustrated by the test and comparison of various fertilizers on growing crops. We do not propose to make our farm an 'experimental farm,' as that term is unusually understood, *i. e.*, a collection of little, minute squares of ground, where curious and fanciful experiments are to be made, such as Liebig might have made in pots of earth in his laboratory. We will rather aim to teach our young men who propose to follow planting or farming as a means of livelihood the most approved and successful methods of raising remunerative crops, as well in the preparation of the soil (often half the battle) and best use of farming implements in all stages of the crops (from seeding to harvesting and preparing for market) as in the supplying of all the requisites of plant food.

"There is a dawn of a new era in the agriculture of our State. Our gifted and distinguished fellow-citizen, Dr. St. Julian Ravenal, has demonstrated, by repeated trials, that sixty to seventy bushels of oats, and other grains proportionately, and from four to five tons of hay, may be raised on an acre of land (by proper treatment and an application of by no means expensive fertilizers) where without such treatment and application hardly a tenth of such yield could be had. Bermuda grass may yet be destined to work a revolution in our agricultural industry. It is now indigenous to our soil, thoroughly acclimated, indestructible by winter frosts or summer suns and droughts, requiring but moderate care to nurse it into a luxuriant growth, with which timothy cannot compare. The marked success which has attended its culture, on a large scale, by Governor Hagood—one of our most enlightened and educated and at the same time practical farmers—has long taken this question of Bermuda grass hay out of the hands of the experimenter and the domain of theory. And in this connection I may be permitted to add that Governor Hagood, as chairman *ex officio* of our board of trustees, takes not only a deep interest in our farming operations, but kindly aids the foreman of the farm with continual practical advice and suggestions. I trust you will pardon me for dwelling at such length on the agricultural feature in our institution, but it seems to me worthy of the extended notice I have given it.

"Mr. Jesse Jones, a thoroughly skilled and unusually ingenious mechanic and machinist, is our master mechanic, and has charge of the workshop, where, under his eye, the student learns the use of all ordinary tools and how to handle them, and how to plan and construct farm buildings, and to make and repair farming implements, &c., and where, gradually, a practical acquaintance with engines, mills, and machinery generally may be acquired.

"When our people shall have become thoroughly awakened to the necessity of providing the means of education of the highest grade to the poorest classes of her citizens free of expense, so that there can never more be even the excuse for the cry that the college at Columbia is 'an aristocratic institution,' 'the rich man's college,' &c., then we may see our legislature, in imitation of the legislatures of our sister States of the South, making provision herself, in addition to the congressional aid by which we are at present solely supported, for enlarging the scope of instruction in our walls, and making the College of South Carolina an institution of high and liberal culture, of which her people may be justly proud, and for which unborn generations of her sons will be grateful."

* * * * * *

"Let there be only a generous rivalry among us to see how much each of us can do towards stimulating the youth of our State to the desire for and the pursuit of that 'higher education' without which a people must inevitably retrograde, not only in intellectual, but in material progress. For if there be one thing in the present age of the world more certain than another, it is that mind rules not only the forces of the social and political world, but to an even greater extent the forces of nature. Show me the nation where the intelligence of the mass of the people is most developed by training, *i. e.*, where thorough education is most diffused, and I will show you a nation most advanced in even material wealth and prosperity. Let us multiply our schools and colleges, then, say I. We cannot have too many of them. In education the aphorism 'Too much of a good thing' does not hold. Who would oppose the building of a new church on the plea that there were churches enough already? Is the plea any stronger in the case of colleges, especially in a State where the young men are growing up in such general illiteracy? No; let us educate—educate in common schools, in private schools, in high schools, in normal schools, in colleges, in universities—everywhere educate! And especially let our mother, the State, extend to the poorest boy on her soil such advantages in the way of education as may enable him to compete in a professional or public career, in any pursuit and in every way, with the richest and proudest in the land."

The number of students for the first session of 1880–'81 was 66, all males, women not being admitted to this college.

COLLEGE AND MECHANICS' INSTITUTE OF CLAFLIN UNIVERSITY.

The other branch of the University of South Carolina is the "Agricultural College and Mechanics' Institute" at Orangeburg.

In the year 1869 an institution was opened for the general instruction of colored youth; this was endowed chiefly by gifts of money from persons in the Northern States, among whom was the late Lee Claflin, of Massachusetts. This school was chartered as Claflin University and has continued with varying fortune until the present time. After the State accepted the agricultural land grant, as already mentioned, the Agricultural College and Mechanics' Institute was organized in 1872 as a coördinate branch of Claflin University. Appropriations were made for some years at irregular intervals, being scarcely sufficient to purchase the agricultural farm. When Governor Hampton came into power the matter assumed a little more regularity, and $5,500 have been appropriated annually from the agricultural fund to sustain the institution.

The faculty of the institute (and of the Claflin University as well) for the session of 1880–'81 was composed of the following persons:

Rev. Edward Cook, A. M., D. D., president, professor of ethics and agricultural topics.
Rev. William H. Lawrence, A. M., professor of Latin, Greek, and German languages and literature.
William J. De Treville, jr., C. E., professor of pure and applied mathematics.
Rev. James H. F. La Roche, A. B., professor of natural science.
James S. Heyward, adjunct professor of mathematics.
Miss Sarah G. Bagnall, preceptor in English literature and French.

The very low standard of attainments among the colored people has obliged the institute to take up the work of education where it is left by the poorly supported and defective common schools of the State. As time has passed some of the pupils have been prepared for the higher courses of study, and every effort seems to have been made to utilize the resources of the university for the benefit of its pupils. At least two-thirds of these are classed as attending the grammar school, which has a course of two years, namely:

First year.—First, second, and third readers; orthography—word primer; arithmetic—progressive primary.

Second year.—Arithmetic—rudiments of written arithmetic; English grammar—language lessons; orthography—word book; geography—primary; reading—fourth reader; penmanship—Reynolds' series.

The earliest and most persistent necessity for the colored people has been well instructed teachers for the public schools; Claflin University has provided, almost since its foundation, a normal school course of three years' duration.

First year.—Practical arithmetic; intermediate geography, completed; new English grammar; dictionary and dictation exercises; school reader No. 5; advanced penmanship.

Second year.—Arithmetic, completed; algebra, begun; English grammar and word analysis; English and Saxon prefixes, suffixes, and derivations; history of the United States; introductory Latin book; Latin and Greek prefixes and derivations; word analysis, parts II, III; drawing and elocution.

Third year.—Algebra, completed; physiology; natural philosophy; chemistry; rhetoric, English history and literature; drawing, orations, and essays.

Pupils completing these courses, or possessing an equivalent training, are admitted to the scientific and agricultural course, which occupies four years. Those who desire to pursue the classical collegiate course omit all the studies of the third normal year, except the algebra, and substitute the following: Harkness' Latin Grammar and Reader; Cæsar's Commentaries; Cicero's Orations against Catiline; Boise's First Book in Greek; Xenophon's Anabasis; Grecian mythology; Grecian and Roman history.

The following list shows the studies pursued in the institute (scientific and agricultural) and the collegiate (classical) courses:

Freshman year.—Higher algebra; plane geometry; rhetoric and composition; physiology; physical geography; French language and literature; bookkeeping; farm and mechanical work; Æneid of Virgil; Cicero de Officiis; Latin grammar and composition; Xenophon's Memorabilia; Homer's Iliad.

Sophomore year.—Solid and spherical geometry; trigonometry, plane and spherical; surveying and navigation; English history and literature; rhetorical exercises; French and German languages; drawing, freehand and mechanical; farm and mechanical work; Livy; Horace, Odes and Ars Poetica; Demosthenes, de Corona; Thucydides' histories.

Junior year.—Conic sections; mechanics; natural philosophy and astronomy; compositions and declamations; French and German languages; Tacitus, de Oratoribus and histories; Greek historians or French and German.

Senior year.—Chemistry; geology, mineralogy. lectures; logic; mental philosophy; moral philosophy; Government Class Book in Civil Polity; orations before the college.

Though the law of 1879 makes the institute a part of the University of South Carolina, it still continues in practice, a department of the older corporation, Claflin University. The grounds and buildings of the institute (aside from those of the university) are worth at least $10,000; these comprise a farm of one hundred and sixteen acres, a large barn, a stable and carriage-house, four dwellings, and two small storehouses. The university proper owns thirty-seven acres, one large brick building containing chapel, lecture rooms, laboratory, and president's quarters, and four dormitories. A grammar school building has been erected recently.

Thus far the double connection of the institute does not appear to have resulted badly, either for its interests or for those of its patrons, the union between the State and the Claflin corporation being both pleasant and profitable.

Admission to all classes, both in the university and the institute, is free to both sexes. The catalogue of 1880–'81 shows 18 male and 2 female students in the collegiate course; 87 men and 39 women in the normal classes, and 150 boys and 92 girls in the grammar school. A recent letter from the president says:

"With what can be earned in the industrial department, a student can get along comfortably with about fifty dollars additional a year. The scholarship is advancing rapidly and the institution is doing a great work for the colored youth of South Carolina.

"It has the confidence and moral support of the white citizens as well as the colored people."

TENNESSEE.

UNIVERSITY OF TENNESSEE, KNOXVILLE.

[Statement of the president.]

* * * The college established in this university, according to the contract made between the trustees and the State of Tennessee and maintained with the income from the national endowment, by act of Congress approved July 2, 1862, is now in a healthy condition and useful operation. The trustees determined from the beginning to conduct it with faithful adherence to the provisions of that Congressional act. They sought, therefore, to provide, first, for instruction in such branches of learning as are related to agriculture and the mechanic arts, "without, however, excluding from the field of teaching other classical and scientific studies, and at the same time including military tactics." Upon this basis the institution has been conducted from 1869 to this time.

The college grounds, buildings, and farm have been provided by the trustees of the university as required of them by the law of the State. The present value of this property is not easily determined with accuracy. It may, however, be placed at $120,000.

The endowments that yield income for the use of the college consist, first, of $9,000, owned by the university for many years past, and which may be applied to building purposes; and, second, of $396,000 in bonds of the State of Tennessee, bearing 6 per cent. interest, and $4,000 in bonds of the same kind, bearing 5 per cent. interest, in which bonds, the proceeds of the sale of the land scrip received by the State of Tennessee from the United States under the act of Congress of July 2, 1862, have been invested. The annual income from this fund, which exists in perpetuity for the maintenance of the college, is $23,960, and cannot be applied to building uses.

The income from college fees for the year ending July 1, 1882, was $2,891.68; the library fund yielded $311.45. The aggregate income for that period from all sources (including cash on hand at its beginning) was $34,890.81.

The expenditure for the year ending July 1, 1882, including payments for the farm, the library, for repairs and improvement of buildings and the construction of gas-works, was $34,383.46.

The expense of the teaching corps, for the same time, was $19.890; the number of instructors was fourteen; the chairs were as follows, viz:

Ethics and evidences of Christianity (filled by the president); agriculture and horticulture; mathematics and mechanical philosophy; chemistry, mineralogy and geology; history and philosophy; English language and belles-lettres; modern languages and comparative philology; ancient languages and literature (assistant); mathematics; military science (the professor being also commandant of cadets). There were also two instructors, one in English and one in ancient languages; one in vocal and instrumental music, and an assistant in analytical chemistry.

The number of students in all departments of the college for the same period of time was 225; all of these were males. No provision has been made, specially, for the instruction of females in technical or industrial branches of learning, nor has any female applied at any time for admission as a student. If such provision were made the applications would probably follow.

The average expense of tuition to students in the preparatory department is $30 a year, and hereafter it will be the same to students in the college proper, to all of whom it is now free.

The State is entitled to 275 scholarships tuition free. Each State senator may fill two of these, and each representative, three. The State appointees have on some principal railroads free transportation one way, and when needful both ways and on another chief road, nearly half rates both ways.

The number of graduates since the receipt of income from the national endowment of July 2, 1862, *i. e.*, since 1871, is 108. Of these there were in 1880—

Teachers	22
Lawyers or students of law	22
Merchants or clerks in mercantile houses	9
Farmers	9
Physicians, dentists, druggists, and medical students	6
Christian ministers, including 1 theological student	3
Business agents, (railroad, insurance, &c.)	3
United States Government clerks	2
Editors and newspaper reporters	2
Tanner and harness maker	1
Attaché of United States minister to Turkey	1
Student at German university	1
Surveyors and civil engineers	2
Unknown, 3; deceased, 1	4
	87
Deduct for twice counted	7
	80

Of the students who have withdrawn from the college without graduating, fewer in proportion to the above have entered the profession of law, more have become farmers, mechanics, traders, clerks, &c., and a considerable number are teachers.

The course of instruction is divided among the following schools, or departments, with the following hours per week in each, for forty weeks, viz:

Departments.	Freshman.	Sophomore.	Junior.	Senior.
1. Mathematics	5	3	2	
2. Applied mathematics and mechanics	3	2	3	5
3. Chemistry and mineralogy	2	3	2	3
4. Natural history and geology	2	3		5
5. Agriculture and botany		3	5	3
6. English language and belles-lettres	3	2	3	
7. History and philosophy			5	5
8. Modern languages—				
German		3	2	
French		2	3	
9. Ancient languages—				
Latin	5	3	2	
Greek	5	3	2	
Philology				2

Preparatory course: One year in mathematics, Latin, Greek, English and elementary science.

Students may take either (1) a science course, (*a*) mechanical, (*b*) agricultural, or (2) a classical course, according to prescribed studies; or (3) an elective course.

The collegiate year is divided into two terms of twenty weeks' each, without intermission between them. The course of study is continuous throughout the year.

The means for practical application of instruction and studies are as follows:

1. *The agricultural department.*—A farm of 260 acres, well stocked and furnished with all needed agricultural implements, machinery, &c., also thorough-bred cattle, 2 Devons (bull and cow), 7 short-horns (2 bulls, 3 cows and 2 calves), and other more numerous cattle. The land is of fair quality, well improved, convenient, and admirably adapted to stock-raising, and for the growth of the grasses, cereals, fruits, and all other crops required to exemplify and enforce the class-room instruction in theoretical agriculture. Several acres are for experimental purposes, and there have been made or are in progress 120 experiments in wheat, 4 in oats, 12 in grass, and 8 in cattle-feeding. Remunerative labor is furnished to students on Saturdays at about 8 cents an hour.

The means of practical instruction in pomology, horticulture, and botany consist of an orchard of 300 fruit trees, including all kinds; a vineyard of one-quarter of an acre; a small hot-house, and a flower-garden.

2. The *department of mathematics and mechanical philosophy.*—Considerable practice is given students in the solution of original and selected problems in all branches of pure mathematics. The graphical solution of problems in geometry, plane trigonometry, and descriptive geometry initiates the course of mechanical drawing. In the school of applied mathematics there are provided two compasses, one transit, one Y level and leveling staff, one plane table and two chains, which are practically used in plane and topographical surveying, surveying of lines for roads and railroads, including running of curves, making sections and profiles for excavations, embankments, &c. In the school of physics and theoretical mechanics the apparatus is sufficient to illustrate all branches of the subjects by experiments, but is not adapted to original investigations.

Topographical drawing is taught (1) with the pen, (2) with brush in colors. Mathematical drawing is taught in shades, shadows, and perspective, with right line, pen, and brush. Instruction is also given in machine and constructive drawing.

There is a small workshop, provided with a work-bench, a kit of carpenter's tools, an iron vise, a turning lathe, a circular saw, and a fret saw, which are used by the professor in preparing appliances for illustrative experiments, and by his students in manufacturing pieces of apparatus.

3. *Department of natural history and geology.*—The means of practical instruction consists of maps, globes, and charts; models of the human body and its various organs; skeletons and preparations in alcohol of various animals, in whole or parts; collections of insects, and lithological and paleontological specimens, two microscopes, and chemical reagents. Physiology and zoölogy are practically taught in the breeding and feeding of domestic animals and the care of them in health and disease.

4. *Department of chemistry and mineralogy.*—The laboratory is large and provided with work-tables sufficient to accommodate the professor, his assistant, and 14 students at one time. It is also well stocked with apparatus and materials for all the requirements of qualitative and quantitative analyses by the gravimetric method and enough apparatus for volumetric analyses, both of liquids and gases.

For assaying and instruction in metallurgy there is a furnace room provided with apparatus and materials necessary for the valuation of ores and for crucible operations.

Practical mineralogy is taught by means of a collection of about 500 minerals. Determinative mineralogy is taught in the laboratory. * * *

THOS. W. HUMES, *President, &c.*

The following letter explains itself:

UNIVERSITY OF TENNESSEE,
Knoxville, Tenn., September 19, 1882.

Rev. THOS. W. HUMES, S.T.D., *President, &c.*:

In accordance with your request I submit changes and improvements in the department of applied mathematics since 1879.

1. The departments of pure and applied mathematics have been separated, each being now under the direction of a full professor.

2. The department of applied mathematics, of which I am professor, embraces the following subjects: Experimental physics, theoretical mechanics, astronomy, surveying, descriptive geometry, shades, shadows, and perspective, civil engineering, topographical drawing with pen and brush, mechanical and engineering drawing, and field practice with instruments in surveying, leveling, laying out of roads and railroads.

3. The physical apparatus has received valuable additions amounting to about $1,000 worth. These additions embrace important pieces of apparatus in illustration of the principles of electricity, magnetism, heat, and light, and an excellent college telescope, the latter costing $350.

4. Since I have been enabled to devote my time and attention exclusively to the branches of applied mathematics, considerable additional work has been done in practi-

cal work and drawing, and the students have made free use of the telescope in observations.

5. A number of graduates in the course of civil engineering have adopted the profession of engineering, and all of them are now in employment and are doing well.

6. The number of candidates for the degree of bachelor of civil engineer in the class of this year is four.

Respectfully,

S. W. LOCKETT,
Professor of Applied Mathematics.

TEXAS.

STATE AGRICULTURAL AND MECHANICAL COLLEGE, COLLEGE STATION.

The object of the State Agricultural and Mechanical College of Texas is to supply theoretical and practical professional training in agriculture and the mechanic arts. The endowment fund consists of $174,000, invested in Texas 7 per cent. gold bonds, and $35,000 in Texas 6 per cent. bonds. The former sum was realized from the investment of the proceeds of the national land grant; the latter from interest accrued on the original endowment previous to the organization of the college. The annual income from the $209,000 is $14,280. This amount is augmented by receipts from matriculation, incidental, and other fees, and by appropriations. The expenses of the teaching staff for the year 1880 were $12,000.

The college employs professors of the following subjects: Moral philosophy and political economy; English language, history, and literature; ancient and modern languages; physics and chemistry; mathematics; mechanics, engineering and drawing; scientific and practical agriculture and horticulture; and military science. A farm superintendent and a foreman of the shops are included among the officers of the college. The number of students in attendance in 1880–'81 was 127. Of these 1 was a senior, 14 were juniors, 29 sophomores, and 83 freshmen. The total attendance increased to 258 during 1881–'82, owing to changes in the length and character of the course of instruction, the provision for State free scholarships, and the wider acquaintance of the people with the college. The scholarships provided by the legislature in 1881 were 93 in number. One-half of the beneficiaries are required to take the agricultural course and the other half the mechanical. They are maintained and instructed free of charge. Maintenance includes board, fuel, washing, and lights.

The college offers a mechanical and an agricultural course of study, each three years in length. The studies common to the two courses during the first year after admission are arithmetic, algebra, geometry, United States history, English grammar, composition and declamation; during the second year, geometry, trigonometry, surveying, physics, chemistry, history, and rhetoric; during the third year, astronomy, geology, English literature, and the constitutions of the State and the United States. Mechanics comes in the second year of the agricultural course and the third of the mechanical.

The special studies of the agricultural course are as follows: First year, breeds of horses, cattle, sheep, and swine; soils, their formation and classification; history of agriculture and structural botany. Second year, practical agriculture, farm irrigation, field crops, fertilizers, tillage, drainage, dairying, and zoölogy. Third year, farm engineering, farm management, nursery business, meteorology, veterinary science, entomology, rural law, and forestry. Practice in the use of farm machinery is given during the first year; in garden, orchard, and farm culture during the second year, and in experimental work during the third year.

The special branches of the mechanical course are drawing, engineering, and shop practice. Drawing is taught through the course, beginning with freehand and mechanical and ending with machine drawing and designing. The engineering instruction is given in the third year, and includes civil engineering, with field work, and the consideration of mills and mill work, the steam engine and iron. The practice of the first year is in the making of elementary constructions in wood and in the use of wood-working machinery; of the second year, in metal work, mill work, steam enginery, and the use of machine tools; of the third year, in special constructions with machines.

Among the means of illustration and practical instruction are mineralogical and geological cabinets, a chemical laboratory equipped for analytical work, a physical laboratory with valuable and extensive apparatus for illustrating the laws and phenomena of which that science treats, engineering instruments, a drawing room supplied with tables, models, and instruments, a farm of 2,416 acres (230 under fence), gardens, orchards, and vineyards, and a series of shops with tools, wood and metal working machinery, and a steam engine. The college building consists of the main edifice, the mess-hall, president's house, and five professors' residences, all of brick, costing about $160,000; two wooden barracks of twenty-four rooms each; a farmer's residence, a bath house, and a stable.

The president of the college in a recent report speaks of its needs as follows:

"For the mechanical students we need larger shops and a greater number of tools, machines, and appliances. For the practical study of the sciences, chemistry, physics, botany, geology, mineralogy, we need a spacious laboratory to itself, with various apartments thoroughly provided with the most approved and latest instruments of physical research, models, specimens, chemicals, &c. The department of civil engineering is suffering badly from the want of more instruments for field work. The library needs the constant addition of new scientific works as they appear, and the regular standard scientific journals. Quarters for 200 more students, for professors and officers, and for the sick; apparatus and material for giving instruction in printing and in the use of telegraph and telephone; live stock for the farm; and the means of artificial irrigation—these are only the most urgent needs which must be satisfied if the college is to do well and profitably the great work which is expected of it by our people."

Of the department of agriculture and horticulture the professor in charge makes the following statements for the year ending June, 1881:

"I have during the whole session given instruction in agriculture and horticulture to those of the older students who have chosen the agricultural course. The class numbered in the first term eight members; three of these left college during the session, leaving only five at present. As laid down in the catalogue of last year, all the freshmen are also in the agricultural course, but being hard pressed with studies in the fundamental branches, it was thought best to defer the technical studies till they were better prepared to take them up. The subjects gone over during the first term in agriculture were: The soil, its constituents, origin and formation, classification, and physical properties. We next completed a course in drainage. Both subjects were taught by lectures. In the second term the class received full instruction in vegetable gardening and irrigation. The former was taught by lectures; for the latter we used Stewart's text-book. It has been my object throughout to make the instruction as practical as possible, and the class room has been complemented by frequent illustrations and outdoor work; especially is this the case with the gardening. It gives me pleasure to add that the class has made very satisfactory progress.

"Practical instruction in farm and garden operations has also been given to students in agriculture for four hours each week during the past term. They have thus grafted a number of pear stock, which were purchased for that purpose, a work which proved highly interesting; they received instruction in the formation and care of hot-beds and cold frames; they assisted in pruning the orchard, in the planting of the seeds and care of vegetables, &c., and they have also had practice in handling plows, cultivators, mowers, and other farm implements.

"The total area under the plow this year is 53 acres, divided between the following crops, viz: Corn, 24 acres; oats, 3 acres; cotton, 2 acres; millet, 3 acres; vegetables and experiment plots, 10 acres; and orchard, 11 acres.

"There are now 25 varieties of grape vines in the garden, of which 20 varieties are from cuttings purchased this spring, and therefore still young plants. The object is to increase the stock by propagation till we can plant a vineyard, and also to add to the number of varieties, so as to compare them together and report upon their merits. The orchard is in a fair condition, and will this year bear a little fruit."

Of the industrial department the following report is given:

"The duties of this department are, to a great extent, planned with reference to illustrating and applying the scientific principles taught in the class room. All instructive labor is regarded as compensated by the instruction given and the skill acquired. Manual labor is not compulsory, but students who desire to help defray their expenses by work can do so by taking part in the uninstructive labor, such as ordinary farm operations, repairing, carpentering, painting, janitor's duties, and stock management, at fair wages. This can be done at extra hours and on Saturdays, without interference with regular studies and duties.

"Instructive and uninstructive duties will be supplied in:

"1. *Agriculture.*—General farm operations.

"2. *Horticulture.*—Garden, vineyard and fruit culture.

"3. *Stock and dairy management.*

"4. *Mechanics.*—Carpentering, fencing, painting, &c.

"Four thousand dollars has just been expended by the board of directors for the equipment of the mechanical department with the necessary tools, machinery, engine, and materials. The shops in which systematic practical instruction is to be given are: (1)

carpenter shop; (2) vise shop; (3) forge shop; (4) steam, wood, and metal working machinery.

"The directors have fixed the maximum rate of compensation per hour in the agricultural department at 15 cents; in the mechanical, at 20 cents.

"The object is to assist worthy students in every way possible, but the college cannot guarantee to any one student sufficient labor to meet all his expenses, as labor can be furnished only as long as the interests of the institution permit it. A small amount of labor is annually expected from each student to assist the professor in the ornamentation and improvement of the grounds. Agricultural students are encouraged to use their spare time in farm work, at fair wages, but will be paid for quantity and quality of work, not for time only. All paid labor will be given by preference to those students needing assistance."

VERMONT.

STATE UNIVERSITY AND AGRICULTURAL COLLEGE, BURLINGTON.

The object of the University of Vermont and State Agricultural College is to furnish the youth of the State opportunities for education in the branches of special importance to them.

The trustees reported its property, exclusive of the Congressional fund, to be estimated in 1882 at $363,000, its lands at $130,000, its buildings at $65,000, and the collections at $50,000. The amount of trust funds was $113,250. The total income for 1879–'80 was $22,110; the expenditure $21,738, of which $17,506 was absorbed by the payment of the salaries of the teaching staff. The proceeds of the national land grant amounted to $135,500. This sum is invested in 6 per cent. State bonds, and the interest is paid to the college by the State treasurer.

The university has faculties of applied science, arts, and medicine. The faculty of applied science consists of the president, who is professor of political and social philosophy, and professors of mathematics, civil engineering, zoölogy, botany and geology, English language and literature, chemistry and physics, modern languages, and military tactics. These professors, excepting those who teach civil engineering and military science, are in the faculty of arts; and their number is increased by professors of Greek and Latin and of intellectual and moral philosophy. A professor of agriculture is to be appointed as soon as a suitable man is found. The faculty of medicine has 26 members.

The summary of students for 1881–'82 is as follows: Seniors, 16; juniors, 14; sophomores, 20; freshmen, 24; unmatriculated students, 3; total, 77. Of these 47 were taking a classical course, 17 an engineering course, 5 a literary-scientific course, 3 a scientific course, 1 a chemical, and 1 a partial course.

The entire college expenses are estimated at from $176.50 to $249 a year—$54 being for tuition and special fees. There are eighteen scholarships, open equally to members of all the collegiate departments.

As has been intimated, instruction is given in the three departments of arts, applied science, and medicine. The first of these has the usual academic course in languages, mathematics, physical sciences, mental, moral, and political philosophy, rhetoric, literature, and history. The second has courses in agriculture and related branches, chemistry, engineering, and mining. Students have full liberty to elect their courses, but beyond this options are not allowed to those who may be candidates for a degree, except that to a limited extent equivalent substitutions may be made by express permission of the faculty.

The department of applied science provides courses of study which fulfill the requirements of the act of Congress granting public land for the maintenance of agricultural colleges. They are in (1) civil engineering, (2) theoretical and applied chemistry, (3) agricultural and related branches, and (4) metallurgy and mining engineering. As the course in engineering is taken by a comparatively large number of students and as the agricultural course indicates the instruction which is afforded to prospective farmers, these two courses are especially worthy of attention. The course in civil engineering is presented in full, and the difference between that and the agricultural course afterward noted. The studies of freshman year are the same for all the scientific courses, and include algebra, geometry, plane trigonometry and surveying, drawing, chemistry, botany, and English studies, including moral philosophy. The special course in civil engineering is as follows:

SOPHOMORE YEAR.—MATHEMATICS: Spherical trigonometry; analytical geometry; calculus. Drawing: Descriptive geometry; plotting; shades and shadows; isometrical drawing; shading and tinting; topographical drawing. Physics: Stewart's elementary lessons.

INDUSTRIAL EDUCATION IN THE UNITED STATES. 233

Astronomy. French or German. English: French on the Study of Words; Shakspere; Chaucer. Field work: Practice with transit and level; topographical surveying.

JUNIOR YEAR.—MATHEMATICS: Geodesy. Mechanics: Weisbach's treatise commenced; resistance of material. Drawing: Linear perspective; plotting; construction of maps; structural drawings. Henck's field book for engineers. Mineralogy, with blowpipe analysis. Physiology. French or German. English: Rhetoric. Field work: Harbor and river surveying; setting out curves; locating a line of railroad, with computations of excavations and embankments.

SENIOR YEAR.—MECHANICS: Strains in bridge and roof trusses; hydrostatics; pressure of earth; stability of walls and arches; hydraulics and hydraulic motors. Drawing: Mahan's stone cutting; graphical statics. Civil engineering: Mahan's building materials; construction of bridges and roofs, roads, railroads, and canals. Geology. English: History and criticism of English literature. Thesis.

The agricultural course differs from the engineering by the substitution of chemistry and physiology for the mathematics, physics, and the larger part of the drawing and field work of the sophomore year; by replacing the mathematics, mechanics, engineering, and drawing of junior year with chemistry, physics, meteorology, and forestry; and by devoting senior year to studies of special use to the farmer. Chemistry is required throughout the year. In the first term, road making, breeding of animals, and the geology and English of the corresponding term of the engineering course are taken; in the second term, political economy; and in the third term, veterinary medicine and surgery, and constitutional law.

The course in metallurgy and mining engineering coincides with that in civil engineering, save that in the last year metallurgy, assaying, and practical mining take the place of special studies in civil engineering. The course in chemistry is presented elsewhere. To meet the wants of young men who cannot leave the farm in the summer or autumn, a course on agricultural subjects is offered for the winter months on condition ten persons desire to enter upon it. The subjects treated would be agricultural chemistry, botany, physics, entomology, stock breeding, dairying, fruit culture, road making, farm accounts, and bee culture. The course is designed to give a general outline of the subjects treated, to point out the true methods of investigation and the most reliable sources of information, and to stimulate and guide private agricultural study.

The university has a library containing over 19,000 volumes; a museum containing some 80,000 specimens, many of them rare and valuable; and a laboratory fitted up with conveniences for manipulation and experiment amply sufficient for those pursuing studies in chemistry.

The agricultural work of the college has passed beyond the instruction of youth and reached the farmers themselves. The faculty have aided in conducting agricultural meetings, giving lectures on veterinary science, fertilizers, the feeding of stock, insects and parasites, social questions, and other matters of general and special interest to the tillers of the soil. Experiments have been conducted, under the supervision of the college, on farms located in different parts of the State. One prominent object was to ascertain the practicability of increasing the fertility of soils by adding those ingredients of plant food which each soil lacks. The results of these and other experiments were published by the leading papers of the State in six articles prepared by one of the professors. They were also published in pamphlet form and extensively distributed. No work undertaken in the interest of agriculture has been more acceptable to the farmers of the State.

The governor of Vermont, in his inaugural message dated October 5, 1882, speaks as follows regarding the University of Vermont and State Agricultural College:

"The act of Congress of July 2, 1862, which gave to Vermont the fund of which the income goes to this institution, provides that this income shall be used for the support of at least one college where the leading object shall be, without excluding other scientific and classical studies and including military tactics, to teach such branches of learning as are related to agriculture and the mechanic arts, in such manner as the legislatures may respectively prescribe, in order to promote the liberal and practical education of the industrial classes in the several pursuits and professions in life. November 9, 1865, the legislature passed an act constituting the present institution, and provided that the course of study should be such as shall render the whole instruction in conformity with said act of Congress. In the succeeding February the trustees, in accordance with law, established a professorship of modern languages, a professorship of chemistry and its application to agriculture and the mechanic arts, a professorship of geology, mineralogy, and mining, and a department of military tactics. The next August a professor of vegetable and animal physiology was appointed, and a course of study established embracing laboratory practice in its application to agriculture, analysis of soils, relations of soil to vegetable productions, botany, forestry, habits of domestic animals, insects injurious to vegetation, and also civil engineering. Professional instructors of military tactics have also been provided, and special winter courses of lectures have been introduced on agricultural chemistry, botany, physics, entomology, stock breeding, dairying, fruit culture, road making, farm accounts, and bee culture, and these courses will be renewed and extended as they are called for. The trustees and officers have been constant and indefatigable in their efforts to comply with the law in letter and spirit.

"At the time of its charter it was an experiment, and many leading men through the State had great fears as to its success, and would have preferred a separate institution. I have conferred with many of them during the past summer, and find that they are now satisfied that the course taken was a wise and judicious one and its results most beneficial, their only regret being the limited number of students who have availed themselves of its privileges. Legislative committees have been appointed to investigate its progress and management, and have found and reported that the trustees and managers have studiously aimed and faithfully labored to comply with their charters and to meet, so far as their means would allow, all the demands for instruction that have been made upon them, and that more than the income derived from the United States fund is annually expended in paying the expenses of the industrial department. The president and professors are always in readiness to respond to calls for public addresses from lyceums, literary, agricultural, and other associations, and in this way do a vast amount of good, and it is to be noted that they uniformly and pointedly enforce the idea of the dignity and nobility of labor.

"Some persons favor an experimental farm to be used in connection with the college, and thoughtlessly reflect on the trustees for not providing one. The United States law provides that not over 10 per cent. of the fund may be expended for land, and that on no pretence whatever shall any part of the land be used for the erection, preservation, or repair of any building. When the State is ready to erect the buildings and assume their preservation we shall doubtless find the trustees ready to provide the land and tutors. Experimental farming had its origin in Prussia thirty years since, and has rapidly extended, until there are now many stations in Prussia, France, England, and our country. They are to be found in our own latitude and climate in neighboring States. Everything of value in the results of this experimental farming is published in agricultural papers, and is easily and cheaply accessible to all. Such work in Vermont would be largely duplicate. Every State that accepted the government fund has largely aided its agricultural college, in some cases to the amount of millions. Vermont has not yet expended a cent. The institution has always kept out of debt, and its management has inspired such confidence that private beneficence is being largely extended to it. Through the liberality of Mr. John P. Howard the old edifice is now being greatly enlarged and almost entirely rebuilt, and the announcement of Mr. Billings's generous gift to the university has just been made public. It has an extensive library, art gallery, laboratory, and a highly successful medical department.

"I respectfully suggest that you take into consideration the propriety of extending some aid to deserving young men of moderate means, to the end that the opportunities here afforded for a higher education may be improved to a greater extent than is now the case. As the senate is based on population, I would mention as one plan that each senator be allowed to name one person residing in his county who should be entitled to tuition in the agricultural college."

VIRGINIA.

Virginia Agricultural and Mechanical College, Blacksburg.

[Statement from catalogues and letter.]

"The objects of the college are to afford a fair, liberal, and practical education to young men who mean to be farmers and mechanics, and to put such education within the reach of many who have not the means to obtain it elsewhere. While the authorities by no means underrate liberal general culture, they hold steadily in view the fact that the mission of this school is peculiar, as designed to meet the wants of the industrial classes. Hence, while reasonable provision is made for the liberal studies, chief attention is given to those that have obvious connection with the needs of the educated farmer and mechanic. Consequently every student is expected to meet the requirements for actual manual labor, so far as such labor is imposed as a part of his education."

The sale of the land scrip donated by the national government produced $285,000, which sum was invested by the board of education in State bonds. By act of the general assembly, approved March 19, 1872, two-thirds of this sum was set apart for the establishment and maintenance of the Virginia Agricultural and Mechanical College. The college was to be located at Blacksburg, Montgomery County, on the conditions that the real estate of the Preston and Olin Institute should be transferred to it and that the county of Montgomery should subscribe $20,000 to its funds. These conditions complied with, the first session began October 1, 1872. After ten years it was deemed necessary to reorganize the institution. This was accomplished in 1882. The expense of the teaching staff is about $14,000, which is two-thirds of the annual income. The original cost of the grounds and buildings was about $100,000.

The number of students in attendance in the session of 1880–'81 was 84; in the session of 1881–'82, 148. The law provides that 200 students from the State may attend free of tuition. Those outside of the State are required to pay $40 per annum. The attendance of students from other States is quite small. The graduates are about 100; they have taken the degree of "graduate in agriculture" or that of "graduate in mechanics;" the degree of A. B. has been added since the reorganization of the college. Probably one-half are engaged in agricultural or mechanical pursuits.

The course of study is framed for those intending to be farmers or mechanics, and to give scientific and literary education and business preparation. It is as follows:

PREPARATORY YEAR.

Arithmetic, English grammar, geography, history of Virginia, orthography, penmanship, elementary algebra, Latin.

JUNIOR YEAR, NEARLY THE SAME FOR ALL.

English grammar and composition, history of United States, Latin, higher algebra, synthetic geometry, elementary physics, elementary course in agriculture, bookkeeping by single entry, commercial calculations, drawing.

INTERMEDIATE YEAR.

Agricultural.—General chemistry, geology, lectures on agriculture, farm practice, rhetoric, history of English language, algebra, synthetic geometry, ancient and modern history.

Mechanical.—Elementary mechanics, algebra, descriptive geometry, drawing, physics, shop practice, rhetoric, English language, ancient and modern history.

Literary and scientific.—Rhetoric, history of English language, French or German, Latin, ancient and modern history, algebra, synthetic geometry, physics, geology, general chemistry.

Business.—Bookkeeping by double entry, business forms, political economy, rhetoric, English language, ancient and modern history, algebra, synthetic geometry.

SENIOR YEAR.

Agricultural.—Lectures on agriculture, horticulture, &c., agricultural chemistry, agricultural botany, agricultural zoölogy, English literature, trigonometry, surveying, farm practice.

Mechanical.—Technical mechanics, industrial chemistry, mineralogy, metallurgy, mechanical drawing, English literature, trigonometry, conic sections, shop practice.

Literary and scientific.—English literature, French or German, Latin, trigonometry, surveying, conic sections, astronomy, psychology, ethics.

Students enter the class for which their preparation fits them, and are promoted as they make attainments ascertained satisfactory by examination.

The course in agriculture of the senior year discusses the formation of soils, the elements necessary to a fertile soil, means of restoring lost fertility, how plants feed and grow, the necessity and methods of drainage, the principles of stock-breeding, and the general business of a farmer's life.

BUILDINGS AND APPLIANCES.

The college is provided with considerable philosophical and chemical apparatus, by the aid of which the lectures on chemistry and physics are illustrated. A farm of over three hundred acres belongs to the college. It is cultivated in part by the labor of the students. Experiments in agriculture, horticulture, stock breeding, and similar matters are made, with a view to the training of the students and the information of the public. The farm is well stocked and has numerous buildings. The other buildings consist of the three principal college structures, five residences for professors, a commencement hall, hospital, and workshops. The latter are provided with a good steam engine and several excellent machines, among them a planer, band saw, spoke machine, and two turning lathes. Much profitable work is done by the students in the shops, by which they gain skill and experience, and supplement their means for obtaining an education.

The students wear a neat and serviceable uniform, and are required to enter the military department and perform its duties, unless exempted for good reasons.

Expenses for a session of ten months, $132.

The college is out of debt and has a large balance to her credit in the treasury.

HAMPTON NORMAL AND AGRICULTURAL INSTITUTE.

EXPLANATION OF THE ACCOMPANYING DIAGRAM.

1. Virginia Hall, 100 by 190 feet, built in 1877: seventy sleeping rooms, chapel, dining room to seat 300, kitchen, laundry, work rooms, shops.
2. Academic Hall, 110 by 75 feet, containing assembly and recitation rooms, office, and attic dormitory.
3. Seniors' cottage, 32 by 60 feet, 30 students.
4. Maple Cottage, 25 by 32 feet, 18 students.
5. Chapel.
6. Principal's residence.
7. Treasurer's residence.
8. Fire department.
9. Residence of farmer and of pastor.
10. Lexington Cottage.
11. Engineer's cottage.
12. Base ball grounds.
13. Hot beds.
14. Barn.
15. Indian girls' building, "Winona Lodge."
16. Raby Lodge.
17. Ex-President Tyler's house.
18. Rev. Mr. Tolman's residence.
19. Indian boys building, "Wigwam."
20. Office and library building.
21. Stone Memorial Building.
22. Students' dormitory.
23. Old workshop.
24. Huntington Industrial Works—saw mill, &c.
25. Machine shop.
26. Indian workshop.
27. Woodbine Cottage.
28. Rose Cottage.
29. ———.
30. Soldiers' monument.
31. Peach orchard, 700 trees.
32. Cherry orchard, 400 trees.
33. Standard pears, 250 trees.
34. Dwarf pear orchard, 400 trees.
35. Grape vines.
36. Nurseries.
37. Apple orchard, 500 trees.
38. Normal school cemetery.
39. Strawberries.
40. The "Marquand" dormitory.

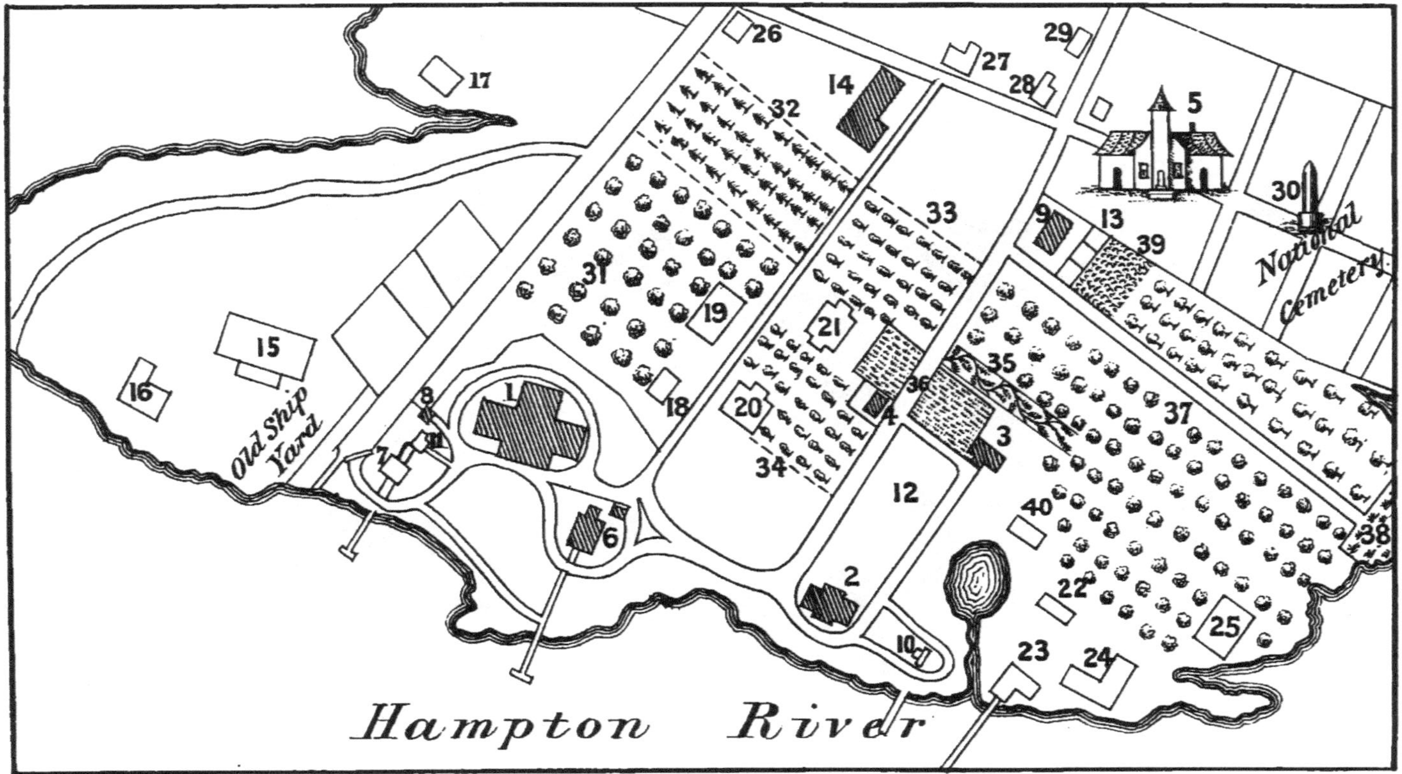

Hampton River
Old Ship Yard
National Cemetery
1
2
3
4
5
6
7
8
9
10
11
12
13
14
15
16
17
18
19
20
21
22
23
24
25
26
27
28
29
30
31
32
33
34
35
36
37
38
39
40

S. EX. 25, 2, 47.

HAMPTON INSTITUTE—VIRGINIA HALL.

HAMPTON NORMAL AND AGRICULTURAL INSTITUTE.

[Statement made October, 1882.]

The Hampton Normal and Agricultural Institute was founded for the instruction of colored youth of both sexes in agriculture and the mechanic arts, and their preparation for the work of teaching among their own race. It has more recently extended its work to the teaching and training of Indian youth. The intention is not to develop the mind of its pupils by collegiate studies, but rather to build up in them a substantial character and habits tending to prosperity. This is done by combining a course of English studies with drill in intelligent manual labor, instructive of itself, promotive of self-reliance and manliness, and helpful to the poor and aspiring negro. The coeducation of the sexes is expected to give the scholars just and appropriate views of their mutual relations. The influence of the school is extended to the masses of the colored people through its graduates, who carry its teachings to the youth of all sections and perform their work with ability and success.

The school is chiefly supported by voluntary contributions from northern friends. It also receives one-third of Virginia's share of the agricultural land grant from the general government. Its sources of revenue are, first, income of agricultural college fund, about $10,000; second, income of school endowment, about $3,500; third, voluntary contributions, about $30,000.

The value of the farms, school grounds, and buildings is $349.283.81; of stock and furniture, $71,080.25; of invested securities, $67,208.46.

The annual expenditure, not including outlays for buildings or cost of 100 Indian students, is $45,000, of which the salaries of officers and teachers is $30,000.

The teachers are as follows: Moral science and agriculture, 1; book-keeping and commercial law, 1; political economy and civil government, 1; mathematics (arithmetic and algebra), 3; English literature and language lessons, 1; grammar and composition, 1; reading and elocution, 1; writing and spelling, 3; history, 1; geography, 1; physiology and hygiene, 1; natural philosophy and chemistry, 1; music, 1; practice-teaching, 1; night school for work students, 5; Indian classes, 8. Industrial teachers, 25; viz, farming, wheelwrighting and blacksmithing, 3; saw-mill and wood-working, 5; engineering, machine shop and knitting room, 1; printing, 1; shoe-making, 1; Indian work shop: instruction in carpentry, painting, tinning, harness making and general repairs, 1, with five assistant teachers; young women's industrial department: sewing and tailoring, 3; cookery, 1; household work, 3.

The enrollment for the school year ending June, 1882, was as follows: colored young men, 239; colored young women, 173; Indian boys, 61; Indian girls, 28; total 501. Average age of young women, 18½ years; average age of young men, 20 years. There was a gain of 106 colored students over the previous year, chiefly among the boarders.

No charge is made for tuition. Board is charged at $10 per month, of which an average of two-thirds is paid in work. Tuition is met by contributions of scholarships from the North.

Scholarships are of two kinds, viz: 1. Permanent, $1,500 each, of which there are thirty-five. 2. Annual, $70 each, of which there are an average of one hundred and eighty, not including those for Indians.

Up to this time, October 23, 1882, 1,886 have been admitted; some of them remained but a few weeks. Including the class of 1882, 456 have graduated. Of these, 23 have died. Not less than 90 per cent. of graduates have devoted themselves to the work of teaching their people. About one-third of the graduates are girls. The proportion of girls in the school is increasing.

The principal said in his report for 1880: "The testimony of southern educational men to the success of our graduates since 1870 has been all that we could wish. They are now in greater demand than ever for the charge of the free colored schools of this and other States; over 20 more than we could supply having been called for this year. From 10,000 to 20,000 children have been taught by them the past year. The majority of them are in the country, with salaries of from $25 to $30 a month, for five or six months, which have of late been paid with promptness. During the off months the industrial training received here gives them resources which they find indispensable." The demand has increased and the applications continue to exceed the supply.

The course of study is as follows:

Junior year: Reading, penmanship and spelling, mental and written arithmetic, geography and map drawing, grammar, and United States history. Instruction in practical farming and the mechanic arts commenced and continued throughout the course, from a day and a half to two days each week. Instruction in sewing and household industries commenced and continued throughout the course, employing the girls from a day and a half to two days each week. Bible lessons commenced and continued throughout the course, on Sunday afternoon from 2 to 3 o'clock.

Middle year: Reading and elocution, penmanship and spelling, arithmetic, grammar, composition and rhetoric, United States history, moral science, physiology, natural philosophy, vocal training. Industrial training as before specified.

Senior year.—Reading, English literature and composition, algebra, book keeping, ancient history, political economy and civil government, theory of agriculture and chemistry, with laboratory work, lectures on Dr. Hopkins's Outline Study of Man, art of teaching. Daily lessons are given to the senior class in the theory and methods of teaching. Members of the class visit the Butler school (a primary school taught on the grounds, and partly sustained by the county as a public free school) for purposes of observation and practice.

A three weeks' institute at the close of the course gives also special preparation for teaching.

A fifteen minutes' talk is given daily to the whole school upon the news of the day, &c. The studies of the Indian classes are rudimentary; teaching is chiefly by the object method. At the close of the school year of 1880, after little over eighteen months' tuition, they were reading simple stories. The girls have the same educational advantages as the boys and are in the same classes. They are also taught sewing and housework by their matron, and share the instructions of the cookery class with the colored girls.

Those of the Indian students who have sufficient knowledge of English enter the regular classes of the school. Three Indian young men graduated very creditably with the class of 1882; another is doing well in the class of 1883; and over a dozen are in the two lower classes—boys and girls.

OPPORTUNITIES FOR INDUSTRIAL EDUCATION.

The students pay about two-thirds of the charges made against them, by manual labor. The value of the work done is not so great as would be that of regular common laborers hired at the usual rates. A loss of from 20 to 40 per cent. is entailed. This expense is warranted by the good which is done in the training of the pupils. The question is rather what can be done for the student than what he can do for the institution. Able bodied farm boys get 8 cents an hour; wages are according to work done.

The following extract from the principal's report for 1882 gives the prominent present and prospective industrial employments of the school:

INDUSTRIAL DEPARTMENTS.

Work details, colored students.

Housework	175	Cookery class	60
Industrial room	65	Laundry	110

No work has yet been provided for day scholars. A girl often works in two departments.

Farm	65	Industrial room	1
Saw-mill	38	Tinsmith	1
Knitting room	7	Painters	2
Engineer's department	9	Cooks	3
Table waiters	35	Carpenters	4
Janitors	12	Shoemakers	3
Office duty	4	Tailor	1
General duty	3	Mail-carriers	2
Blacksmith	1	Wheelwrights	3
Printing office	3	Stock farm	10
Commissary department	1	Brickmakers	4
Watchmen	2	Harness-makers	2

Day scholars on orderly duty, 13. Total earnings last year, $24,898.37.

Indian students.

Housework	15	Industrial room	28
Cookery class	20	Wheelwrights	4
Farmers	8	Painters	2
Carpenters	41	Engineers	5
Shoemakers	11	Butchers	2
Tinsmiths	7	Harness-makers	4
Blacksmiths	3	Printers	2

Indians have a monthly allowance of from $2.50 to $5.00 for their labor, according to the time and value of it. It is not included in the above total; with this they purchase a portion of their clothing. This is to teach them the use of money. As a rule they work half days, studying the other half, and have holiday on Saturdays.

Indian apprentices are slow, and, owing to ailments, not very regular; but they are neat, interested in their work, and learn easily.

AGRICULTURE AND MECHANICS.

The number of colored students employed in agriculture was 83; earnings last year, $6,025—to be increased this year.

This department has two farms, one of 190 acres, connected with the school, and another 4½ miles distant, of 350 acres, called "Hemenway Farm" a gift, to which has recently been added, by purchase, another of 250 acres adjoining; both are well adapted for stock and grain.

The last named, of 600 acres, is in charge of Mr. Charles H. Vanison, a graduate, and is cultivated entirely by work students. On the former, Mr. George Davis, also a graduate, assists Mr. Howe, the general manager.

Agriculturally the school is well appointed; nearly complete, with land, outfit, machinery, and stock. There remains only a debt of $2,500 on the last purchased farm, half its cost. Brick-making and the wheelwright and blacksmith shops are in this department.

Total number of colored students employed in mechanics 82; number of Indians employed, 61.

THE HUNTINGTON INDUSTRIAL WORKS,

comprising a steam saw-mill and wood-working establishment, were the gift of Mr. C. B. Huntington, of New York, costing in all over $30,000, and affording to industrious young men without means the opportunity of getting an education and learning a good trade.

Colored students employed --- 38
Earned last year -- $3,535

Earnings will be increased this year. The capacity of the mill per day is fifteen thousand feet of lumber. Every year a class of from fifteen to twenty destitute, ignorant, but earnest young men, enter the mill for one year steady work of ten hours. Of the most promising, a few are selected for a two years' apprenticeship in the wood-working shop in the second story. They are "work students," studying two hours every night till they enter the regular course, and then are employed two days each week, studying four days throughout the three years' course, being able to save from one year of steady work at the mill $60 to $70 and in two years $140 for school expenses. They are the poorest class, but ask no charity.

About one-fourth drop out for various reasons. Those who graduate are valuable men. The mill is doing a good business, preparing and selling building material of all kinds. It creates fine opportunities for young men to work their way, and may well be a source of gratification to its generous founder.

ENGINEERING.

Number of students employed ----------------------------------- 13
Earned last year -- $1,130 74

and increasing. This branch has been established eight years, but has never had suitable quarters. It has piped all the principal buildings for steam, water, and gas, connecting them by an underground system of steam pipes 1,500 feet in length, which works admirably; made 300 bedsteads out of gas pipe; attends to ten boilers and four steam engines, and repairs machinery.

A gentleman has just offered $4,000 for a new brick workshop 60 by 40 feet, two stories, in which a bone mill and grist mill can be placed to great advantage.

We have long ground bones, but never satisfactorily, owing to poor machinery, and could save about $35 a month by grinding our own meal.

Considering the probable growth of the shop, a suitable steam engine, boiler, lathes of various kinds, shafting, pulleys, drill press, planer, grist mill, and bone mill would cost $10,000.

Such a machine shop would add to the educational powers of the institute and provide much-needed opportunities.

GENERAL STATEMENTS.

Agriculturally the negro is going ahead, for he is the laborer of the South; he is buying farms at $5 an acre, and covering the land with his small holdings.

Mechanically he is losing ground, for there is no way for him to acquire the needed skill. The majority, however, are not adapted to mechanics. For all that, they are capable of producing an excellent mechanical class. The shops, North and South, are, as a rule, closed to them.

The present generation of colored mechanics were nearly all trained in slavery.

In general, it may be said of the industries of schools which teach the trades in connection with studies, that, if given the building and outfit and salaries of foremen, they will take care of themselves.

Our problem is to turn to account the labor payments of students, who, last year, earned $24,898.37, being paid at the rate of from 4 to 8 cents per hour. This year it will be more.

From their standpoint it is fairly earned. From ours, at least one-fourth of it, say $6,000, is a direct drain on our resources. We give much employment regardless of pecuniary profit; the welfare of the student is made paramount; instruction is primary to production. The student learns, but the school loses.

This $6,000 must be had to pay for board and clothing. Shall it be received as a charity or a wage-money? The difference is wide. We choose the latter, though it would be easier to get it by an appeal to the benevolent in the name of poverty. We ask the benevolent to maintain a work that within itself takes care of the student and develops self-reliance and manual skill, and preserves his self-respect and dignity.

This is not the way to make polished scholars, but it makes men.

Last year's total charges to students (for board, &c.,) were $30,679 96
Last year's payments by students:
    In labor 24,898 37
    In cash 4,025 37
Aid in direct charity 2,159 29
       Total 31,083 03

The surplus of students' credits is owing to the fact that the ninety work students who attend night class only, working the whole of every week day, are laying up their earnings by agreement, so as to have a fund from which to meet their cash payments when they enter the regular course. As students have increased, charity has decreased, as follows:

Session of 1878–'79, 254 students; direct aid $2,452 19
Session of 1879–'80, 293 students; direct aid 2,491 04
Session of 1880–'81, 321 students; direct aid 2,159 29

Average students' labor is not up to that of outside labor. The student's chief ambition is for book knowledge. He works because he must; his muscles are not tough; life is not fully serious to him, for all its responsibilities are not upon him. There is a humanity in the school that he may unconsciously count on.

Many, however, either flinch from work or break down under it. The way to make men is to train the head and the hand together. This is the most difficult, the most costly problem in education, but it pays. The better the product the more it costs.

RESULTS OF INDIAN EDUCATION.

Our Indian workshop has completed, for the Indian Department in Washington, to be used in the West, 2,000 pairs of shoes, 70 sets of double plow harness, and 500 dozen articles of tinware, and hopes to supply something more.

The interesting fact of the year has been the return, after three years' training, of thirty-one Indians—five of them girls—to their homes in Dakota. One went to Indian Territory.

They were brought here by Capt. R. H. Pratt, in November, 1878, by order of Secretary Schurz, and returned October 1, 1881.

They are employed at salaries of from fifteen to twenty dollars a month and rations, as follows: Farmers and herders, 7; teachers, 3; carpenters, 9; blacksmiths, 2; office boy, 1; issue clerk (for rations), 1; shoemaker, 1.

One is out of health and one was killed by accident.

They are settled among the Sioux agencies on the Upper Missouri, thus: At Yankton agency, six—four boys and two girls. These are favorably reported upon by the Rev. J. P. Williamson and Rev. Joseph Cook, missionaries. The former says:

"So far they have all run well. I have not heard a slander against one of the number.

They attend church regularly; they are recognized as leading spirits among the Christian youth; their appearance is always creditable." He says: "Not one white boy in sixteen would do his work or teach as well as David Simmons."

The latter writes less favorably of the two girls, who live in the camp with their mothers.

Five are at Lower Brûlé, of whom three had not been doing well. Major Parkhurst, agent, has just written as follows:

"All the returned boys from Hampton have come to time, and are now at work. They were 'tired of doing nothing,' and concluded 'to come under the yoke.'"

Three boys and one girl are at Crow Creek, the latter keeping her father's store and accounts, but not under the best of influences. The two shopboys, carpenters, are reported as "doing all that could be expected," and the teacher as "doing splendidly." They are exerting a good influence on the Indians around them.

Five boys are at Cheyenne River Agency. One is an assistant teacher; the rest are mechanics. "All are doing splendidly," reports Major Love, agent. Mr. Kinney, missionary, writes, "Your boys are doing very nicely."

Two boys and one girl are at Standing Rock Agency. Major McLaughlin, agent, writes: "Both the young men are doing well." A lady missionary reports that "The young men are doing first rate; they are quite conscientious workers, and have the respect of every one." The girl has poor prospects.

Five boys and one girl are at Fort Berthold Agency. The girl writes: "Hard out here to be good woman." She is doing well, however. Three of the boys give good satisfaction as workers; two have gone to school at Santee.

The latest reports upon them are the most hopeful. Those who have separated themselves from camp-life, and occupy decent rooms at the agencies, have done the best. Girls cannot do this, and suffer in consequence. Forty new pupils from the same agencies are here, and will, we hope, in two and one-half years re-enforce them. Will they hold out? Their relations with the school are most pleasant; there is constant correspondence, and we hope to help them, even from here. A probation of six months is short, and not conclusive, but it gives ground for hope.

The new Indian girls' building, to which the name "Winona (Elder Sister) Lodge" has been given, is finished, and has cost $30,000. Probably it is the most complete provision ever made for such a purpose. Our thirty Indian girls will be increased to at least fifty next fall.

S. C. ARMSTRONG, *Principal.*

The following article from the American Missionary by the principal of Hampton Institute, General S. C. Armstrong, gives a brief and comprehensive view of the work and duty of Indian education in the east:

At Hampton there are ninety and at Carlisle there are nearly three hundred Indians—boys and girls—who are learning civilization as an object lesson, and are themselves an object lesson to the centres of intelligence and wealth, where are the sentiment that inspires and the means that provide for the combined practical and spiritual teaching of the red man. They suffice, perhaps, for a tangible proof of the Indian's capacity, of which the need was great; their effect upon public sentiment has been marked. The result with these Indians has, so far, proved satisfactory. Scattering these pupils among the farmers of Massachusetts and of Pennsylvania for a portion of the year has had such a good effect mutually that five hundred more might well be so placed in various States, under the care of special agents, with proper rendezvous where the sick or unsatisfactory might be kept with a view to returning home, say, 10 per cent. of the entire number.

The negro institutions at Nashville, Tenn., at Talladega, Ala., and elsewhere could do excellent work for them. The aims and methods of most white schools render them unfit for Indians.

We have found the weak point of the race to be physical, not mental or moral. They can endure the hardships peculiar to the plains, but not steady work from day to day. They are tainted with inherited disease; the lungs are their weak point. They are sinewy but not muscular; however, as a race they hold their own with favorable surroundings, are not decreasing seriously, if at all, and will not settle the problem by dying out.

Mechanically they have proved apt to learn, but slow to execute. Our Hampton Indian workshops have this year supplied the Indian department with two thousand pairs of men's brogan shoes, five hundred dozen articles of tinware, and seventy-five sets of double plow harness, which were pronounced by the inspectors well made and satisfactory. Carlisle has done more.

Both girls and boys take quickly and kindly to neatness and to industrial pursuits, as well as to books. They are as eager as the negroes for knowledge, and become more and more so as they advance. Want of ambition is the least of their troubles. Teaching them is hard work, but interesting and stimulating in the highest degree.

They resent injury, but are not revengeful; not a sign of treachery in nearly five years. Religiously they are, I believe, the most hopeful of the heathen races. The vastness and the grandeur of the West has affected them as desert life has the Arabs; they are remarkably oriental in customs and ideas. They worship no fetish, there are no idols to break, but they have a crude faith to be cleared, dim eyes to be opened.

Christian efforts, under the care of Archdeacon Kirby of the Episcopal Church, have evangelized ten thousand Indians of British America, in their simple natural life. The mixed, harassed condition of our own makes the work far more difficult.

The mingling of races at Hampton has worked well; they are mutually helpful and stimulating. An Indian classmate is kindly, thoughtfully treated by his colored compeers. A race that has been led is leading another. The "house-father," chief of our sixty Sioux boys, is a negro. With perhaps finer mental and moral texture, the red race does not produce half enough to feed itself; the rougher, stronger blacks have not thrown a pauper upon the country, and raise raw material for the mills of Christendom. With benevolent intentions we have diminished and weakened the one; using the other only for selfish purposes, it has multiplied and grown stronger. Bringing both races under the care of the American Missionary Association is most fitting and wise. Both are peculiarly the concern of the American people, are providentially committed to our care, and are a part of us. In doing for them we are doing for ourselves, our children, and our country.

On the Indian girl rests most heavily the weight of past and present influences. When, in October, 1881, I took 25 Indian boys and five girls back to their Dakota homes, after three years' training at Hampton, the former were readily placed in rooms by themselves, away from the camp, employed in agency workshops at the trades they had learned, and thus helped on greatly. The girls could not be so isolated; they had no trades, and though they could make their own garments and do housework, there were not suitable situations for them; they returned to their mothers and grandmothers, who might sell them to the brave who would pay the highest price in ponies for them.

One of the five, an earnest Christian, wrote: "Hard to be good woman out here." She finally married a white man of good repute. Another is reported as a most satisfactory house servant in the family of a missionary; another keeps her father's store and books. He is one of the best and most thrifty of Indians; but the family live in one room in a log house. Two others, younger, are waiting an opportunity to return to Hampton for two years' more training, with a view to becoming teachers.

Teaching is the career for Indian girls, as it has been the one way for colored girls of the South to be more than drudges; there it is the only field for a womanly ambition. The increase of educational work for Indians creates some hope for their girls, on whom rests the future of their race.

There is a tendency to increase our Indian's course of study to longer than three years. One set having returned, the Indians, whose parental feelings are tender and strong, are more trustful of us, and readily consent to a longer absence of their children. One boy has already returned at his own expense, and another is saving his money for the purpose, both to learn more and to perfect themselves in their trade of shoemaking. The sooner the Indian can stand without government aid the better. Any boy can return who will pay his way back. This gives a motive to work, and creates appreciation of his opportunities.

For the practical necessities of Indian life their training should be practical.

We give half the day to study and half to labor. An education which does not fit them to take care of themselves may do them more harm than good.

I think that when charity and the government are linked together for Indian work the former should erect the buildings and maintain the teachers, the latter supply the wants of the body. United States beef and flour and shoes are as good as anybody's, but government employés, as our civil service stands, are not the men to elevate the Indian. The telling factor in all work for men is the person who does it. Unless that shall be supplied from the pure fountains of our Christian civilization it will not, as a rule, be supplied at all. I refer to the educational work at the agencies; there the government day and boarding schools should be strictly responsible to the controlling power, and their moral value will be that of the agent in charge. Missionary institutions should stimulate these, and should be conducted by superior men and women directly responsible to their Eastern supporters. I call it sham missionary work to send out Christian teachers to be supported on public pay. The churches who do that, and some do, are doing nothing. Let us first send our own teachers for the Indians, and then fit them to become their own teachers; to make the teachers is to make the people.

The free negro schools in the South are vitalized by a number of strong central institutions under northern men that train the picked growth of the race as teachers. This is, I think, the true relation of eastern charity to the Indian. There should be an excellent boarding and industrial school at each important agency for this purpose. Getting $15 a month of Government for food and clothing for each pupil need not in the least weaken the independence or morals of teachers. The friends of the Indian will do the rest. The situation is critical, the opportunity is great; the rising tide of public sentiment, the movement at Washington, the eagerness as well as the exigency of the red man mean much.

But this work needs a leader; it will drag if thrown on an overloaded man. The man is as much as the money; the one will bring the other, both by wise appeals and good work that will commend itself to the country. For more than a century Indians rejected our civilization; now their thinking men—for they are a race of thinkers—forecast the future and wish their children taught the white man's way as their only hope. They do not choose this; they are compelled to it. Hundreds, thousands, are waiting for an education. They beg for what they once refused.

RESULTS ATTAINED AT HAMPTON.

But the work of Hampton Institute is more largely with the colored people, and there need be no better evidence of the thorough and practical education they are there receiving than the report of the last examining committee and large percentage (61.4) of correct answers to questions submitted to the last senior class by Mr. George A. Walton, one of the committee. Portions of the report are here presented, together with a list of the questions mentioned:

Connected with the Normal Institute is the Butler school, which serves as a training or practice school for the students of the Normal. This school is in charge of the teacher of methods in the institute, and affords a fine opportunity for training in the art of teaching. There each student spends a portion of his senior year, not simply in observing, but in acquiring skill by the practice of his art. A "kitchen garden," as it is called, has been introduced into this school; this consists of practice in the various duties belonging to housekeeping, such as sweeping, dusting, laying and tending table, washing, and so on. These operations are practiced under direction of the teacher, by all the pupils, sets of miniature utensils being furnished for the practice. Thus the ordinary exercises of the school are supplemented by training in those habits of order and neatness so conducive to comfort, culture, and happiness in the home. Thus furnished, the student of Hampton graduates with an outfit which must place him in the front rank of the teaching profession in the section of the country where he is called to labor.

Nor does this growth cease with his graduation. By a plan, so far as known to the committee, peculiar to Hampton, the former graduates of the school take the principal parts at commencement; six of the exercises of this year were by graduates of the class of 1881, one was by a graduate of the class of 1873. For practical wisdom and breadth of comprehension, these parts could nowhere be excelled by any class of students of equal opportunities. All were delivered with force and expression, and must have convinced the most skeptical that the problem of the future of his race is solved when the colored man is furnished with an education and an equal chance to labor. Less time than we desired was given to examining the methods and estimating the results of the industrial education, which is a leading feature of the Hampton Institute. Enough, however, was seen to show that manual labor, as a means of mental and physical training, is an essential. Each student is required to give at least two days a week to this department. Some are engaged in working upon the land, of which there are about 600 acres of tillage; others work at the various trades. The students make long days, but with the varied employments, little fatigue is experienced, and good health is the rule. Thus, in addition to the knowledge and discipline received in the school proper, every student leaves the institution with the ability to support himself by some useful employment.

The industrial pursuits are calculated to exercise the students' active powers or faculties, as distinguished from their passive powers or capacities. In this respect these pursuits supplement in a remarkable degree the training received by the ordinary school processes. The complaint frequently made that the student is unable to do anything when he leaves school, is too often true; with such training as is received at Hampton this complaint is not likely to be made, for it will not be true. This would be inferred from the nature of the case, but it is actually shown in the service the graduates are able to render. The treasurer's clerks are graduates of Hampton, doing their work with accuracy and dispatch; the overseers on both the farms run by the institution are graduates of the school, as is also the head of the tailoring department. Over 90 per cent. of all the graduates have taught in the schools of Virginia or other States. One is principal of a normal school in Alabama, while three-fourths of all the graduates have chosen teaching as a profession. Others, not in schools, are filling positions of trust and responsibility; nearly all who teach report Sunday schools connected with their day schools, and some have founded temperance societies.

Thus it will be seen that, wherever they go, the graduate teachers become the leaders among their people.

And so, through this and similar institutions throughout the South, the problem of good citizenship presented by negro suffrage is solved. Give the colored man a good education and a fair chance and he will surely become a good citizen and win for himself and his race honorable distinction. The figures in this problem are the slaves themselves; the solution depends on liberal endowments and efficiency of management, such as is seen at Hampton.

Though the colored race has been chiefly considered in the report and though the evidence is less cumulative in the case of the Indian, from what is known there is every reason to believe that, admitted to equal privileges and charged with the same responsibilities, the same results are to flow to the red man. The committee heartily concur in the statement in General Armstrong's report for the academic year just closed: "Our four years' work for Indians satisfies us that their progress is a question not of capabilities, but of opportunities. Universal education means peace and prosperity to the red man. Justice and humanity call for it, and common sense suggests that paying $800 in three years for the education of an Indian is better than paying $1,000 a year for each soldier sent to fight him."

So the question what shall be done with the emancipated slave and the "savage Indian" is solved not by extermination, but by mental discipline and a training of their powers to various forms of labor.

QUESTIONS.

I.

ARITHMETIC.—How many bushels of potatoes in a rectangular bin 10 feet square at the bottom and 2½ feet deep, allowing 1¼ cubic feet to a bushel?

LANGUAGE.—Write a telegram to some person at home, stating that you have arrived at New York and naming the day you expect to reach home; also naming the railroad by which you are to come.

GEOGRAPHY.—(1) Name some country in about the same latitude as New England, which has a warmer climate. (2) What are some of the causes that affect the climate of a country?

II.

ARITHMETIC.—Two bushels one peck of seed peas were put up in bags, each holding three-fifths of a gill; how many bags were required?

LANGUAGE.—Correct the following sentence, if incorrect, and state the reason for the corrections:

Samuel or John have worked here last year; i do not know as either of them are here now.

GEOGRAPHY.—Name a port to which vessels sailing from Boston go for (1) sugar and molasses, (2) raw hides, (3) coffee. (4) Write anything you know about any of these articles.

III.

ARITHMETIC.—A square lot of land was inclosed by a fence at a cost of $40. If the fence cost $0.62½ per rod, what was the length of one side of the lot?

LANGUAGE.—Correct the following sentence, if incorrect, and parse "laid" and "by:"

A peck of these kind of peas were laid by for planting.

GEOGRAPHY.—Name the bodies of water upon which are situated (1) Boston, (2) Springfield, Mass., (3) Philadelphia, (4) Chicago. (5) Describe any of these cities.

IV.

ARITHMETIC.—How many yards of carpeting three-fourths of a yard wide are required to carpet a floor 16½ feet long and 9 feet wide, allowing nothing for waste?

LANGUAGE—Correct the following sentences, if incorrect, and parse "ought:"

Ought a pupil to whisper in school i don't think they had.

GEOGRAPHY.—(1) Name three important exports of the Southern States. (2) Tell where they are produced and anything you know about any of them.

V.

ARITHMETIC.—How many cans, each holding 1½ pints, will be required to hold 7 gallons 2 quarts of preserves?
LANGUAGE.—(1) What is the subject of a sentence? (2) Give an example of a simple sentence; (3) of a compound sentence; (4) of a complex sentence.
GEOGRAPHY.—(1) Name five of the largest rivers of North America, and tell into what each flows. (2) State anything you know about any of these rivers.

VI.

ARITHMETIC.—If 2 boys can shovel a snow-path in 24 minutes, in what part of an hour can 3 boys shovel it?
LANGUAGE.—Write a short letter to your father, describing your school and your work.
GEOGRAPHY.—(1) Which is farther north, Albany or Paris? (2) Name in order the bodies of water you would pass through in going from Albany to Liverpool. (3) Describe any of the above named cities.

VII.

ARITHMETIC.—Find the bank discount on $600 from July 15 to the 5th of August next following, the rate being 5 per cent.
LANGUAGE.—Write a letter to a manufacturer, ordering goods sent you by some particular express.
GEOGRAPHY.—(1) Through what zone does the equator pass? (2) How many degrees in width is this zone? (3) What countries lie mainly in this zone?

VIII.

ARITHMETIC.—Bricks are 8 inches long, 4 inches wide, and 2 inches thick. How many bricks will it take to build a wall 20 feet long, 10 feet high, and 18 inches thick, allowing one-fifth of the wall to be cement?
LANGUAGE.—Correct the following sentence, if incorrect: (1) Each board of officers keep their own accounts. (2) Make out a bill against your teacher for a hat, and receipt the bill.
GEOGRAPHY.—(1) Draw an outline map of your own State, and locate your own town. (2) Write a brief description of your town, naming in order the towns which surround it.

WEST VIRGINIA.

WEST VIRGINIA UNIVERSITY, MORGANTOWN.

[Statement obtained from catalogues, &c.]

The proceeds of the land grant to West Virginia were supplemented by appropriations from the State and aid given by the town in which the agricultural college was to be located. The original institution was named the West Virginia Agricultural College, but after it had been fully adopted by the State an act was passed requiring it to be known as the West Virginia University. It is announced that its design is "to educate, inform, and discipline the student's mind, to strengthen his moral principles, and supply such general and generous as well as special culture as will best prepare him for success and usefulness in any pursuit or profession in life."

The value of its grounds, buildings, and apparatus is estimated at $175,000. Its productive funds amounted to $110,000, the annual income of which is $6,500. The State appropriation for 1881 was $16,500.

The faculty has 12 members. The department of agriculture, chemistry, and physics has been recently furnished with a commodious and well appointed laboratory of theoretical and practical chemistry.

The students in attendance in the school year 1881–'82 were 177 in all the departments. Of these 102 were preparatory and 75 collegiate students. Nearly all of them were residents of West Virginia, only 18 being from other States. The tuition in the preparatory departments is $5 each term, and in other departments $8. There are three terms a year. The number of graduates previous to 1883 was 78.

The instruction thus far provided for in the university is embraced in 5 departments, namely: classical, scientific, agricultural, engineering, and military; there are also law, medical, and preparatory departments. The classical course is similar to the academic course of other colleges. The scientific course gives special prominence to chemistry, and agriculture is among the studies prescribed. The department of engineering has the studies common to such a course, being the same as the scientific course up to the senior year. In the military department there are daily drills by the cadets, and military science is systematically taught. The studies include among others cavalry and artillery tactics, military history, military engineering, the strategy and art of war, military law and court-martial, and ordnance and gunnery. Dress parade, reviews, inspections, and guard mountings are held as often as deemed expedient. The law provides that five cadets may be appointed in each senatorial district in the State. These are educated free of cost for tuition, books, stationery, &c. The cadets may pursue their studies in any department of the university, subject to general regulations. The drill occupies one hour on each of four days in the week. The cadets must be between sixteen and twenty-one years of age.

The studies of the agricultural department are embraced in a two years' course, and those who complete them creditably receive a certificate to that effect. Agricultural instruction is given largely by lectures. The subjects treated by these in the first year include the chemistry, structure, and physiology of plants, air, water, and soil; tillage, draining, and manuring; domestic animals; foods; agriculture; products; gardening and the culture of fruits and vegetables. In the second year topics directly treating of farm operations, including the raising of crops, the care of domestic animals, rural economy, the history of agriculture, and entomology are made the subjects of lectures. The law department includes courses for two years of nine months each, and leads to the degree of bachelor of law. The medical department is also open during the entire university session of nine months. In the two departments last named instruction is given principally by means of lectures and practical exercises by the students.

WISCONSIN.

UNIVERSITY OF WISCONSIN, MADISON.

[Statement obtained from catalogues, letters, &c.]

The University of Wisconsin was organized in 1848, and reorganized in 1866. By the act of reorganization its object was declared to be "to provide the means of acquiring a thorough knowledge of the various branches of learning connected with scientific, industrial, and professional pursuits."

The endowment consists of the university fund, $226,460.78; the agricultural college fund, $267,330.86; the Johnson endowment fund, $5,000; and the Lewis medal fund, $200. The value of the grounds, buildings, and apparatus is $455,000. For the year closing with September, 1881, the income was as follows: State appropriation, $44,558.27; from productive funds, $31,749.38; students, $5,933.43; entire income, $82,669.81. There are 4,210 acres of university land and 4,359 acres of agricultural college land remaining unsold.

The faculty consists of a president, 19 professors of the colleges of arts and letters, 7 professors of the law faculty, 11 instructors, and 5 other officers.

The collegiate professorships are as follows: Mental and moral philosophy; mathematics; Latin and history; Latin; Greek language and literature; astronomy; civil polity and political economy; physics; chemistry and agriculture; German language and literature; English literature; geology; mining; metallurgy; Scandinavian languages; rhetoric and oratory; French language and literature; zoölogy; civil and mechanical engineering; botany and agriculture; music; military science and tactics.

The number of students in attendance during the collegiate year closing in 1882 was 398, classified as follows:

	Seniors.	Juniors.	Sophomores.	Freshmen.	Total.
Resident graduate					1
Ancient classical course	18	11	19	18	66
Modern classical course	16	18	15	22	71
Scientific course	20	9	8	24	61
Civil engineering course	3	5	11		19
Mechanical engineering course		2			2
Metallurgical course	3				3
Agricultural course		1		2	3
Total					228
Special students					116
Law students					50
Greek class					6
Grand total					398

There is preparatory work in Greek only.
Tuition is free to residents of the State; $18 to others.
There are ten scholarships, for the present limited to students speaking one of the Scandinavian languages. Their annual value is $50 each.
The graduates number 877; collegiate, 570; law, 307. Of the collegiate graduates 430 are men; 140 women.
Degrees have been conferred as follows: A. B. (ancient classical course), 129—121 on men, 8 on women; L. B. (modern classical course), 66—33 on men, 33 on women; S. B., 228—160 on men, 68 on women; C. E. B., 21; M. B. (mining), 7; M. E. B. (mechanical engineering), 1; agriculture, 1.
The eight courses of study in the colleges of arts and letters are termed respectively the ancient classical, modern classical, general science, agricultural, civil engineering, mechanical engineering, mining, and metallurgical courses.
The ancient classical course corresponds to the usual academic course of other colleges.
The modern classical course substitutes French or German for Greek.
The general science course is, after the first year, chiefly elective, and election of studies may be made from all the leading departments of mathematical and physical science, and the modern languages.
The civil engineering course provides such instruction as shall fit its students to develop into capable engineers.
The mechanical engineering course is accompanied throughout by practice in the machine shop.
The mining and metallurgical courses are nearly alike, the variation being in giving special prominence to chemistry in the latter. The two courses may be united and accomplished by an able and diligent student in the usual time allotted to a single course.
The agricultural course is supplemented by experiments in agriculture and horticulture on the university farm.
The courses in agriculture and mechanical engineering deserve extended notice, as being the ones which most directly teach industries.
The course in mechanical engineering was established in 1877. The studies of the first year are the same as those in the course in general science, with one exception. The special studies of the second year are chemistry, drawing, and the elements of machines; the third year, drawing, resistance of materials, the steam engine and machinery, and mill work; the fourth year, drawing and the steam engine continued, metallurgy, hydraulics and hydraulic motors, and machine designing. Shop practice is continued throughout the course.
The course in agriculture, extending through four years, is designed to meet the wants of such young men as may desire a college education and yet have it tend in the direction of the farm.
One language is taught in this course, namely, German, by which the way is opened to a direct knowledge of the work of the agricultural experimental stations of Germany. In this course some eight terms in all are spent in the study of chemistry, and practice is given in analysis of agricultural products, both qualitatively and quantitatively. Next to chemistry stands botany, which is taught during four terms, and comprehends a study of not only our common plants but a familiarity with the wild and cultivated grasses, and as full a consideration as time will permit of the noxious fungi. Among studies requiring from one to two terms might be named zoölogy, physics, and geology. Agriculture as a study comes in the last year of the course, at a time when the student is well prepared by previous preparation to take up such subjects as stock breeding, stock feeding, rotation of crops, drainage, &c. Students completing the course are given the degree of bachelor of agriculture.
Since the requirements for admission into this course are above the ability of many young men who are desirous of devoting some time to study in this direction, special students in agriculture are admitted upon passing examination in the common English branches. Special students may pursue any studies of the course for which they are prepared.
It is most evident, however, that the scope of an agricultural department is quite limited if its effort ends with giving instruction to the pupils at hand. Cognizant of this fact, and desirous of extending its usefulness to the many intelligent farmers of the State who are otherwise ignored, the board of regents established the experimental farm. For a series of years the farm was largely devoted to making tests as to the productiveness of the various varieties of field crops. Among the experiments, running through several years, was that of the endeavor to find a winter wheat suited to Southern Wisconsin. The value of the Fultz and Clawson were early demonstrated for this purpose.
In 1881 the legislature appropriated $4,000 for experiments in amber cane and the ensilage of fodders. In 1882 it appropriated $2,000 for a continuance of this work. It is yet too early to predict the results of these experiments as a whole, but those of the first

year with amber cane were permanently successful as compared with results obtained in this direction elsewhere. In 1881 about 1,200 pounds of good raw sugar were made, and this was refined into good brown and white sugar. The yield per acre varied from 700 to 1,000 pounds of sugar, in addition to from 80 to 100 gallons of syrup and 30 bushels of seed.

In the ensilage of fodders no very satisfactory data were obtained, but at present it would seem that this season we have all the facts necessary to ascertain the value of this method of preserving fodder in our State.

The university is open to females under such regulations as the board of regents may deem proper. They are received in all respects on the same terms as young men.

The university is provided with extensive and valuable geological and mineralogical cabinets, and collections in natural history; also with well selected philosophical and chemical apparatus.

There are also chemical, zoölogical, physical, mineralogical, and assay laboratories, well supplied with apparatus and material, affording excellent facilities for the prosecution of studies in the several departments of science.

When the course in mechanical engineering was established, the work of fitting up a machine shop, in which instruction in practical mechanics and machine construction might be given as a supplement to that of the class room, was undertaken. A room 38 by 40 feet, 14 feet high, was set apart for the shop. Machinery and tools of the most approved kinds were procured. Among them were a planer, two engine lathes, a hand lathe, a milling machine, an upright drill, and a full complement of benches and bench tools. The motive power is furnished by a thirty horse power steam engine. Ten hours per week is required throughout the course.

The method of instruction is a combination of the Russian system with that followed at the Worcester (Mass.) Free Institute. Much practical work is done in the shop. One of the articles in process of construction in 1880 was an engine for the State Capitol.

Each student is required to construct the model of a machine previous to his graduation.

APPENDIX B.

STATISTICS OF INSTITUTIONS ENDOWED WITH THE NATIONAL LAND GRANT.

Name.	Location.	Date of charter.	Date of organization.	President.	Instructors.	Preparatory department. Students.	
						Male.	Female.
State Agricultural and Mechanical College.	Auburn, Ala	1872	1872	Rev. I. T. Tichenor, D. D.	1	47	
Arkansas Industrial University.	Fayetteville, Ark	1871	1871	General D. H. Hill	a6	a321	
University of California	Berkeley, Cal	1868	1869	William T. Reid, A. M.	0	0	0
State Agricultural College	Fort Collins, Colo.	1877	1879	Charles L. Ingersoll, M. SC.			
Sheffield Scientific School of Yale College.	New Haven, Conn	1701	1847	Rev. Noah Porter, D. D., LL. D			
Delaware College	Newark, Del	1867	1870	William R. Purnell, A. M., LL. D.			
State Agricultural College.b	............, Fla.						
University of Georgia:							
Georgia State College of Agriculture and Mechanic Arts.	Athens, Ga	1872	1872	Rev. P. H. Mell, D. D., LL. D. (ex officio).			
Southwest Georgia Agricultural College.	Cuthbert, Ga	1879	1879	V. T. Sanford, A. M.		130	
North Georgia Agricultural College.	Dahlonega, Ga	1871	1873	Hon. D. W. Lewis	2	129	
Middle Georgia Military and Agricultural College.	Milledgeville, Ga		1880	W. S. Dudley, M. D	5	151	167
South Georgia Agricultural College.	Thomasville, Ga	1879	1879	O. D. Scott		171	
Illinois Industrial University.	Urbana, Ill	1867	1868	Selim H. Peabody, PH. D., LL. D.	3	60	11
Purdue University	La Fayette, Ind.	1872	1874	Emerson E. White, A. M., LL. D.	2	129	
Iowa State Agricultural College.	Ames, Iowa	1869	1869	A. S. Welch, LL. D	2	10	5
Kansas State Agricultural College.	Manhattan, Kans.	1863	1863	George T. Fairchild, A. M.			
Agricultural and Mechanical College of Kentucky.	Lexington, Ky	c1865	1866	James K. Patterson, PH D., F. R. H. S., F. S. A.	6		
Louisiana State University and Agricultural and Mechanical College.	Baton Rouge, La.	1853 1874	1860 1874	William Preston Johnston.			
Maine State College of Agriculture and the Mechanic Arts.	Orono, Me	1865	1868	M. C. Fernald, A. M., PH. D.	0	0	0
Maryland Agricultural College.	College Station, Md.	1856	1859	William H. Parker		6	
Massachusetts Agricultural College.	Amherst, Mass	1863	1867	Hon. Paul A. Chadbourne, D. D., LL. D.			

a Report of normal department is here included.
b Location not fixed, and college not organized at last report, 1880.
c As a department of Kentucky University; new charter in 1880.

STATISTICS OF INSTITUTIONS ENDOWED, &c.—Continued.

Name.	Location.	Date of charter.	Date of organization.	President.	Instructors.	Preparatory department. Students. Male.	Preparatory department. Students. Female.
Massachusetts Institute of Technology.	Boston, Mass.	1861	1865	Francis A. Walker, PH. D.			
Michigan State Agricultural College.	Lansing, Mich.	1855	1857	T. C. Abbott, LL. D.	0	0	0
University of Minnesota	Minneapolis, Minn.	1868	1867	William W. Folwell, LL. D.		44	27
Alcorn Agricultural and Mechanical College.	Rodney, Miss	1871	1872	Rev. H. R. Revels, D. D.	5	170	
Agricultural and Mechanical College of the State of Mississippi.	Agricultural College, Miss.	1878	1880	Stephen D. Lee	3	154	
University of the State of Missouri.	Columbia, Mo.	a1839	a1840	Samuel S. Laws, A. M., M. D., LL. D.			
School of Mines and Metallurgy.	Rolla, Mo	1870	1871	Charles E. Wait, C. E., M. E., director.	2	25	
University of Nebraska	Lincoln, Nebr.	1869	1871	Henry E. Hitchcock, PH. D., acting chancellor.		91	92
University of Nevada b	Elko, Nev		1874	Hon. John S. Mayhugh, (president of board of regents.)	2	22	26
New Hampshire College of Agriculture and the Mechanic Arts.	Hanover, N. H.	1866	1866	Rev. Samuel C. Bartlett, D. D., LL. D.			
Rutgers College	New Brunswick, N. J.		1865	Rev. W. H. Campbell, D. D., LL. D.			
Cornell University	Ithaca, N. Y.	1865	1868	Andrew Dixon White, LL. D.			
University of North Carolina.	Chapel Hill, N. C.	1789	1875	Hon. Kemp P. Battle, LL. D.			
Ohio State University	Columbus, Ohio	1870	1873	W. Q. Scott	7	74	19
Corvallis College	Corvallis, Oreg.	1868	c1865	B. L. Arnold, A. M.			
Pennsylvania State College.	State College, Pa.	1854	1859	George W. Atherton, A. M.	5	66	19
Brown University	Providence, R. I.	1764	1765	Rev. E. G. Robinson, D. D., LL. D.			
South Carolina College of Agriculture and the Mechanic Arts.	Columbia, S. C.	1878	1880	William Porcher Miles.			
Claflin University and South Carolina Agricultural College and Mechanics' Institute.	Orangeburg, S.C.	{1869 1872}	{1870 1874}	Rev. Edward Cook, A. M., D. D.	3	d201	b115
University of Tennessee and State Agricultural College.	Knoxville, Tenn.	{1807 1869}	{1809 1869}	Rev. Thomas W. Humes, S. T. D.	3	92	0
State Agricultural and Mechanical College of Texas.	College Station, Tex.	1871	1876	John Garland James	0	0	0
University of Vermont and State Agricultural College.	Burlington, Vt.	{1791 1865}	{1800 1865}	Rev. Matthew H. Buckham, D. D.			
Virginia Agricultural and Mechanical College.	Blacksburg, Va.	1872	1872	Thomas N. Conrad, A. M.		12	0
Hampton Normal and Agricultural Institute.	Hampton, Va.	1870	1868	Gen. S. C. Armstrong, principal.	4	e76	e47
West Virginia University	Morgantown, W. Va.	1867	1867	Hon. W. L. Wilson		102	0
University of Wisconsin	Madison, Wis.	1848	1849	Rev. John Bascom, D. D., LL. D.		f6	

a Missouri Agricultural and Mechanical College, a department of this university, was chartered and organized under the national grant in 1870.
b Preparatory department only organized.
c Organized as an agricultural college in 1872.
d Of these 97 males and 39 females are normal students.
e Besides 48 boys and 26 girls in Indian classes.
f Preparatory Greek class.

Statistics of institutions endowed with the national land grant—Continued.

Name.	Number of faculty.	Whole number of students.	Collegiate department.																		Number of students in partial course.	Number of Graduate students.	Number of scholarships.	Number of years in full course of study.	Number of weeks in scholastic year.	Annual charge to each student for tuition.
			Students in classical course.								Students in scientific course.															
			Freshman.		Sophomore.		Junior.		Senior.		Freshman.		Sophomore.		Junior.		Senior.								
			Male.	Female.	Male.	Female.	Male.	Female.	Male.	Female.	Male.	Female.	Male.	Female.	Male.	Female.	Male.	Female.							
Alabama State Agricultural and Mechanical College	11	135	19	3	7	1	12		6	2	63		34		23		15	1			a1,134	4	40	30
Arkansas Industrial University	11	120	32	8	23	7	14	5	5	2	2	0	3	1		1	14		64	16	0	4	40	60
University of California	38	246									21	0	16	0	17	0	47	0	79	1	30	4	40	60
Colorado State Agricultural College	8	56			4	2					15		7		4		7		5		30	3	36	100,150
Sheffield Scientific School of Yale College	29	207											63		56				1			3	37	60
Delaware College	8	54	4										7		4		7	0			(e)	4	39	
Florida State Agricultural College d																								
University of Georgia:																								
Georgia State College of Agriculture and Mechanic Arts	8	39									18		7							9	(e)	4	40	(e)
Southwest Georgia Agricultural College	4	25									(18)		(13)		(11)		(6)			3		4	42	f10
North Georgia Agricultural College	6	48																		3		4	40	f10
Middle Georgia Military and Agricultural College	5	37																				4	40	f10
South Georgia Agricultural College	5	14																				4	36	0
Illinois Industrial University	23	281									6	24	8	19	33	16	31	4	10		(0)	4	39	f10
Purdue University	12	160									63	17	72	6	7	1	10	1	6	3	0	4	37	0
Iowa State Agricultural College	20	211									30	27	12	15	15	12	19	5	1	3	g184	4	38	14
Kansas State Agricultural College	i14	h312									70		42						3			4	37	0
Agricultural and Mechanical College of Kentucky	10	i4220																				4	38	15
Louisiana State University and Agricultural and Mechanical College.	68	i159																			(0 3,4		39	0
Maine State College of Agriculture and the Mechanic Arts	9	m90																			1	4	36	30

c To residents of State.
d Location not fixed and college not organized at last report, 1880.
e Tuition in July, 1881, was made free; annual fees, $15.
f Incidental fees.
g State appointments.
h Matriculation and incidental fees.

a 600 beneficiaries, 400 normal students, 1 honorary appointment from each of the 74 counties, and 60 additional from the State at large.
b Free in all departments of university proper; students in preparatory department without normal or beneficiary appointment pay $30 per annum, and all students pay $5 matriculation fee.

i Total for all departments.
j 224 males and 88 females.
k 249 males and 71 females.
l Each legislative representative district is entitled to send four properly prepared students free of tuition, and each county four normal pupils.
m 87 males and 3 females.

252   INDUSTRIAL EDUCATION IN THE UNITED STATES.

Statistics of institutions endowed with the national land grant—Continued.

Name.	Number of faculty.	Whole number of students.	Students in classical course.								Students in scientific course.										Number of students in partial course.	Number of graduate students.	Number of scholarships.	Number of years in full course of study.	Number of weeks in scholastic year.	Annual charge to each student for tuition.
			Freshman.		Sophomore.		Junior.		Senior.		Freshman.		Sophomore.		Junior.		Senior.								
			Male.	Female.	Male.	Female.	Male.	Female.	Male.	Female.	Male.	Female.	Male.	Female.	Male.	Female.	Male.	Female.							
Maryland Agricultural College	7	49	11								5		7		12		25		8	8	(a) 17	4	40	(a) $36
Massachusetts Agricultural College	10	113	5		18		7		10		19	1	13	2	13		52	1		8	10	4	39	d200
Massachusetts Institute of Technology	40	6300		6	5	8		5		13	66	2	31	2	20		22	2	226	15		4	36	0
Michigan State Agricultural College	20	216			18	6	2		10	3	79	2	54	3	31	2	28	1	17	2		4	37	0
University of Minnesota	22	162			5						14	2	21		5		8		47			4	38	0
Akorn Agricultural and Mechanical College	3	15																				4	39	0
Agricultural and Mechanical College of the State of Mississippi	9	150									66		40		10		8		14	2	0	4	39	0
University of the State of Missouri	21	f435	6	5	22	6	23	5	26	6	4	1	1						45	0		3	38	20
School of Mines and Metallurgy	8	57			18		19		18		7	2	13	3	6	1	2		34	4		3	37	20
University of Nebraska	16	101							m62													3	42	0
University of Nevada																								
New Hampshire College of Agriculture and the Mechanic Arts	K7	41	6		4		5		1		18				13		10		8	0	34	3	37	30
Rutgers College	17	143	16		22		23		26		18		4		8		10		10	6	40	4	36	75
Cornell University	48	384	10	5	18	6	19	5	18	6	63	10	57	7	42	5	30	5	35	23	132	4	38	75
University of North Carolina	13	195																	47	8	99	4	40	55
Ohio State University	16	124					m50		m52		7	1	11	1	18	1	19		63	2		4	37	115
Corvallis College	5	150																					40	30
Pennsylvania State College	12	60																	8		60	6	40	0
Brown University	18	264	m85		m68		m50		1		15	3	8	2	8	1	10			5	50	4	40	100
South Carolina College of Agriculture and the Mechanic Arts	4	68																			m73	4	40	0
Claflin University and South Carolina Agricultural College and Mechanics' Institute	7	23	9		6	2	5		1															0
University of Tennessee and State Agricultural College	11	141									213		32		13			3		0	275	A	33	30
State Agricultural and Mechanical College of Texas	8	258	13	3	13	1	10		10	3			6		4				3	0	93	4	40	63
University of Vermont and State Agricultural College	10	77									8										18	4	38	45

Virginia Agricultural and Mechanical College	8	94						46	22	10	4		200	4	43	p40
Hampton Normal and Agricultural College	a18	303						95	71	44	30	36	27		215	3	57	0
West Virginia University	12	75	19	24	9	19	25	9	22	1	24			(r)	4	41	15-24
University of Wisconsin	31	342	20	19	24	9	19	25	9	22	3	17	2	16	1	24	2	119	1	10	4	38	c6

a Students from Maryland and the District of Columbia were received free of tuition until 1881–'82; since then all students pay $75 per annum.
b Actual number of students; 15 are twice named in the classification given.
c 39 of these are in the School of Mechanic Arts and 49 in the Lowell School of Practical Design.
d $150 in School of Mechanic Arts.
e To residents of State.
f Exclusive of the Mining School at Rolla, and the Schools of Law and Medicine at Columbia.
g $30,000 aid fund.
h Two years only in the Agricultural and Mechanical College.
i Tuition and incidental fees.
j Preparatory department only organized.
k There are also ten occasional lecturers.
l Incidental fees.
m Includes students taking scientific and select courses.
n The income of the $50,000 received from the national grant pays tuition fees of scholars, forty-six in 1880 receiving its aid.
o There are three years in the scientific and agricultural courses.
p To non-residents.
q There are also two teachers in the normal department, seven in the Indian department, eight officers and instructors in the women's industrial department, and eight in the men's industrial department.
r Sixty cadets are educated free of cost for tuition, books, stationery, &c.

254 INDUSTRIAL EDUCATION IN THE UNITED STATES.

Statistics of institutions endowed with the national land grant—Continued.

Name.	General library. Number of volumes.	General library. Number of pamphlets.	General library. Increase in last school year in books.	Number of volumes in society libraries.	Property, income, &c. Value of grounds, buildings, and apparatus.	Property, income, &c. Amount of productive funds.	Property, income, &c. Income from productive funds.	Property, income, &c. Receipts for the last year from tuition fees.	Property, income, &c. Receipts for the last year from State appropriation.	Property, income, &c. Received from all other sources.
Alabama State Agricultural and Mechanical College	2,000		13		$75,000	$253,500	$20,280	$2,000	$5,000	
Arkansas Industrial University	1,476				170,000	130,000	16,400	200	30,600	
University of California	16,000	4,000		1,000	865,000	1,071,204	99,216		(b)	
Colorado State Agricultural College	150	400			55,000	(a)				$16,706
Sheffield Scientific School of Yale College	5,000				200,000	665,000	12,564	17,798	0	
Delaware College	6,000	500	25	3,500	75,000	83,000	4,980	500		
Florida State Agricultural College						121,400	10,004			
University of Georgia:										
Georgia State College of Agriculture and Mechanic Arts	d15,000		c340			f242,202	9,914			
Southwest Georgia Agricultural College	500				20,000		2,000			
North Georgia Agricultural College	3,000				25,000		2,000	1,800		
Middle Georgia Military and Agricultural College					9,000		2,000			
South Georgia Agricultural College										
Illinois Industrial University	12,942	2,500	425	0	450,000	319,178	20,660	0	26,610	29,191
Purdue University	2,065	1,030	262	0	250,000	340,000	17,161	0	4,500	5,138
Iowa State Agricultural College	6,000	25	300	0	500,000	600,000	45,000		24,000	
Kansas State Agricultural College	3,050	520	150	300	125,000	386,165	25,780	2,500	16,000	3,111
Agricultural and Mechanical College of Kentucky					110,000	165,000	9,900	0	10,000	0
Louisiana State University and Agricultural and Mechanical College	17,000	2,000		0	400,000	318,313	14,500			
Maine State College of Agriculture and the Mechanic Arts	4,105	750	131	1,500	145,000	132,500	7,500	2,000	3,000	g12,000
Maryland Agricultural College					100,000	112,500	6,978	4,601	6,000	6,379
Massachusetts Agricultural College	2,320	300	200		265,772	275,000	13,865			
Massachusetts Institute of Technology				300	1,315,727	267,000	16,672	48,857		
Michigan State Agricultural College	6,000				358,472	325,038			667,164	
University of Minnesota	15,000	1,000	600	0	220,000	575,000	35,000	0	23,000	
Alcorn Agricultural and Mechanical College	2,000	600			175,000	113,375	6,000	0	2,000	
Agricultural and Mechanical College of the State of Mississippi	830	350			125,000	113,757	6,679			
University of the State of Missouri	12,377	13,050	204		150,000	460,000	27,500	11,296	j120,000	27,000

INDUSTRIAL EDUCATION IN THE UNITED STATES.

Institution							
School of Mines and Metallurgy	1,750	1,000	72	46,660	55,000	800	7,500
University of Nebraska *k*	4,000			150,000			28,000
University of Nevada *l*				25,000			6,000
New Hampshire College of Agriculture and the Mechanic Arts	2,000	225		100,000	90,000		*n*6,950
Rutgers College	9,700	3,500	1,300	400,000	100,000	3,270	
Cornell University	42,950	12,250	1,300	942,975	303,129	14,750	5,000
University of North Carolina	7,000	3,000		250,000	1,264,009		6,701
Ohio State University	1,900	500	16,000	500,000	142,500	*p*3,798	7,998
Corvallis College	200			10,000	27,886	1,300	66,500
Pennsylvania State College	8,000			632,000	559,628		8,272
Brown University	53,000	17,000	575		60,000		0
South Carolina College of Agriculture and the Mechanic Arts	20,500	1,000			500,000	30,806	
Claflin University and South Carolina Agricultural College and Mechanics' Institute	1,200			25,000	645,973		
University of Tennessee and State Agricultural College	3,334	390	83	10,000	*q*191,800		
State Agricultural and Mechanical College of Texas	1,090	300		120,000	469,000	*r*2,862	311
University of Vermont and State Agricultural College	19,400		1,015	212,000	209,000	3,358	
Virginia Agricultural and Mechanical College	700	200	0	245,000	248,750	100	6,521
Hampton Normal and Agricultural Institute	1,500	640	450	100,000	360,000	3,500	
West Virginia University	5,000	300	250	420,364	*s*67,208	6,500	$10,000
University of Wisconsin	10,000	1,400	510	175,000	110,000		16,500
				455,000	498,992	5,933	30,000
							44,558
							430

a Endowment is the Congressional grant to agricultural colleges, amounting, in Colorado, to 90,000 acres, but not yet sold.
b One-fifth of 1 mill tax, amounting to about $20,000 for the year 1881; there was also a special appropriation of $5,000 for building in that year.
c This includes a large amount of funds received during the past year from the estate of the late Joseph E. Sheffield, no income from which appears in the column of income given.
d Location not fixed and college not organized at last report, 1880.
e University library.
f Entire proceeds of the sale of land scrip, the income of which, $17,914, is, by various acts of the legislature, divided between the State College at Athens and the branches at Cuthbert, Dahlonega, Milledgeville, and Thomasville.
g Average yearly income from students' board bills.
h Fifty-four thousand dollars additional are invested in permanent property.
i For two years; this includes interest on the agricultural fund, which is held by the State as a trust fund for the institution.
j Special appropriation by the legislature of 1882–'83 for the placing of the college on a permanent basis.
k Preparatory department only organized.
l For two years.
m Interest on the $116,000 received from land grant.
n Income from agricultural fund only.
o Includes receipts from tuition.
p From incidental fees.
q This sum is the agricultural fund, and its income is divided between the institution under consideration and that next mentioned.
r Includes all college fees.
s Does not include amount arising from sale of Congressional land grant.
t Income from land grant.

APPENDIX C.

DESCRIPTIONS OF THE WORCESTER COUNTY FREE INSTITUTE OF INDUSTRIAL SCIENCE, WORCESTER, MASS.; THE STEVENS INSTITUTE OF TECHNOLOGY, HOBOKEN, N. J.; AND THE POLYTECHNIC AND MANUAL TRAINING SCHOOLS OF WASHINGTON UNIVERSITY, SAINT LOUIS, MO.

WORCESTER COUNTY FREE INSTITUTE.

[Statement by Principal C. O. Thompson.*]

This institution arose from a conviction on the part of its founders that there is need of a system of training boys for the duties of an active life which is broader and brighter than the popular method of "learning a trade," and more simple and direct than the so-called "liberal education." It is the undoubted opinion of the managers of the institute, and of all who have watched its operation, that the connection of academic culture and the practical application of science is advantageous to both in a school where these objects are started together and carried on with harmony and equal prominence. The academy inspires its intelligence into the work of the shop, and the shop, with eyes open to the improvements of productive industries, prevents the monastic dreams and shortness of vision that sometimes paralyze the profound learning of a college.

GENERAL IDEA.

The institute offers a good education—based on the mathematics, living languages, physical sciences, and drawing—and sufficient practical familiarity with some branch of applied science to secure to its graduates a livelihood. It is specially designed to meet the wants of those who wish to be prepared as mechanics, civil engineers, chemists, or designers for the duties of active life.

ORGANIZATION.

The training of students preparing for mechanical engineers occupies three and a half years; that of all others three years, of forty-two weeks each. There are therefore four classes, viz, apprentice, junior, middle, and senior.

ENDOWMENTS—FUNDS—EXPENSES.

John Boynton, of Templeton, gave	$100,000
Interest before use on this gift	27,000
Ichabod Washburn, of Worcester, gave	130,000
Stephen Salisbury, of Worcester, gave	250,000
City of Worcester, by citizens	67,000
State of Massachusetts	50,000
Total endowment	624,000
Income from tuition paid by non-resident students a year	1,500
Value of Boynton Hall and equipment other than chemical and physical apparatus	75,000
Value of Washburn machine shop and its equipment	55,000
Value of grounds (seven acres) and one dwelling-house	25,000
Annual income	24,000
Annual expense of teaching staff	21,500

INSTRUCTORS.

Charles O. Thompson, A. M., Ph. D., principal, and professor of chemistry.*
George I. Alden, B. S., professor of theoretical and applied mechanics.
George E. Gladwin, professor of drawing.

---

*Professor Thompson has resigned and Rev. H. T. Fuller, A. M., has been appointed principal.

INDUSTRIAL EDUCATION IN THE UNITED STATES. 257

John E. Sinclair, A. M., professor of higher mathematics and civil engineering.
Alonzo S. Kimball, A. M., professor of physics.
Edward P. Smith, A. M., professor of modern languages.
Thomas E. N. Eaton, A. M., junior professor of mathematics.
Milton P. Higgins, B. S., superintendent of machine shop.
Walter U. Barnes, B. S., assistant in chemistry.
Aldus M. Chapin, C. E., instructor in field work.
Paul A. Chadbourne, D. D., LL. D., lecturer in geology.
Number of students, all boys, 93; average age at entrance, eighteen and three-quarters years.

The institution is open to all qualified applicants regardless of locality, and students are in attendance now from Pennsylvania, Maine, Connecticut, New Hampshire, Rhode Island, Ohio, Texas, California, Minnesota, the District of Columbia, and Chili. But all residents of the county of Worcester and 23 residents of Massachusetts and not of Worcester County are entitled to free tuition. Others pay $150 per annum.

SCHOLARSHIPS.

Resolve of Massachusetts Legislature, approved May 10, 1869.

Resolved, That there be allowed and paid out of the treasury of the Commonwealth the sum of $50,000 to the Worcester County Free Institute of Industrial Science. And in consideration of this grant, said institution shall annually receive twenty pupils, and instruct them during the entire course, free of tuition; such pupils to be selected by the board of education from the different counties in this Commonwealth, except that none shall be taken from Worcester County.

Three students from that part of Norfolk County, viz: from the towns of Bellingham, Foxboro', Franklin, Medway, Walpole and Wrentham, which formerly made part of the ninth Congressional district, may receive free tuition in accordance with the terms of the gift of Hon. George F. Hoar.

Applications for these scholarships are filed at the institute as soon as received. After the entrance examination, successful candidates receive the scholarships in the order of application.

GRADUATES.

Summary of employments of graduates, liable to daily change.

Whole number of mechanical engineers ---------------------------------- 88
All others --- 98
                                                                       ———
                                                                       186

Of the mechanical engineers, 26 are journeymen; 21 are superintendents, foremen, or proprietors of manufacturing establishments; 10 are draughtsman; 5 are mechanical or civil engineers; 3 are farmers; 1 is a chemist; 18 are engaged in miscellaneous business, generally in manufactures; 1 is dead; total, 88.

Of the graduates from other departments, 36 are civil engineers; 3 are superintendents or foremen; 11 are teachers; 7 are draughtsmen or designers; 3 are journeymen mechanics; 6 are chemists, assayers, or apothecaries; 1 is a farmer; 27 are engaged in miscellaneous occupations in active business; 4 are dead; total, 98.

Inasmuch as a large number of those reported as engaged in miscellaneous business are really in positions in factories and mills with a certain prospect of promotion, and where their technical training is indispensable, it is correct to say that 90 per cent. of the graduates of the institute are occupying positions for which their training directly prepared them.

Note.—All graduates are urged to begin life at the bottom and depend upon their education for *speedy advancement.*

OUTLINE OF THE COURSE OF STUDY.

Recitations and practice are assigned to the classes according to the following scheme, the figures indicating hours per week:

FIRST HALF-YEAR.

Seniors.—Theoretical mechanics, 5; French or German, 3; English, 2; chemistry, 2; physics, 4; mechanical drawing, 6; practice, 10. *Middlers.*—General geometry, 5; de-

S. Ex. 25——17

scriptive geometry, 3; German, 2; English, 1; chemistry, 4; free drawing, 2; mechanical drawing, 6; practice, 10. *Juniors.*—Algebra, 4; geometry, 4; German, 2; English, 1; chemistry, 2; free drawing, 6.

SECOND HALF-YEAR.

Seniors.—Applied mechanics, 5; French or German, 3; English, 2; chemistry, 4; mechanical drawing, 6; practice, 10. *Middlers.*—Calculus, 5; German, 3; English, 1; physics, 4; free drawing, 2; mechanical drawing, 6; physics, 4; practice, 10. *Juniors.*—Trigonometry, 4; algebra, 4; German, 3; English, 1; chemistry, 4; free drawing, 6; practice, 10. *Apprentices.*—English, 5; free drawing, 10; shop practice, 39.

INSTRUCTION TO WOMEN.

Several women have enjoyed the full advantage of the institute, receiving instruction in return for service as assistants in the office.

The third supplement of Watts's Dictionary of Chemistry, London, 1879, page 426, sets out the work of Miss Mary F. Reed as an original contribution to knowledge.

This work was done in this laboratory, and is the only original woman's work in chemistry, so far as I know, which has secured notice in Watts's Dictionary.

BUILDINGS, WORK-ROOMS, SHOPS, LABORATORIES, ETC.

Rooms and utensils.—Boynton Hall is a commodious granite building, 146 feet long by 61 feet wide, built by the citizens of Worcester. It contains a chapel capable of seating four hundred persons; a lecture room, in the rear of which are a store room and private laboratory, with store and balance rooms; furnished with all the tables, reagents, &c., necessary for the students' use; a laboratory, fully equipped for instruction in chemistry; a physical laboratory, furnished with power from the shop and adapted to the use of students in the practical solution of problems in physics, containing Willis's apparatus, complete working machines to illustrate the movements of the link and valve; C. H. Morgan's machine for showing the correct forms of cams and their movements; models of bridges, thermic, optical, and galvanic apparatus to meet every want; two commodious drawing rooms, one for freehand, the other for mechanical drawing, with model rooms, where are the best French and English plates, manuscript drawings, models, casts, &c., a designer's room, commodious recitation rooms, and office room. There is also a full set of instruments for the use of the civil engineers. Through the generosity of a constant friend the institute has come into possession of the celebrated Chevallier universal microscope, which was imported by the late Francis Peabody, esq., of Salem.

The Fairbanks testing machine, which was on exhibition at the Centennial and received an award, has been added to the apparatus of the physical laboratory for the purpose of instruction. This machine has a capacity of 52,000 pounds, and is of universal applicability to the determination of the strength of materials.

Books.—There is a small library of books of reference at the institute. Through the liberality of the trustees of the Green library, which contains 45,000 volumes, students share in its use with the citizens of Worcester. All new standard works in technical literature are promptly added to this library as they appear.

The library of the American Antiquarian Society, of 60,000 volumes, is accessible to students.

Practice.—The Washburn machine shop offers unusual facilities to students in this department for obtaining a practical knowledge of the use of tools and the management of machines. The shop is equipped with the best tools and machinery for the working of iron and wood, and is managed by a superintendent, who employs a sufficient number of skilled workmen. The students spend their practice hours in it as apprentices. Besides the general training in drawing, the mechanical engineers have special instruction during senior year in making working drawings of machines, determining the strength, dimensions, and proper proportions of machines from numerical specifications and in the laws of motors. It is the main purpose of the shop to carry out the wise and comprehensive plan of its founder, the late Hon. Ichabod Washburn, of Worcester, as expressed in the following extract from his letter of gift, dated March 6, 1866:

"There shall be a machine shop of sufficient capacity to employ 20 or more apprentices, with a suitable number of practical teachers and workmen in the shop to instruct such apprentices, and provided with all necessary steam power, engines, tools, apparatus and machinery of the most improved models and styles in use, to carry on the business of such machine shop in all its parts as a practical working establishment. There shall be a superintendent of such shop, who shall be appointed and subject to be removed by the trustees, who shall be a man of good morals and Christian character, having a good English [education, a skilfull and experienced mechanic, well informed and capable of teaching others in the various parts and processes of practical mechanism usually applied or made use of in the machine shops of the country, who shall devote his time and attention to the management and business of the shop, purchasing stock, making contracts for the manufacture and sale of machines, and other work usually done in machine shops, subject to such rules as the trustees may prescribe, and having charge of the proper financial concerns of the shop, hiring necessary workmen, and discharging the same at his discretion, and shall see that the apprentices are suitably taught in all the departments of practical mechanism, working of wood and metals, and use of tools, so as to make them, so far as may be, skilled workmen, and fitted to carry on business for themselves after they leave the shop at the expiration of their apprenticeship.

"He shall, moreover, have a care and oversight over the apprentices, such as a faithful master would exercise, to the end that they may cultivate habits of industry, good conduct, and attention to their studies."

The shop is a three-story brick building, 100 feet long by 40 feet wide, with a wing 65 by 40 feet, for engine, boilers, and blacksmith shop. These rooms are all equipped according to the directions of the benevolent donor.

Students who desire instruction in mechanics according to the present arrangement must enter the apprentice class, unless they have already attained adequate proficiency in the use of tools and machinery.

As much variety as possible is sought in the kind of work assigned to students. In general the apprentice class learn something of the use of wood-working tools and machinery; the junior, middle, and senior classes work mainly on iron.

Practice in the machine shop and drawing room is given in manufacturing the products enumerated in the catalogue. It comprises—

IN THE WOOD ROOM.

Benchwork.—This includes a great variety of manipulation, under constant instruction, in laying out work with knife and pencil, the use of the planes, the handsaws, chisels, gouges, squares, gauges, and other tools.

Wood turning—with the use of the various turning tools, on hard and soft woods.

Machine sawing—with large and small circular saws, and scroll-saws.

Machine planing—with the cylinder and Daniels planer.

Machine boring, the use of the shaping and moulding machines and the auxiliary manipulations of all the machinery used.

IN THE IRON ROOM.

Benchwork.—Filing and chipping, preparing work for lathes, tapping, reaming, scraping, and fitting plane surfaces, finishing with oilstone and emery cloth.

Work with speed lathe.—Drilling and countersinking, filing and polishing, hand-tooling.

Work with engine lathe.—Instruction in the use and care of lathe and turning tools, squaring up, the proper and maximum speed for cutting metals, turning to exact size, the use of the calipers, a variety of turning, both heavy and light, cutting threads, squaring up and finishing nuts, chucking straight holes, reaming, inside boring, boring with boring bar, fitting bearings, &c.

Drilling—with speed-lathe, upright and traverse drillers.

Milling—Use of universal milling machine, milling nuts, bolt heads and studs, cutting splines, fluting taps and reamers, milling to size and line, cutting gears.

Planing—Instruction in the use of the planer, planing surfaces and bevels.

Work with screw machine—Making machine bolts with revolving head screw machine, cutting up stock, making screws and studs and tapping nuts.

Tool making—The correct forms of turning-tools and the principles of grinding them, making taps, dies, reamers, twist drills, countersinks, counterbores, mills, milling machine cutters, mandrels, boring bars, chuck drills, centres.

Management of steam—Care of the boilers and engine, including the work of firing, the care and the control of the steam pressure, the water supply; also the care and manipulation of the steam pump and injectors. This practice in the steam department is under the constant oversight of the engineer.

Designing and constructing.—At some point in senior year, after the students have each accomplished the practice just specified, they will receive instruction in designing machinery and undertake the building of one or more complete machines from their own drawings. These drawings, though made from definite specifications, are intended to afford ample field and scope for the personal responsibility and originality of each student in making correct design and arrangement of the parts of the machine in hand. While this work is not copying, it must not depart essentially from the best practice among manufacturing mechanics. The present senior class are constructing a Corliss engine.

CIVIL ENGINEERING.

The civil engineers join the mechanical engineers in the study of theoretical mechanics.
In applied mechanics they solve problems relating to the stresses and strains in girders, roofs, and trusses, the suspension bridge, the stability of the arch, the strength of boilers, pipes, and thick hollow cylinders, deflection and designing of beams, the stability of dams, reservoir walls and retaining walls, the pressure of earth and stability of earth foundations, the energy of liquids in motion, the construction of water-wheels, and other problems relating to engineering structures.

PRACTICE.

A full equipment of transits, levels, chains, &c., is provided for the instruction of the students in practice in the different branches of civil engineering.
The junior class study Gillespie, solve problems in the field, in mensuration, triangulation, leveling and general topography. All field notes are carefully plotted and reported.
The middle class, after studying Henck's Field Book and Davis's Earth Work, proceed with a practical application of the information thus obtained to locating highways and laying out lines of railroads, setting slope stakes, and making calculations for excavations and embankments.
The senior class study Mahan's Stereotomy with practical problems, Gilmore's Limes, Hydraulic Cements and Mortars, and Gilmore's Roads, Streets, and Pavements.

CHEMISTRY.

The general course in chemistry is calculated to give every student a clear understanding of the general principles of the science, and is taught to all students by means of laboratory manipulation and class-room drill.
This course begins with twenty lectures, followed by ten two-hour lessons in laboratory manipulation in the first half of junior year. During the second half the class have sixty recitations in Barker's Chemistry.
In the first half of middle year, forty two-hour lessons are given in wet analysis.
In the first half of the senior year twenty lessons in organic chemistry are given; in the last half, a course is given in the use of the blowpipe and determinative mineralogy, followed by lectures on metallurgy.

PRACTICE.

Practice in the chemical laboratory, for those who intend to be practical chemists, includes, in addition to the general course, the following subjects:
Junior class.—Blowpipe analysis, beginning with dictation lessons in the use of the blowpipe with its auxiliaries, and concluding with the determination of fifty minerals according to Dana's classification.
Qualitative analysis, dictation lessons, and examination of fifty mixtures.
Middle class.—Use of the balance, and gravimetric problems with use of Fresenius' quantitative analysis.
Volumetric analysis with use of Sutton's text-book.
Senior class.—Blowpipe assaying of gold, silver, mercury, lead and copper; furnace assaying of gold, silver, lead and iron. Analysis of iron, steel and slags, milk, beer, water and fertilizers.

PHYSICS.

All students receive instruction in the subject of general physics, which is amply illustrated. Students who are qualified by previous mechanical training, or by special aptness or taste for physical research, may practice in the physical laboratory.
The entire course in this department offers to the student facilities for the acquisition of an exact knowledge of the elementary principles of physics.

PRACTICE.

Students in this department, in addition to the general course, spend their practice hours in the physical laboratory.
The laboratory possesses a collection of apparatus specially constructed for the practical solution of physical problems, among which are the Fairbanks testing machine, dynamometers, apparatus for determining the tension of steam, latent and total heat of vaporization, a model boiler and fittings for determining the efficiency and economy in use of boilers, &c.

STEVENS INSTITUTE OF TECHNOLOGY.

The students perform experiments involving measurements in each branch of the science treated in the lectures of the general course. The strength of materials, the fall of bodies, the pressure and flow of liquids and gases, the vibration of sounding bodies, focal distances of lenses, indices of refraction, latent and specific heat, tension of vapors, resistance of telegraphic wires and cables, electro-motive force of batteries, and strength of currents are among the problems assigned for laboratory practice.

Experimental investigations are carried on by the students under the direction of their instructor, and experience has shown that as a means of discipline special researches of this kind are more valuable than systematic work following a text-book.

DRAWING.

All students are taught freehand drawing. By carefully studied exercises in outline drawing, shading and coloring, from copies, models and casts, and by blackboard work, discipline of the sense of form and proportion is secured, and an ability to delineate objects is acquired which is of great value in all departments of applied science.

In the mechanical drawing-room instruction is given in the use of instruments, shading and coloring, plane and isometric projections, and the theory of shades, shadows and perspective. All drawing is done under the eye of the instructor.

PRACTICE.

Students who evince marked power in drawing are admitted to practice in this department.

A course of lessons is devised for each student in practice, preparatory to designing for textile fabrics, lithography, &c. Students enjoy access to collections of illustrations and examples. Students who practice in drawing join the civil engineers in the study of stereotomy.

The course in drawing is the best preparation for the business of a designer, whether for prints, fresco, and ornamental painting, or any other similar art.

Every student in the department of mechanics, in addition to the work just specified, is required to make at least one complete set of working drawings in the shop under the direction of the superintendent, for use in the shop.

STEVENS INSTITUTE OF TECHNOLOGY.

The Stevens Institute of Technology, Hoboken, N. J., is a school of mechanical engineering. It owes its foundation to the bequest by the late Edwin A. Stevens of a valuable lot of ground in Hoboken and several hundred thousand dollars (about $650,000) for the establishment of "an institution of learning for the benefit, tuition, and advancement in learning of the youth residing from time to time, in future, within the State of New Jersey." The executors of the will determined what should be the nature of the instruction given. The endowment of the institute is about the same as at the time of its opening in 1871. Its grounds, buildings and apparatus are valued at $400,000; its productive funds amount to $410,000; the income from them for the year 1880 was $30,000, and the income from tuition fees was $13,840.

The faculty consists of a president, and professors of physics, mechanical engineering, mathematics and mechanics, mechanical drawing, chemistry, languages, belles-lettres, and experimental mechanics and shop work. Its members have supplemented the work of teaching by making original investigations and contributing largely to scientific and technical literature. The students in attendance in 1880 numbered 144, of whom 20 were seniors, 25 juniors, 46 sophomores, and 53 freshmen.

The expenses of the student for tuition are $150 per annum if he reside at the time in New Jersey; $225 if he come from any place outside the State, New York City, for example. In the chemical laboratory he must pay for injuries to apparatus, and in the department of shop work for the material used, the cost of which is estimated at $65 for the entire course. The tuition of a limited number of students is covered by scholarships, as follows: One scholarship each year is given to the graduate of the high school connected with the institute who passes the best examination at the end of the spring term. Three scholarships each year are given to recommended graduates from the public schools of Hoboken.

Previously to 1881, 83 young men had graduated. Nearly all of them took the degree of mechanical engineer, and immediately engaged in professional work in desirable places. The president of the trustees of the institute recently said: "Our graduates have borne splendid testimony to the men who have trained their minds and their hands to work.

Wherever they have gone they have made their mark. There is an air of serious earnestness about them in their course of study that shows even to the casual observer that they are here for work; and when they go out from us they show that they have been trained to work with head and hands."

COURSE OF STUDY.

The full course of study covers four years, each year being divided into a preliminary term of one month (during which the sophomore, junior, and senior classes devote eight hours a day to experimental mechanics and shop work) and three regular terms of combined lecture, recitation, and shop work. The following plan of instruction is given in the catalogue:

The plan of instruction which has now been successfully pursued for ten years is such as will best fit young men of ability for positions of usefulness in the department of mechanical engineering and in those scientific pursuits from which this and all the sister arts are daily deriving such incalculable benefits. With this view there is afforded:

(1.) A thorough training in the elementary and advanced branches of mathematics and their application to mechanical constructions.

(2.) The subject of mechanical engineering, including theory and practice in the construction of machines, forms a distinct department, under the charge of professors experienced in the practical relations of this subject, who devote their entire attention to this branch.

A mechanical laboratory has been instituted as an adjunct to this department, in which students are permitted to study the materials of construction during the process of testing, which is at nearly all times in progress, and frequently to take part in such work. They are given opportunities to take part in tests of steam engines, boilers, and other operations carried on in this laboratory, and engage in the construction of machinery and other work done in the workshop. Much of this work is made from designs produced by students, and some machines here used are the work of students entirely.

(3.) The subject of mechanical drawing (which may well be called the language of engineering) forms a separate department, to which much time and attention is devoted.

The course comprises the use of instruments and colors, descriptive geometry, shades, shadows, and perspective, and the analysis of mechanical movements, the principles involved being at once and continuously applied in the construction of working drawings from measurements of machines already built, as well as in making original designs.

(4.) Arrangements of an unusually perfect character have been made, to give a thorough, practical course of instruction in physics, by means of physical laboratories, in which the student is guided by the professor of physics, in experimental researches bearing upon the subjects of his special study.

Thus the student will experimentally study those methods of making measures of precision which are used in all determinations in physics; he will measure for himself the tension of steam at various temperatures, and construct the curve showing their relations; he will determine the electrical resistance of several conductors and insulators, and so on through the subjects of physics.

By such means as these not only will facts and laws be impressed in a manner which no other process can approach, but a training will be given in methods of investigation which will be invaluable for the mastery of the always new and varied problems of actual work.

(5.) The subject of chemistry is taught chiefly by experimental work in the laboratory, with accompanying lectures and class room instruction. It is believed that in this manner only can students be made thoroughly conversant with the subject.

(6.) The French and German languages form an essential part of the course of instruction, since they are indispensable to the engineer and man of science as the vehicles of a vast amount of information, and also as affording that kind of mental culture which mathematical and physical science, if followed exclusively, would fail to supply.

(7.) A department of belles-lettres furnishes the means of cultivating literary taste and a facility in the graceful use of language, both in speaking and writing, which are as desirable in the engineer and man of science as in the classical student.

INDUSTRIAL DEPARTMENTS.

The departments of physics, mechanical drawing, and mechanical engineering have a direct bearing upon the industrial work of the institute, and therefore are worthy of special description.

The department of physics is organized for purposes of instruction and original research. The instruction of the first year is upon the inductive method of research, the general properties of matter, inductive mechanics, pneumatics, the laws of vibratory motion, acoustics, and light. The second year is devoted to the study of heat, light, mag-

REAR VIEW.

PHYSICAL LABORATORY.

netism, and electricity. During the third year the professor of physics lectures upon the modes of making exact measures, shows the application of these measures in the various departments of science, and explains the construction, the methods of adjustment, and the manner of using instruments of precision. The fourth year is spent in the physical laboratories upon experimental investigations, schedules of which are prepared by the professor.

The physical laboratory is provided with a complete outfit of all instruments of research and exact measurement, including numerous forms of dividing engines, cathetometers and comparators, spectroscopes, microscopes, electrometers, galvanometers, electric resistance coils, &c. Among recent additions is the original circular dividing engine of James Ramsden.

The department of mechanical drawing was so organized as to make the course of instruction thorough, practical, directly useful, and comprehensive. The foundation of future acquirement is secured by practice in the simple drawing of lines. Elementary studies of projection are afterward taken, the method adopted being that of beginning by making the drawings of a solid object bounded by plane surfaces in varied positions and proceeding to more complex forms. The next step is the drawing of parts of machines from actual measurements and the study of descriptive geometry. Shades, shadows, and perspective are not of primary importance to the mechanical engineer, and therefore are not long studied. More attention is paid to practical exercises in the plotting of mechanical movements, the drawing of the various forms of gearing, and the construction of curves representing varied motion and the like. The course also includes some actual planning. A subject is assigned or selected. The student proceeds to actual work upon it, makes a skeleton diagram of the movement, sketches in the proposed arrangement of parts, calculates their strength and proportion, modifies the original plan accordingly, draws each part in detail and finally makes a general plan of the completed design.

The department of mechanical engineering provides thorough instruction in those subjects which belong exclusively or preëminently to that field of study, and supplies such practice as gives a knowledge of appliances, processes, and methods necessary to the construction of such mechanical designs as the student may be taught to originate. The workshop course consists of (1) carpenter work and wood turning, mill wrighting and steam fitting, which are pursued by the freshman class; and (2) machinist work, blacksmithing, moulding and founding, and pattern making, which are pursued by the sophomore and junior classes. In the carpenter shop the student is first taught the preparation of tools for work and afterward given some twenty exercises in planing, sawing, framing, &c. The instruction in wood turning is upon the care and management of the lathe, the production of prescribed forms and figures, and the behavior of different woods while being operated upon. The practice in millwrighting and steam fitting is likewise thorough and complete.

The machinist work includes eleven exercises in vise work; ten in planing, besides six preliminary exercises in the management of the machine; familiarization with the movements and management of milling machines, ten exercises in their regular use, and eight in gear-cutting; sixteen exercises in drill press work; miscellaneous drilling by hand; and some forty exercises with the metal lathe. The course is finished by the student being sent to examine the kind, size and use of tools and machines employed in various manufactories and mills, and the methods adopted in the production of heavy machinery. The courses in blacksmithing, moulding, and founding, and pattern making are arranged with similar care. The institute has been provided for a considerable time with a machine and carpenter shop, an iron and brass foundry, and a blacksmith shop. It has increased their equipment from time to time.

In 1881 a new machine shop was fitted up and presented to the institute by President Morton. A description of this is given as follows:

"The building occupied by this shop is 50 feet by 80 feet on the floor, with a high open roof, and galleries running around all four sides.

"A Buckeye engine, placed near the center, drives two lines of shafting which run along the fronts of the galleries, and from these belts pass off to the countershafts of the various machine tools.

"A spiral stairway gives access to one of the galleries near its center, where is placed the tool room, in which is systematically arranged all the small tools, such as drills, cutters, taps and dies, mandrils, gauges, &c., which are used with the machine tools.

"The machine tools on the main floor consist of fourteen lathes of different sizes, from one of 22 inches swing and 12 feet bed downward, all by different makers, and thus presenting a wide range of variation in style and structure; two planers, with beds 20 inches by 5 feet; two drill presses; and one universal milling machine. There are, besides, grindstones and emery wheels, driven by power, and a large number of vises, work benches, sets of wood working tools, and all other accessories."

A mechanical laboratory was established in 1875, in which have been tested steam boilers and engines, the value of lubricants, the strength of building materials, the physical and mechanical properties of iron and steel, and many other structures and substances. The other laboratories are also thoroughly furnished, and collections illustrative of the sciences are not wanting.

WASHINGTON UNIVERSITY.

[Statement from latest reports and catalogues.]

Washington University, Saint Louis, Mo., was founded in 1853. It is intended to embrace the whole range of university studies, except theology, and to afford opportunity of complete preparation for every sphere of practical and scientific life. Seven departments have been established, viz: Smith Academy, in which primary, secondary, and preparatory instruction is given; Mary Institute, a female seminary located apart from the central university; the college proper; a school of fine arts; a law school; a manual training school; and the O'Fallon Polytechnic Institute. In this polytechnic school there are courses in civil engineering, mechanical engineering, chemistry, mining and metallurgy, and building and architecture. They extend through four years, and are intended to prepare for professional work in the departments of engineering, chemistry, and architecture. The studies are the same for all the courses during the freshman and sophomore years. They include higher mathematics, surveying, drawing, descriptive geometry, physics, chemistry, history, modern languages, English studies, and shop work. The courses are so arranged for junior and senior years as to include only studies directly contributing to training in the professions to which they are preliminary. The course in chemistry has only geology, mineralogy, and political economy, in addition to distinctly chemical work. The course in mining and metallurgy consists principally of technical studies, such as the occurrence of minerals, the opening and ventilation of mines, accidents, the transportation and preparation of ores, furnaces, fuels, metallic compositions, and processes employed in manufacturing.

The courses in civil engineering, mechanical engineering, and building and architecture include many subjects common to all. These are, in junior year, differential calculus, descriptive geometry, drawing, chemistry, English composition, and shop work; in senior year, mechanics, drawing, political economy, and shop work. The civil engineering course is accompanied by laboratory and field practice, and includes practical astronomy. The course in mechanical engineering gives special prominence to shop work; that in building and architecture, to designing, modeling, architectural drawing, and engineering.

DEPARTMENT OF ENGINEERING—APPLIANCES AND METHODS OF STUDY.

The institute has a choice and extensive collection of photographs, models, and other appliances illustrating the principles of civil and mechanical engineering. Its laboratory of mechanical engineering is large, and equipped for testing boilers, engines, and machinery in general. The shops of the manual training school are open to the students, and the use of tools for working word and iron is systematically taught.

The instruction in all branches of study is given from text books when practicable, and supplemented by lectures and practical work.

Every effort is made to give the best engineering practice, both European and American, and to keep pace with the great advances made on all sides in every department of physical science. Special prominence is given to the use of graphical methods which are most advantageously employed in supplementing the processes of computation. Advantage is taken of the opportunities afforded by the city and the vicinity for the study of manufactories, machinery, and engineering works.

DEPARTMENT OF MINING AND METALLURGY.

This branch of the institute was organized in 1871. The instruction is given by means of lectures and recitations on various subjects pertaining to the course; practical work in the physical, chemical, and metallurgical laboratories; field work in geology; projects, estimates, and plans for the establishment of mines and metallurgical works; and the examination of mines and manufacturing establishments. The collections of the department are increasing rapidly, and now include a series of models of crystals and specimens illustrating the various minerals and rocks and their associations, ores, coals, petroleums,

INDUSTRIAL EDUCATION IN THE UNITED STATES. 265

fire clays, and building materials; botanical and zoölogical forms; characteristic fossils of the different zoölogical ages; metallurgical products, &c. Special facilities are offered for critical studies in microscopic lithology.

The following is a statement of the number of specimens in collections in September, 1882:

Crystal models	250
Minerals	15,000
Rocks	5,000
Microscopic preparations (rocks and minerals)	1,000
Fossils	40,000
Casts of large animals	250
Corals and shells (modern)	2,500
Zoölogical	300
Botanical	1,000
Archæological	1,500
Metallurgical	3,000
Total	69,800

The assay laboratories are completely furnished with crucible, scorification, and cupelling furnaces, and everything necessary for practical work in the assay of the principal ores. From a large stock of these obtained from various parts of the country the students are required to make a large number of assays.

In the numerous finely equipped chemical laboratories a practical course is pursued in connection with lectures on qualitative and quantitative analysis. The students are required to make tests and full analyses of coals, limestones, ores, clays, technical products, &c. An assistant is in constant attendance in the assay and metallurgical laboratories, to aid in the practical work assigned.

During the summer vacation the students are required to visit some mining or metallurgical district, and at the opening of the following term they hand in a journal of travels, with a report of the operations conducted in the region visited, illustrated with drawings. Before receiving their degree (engineer of mines) they execute plans for the establishment and working of mines or smelting-works under given conditions, with drawings, estimates, and written memoirs.

PHYSICAL LABORATORY.

The physical laboratory is provided with large tables fitted up for the purpose of enabling the students to perform certain assigned experiments in mechanics, pneumatics, heat, optics, acoustics and electricity. These experiments are increasingly elaborate as the student advances, and their purpose is to give an insight into the methods and means used in physical investigation.

DRAWING DEPARTMENT.

With the beginning of the freshman year freehand drawing from the "round" or solid is practiced, first in outline, then in shading with charcoal. In the first stages of freehand shading there is but little attempt made at finishing work; the student is urged to gain the power of expressing rapidly a clear idea of the object before him by means of his drawing rather than to attempt an artistic production.

Instruction in the conventional use of color and the use of the brush in shading as applied to mechanical and architectural drawing is taken up at this stage of the work.

Regular students of the sophomore class use as models during the time allotted to freehand work parts of machinery, casts of ornaments, &c. During the first term they spend some time in sketching from nature. The time devoted to mechanical drawing is spent in line and brush shading, lettering, &c.

During the second term the time is devoted to machinery, architectural, and map drawing. Recently a course in sepia painting has been partly introduced in the work of this class.

The junior class in civil engineering work from models, arches, &c., finishing with pen and ink, India ink with brush, and also practice sepia and water color painting.

The senior class in civil engineering devote the time allotted to drawing in finishing drawings from actual measurement and the designing of structures. The drawings are executed with pen and ink, brush-shading in sepia or India ink and water color.

The course pursued by the classes in mining engineering differs only in the objects used as models. The juniors execute drawings of profiles, crystals, plans, and sections of mines and mining machinery, furnaces, apparatus, and machinery of smelting works. Seniors execute similar work from actual measurement and constructions.

MANUAL TRAINING.

In the enumeration of studies the word "shopwork" is used to cover the systematic course of instruction and practice in the use of the more common hand and machine tools. As at present arranged "shopwork" is required of all engineering students, and is available to all others. Generally four hours per week are given to the shop, the practice lasting a year in each one of the four shops: carpenter shop, turning shop, blacksmith shop, and machine shop. It is believed that the value of the training which students can obtain in from four to twelve hours a week of shop work is abundantly sufficient to justify the expense of materials, tools, and expert teachers, whatever may be their plans for the future. No branch of study has been omitted from the theoretical work on account of the shop practice. The standard of scholarship has not been lowered. The knowledge of practical matters and the ability to use tools do not displace but supplement abstract and theoretical work.

MANUAL TRAINING SCHOOL OF WASHINGTON UNIVERSITY, ST. LOUIS, MO.

The manual training school of Washington University was established as a separate and independent department of the university in June, 1879, and opened in September, 1880. It owes its existence to the conviction on the part of its founders that the interests of Saint Louis demand for young men a system of education which shall fit them for the actual duties of life in a more direct and positive manner than is done in the ordinary American school. Its plan is outlined in Article II of the ordinance establishing it, which is as follows:

OBJECT.

"Its object shall be instruction in mathematics, drawing, and the English branches of a high school course, and instruction and practice in the use of tools. The tool instruction, as at present contemplated, shall include carpentry, wood-turning, pattern-making, iron chipping and filing, forge work, brazing and soldering, the use of machine shop tools, and such other instruction of a similar character as it may be deemed advisable to add to the foregoing from time to time. The students will divide their working hours as nearly as possible equally between mental and manual exercises. They shall be admitted on examination at not less than fourteen years of age, and the course shall continue three years."

STUDIES.

Applicants for admission must pass a good examination in the leading rules of arithmetic, common school geography, spelling, and penmanship, and the writing of good English.

The arrangement of studies and shop work by years is substantially as follows:

First year: Arithmetic completed, algebra to equations, the structure and use of the English language (or Latin), history of the United States, physical geography, mechanical and freehand drawing, penmanship, carpentry and joinery, wood carving, wood turning, and pattern making.

Second year: Algebra through quadratics, plane geometry, natural philosophy, English history (or Latin continued), English composition and literature, principles of mechanics, penmanship, drawing (line-shading and tinting machines, freehand detail drawing), blacksmithing, and use of machine tools.

Third year: Solid geometry, plane trigonometry and mensuration, English composition and literature, history or French, ethics and political economy, book-keeping, machine and architectural drawing, study of the steam engine, benchwork and fitting, work in the machine shop, and the execution of a project preliminary to graduation.

The course in drawing has three general divisions: First, freehand drawing, designed to educate the sense of form and proportion, to teach the eye to observe accurately and to train the hand to delineate rapidly the forms either of existing objects or of ideals in the mind; second, mechanical drawing, including the use of instruments, geometric constructions, the arrangement of projections, elevations, planes and sections, and the various methods of producing shades and shadows with pen or brush; third, technical drawing, illustrating conventional colors and signs, systems of architectural or shop drawings, and at the same time familiarizing the pupil with the proportions and details of various classes of machines and structures.

SHOPS.

The school has 2 carpenter, 2 turning, 1 blacksmith, and 1 machine shop, each having accommodation for 20 pupils. Four classes of that size can be taught daily in each. Every pupil in the woodworking shops has a set of edge tools for his exclusive use. Other tools, such as squares, hammers, wrenches, &c., are provided for the use of each class in succession.

[S. Ex. 25——face p. 266.] THE MANUAL TRAINING SCHOOL OF WASHINGTON UNIVERSITY.

INDUSTRIAL EDUCATION IN THE UNITED STATES. 267

Each carpenter shop contains 20 benches, vises, and sets of tools for use in common, a power grindstone, the instructor's desk and bench, settees for the class, and the requisite quota of clamps, glue-pots, &c. A double circular-saw machine is provided for getting out stock ("blanks" for class use) and jobbing.

Each turning shop contains 20 speed lathes, 12-inch swing and 5-foot bed, with complete equipment of face plates, chucks, &c., for 60 pupils; and each shop contains several 8-foot benches for pattern work, a power grindstone, and a moulder's bench and tools for illustrating practically the use and handling of patterns for foundery work.

The blacksmith shop has its full equipment of 20 forges, anvils, tubs, and sets of ordinary hand tools. Ten sets of heavy tools suffice for 20 pupils, as they may work in pairs as "smith and helper." The blast is supplied by a fan blower, and a powerful exhaust fan keeps the shop reasonably free from smoke and gas. In connection with one of the larger forges is a hand-bellows, which can be used when the engine is not running. As every shop exercise lasts two hours, the shop readily accommodates eighty pupils a day.

The machine shop possesses an equipment of 7 engine lathes of 14-inch swing and 5-foot bed; 4 speed lathes; a post drill; a planer, 21-inch by 5 feet; a 25-inch goose neck drill; a shaper of 15 inches stroke; and a large power grindstone. Ten vises and benches, with 40 drawers, afford opportunity for benchwork. It is furnished for a class of 20 students at once. The Corliss engine occupies a part of this shop. It has a 14-inch cylinder and 24-inch stroke, and runs at the rate of 65 revolutions per minute. The engine was built specially for the school by Messrs. Smith, Beggs & Rankin, of Saint Louis. This equipment of steam power furnishes to pupils of the third-year class the means of becoming familiar with such machinery on a scale unsurpassed.

DETAILS OF SHOP INSTRUCTION.

The shop instruction is given similarly to laboratory lectures. The instructor at the bench, machine, forge, or anvil, executes in the presence of the whole class the day's lesson, giving all needed instruction and illustrations. The pupils make notes and sketches as necessary, and questions are asked and answered that all obscurities may be removed. The class then proceeds to the execution of the task, leaving the instructor to give additional help to such as need it. At a specified time that lesson ceases, and the work is brought in, commented on, and marked. It is not required that all the work assigned should be finished; the essential thing is that it should be well begun and carried on with reasonable speed and accuracy.

The shop-training is gained by regular and carefully-graded lessons, designed to cover as much ground as possible, and to teach thoroughly the uses of ordinary tools. This does not imply the attainment of sufficient skill to produce either the fine work or the rapidity of a skilled mechanic; this is left to after years. But a knowledge of how a tool or machine should be used is easily and thoroughly taught. The mechanical products or results of such lessons have little or no value when completed, and they are generally used as new material for more exercises.

In the first place, the main object of one or more exercises is to gain control and mastery of the tool in hand, and not the production of a particular model. The use of the tool may be well taught by a large variety of exercises, just as a knowledge of bank discount may be gained from the use of several different examples. No special merit can be claimed for a particular example; neither can a particular model or series of models have any great value. No good teacher is likely to use precisely the same set twice.

Again, the *method* of doing a piece of work, and not the finished piece, may be the object of a lesson. The exercises by which certain methods of using tools are to be taught often depend upon varying circumstances, such as the quality of the material, the age of pupils, and their knowledge of working drawings.

HOW THE USE OF TOOLS IS TAUGHT.

The tools are not given out all at once; they are issued as they are needed, and to all members of a class alike.

I.—CARPENTRY.

In carpentry work the tools used are the cross-cut, tenon, and rip saws; steel square, try square, bevel and gauge, hammer, mallet, rule and dividers, oil stones, and slips; and among edge tools the jack and smoothing planes, chisels, knife and gouges. Braces and bits, jointer planes, compass saws, hatchets, and other tools are kept in the shop tool closet to be used as needed.

The saw and the plane, with the square and gauge, are the foundation tools, and to drill the pupils in their use numerous lessons are given, varied only enough to avoid monotony. The pupil being able to plane a piece fairly well and to keep to the line in sawing, the next step is to teach him to add the use of the chisel in producing simple joints of various kinds. The particular shapes are given with the intent to familiarize the pupil with the customary styles and methods of construction.

The different sizes of the same tool, chisels for instance, require different care and methods of handling, and the means of overcoming irregularities and defects in material form another chapter in the instruction to be given. With the introduction of each tool the pupils are taught how to keep the same in order. They are taught that sharp tools are absolutely necessary to good work. To make them realize this is a difficult task.

II.—TURNING.

Five or six tools only are used, and from previous experience the pupils know how to keep them in order. At first a large gouge only is issued, and the pupils are taught and drilled in its use in roughing out and producing right line figures; then convex and concave surfaces; then in work comprising all these—all in wood turning with the grain. A wide chisel follows, and its use in conjunction with the gouge is taught. After this a smaller gouge, chisel, and parting tool, and a round point are given, and a variety of shapes are executed. Next comes turning across the grain; then bored and hollow work. Next, chucking and the various ways of manipulating wood on face-plates, chucks, mandrels, &c. Finally, turning of fancy woods, polishing, jointing, and pattern work.

III.—FORGING.

Work in the blacksmith shop is in one essential feature different from any other kind. Wood or cold iron will wait any desired length of time while the pupil considers how he shall work, but here comes in temperature subject to continual change. The injunction is imperative to "strike while the iron is hot," and hence quick work is demanded—a hard thing for new hands. To obviate this difficulty bars of lead are used, with which the lesson is first executed, while all the particulars of holding and striking are studied. The lead acts under the hammer very nearly like hot iron, and permits of every operation of the blacksmith's shop, except welding.

The various operations of drawing, bending, upsetting, punching, welding, tempering, &c., are learned in connection with the fabrication of hooks, stirrups, chains, swivels, tongs, and other tools.

One of the most difficult lessons in the art of the smith is that of managing the fire. The various kinds of heat are explained and illustrated, and habits of economy of both iron and fuel are inculcated.

IV.—IRON CUTTING.

The course in the machine shop begins with the chisel and the file. The series of lessons in vise work covers chipping and filing. The size, shape, quality, and use of cold chisels are studied as well as their construction at the forge. Large models of drawings are used to show the nature of files, and the various kinds of files are used upon exercises designed to call out their special points.

Then comes the cutting tools of lathes, drills, and planers, and the multiform uses of the various machine tools. The exercises are numerous and greatly varied. They all involve only light work, no attempt being made to teach the manipulation of heavy pieces. A boy accustomed to plan and reason soon learns such things. It can not be claimed that the student workmen become skilled mechanics in any of the shops, though it is insisted that every step shall be clearly understood and fairly executed. The rapid progress of boys to whom all subjects are presented in logical order, with clear and full explanations, and who work under the continual guidance of an expert teacher, and only two hours at a time, during which their interest is fully sustained—the progress of boys under such conditions is most surprising to those who compare the work produced here with the performances of ordinary apprentices of the same number of hours.

STUDY AND MANAGEMENT OF STEAM.

The steam-generating apparatus of the university consists of a battery of three large steel boilers, set and furnished in the most approved manner. These boilers furnish heat for the entire group of university buildings, as well as steam for the engine in the shop. The engine is of the best pattern and superior workmanship, and is capable of about sixty horse-power. During their third year the pupils make a careful study of the engine and furnaces, and are practiced in the management and care of them both.

PROJECT FOR GRADUATION.

Before receiving a diploma of the school, each student must execute either alone or jointly with others, a project satisfactory to the faculty of the school. The project con-

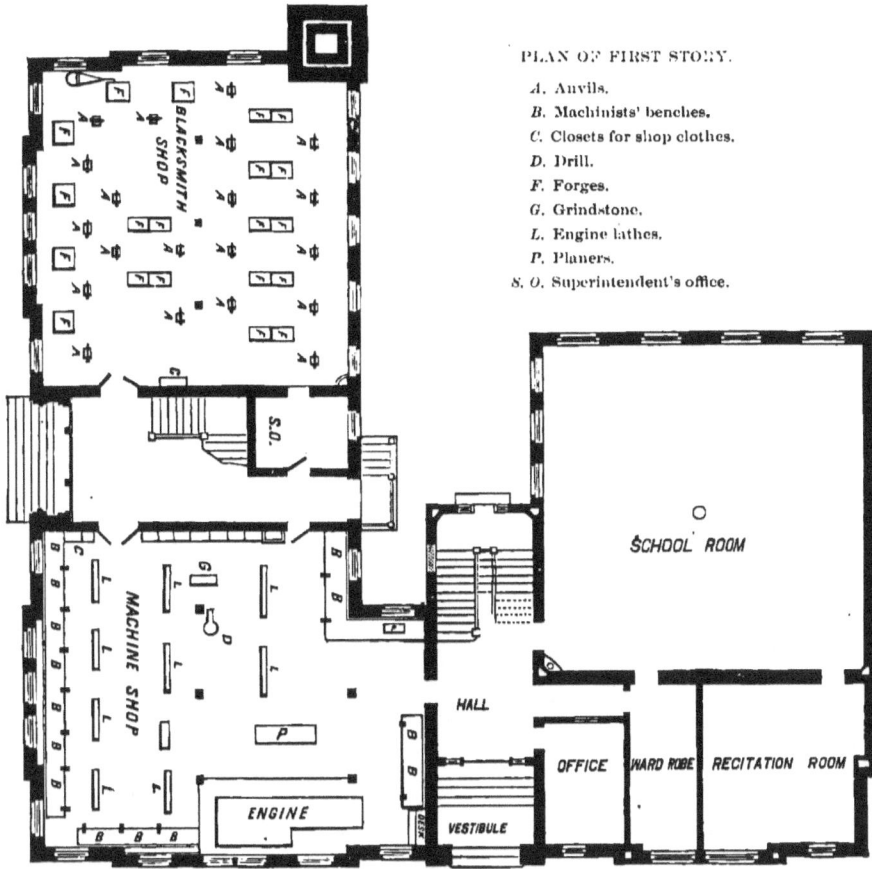

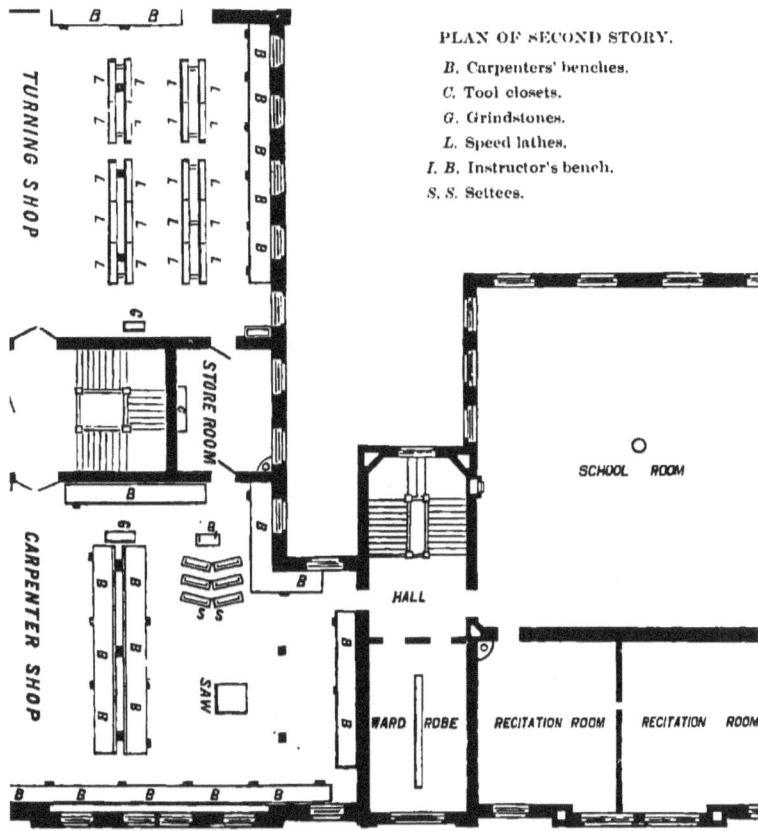

sists of the actual construction of a machine. The finished machine must be accompanied by a full set of the working drawings according to which the machine is made. If it is not feasible to construct the patterns for castings of such machines, proper directions for their construction must accompany the drawings.

ENLARGED SCHOOL BUILDING.

A perspective view of the school building and the arrangement of the three floors are shown in the accompanying cuts. It will be noticed that the original building, which has been used for the first two years of the school, is to be henceforth wholly devoted to the interests of shop work, while all needed study, recitation, and drawing rooms are supplied in the recent addition. The enlarged building has a frontage on Washington avenue of 106 feet 4½ inches, and on Eighteenth street of 100 feet.

THE RESULTS OF EXPERIENCE.

The catalogue of Washington University for 1881–'82, issued in December, 1881, also contains the following statement:

The managers of the school are abundantly confirmed in their views as set forth in the prospectus two years ago by the experience of the school during its first year and a half.

From the first the school has been well patronized, and vacant seats have been few; at times every seat has been filled. The school was opened with sixty seats, all for a single class.

The entire number of students enrolled during the first year was 60. The number of seats was increased to 100 during the last summer. The number of students enrolled thus far this year is 102, of whom 42 were members of the school last year.

The zeal and enthusiasm of the students have been developed to a most gratifying extent, extending into all the departments of work. The variety afforded by the daily programme has had the moral and intellectual effect expected, and an unusual degree of sober earnestness has been shown. Success in drawing or shop work has often had the effect of arousing the ambition in mathematics and history, and *vice versa*.

Progress in the two subjects, drawing and shop work (and we had little previous knowledge of what could be done with boys as young as those of the first year class) has been quite remarkable. To be sure there was no doubt of the final result, but the progress has been more rapid than it seemed reasonable to expect. The second year class contains already several excellent draughtsmen, and not a few pattern makers of accuracy and skill. The habit of working from drawings and to nice measurements has given the students a confidence in themselves altogether new. This is shown in the readiness with which they undertake the execution of small commissions for the interest of the school or for the students of other departments. In fact, the increased usefulness of our students is making itself felt at home, and in several instances the result has been the offer of business positions too tempting to be rejected. This drawback, if it can be called one, the school must always suffer. The better educated and trained our students become, the stronger will be the temptations offered to them outside, and the more difficult it will be for us to hold them through the course. Parents and guardians should avoid the bad policy of injuring the prospects of a promising son or ward by grasping a small present pecuniary advantage at the cost of far greater rewards in the future. From the testimony of parents (and by a circular all were invited to give frank expression to their views), the physical, intellectual, and moral effect of the school is exceedingly satisfactory. The *unanimous* response is, an unusual interest and pleasure in school, and very generally an increased fondness for such books and periodicals as the Scientific American. A few boys who had never shown any interest in tools have developed into good and enthusiastic workmen. As a rule the good scholars are the good mechanics.

SUCCESS OF THE RUSSIAN PLAN.

In another important respect our expectations have been more than realized, namely, in our ability to introduce class methods in giving instruction in the theory and use of tools. All divisions in the shops have thus far been limited to 20 pupils, and as a rule all members of a division have just the same work.

The exercises have been two hours long, though often the students have asked for longer work. It is but due to the pupils of the school to say that they have uniformly seconded all efforts looking towards good order and good manners. No little surprise has been expressed by visitors at seeing how quietly and independently twenty boys can work for a couple of hours in the same room. An examination of the rules given below will show the care and consideration expected of all during shop practice. Though all classes handle keen-edged tools, no serious accident has happened, and very rarely have small injuries been received.

COST OF TOOLS.

The cost of our equipment of tools, &c., has been quite heavy, and the generosity of our friends has been put to the test. Over $30,000 have been paid for tools and furniture. It is exceedingly gratifying to the management of the school to be able to report that no call for money for needful apparatus has failed of a favorable response.

REGULATIONS FOR PRACTICE HOURS IN THE WORKSHOPS OF THE MANUAL TRAINING SCHOOL.

"1. When dismissed for shop work, students will go directly to the shop assigned.

"2. During practice hours students must give their undivided attention to the work assigned, not leaving it to clean up till the ringing of the first bell.

"3. All singing, whistling, and lounging on the benches is strictly forbidden; students should talk only when it is necessary, and then in a low tone.

"4. During the regular hours private work can not be permitted. At other times, such work, if of a suitable character, may be allowed, at the option of the instructor.

"5. Students should clean, and return to its place any tool taken from the tool cases as soon as they are through using it.

"6. Promptly upon the ringing of the first bell work should cease; the tools should be put in their proper places, and the bench or machine cleaned, before leaving the room to wash up. Unfinished work should be put in the drawers, or in such places as the instructor may direct. The tool drawers should always be left clean and in order.

"7. Students will be admitted only to such shops as their work calls them, and at the hours assigned, except by permission of the instructor.

"8. The circular saws are not to be used except when specially directed by the instructor.

"9. Students are expressly forbidden to stand around the saw table while the saws are in use.

"10. When directed to use a saw, do not raise it higher than is necessary to cut through the stock.

"11. Avoid passing the hands beyond the saw; use a stick to push small pieces between the saw and the guide. Too much care cannot be exercised in all things pertaining to the use of machines.

"12. When a student has finished the work assigned him, and he sees that the instructor is not engaged, he may go to him for further instructions; otherwise he will remain quietly at his place.

"13. Students must promptly report to the superintendent any loss or breakage of either tools or furniture. Losses and injuries which are the result of gross carelessness or disobedience of orders should be paid for by the students responsible for them."

STATEMENT OF CONDITION SEPTEMBER 27, 1882.

The entire building is completely equipped. It is proposed to admit 100 new pupils annually. This number will diminish to about 80 the second year and 60 the third year. Hence the maximum number of pupils is 240. Ninety new pupils have been admitted the present year. The entire number now in school is 130.

There are nine divisions in the shops. There are 9½ teachers on an average in the school, not including the director, who hears no regular class.

The daily programme of the school is as follows:

Daily programme.

Class.	Division.	9 a. m. to 11 a. m.	11 a. m. to 1 p. m.	1 p. m. to 1.20 p. m.	1.20 p. m. to 3.20 p. m.
Third year.	A	Physics, geometry..	Machine shop........		French, drawing.
	B	Machine shop.........	Mechanics, geometry.		History, drawing.
Second year.	A	Algebra, physics.....	Blacksmith shop.....		Drawing, English history.
	B	Blacksmith shop....	Algebra, physics.....		English history, drawing.
	C	Algebra, English history.	Blacksmith shop.....		Drawing, physics.
First year.	X	Carpenter shop........	Drawing, physical geography.	Recess.	Arithmetic, English grammar.
	R	Drawing, Latin......	Carpenter shop.......		Arithmetic, physical geography.
	Q	Arithmetic, drawing.	Carpenter shop.......		Physical geography, Latin.
	N	English grammar, physical geography.	Arithmetic, drawing.		Carpenter shop.
	K	Carpenter shop.......	Arithmetic, English grammar.		Drawing, physical geography.

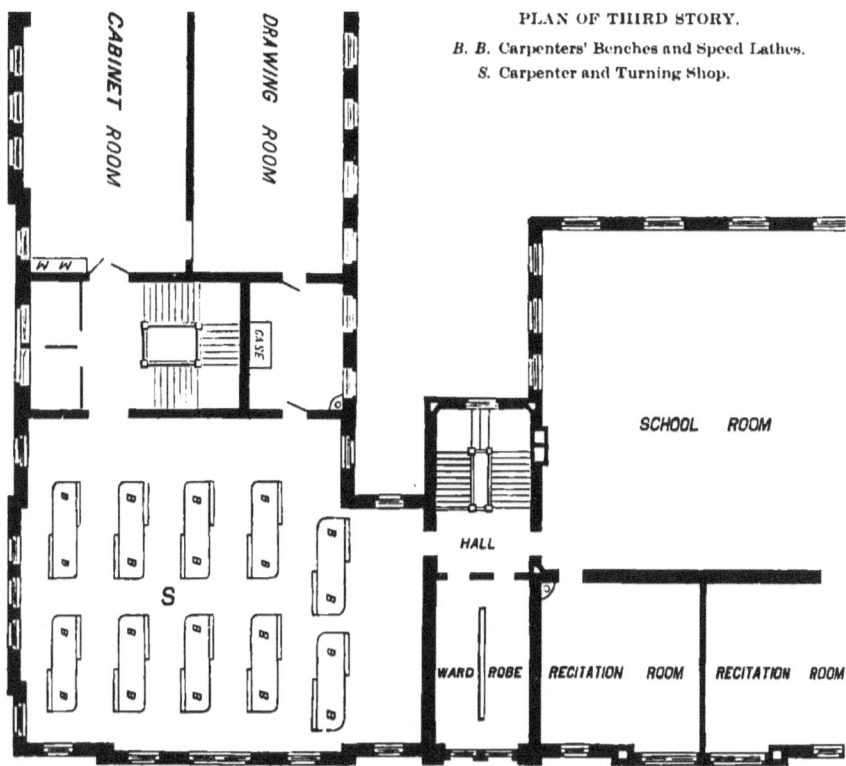

PLAN OF THIRD STORY.

B. B. Carpenters' Benches and Speed Lathes.
S. Carpenter and Turning Shop.

[S. Ex. 25——face p. 270.]

NOTES.—All drawing exercises are one full hour long.

Recitations of third year class are 60 minutes; all other recitations are 40 minutes.

Third year class, A division, have United States Constitution twice in place of physics and once in place of geometry per week.

Whole third year class have English literature once a week in place of French or history.

Second year class have studies in literature once a week in place of history, and composition and spelling in the place of physics.

First year class omit arithmetic, physical geography and English grammar, once a week, to give place for spelling, penmanship, and composition.

APPENDIX D.

SPECIAL EFFORTS FOR THE EDUCATION OF CARRIAGE MAKERS.

NOONDAY CLASS OF CARRIAGE BUILDERS' APPRENTICES AT THE FACTORY OF BREWSTER & CO. (OF BROOME STREET), NEW YORK.

[Description by J. L. H. Mosier, esq.]

In the latter part of January last, while debating with myself what to do to insure success, the happy thought of noon hour studies came to my relief. I would make education compulsory. I began with calling them together for reading only; at a later period I furnished them with paper and caused them to write a full "foolscap" page at home every week, and to present the same to me on Mondays or Tuesdays. I gave each boy a small pass book and instructed them how to keep account of the wages earned by them—simple debit and credit. Later on I gave them simple lessons in perspective drawing. I made the sketches, and to advance my clerk he copied them; each boy receives a copy and six slips of paper; there are five or six sketches. He must copy the sketches on both sides of one slip each week and present them. If he has made sufficient progress when the six slips are filled, we give him advanced sketches to copy; if the reverse, he is kept at the old one until he is perfect. Marks are scored for being late or absent and for a lack of deportment. The reward is one term at the technical school of carriage builders, three nights per week for seven months.

This year I shall introduce arithmetic and a higher grade of bookkeeping. I have also caused them to elect a president, and vice-president, and secretary, and shall also give them a little parliamentary training.

In engaging a boy I give him and his parents a brief outline of what I have here related, and make it a part of the contract, verbal; a failure to comply means dismissal.

Thus far I have met with better success than I anticipated, enough to encourage me in my good work. Brewster & Co. furnish stationery, &c. As class books we have The Hub, Carriage Monthly, and the Blacksmith and Wheelwright, which are given the class, gratis, by the publishers of the journals mentioned.

EVENING CLASS FOR CARRIAGE MECHANICS AT NEW HAVEN, CONN.

[Description by George A. Hubbard, instructor.]

Several years ago, upon coming to this city from Central New York, I found that the construction of carriage bodies was of a decidedly complicated nature, and involved some of the most intricate geometrical problems in the preparation of the plans and drafts laid out for the workmen. Wishing to fathom what were then mysteries to me, I paid an experienced workman for explanations. These were given in so crude and incomplete a manner that I resolved to exert myself and, if possible, establish a class or school where instructions pertinent to the wants of carriage mechanics might be given. With that object in view I have studied during my spare time to get the matter in as simple and clear a form as possible.

Most of the pupils, after a hard day's work, walked about two miles, both in coming and returning from the session. One came from a distance of over three miles, walking most of the time, and was absent only four evenings during the session. When you consider in connection with this exertion the laborious nature of the work performed during the day of ten hours' duration, you will form some idea of the disposition manifested by the pupils to acquire knowledge. The ages of the pupils run from eighteen to thirty-three years, with but two exceptions over twenty years.

Being myself a mechanic and laboring each day, I found the exertion for the session of 1881–'82 too much, and for the session of 1882–'83 I deemed it prudent to form but one class of 12 pupils two evenings a week, the pupils being selected through priority of application, there being in all between 25 and 30 applications for membership. The session opened the first Tuesday in October, and is now proceeding satisfactorily. In the construction of carriages there are brought into practical application artistic designing; mechanical and geometrical drawing; mechanics; knowledge of wood, iron, steel, cloths, leather, upholstering material, paints, oil, and varnish; chemical action of atmospheric changes upon the different materials used, both in process of completion and in the finished vehicle; draft of vehicles; and, lastly, mechanical skill.

In addition to the annual session I have formed a permanent session, open to all of my pupils, meeting regularly every other Wednesday evening through the year, for the purpose of considering mechanical topics. As an aid I have begun a cabinet of materials entering into the construction of carriages, both in the natural—such as woods and ores—and merchantable form. My library relating to carriages is now one of the best in this country.

[Among the volumes relating to carriages are: Draftbook of Centennial Carriages; Book of Carriage Drafts; World on Wheels, by Stratton; Carriage Builders' Reference Book; History of Coaches, by Thrupp; The Underwork of Carriages, by Budd; Carriage Makers' Manual, by Ware; Carriage Painters' Manual, by Gardner; Construction of private Carriages in England, by Hooper; Coach Body Makers' Guide, by Mattison; The Hub, 11 volumes; Carriage Monthly, 15 volumes; New York Coach Maker, 9 volumes; Harness and Carriage Journal, 2 volumes; Blacksmith and Wheelwright, 6 volumes; Coach Painter, 3 volumes; Le Guide du Carrossier, 3 volumes; Saddlers, Harness and Carriage Gazette, 3 volumes.]

REPORT OF THE COMMITTEE ON TECHNICAL EDUCATION.

PHILADELPHIA, *October* 18, 1882.

To the members of the Carriage Builders' National Association.

GENTLEMEN: Since making our last report to you in Cincinnati, just a year ago, the second term of the Technical School for Carriage Mechanics has closed and the third term fairly opened; and we now have the pleasure of presenting a brief review of the progress of the school during the season of 1881–'82, and of indicating the prosperous beginning which has been made in its work for the season just opened.

The second term opened on October 4, 1881, when the class was removed, together with all the classes of the Metropolitan Museum of Art Schools, to the new and more convenient location at Nos. 214 and 216 East Thirty-fourth street, New York, and continued until May 30, 1882, covering a period of about eight months. Three evening lessons were given each week during the time named, excepting the month of January, when there were two lessons per week. The total number of sessions thus numbered 100, and it is worthy of special note that the instructor, Mr. John D. Gribbon, was never once absent.

The term opened with 26 pupils on the roll (against 22 at the close of season of 1880–'81), which number increased to 40 at the end of October, 47 at the end of March, and 49 at the end of the term. These were divided among the different mechanical departments as follows: 14 journeyman bodymakers, 17 apprentice bodymakers, 2 journeyman blacksmiths, 2 apprentice blacksmiths, 2 journeyman painters, 2 apprentice painters, 1 superintendent, 1 journeyman wheelmaker, and 8 office men.

The widening influence of the school was indicated by the distance from which many of the pupils came in order to utilize its advantages, 29 of the pupils being from New York City, while the remainder were divided among the following localities, namely: Long Island, 7; Newburgh, N. Y., 1; New Jersey, 1; Ohio, 2; Kentucky, 1; Iowa, 1; Massachusetts, 3; Delaware 1; Connecticut, 1; and Canada, 2. Some of the pupils from a distance who were obliged to discontinue attendance were supplied by the instructor with drawings and lesson papers, by which they were enabled to continue their studies at their homes.

It being found impossible for the instructor to attend to the demands of all the pupils, an assistant instructor, Mr. John C. Konrad, was selected from among the more experienced pupils, who rendered valuable assistance to Mr. Gribbon.

The attendance during the second term ranged as follows, namely: During October, 1881, the average number present was 24; November, 24; December, 21; January, 25; February, 18; March, 18; April, 18; and May, 21; or 21¼ as the average for the season. The decreased average during February, March, and April was no doubt partly owing to the activity of business in the shops, and the consequent working overtime. The attendance on Saturday nights, however, was unsatisfactory throughout the season, and materially reduced the general average; and we have taken steps to remedy this difficulty by altering the class nights during the present season to Monday, Wednesday, and Friday, by which means it is hoped and expected that the average of attendance will be materially increased. We understand, however, that the above statement of attendance compares favorably with that of other similar evening classes in New York, where the pupils are actually engaged during the day in mechanical pursuits.

Blackboards were provided for such pupils as were sufficiently advanced to make use of them, and creditable working drawings in full size were produced by Messrs. Pease,

Oak, Donovan, Mondin, and Campbell. Some of these drawings have been reproduced in full size on roll paper, and are for your inspection in another part of the building.

The progress of the pupils is thus reported upon by the instructor, Mr. Gribbon, who says: "I consider that the scholars made creditable progress during the second term, taking into consideration the fact that nearly all of them had received no previous instruction in drawing of any kind, or in geometry;" and he adds: "I consider it a great loss to the apprentices that they have not been taught the first principles of geometry in the public schools before trying to learn a trade, for there is so little manual labor nowadays in consequence of the general use of machinery, that a boy requires to be more intelligent and to have a better mental training in order to make a place for himself in the trade than in the days of long apprenticeship."

After due consideration, it was decided to give certificates to such pupils as showed special aptitude and application during the term. The following form was adopted: "Certificate of progress awarded to ———, of ———, for regular attendance, diligent study, and commendable progress, while a pupil in the class in carriage drafting and construction connected with the Metropolitan Museum of Art Schools of New York, from ——— to ———." Twenty-three certificates of this character, printed in attractive form, and duly signed by the committee and the instructor, and also stamped with the seal of the association, were awarded during the second term. Similar certificates will also be given during the current season.

In addition to the one hundred regular class nights, four evenings during the season were devoted to lectures upon mechanical topics, namely: Wednesday, December 7, 1881, lecture by Mr. Chauncey Thomas, of Boston, on "Novelty and expression in design;" Wednesday, January 25, 1882, lecture by Mr. J. L. H. Mosier, of New York, on "Fracture of iron and causes thereof;" Wednesday, March 8, 1882, lecture by Mr. J. L. H. Mosier, of New York, on "Sound and its relation to wheeled vehicles;" and Wednesday, May 17, 1882, lecture by Mr. Howard M. Du Bois, of Philadelphia, on "The whys and wherefores in wheel making," at all of which there was a full attendance of the pupils. The committee owe special thanks to the above named gentlemen for their courtesy in freely giving these interesting and instructive lectures.

The third term for the season of 1882–'83 was opened on the evening of Monday, October 9, when twenty-six pupils were enrolled, the same number as at the beginning of the previous term, divided among the different departments as follows: Bodymakers, 17; blacksmiths, 5; gearmaker, 1; office men, 2; and carriage draughtsman, 1. Various improvements in the working facilities have been introduced during the summer vacation, including a rearrangement of the tables and gas jets, and the introduction of four new blackboards and an additional case in the museum for the reception of models.

The class is continued at the same location as last year, and under the same arrangement with the committee of the Metropolitan Museum of Art, to whom we pay $1,200 annually, and allow all fees received from pupils; in consideration of which a suitable class room is supplied to the carriage class, now second in size and importance in the school, together with lighting, heating, and superintendence, and all necessary working facilities. Mr. John D. Gribbon, by a unanimous vote, has been retained as instructor, and he will be assisted as before by Mr. John C. Konrad. The term will be continued until May 26, 1883, or thirty-two weeks, with three lessons per week, the tuition fee to pupils being placed at the nominal rate of $5 for the season.

It is proposed to continue the series of technical lectures by experts, though arrangements have not yet been perfected for the course; and we take this opportunity of suggesting that any member of the association who feels disposed to address the class on any mechanical subject connected with the trade, or who can assist us to secure the services of any expert known to him, will greatly oblige the committee by communicating with them on the subject, as a growing conviction is felt that such lectures can be made an important and valuable feature of the school work.

The committee would also invite your attention to the need of increasing the working facilities of the school by making constant additions to its technical library and museum. Accessions of some importance have been made during the past year to both these departments, special acknowledgment being due to Mr. J. L. H. Mosier and his associates connected with the Brewster Carriage Works, Broadway and Forty-seventh street, New York, for a gift of 36 volumes; and to Mr. H. M. Du Bois, and Messrs. Hoopes, Brother & Darlington, for specimens of wheels and parts of same. The usefulness of the library would be largely increased if many of the pamphlets, periodicals, and collections of carriage drawings should be bound into volumes, and it is hoped that a sufficient surplus will be derived from your subscriptions this year toward the school fund to authorize the committee not only to forward the work of binding, but also to purchase many additional text books and works of reference, the need of which is now keenly felt. To better illustrate the requirements of the school in this regard, and to enable you to judge of what has already been accomplished in this direction and to perceive what further contributions will be most acceptable, a printed catalogue of the books, pamphlets, and periodicals now in possession of the school will be distributed among the members of the association at this convention; and gifts of any additional works of technical interest which the study of this catalogue may suggest to you are earnestly invited.

We also take the liberty of suggesting that any of the parts of carriages exhibited by the members of the association at this convention which exhibitors may feel disposed to present to the school will be thankfully received by the committee and duly deposited in the museum of models.

Before closing this our annual report we take pleasure in alluding to the successful continuance of two similar classes for the instruction of carriage mechanics now in successful operation in New Haven, Conn., and New York City, namely: Mr. George A. Hubbard's class for carriage draughtsmen, in New Haven, and Mr. J. Polya's class for carriagebody makers, at No. 1295 Broadway, New York. We are pleased to learn that both these classes have met with marked success during the past year, and that courses of study similar to those already pursued will be continued during the present season.

Respectfully submitted.

Signed by the committee on technical education:

JNO. W. BRITTON, *Chairman.*
WILDER H. PRAY, *Treasurer.*
WM. D. ROGERS.
LOWE EMERSON.
CHAUNCEY THOMAS.
WM. N. FITZ GERALD.
GEO. W. W. HOUGHTON, *Secretary.*

REPORT OF THE TREASURER OF THE TECHNICAL SCHOOL.

SUMMARY.

Total single subscriptions	$3,770 90
Total yearly subscriptions	5,520 00
Paris scholarship	500 00
Grand total	9,790 90
Amount due and unpaid	405 00

RECEIPTS.

Single subscriptions	3,790 90
Yearly subscriptions	3,325 00
Paris scholarship	500 00
Interest on deposits	142 31
Rebate on school payments	11 15
Total receipts	7,769 36
Total disbursements	4,432 83
Cash on hand	3,336 53
	7,769 36

RESOURCES.

Cash on hand	3,336 53
Subscriptions due and not paid	405 00
Subscriptions not due	1,620 00
	5,361 53

APPENDIX E.

SCIENTIFIC INSTRUCTION IN WELLESLEY COLLEGE; THE INDUSTRIAL TRAINING OF WOMEN IN LASELL SEMINARY, THE IOWA AGRICULTURAL COLLEGE, AND THE ILLINOIS INDUSTRIAL UNIVERSITY; A HISTORICAL SKETCH OF THE NEW YORK SCHOOL OF COOKERY; THE WORK OF MISS MARIA PARLOA AS A TEACHER OF COOKERY; "COOKING SCHOOLS IN THE SOUTH; AND THE NEW CENTURY EVENING CLASSES FOR WOMEN."

COURSE OF INSTRUCTION IN SCIENCE IN WELLESLEY COLLEGE.

The scientific course is arranged for students who desire to give the four years of college life to the pursuit of the natural, physical, and mathematical sciences and the studies necessarily connected therewith. The course as laid out gives opportunities for scientific study which are substantially the equivalent of those given to young men in the best scientific and technical schools.

In the department of chemistry and mineralogy there are two laboratories, a lecture room, and a storeroom for apparatus. The chemical laboratory is furnished with apparatus, cupboards, and drawers for ninety-six students, working in divisions. The desks are furnished with sinks, gas, and hot and cold water. The laboratory is provided with a number of convenient hoods for manipulation of noxious gases.

After studying chemistry a year, the students commence the course in mineralogy. This embraces the various topics comprehended under morphology, the physical properties of minerals, and the chemical reactions employed as tests. In the mineralogical laboratory every convenience for blowpipe analysis is provided. From 20 to 30 determinations (according to Brush) are required. Students can also determine as many other minerals as they desire.

Throughout the course they study minerals, and become familiar with their chemical and physical properties by careful observation and comparison, with the aid of the blowpipe, the microscope, and chemical reagents. They have access to the cabinet collections and use specimens in the class room.

The study of crystallography is taken up in connection with mineralogy. This is aided by a collection of models of crystal forms and a collection of typical crystals.

The study of lithology follows. There is a large collection of rocks specially arranged for this course. An important branch of this study is carried on with the aid of the compound microscope, the polariscope, and a collection of microscopical sections of typical rocks and their constituent minerals.

The department of physics occupies a convenient lecture room, with lantern and *porte-lumière* constantly in place for the illustration of lectures or the projection upon the screen of minute experiments. Water, wires from the battery, oxygen and hydrogen, and illuminating gas are furnished at the lecturer's desk. There are a professors' laboratory, for the preparation of experiments, and an extensive students' laboratory, supplied with instruments for quantitative work. One dark room is supplied with a Bunsen's photometer for measuring the candle power of lights, and with apparatus for spectrum analysis, &c. Another room is fitted up for an electrical laboratory, and supplied with a Wheatstone's bridge and resistance coils, Thomson's mirror galvanometer and lamp stand, and other apparatus necessary for electrical measurements. There is also a battery room and a room for photography.

Physical astronomy is an elective study of the senior year. The basis of instruction is given by lectures, illustrated by globes, charts, and lantern slides. The lectures are supplemented by the constant use of the works in the astronomical library and by observations with the telescope. Every student is required to observe the moon at several phases, and to identify certain prominent craters and seas; also, to observe the sun and planets and certain nebulæ and clusters. Especial attention is given to spectroscopic astronomy and the constitution of the sun.

In botany instruction is given by recitations, lectures, and by practical work in the laboratory. Compound microscopes are furnished by the college for the use of all the classes. The students have access at all times to the herbarium and the botanical library. Plants from the greenhouse are supplied during the winter.

In biology the full course extends through two years, and consists almost entirely of laboratory work. Every student is provided with a microscope and two or three objectives The laboratory possesses lenses of the highest power, and each student is furnished with a complete set of dissecting instruments, and a case of twenty reagents and coloring fluids for testing the nature and properties of the objects studied. After a lecture upon the subject of the day, the students repair to their respective tables, each of which is provided with the organism or tissue to be studied. Drawings are made of their dissections and preparations, and these are accompanied by written descriptions, together with notes of physiological action, &c.

There are in constant use in the different scientific departments 65 microscopes of various patterns, according to the work to be done; also a microscope especially adapted to the study of rock sections, and a polari-microscope. There is a large battery of objectives, ranging in power from 1.25 inches down, and a variety of accessory apparatus.

There are, in addition to the general library of 20,000 volumes, five special libraries, viz, the botanical, that of biology and zoölogy, the chemical, that of the physical department, and the Gertrude library for biblical study. A large reading room is also supplied with newspapers, periodicals, and more than a hundred literary reviews and magazines, and the best scientific journals of every kind published in the United States, England, Germany, and France.

INDUSTRIAL TRAINING IN LASELL SEMINARY, AUBURNDALE (NEAR BOSTON), MASS.

Thorough instruction in cooking has been given in this school for six years by Miss Parloa and Mrs. Daniels, of Boston, and for five years lessons have been given in dress cutting and fitting, after Taylor's system, and in millinery by experienced city workers. The primary object has been to qualify the pupils to supervise every department of home interests; to present them in an attractive aspect; to elevate them to their true place, as likely to be in any well-ordered home most important prerequisites in the fulfilment of duty. At the same time the instruction is so thorough technically as to be available if necessary for any service. Classes are formed in each branch of work, in which the pupils are demonstrators, the teacher supervising if more special instruction is desired. Both these and the general lectures are entirely apart from the domestic department of the school, as in the chemical lectures or other laboratory work, which they follow in general style of presentation.

Miss Parloa's lessons given on Saturday afternoons, were free, and attended by the whole school. A programme for the entire course of lessons is issued at the beginning of the year, each lesson containing a variety of substantial and dessert dishes. Miss Parloa prepares these at a table on a low platform, and cooks, as may be necessary, at a stove on the same platform, in near view of her audience, explaining as she works. The various dishes disappear in an assembly of school girls ready with spoon and napkin, as well as with note book; and the whole bears the appearance of a recreation rather than a task. The interest has been surprising, even to those who had the most sanguine faith in ultimate success. The circular issued for this year contains extracts from notices by the press in every part of the country, representing every variety of interest, and expressions from the homes to which the pupils belong of great gratification with the interest awakened and the success in repeating the processes learned at school.

The dressmaking work is done by the pupils themselves, in classes of six, in one of the usual recitation rooms. At the junior socials fair hostesses have received their invited guests in dresses fitted and made in connection with this class, entertained later in the chapel with the usual literary exercises, and led the way to a tastefully arranged table, where they served sandwiches, a variety of delicious cake, coffee, and ice creams, entirely the work of their own hands.

As we learn, recently a whole side of beef was cut up, as furnished for the best private tables, and a thorough lesson given in the uses and prices of the various pieces. It is a part of the plan to impart practical knowledge of materials in market and shop, to encourage the development of judgment and skill for all the needs of household life.

A little time steadily given through a year to the cultivation of practical intelligence in these matters is found to detract in no way from the usual school requirements, while it builds a broad, easy way over the gulf which lies for many a girl between her school and her married life.

"My daughter has improved in so many ways," is a frequent comment of mothers. "She has brought home an interest never apparent before in all our home work." This is what was most desired to bring the girl's mind into relation with life as it is likely to be for her, to bring her highest scholarly acquirements to enrich her home life.

The principal is more than satisfied of its practicability, and so much considers the experiment an established and gratifying success that a practice kitchen and dining room, with all appliances of the best cooking schools, were provided in the new wing added last year.

In all the departments of home instruction there is eager interest on the part of pupils and assurance of the best success.

DEPARTMENT OF DOMESTIC ECONOMY IN THE IOWA AGRICULTURAL COLLEGE, AMES.

[By Mrs. Mary B. Welch, lecturer on domestic economy.]

The first instruction in this department was given in 1872 by a course of lectures to the junior girls on matters connected with housekeeping. In 1877 the trustees added a course in cooking, and provided and furnished a kitchen for the use of the class. For the last four years, therefore, lessons in cooking have been given to the junior class, in connection with lectures on such subjects as house furnishing, care of the sick, care of children, management of help, dress, &c. Physiology and domestic chemistry are carefully taught as a part of the course in domestic economy.

In 1879 the course was further extended by the addition of sewing and laundry work. These have been taught with fair success for two years. Many of our students, however, have been able to pass them by examination, and it was found difficult to arouse the same degree of interest in either as in cooking. There has been a steadily increasing demand for instruction in the latter, and the course has been reorganized for this year so as to give the cooking lessons to a larger number of students. These lessons were formerly confined to the juniors, on account partly of want of room in the small kitchen provided by the board, and partly on account of lack of drill in chemistry in the preceding years. At the last session of the legislature larger rooms were assigned to the department, and the present plan arranges for progressive lessons to the freshman, sophomore, and junior classes.

The young women of the freshman class prepare, under my instruction, the noonday meal for one table in the main dining hall, where two hundred students are boarded. The housekeeper furnishes the bill of fare for the day, and sends to the practice kitchen sufficient material for a dinner for ten persons, which is cooked and served by the teacher and her class. Not more than five work at once, and thus each receives careful supervision and can get actual practice at every lesson. In this way the class is taught plain cooking—how to prepare meats, vegetables, and simple desserts. The dinner cooked at the last lesson is a fair sample of the daily work. It consisted of roast beef, mashed potatoes, stewed tomatoes, and apple dumplings. While the work was going on the teacher explained not only the culinary processes, but told the class also something about the value of beef as a food, the best cuts, how to tell good beef from poor, the marks of disease, something also about the history and food value of the potato and apple, the tests for good flour, and the composition and action of baking powder.

In order to get time for this minute instruction to so large a number, the laundry work and sewing were necessarily abolished and the sophomores are given the lectures, which have been extended to embrace not only those matters which relate strictly to housekeeping, but more comprehensive information on hygiene, the laws of good breeding, and those things which go to make a home beautiful as well as clean and convenient. The class is required to take notes, and in connection with the lectures do a good deal of careful reading and write several essays each on the topics treated of.

Finally, to the juniors is given a more elaborate course in cooking. Great pains is taken in that year to explain as carefully as may be the nutritive value of different foods, tests for adulterations, the combination of the several classes of food in bills of fare so as to be most valuable, &c. Together with the theory is given thorough practice in both plain and ornamental cookery. Bread and soups are made the subjects of special drill, while salads, side dishes, pastry and cake, carving, boning, and garnishing are also most thoroughly taught. A few lessons are given in the preparation of food for the sick, and these are dwelt on with special emphasis.

The interest of the students in the department of domestic economy has been constant and lively, while the board of trustees, the college faculty, and the patrons of the school have united in encouraging its development. It is acknowledged to have met a long-existing want and to have done real service to the young women of the State. It has not only given them manual skill, but it has also increased their respect for all branches of such labor, and added dignity to that part of their life work hitherto considered as menial drudgery. The promise for the future is most encouraging. Stimulated by the enthusiasm of her pupils, strengthened by the good will of her fellow teachers, and aided by the generous appreciation and liberal policy of the board of trustees, the teacher of domestic economy looks forward with sure faith to the fullest development of her department.

THE SCHOOL OF DOMESTIC SCIENCE OF THE ILLINOIS INDUSTRIAL UNIVERSITY.

[By Mrs. John M. Gregory.]

This school was formally opened in Urbana, 1874, being the first college course of high grade in domestic science organized in the United States, if not in the world. With no precedent to guide, few or no text books on the subject to furnish material aid, with an incredulous public opinion to contend against, and opposition in most unexpected quarters to meet, the undertaking at the outset seemed formidable enough. But the six years that have intervened have sufficed to overcome many obstacles and demonstrate the practical value of the work.

The school was the outgrowth of a conviction that a rational system for the higher and better education of women must recognize their distinctive duties as women—the mothers, housekeepers, and health keepers of the world—and furnish instruction which shall fit them to meet these duties.

As set forth in the catalogue, it was the aim of the school to give to earnest and capable young women a liberal and practical education, which should fit them for their great duties and trusts, making them the equals of their educated husbands and associates, and enabling them to bring the aids of science and culture to the all important labors and vocations of womanhood.

This school proceeded upon the assumption that the housekeeper needs education as much as the house builder, the nurse as well as the physician, the leaders of society as surely as the leaders of senates, the mother as much as the father, the woman as well as the man. We discarded the old and absurd notion that education is a necessity to man, but only an ornament to woman. If ignorance is a weakness and a disaster in the places of business where the income is won, it is equally so in the places of living where the income is expended. If science can aid agriculture and the mechanic arts to use more successfully nature's forces and to increase the amount and value of their products, it can equally aid the housekeeper in the finer and more complicated use of those forces and agencies in the home, where winter is to be changed into genial summer by artificial fires, and darkness into day by costly illumination; where the raw products of the field are to be transformed into sweet and wholesome food by a chemistry finer than that of soils, and the products of a hundred manufactories are to be put to their final uses for the health and happiness of life.

The purpose was to provide a full course of instruction in the arts of the household, and the sciences relating thereto. No industry is more important to human happiness and well being than that which makes the home. And this industry involves principles of science as many and as profound as those which control any other human employment.

In the fall of 1874 the writer of this article was called to take charge of this school, which then existed only in name. During the first year she gave much time to mapping out and preparing a course of study, which was presented for the first time in the catalogue of 1875–'76, substantially as follows:

COURSE OF DOMESTIC SCIENCE

Required for degree of B. S. in school of domestic science.

FIRST YEAR.

1. Chemistry; trigonometry; drawing (full term); British authors.
2. Chemistry; designing and drawing; American authors.
3. Chemistry; designing and drawing; rhetoric.

SECOND YEAR.

1. Botany; physiology; German or English classics.
2. Food and dietetics (simple aliments); botany and greenhouse; German or English classics.
3. Food and dietetics (compound aliments and principles of cooking, &c.); zoölogy; German or English classics.

THIRD YEAR.

1. Domestic hygiene; ancient history; German or French.
2. Physics; mediæval history; German or French.
3. Physics or landscape gardening; modern history; German or French.

FOURTH YEAR.

1. Household æsthetics; mental science; history of civilization.
2. Household science; constitutional history; logic.
3. Domestic economy; usages of society, &c.; political economy; home architecture; graduating thesis or oration or essay.

It will be seen in the above that the technical studies do not begin until the second term of the sophomore year. There are two reasons for this arrangement: First, the very evident one that the applications of a science must be preceded by and based upon a knowledge of the theory and general principles of that science. For instance, no truly scientific study of food and dietetics could be entered upon until the pupils had acquired a knowledge of general chemistry, qualitative and quantitative analysis, as also some knowledge of plant structure, and skill in manipulating the microscope. A second reason for placing the technical studies late in the course is that the students may bring to this work greater maturity of mind.

No other one science is more constantly applicable to the necessities of every-day life than chemistry. Hence it was made a prominent feature of the course, either under the form of general chemistry with laboratory practice, or in the study of foods and their analysis. Moreover, laboratory practice is calculated to develop that patient, careful attention to minutiæ, and appreciation of exact weights and measures, which is quite as essential to definite results in the kitchen as in the laboratory. A habit of searching for the causes of failure, formed in the laboratory, will yield good results in the kitchen. George Eliot makes one of her characters in "Adam Bede" say: "A woman will make porridge every day for twenty years and never think of measuring the proportion between the meal and the milk; a little more or less she'll think doesn't signify. The porridge will be awkward now and then; if it's wrong, it's something in the meal, or it's something in the milk, or it's something in the water. Look at me; I make my own bread, and there's no difference between one batch and another from year's end to year's end; but if I'd a woman in the house I must pray for patience at every baking of the bread if it turns out heavy. It's an impious, unscriptural opinion to say a woman's a blessing to a man now; you might as well say that adders and wasps are blessings, when they are only evils belonging to this state of probation." Not so bad as that, Mr. Massey. She simply needs to be educated. Man's contact with the world has taught him to give "pounds and ounces as to quantity," where woman gives only approximative handfuls.

The other corner stones of the course are anatomy, physiology, and hygiene. No other acquisitions can atone to young women for the lack of a thorough practical knowledge of these. Woman, much more than man, has suffered from lack of proper instruction in school courses in these vital sciences.

Mathematics is required in the course only through trigonometry, this being as far as required by any subsequent study in the course, and as far, in all probability, as will be needed by young women in after life.

TECHNICAL STUDIES.

The work in the technical studies was necessarily conducted by lectures, class demonstrations, and readings. The students were thus made acquainted with the best literature on the subjects treated. The university library, with its wide range of carefully selected scientific works and annual appropriations for the purchase of new books, afforded excellent opportunities for the students to consult authorities.

Food and dietetics.—This study occupied two terms. The work began with a study of the simple aliments, such as *starch*, the structure of its grains in different plants, shown by the microscope; test, action of heat, water and other agents upon it; digestibility and dietetic value; *sugar*, kinds, sources from whence obtained; tests, relative sweetening values, processes of manufacturing and refining; effects of heat, acids, and other agents upon it, and means of judging quality; dietetic value. The hydrocarbons, the nitrogenous group, and saline principles were studied in the same manner, care being exercised to bring into prominence, appropriately grouped, all the physical and chemical properties having a practical bearing upon the preparation of foods to secure their highest dietetic value.

This preliminary work prepared the students for the more complicated study of the compound aliments and the general principles of cooking and dietetics. The *cereals* furnished the themes for a number of instructive lectures. The structure of the wheat grain was shown under the microscope, and also by means of one of Doctor Auzoux's admirable *papier mâché* models. A knowledge of the physical properties and composition of the different parts of the grain made clear the transformations produced in the processes of grinding and bolting, and showed the comparative nutritive value of the different products of milling. This was followed by lectures on bread-making by fermentation and by the use of chemicals, the advantages and disadvantages of the two methods. The yeast plant was studied under the microscope, and the effect of different temperatures upon it noted. The qualities of good bread, the chemical transformations that take place in rendering the dough light, the temperature required for baking, the methods of determining the temperature of the oven, the digestibility of bread as influenced by its freshness, lightness, and sweetness, and other related topics, were subjects in which the students became much interested. They often expressed great pleasure and surprise to find so many and such profound principles of science bearing upon so common an art as breadmaking. They left the subject, no longer to regard the difference between good and bad bread as a matter of "luck," but as dependent upon the intelligent application of scientific principles; principles as much under human control as are those which regulate the action of a steam-engine. The world readily concedes that knowledge is essential to success in controlling a locomotive, but it is slow to see that it is equally essential to success in the management of a bake oven. In a little, well-directed study of the chemistry and philosophy of bread-making may be acquired useful principles that women are left to find out for themselves, as a rule, through experience, which, too often, means months of sad failure and impaired health.

We are apt to regard the common vegetables of our gardens as devoid of interest and unworthy of study. This is because of our ignorance. Take for example the Irish potato (*Solanum tuberosum*). Look into its history, study its chemistry and philosophy, and what a volume of political economy, national destiny, practical truth, and anecdote is opened up. From a mere curious exotic planted in Sir Walter Raleigh's garden in 1586, so disappointing that he ordered his gardener to "pull up the worthless weed," it becomes one of the most widely diffused plants, struggling for existence even within the arctic circle. It has added millions to the populations and wealth of Europe. A single failure of the potato crop left Ireland in a famishing condition, reducing its population, it is said, from eight or nine millions to five millions. The potato famine in Ireland was but one of Heaven's great hygienic teachers, confirming two great natural laws, viz.: 1. Rotation of crops. Plants long cultivated on the same soil fail at least. 2. Variety in diet. Long ago it was written "Man cannot live by bread alone." This contains a dietetic as well as a spiritual truth, even more applicable to the potato than to bread.

The discussion of the potato and other vegetables common upon our tables, afforded many a topic of as much interest as importance. The composition, chemical changes in cooking, various methods of preparation, and dietetic uses and value were thoroughly studied.

The potato is defective in nitrogenous principles, fat, and mineral matter. In this is to be found an explanation of the enormous consumption of potatoes by the Irishman.

Tea, *coffee*, and *cocoa* furnish topics for a number of practical lectures, treating of the different kinds, their comparative values, composition, properties, effects upon the system, &c. The best way to teach one how to make good coffee is to begin by teaching the properties of its constituent principles. This known, good results are insured or failures will be speedily corrected. For example, know that the peculiar aroma upon which the goodness of coffee so largely depends is dissipated by long boiling or continued exposure to the air and one will not make the common mistake of roasting, grinding, and leaving coffee long exposed to the air before using, or allowing it to boil until the aroma is dissipated and the residuum but a bitter dose.

That questionable food, alcohol, was impartially considered in the light of the latest and most reliable scientific investigations, and the highest authorities were questioned in regard to its effects upon the system in extremes of heat, cold, hunger, severe mental or physical labor, its medicinal value, &c.; and then all the force of moral considerations was brought to bear upon this instrument of evil that so baffles scientific certainty, that is so delusive in the exquisitely cut wine-glass, this will-o'-the-wisp that lures men on to ruin and is the direct or indirect cause of so many woes.

The time has come when women should be educated for battle with king alcohol. Young, impressible womanhood must drink from the springs of learning, that their eyes may be opened to a full realization of the nature and strength of this evil, to a perception of its chief strongholds and its vulnerable points. They must be led to see that prenatal influences are largely responsible for the intemperance of the world; that bad bread, unwholesome food, insufficient nutrition, and improperly selected diet create a want in the system, which, not being understood, often seeks gratification in the wine cup. We shall never get the upper hand of intemperance until we have gone back of the saloons, in search of the causes that gave it birth; till we have entered the homes, and taught those who preside over them the strong moral influences exerted by good bread, wholesome food, and healthful, attractive homes. Says an English philanthropist of extended observation, "The more we investigate the social evils of the day, tracing them to their causes, the more convinced shall we be that reform to be healthful must proceed from within rather than from without. If we wish to purify and elevate the national life we must begin, therefore, in the home. And if we wish to reform the homes of the people we must train aright those who for good or for evil will preside over them."

Animal foods open up a wide field for interesting study and research. The importance of a mixed diet, the composition and nutritive value of different meats, the average market price and economical value of different parts of the beef, methods of cooking with reference to comparative economy and healthfulness, temperature required, means of judging of the quality of meat, the use of the microscope in detecting the presence of trichina and other parasites, thorough cooking as a safeguard against these parasites, and its antiseptic action when meat is tainted, were among the topics discussed, and are sufficient to show the magnitude and importance of the subject.

We need no better argument for the importance of instructing the people on these subjects than is furnished by the official reports of the enormous quantity of diseased and unwholesome meat that annually finds its way into the markets, in spite of health officers and inspecting boards. Boards of health, however vigilant, will labor with tied hands until they find in educated housekeepers efficient colaborers.

Milk, a typical food, its analysis, examination under the microscope, varying composition as influenced by breeds of cows, their treatment, and food, and by climate, &c., the philosophy of butter making, temperature for setting the cream and for churning, importance of cleanliness, duration of churning, working, washing, and salting butter, and other related topics were discussed.

When it is so comparatively easy to make good butter it seems a pity that ignorance should be allowed to serve us a dyspeptic article. But many a farmer's wife does not know what good butter is, much less the methods of producing it.

FOOD MUSEUM.

To aid in this study of food and dietetics, the nucleus of a food museum was begun, with the purpose of developing it, when the requisite funds could be secured, somewhat on the plan of the food collection of the Bethnal Green Museum, London, where the labors of Playfair, Huxley, Frankland, and Church are doing so much to instruct the public in this hitherto neglected department of education. The London food collection is a grand object-lesson on the materials and processes of every-day life to the multitudes who visit it. Specimens of all the important human foods are gathered from the various quarters of the globe, and the composition of the most important foods is shown by what is termed "displayed analyses," enabling the eye to take in at a glance the relative proportion of the various constituents of a given food.

Colored charts, drawings, and diagrams attract the eye and fix the attention, teaching even the most illiterate useful lessons on the composition and physiological functions of foods, and guarding them against adulterated and spurious articles. Numerous water analyses are so shown as to enforce the necessity for pure drinking water. Filters of different kinds and the materials used in their construction are exhibited, and the actual process of filtering through sand, gravel, and charcoal is displayed. In short, in every department of this great museum the endeavor has been to make the food collection tell its own story in a most forcible and practical manner. It is a matter of reproach to the United States that hitherto little or nothing in this direction has been done here, either in a public or private way.

It was also the as yet unfulfilled purpose of the school of domestic science to have a kitchen museum, fitted up with the most approved modern conveniences, partly for experimental purposes in connection with class lectures and partly as a means of illustrating the most convenient arrangement for a kitchen, showing the great economy in time and strength that would result from having kitchens properly planned and arranged.

Hygiene.—In addition to the study of advanced anatomy and physiology, this school provided for its young women a special course of lectures, extending through a term, on the hygiene of the home, embracing such topics as the location of dwellings, good drainage, uncleanliness as a cause of disease; the necessity for good ventilation, pure water, and abundant sunlight; bathing, exercise, and other conditions of health; the construction, material, and hygiene of dress; the principles of nursing the sick. Lectures were also given on the anatomy, physiology, and hygiene of the female pelvic organs, under the conviction that it is through the want of this knowledge that so many women become confirmed invalids. The teacher, delicately, cautiously, prayerfully, and with reverential tread, endeavored to lead her pupils into paths which show the grander possibilities for humanity through an enlightened motherhood. The young women were taught to look upon disease as the penalty for disobedience to inexorable natural laws; that among the many causes which combine to rob woman of her birth-right, good health, one of the most potent is her very unhygienic dress. And it was not found impossible to secure, if not a radical, at least a very sensible reform in the dress of the members of the class.

From one-seventh to one-fourth of all children both fail to pass their first year, and 25 to 40 per cent. perish before they have completed their fifth year, we are told.

We appeal to physicians to stay this terrible "slaughter of the innocents," but with a grave shake of the head they tell us they are all but powerless in the matter, and that our future hope must look mainly to a more enlightened motherhood. But, full of old time prejudices, we are slow to act. Says Rev. Charles Kingsley, "Would to God that some man had the historical eloquence to put before the mothers of England the mass of preventable suffering, the mass of preventable agony of mind and body which exists in England year after year; and would that some man had the logical eloquence to make them understand that it is in their power, in the power of the wives and mothers to stop, as I believe, three-fourths of it."

What is true of England is true of America.

"To tens of thousands that are killed add hundreds of thousands that survive with feeble constitutions and millions that grow up with constitutions not so strong as they should be, and you will have some idea of the curse inflicted on their offspring by parents ignorant of the laws of life."—(Herbert Spencer.) Is anything more needed to show the importance of introducing into courses of study for girls the lectures outlined above?

The following is from a board of health report: "The records of infant mortality offer a melancholy illustration of the necessity of the mother's previous preparation for the care of her children. The first-born die in infancy in much larger proportion than their successors in the family. The mother learns at the cost of her first child, and is better prepared for the care of the second, and still better for the third and fourth, whose chances of development into full life and strength are much greater than those of the oldest brothers and sisters." "Think of the mother learning at the cost of her first child,' and of the absurd young mother learning beforehand, and choose between. Also, please compare the 'previous preparation,' here recommended with the mere bureau-drawer preparation which is the only one at present deemed necessary." (Mrs. Diaz.)

What knowledge can be of higher value than that which "aims to render growth more perfect, decay less rapid, life more vigorous, and death more remote," by the control it gives over the causes of disease? Strange that the question should need asking. "Stranger still that it should need defending," says Herbert Spencer.

All are ready to concede our need of a physical reformation, but few are prepared to do anything to bring it about. Only physicians seem to have any just conception of the great number of preventable diseases that year after year are desolating our homes. Not until our schools and colleges shall more generally unite their efforts with those of physicians and health boards, can we hope for any very marked progress in sanitary reform. If women were properly educated they could do in this sanitary work what cannot be done by men.

, Within the last few years sanitary science has attained proportions too vast to admit of its being summarily disposed of in the meager "hints on health" usually appended to text books on physiology. Physiology and hygiene are sciences so vast in importance and extent as to merit being more generally dignified in colleges by separate professorships.

Especially do girls need to have the gospel of good health preached to them and lived before them daily. It cannot be true that Michelet is right when he asserts that women are essentially diseased. It cannot be true that the Divine Architect, every where else so wise a builder, so accurate in His estimates, so judicious in apportioning means to their ends, has here alone made the burden too heavy for the support, the aspirations too great for the capacities. It may be true that at present disease is the rule among women and health the exception; but let us not make the mistake of charging the fact to a blunder in the original formation of woman. To do so is to defeat the possibility of our attaining to anything better. When we are better educated this matter will surely be righted, and only then.

We profess to believe that education should include the whole man, physical, moral, and intellectual; but is not the attention given to physical education, as a rule, disproportionate to our professed belief in its importance? Culture of the intellect too often stands for the whole of education, and girls especially have grown to look upon matters pertaining to physical education as unworthy their attention.

Household esthetics.—The following were the general topics embraced in this study: General principles of taste as applied to ornamentation, requisites of furniture, wall and ceiling decoration, treatment of floors, selection of carpets, ceramic art, and the esthetics of dress. The university library furnished many valuable and rare works on household and decorative art for reference.

If, as Keats tells us, "A thing of beauty is a joy forever," then a study which seeks to secure more beauty in our homes, and so multiply joys, should take no mean place in the education of girls.

In the study of household esthetics one of the first points we endeavored to impress upon the girls was that women are not "instinctively authorities on all matters pertaining to taste" any more than upon metaphysical points, but that they may become such by much the same means as they would adopt to become proficient in metaphysics or literature, viz, by well directed study and effort. We referred them to art critics, who charge the decline in art largely to the false models kept so constantly before the eye, and so led them to appreciate the importance of having the objects by which we are surrounded in the home beautiful and in good taste. We taught them that a reform in woman's dress is demanded not only on the ground of health, but for well-defined esthetic reasons. In the art gallery we showed them the Venus of Milo in the majesty of her perfect womanhood, and noted her comparative chest and waist measure. We pointed to her as the model female form before which every true artist bows.

Through the influence of certain very helpful articles in some of our popular magazines, quite a general desire has been created to attain to something better than we have yet known in this direction in our homes. But by what means may girls acquire this knowledge? When one stops to think of it seriously, the marvel is not that women so generally offend in this respect, but rather that we should see even so much good taste displayed as we do, since it is only as a new departure in education that this subject constitutes any part of a course of study for girls.

In one term it is not possible to turn out finished art critics, but in this time, a teacher full of the spirit and importance of the subject can do much towards awakening thought and giving direction to future study.

Our manufacturers will not supply us with artistic domestic articles till there is a demand for them by appreciative consumers. And this demand will not be made until our systems of education give the impulse.

The same amount of time that is now devoted by girls, irrespective of native aptitude, to dabbling in water-colors and oils, and to constructing cardboard air-castles, that have no real or apparent use, or, as Anna Brackett puts it, in "crocheting covers for covers, and covers for covers of covers," concentrated upon a vigorous, well-directed study of the principles of ornamentation, would do far more towards permanently beautifying our homes, walls, floors, chairs and tables, our daily lives, than we can ever know, so long as woman's leisure is given to those ephemeral productions that are so sadly out of place in a world where moth and dust doth corrupt, and where time is so valuable and opportunity so limited.

Under the name *household science* the following topics are treated: The principles of heating and ventilation, kinds and comparative values of different fuels, usual methods of heating dwellings, grates, stoves, furnaces, hot water and steam apparatus, culinary utensils, their most approved forms, properties of the materials of which they are made, iron, tin, copper, brass, &c., contaminations of food liable to occur from carelessness or from ignorance of the properties of certain metals, preservation of foods, chemistry of illumination. The adulteration of foods is treated by lectures and laboratory practice in testing foods.

Does it sound utopian to speak of the value to the housekeeper of skill in manipulating the microscope? Ah! but the utopian ideas of one age very often become the blessings of their successors, and the future may show that housekeepers who in their college days had the keenness of their sight multiplied from fifty to one thousand times in testing foods for adulterations and impurities, will consider a Zentmeyer's grand American microscope quite as indispensable to their households as a Chickering grand piano, a safe guarantee, aided by a knowledge of chemistry, that they will not give their children a stone when they ask for bread, or put poisoned confections in their darlings' stockings at Christmas time.

Domestic economy, as taught, included lectures on the conservation of the forces of the household, on expenditures, and on the management of servants. A series of lectures were given on the government and instruction of children.

If a knowledge of political economy be of service in the production and distribution of wealth, a knowledge of domestic economy is no less serviceable in securing a right use of that wealth. If a knowledge of the former is necessary for those who sit in parliaments and legislative halls, how much more necessary is a knowledge of the latter to those who rule over the homes and give to mind its first and most lasting impressions.

Plato taught us that the beginning is the chiefest part of every undertaking. We are very fond of saying "As the twig is bent the tree's inclined;" "She who rocks the cradle rules the world;" that what Napoleon needed to secure the welfare of France was "good mothers." Such expressions have long formed the key-note of addresses to young women, graduating from courses of study in which no instruction was given upon those all-important duties we all agree in declaring to be hers. If there be truth in these beautiful sayings why not act upon them in shaping courses of study for girls? Herbert Spencer pertinently asks, "Is it, then, that the unfolding of a human being in body and mind is so comparatively simple a process that any one may superintend and regulate it with no preparation whatever? If not—if the process is with one exception more complex than any in nature, and the task of administering to it one of surpassing difficulty, is it not madness to make no provision for such a task? Better sacrifice accomplishments than omit this all-essential instruction."

Domestic economy well taught and intelligently practiced would save many a home from that worst of bankruptcies—the bankruptcy of peace, health, and happiness.

Etiquette.—The following topics were treated by lectures and discussions: Importance of a proper study of the rules of politeness and of the usages of good society; intimate relation of morals and manners; politeness but the embodiment of the golden rule; good manners not a thing to be put on with the Sunday dress, but to become a part of us by habitual use; etiquette of the home circle of the first importance; behavior in public places; visits, calls; hospitality a duty; dress, "cleanliness next to godliness;" forms of introduction; salutations; grace in personal bearing; the laws of conversation; sincerity in manner and speech cultivated; slang phrases, high-sounding adjectives, scandal, gossip, &c., to be avoided.

Home architecture.—We have no statistics to show the exact saving in time that would be secured to the world by having properly planned and constructed houses. But, doubtless, if the sum total of the time and energy lost to women in taking unnecessary steps in the course of the preparation of a meal from the inconvenience of absent or misplaced closets and doors that open the wrong way, from the vexation of spirit caused by smoky chimneys, the nervous and physical exhaustion due to stairs so constructed as to endanger life and limb, the impaired vitality, depression of spirits, days lost in sickness from rooms that cannot be properly ventilated and lighted could be presented to the social economist the showing would be something truly startling to him.

Women are the chief sufferers from these causes, but at present there seems no redress for them. He is a rare builder who is willing to concede that the average woman knows anything about how a house should be built. In very many cases we fear he is right. Many a woman has found when she attempted to direct these matters that she knew too little of architectural principles to be able to express her desires in an intelligible form. May we not in educating girls do something toward securing in the future houses for the people better adapted for homes? We believe so. In our school of domestic science the professor of architecture gave a series of lectures to the girls upon home architecture, including such topics as the principal architectural styles, general characteristics of exteriors, chief requisites of interiors, requirements of different apartments, sanitary requisites, cellars, walls, water supply, light, and convenience. To make the work as practical as possible the pupils were required to present drawings of original plans, and were taught how to make these drawings to a scale, and with a proper use of lines, shading, and colors.

The professor of horticulture taught them the general principles of landscape gardening, the kinds and uses of trees, shrubs, grass, and flowers, the construction and laying out of drives and walks, location of buildings, &c. The pupils first drew from copy, then, after the actual study of some locality with its environs, designed and drew full plans for its improvement. In the conservatory they had practice in the propagation and care of flowering and other ornamental plants. The young ladies took hold of this work with an enthusiasm which showed that they appreciated its value, and we believe that they will find in after life that the few weeks thus spent in their college days will bring them larger returns than if devoted to making copies of imaginary landscapes in oil and in manufacturing bouquets in water colors, or even in digging for Greek roots.

At the end of the course an original thesis was required on some subject bearing upon the technical studies of the school. The following are among the subjects selected by those who have graduated from this school: Art in the Home, Adulterations of Foods, Wheat, Chemistry of Foods.

Those who complete the full course receive the degree of B. S. in the college of natural science.

Such, in outline, was the technical part of the education given in this school of domestic science and the main principles on which it was based. Its results are yet to be told by the lives of its students; but enough has been seen to inspire the desire for the continuance of the experiment and for its extension in all the higher institutions of learning where women are educated. The sun of this nineteenth century, which has witnessed so much of progress in bringing the power of education to bear upon the work and well being of men, will not set till it has seen the school and college fling helpful light into the home and household—the work and well being of women.

THE NEW YORK SCHOOL OF COOKERY.

This school was founded in 1876 by Miss Juliet Corson. The first lessons were given in the ladies' course, where the instruction covered (1) the preparation of plain and inexpensive articles of food in palatable and attractive forms; (2) the dressing of the remains of food in side-dishes suitable for breakfast and luncheon; (3) the elaborate and delicate dishes of artistic cookery.

In 1877 the plain cook's course was instituted for the purpose of teaching the principles of plain family cooking to young housekeepers in moderate circumstances, to young women employed as domestics, and to the wives and grown daughters of workingmen.

In 1878 the first and second artisan courses were planned for the instruction of the children of working people in cooking the cheapest kinds of food in simple and nutritious dishes.

The number of lessons given in the above-named courses from 1876 to 1881 was 740; the attendance, ranging through all social classes, was over 7,500 persons. In 1879 Miss Corson's illustrated lectures in the Cooper Union Saturday evening course were attended by about 5,000 people.

An important fact in connection with this instruction is that it has frequently been given in direct connection with young ladies' schools. In Montreal a special course of lessons was given to the pupils of the high school, under the supervision of the board of school commissioners, and many of the pupils of Mrs. Mercer's young ladies' school attended the lessons given before the Ladies' Educational Association.

Lessons were given in Farmington, Conn., before the pupils of Miss Porter's school. In Washington some of the lessons were attended by the scholars of Park and Mount Union Seminaries, Miss Ross' and Miss Osborne's schools, the pupils of the city normal and high schools, of the Spencer Business College, and the advanced grammar school.

During the year 1881 a class from Miss Brown's young ladies' school, of New York, has been regular in its attendance at the school of cookery. Two comprehensive lessons in cookery for the sick and convalescent were given in December, 1880, to the pupils of the training school for nurses attached to the New York Charity Hospital.

During the spring and early fall seasons Miss Corson gives lessons outside of New York, and has found large and interested audiences at Montreal, Canada; Washington, D. C.; Indianapolis, Ind.; Peoria, Ill.; Cedar Rapids, Iowa; Farmington, Conn.; Syracuse, N. Y.; Pittsfield, Mass., and Hartford, Conn.

Miss Juliet Corson also gives the following account of her work during the past two or three years:

During the season of 1880–'81 my local teaching comprised 144 lessons to twelve private classes of ladies, where the attendance numbered 120; 50 private lessons to individuals; 21 lessons to mixed classes, where the attendance reached the number of 150; 17 public lessons to cooks, attendance, 166; and 50 lessons to the children of working people, where the average attendance at each lesson was 8. One of the private classes was composed of quite young ladies, the pupils of Miss Annie Brown's school, No. 22 West 56th street, New York.

In December, 1880, I gave two lessons on the preparation of food for the sick and convalescent before the pupils of the Training School for Nurses attached to the Charity Hospital of New York. The class consisted of 30 nurses; the commissioners of charities and corrections and the resident and visiting physicians of the public institutions on Blackwell's Island were present.

The first lessons of the next season (1881–'82) given away from New York were at Pittsfield, Mass., for the Ladies' Art Association, and consisted of six lessons in general cookery to the ladies of the town and the pupils of Maplewood Institute for Young Ladies, the attendance being about 100, and six free lessons in economical cookery to working people, with an average attendance of 50.

The second course of outside lessons was given at Hartford, Conn., under the auspices of the City Mission, Mrs. Virginia T. Smith, superintendent; there were twelve lessons to ladies at Cheney Building, where the attendance numbered about 150, and twelve free lessons to working people at the Morgan Street Mission, to a class of about 50.

At the close of March, 1881, I resigned my connection with the charity department of the New York Cooking School, and continued my usual line of instruction as in previous years.

In April, 1881, I gave twenty-four lessons to ladies at Saint Louis, Mo., for the benefit of the Women's Christian Association of that city; the average attendance was about three hundred in the public class and fifty in a special private class. The president of the association, Mrs. C. R. Springer, in a letter dated May 29, 1881, says: "We cleared over $1,200. Have any people done better financially?"

From Saint Louis I went to Chicago, Ill., where I gave one lecture on Domestic Economy in Fairbank Hall, one free evening lesson to about five hundred working people, and eighteen public lessons to ladies.

In May, 1881, I gave six lessons to ladies, under the auspices of the Diet Dispensary of Cleveland, Ohio, to an audience of about one hundred.

In the same month, at Northampton, Mass., I gave seven lessons to a class of about one hundred and fifty ladies, one evening lesson to the students of Smith College, which was attended by President Seelye and the faculty of the college, and one evening lesson to working-people.

In June, 1881, I gave six lessons in cookery for invalids to the pupils of the New York State Training School for Nurses, in Brooklyn, Long Island, N. Y.

In September I went to Concord, Mass., at the invitation of Miss Ellen T. Emerson, and, under the management of that lady and Mrs. Judge Hoar, I gave six lessons to ladies, six lessons to cooks, and six free lessons to working people, in the old Concord school-house. These lessons were the inaugural series of the Concord Cooking School.

In December, 1881, I accepted the invitation of Captain R. H. Pratt, U. S. A., to visit the government Training School for Indian Youth, at Carlisle Barracks, Carlisle, Pa. At that time I gave a course of lessons to the Indian girls, some of whom did not speak or understand English, but all proved attentive and intelligent pupils.

The following extract from the paper published at the training school gives the local impression of the result of the lessons, and it is borne out by subsequent reports from the school, received from Captain Pratt during the past summer. A further indication of the genuine nature of the interest felt by the Indian girls is the pleasure they evinced when I promised to write an Indian cookery-book for them. They at once began to make lists of their cooking utensils and food supplies for my guidance. This book is now in hand. The following is the extract from The Big Morning Star:

"We were indeed glad to accept Miss Corson's generous offer to give our girls a course of lessons in cookery. Her teaching was simple and practical, and admirably adapted to the capacity of our Indian pupils. A table was placed ready for the lesson; in front of it were grouped the girls, and back of it stood Miss Corson, calling to her aid from time to time eager volunteers from the class. Beginning with the importance of absolute cleanliness the table was scoured, the utensils to be used were rubbed and polished until they shone. Only such materials and utensils were used as she learned from the girls they could get at their homes. Miss Corson's experience at the New York School of Cookery, where she has done so good a work in training poor children, enabled her to use such simple language, such telling gestures that even those with the least knowledge of English could follow and understand her teaching. Usually she had two or three dishes in course of preparation at once. A little girl washed potatoes, rubbing each carefully with a bit of rag, and deftly imitating Miss Corson, as she showed her how to pare a ring of skin from each, and then to boil them just long enough, so that they should be dry and mealy, slipping readily from their loosened jackets. Meantime another girl peeled more potatoes, and following her teacher's example neatly removed a thin, transparent paring, and cut out defects, and while she did it the whole class received a lesson in avoiding wastefulness. After each step in the lesson Miss Corson questioned the class as to what had been done and why it was done. In this way from plain and meagre materials very palatable dishes were prepared. It was a most interesting sight; the earnest watchfulness of the girls who looked on; the self-important little airs of the girls who carried out the lessons as they bent over the table and peered into the saucepans bubbling on the range. They made soups and stews; they baked and broiled; and even the much maligned frying-pan was brought into requisition, as Miss Corson taught them that it was possible to fry things without making them greasy and indigestible. As each dish was prepared she told them what other materials could be used in the same way. The pleasure of the girls in receiving this training was shown by their expressions in their home letters. * * * Miss Corson says she found the Indian girls as quick, and apt and enthusiastic as any pupils she has had. The desire to become good housekeepers became more eager from her pleasant teachings, and we are sure that when she comes again, as she has promised, she will find that they have not lost what they learned, and are ready to go on as far as she will take them."

The New York season of 1881–'82 was conducted as usual, instruction being given to both ladies and cooks, with the average attendance at the various lessons. During this season a course of twelve lessons to ladies and one free lesson to workingwomen was given at the Industrial Restaurant, No. 112 Lexington avenue, Brooklyn, N. Y. The class numbered about twenty.

In March, 1882, a course of six lessons in cookery for invalids was given before the physicians and nurses attached to the nurses' training school of the Brooklyn City Hospital, of which Mrs. Seth Low is president. The class numbered about fifteen.

In April a course of seven lessons to a private class of forty ladies was given in Stamford, Conn., under the management of Mrs. Schuyler Merritt.

It affords me great satisfaction to be able to make a favorable report of my connection with the Lake Erie Female Seminary, at Painesville, O. My first instruction there was given in the form of a course of six lectures on food and digestion, in the autumn of 1881, which were attended by about one hundred and forty of the pupils of the seminary and many of the ladies of Painesville. These lectures were followed by a course of practical lessons in cookery in the autumn of 1882, attended by the entire school. The young ladies took an active part in the preparation of the various dishes, and the most excellent results are reported by Miss Mary Evans, principal of the seminary. These lessons in cookery form part of the regular course of instruction at the seminary.

The season of 1882–'83 in New York was begun in November, 1882, and is not yet finished. The usual instruction is being given to ladies and cooks, with the usual success. My labors among the working-people this season include the writing of a "Dietary for Workingmen," published in the workingmen's paper, the DAILY NEWS of New York; the revision of a paper on Domestic Economy for the Charity Organization Society of New York; the teaching of soup making to a woman chosen by Miss McBryde, of the Church of the Holy Trinity of this city; this soup is sold to the poorer members of the church and its missions at the cost of production. I am also giving a course of free lessons in economical cookery to these workingwomen at the same church.

In February of the present year I shall give a course of six lessons at Plainfield and at Morristown, N. J., assisted by Mrs. Thomas H. Taylor, who proposes to establish a cooking school at Plainfield.

In conclusion, I beg leave to call attention to a series of articles on "Dietetics," now appearing in Harper's Bazar; the subject is important, and has not yet been treated in an adequate manner. These articles will be republished in book form, probably during the present year.

JULIET CORSON,
Superintendent of the New York School of Cookery.

THE WORK OF MISS MARIA PARLOA AS A TEACHER OF COOKERY.

INDIVIDUAL WORK.

Each year the interest increases. I am constantly obliged to turn away applicants for admission to private classes. The public lectures were never better attended, but I am able to deliver only two a week; so much of my time is occupied in giving instruction outside of my own school. During the past year I have lectured thirteen times before the ladies of Springfield and three times before the working-women in the evening. At these lectures there were large audiences, and after I had completed my work in the city several cooking clubs were formed. At Lowell I gave nine lessons. Much interest was manifested, and a cooking school for working-women and children, with a few classes for ladies, is to be begun this month. A course of lectures on physiology, hygiene, and nursing was arranged for the working-women of Providence, R. I., and I gave three talks on cookery. These were largely attended, about 500 people being present at one on marketing. It is confidently hoped that a school will soon be established in Providence. A resident at Manchester-by-the-Sea employed me to give three lectures there this summer, and at the close of the series there was a call for more, but I had not the time for the lessons. I am now engaged to lecture at Taunton and expect to go also to Worcester. At Lasell Seminary, Auburndale, the work goes on prosperously. There is a course of twelve lessons during the school year, given by myself on alternate Saturdays, and there are practice classes, taught by the wife of the principal. Last year there was but one class, but there are now three. The girls take a deep interest in this study and demonstrate in their homes their ability to carry out the instruction received. During the present term is to be introduced, as a text book, "The First Principles of Household Management and Cookery, by Maria Parloa." Plans have been drawn for a model practice-kitchen. This is to be made as complete as possible, so that in one school at least have the most sensible preparations been made for the permanence of object lessons in cookery.

THE BOSTON COOKING SCHOOL,

which was started about three years ago by a special committee of ladies from the Woman's Educational Association (under whose auspices the Harvard examinations for women were inaugurated, and the Boston Art School and the women's department at the Massachusetts Institute of Technology were established—and they are now successfully carried on), is doing a broad work. Here there are classes taught by Mrs. D. A. Lincoln, whose time is fully occupied; classes of ladies and cooks, and of girls from the Horace Mann School for Deaf-Mutes. A normal department has been opened this year, in which I am the teacher. Already a number of pupils in this department have been assured of situations as teachers as soon as they are prepared to accept them.

The Boston Cooking School has established branches for poor women and children. In

INDUSTRIAL EDUCATION IN THE UNITED STATES. 289

1880 a demonstration lesson was given on one evening of every week, and several practice lessons were given during the week. This branch school is supported entirely by contributions. Last year about three thousand persons were present at the lessons, sometimes more than two hundred women attending at one time.

At the South End the second branch was started, and is supported by ladies of the South Congregational Society. Lessons are given in the vestry of the church. Though there is as yet only one lesson a week the interest grows steadily. These schools are doing great good among the poor.

OTHER MATTERS.

Miss Joanna Sweeney, who has given lessons in Boston six or seven years, has as many private classes as she is able to receive.

Madame Favier continues her private classes. At the rooms of the Young Women's Christian Association there are classes of school girls on Saturdays.

It thus appears that the interest here is not decreasing. On the contrary it is certain that there would be many more pupils if there were enough competent teachers.

MARIA PARLOA.

Information has recently been received from Miss Parloa of her work subsequent to that already described. It is as follows:

My last report to the Bureau of Education was made in the summer of 1881, when I was about to close my school in Boston, after a pleasant experience of four years in it, and seek a new field. In the fall I went West, and gave courses of six lectures or lessons at Chicago, Ill, twelve at Evanston, in the same State, and twelve at Milwaukee, Wis. The interest taken in my work was not so great as I had expected, although before the courses were finished it increased considerably. Returning in the spring to the East, and visiting New York, I gave a series of lessons under the auspices of the New York Cooking School. The audiences were large, and much interest was manifested. This work occupied Mondays and Tuesdays; on the other days of the week I lectured twice at West Winsted, Conn., and twice at Waterbury, and the patronage of both series was gratifying. In a month's time there were given ten lessons in New York, six in Winstead, and seven in Waterbury. At the end of these engagements a call to Buffalo, N. Y., took my attention. Ladies of that city had arranged two courses of lectures, one for the morning, for the benefit of themselves and their friends, and the other for the evening, for cooks. Plans also were made for three special evening lectures to working people. In the three weeks of my stay in Buffalo I gave thirty-three lessons. At all times the attendance was large, but it was particularly large at three free lectures, when it was necessary to turn hundreds of persons away, and at the lecture on marketing, which was so popular that it was repeated, by request, in a more spacious hall. At one lecture in Buffalo the audience numbered nine hundred. Much hope was expressed that a permanent school of cookery would be established, but I think it has not. From Buffalo I went, early in May, to Orange, N. J. Both there and at Newark I gave six lessons, two a week at each place. The other days of the week I spent at the Charity Hospital; Blackwell's Island, New York, giving instruction in sick-room cookery to the nurses and young physicians connected with the hospital and the training school for nurses. It was June before this labor was finished. In the early summer I prepared additional matter for my "First Principles of Household Management and Cookery" and then gave at Windsor, Vt., a course of lectures arranged by Miss Mary Evarts. At all lectures general information is given in regard to kitchen work and cookery and dishes are made in the presence of the audience.

During my stay in New York I became impressed by the vastness of the field, the great need of work and the desire for knowledge, and so, abandoning plans made for a European trip for purposes of study, I determined to establish a practice school in the metropolis of the country. I hoped to live to see cooking schools as practically and firmly founded in New York as in Boston. This I say not of any local pride, but because the work has received careful attention there for many years and has grown steadily on this account, so that it is now on a sure foundation, and appears likely to go on forever.

Having leased the house No. 222 East 17th St., New York, for a long term, I have had it so altered and furnished as to be commodious in every way for my purposes. Especially is it bright and inviting, so as to enhance the attractiveness of the work to be done. School was opened October 30, and every week there are given two public demonstration lessons. Thus far these have been well attended. There are several practice classes, in which the ladies do the work. Some of these I teach and some are taught by my assistant. The ladies who patronize the lectures and classes are of all ages, from the young girl to the white-haired matron, and a gratifying fact is that many report successful work at home. The nurses of the training school of the New York Hospital are soon to begin taking a course of private lessons in cooking for the sick. I have lately given a series of lectures at Albany, N. Y., and two lessons at Orange, N. J., for the benefit of a hospital. This week I begin a course of twelve lessons at New Haven, Conn.

And so the work goes on. The school, as was the case in Boston, is entirely under my own management and maintenance. The expenses of the establishment are heavy enough to preclude my doing such charitable work as I would like to do and as is possible in those schools which are partly supported by subscriptions. The real need of the country, as I wrote you in 1879, is a national training school of cookery, where women and girls could receive a thorough education in physiology, chemistry, hygiene, and cookery. No private enterprise could give the same return as such a national school. When we have an institution of this kind, whose benefits are within reach of persons of small means, the work will go forward as it should.

REPORT ON COOKING SCHOOLS IN THE SOUTH.

WASHINGTON, *May* 9, 1881.

SIR: Cooking schools at the North have long since justified their existence, but that the South had room for them, or that it would even allow them foothold, had been doubted by all who imagine they knew southern characteristics and the inherited inaptitude for personal labor of any sort.

"A cooking school in the South! It can't be done;" insisted wise heads when the project was first unfolded. Prejudice will be too strong for you. Old conditions are powerful enough still to make personal labor a degradation, and you will not find a dozen people enlightened enough to care for or understand the virtue in such an undertaking."

SCHOOL AT RALEIGH.

In the mean time the said undertaking was progressing at Raleigh, N. C., with as much energy as was consistent with the modes of work prevalent there. The head of a flourishing school for girls located at that point—a man of unusual energy and in many points of advanced ideas upon education—had decided upon introducing the new branch, and a large and airy class room, fitted up in the best manner with every needed appliance for successful lessons, was organized. A few indorsed the movement, but for the most part it was regarded from the standpoint of the old Israelites—a standpoint as popular to-day as then—"all they that passed by did wag their heads for scorn." With the 1st of October, 1879, the course began, a class being formed from the very few in the city who had become interested, while two lessons weekly were given in the school itself. The names from this source had come in slowly, seven only expressing any willingness to "take," and even these hesitating and doubting if they were not in some mysterious manner to be betrayed into "niggers' work."

The first lesson settled this question. The class quadrupled and had to be limited as to numbers, and from October to May worked not only steadily but enthusiastically, accomplishing far more than had been expected for it. Utterly ignorant as most of them were in the beginning, and requiring to be taught details which come by intuition to the New England girl, within four months they were able to give a supper to the trustees of the school, not so elaborate in character as perfect in preparation, and at the end of the session each one was mistress of certain points which must inevitably redeem any home she enters from the curse of food ruined in the preparation. To make the best bread, brown and white, boil a potato perfectly, make coffee and tea as perfectly, and roast or broil or stew the rather dubious meat supply in the best and most savory way, may seem a small accomplishment, unless one knows something of what the southern dietary is, and has tested personally all the miseries involved in three meals daily of saleratus-biscuit or corn-pone, and bacon or beef fried to the consistency and flavor of old leather. Beginning with the southern antipathy to cold bread, the class quickly found that the amount prescribed for the lesson was by no means sufficient to meet the demand for it, and a keen rivalry began as to who should make the handsomest loaf. Household science generally made part of the course. Familiar talks and papers on all phases of this subject stimulated interest, and in addition a topic was given weekly—usually the history of some ingredient in the day's lesson. As the line of work came to be understood, inquiries came from various parts of the State as to its practicability and success. The classes for the towns-people had been well filled by enthusiastic learners, and in three months the "Raleigh cooking school" had no further need to question its future, but knew itself an assured success.

Some 45 lessons were given in the school girls' six months' course, a written examination ending it, and certificates of degrees of proficiency being given. Three courses of twelve lessons each were given to ladies' classes from the city, and in March, 1880, a course was also given to a large class in Charlotte, N. C., and arrangements were made for organizing a school at Staunton, Va.

COOKERY FOR THE DEAF AND DUMB.

So recent is the interest in the questions of the education of the deaf and dumb, that to prove them susceptible of training at all has seemed a sufficient accomplishment. Each institution has had, in addition to the regular school course, its set of workshops, and the poorer boys, to whom some trade is a necessity, have learned basket and broom making, carpentering, &c., while the girls have been taught mattress making and sewing in general, as the only occupation open to them. For these girls, hedged in on every side, I would speak as in all senses more helpless, and appealing even more strongly than their brothers for training, and for some more potent weapon of defence in their journey through the world than the needle has ever proved.

Before giving details, there are several points to be considered, one or two of which are urged as objections to any general adoption of the new system.

Necessarily, institutions for the deaf and dumb must be filled with pupils from the lower, and often from the lowest, grades of society. Poverty, drunkenness, and disease own these unfortunates as offspring, and to many of them, gathered in from poorhouses and jails, or from homes where deepest want and degradation have ruled, the first knowledge of plentiful and wholesome food, of personal cleanliness, of kindness, or of any sense of brightness in life comes from their introduction to the asylum.

But, however clouded their intelligence, they prove, almost without exception, easily guided, keenly susceptible to sympathy, and reaching out with intense eagerness for any clew to the unknown life about them. No one who has worked among them can be insensible to the demand made by these shut-in souls, whose only avenue to understanding is the eye, and whose very presence is an appeal for all the light and help we may give.

So long as the asylum offers them a home, they are secure; but when the term of years in which the State provides for them has expired, what is the outlook? One or two, perhaps more, from each graduating class, are likely to become teachers; but the field is a limited one, and only very unusual intelligence admits of this possibility. A few others, from prosperous or comfortable homes, will return to be cared for by parents, till the chances and changes of life turn them over to the uncertain mercies of their nearest relatives. But the large majority are homeless, and must depend upon themselves. To such, only positions as seamstresses or nurses are open. For the latter field they are in many points unfit, while the former is already overcrowded.

Work for women is in all cases hard to find and poorly paid. If this be so where full faculties go begging for it, how doubly is it so where communication must always be limited and hampered, and where training grudgingly given to the best fitted recipient would be withheld altogether from these, because demanding time and patience beyond the will of the employer.

Household service suggests itself as the only opening. But the instinctive prejudice against manual or rather menial labor which seems the American woman's instinct crops out as strongly in the deaf-mute as in the shop girl, who would rather stand fourteen hours daily behind a counter than one hour behind a cooking stove or wash tub. This prejudice, too deeply rooted at the North, is intensified at the South by every influence of inheritance and present surroundings. Until a new sense of the dignity of labor has reached the masses in the only way possible, that is through its indorsement by the better class, the work of overcoming such prejudice will be difficult and well-nigh impossible.

The perplexed philanthropist who has studied the limitations of his work dismisses the matter as settled when he has said, "Let them become cooks or housekeepers." He leaves the topic with the comfortable sense that "fiat cooks" is as potent a watchword as "fiat money" to the Greenbackers.

No popular delusion is more deeply rooted than the idea that all women take as instinctively to housekeeping as a duck to water. The bookkeeper, the merchant, the artisan admits the necessity of preliminary training, and submits to the inevitable apprenticeship with a patience born of the knowledge that only by and through training can any successful result be accomplished. But that the myriad details of housekeeping—the ordering of a home—the preparation or direction of the preparation of food, demand anything more than some instinctive sense is seldom admitted, such sense being supposed to come at the required time, whether previously developed or not. Women themselves are partially responsible for this theory, and announce that given a home any woman can oversee its details.

On this theory girls remain untaught, even where teaching would be easy. But it is always harder to do justly than to love mercy, and always more work is involved in teaching unskilled hands than in using one's own. And even where there is an honest intention to teach days and months slip by. Any time will do, and "any time" ends in no time. If this is the case where teaching would be comparatively easy, how much more so where limited capacity and hopelessness of full communication and understanding still further complicate the work.

The home thus giving no surety of such training, and the homeless having even less possibility of the desired knowledge, the State must provide some means by which its wards may be saved from finally returning upon its hands as paupers. But the limitations of work already referred to have made the question a perplexing and baffling one to all who have sought its solution.

The solution must be found in opening up new and suitable avenues of employment, and of these, scientific and practical cookery offers one of the most useful and appropriate.

A year of quiet work in a class of ten, in the Institute for the Deaf and Dumb, at Raleigh, N. C., has shown what can be accomplished in a new industry, which, it has now been demonstrated, may form a part of the ordinary school training without interference with the usual course or any lengthening of the time required for its completion.

With the establishment and full success of the South Kensington Cooking School, followed shortly with equal success by those of New York and Boston, came the thought to one of the trustees of the North Carolina Institute for the Deaf and Dumb, that such schools might be a possibility for them. He was a man of broad culture and strong humanity, with whom thought and action marched hand in hand. No time was lost in suggesting the innovation, but in a conservative, slow-moving community, hampered by legislative stupidity, always more ready to work for future election than for public good, it was a long and tedious process. Aided at last by the warm coöperation of the principal, and stimulated by the fact that a cooking school had been projected and organized in connection with a large and liberally managed school for girls, known as Peace Institute, the necessary steps were at last taken. A room was fitted up with all essential appointments, and the superintendent of the Raleigh Cooking School, the first one in the entire South, was called upon for a course of lessons.

Beginning with many misgivings as to their success, yet with a faith that could not doubt their practicability for, at least, the most intelligent of the class, a month had not passed before suspense gave place to certainty. The class, the ten members of which were chosen from among the most intelligent pupils, was still of varying capacity. One or two were slow to understand, and awkward in execution. But the dullest face brightened as the lesson began. The least movement of the teacher was copied with Chinese minuteness. To a portion of the class, coming from homes where bacon and saleratus biscuit or corn-pone had been the chief diet, and where the range of cooking utensils are as limited as the food supply—not only the appointments of the room, but the articles to be cooked, were all mysteries. They were soon mastered, however. The quick eyes and ready hands speedily took possession of the new knowledge. A young teacher, chosen as interpreter, made all questionable points plain, and by her own careful preparation of her class-book gave a model, which all followed with greater or less success. Immediate objections were made by some of the parents, who looked upon the new departure as something designed to degrade their children, and who protested loudly that they should not do "niggers' work." But, as representatives of the best families had been chosen, this statement sufficed to quiet them, and the rapidly growing interest of the girls themselves completed the work.

Realizing that a portion of the system in use in the practice class of the cooking school proper must be set aside here, and that, with these limited intelligences, the physiology and chemistry of food could find little or no place, it became the superintendent's aim to form a set of lessons which should include chiefly simple and economical dishes perfectly prepared, and thus to lay a foundation on which each might build as circumstances might indicate. To this end breadmaking in all its forms, the best cooking of meats and ordinary vegetables and simple sweets, made up the greater part of the work. So unexpected were the results that within three months the class prepared the largest portion of a supper for the trustees, the delicate quality and serving of which were the best answer to any doubt that may still have lingered as to the efficacy of the new system.

With the close of the session in June, 1880, ten young girls left the institute with a well tested and established knowledge of principles in cookery, which will in time redeem whatever home they may enter from the curse of the inevitable ill-health and consequent ill-regulated thought entailed by the wretched cookery of the past. With her own hands each one had made, often enough to assure future certainty, bread, both white and brown; coffee and tea; had broiled a steak, and prepared meats in various ways—good soups and simple desserts—besides solving the mystery of cooking perfectly a boiled potato. Two or three of the class showed a special aptitude for the work, and having learned to their surprise that a lady could handle pots and pans, yet remain a lady, are ready now for places from which a year ago they would have shrunk. Small as this entering wedge may seem its effects are incalculable. The cooking school means for the future of each pupil the largest result from the smallest expenditure; a knowledge which will make the cheapest and simplest food savory and palatable, and which, carried out, must end much of the chronic dyspepsia and general ill-health from which all suffer. Household labor dignified, its appliances made more perfect, and delicacy and order and daintiness ruling, in place of the dirt and wild confusion supposed to be the inseparable concomitants of all southern kitchens, a new race of servants will arise, and the generation of old family servants, fast passing away, and whose loss is daily mourned, will be replaced by a class to whom waste will be well-nigh impossible, and who will revolutionize old fashions, not by destruction but by reconstruction. Comfortable and adequate support need never fail the owner of this knowledge, and bondage to the needle will cease once for all. The session of 1880–'81 has had a building specially adapted to the purpose, the former one being slightly cramped, and a larger class were allowed the advantage of the course, an assistant trained last year having taken efficient charge of it.

The work is only in its infancy, but gives fullest promise of vigorous growth, and it is the superintendent's earnest wish and hope that it may not be confined to the Raleigh Institution, but may be attempted in others.

COOKING SCHOOLS AT STAUNTON, VA., AND WASHINGTON, D. C.

The school at Staunton, Va., opened the 1st of November, 1880, and continued to April 1, 1881, some forty lessons having been given to a class of about 30 school girls, and one course to a ladies' class. While retaining the general oversight of these schools, the headquarters of the superintendent will be hereafter in Washington, the Washington School of Cookery having been formally opened at 1323 H street, northwest, the workings of which will be on much the same plan as the Boston Cooking School, though modified by experience of special needs. A diet kitchen has also been organized in connection with the school, and Washington will, it is believed, admit of as representative work as has been accomplished in other cities.*

Beginning work in this field with the intention of using Miss Corson's system, it was very soon found impracticable. It demands the choicest supply our large city markets can afford, and the meat dishes have too characteristic a French flavor to be liked by those unaccustomed to French cooking. Miss Corson's admirable clearness of statement and dexterous handling can always be imitated to advantage, but practical work is better accomplished on Miss Parloa's theories. My own course based itself more and more on my experience as a housekeeper, both at South and North, and aimed at last simply to utilize to the best advantage the food supply of the place in which work must be done, with a constant effort to improve the nature of that supply, though the difficulties hedging about not only this but many other features of the work are more than it is worth while to consider here.

Finding, as before stated, no manual which met the need of classes, it became necessary to prepare one; and the publishers, Messrs. Fords, Howard & Hulburt, of New York, issued in February of the present year "The Easiest Way in Housekeeping and Cooking," adapted to domestic use or study in classes. In this I have aimed to cover the ground constantly talked over in all my class-work, and in small space to make a practical hand-book of household science. There are many most excellent authorities for the trained housekeeper, Marian Harland, Mrs. Henderson, Miss Parloa, and many others having made trustworthy and valuable books, but still not adapted to class use.

Interest is spreading so steadily that cooking schools must shortly be found in every city, North or South, where real progress is known, and the cooking school should and must include some knowledge of domestic science both in detail and as a whole.

HELEN CAMPBELL,
Superintendent of the Washington School of Cookery,
1323 H Street, Northwest.

Hon. JOHN EATON,
Commissioner of Education.

---

*The cooking school in Washington is in a prosperous condition. It is composed of mission classes, a diet kitchen, and pay classes. The latter are for (1) cooks, (2) nurses, and (3) ladies. The mission classes are conducted by Miss Lizzie Gammill; the diet kitchen and pay classes by Mrs. R. A. Baker. Mrs. A. L. Woodbury has a supervision of the school, and makes it a place for the free instruction of the poor children of the city in this branch of household economy.

NEW CENTURY EVENING CLASSES FOR WOMEN.

The evening classes, conducted by members of the New Century Woman's Club of Philadelphia, include the following: Monday, German; Tuesday, cutting and fitting, sewing, physiology, elocution, French; Wednesday, arithmetic, literature; Thursday, cooking; Friday, book-keeping, writing, German, spelling; Saturday, French, grammar. The subjoined letter explains fully the origin and management of these classes:

PHILADELPHIA, *January* 29, 1883,
1112 *Girard Street.*

DEAR SIR: Your letter received in regard to New Century Evening Classes for Women in Philadelphia.

These classes were started last winter, as an experiment, by a few of the members of the New Century Woman's Club of Philadelphia. They are offered only to persons of limited means, whose day hours are occupied. The rooms of the club house are used for class-rooms, and the teaching is done mainly by club members. A few of the studies cost from 5 to 10 cents a lesson; but the rule is 50 cents for 24 lessons. The class of applicants ranges from house servants, laundresses, &c., up to teachers, a large proportion being saleswomen, clerks, cash-girls, &c. Last winter we had 226 pupils; this season, over 400; and the demand for such instruction being larger than we can supply, the pressure has resulted in the opening of several other such centers, working on precisely the same basis.

Several of the higher branches are not so superfluous as might at first appear, French, and especially German, being much in demand in stores. Embroidery is used in making articles for sale, drawing directly put to designs for embroidery, illuminating, &c.

The attendance after the first week or two, in which a few drop out and are seen no more, is remarkably steady, and we think it an encouraging fact that so many young women are willing, after a day of hard work, to devote the evening to mental improvement.

In connection with the classes, a course of Saturday lectures to women is in progress, chiefly on domestic subjects—"How to wash the baby," "How to cook for the sick," "What to do till the doctor comes," &c. We have also just started a society called "The New Century Women's Guild," with parlor, library, magazines, music, &c., to be always open to members at cost of $1 a year, as a place of recreation and also a center for whatever projects in the interests of women may grow out of it.

Yours, respectfully,

ELIZA S. TURNER.
Chairman Committee on Evening Classes in New Century Club.

Hon. JOHN EATON,
Commissioner of Education.

APPENDIX F.

INSTRUCTION IN CHEMISTRY IN INSTITUTIONS ENDOWED WITH THE NATIONAL LAND GRANT WHICH HAVE SPECIAL COURSES IN CHEMISTRY.

[Principally from Circular of Information No. 6, 1880.]

UNIVERSITY OF CALIFORNIA.

To students in the classical course lectures upon chemistry are delivered during the first half of the junior year. Students in the literary course take chemistry both in the lecture room and the laboratory throughout the sophomore year and may continue it as an elective in the first junior term.

In the several scientific departments a course of general and theoretical chemistry is given during the latter half of the freshman and the whole of the sophomore year. It embraces the elements of both inorganic and organic chemistry, and includes lectures, recitations, and laboratory work. The last is of an elementary character. In the college of mining, analytical chemistry, both qualitative and quantitative, is studied through the junior and senior years. In the college of agriculture the advanced lectures to the juniors are also given, together with a course upon organic chemistry in the senior year. Chemical analysis, with its special bearings upon agriculture, is carried through both the junior and the senior classes, and the juniors have also special instruction in agricultural chemistry. In the college of chemistry the entire four years' course of study leading to a degree is as follows:

Freshman year.—Algebra, solid geometry and conic sections, trigonometry, analytical geometry, rhetoric, composition, French or German, and elementary chemistry.

Sophomore year.—German or French, physics, inorganic and analytical chemistry, blowpipe analysis, general botany, industrial botany, and descriptive geometry.

Junior year.—History, zoölogy, political economy, surveying, physics, analytical chemistry, mineralogy, and theoretical chemistry.

Senior year.—Physiological, analytical, and organic chemistry, metallurgy, mineralogy, assaying, geology, physical laboratory, and thesis.

Students taking this course spend at least fifteen hours a week in the laboratory during the junior year and twenty hours a week during the senior year. Practical instruction in electrometallurgy is given to such students as desire it. Special students in chemistry are received.

The laboratories are open daily, including Saturdays. The room for quantitative analysis has accommodations for thirty-two students. Adjoining it are the laboratory and study of the professor, the balance room, and the fusion room. Below is a room for qualitative analysis, also with accommodations for thirty-two students. Adjacent to this is a room devoted to work in elementary chemistry. A charge of $15 a term is made for chemicals used in analysis. Breakage is also charged for.

YALE COLLEGE—SHEFFIELD SCIENTIFIC SCHOOL.

Chemistry in its different branches is the principal study of the chemical course. The other subjects, which in respect to the amount of time devoted to them may be termed the minor studies, besides contributing something toward a general scientific education, are for the most part connected with the main object of the course. A knowledge of French and German sufficient to render available the chemical literature of those languages is indispensable to the advanced student. Mineralogy is so intimately connected with chemistry that it may properly be termed the chemistry of natural inorganic compounds, while a knowledge of the more important elements or outlines of geology may be considered of sufficient value in itself to repay the student for the moderate amount of time required for its acquisition.

The freshman year, being designed to fit the student equally well for any of the courses which he may choose at the beginning of the junior year, must necessarily include some studies which are not absolutely indispensable as a foundation to his future course. The chemistry, physics, German, and in part the mathematics of this year may be regarded as strictly preparatory to the chemical course.

Junior year.—During a greater part of this year instruction is given by means of text-books and recitations in chemical philosophy or "theoretical chemistry." This may be considered as a continuation of the elementary chemistry studies during the freshman year. Throughout the year the student spends four consecutive hours in the chemical laboratory five days of every week. On one day of the week exercises in mineralogy take the place of chemistry. The laboratory study is devoted to a systematic course in analytical chemistry except during a part of the summer term, in which analytical chemistry is replaced by experimental work in organic chemistry. This work consists of the preparation by synthetic methods of a series of organic compounds, and is designed as a preparation for the systematic study of that branch of chemistry which is carried on during the senior year. French and German are studied throughout the year.

Senior year.—During this year also about four hours daily are given to the study of analytical chemistry in the laboratory. At the end of the first term the student is familiar with the most important general analytical methods. The subject of his laboratory work during the second term is to a great extent optional. He may, if desirous, gain experience in the assaying of ores or analysis of some particular class of products with a view to its technical application; or he may devote his time to original research on some subject of scientific interest. Not less important, although requiring less time, is the study of organic chemistry. On account of the lack of a suitably-organized laboratory for organic chemistry, experimental work which, under favorable circumstances, would be highly desirable, is not carried on in connection with this study during the senior year. Lectures in zoölogy are attended during the first term and recitations in geology during the year. These exercises, together with three lessons weekly in French, fully occupy the time not required for chemical studies.

Method of instruction.—In most of the studies of the course instruction is given by means of text-books and recitations in the usual manner, which requires no particular explanation. In regard to analytical chemistry, to which more time is allotted than to any other single branch of study in the course, it may be observed that it is intended to serve two purposes. It is to be used by the advanced student as a means of investigation in scientific or technical researches. The beginner, however, derives from its study advantages of another kind. The knowledge of the properties of chemical compounds and familiarity with chemical reaction gained by experience in the laboratory, and the development of the reasoning faculties by the application of this knowledge in analytical processes, enable the student to generalize and classify chemical phenomena and aid him to understand the more abstract theories of chemical philosophy. The method of instruction adopted is conformed to this view of the uses of the study. Text-books are used and recitations are required, but the more important part of both study and instruction is performed in the laboratory. In order to solve the problems which are thus presented, the student, aided by books and instructors, must learn both principles and their application.

Graduate work.—This school has been constantly increasing the facilities which it offers to graduate students for the study of different branches of chemistry. The laboratories for analytical and physiological chemistry are open seven hours daily for their use. They may begin with a course in quantitative analysis or with more advanced work, according to their previous preparation. Each one receives separately in the laboratory all assistance necessary to enable him to advance in proportion to his ability and diligence. Recitations in quantitative analysis accompany laboratory work during the first term of the year. Graduates may also, if desirous, attend any of the recitations or exercises belonging to the above described chemical course. After suitable preparation the undertaking of original investigations is encouraged. (The work of this kind carried on in our laboratories has afforded, it is believed, the most valuable training possible for the student and has often resulted also in the production of contributions to science of considerable value.)

Laboratories.—The chemical laboratories of the school may be designated according to their special uses as follows:

1. A laboratory for elementary chemistry, used exclusively for instruction of the freshman class.
2. A laboratory for qualitative analytical chemistry.
3. A laboratory for quantitative analytical chemistry and various chemical investigations.
4. A laboratory for physiological chemistry. An additional room in the basement of Sheffield Hall is fitted up with furnaces and apparatus necessary for assaying of ores in the dry way, while the practice required in determinative mineralogy is carried on in a laboratory arranged especially for this purpose in the Peabody museum.—(Sixteenth annual report.)

The special report on chemistry and physics, from which the statements of this appendix are generally taken, says: "Blowpipe analysis is taught in all the regular courses. In the engineering courses this study is taken by the seniors. Other courses have it in the junior year. Students in the courses of 'natural history' and 'biology' have instruction in qualitative analysis during the first junior term. In the latter course toxicology and physiological chemistry are taught through the second junior term. Juniors in the agricultural course take the chemistry assigned for the same time to the chemical students. In the senior year they have agricultural chemistry."

UNIVERSITY OF GEORGIA.

There are two classes in chemistry, the junior and the senior. The students of the junior class study general chemistry, meeting the professor three times a week for ten months. Subjects are taken up in the following order: (1) The non-metallic elements; their history and their combinations with each other. (2) The principles of chemical nomenclature, symbols, and notation; the general principles of chemical philosophy. (3) The metals; their history, combinations, &c. (4) Organic chemistry. Text book, Fownes. This course is illustrated experimentally, and practical applications of the several subjects are duly noted. The senior class meet also three times a week for ten months, and study organic, industrial, and agricultural chemistry. Industrial chemistry is taught by lectures, illustrated by specimens, models, and drawings. The lectures upon agricultural chemistry begin about the 1st of March, and are free to the public, in accordance with the terms of the Terrell endowment. In this course the following subjects are presented: (1) The chemistry of the plant; (2) the anatomy and physiology of the plant; (3) the chemistry of the atmosphere; (4) the chemistry of the soil and its physical properties influencing agriculture; (5) means of improving the soil and influencing the growth of plants (farmyard manures, commercial fertilizers, &c.).

There is also a class for practical work in the laboratory. This class meets three times a week, spending on each occasion from two to four hours in actual practice. A thorough course of manipulation, blowpipe analysis, qualitative and quantitative analysis, is thus offered to students of the university.

The following course of study leads to the degree of bachelor of chemical science:

Freshman class.—English, algebra, geometry, drawing, history, botany.

Sophomore class.—English, algebra and geometry completed, history, book-keeping, geometrical drawing, elements of mechanics, trigonometry, mensuration and surveying (with practical exercises), botany, zoölogy, agriculture.

Junior class.—General chemistry; laboratory practice in manipulation, blowpipe analysis, and qualitative analysis; physics; English and English literature; French; German.

Senior class.—Industrial chemistry, including mining and metallurgy, chemical manufactures, &c.; agricultural chemistry; quantitative analysis, gravimetric and volumetric; physics; astronomy; French; German. The student is obliged to spend at least five hours a day in the laboratory six days of the week.

In the agricultural course the students are engaged in the laboratory six hours a week through the junior and senior years. Their work is necessarily in those portions of chemistry most directly related to agriculture.

The city of Athens contributed $25,000 for the erection of a laboratory building. This is a three story structure with a basement covering an area of one hundred by fifty feet. The entire first floor and basement are occupied by the department of chemistry, and contain analytical laboratories, balance rooms, an assay room, a room for microscopic and spectroscopic work, an industrial museum, store rooms, engine room, workshop, printing office, &c. The second floor contains a lecture room and museum for the department of agriculture, with an apparatus room, working room, and lecture room for the department of physics. The third floor is devoted to the department of engineering and drawing. The laboratories are open to students the whole of each day. A fee of $15 is charged to each student for the use of chemicals. A common set of ordinary apparatus is furnished at a cost not exceeding $10. Special students may, by permission of the faculty and payment of a fee of $35, take a course of chemistry alone, including lectures and laboratory practice.

The industrial collection of the university is quite extensive, numbering over four thousand items. It well illustrates the applications of chemistry to the useful arts and is made a prominent feature in the organization of the chemical department.

A few researches are reported upon such subjects as analysis of the cotton plant, of Georgia marls, tests of strength of Georgia timber and iron, and so on. The university was founded in 1800, and the sciences were taught from the beginning. In 1870 laboratory work was introduced, and it has since been made a part of the regular college curriculum. Chemistry and physics are not taught in the elementary schools of Athens.

ILLINOIS INDUSTRIAL UNIVERSITY.

In the schools of agriculture and horticulture, chemistry is taught throughout the freshman year and agricultural chemistry during two sophomore terms. The latter is pursued in connection with laboratory practice in the analysis of soils, fertilizers, foods, &c. The school of architecture has but one term of chemistry, with laboratory practice, in the junior year, while the schools of civil and mechanical engineering have double this amount. Students in mining engineering take chemistry, with laboratory practice, through two junior terms and the entire senior year. This laboratory practice covers qualitative and quantitative analysis, with assaying and blowpipe work, and is arranged with special reference to the needs of miners and metallurgists. In the school of natural history chemical instruction is given through the freshman year. In the two specially linguistic schools it is required for one junior term, but the school of English and modern languages offers an additional term as an elective. There is also a school of chemistry, in which a regular four years' course of instruction is provided. In this course text book recitations upon the principles of chemistry and chemical physics occupy six weeks of the first term. Through the remainder of the first year recitations alternate with laboratory practice. During the next three years each student is expected to work two hours daily in the laboratory, five days in the week. In order to graduate he must make an original investigation and present a thesis. Students who pursue chemistry incidentally to other courses work two consecutive hours daily in the laboratory during as many terms as their special "school" may require. The full course for a degree in the school of chemistry is as follows:

First year.—First term: Trigonometry, advanced geometry, British authors or French, chemistry with laboratory practice (the latter in qualitative analysis). Second term: Analytical geometry, American authors or French, chemistry, and qualitative analysis completed. Third term: Calculus or freehand drawing, rhetoric, French (optional), organic chemistry, and quantitative analysis.

Second year.—First term: Physiology or botany, German, quantitative analysis. Second term: Zoölogy or botany, German, volumetric analysis, alkalimetry and acidimetry, analysis of corn or other grain. Third term: Zoölogy, German, preparation of salts, acids, &c., electroplating.

Third year.—First term: Mineralogy, German, ultimate organic analysis, analysis of urine. Second term: Physics, German, blowpipe analysis and determination of minerals; assaying, both dry and humid, of gold, silver, and lead ores. Third term: Physics, German, photography, including the preparation of photographic chemicals.

Fourth year.—First term: Mental science, meteorology and physical geography, gas analysis, analysis of mineral waters. Second term: Constitutional history, logic, toxicology, including the microchemistry of poisons. Third term: Political economy, geology, original research, and thesis.

The purely chemical portions of this course are somewhat variable, in order to accommodate the needs of students who intend to become pharmacists, agriculturists, metallurgists, &c.

PURDUE UNIVERSITY.

Chemistry is required, with laboratory practice, two hours a day throughout the junior year. Inorganic chemistry occupies two-thirds of the time and organic chemistry one-third. No set text books are employed. The course includes theoretical chemistry, the elements of synthetical chemistry, qualitative analysis, and crystallography. Students use the balance and apply the principles of stoichiometry from the first. Definite quantities of substances are used, and the product of each reaction is weighed or measured, the actual quantities thereof being compared with the theoretical.

There are also two years of elective study, arranged as follows:

First year (second year from the beginning).—First term: Lectures on qualitative analysis, five hours a week; laboratory practice, ten hours a week. Second term: Lectures on qualitative analysis continued; soils, minerals, and fertilizers; principles of quantitative analysis; instruction five hours, laboratory work, ten hours a week. Third term: Quantitative analysis continued; general review of principles of analysis; time allotted as before.

Second year (third from the beginning).—Mineralogy, descriptive, mathematical, and determinative; metallurgy and assaying; organic chemistry, lectures, recitations, and laboratory work. Special reference is made to technical applications. Students taking this year's course are expected to spend from six to eight hours a day in actual laboratory practice.

MAINE STATE COLLEGE OF AGRICULTURE AND THE MECHANIC ARTS.

In this college there are five regular courses of study, as follows: (1) in agriculture, (2) in civil engineering, (3) in mechanical engineering, (4) in chemistry, and (5) in science and literature. Special students are also received.

Chemistry is required of all regular students through the sophomore year. The students in agriculture continue the study during the junior year and the candidates for a chemical degree carry it on to the end of the course. In the first sophomore term there are daily recitations in general chemistry, based upon Roscoe's text book. These are supplemented by lectures. During the first junior term, the students in courses 1 and 4 recite daily together in agricultural chemistry. Through the second junior term and the whole senior year, the chemical students have daily recitations from Naquet's Principes de chimie, the latest French edition.

In courses 1 and 4 at least two hours daily through not less than nineteen weeks of the sophomore year are spent upon qualitative analysis in the laboratory. Quantitative analysis, at least two and a half hours daily, runs through the junior and senior years in course 4, but only through the junior year in course 1. The work done in quantitative analysis covers the usual ground of gravimetric and volumetric determinations, including assaying for gold and silver. Special attention is necessarily paid to agricultural analysis. Organic combustions and the more difficult analyses of complicated minerals, cast iron, and so on are undertaken by post graduate students. Four original researches in chemistry have been published from this college.

The laboratory facilities are good. The laboratory building contains two apparatus rooms, a lecture room, a cabinet, a library and weighing room, a recitation room, and rooms for analytical purposes. The general laboratory room measures 35 by 60 feet, is provided with gas and water, and accommodates thirty-two students. There is the usual supply of apparatus and chemicals.

MASSACHUSETTS INSTITUTE OF TECHNOLOGY.

A certain amount of chemistry is required of all students who are candidates for degrees, namely, all the inorganic portion of Eliot and Storer's Elementary Manual, and, in qualitative analysis, a knowledge of general methods, with the ability to identify the various metallic elements in simple compounds and to prove the presence or absence of the commoner acids. Both general chemistry and qualitative analysis are taught by lectures and laboratory practice during the first school year. Students who pursue courses in chemistry, mining, metallurgy, physics, or natural history continue the study of qualitative analysis in their second year, the laboratory work being supplemented by lectures. In the second term of the same year they take up quantitative analysis. Chemical philosophy is taught to the students in chemistry and physics, partly by lectures and partly by recitations upon the basis of Cooke's text book. Strictly chemical students follow the preceding course with the study of organic chemistry, Schorlemmer's work being used as a basis for the lecture room exercises. Parallel with the latter there is a course of laboratory instruction, and some organic research is usually undertaken as thesis work. Other lines of investigation may, however, be chosen. Industrial chemistry is taught by lectures and laboratory practice, and instruction in physiological chemistry is also provided.

Candidates for a degree in chemistry have three courses of study open to them, all being identical in the first year. Course A runs as follows:

Second year.—First term: Qualitative analysis, analytical geometry, physics, English history and literature, German. Second term: Quantitative analysis, chemical philosophy, differential calculus, physics, English history and literature, German.

Third year.—First term: Quantitative analysis, microscopy, physical laboratory, constitutional history, German. Second term: Quantitative analysis, industrial chemistry, drawing, physical geography, dynamical geology, physical laboratory, political economy, German.

Fourth year.—First term: Organic chemistry, metallurgy, history of chemistry and allied sciences, abstracts of memoirs, applied physics, optional studies. Second term: Studies for this term, including thesis work, are specially assigned to each student.

In courses B and C mathematics is dropped at the close of the first year, being replaced by the natural sciences. Course B is for students who prefer a larger amount of the last named studies, and course C for those who intend to pursue industrial chemistry. The laboratories for qualitative and quantitative analysis were established in 1865. That for organic chemistry was started in 1877. The laboratory for industrial chemistry has been equipped during the past year, 1878–'79. No list of researches has been prepared, although a considerable amount of good work has issued from the institute.

RUTGERS SCIENTIFIC SCHOOL.

In this school there are two regular courses of study, extending through four years, one in civil engineering and mechanics, the other in chemistry and agriculture. There is also a special course of two years in chemistry, with opportunity for post graduate work. Through the sophomore years, students in both of the regular courses attend lectures upon theoretical and inorganic chemistry, using Barker's text book. The seniors in the engineering course also hear two terms of lectures upon organic chemistry and one term upon chemical physics. For the students in chemistry and agriculture, chemical instruction is given both in the junior and in the senior years. The juniors have determinative mineralogy and analytical chemistry, while the seniors continue their laboratory practice and hear lectures upon agricultural chemistry and chemical physics. According to the catalogue, the laboratory work of the last senior term seems to be devoted to a thesis. The special course of chemistry is as follows:

First year.—First term: Inorganic chemistry, stoichiometry, blowpipe and qualitative analysis, French, physics, thesis. Second term: Inorganic chemistry, qualitative analysis, physics, French, thesis. Third term: Inorganic chemistry, qualitative analysis, French, thesis.

Second year.—First term: Organic and applied chemistry, stoichiometry, quantitative analysis, physics, German, thesis. Second term: Organic and applied chemistry, quantitative analysis, physics, German, thesis. Third term: Geology, applied chemistry, mineralogy, German.

In all the lecture courses the students are required to take notes and to submit them to the inspection of the professor. Problems are given out for solution continually. In the laboratory a written report of every analysis is required. Rigid written and oral examinations are held at the end of every term. Original research on the part of advanced students is encouraged to the utmost. Post graduate students are taken in as subassistants and receive a certain compensation for their work; they thus acquire that most valuable discipline which teaching alone can give.

CORNELL UNIVERSITY.

The instruction in chemistry is substantially as follows: *General chemistry:* Sixty lectures inorganic and twenty-four organic, covering three terms of work. The organic chemistry is elementary. *Laboratory practice:* This begins with a course of exercises in elementary chemical manipulation. As little assistance as possible is given the student, to whom are left the result of each experiment and its interpretation. A written report of all work is daily handed to the instructor for criticism. After the usual qualitative course, quantitative analysis is taken up. Work is here laid out with reference to the future needs of individual students, whenever it is possible to do so. Those who are preparing for some application of chemistry to industrial processes are directed as early as possible towards original investigation in the line of the industry specified. Instruction in blowpipe analysis, determinative mineralogy, and assaying is given in the appropriate rooms at all laboratory hours. *Industrial chemistry:* Two series of sixteen lectures each occupy the third terms of two successive years. A collection of raw materials, waste, and finished products is being made to illustrate chemical industries and to exhibit before the class. The study of this material in detail is an essential feature of the course. Printed synopses of the lectures and copies of all diagrams used to illustrate them are given to each student who attends them. *Agricultural chemistry:* The course of instruction includes about sixty lectures and a large amount of laboratory practice. *Medical chemistry:* Students who intend to pursue the study of medicine receive a course of laboratory instruction in qualitative and quantitative analysis, the latter being especially in the line of the animal secretions. *Chemical philosophy:* Cooke's treatise is used as a text book, and special attention is paid to the problems contained in it. Lectures are also given upon recent developments of the subject, and the reading of Wurtz's History of Chemical Theory is required. *Higher organic chemistry:* Advanced instruction is given by lectures and recitations, the text book for the latter being either in French or in German. During the past year the second volume of Naquet's Principes de chimie has been used.

The laboratory rooms open to students are as follows: (1) the general laboratory for introductory and qualitative work; (2) a special laboratory for general quantitative analysis; (3) a special laboratory for agricultural and medical quantitative analysis; (4) a blowpipe room; (5) an assay room; (6) a room for spectroscopic and other optical work in chemistry; (7) a room for weighing and for the analysis of gases; and (8) a reading room. The last named room is well provided with chemical journals and works of reference.

All chemicals needed for experimental or analytical work are directly accessible to students. Gases are drawn from appropriate stop cocks in the general laboratory, at a table provided with pneumatic troughs. Hydrogen and sulphydric acid are carried to the different rooms of the laboratory from generators in charge of the curator. Richards's jet aspirator is used for water blast and filter pumps, one of the latter being attached to every working table in the quantitative laboratories. These rooms are also fitted with steam evaporating baths, drying closets, self regulating air baths at different temperatures, batteries for electrolytic determinations, and so forth. The laboratories are open five days in the week from eight o'clock until five, and students are permitted to arrange their working hours according to their own convenience. But not less than two hours of continuous work can be taken at any time. Chemicals, apparatus, and gas are supplied to students at current prices.

A chemical and physical society has been organized by the special students in chemistry and physics for the reading of original papers and the general discussion of appropriate subjects. It meets semi-monthly in the laboratory building.

UNIVERSITY OF VERMONT AND STATE AGRICULTURAL COLLEGE.

The classical students take chemistry in the second third of the sophomore year. The instruction is given by experimental lectures. A little laboratory work sometimes is taken as an extra. Students in the literary-scientific course may take chemistry in place of Greek. Engineering students receive three terms' instruction, lectures in the first freshman term and laboratory work in the second and third.

The agricultural and chemical students have chemistry throughout the course, except in the third term freshman and junior years. Even in these terms, however, a little chemical work may be done. The course of study is about as follows: Freshman year: First term, lectures on descriptive chemistry; second term, theoretical chemistry and laboratory work, the former being taught by recitations from Barker's text book and the latter consisting of exercises in manipulation and the preparation of chemical products; third term, blowpipe analysis. Sophomore year: First and second terms, qualitative analysis (Fresenius); third term, quantitative analysis. Junior year, first and second terms, quantitative analysis continued, both gravimetric and volumetric. In the second term, assaying and metallurgy are optional. Senior year: First term, recitations in organic chemistry and laboratory work. In the second and third terms, the agricultural students study agricultural chemistry. The chemical students do organic laboratory work in the second term, and during the third they take analytical, organic, or technical chemistry, according to option.

APPENDIX G.

INDIAN INDUSTRIAL SCHOOLS.

TRAINING SCHOOL FOR INDIAN YOUTH AT CARLISLE, PA.

UNITED STATES INDIAN SERVICE,
TRAINING SCHOOL FOR INDIAN YOUTH, CARLISLE BARRACKS,
Carlisle, Pa., January 22, 1883.

DEAR SIR: In compliance with your request I herewith furnish you a brief history of the Carlisle school and some account of its industrial features. In the spring of 1875 74 Indian prisoners were sent to Florida from the Indian Territory. At the instance of General Sheridan the War Department placed me in charge of those prisoners, they having been under my care at Fort Sill. They were from the Cheyenne, Arapahoe, Kiowa, and Comanche tribes, and were selected for this banishment because of well known offenses against the peace of the frontier. Some of them were guilty of the most outrageous crimes. Years of army service among the Indians and observation of their treatment had led me to favor giving to the Indian a broader chance, and to form a desire that he might be brought more in contact with the peaceful and industrious side of civilized life. Before the prisoners were started from Fort Sill, therefore, I wrote to my superiors urging that they be educated and trained industrially during their imprisonment. Soon after reaching Saint Augustine I wrote repeatedly to the War Department urging that some locality with more industrial surroundings be selected and the prisoners be transferred. This was denied, and I then set to work to make the best use of the elements to be found in the sleepy old Spanish town.

With no means I was forced to seek the coöperation of charitable and missionary folks. Miss S. A. Mather, Mrs. King Gibbs, Mrs. Couper Gibbs, of St. Augustine, and Mrs. Dr. Caruthers, of Tarrytown, N. Y., winter residents of St. Augustine, volunteered to teach and did teach the classes of those grown Indian men for two years and a half, giving them about an hour of instruction daily. Industrially, there was little practical opportunity, but numbers were placed at work for different periods in saw-mills, at picking oranges, as hostlers, grubbing the land, boating, and whatever could be found in connection with their own necessities and comfort in the old fort. Twice we boated pine logs from a distance and constructed log houses within the fort, riving the clap-boards, building stick chimneys, chinking and daubing, that they might learn to construct houses, to replace the skin tepes. Some of them advanced rapidly in acquiring literary, English speaking, and industrial knowledge. Others were very stupid. One of the most satisfactory results in the labor line was in placing five men to grub five acres that had intimidated other laborers, both white and black. The undergrowth and roots to be removed were of the most dense and appalling kind, and yet the Indians stuck to it until they had made a complete success of it, notwithstanding their blistered hands. A good evidence of the success of our labors was a petition to Congress, signed by a very considerable number of the laboring class and others of the community, asking that I be forbidden to put the Indians out to labor in competition with other classes, as I was taking bread from the mouths of those who were dependent upon such labor for their living, &c. In the spring of 1878 the authorities at Washington determined to release the prisoners and permit them to return to their homes. There were 22 of them who preferred to remain east and get a better knowledge of civilized life and more education before going home. The expenses of these 22 young men were assumed by charitable people. General S. C. Armstrong, of the Hampton Normal Institute, received 17 into his institution, and 4 went to Paris Hill, near Utica, N. Y., under the immediate charge of Rev. J. B. Wickes, an Episcopal clergyman, encouraged by Bishop Huntington, all the expenses being defrayed by Mrs. Burnham. One was taken to Tarrytown, N. Y., in Dr. Caruthers's own family. Hampton Institute is an industrial school, and furnished the most reasonable and practical education of any institution I was able to find. The remainder of the party were returned to their respective agencies, and such was the effect of their training in Florida during their three years' absence that they at once became the best element for progress in their tribes. At this time, while a few have gone back to the blanket condition (most likely from necessity, because no other way was open to them), there is abundant testimony in the reports of their respective agents during the past four years that they continue to form a useful and leading industrious element among their people.

A few weeks after the arrival of the party at Hampton Institute General Armstrong was so favorably impressed with the conduct and progress of the 17 he had received that he was willing to accept 50 more, including girls. Mr. Schurz and Mr. McCrary, then Secretaries of the Interior and War Departments, accepted the proposition, and I was sent in the fall of 1878 to Dakota and brought away 49 children from six different agencies of the Sioux, Gros Ventres, Mandan, and Arickeree tribes. These, together with the former Florida prisoners, were placed under training in all the varied systems of literary and industrial pursuits Hampton Institute so liberally provides for its colored pupils. Side by side with those colored pupils the Indian boys and girls, in perfect harmony with the new life, demonstrated their capacity to hold their own in improving the best of chances. It was very much desired by the friends of this new move, and particularly General Armstrong, that I should remain with them, and a clause was introduced in the Army appropriation bill, which passed Congress in the spring of 1879, for the "detail of one officer not above the rank of captain for duty with reference to Indian education."

It was a theory I had advocated for several years, that to get the best results in our educational work among Indian children as many as possible should be removed from reservation and tribal influences and placed in an atmosphere of civilized life. To this end I had urged the use of vacant military posts and barracks as furnishing, without much cost in changing and improving buildings, places for making a beginning, and I now proposed to the Interior and War Departments to undertake the education of 250 to 300 children at the old military barracks at Carlisle. This proposition was accepted.

After many preliminaries I was sent in September, 1879, to the Rosebud and Pine Ridge Agencies in Dakota, whence I brought away 84 children, and immediately after went to the Indian Territory, and from the Kiowa, Cheyenne, Pawnee, and other tribes brought 52 more. To these were added 11 from the Hampton Institute of the young men who had been with me in Florida. The school was opened on the 1st of November, with 147 students. From time to time children from various western tribes came in, and at the end of July, 1880, we numbered 239 children, about one-third girls. At the end of the second year, October, 1881, we had increased to 295. At the present time we number 379, 132 girls and 247 boys. From the beginning our principle has been to place the most emphasis on industrial training, next English speaking, and then literary training. To accomplish the first we very early in the work established shops for mechanical instruction in carpentry, black-smithing, wagon-making, harness-making, tailoring, tin-smithing, shoemaking, printing and baking, and our farm of 115 acres gave some scope for agricultural training. We have avoided theory in our industrial training and adhered to practice, being governed to a great extent by the old apprentice system. We have at the head of each branch a skilled mechanic as practical instructor, and as nearly as possible we pursue the methods of trades-people in their instructions to apprentices. We give half of each day to work and the other half to school, and have found that our progress is proportionately greater in each than it would be if the attention was directed to either the one or the other for the whole time. Under this system we have under training as carpenters 13 boys; as wagon-makers and blacksmiths, 15; as harness-makers, 15; as shoemakers, 19; as tailors, 12; as tinners, 11; as printers, 5; as bakers, 3; and every boy not engaged at some trade is required to work during the season upon the farm. Such products of our labors as we are not able to make use of for the school are purchased by the Indian Department and shipped to agencies. We think our boys as forward in capacity for receiving instruction in each of the several branches as the average white boy. In the blacksmith shop our apprentice boys, after two years' instruction, are able to iron a wagon, repair a plow, shoe a horse, &c. In the wood-working department they are able to get out all the different wood parts of the wagon ready for the blacksmith; in the tin-smithing, to construct coffee-pots, buckets, pails, pans, cups, &c.; in the harness-making, to cut out and manufacture harness; in the tailoring, to cut out and manufacture clothing; in shoemaking, to repair and manufacture boots and shoes; in printing, to set up and distribute type and make up forms; in baking we have no other help than Indians. We give to our girls instruction in the various industries of the sex. In cooking, sewing, housework, laundry work, &c., they are apt pupils.

One of the most useful features of our work has been to place our boys and girls in private families, principally among farmers, where they perform the same kind of labor and are subjected to the same home and industrial influences as white children of their own age. This has led to the most beneficial results. The children take on English speaking and the industries of civilized life very speedily. During vacations we place out all we can spare from our own work, and during the winter we allow a considerable number to remain and attend the public schools in the several neighborhoods, they being required to do such work mornings and evenings as they are capable of, and so pay for their board and clothes. By this course we are enabled to train a considerably larger number of pupils than we are allowed appropriation for. It is plain that the real hindrance to Indian progress is found in the fact that they are kept entirely separated from the other masses of our population, and by every act of our Government and every sentiment of its people, societies, missionary and other, made to feel that they are a separate people and must so remain forever. With their education in separate schools, with their home life on prison reservations, with their liberty of coming and going restricted to these reservations, with all their aspirations and ambitions so limited there can be no healthy growth. To overcome these difficulties the Indian mind and the mind of the public, as well as of Congress, must be educated to grant to them the enlarged privileges accorded to all other races. The boy will never learn to swim until he goes into the water, and the experiences of industrial and civilized life, through its associations and competitions, will determine for both Indian and white his true status. We have had quite enough of the Sioux, Cheyenne, Comanche, &c., as Sioux, Cheyenne, Comanche, &c. We can end their existence among us as such separate people by a broad and generous system of English education and labor training which will reach all the 50,000 children, and in a very few years remove all our trouble from them as a separate people and as separate tribes, and instead of feeding, clothing, and caring for them from year to year, put them in condition to feed, clothe, and care for themselves. Our experiences in many individual cases in the last few years make it very evident that not only may we fit the Indian to take care of himself in his own home, but may fit him to go and come and abide in the land wherever he may choose, and cease to be a savage.

We appreciate the difficulties of the return of our pupils to the great mass of uneducated and savage influence, but it must be borne in mind that the conditions of the Indians have entirely changed within the past decade. They are now hemmed in on all sides by the aggressive white population, their reservations are reduced to very small limits, and the passage of railroads through them, and the constant going and coming of white men, have so brought them in contact with civilized life that by those means and influences alone a great deal of pressure is brought to bear upon the tribes in general. So our returned pupils, instead of becoming isolated on their return to their people, become mediums of communication between their people and this surrounding civilization; and, whereas a few years ago an educated Indian returning to his people found himself entirely separated and useless as an educated and civilized man, he now finds himself a valuable medium for helping his own people to meet the overpowering wave of civilization that is upon them.

We have returned from Carlisle in round numbers about two hundred pupils since we began our work. I am safe in claiming that two-thirds to three-fourths of these returned pupils are exerting a most valuable influence on their tribes. Many of them are used by the agents in the schools and in the workshops and even in the offices of the agency. We have an instance where a young Sioux, after three years at Carlisle, has so fitted himself in his penmanship and knowledge of office duties as to get a salary of $60 a month as an assistant clerk. One of our graduates has charge of the discipline and management out of school hours of the boys in a school of 125 pupils. From the agent, from the teachers, and from the superintendent of the school I have the most flattering encomiums. Others are employed as blacksmiths, carpenters, harnessmakers, and shoemakers after having acquired some knowledge of these trades in our Carlisle school, and are standing examples to their people of the utility of civilized knowledge and occupations.

I would however revert to the original idea and that is the absorption of the Indians in our population the same as that of all other races that come from foreign shores to us. We must build forward and as rapidly as possible to the day when we shall have no exclusive schools for Indians, but when Indians shall enter into our school systems and into our labor systems the same as the other races; and it is not a very great matter to accomplish this result. We have upward of fifty millions of people, and we have only 261,000 Indians, one Indian to every two hundred of our population. There is not the same race prejudice against the Indian as against some other peoples. Indeed the whites may well be reminded that many now classed as Indians are more Anglo-Saxon than Indian. Besides, many traits of Indian character have always received the commendation of the Saxons.

The effect of our observation and experience in this work is to make us more and more confident of the successful result of well-directed industrial Indian education.

Very respectfully, your obedient servant,

R. H. PRATT,
First Lieutenant Tenth United States Cavalry, Superintendent.

Gen. JOHN EATON,
Commissioner of Education, Washington, D. C.

THE INDIAN SCHOOL AT FOREST GROVE, OREGON.

[From the Oregonian.]

The Indian Industrial and Training School at Forest Grove dates from the year 1879. In this year the appropriation of $5,000 was conditionally secured for the establishment of an Indian training school and Capt. M. C. Wilkinson, an energetic and enthusiastic advocate of this method of dealing with and settling the Indian problem, was placed in charge of the work. This amount was by the Secretary of the Interior set apart for the purpose designated from the civilization fund created from the sale of Indian land in Kansas and was not a Congressional appropriation. Its conditions required the school to be in progress with an attendance of 25 pupils by the following July. Captain Wilkinson went immediately to work. A site was secured adjoining the town of Forest Grove on the northwest, consisting of four acres of land in a state of primeval wildness. Here ground was broken for the school in November, 1879, and the work was pushed forward with so much energy that on the 26th of February, 1880, the school opened with 18 pupils, gathered from the Puyallup tribe. With this first sum of $5,000 a clearing was made and a building 60 by 32 feet, two stories high, with a wing or addition 30 by 30 for kitchen, laundry, &c., was erected; the children were gathered from their homes, subsistence and stores were purchased, and employés paid for one year.

A nucleus was now formed around which industrial forces began to rally. In 1880 an appropriation of $10,000 was granted from the same fund, and another building of the same dimensions as the first was constructed by the labor of the Indian boys alone. Added to this building was a wood shed and wash room 24 by 15 feet. The four acre tract was cleared of trees and undergrowth, leveled, and inclosed with a substantial board fence, which, together with all buildings and outbuildings, was neatly whitewashed. Sidewalks were laid around the buildings and cross-walks between the two, these greatly aiding in keeping the floors clean. These buildings present on the outside an appearance precisely similar, and stand a distance of perhaps 200 feet apart. On the ground floor of the first are the school rooms, chapel, and boys' sitting room. The school rooms have comfortable seats and the same appliances in the way of maps, charts, blackboards, &c., that are usually found in the district school house. In the upper story of this building is the boys' dormitory, an apartment extending the entire length of the main building, passably well ventilated and kept scrupulously clean. The beds are placed in two rows, six feet apart, furnished with good mattresses and pillows and made comfortable by gray blankets. Two boys occupy each bed. The bedsteads are home made, or rather "school made," being the work of the boys themselves, under direction of Captain Wilkinson.

The second building contains on the ground floor the school dining room, the sewing room, and the matron's and superintendent's private apartments. On the upper floor is situated the girl's dormitory. This is divided into rooms, in each of which is a double bed, stand, &c., the older girls occupying the rooms in pairs. There is also an extension of this dormitory, arranged like that occupied by the boys, where the younger girls sleep.

The long tables in the dining room are neatly covered with white oil cloth, and when laid with linen washed and ironed by the Indian girls, and laden with well cooked vegetables, raised by the Indian boys, and surrounded by both girls and boys neatly clad and dining after the manner of civilized people, they present in themselves an encouraging picture of civilization.

As an individual instance of the great transformation effected in these heretofore untutored children of nature, the writer's attention was called to the Spokane girl who has charge of the table linen and general supervision of the dining room. It is stated that upon her arrival at the school some two and a half years ago she was a complete specimen of the wild, untidy Indian girl of the border, unable to speak a word of English, and was withal unusually repulsive in her appearance. So ready a pupil has she become in the ways of civilization that she is now as neat as any country lass; is careful and painstaking in the labor assigned her, speaks English quite intelligently, and is polite and engaging in her manners. Her case is but a single instance of the progress made by the girls in the art of civilized home making; and when these, after their term expires, are returned to their people the hope is certainly not without reason that their influence in cultured, womanly ways will be of vast benefit. The work and government of the house and school are thoroughly systematized and each department is placed under the charge of careful, competent, and thoroughly trained assistants, the whole being at present under the management of Mrs. Gertrude B. Wilkinson.

The employés are a clerk and superintendent, a matron, two teachers, a farmer, seamstress, blacksmith, shoemaker, and carpenter, who each supervise their special branch of industrial education. In conducting the school cleanliness and obedience are the first rules, and that these are carefully enforced is apparent to the visitor.

The sexes are kept strictly separate in play and work, the dividing line between the two buildings and play grounds being indicated by a row of flower beds, being called by Captain Wilkinson the "dead line," but renamed by Mrs. Wilkinson the "life line," it being explained by this lady to the pupils, in her pleasant and convincing way, as the moral life of the Indian to observe strictly the social and moral conditions without which it is impossible for any people to be healthful, happy, and prosperous. Efforts are made to break up all tribal associations, those of race being deemed ample to hold the Indians in bonds of fraternal sympathy. Among the first things insisted upon is the use of the English language. So far as can be avoided, no "Indian talk" is allowed, and by strict attention to this matter the pupils are usually able, often in three or four months, to communicate tolerably well in English. Progress is made here to a certain extent, after which for a time advancement seems to cease altogether, until the pupil is taught to "think in English," thus making the language his own instead of a mere medium whereby his thoughts in the language of his tribe are conveyed. When this point is established the progress is more rapid, and is indeed in most cases quite satisfactory. In the schools the rudimentary elements of education are taught by oral and written methods and object lessons, each being patiently applied. As at present arranged each pupil spends a half day in the school room and a half day in the shops or work rooms. This rule is absolute, no pupil being excused except for illness. In industrial pursuits the boys are taught blacksmithing, shoemaking, carpentering, wagonmaking, and farming. The blacksmith and shoe shops are located in the center of the village of Forest Grove. There are in the first seven apprentices, and the cash received for their labor for the fiscal year ending June 30, 1882, was $1,038.50.

These boys are strong and muscular, work at the forge and wield the sledge with a will, and learn readily. In the shoemaker's shop are eight apprentices. These made shoes for the school from the 1st of March to the 31st of August, 1882, to the value of $212.25. The cash received for labor for the same period amounted to $133.95. In carpenter work during the two months preceding the last report made by Captain Wilkinson, thirteen boys built two dormitories 32 by 32 feet, 24 feet high; a sick ward, double walled, 25 by 36, 12 feet high; an addition to the kitchen, 14 by 28 feet, and in the same time made seven bedsteads. These boys did all the work, putting it together in a substantial and workmanlike manner, the carpenter of course directing. Last spring a tract of 45 acres of land was rented and 10 boys were put under the direction of the farmer. Of the tract 14 acres were pasture land, from which was harvested 10 tons of hay. On the residue was raised 5 bushels of onions, 300 dozen green onions for table use, 96 bushels of beans, 340 bushels of potatoes, 120 dozen cabbage, 150 bushels of apples, 6 bushels of plums, 10 bushels of pears, 56 bushels of peas, 153 bushels of beets, 154 bushels of turnips, 1,272 dozen ears of green corn and 10 bushels of tomatoes. The boys in addition to their work in the garden during the summer built a sewer 750 feet long and 4½ feet deep, cut 50 cords of wood for winter use and labored as opportunity offered in the neighboring harvest fields. It will be seen that the industrial progress of the boys is rapid and is of a varied character.

The girls on entering the school are first started at the wash-tub, the fitness of this being obvious, as personal cleanliness is unknown to them in a savage state. This is followed by instruction in ironing, dishwashing, preparing vegetables for cooking, sweeping, scrubbing, cookery, chamberwork, sewing, and mending. During the year ending June 30, 1882, they had, under direction of the seamstress, made 1,118 garments and had kept their own and the boys' clothes in repair, besides attending to their studies and taking their turn at housekeeping details. The most judicious care is exercised over the morals of all the pupils, their instruction in ways of modesty and virtue being not the least of the teacher's care. All pupils, unlesss ill, attend divine service every Sunday, and have on stated evenings prayer meetings and other religious exercises in their own chapel-room.

Their deportment during these services is usually good, as is also their deportment about the school, shops, and grounds. It is not claimed that Indian boarding schools are doing more than pioneer work. In their management there is neither precedent nor text-books to follow. From the first the school at Forest Grove has been hampered for means. The first three appropriations of $5,000, $10,000, and $15,000 from the civilization fund, as before stated, were supplemented last year by a Congressional appropriation of $30,000.

Want of funds has prevented the use of many conveniencies which are considered necessary to the proper management of a private family and which are even more essential to the smooth working of a large household. Too often the ingenuity of teachers is taxed to see how they could manage to do without instead of how they could teach the pupils to use the appliances of civilized life. The time heretofore allotted to the students for instruction in the training school was three years. It is apparent that to return immature youth to heathen homes after only three years' training in ways of civilization under specially favorable conditions is a hazardous experiment. Justice and true economy alike require a supplemental course of at least two years to give the new habits formed time to take deeper root. Hence hereafter Indian parents will be expected to surrender their children for five instead of three years.

There are at present under instruction in the school 91 pupils, varying in age from 10 to 20 years. Of these 54 are boys and 37 girls. Twelve tribes are represented, as follows: Chehalis, 6; Alaskans, 12; Nesquallies, 3; Oyster Bay, 2; Pitt River, 2; Piute, 1; Puyallup, 22; Spokane, 18; Snohomish, 1; Umatilla, 10; Warm Springs, 2; Wascoes, 12.

As has before been stated, efforts are made to abolish all tribal associations, and so successfully that one or two representatives of several tribes feel quite as much at home as those that are represented by large numbers.

The great need of the school at present is land. The four acres occupied belong to Pacific University, and efforts will be made the coming year to lease for a long term of years or to buy the site occupied. To earn the Congressional appropriation of $30,000 it will be necessary to have 147 pupils under tutelage for a year, and to accommodate the increased number the superintendent is now making important additions to the buildings. Captain Wilkinson, who had been in charge of the work from its inception, was a few months since ordered to join his regiment at Missoula and was thus compelled to relinquish the work. This removal is greatly to be regretted at the present stage of affairs, as it will be almost impossible for any one else to take up the work and carry it forward in detail without more or less loss of time. The Department of the Interior has, however, done the best possible thing under the circumstances, in placing Mrs. Wilkinson in charge. She has been from the first an enthusiastic worker, has shared fully all of her husband's plans, and has once visited Washington in the interest of the school.

It was thought best to separate the school proper entirely from Pacific University. This has accordingly been done and Lieutenant Pierce detailed to succeed Captain Wilkinson as professor of military tactics in the university. A visit to the Indian industrial school at Forest Grove will well repay the curious, the skeptic, or the humanitarian. The visitor who inspects it and learns from its workings cannot fail to be impressed favorably with the civilizing effects upon the Indian youth, and will look with interest as the years go on for a chronicle of the good results which can scarcely fail to follow this educational effort.

An account of Indian education at Hampton Institute, Virginia, has already been given in connection with the description of that institution in Appendix A.

INDEX.

The extended statements in the appendixes respecting individual institutions usually contain facts about (1) their objects; (2) finances; (3) faculties; (4) students; (5) scholarships; (6) courses of study; and (7) buildings and appliances. Entries under these headings were not generally made in indexing the appendices. Reference to the respective institutions will guide the reader to information on these subjects.

A.

	Page.
Abbot, President T. C., his opinion of manual labor	28
Agassiz, Professor, his opinion of the Massachusetts Agricultural College	142–157
Agricultural and Mechanical College of Kentucky, account of	129–134
scholarships	21
Agricultural and Mechanical College of Mississippi, account of	168–171
manual labor	27
Agricultural and Mechanical College of Missouri, account of	175
Agricultural and Mechanical College of Texas, account of	230–232
scholarships	22
shop practice	31
Agricultural College and Mechanics' Institute, Claflin University, account of	226, 227
Agricultural colleges, courses of study	24–28
faculties	19, 20
finances	17–19
graduates	23
objects	8–16
principles determining their establishment and organization	13–15
reports required of	7
results	34
statistics	249–255
students	20
tuition and scholarships	21–23
work of	3–6
Agricultural department, University of Tennessee	229
Agricultural experiments	29
Agricultural experiment station in Connecticut	95
in New Jersey	183
in North Carolina	208
in Ohio	211
Agricultural instruction in Louisiana University	131
Agricultural schools in Europe, comparison of American schools with	5, 6
Agriculture, college of, Illinois Industrial University	105, 106
University of Minnesota	163
Agriculture, courses and instruction in, Brown University	223
Bussey Institution	36
Cornell University	185–187
Kansas Agricultural College	125
Maine State College	133
Michigan Agricultural College	159
Mississippi Agricultural College	170
Ohio State University	210, 211
Pennsylvania State College	217, 218
Purdue University	112
Rutgers Scientific School	181, 182
Sheffield Scientific School	96
Texas Agricultural and Mechanical College	230, 231
University of California	89
University of Georgia	100
University of Nebraska	177
University of Wisconsin	247
Vermont Agricultural College	233
West Virginia State University	246

310 INDEX.

	Page
Agriculture, relations of science to	4
Agriculture, school of, Iowa Agricultural College	119
Agriculture, studies in	26
in University of North Carolina	207
Agriculture, study of, in Alabama Agricultural College	82
Agriculture, work in, at Hampton (Va.) Institute	238, 239
Aid to students in agricultural colleges	22
Alabama Agricultural and Mechanical College, account of	81–84
mining engineering	32
Alcorn Agricultural and Mechanical College	171
American Institute of Instruction, recommendations of committee on industrial education	56
American principles, preservation of	77
Apprentices, instruction for carriage builders'	272
Apprenticeship, condition of	8–10
lack of, being supplied	75
reasons for decay of	10
unnecessary extension of	156
Architecture, course in building and, in University of Georgia	101
Architecture, course in, in Cornell University	189
Massachusetts Institute of Technology	144
University of Minnesota	165
Architecture, instruction in home	285
Architecture, school of, Illinois Industrial University	107
Arkansas Industrial University, account of	84–86
Armstrong, General S. C., report of Hampton Normal and Agricultural Institute	237–241
on Indian education in the East	241–243
Art, course in industrial, Purdue University	115
gallery of, Illinois Industrial University	108
school of, Illinois Industrial University	108
schools of, Cooper Union	39
Artisans, powers necessary to	56
Art School, Massachusetts Normal	35
Atkinson, Prof. Edward, on the need of educating the operative	75
Atlanta University	103

B.

Badger, Rev. Henry C., remarks on Cornell University	197
Battle, Hon. Kemp P., statements respecting University of North Carolina	208
Bavaria, higher agricultural education in	6
Boarding-houses, licensing of, in South Carolina	22
Boston, Mass., evening drawing schools	50
introduction of manual labor into its schools	54–55
sewing in its schools	60
Boston Industrial School, work of	54
Brewster & Co., instruction of apprentices with	272
Brown University	221–223
Bussey Institution	36

C.

California, University of. (See University of California.)	
Campbell, Helen, on cooking schools in the South	290–293
Carlisle Barracks, Indian school at	302–304
Carpentry, instruction in, in Kansas Agricultural College	127
in manual training school, Saint Louis	267
Carpentry and joinery, course in, in Purdue University	114
in Massachusetts Institute of Technology	150–151
Carriage Builders' National Association, report of its committee on technical training	273–275
Carriage-makers, instruction of	272–275
Carriage mechanics, evening class for, at New Haven	272
technical school for	51
Carriages, library of works relating to	273
Case School of Applied Science	41
Chambers, Prof. W. H., statement of agriculture in Alabama Agricultural College	82

INDEX.

	Page.
Chandler scientific department of Dartmouth College	37
Chancy, Rev. George L., his idea of school shops	55
Chemistry, courses in, in agricultural colleges	32
Chemistry, instruction in, in Alabama Agricultural College	83
Arkansas Industrial University	86
Cornell University	192–194, 300
Illinois Industrial University	107, 297
Kansas Agricultural College	126
Maine State College	133, 135, 298
Massachusetts Institute of Technology	144, 299
Michigan Agricultural College	159
Ohio State University	210
Purdue University	116, 298
Rutgers Scientific School	181, 299
Sheffield Scientific School	295–297
University of California	90, 295
University of Georgia	101, 297
University of Missouri	174
University of North Carolina	206
University of Vermont	301
Worcester County Free Institute	261
Chemistry, instruction in agricultural, in Cornell University	186, 193
University of Minnesota	164
Chemistry, value of, to industries	13
Chemistry and mineralogy, department of, in University of Tennessee	229
Chemistry and physics, course in, in Pennsylvania State College	217, 218
Chemnitz, Saxony, industrial education in	45
Children, industrial instincts of	46
removal of, from school to work	48
Citizenship, education for, needed in America	5
Civil engineering, instruction in, in Cornell University	190–191
Maine State College	134
Massachusetts Institute of Technology	143
Ohio State University	210
Pennsylvania State College	218
Rutgers Scientific School	181
Sheffield Scientific School	95
University of Minnesota	165
Worcester County Free Institute	260
See also Engineering.	
Civil engineering and mechanics, course in, in Rutgers Scientific School	181
Claflin University	226, 227
Classification of students of Ohio State University	212
Colorado Agricultural College, account of	91–93
department of drawing and mechanics	30
manual labor	27
Colorado State School of Mines	35
Colored youth, education of, at Hampton, Va.	237–245
Columbia College School of Mines	39
Cookery, instruction in	277, 278, 279–282, 285–293
New York School of Cookery	285–288
See Domestic Science.	
Cooking schools in the South	290–293
Cooper Union for the Advancement of Science and Art	38
School of Telegraphy of	72
Cornell University, account of	183–204
instruction in chemistry	300
instruction in horticulture	73
shop practice	31
Corson, Miss Juliet, her account of New York School of Cookery	286–288
Corvallis College	213
Course of study in Colorado Agricultural College	92
Courses of study in colleges of agriculture and the mechanic arts	24–34
Crime, diminution of, through industrial education	76

D.

Dairying, instruction in, in Kansas Agricultural College	127
instruction for women in	73

312   INDEX.

	Page.
Dairy of Iowa Agricultural College	119
Dartmouth College, scientific and engineering branches of	37–38
Deaf and dumb, instruction of, in cookery	291
Delaware College	97–98
Design, school of, Massachusetts Institute of Technology	73, 146
Designs, value of attractive	13
Domestic economy, department of, Iowa Agricultural College	121, 278
instruction in, in Kansas Agricultural College	127
Domestic science, instruction in	63, 277–293
school of, Illinois Industrial University	109, 279–285
Drawing, course in, in manual training school, Washington University	266
Purdue University	115, 116
Sheffield Scientific School	96
University of Georgia	101
Drawing, department of mechanical, Stevens Institute of Technology	262, 263
instruction in, in Worcester County Free Institute	261
instruction in freehand, in Cornell University	192–204
value of, in industries	13–74
value of, to mechanics	48
Drawing classes in mechanics' institutes	40, 42
Drawing department, Washington University	265
Drawing in evening schools	49–52
Dwight School, Boston, shop practice at	55

E.

Economy, encouragement of students in	22
Electrical engineering, instruction in, in Massachusetts Institute of Technology	145
Elizabeth Aull Seminary, school of home work of	63
Engineering, college of, Illinois Industrial University	106
Engineering, course in, in University of California	90
University of Georgia	101
Engineering, department of, Washington University	264
Engineering, instruction in, Alabama Agricult'ral College	82
Engineering, school of, Iowa Agricultural College	120
Purdue University	116
University of Missouri	174
See, also, entries under Civil engineering, Mining and metallurgy, and Mechanical engineering.	
Engineering and surveying, instruction in, in North Carolina University	207
Engineering, museum of, Cornell University	203
Esthetics, instruction in household	283
Etiquette, instruction in	285
Evening classes for women, New Century Woman's Club of Philadelphia	294
of Franklin Institute	42
of Ohio Mechanics' Institute	40
of Spring Garden Institute	42
Evening drawing schools	49–52
Evening High School of New York, purposes and occupations of its students	47
studies in	48
Evening school of science, Cooper Union	39
Evening schools	47–52
Excursions of students of Columbia College School of Mines	39
Experimental farm, advisability of procuring, in Vermont	234
Experimental work, Colorado Agricultural College	93
Massachusetts Agricultural College	141
New Hampshire College of Agriculture and the Mechanic Arts	180
Purdue University	113
University of Minnesota	167
University of Wisconsin	247
Experiments, agricultural	28
Experiment station in North Carolina	208
Ohio State University	211
Rutgers Scientific School	183

F.

Fairchild, President Geo. T., his report of Kansas State Agricultural College	123–129
Farmers, demand of, for agricultural schools	4

INDEX. 313

	Page.
Farmers' institutes, at Pennsylvania State College	219
in Colorado	91
Farmers' lecture course, University of Minnesota	165
Farms of agricultural colleges....86, 93, 109, 123, 124, 136, 138, 141, 160, 165, 169, 175, 177, 179, 182, 201, 212, 221, 227, 229, 231, 235, 239	
Finances of colleges of agriculture and the mechanic arts	17–19
Foley, Thomas, remarks on manual training	156
Food and dietetics, instruction about	280
Forest Grove, Oreg., Indian school at	305–307
Forging, course in manual training school, Saint Louis	268
Massachusetts Institute of Technology	151, 155
in Purdue University	114
Foundry course, Massachusetts Institute of Technology	151, 154
Franklin Institute	41

G.

Geological and natural history survey of Minnesota	167
Georgia State College of Agriculture and the Mechanic Arts, account of	99–102
German technical instruction compared with American	7
Gloucester, Mass., manual training at	53
Goss, Prof. M. F. M., his account of mechanical instruction in Purdue University	114
Graduates of colleges of agriculture and the mechanic arts	23
of industrial institutions, the ends served by them	76
of the Alabama Agricultural and Mechanical College	81
Hampton (Va.) Institute	243
Illinois Industrial University	105, 110
Iowa State Agricultural College	118
Maine State College	133
Massachusetts Agricultural College	140
Massachusetts Institute of Technology	143
Michigan Agricultural College	159
Pennsylvania State College	215
Rutgers Scientific School	182
University of Minnesota	162
University of Tennessee	228
Worcester County Free Institute	257
Gregory, J. M., tribute to, by regent of Illinois Industrial University	110
Gregory, Mrs. J. M., her account of the school of domestic science, Illinois Industrial University	279–285

H.

Hampton Normal and Agricultural Institute, account of	236–245
domestic instruction	64
manual labor	28
statistics of graduates	24
Hardaway, Prof. R. A., his reports on engineering and military instruction in Alabama Agricultural College	82, 83
Harvard University, course for women at	58
scientific departments	36
Hill, Gen. D. H., his report of Arkansas Industrial University	84–85
History and political science, instruction in, in Cornell University	197–200
Home architecture, instruction of women in	285
Horticulture, instruction in, in Cornell University	186
Kansas Agricultural College	126
University of Minnesota	164
instruction of women in	73
studies in, in Illinois Industrial University	106
Hubbard, George A., his description of his evening class	272
Humes, President Thomas W., his report of University of Tennessee	227–229
Huntington, Miss Emily, her kitchen garden system	62
Huntington industrial works of Hampton Institute	239
Hygiene, instruction of women in	282

I.

Illinois Industrial University, account of	103–110
instruction in chemistry	207

314   INDEX.

Illinois Industrial University—Continued.   Page.
   mechanical engineering 30
   mining and metallurgy 32
Indian education at Hampton (Va.) Institute................................ 240–243
Indian girls, instruction of, in cookery....................................... 287
Indian industrial school at Carlisle, Pa 302–304
   at Forest Grove, Oreg... 305–307
Indian instruction in the East.. 241–243
Industrial college of University of Nebraska 177–178
Industrial education, need of, in America 41
   promised results of... 74
Industrial education in agricultural colleges 24–34
   in schools other than those endowed with the national land grant 34–57
Industrial work in evening schools 47
Industries, increasing value of American 74
Instructors, large number of, in foreign technical schools...................... 7
Instructors in colleges of agriculture and the mechanic arts 19, 20
Iowa State Agricultural College, account of................................. 118–123
   manual labor 28
   shop practice 30
Iron cutting, instruction in, in manual training school, Saint Louis........... 238
Iron working in Worcester Free Institute...................................... 259
Investigations, agricultural, at Massachusetts Agricultural College........... 141

J.

John C. Green School of Science 38
Journal of Franklin Institute 41
   of Ohio Institute 40

K.

Kansas State Agricultural College, account of.............................. 123–129
   instruction for women 64
   instruction in agriculture 25
   manual labor 27
   objects 15
Kentucky Agricultural and Mechanical College 129–131
Kindergarten work, a preparation for industries............................. 45–47
Kitchen garden at Hampton (Va.) Institute.................................... 243
Kitchen gardens 62

L.

Laboratories of Illinois Industrial University 109
   Iowa Agricultural College.. 123
   Massachusetts Institute of Technology 147
   University of Georgia.. 99
Labor, manual, in agricultural colleges..................................... 27, 28
   Colorado Agricultural College 95
   Cornell University 185
   Hampton (Va.) Institute 238–240, 243
   Iowa State Agricultural College 123
   Kansas Agricultural College.. 128
   Maine State College.. 135
   Michigan Agricultural College... 159, 160
   Mississippi Agricultural College 170
   Texas Agricultural and Mechanical College.................................. 232
Laborers, effect of elementary education on.................................... 47
   elevation of, through education 74
   skill needed by 12
Ladies' department of University of Minnesota 174
Land, Congressional grant of... 16
Lasell Seminary, industrial training in....................................... 277
Lawrence Scientific School 36
Lecture course for farmers, University of Minnesota.......................... 165
Lectures, instruction by... 7
Lectures of Franklin Institute... 42
Lehigh University, school of technology....................................... 43

	Page.
Leland, Charles G., his circular on industrial art	47
Lewis College	44
Literary and scientific departments, relations of, in Rutgers College	180
Living, cost of, diminished by education	75
Lockett, Prof. S. W., his letter on applied mathematics in University of Tennessee	229
Louisiana State University and Agricultural College	131–132
Lowell Institute, lecture courses of	146

M.

MacDonald, George, his opinion of industrial occupation	75
Machine shop of Stevens Institute of Technology	263
Worcester Free Institute	258
Machine work, instruction in, in Purdue University	114
Maine State College of Agriculture and the Mechanic Arts, account of	132–136
graduates	24, 133
instruction in chemistry	298
manual labor	27
shop work	30
Manual labor. (See Labor.)	
Manual training in public schools	52, 54–56
Manual training school, Massachusetts Institute of Technology	147
Washington University	266–271
Manual training schools, effect of, on their students	75
Manufactures, improvement of American	44
improvement of, through industrial education	74
Marvel, Mr. L. H., his account of manual training at Gloucester, Mass	53
Maryland Agricultural College	136–138
Maryland Institute	52
Massachusetts Agricultural College	139–142
method of instruction	25
Massachusetts Institute of Technology	142–157
instruction in chemistry	299
mining and metallurgy	33
school of practical design	73
shop work	30
Massachusetts Normal Art School	35
Mechanical engineering, courses and instruction in, Cornell University	31, 187–188
Illinois Industrial University	30, 106
Iowa Agricultural College	30, 120
Louisiana State University	131
Maine State College	30, 134, 135
Massachusetts Institute of Technology	30, 143, 147–157
Ohio State University	31, 210, 211
Purdue University	30, 113
Sheffield Scientific School	96
Stevens Institute of Technology	263
Texas Agricultural and Mechanical College	31, 230, 231
University of Minnesota	165
University of Wisconsin	247
Mechanical laboratory of Cornell University	203
Mechanical work in Spring Garden Institute	42
Mechanic arts, college of, University of Minnesota	165
colleges of agriculture and mechanic arts, statistics of	249–255
courses of study in	29–34
instructors in	20
School of, Massachusetts Institute of Technology	146, 147–157
University of California	89
Mechanics, education needed by	11
their desire for technical education	4
Mechanics and civil engineering, course in, in Rutgers Scientific School	181
Mechanics and drawing, department of, in Colorado Agricultural College	92
Mechanics' institutes	40, 41–43
Metallurgy. (See Mining and metallurgy.)	
Method of instruction in manual training school of Washington University	267
Metropolitan Museum of Art, evening classes of	52
Middle Georgia Military and Agricultural College	102

	Page.
Michigan State Agricultural College, account of	158–163
instruction in agriculture	25
Military department of Mississippi Agricultural College	171
Military instruction in Alabama Agricultural College	83
Arkansas Industrial University	85
Kansas Agricultural College	128
Military science in Cornell University	188
instruction in, in Illinois Industrial University	107
Iowa Agricultural College	122
Miller Manual Labor School	53
Miller school of agriculture, zoölogy, and botany, University of Virginia	44
Milwaukee College	59
Mining, instruction in, in Alabama Agricultural and Mechanical College	32
Arkansas Industrial University	85
Cornell University	191
Massachusetts Institute of Technology	33, 144
Ohio State University	33, 210
University of California	90
Mining and metallurgy, courses in	32–34
department of Washington University	264
instruction in, in Illinois Industrial University	32
University of Vermont	233
Mines, Colorado School of	35
Mines and Metallurgy, Missouri School of	175–176
Minnesota, University of. (See University of Minnesota.)	
Mississippi Agricultural and Mechanical College, account of	168–171
manual labor	27
Missouri State University	172–176
Modeling in industrial art department of Purdue University	115
Mount Holyoke Female Seminary, labor in	63
Mosier, Mr. J. L. H., his account of noonday class of carriage-makers' apprentices	272
his labors for working youth	51
Museum of Bureau of Education, exhibit of school sewing work at	62
Museum of engineering, Cornell University	203
Museums of University of California	88

N.

	Page.
Naillen, A. van der, his school of engineering	34
Natural history, instruction in, in Cornell University	194–196
Natural history, school of, University of Missouri	174
Natural science, college of, Illinois Industrial University	107
Naval achitecture in University of Michigan	37
Towne Scientific School	43
New Century Woman's Club of Philadelphia, evening classes of	294
New Hampshire College of Agriculture and the Mechanic Arts	178–180
New Jersey Bureau of Statistics of Labor and Industries, replies of workmen to	4, 8
New Jersey College for the benefit of Agriculture and the Mechanic Arts	180–183
New York School of Cookery	285–288
Nichols, Dr. James R., his opinion of education at the Massachusetts Agricultural College	142
North Carolina, influence of the State University	208
University of. (See University of North Carolina.)	
North Georgia Agricultural College	102
Nurses, training schools for	64–72

O.

	Page.
Objects of colleges of agriculture and the mechanic arts	8–16
O'Fallon Polytechnic Institute, Washington University	264–266
Ohio Mechanics' Institute	40
Ohio State University, account of	200–213
mining engineering	33
practice in mechanics	31

P.

	Page.
Page, James A., report of shop at Dwight School, Boston	55
Palfrey, Gen. J. C., his opinion of drawing	48
Pardee scientific department of Lafayette College	41
Paris Carriage-makers' Society, school of	51
Parloa, Miss Maria, work of, as a teacher of cookery	288–290
Pattern-making, instruction in, in Purdue University	114
Patterson, President J. K., on the position of the Agricultural and Mechanical College of Kentucky	130
Peasants, prosperity of, around Gröningen, Holland	75
Pennsylvania State College	214–221
Physics, apparatus for, in University of Georgia	99
Polya, Mr. J., his drawing school for carriage-makers	51
Practical work before technical training	49
Practicums of Pennsylvania State College	219
Pratt, Lieut. R. H., his account of Indian education at Carlisle, Pa.	302–304
Printing, instruction for women in	73
instruction in, in Kansas Agricultural College	128
Prizes offered by Agricultural and Mechanical College of Missouri	175
Public schools, connection of Illinois Industrial University with	110
connection of University of Minnesota with	6
manual training in	52, 54–56
Purdue University, account of	110–118
instruction in chemistry	298
manual labor	27
scholarships	21
school of mechanics	30

R.

Ravenel, Dr. St. Julian, his experiments in agriculture in South Carolina	225
Rensselaer Polytechnic Institute	40
Rockford Seminary	59
Rose Polytechnic Institute	35
Ruffner, Hon. W. H., his remarks on the Michigan Agricultural College	160
his statement about Delaware College	98
Runkle, Prof. John D., his account of the School of Mechanic Arts at Boston	147–157
his enumeration of studies in the Royal Agricultural Academy at Hohenheim	26
his statement of the principles of the Russian system of shop practice	32
on differences between foreign and American technical schools	7
Russell, Mr. J. S., his estimate of the practical education of woman	58
his list of agricultural studies	26
lessons from his work on technical education	11
Russian system, principles of	32
Rutgers Scientific School, account of	180–183
instruction in chemistry	299

S.

Salaries, relation of, to total expenses of agricultural colleges	18
Scholarships in agricultural colleges	21
School of mines and metallurgy in Missouri	33, 175–176
School-shop connected with Dwight School, Boston	55
Science, relations of, to agriculture	4
summer school of, University of Minnesota	168
Secret societies, not allowed at Purdue University	117
Sewing, instruction in	59–62
in Kansas Agricultural College	128
Sheffield Scientific School, account of	93–97
instruction in chemistry	295–297
mining engineering	32
Shop practice at Massachusetts Institute of Technology	146, 151–157
Worcester County Free Institute	258
Shops, equipment of	147–150
Shops, practice in	30–31
Shops and shop courses (illustrated) of the Massachusetts Institute of Technology	148–157

	Page.
Shops of Cornell University	203
Illinois Industrial University	109
Kansas Agricultural College	125
manual training school, Washington University, Saint Louis	266–267
University of Minnesota	166
Shop-work, methods of	31
Shop-work in Purdue University	113, 114
Skilled labor, economy of	11, 12
Smith College	59
South Carolina College of Agriculture and Mechanics	224–227
South Georgia Agricultural College	103
Southwest Georgia Agricultural College	102
Special students, provision for, in Iowa Agricultural College	119
Springfield, Mass., evening drawing school	50
Spring Garden Institute	42
Summer school of science, University of Minnesota	168
Superintendents, qualifications necessary to	12
Statistics of institutions endowed with the national land grant	249–255
Steam, study and management of, Manual Training School, Saint Louis	268
Stenography, instruction in	72
Stetson, Mr. C. B., his conclusions on value of technical education	12–13
Stevens Institute of Technology	261–264
Straight, Prof. H. H., on industrial education	56
Stubbs, Prof. Wm. C., his report on chemistry in Alabama Agricultural College	83

T.

Taxation for schools in Chemnitz, Saxony	45
Technical education, moral effects of	11
social effects of	11
value of	12–13
Technical education in Europe and America contrasted	7
Technical schools, expensiveness of	17
value of, to Chemnitz	45
Technical training, actual work a preparation for	49
Telegraphy, instruction in, in Kansas Agricultural College	128
instruction of women in	72
Tennessee, University of	227–230
Tenney, President E. P., his remark on industrial education in the West	13
Texas State Agricultural and Mechanical College	230–232
shop work	31
Thayer School of Civil Engineering	38
Thompson, Charles O., his account of the Worcester County Free Institute	256–261
Thompson, Prof. S. R., his statement about the University of Nebraska	177–178
Thwing, Mr. Charles F., on illiteracy and want of trade education in criminals	76
Tichenor, Rev. I. T., his report of the Alabama Agricultural College	81
Towne Scientific School	43
Trade, extension of American	44
Trades, how learned	8–10
Training schools for nurses	64
Trenton Art School	52
Tuition in colleges of agriculture and the mechanic arts	21
Turning, instruction in, in Manual Training School, Saint Louis	268
in Massachusetts Institute of Technology	151, 152

U.

Union College, School of Civil Engineering	40
Universities, relation of State, to practical education	14
University of California, account of	86–91
college of mining	33
instruction in chemistry	295
University of Georgia	98–103
instruction in chemistry	297
University of Michigan, engineering courses in	37
University of Minnesota, description of	164–168
relation of, to public schools	6

INDEX. 319

	Page.
University of Missouri, account of	172–176
domestic instruction in	64
University of Nebraska	177–178
University of Nevada	178
University of North Carolina	204–208
assignment of scholarships	21
University of Pennsylvania, Towne Scientific School	43
University of South Carolina	224
University of Tennessee	227–230
University of Vermont and State Agricultural College, account of	232–234
instruction in chemistry	301
University of Virginia	44
University of Wisconsin, account of	246–248
mining engineering	33
mechanical engineering	31

V.

Vacation study, Columbia College School of Mines	39
Vaccine lymph, station for, in Louisiana	132
Vassar College	59
Vermont, University of. (See University of Vermont and State Agricultural College.)	
Veterinary museum of Cornell University	202
Veterinary science, instruction in, in Cornell University	186
Illinois Industrial University	106
Maryland Agricultural College	138
instructors in	19
school of, Iowa Agricultural College	121
Virginia Agricultural and Mechanical College	234–235
agricultural studies	26
Virginia Military Institute	44
Vise work in iron, in Purdue University	114

W.

Wages increased by education	75
Walton, Mr. George A., his examination of students of Hampton Institute	243–245
Washington University	264–271
Webster, Daniel, his enumeration of American political principles	77
Welch, Mrs. Mary B., on instruction in domestic economy in the Iowa Agricultural College	278
Wellesley College, instruction in science in	276
West Virginia State University	245
White, President E. E., his remarks on students' expenditures	22
White, President A. D., his remark on the vitality of the demand for practical education	5
Wilkinson, M. C., his work in Indian education	305–307
Wines, Dr. E. C., prison statistics from	76
Wisconsin, University of. (See University of Wisconsin.)	
Wives, education of	58
Woman, scientific and industrial education of	57–74
Women, industrial and scientific instruction for	273–294
Women, instruction for, in Massachusetts Institute of Technology	145
Wood turning, course in, in Purdue University	114
Wood working in Worcester Free Institute	259
Worcester, Mass., evening drawing schools of	50
Worcester County Free Institute	256–261
Workshop regulations	270
Wright, Col. Carroll D., on the improving condition of laborers	75

Y.

Yale College. (See Sheffield Scientific School).

Z.

Zoölogy, instruction in, in Cornell University	195

www.ingramcontent.com/pod-product-compliance
Lightning Source LLC
Chambersburg PA
CBHW030005240426
43672CB00007B/837